A-D 10/16 £76.99

FORENSIC FOOTWEAR EVIDENCE

CRC SERIES IN
**PRACTICAL ASPECTS OF CRIMINAL
AND FORENSIC INVESTIGATIONS**

VERNON J. GEBERTH, BBA, MPS, FBINA *Series Editor*

Forensic Pathology, Second Edition
Dominick J. Di Maio and Vincent J. M. Di Maio

The Practical Methodology of Forensic Photography, Second Edition
David R. Redsicker

Quantitative-Qualitative Friction Ridge Analysis: An Introduction to Basic and Advanced Ridgeology
David R. Ashbaugh

Footwear Impression Evidence: Detection, Recovery, and Examination, Second Edition
William J. Bodziak

The Sexual Exploitation of Children: A Practical Guide to Assessment, Investigation, and Intervention, Second Edition
Seth L. Goldstein

Practical Aspects of Munchausen by Proxy and Munchausen Syndrome Investigation
Kathryn Artingstall

Practical Fire and Arson Investigation, Second Edition
David R. Redsicker and John J. O'Connor

Interpretation of Bloodstain Evidence at Crime Scenes, Second Edition
William G. Eckert and Stuart H. James

Investigating Computer Crime
Franklin Clark and Ken Diliberto

Practical Investigation Techniques
Kevin B. Kinnee

Friction Ridge Skin: Comparison and Identification of Fingerprints
James F. Cowger

Tire Imprint Evidence
Peter McDonald

Practical Gambling Investigation Techniques
Kevin B. Kinnee

FORENSIC FOOTWEAR EVIDENCE

William J. Bodziak

CRC Press
Taylor & Francis Group
Boca Raton London New York

CRC Press is an imprint of the
Taylor & Francis Group, an **informa** business

CRC Press
Taylor & Francis Group
6000 Broken Sound Parkway NW, Suite 300
Boca Raton, FL 33487-2742

© 2017 by Taylor & Francis Group, LLC
CRC Press is an imprint of Taylor & Francis Group, an Informa business

No claim to original U.S. Government works

Printed and bound in India by Replika Press Pvt. Ltd.

Printed on acid-free paper
Version Date: 20160421

International Standard Book Number-13: 978-1-4398-8727-1 (Hardback)

Visit the Taylor & Francis Web site at
http://www.taylorandfrancis.com

and the CRC Press Web site at
http://www.crcpress.com

To my wife Shirley, and our family: Bill, Betsy, Peyton and Griffin; Leslie, Dustin, Haley and Ryan; and Chuck, Carey, Will and Jordan.

Contents

16   Examination of Crime Scene Impressions with Known Footwear   365

Series Editor Note

This textbook is part of a series titled "Practical Aspects of Criminal and Forensic Investigation." This series was created by Vernon J. Geberth, a retired New York City Police Department lieutenant commander who is an author, educator, and consultant on homicide and forensic investigations.

This series has been designed to provide contemporary, comprehensive, and pragmatic information to the practitioner involved in criminal and forensic investigations by authors who are nationally recognized experts in their respective fields.

Preface

After having written much on the topic of footwear evidence, working in the private sector over the past 18 years has provided me with additional information and experiences along with a better understanding of the applications and use of this evidence. This book includes new topics, updated research, and a more transparent view of how this evidence should be treated and evaluated. Footwear marks and impressions are among the most commonly produced forms of evidence produced at the scene of a crime. As technology changes, the capabilities of forensic science continue to evolve. Stronger alternate lights sources and lasers, higher quality lifting films, easy to use snow casting products, new chemical reagent formulations and techniques, and higher resolution digital cameras have provided an increased ability to detect, recover, and utilize this evidence. High-resolution scanners, comparative software programs, and computer enhancement techniques have improved the capacity to both conduct and report examinations. Investigators are increasingly organizing scene marks and impressions in an automated and more efficient way that often enables them to quickly link multiple crime scenes with repeat offenders. While newer resources and technology have enabled greater utilization of the evidence, the physical comparison and evaluation of that evidence must still be conducted by someone with a foundation of knowledge and experience about footwear and the value of the features evident in a crime scene impression. With over 44 years of work in this field, I have conducted detailed comparisons between known footwear and all forms of forensic footwear evidence in many thousands of cases; had hundreds of consultations with both prosecution and defense counsel; have reviewed testimony of footwear experts and investigators in prior convictions under appeal; and have interacted with crime scene technicians, examiners, and investigators in classes and forensic forums in both the United States and other parts of the world. In writing *Forensic Footwear Evidence* it is my intention to share that foundation of knowledge and experience to provide novice and experienced examiners, crime scene technicians, investigators, prosecution and defense counsel with a comprehensive source of information on this topic.

Acknowledgments

Writing a book of this size cannot be undertaken without the assistance, knowledge, experiences, and contributions of others. My special and sincere thanks to those who provided considerable time and support in this endeavor, including Lesley Hammer, Herb Hedges, Jim Wolfe, Ron Mueller, Jim Streeter, Mike Gorn, Matt Johnson, Christine Snyder, Shelly Massey, Cindy Homer, Jacqueline Speir, Isaac Keereweer, Phil Gallant, Theo Velders, Patrick van Vilsteren, and Gerrit Volckeryck. In addition, I also extend my appreciation to members of the Scientific Working Group for Shoe Print Evidence (SWGTREAD 2004–2013) and to others who have conducted research and published in scientific journals regarding footwear evidence.

About the Author

William J. Bodziak has spent over 44 years in the field of footwear and tire evidence. He began his training in the evaluation of footwear, tire, and questioned document evidence when transferred to the FBI Laboratory as a Supervisory Special Agent in 1973. In that capacity he examined evidence in thousands of criminal cases until his retirement in 1998 and, since, in the capacity of a private examiner. While in the FBI laboratory, his casework experiences included critical evidence in major investigations, including the bombing deaths of a federal judge in Alabama and a civil rights worker in Georgia in1989, the O.J. Simpson criminal and civil investigations in 1995, and the 1995 Oklahoma Bombing case involving Timothy McVeigh and Terry Nichols.

Mr. Bodziak created the first technical conferences on footwear and tire evidence held in 1983 and 1984 and taught the subsequent Forensic Footwear Courses at the FBI Academy which began in 1985. He organized the first International Symposium on Footwear and Tire evidence at the FBI Academy in 1994 that involved over 230 examiners from 30 countries. He has provided instruction in the forensic examination of footwear and tire evidence both at the FBI Academy as well as over 100 other locations throughout the United States and other countries. His experiences have included hundreds of sworn testimonies in the United States, as well as in courts in Canada, South Africa, Israel, Guam, Saipan, Puerto Rico, and the US Virgin Islands. Mr. Bodziak holds an undergraduate degree in biology and a Master of Science in Forensic Science. Mr. Bodziak previously authored *Footwear Impression Evidence: Detection, Recovery, and Examination* (2000) and *Tire Tread and Tire Track Evidence: Recovery and Forensic Examination* (2008). He has also authored chapters in other books as well as articles in professional journals in the areas of questioned documents and footwear and tire tread impression evidence. He was conferred status of a fellow of the Questioned Document section of the American Academy of Forensic Sciences where he served as both secretary and chairman of that section. He has been a member of the American Society of Questioned Document Examiners and a Certified Diplomate of the American Board of Forensic Document Examiners. He is a distinguished member of the International Association for Identification where he is a Certified Footwear Examiner and has served as the chairman of the Footwear and Tire Track subcommittee. From 2004–2013 he served on the Scientific Working Group for Shoe Print and Tire Track Evidence.

General Information about Footwear Evidence

1

Along with DNA and fingerprints, it was reported in the United Kingdom, that the most frequently encountered evidence at scenes are footwear marks and impressions.[*] Although common sense would reason the same would be true anywhere, the usage and recovery of this form of evidence have not achieved their full potential everywhere in the world.

The possible presence of both visible and latent shoe impressions must be in the minds of first responders and crime scene investigators. Obviously, there are sometimes other priorities: What type of crime was it? Is the perpetrator gone and is the scene secure and safe? What is the condition of any victim? Is medical assistance or a medical examiner needed? Once these priorities are attended to, the focus must quickly shift to the preservation and recovery of physical evidence. New questions arise. Is the type of crime committed one where physical evidence like fingerprints or shoe prints is essential to the proof of facts regarding the crime? Was there a forced point of entry where footwear impressions might be found outside as well as inside that location? Was there broken glass inside a broken window that contains a latent shoe print? Was there a kicked-in door? Is the flooring inside the point of entry light or patterned so it may conceal the possible presence of highly detailed latent footwear impressions? Was the crime a burglary or home invasion, meaning the perpetrators may have been at the scene for an extended period of time, or was it a more sudden and deliberate crime like a shooting made from outside, making it unlikely the perpetrator ever walked inside? Was there a bleeding victim where the perpetrator may have tracked through the victim's blood? Was it a burglary where the entire house or business was ransacked, with many pieces of paper strewn across the floor that may have been taken from drawers or a safe during the crime and may contain latent prints of the perpetrator's shoes? Is it possible that impressions exist outside in soil or snow in the directions from which the perpetrator approached or departed the scene? Is there a need to take photographs of the shoes of first responders so their shoe prints can be eliminated and to allow for revealing which shoe impressions were those of the perpetrator?

The successful detection and recovery of all evidence at crime scenes are two of the most difficult challenges in law enforcement. The dedicated personnel who accept these challenges and devote their time and efforts to detecting and recovering evidence are sometimes praised but have, at times, been the subject of harsh criticism. It is always easy to be critical, as one well-known author was in his description of a famous crime scene as follows:

> To summon up a ghastly remembrance of police tipstavery, bend your glance backward to the opening chapter of the Lindbergh case. Do you remember—could anyone ever forget—the foaming and senseless cataract of gorgeously uniformed state troopers that descended on the Lindbergh home in motorcycles, roared up and down the road trampling every available clue into the March mud, systematically covering with impenetrable layers of stupidity every fingerprint, footprint, dust trace on the estate? ... What wouldn't Prosecutor Wilentz have

---

[*] National Policing Improving Agency (NPIA), Footwear Marks Recovery Manual, 2007, UK.

given for a long conclusive fingerprint on the crib, windowsill or ladder? How effectively he could have introduced a moulage reproduction of that footprint under the nursery window! … A European prosecutor would have had all of these aids as a matter of routine; the first investigator who reached the scene would have protected with his life (and reputation) that footprint in the mud. But our handsome American troopers, densely packed in motorcycle array, Humpty-dumptied the problem so completely that no subsequent forensic glue, however skilled, could ever piece it together again.

H. M. Robinson
Science Catches the Criminal, Blue Ribbon Books, New York, 1935, pp. 286–287

The degree of factual accuracy in Robinson's words is unknown, but much has happened over the many decades since those words were published. Technological advances in equipment and materials, formalized protocol, research, and better training and materials have resulted in immense improvements and efficiency in the recovery of evidence from the scene of a crime.

Footwear Evidence Past and Present

Humans have been making important observations and conclusions about impressions of feet and shoes as long as they have existed and certainly way before records were kept. The acquired observation skills and accumulated knowledge of hunters in both ancient and modern times provided them with increased success when tracking animals for their survival. A parallel set of observation skills, and methodology relating to the footwear of individuals, is used in establishing a perpetrator's presence at the scene of a crime. Written transcripts from old court proceedings describe how shoe marks left at scenes have been compared with a suspect's shoes and used as evidence for hundreds of years. The proceedings of the Old Bailey, London's Central Criminal Court, London, England, offer numerous examples.* One case from July 1697 involved a murder, of which the transcript reads:

> …opening the shutters, found a great deal of blood, and the print of a slipper in the blood: and they sent for a Constable…but the French woman, who some time after was apprehended in Rupert Street; and in her lodging, in a trunk, they found most of the goods, and one of the slippers that was bloody ….[†]

Another example from these records involves a case of grand theft on July 10, 1765. The transcript reads, "I put Laurence's foot into the print of a foot in the mould in my garden, and it fitted exactly."[‡] In addition, another case's transcript from 1884 states:

> I took the prisoner to the station, where he took his boots off by my direction—I went with them to the prosecutor's house—I found one footmark close to the gate, and one close to where the struggle took place, and two inside the stable gate, not far from where the

---

* www.oldbaileyonline.org can be searched for proceedings from court cases between 1674–1913.

† Margaret Martell, Murder, Theft; transcripts from the Proceedings of the OLD BAILEY, London's Central Criminal Court, London, England, July 7, 1697. (see http://www.oldbaileyonline.org/browse.jsp?id=t16970707-46-off242&div=t16970707-46&terms=slipper#highlight)

‡ Henry Laurence, John Fluty, Theft > grand larceny, Theft > grand larceny, 10th July 1765. Transcripts from the Proceeding of the Old Bailey, London's Central Criminal Court, London, England, July 10, 1765. (See http://www.oldbaileyonline.org/browse.jsp?id=t17650710-29-off160&div=t17650710-29&terms=foot|mould#highlight.)

struggle took place, leading from the stable yard into the Avenue Road, the way the prosecutor said the men ran in   I made marks with the boots by the side of those footmarks;
they corresponded in size and shape—the prisoner's left boot had had a toe tip with nails
under it, and they corresponded with marks in footprints—on the right boot there was no
toe tip, but a tip on the heel—I found corresponding marks for both right and left.[*]

Many of these old references do not involve the recovery of the evidence, but situations where the police compared the suspect's shoe directly alongside of the impression
at the crime scene. One such case was the Richardson case from Kirkcudbright, Scotland
in 1786.[†] This case involved the fatal stabbing of a young woman. The investigator trailed
the footprints leaving the scene, noting the perpetrator's shoes were heavily nailed and
patched. Tracings were made of these impressions and later the shoes of Richardson were
identified as the source. In Figure 1.1, a tracing of a shoe print from that crime scene

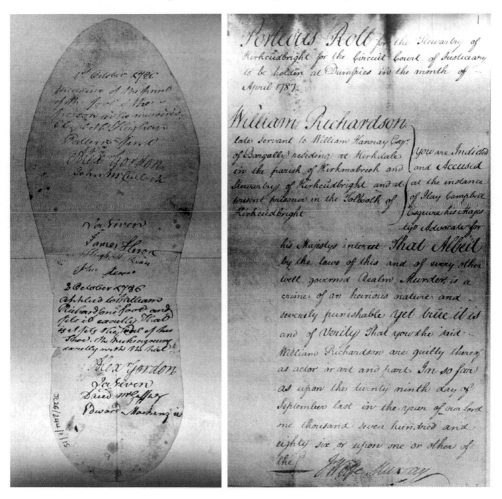

Figure 1.1 Two documents from the Richardson case in 1786. Cases then predated photography; thus measurements, notes, scene tracings, and on-scene comparisons were relied on.

[*] David James Wilby, Violent Theft > robbery, 29th December 1884. Transcripts from the Proceedings of
the Old Bailey, London's Central Criminal Court, London, England, December 29, 1884. (See http://www.
oldbaileyonline.org/browse.jsp?ref=t18841229-184.)
[†] Robinson, H. M., *Science Catches the Criminal*, Blue Ribbon Books, New York, 1935, pp. 18–19.

appears on the left. On the right is the court document from April 1787. The words on the tracing read at the top "1st October, 1786 measure of the print of the foot of the person who murdered Elizabeth Hughan." In the heel the words read, "2 October 1786 applied to William Richardson's foot and fits it exactly. That is it fits the sole of the shoe. The nicks agreeing exactly with the heel."

What is obvious from the review of older transcripts was that no trained forensic examiners existed, but instead, comparisons were carried out by investigators at the scene, often by placing the shoes of suspects alongside the crime scene impression. It was not until many years later that photography, casting, and lifting became a common practice and that police forces had access to someone possessing some level of formalized training to conduct the comparisons.

What Footwear Impressions Contribute to Investigations

The investigative value of footwear evidence is greatest during the first hours of the investigation. Digital photographs revealing the sole design of an impression recovered from a scene can be a great asset to investigators when interviewing suspects or witnesses and conducting searches. This awareness and practice facilitate the recovery of footwear of suspected individuals for later forensic analysis. The forensic examination encompasses the class characteristics of design and physical dimension, the condition and features of general wear, and randomly acquired characteristics, such as cuts and scratches or stones or other debris held in the outsole tread. In many cases, differences in class characteristics enable exclusion of footwear. In instances of inclusion, the degree of detail retained in a crime scene impression may or may not be sufficient to identify the shoe but can still provide various levels of association with the shoes of the accused. When diluted among the billions of shoes owned in the US and the many thousands of different sole designs in the marketplace, any specific design and dimension of a shoe's outsole alone will be representative of a very small fraction of 1% of the general footwear population.

Footwear impressions also may assist in determining the number of suspects and their path into, through, and away from the crime scene. They may be used to corroborate or refute information provided by witnesses or suspects. Involvement of an individual in the crime may sometimes be established based on the composition and/or location of the impressions alone. For instance, leaving isolated impressions in a remote field alongside the victim's body or leaving impressions on top of a bank counter can offer significant proof of involvement. One memorable case involved a perpetrator who staged a break-in to his own house through a basement window for producing his alibi regarding the murder of his wife. The detective investigating the case noticed shoe prints in the newly fallen snow that exited the rear door and then led directly to the broken basement window, an unlikely path that clearly disputed the alibi and ultimately led to a confession. In the majority of cases, simply the proof that a person's shoes produced impressions at a crime scene where they otherwise had no legal access may constitute highly relevant evidence that can contribute toward proof of that individual's presence and/or involvement in the crime.

How Effectively Is Impression Evidence Used?

Although the use of footwear evidence has been in practice and accepted in court as far as written records can be found, not all law enforcement agencies give this form of evidence the emphasis they should. This is a complicated issue but one that needs to be put forth for discussion and awareness. The many reasons listed hereafter are some that may explain or account for the underutilization of this evidence, not only in the US, but in other countries as well. Not listed in any order of importance and not all applying to every law enforcement jurisdiction, they are nevertheless provided to explain some of the reasons some police agencies may not be realizing the maximum value of this evidence.

The Very Large Number of Investigative Jurisdictions in the US

A 2008 US Department of Justice census found there were 17,985 separate law enforcement agencies in the United States. Included among those were 12,501 local police agencies, 3063 sheriff departments, and 50 state law enforcement agencies.[*] The large number of separately run and budgeted departments creates logistical problems that are different from those in smaller countries, particularly when addressing the many issues involving crime scene response, training, and policy. Yet these departments, by law, are the reactive agency that responds to crime scenes in their jurisdictions, collects evidence, and conducts investigations. This large number of agencies makes interaction and sharing of crime scene intelligence between law enforcement agencies most difficult.

Less Emphasis on Repeatable Offenses in the US

Some agencies in the US actively recover forensic evidence from all scenes of crime including repeatable offenses such as burglaries. Repeatable offenses often involve the same individual producing impressions with the same shoes at multiple crime scenes. If these scenes are not processed for evidence, the ability to enter impressions into a database to link those crime scenes, a practice known as footwear intelligence, is eliminated. A great many agencies, particularly in larger cities, are so consumed with homicides, assaults, drug crimes, and other priorities, they are unable to process the scenes of less serious but repeatable forms of offenses and thus are not able to link crimes through associations of footwear impressions.

Limited Resources

In general, the limits any police force has with regard to its human and financial sources will drastically influence its ability to respond to and process crime scenes. For this reason alone, it is possible some departments only photograph footwear evidence, making no attempt to cast, lift, or enhance impressions. This diminishes the recovery and effectiveness

---

[*] US Department of Justice, Census of State and Local Law Enforcement Agencies, 2008, published July 2011, NCJ 233982, p. 2.

of this evidence. The training of crime scene technicians in both the recovery methods and potential value of footwear evidence is also critical to its recovery and use in solving crimes. Many departments provide little or no external training while at the same time their internal training in this discipline may be outdated, inadequate, or even nonexistent.

Limited knowledge in the investigative and legal community: Forensic footwear experts are the most knowledgeable persons familiar with all facets of footwear evidence and are the primary source of information for other law enforcement personnel and attorneys. Part of their duties should include the communication and sharing of their expertise, whether it is teaching crime scene investigators, supporting detectives in their investigation as it relates to footwear evidence, or explaining the strength and relevance of their examination findings to the legal community. The long-term effect of the underutilization and limited knowledge of footwear evidence on the overall law enforcement community is merely a further discouragement and deterrent for the crime scene officer to search for it, for detectives to understand its value, and for prosecutors to utilize it.

Lack of Aggressive Approach to Locating Impressions at the Scene

Because the location of latent or barely visible footwear impressions on ground level substrates makes them more difficult and challenging to find, an aggressive approach and effort are required to find these impressions. Many responders have limited experience searching for footwear impressions or simply do not allocate the time and effort needed to do this. What is not looked for will not be found. There is also the fallacy that whenever first responders have walked through the scene prior to it being processed, any and all footwear impressions of the perpetrator are immediately lost. Consequently, certain areas of the crime scene may be ignored simply because those areas have been tracked over and it is presumed any impressions of the perpetrator were destroyed. This presumption is simply not valid. Although the general area that contains the perpetrator's impressions may have been walked over many times, the impressions themselves may not necessarily have been destroyed. Even if a particular impression were stepped over, the untouched portion of that impression would be just as valuable as any partial impression. Figure 1.2 depicts a photograph taken at a crime scene where the perpetrator and responders tracked over the same areas through a recent and thin layer of snowfall. The impressions of the perpetrator as well as first responders who tracked over the same area are obvious, and observant investigators were able to easily eliminate the impressions of the responders and recover the impressions of the perpetrator. Most of the impressions of the perpetrator were not even touched by other footwear in spite of the subsequent heavy foot traffic.

Footwear Experts Often Share Their Time with Another Separate Forensic Specialty

The community of footwear examiners in some countries, particularly in the US, is largely made up of examiners who are also trained in other forensic disciplines, meaning they must divide their time with other forms of evidence such as fingerprints, trace evidence, firearms, tool marks, and questioned documents. Some may also devote considerable portions of their day to other responsibilities such as crime scene processing and general law

Figure 1.2 A snow-covered walkway leading to the crime scene visibly recorded the steps of the perpetrator as well as several first responders whose shoe designs could be excluded. Most of the impressions of the perpetrator's shoes survived.

enforcement duties. Few laboratories in the US have examiners who are totally dedicated to the examination of footwear and tire evidence. This affects the depth of the examiner's experience as well as the time he spends on research, continuing education, presentations at scientific meetings, and the resulting overall use and emphasis of this form of evidence within the examiner's jurisdiction.

The Formation of Footwear Impressions

Each time a person takes a step, their footwear makes direct physical contact with the substrate. In many of those instances impressions are produced that have replicated excellent detail. While most responders readily accept the potential for the presence of latent fingerprints on a variety of surfaces at a crime scene, they don't always recognize the equal and perhaps even greater chance that latent footwear marks could also be present. Why say "greater" chance? One reason is because many perpetrators wear gloves during the commission of the crime, thus leaving no fingerprints at all. Another would be the fact that in the commission of some crimes, a perpetrator may be simply moving through a scene, not touching anything with their hands, thus their feet makes contact with the substrate more than the friction ridge portions of their fingers or hands. With every step that is

Figure 1.3 On the left, a shoe that has stepped in a red substance redeposits that substance on the substrate in subsequent steps in the form of a transfer impression. The transfer impression is a positive likeness of the raised areas of the outsole that made contact with the substrate. On the right, a shoe steps in shallow soil, producing a three-dimensional impression.

taken, whether in soil or snow, on a concrete or tile floor, on broken glass, a wooden window sill, a piece of paper, a bank counter, or on countless other objects and materials, the potential exists for replications of the characteristics of the shoe outsoles in either visible or latent forms.

Two-dimensional footwear impressions are most often a result of the transfer of materials acquired by the shoe during prior steps that are redeposited to the substrate in the form of what is known as a transfer impression. Figure 1.3 includes a transfer impression where a shoe has tracked through a red substance, has acquired that red substance on its outsole, and has now transferred that substance back to the substrate. Transfer impressions are positive impressions inasmuch as they represent a positive likeness of the design of the outsole. Figure 1.4 depicts a transfer impression and the heel of the shoe that produced it, showing how the impression represents the portion of the sole that made it. Void areas on the outsole, indicated with an arrow, will reproduce similarly as a void area in the transfer impression. Transfer impressions of this type include the transfer of moist or dry materials. Figure 1.5 depicts two transfer impressions. One is a wet origin impression made with a moist muddy sole. Impressions that involve moisture are known as wet origin impressions and will penetrate or otherwise bond more firmly to the substrate. The other is a dry origin impression made with an exterior dry soil residue. Those that involve dry materials transferred to a dry receiving substrate are known as dry origin impressions. Because dry origin impressions do not usually bond firmly to the substrate, they are more fragile. The arrow in Figure 1.5 shows an area that was intentionally wiped with a finger to demonstrate the fragile nature of dry origin impressions.

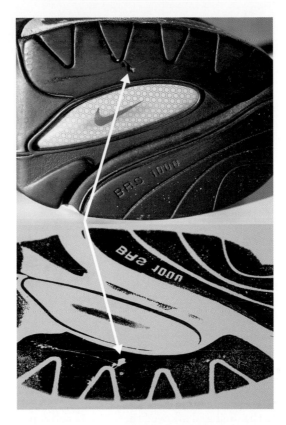

Figure 1.4 An example of the heel of a shoe and a transfer impression made by that heel. Note that void areas such as grooves, lettering, cuts, and scratches have not made contact with the substrate and similarly appear in the impression as void areas.

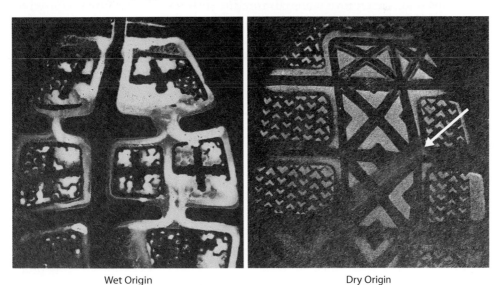

Wet Origin   Dry Origin

Figure 1.5 Wet and dry forms of transfer impressions. On the left is a soil-based wet residue impression and on the right is a dry soil–based residue impression. Wet origin impressions bond to the substrate. On the right the arrow points to an area of the dry origin impression where a finger swipe was intentionally made to demonstrate its delicate nature.

Figure 1.6 A negative impression made on a bench top that contained an accumulation of dust. The shoe outsole removed the dust and allowed the white bench top color to show through.

A less often encountered form of two-dimensional impression occurs when the contact areas of a shoe's outsole remove material from the substrate. This is often referred to as a negative impression. The crime scene impression in Figure 1.6 is a negative impression produced on a bench top that contained a thick accumulation of dust. When the perpetrator stepped on this, the raised area of his shoe's outsole removed the dust, allowing the color of the bench top surface to show through.

Three-dimensional impressions like those shown in Figure 1.7 result when an outsole permanently deforms substrates such as sand, soil, mud, and snow. Three-dimensional impressions are normally shallow but can be deeper if the substrate conditions allow. Three-dimensional impressions provide representation of additional portions of an outsole and its characteristics not always replicated in two-dimensional impressions.

Variations in Impression Detail

Although the way that a shoe replicates its outsole appears superficially simple, each step and impression produced are affected by many factors. The impression-making process is not a perfect one and like other compound events, there will always be variations between multiple subsequent impressions of a shoe. This is normal. The variations involve both the quantity and completeness of each impression as well as the quality of detail replicated. The movement of the shoe itself is subject to variations in its precise motion, speed, and force as it strikes the ground slightly differently with each step, subject not only to the

Figure 1.7 Uneven substrates and stones prevent complete contact between the shoe and substrate and are examples of natural and normal interferences in the production of footwear impressions. The details in the remaining areas represent the shoe that produced them.

biomechanics of the wearer but also to external forces, interferences, and influences. Firm non-giving substrates can be smooth, slippery, rough and uneven, wet or dry, and non-porous or porous. Likewise, impressions in compactable substrates such as sand, soil, mud, or snow may provide conditions that provide firm support, while others give way and allow the shoe to penetrate more deeply into the substrate. Similar variations occur with regard to the materials acquired on the outsole that are subsequently transferred in the form of an impression, comprised of countless dry and moist residues, dust, mud, blood, or greasy or oily materials. In the end, variables for both two- and three-dimensional impressions provide a range of footwear impressions that vary extensively in their quantitative and qualitative characteristics. Interferences also affect the precise quantity and quality of replication. Interferences include stones, sticks, debris, air pockets, unevenness or texture of the substrate, wet or sticky substances, or any other material that interferes with or obstructs the quantity or quality of an impression's replication. Figure 1.7 depicts an impression made in a rocky soil mixture on an uneven substrate. The unevenness of the substrate combined with the obstruction created by many rocks has prevented a more complete recording of the shoe outsole. In spite of those interferences, some detail of the outsole, including some lettering on it, has been retained and the impression is still of significant value for comparison with footwear.

Figure 1.8 depicts two sequential two-dimensional impressions produced by the same heel adjacent to one another on a tile floor. Each impression was enhanced with black fingerprint powder. In the impression on the right, as indicated by the arrows, there is a void

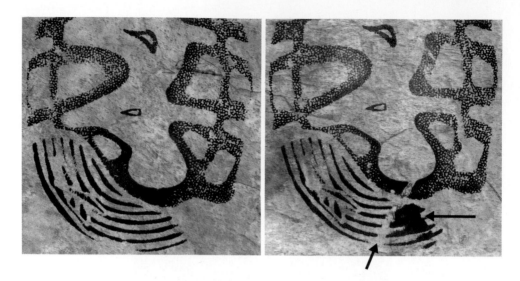

Figure 1.8 Two impressions sequentially produced by the same heel on a tile floor and developed with fingerprint powder. Variations normally occur between impressions, as the precise set of circumstances surrounding impressions is never exactly the same. The arrows on the impression on the right show two features that do not exist in the impression on the left.

area running through the pattern and there is also a solid black area. The void area was the product of a piece of debris that was between the heel and the floor when that impression was made. Consequently, the heel did not transfer its detail to the floor beneath that debris; thus, that area did not attract any fingerprint powder and now appears as a void area in that impression. To some it may appear as if the heel that produced that impression had a cut in it, but that was not the case. The solid black area was due to a sticky substance that was already present on the floor, unrelated to the impression process, but attracted the powder. Neither of these features appears in the impression on the left, as these two interferences did not exist between the heel and substrate in that impression.

Other examples of variations in the impression-making process are illustrated in Figure 1.9, showing six impressions made with the same shoe on various substrates, including (1) a granular and rocky soil, (2) with a dusty outsole on newspaper that was lifted electrostatically, (3) a lift of a soil-based impression on tile, (4) an impression in uneven dark sandy soil, (5) a bloody impression on concrete, and (6) a cast of an impression made in a soil and grass mix. Even though the same shoe made each of these, considerable variations exist between these impressions. The makeup and amount of the contaminant transferred (dirt, dust, blood), the nature of the contaminant (liquid or solid, fine or coarse) the color of the receiving substrate, the nature of the substrate (clay soil, sand, rocky soils, snow, tile, wood, paper), the texture and condition of the receiving substrate (glass, fabric, carpet, tile floor, and concrete), the moisture condition of the substrate (damp, wet, dry), the outsole condition itself (smooth, rough, worn, wet, dry, rigid, soft), and the dynamics of the interaction between the shoe and substrate (foot movement, uneven or unstable substrates) are just a few of the factors that affect the resulting detail replicated in any impression.

Variations also occur during the process of making known impressions, regardless of the method or methods used. Figure 1.10 depicts enlarged areas of two design elements taken from two known impressions of an outsole. Even though these impressions were made in a standardized way, one right after the other, they will still have very minor

Figure 1.9 Six impressions made by the same shoe demonstrate normal variations that occur due to different substrates and conditions.

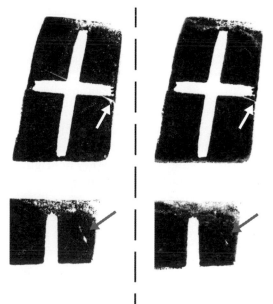

Figure 1.10 Minor variations between multiple known impressions of the same area of one shoe are normal for the same reasons they occur in crime scene impressions. Two examples are indicated with arrows.

variations. Two of those variations are indicated with arrows and illustrate how two random cuts are represented depending on the amount of ink and pressure. Known impressions are covered in Chapter 11.

The Effect Recovery Methods Have on Detail

Variation in detail that relates to the recovery process is a separate issue from variations that normally occur between multiple impressions at a crime scene. Impressions produced by the perpetrator at the scene are what they are. Their detail can range from very poor to excellent. Police and crime scene technicians have no control over that. However, they do have control over the recovery of these impressions. Unfortunately, not all crime scene personnel responsible for recovery of this evidence have been afforded the same training, equipment, materials, and experience. Consequently, impressions of the same detail at one scene may not be recovered with the same degree of success at another. Although not excusable, it is a reality that is obvious to forensic footwear practitioners. Poorly recovered evidence has a great impact on forensic examination results. For the prosecution, poor recovery methods and practices limit the potential that evidence might contribute to the case. For the defense, limitations of recovery can potentially prevent documentation of exculpatory evidence.

General Guidelines for the Recovery of Footwear Evidence

As a general procedure, whenever possible, the recovery of the original item containing the impression should be made as long as doing so will not damage it. This might include pieces of paper stepped on while a bank robber jumped onto the bank counter, a stepped-on piece of broken glass on the floor, or a piece of stepped-on cardboard containing muddy shoe marks. In serious crimes, it might also include actually removing larger pieces of wood or tile flooring, particularly if the ability to enhance those impressions at the scene is either not possible or available. A study in Finland reflected that best examination results were obtained when the shoeprints submitted to the laboratory consisted of the original evidence, in which case, definite identifications were reached in 19.7% of the cases and probable conclusions in another 20.2% of that evidence.[*] In a study reported in 1994, positive identifications in footwear impression cases overall were made in 24% of the cases, with some form of corroboration in an additional 56% of the cases. Out of those identifications, original evidence, in the form of paper, glass, and other stepped-on objects, accounted for the majority of identifications.[†] These results are not surprising, as the recovery of original impressions provides far greater time and resources in a laboratory environment to record and enhance their detail.

If and when the original impression evidence cannot be removed, there are many techniques, materials, and methods used to recover those impressions. Because of the

---

[*] Majamaa, H., Ytti, A., Survey of the conclusions drawn of similar footwear cases in various crime laboratories, *Forensic Science International*, 82(1):109–120, 1996.

[†] A UK study reported by David Baldwin in 1994, exact cite unknown.

innumerable combinations of impression forms and substrates, no single technique or enhancement process will be appropriate for the recovery of all or even a majority of footwear impressions. The following chapters on photography, casting, snow casting, two-dimensional impressions, and enhancement provide useful information regarding the best practices and materials for recovering footwear evidence. Some general guidelines to follow are

Always Take General Crime Scene Photographs. They provide a record of the original appearance and/or location of the impression. Use numbered or lettered identifiers to assist in this documentation and to cross-reference in written notes as well as any examination quality photographs, lifts, or casts that are subsequently made.

Make Notes and Crime Scene Sketches as Needed. These should include the same letters or numbers as the various identifiers used in the general scene photographs. Notes should include information that supplements the photographs, such as the date recovered, exact whereabouts, and conditions and circumstances surrounding the footwear impressions.

Remove Items Containing Impressions from the Scene. All original impressions should be removed from the scene if and when it is possible to do so without compromising the evidence. These would include pieces of paper, glass, and other easy to remove items. In crimes that are more serious or situations where the necessary expertise and materials are not available, consideration should be given to removing larger items such as kicked doors or sections of flooring to enable better processing of the evidence later in a laboratory environment.

Take "Examination Quality" Photographs. These are close-up photographs taken from directly over the top of the impression, with the camera's sensor plane parallel to the impression, and with a scale alongside the impression. They are taken specifically for recording the maximum amount of detail to be used later in a forensic comparison with shoes. The same identifier numbers or letters should be included in these photographs as were used in the general scene photographs.

Follow Photography with Casting or Lifting and/or Enhancement. Photography should always be followed with attempts to enhance and/or lift two-dimensional impressions or by making casts of three-dimensional impressions. The same identifier numbers or letters should be used on those lifts and casts as were used in the general scene photographs.

The Age of Impressions

The life expectancy of footwear impressions can range from a brief moment to numerous years. Exterior impressions in snow, sand, and soil begin to degrade soon after they are made. The speed and extent of that degradation will depend on time; weather factors such as temperature, wind, and rain; destruction by other footwear traffic; and the composition of the substrate. Interior impressions in residue, dust, or blood, if not cleaned up or altered through physical contact, may last for much longer periods of time.

There is no method to analyze a footwear impression and determine its precise age. Impressions simply don't degrade or change in such a precise and predictable manner to

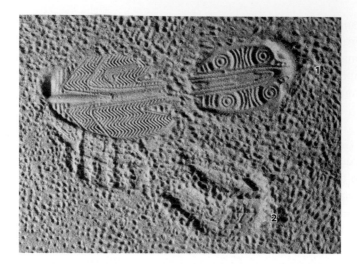

Figure 1.11 An older impression (2) is weathered like the surrounding substrate, but is later tracked over by a more recent impression (1).

allow a distinction that they are 1 hour versus 2 hours versus 36 hours old. Limited age determinations of impressions are sometimes possible in those cases where that impression can be placed on a timeline based on common sense and/or factual information. For instance, impressions made as a result of tracking through the victim's blood obviously occurred during or after the bleeding. Impressions that resulted from stepping on papers spilled from within a burglarized safe or drawer obviously occurred during or after the burglary. Footwear impressions on bank counters, in all likelihood, are less than 24 hours old, since most bank counters are routinely cleaned and polished at least once every day. This type of aging, although not expressed in minutes or hours, can still be of some value and the proof of facts in an investigation. Other observations can also offer evidence of a general timeline. Some impressions at the same scene may appear older in contrast to others that appear to be fresh. Figure 1.11 depicts a fresh impression in sand that has cut through and obliterated part of the older impression. Note the older impression (2) and the surrounding substrate have indentations of raindrops but the fresh impression (1) occurred after the rain. In a crime freshly committed, the fresh impression may be important while the weathered impression may not. Alternately, for a crime that took place three days prior based on the condition of the decedent or other factors, the weathered impression may be the most important.

Other relative time references may involve objects that could not have been stepped on prior to the crime such as the glass from a broken window at the point of entry, as depicted in Figure 1.12. More specific time references may involve surveillance cameras that document a person wearing a style of shoe at a particular recorded time and may even include photographs or video showing where the perpetrator has stepped. Figure 1.13 is a photograph taken by a video surveillance camera during a bank robbery. The video camera system has documented where and when the perpetrator jumped onto the bank counter.

Every crime scene provides a different set of circumstances, but the crime scene investigator, while still at the scene, should be observant and document anything related to the issues of age, including what objects were stepped on and the timeline, and sequence of any impressions, as those may impact the relevance of that evidence.

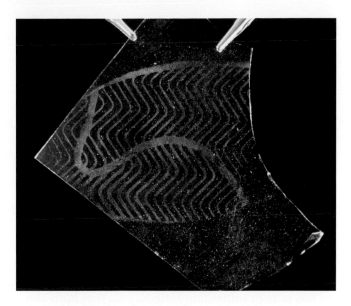

Figure 1.12 A case example of a positive impression on broken glass produced during commission of a crime.

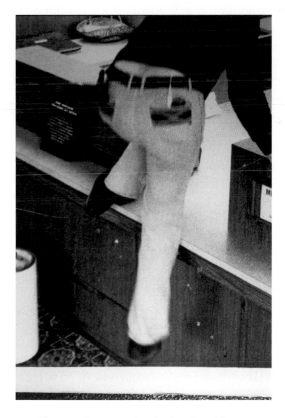

Figure 1.13 A video surveillance photograph of a bank robber jumping over the bank counter not only provides a time reference but also provides important information about where the perpetrator has stepped. Reviewing video surveillance is a useful resource to assist in the detection and recovery of footwear evidence.

The Scene of the Crime and Preservation of Evidence

Wherever he steps, whatever he touches, whatever he leaves even unconsciously, will serve as silent witness against him. Not only his fingerprints or his footprints, but his hair, the fibers from his clothes, the glass he breaks, the tool marks he leaves, the paint he scratches, the blood or semen he deposits or collects—all of these and more bear mute witness against him. This is evidence that does not forget. It is not confused by the excitement of the moment. It is not absent because human witnesses are. It cannot perjure itself. It cannot be wholly absent. Only its interpretation can err. Only human failure to find it, study, and understand it can diminish its value.

Paul L. Kirk
Crime Investigation, John Wiley & Sons, 1953

The above-cited famous quote of the late Paul L. Kirk, professor of criminalistics at the University of California, is often used to remind us of Dr. Edmond Locard's "Exchange Principle."* Locard's principle holds that the perpetrator of a crime brings something into the crime scene and leaves with something from it, and that both can be used as forensic evidence. However, as any crime scene technician or investigator will tell you, the task of finding every trace of evidence is not only a great challenge, but also its success will be a product of training, experience, resources, diligence, and time. Approaching a crime scene with the attitude and recognition that footwear evidence can be present will increase the success of finding both patent and latent impressions.

Although some foot traffic of first responders is unavoidable, there is still great potential for locating and recovering most impressions. When a cursory visual examination fails to reveal impressions, the crime scene investigator should continue to aggressively search for latent or faint impressions using tools such as high-intensity oblique light, alternate light sources, electrostatic lifters, and other detection and enhancement methods.

The perimeters of interior and exterior areas should be secured to prevent foot traffic other than of those who are actively recovering evidence. The practice of maintaining a crime scene log that documents all persons who entered a scene is a great practice, not only if documentation of their shoes for elimination is needed, but also to act as a deterrent for anyone who wishes to but has no reason to enter the scene.

The use of stepping plates strategically placed in critical areas of the scene allows crime scene technicians to minimize stepping on the actual scene substrate. An example of the use of stepping plates is provided in Figure 1.14. Alternately, some crime scene technicians employ booties to cover their shoes to prevent adding additional patterns to the scene. Common sense and resourcefulness should be used to establish a minimally intrusive route into, through, and out of the crime scene you are processing.

Figure 1.15 is a diagram of a crime scene involving a hypothetical burglary and homicide that illustrates some of the ways footwear impressions are typically produced. Beginning outside of the forced point of entry an impression made in soil lies beneath the broken garage window (1), while latent shoe impressions were transferred to pieces of broken glass just inside (2). As the perpetrator tracked through the garage and a storage room,

---

* Dr. Edmond Locard (1877–1966) was a French pioneer in forensic science.

Figure 1.14 The use of stepping plates allows crime scene technicians access to the scene while minimizing interference with impression and other evidence. Plates provided courtesy of TriTech Forensics, www.tritechforensics.com, 2014.

his or her shoes picked up dust and residue from the dirty floor (3). As the perpetrator continued into the next room, the shoes transferred that dust and residue back onto the finished nonporous wood floor (4). The perpetrator now entered a carpeted room where the shoes acquired a very thin coating of dust from the carpet. During the ransacking of a desk drawer, papers were knocked to the floor and stepped on, transferring latent but highly detailed dry dust impressions to the paper (5). As the perpetrator moved around in the area of the bleeding victim, he or she stepped in the blood and subsequently tracked a series of blood impressions across the carpet and onto the covered front porch when exiting (6). Finally, the perpetrator stepped on newly fallen snow sticking to the front walkway when leaving the scene (7).

The examples provided in this hypothetical scene, as well as many others, occur every day at crime scenes. Crime scene investigators familiar with the variety of ways that footwear impressions can be formed are able to approach a scene visualizing the various substrate materials (carpet, tile, wood, snow, dirt) and their condition (clean, dirty, wet, dry) and realize the potential for impression-rich areas. Referring to Figure 1.15, it is not unusual in an actual case to learn that only the most obvious and visible heavy blood marks such as those on the carpet at area 6, the impression in soil at area 1, and the impressions in snow at area 7 were found and photographed with no further processing, lifting, or casting taking place. In many instances, the other impressions would not be found. On the other hand, a person well trained and experienced would process the scene more methodically. They would recognize the potential for finding latent shoe marks on the pieces of glass at area 2, subjecting the glass pieces to a detailed inspection with proper lighting, and preserving them for examination and enhancement. They would see the dirty condition of the floor at area 3 and understand the potential of locating both impressions in the dust in area 3 as well as latent dusty transfer impressions as the perpetrator continued to walk upon and deposit that dust onto the clean wood floor in area 4. The experienced crime scene investigator would use oblique lighting and/or electrostatic and/or other lifting techniques in that area to locate and recover latent impressions. They would also immediately

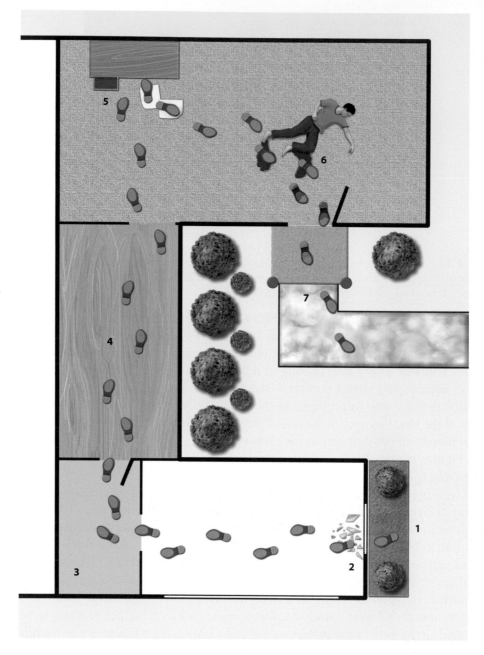

Figure 1.15 This hypothetical crime scene depicts many areas where footwear impressions are routinely produced.

recognize the value in the pieces of paper on the ground at area 5, understanding that if the perpetrator had stepped on them they would almost certainly contain highly detailed latent shoe prints. The examiners would either treat the papers electrostatically at the scene or preserve the papers for treatment later in the laboratory. They would then recover the heavier visible impressions in blood near the victim, but also recognize that they are often the least detailed, and in subsequent steps onto the porch the perpetrator's blood-soaked outsoles would have deposited thinner bloody shoe marks that would reveal greater detail after enhancement with chemical reagents. They would also be sure to cast the impressions in soil at area 1 and in the snow at area 7 after the proper photography of those impressions.

This hypothetical example is provided to make two important points: first, much of the highly detailed footwear evidence is latent and requires specific techniques and an aggressive approach to successfully locate and recover; and second, when crime scene technicians are equipped with the proper materials, knowledge, and experience, they can recognize the full potential of various areas and conditions at a scene that contains latent footwear impressions that would otherwise go undiscovered.

General Search Methods

Although some impressions are clearly visible at a crime scene, search methods for two-dimensional impressions, many of which are latent, require more diligence to find and recover. To be thorough, as well as to maintain control, it is much more manageable to methodically search for impressions in one small area or room at a time. The initial use of an intense oblique light source works well for detecting dust and residue transfer impressions on smooth surfaces like tile or wood flooring, countertops, and other nonporous substrates. Portable LED lights or alternate light sources (ALS) are commonly used to provide oblique light, but any high-intensity light source can be effective. Whenever possible, the room should be darkened and the high-intensity oblique light should be positioned at a low angle of incidence to graze the ground. Figure 1.16 illustrates this method, for which an ALS, LED, or other high-intensity light source can be used. Holding the light too high will not provide the same degree of success. Oblique light usually does not work as well and often not at all on textured surfaces like paper, raw wood, cardboard, or carpeting, so failing to find impressions on those substrates does not mean they are not present. Even when on smooth substrates many latent impressions in very fine dust, residue, or blood are so

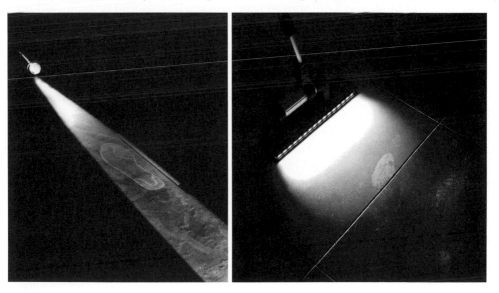

Figure 1.16 The use of a high-intensity ALS and LED oblique light sources in a darkened area will reveal footwear evidence that is not visible in normal ambient light. These are most effective when the light grazes the floor.

faint that high-intensity and oblique lighting will not reveal them. That same intense light source can also be used to bounce light off of the substrate at different angles from opposite sides of a room to detect some impressions that only appear with reflected light. In the end, despite the use of high-intensity light, some latent impressions will still not be visualized.

An additional nondestructive detection tool to search for latent impressions is the electrostatic lifter. Electrostatic lifting transfers dry origin dust and residue impressions to a black film, enabling the recovery of many impressions that otherwise would go undetected. It is routinely used to search large areas where the perpetrator potentially tracked dry dust or residue from one surface (dusty porch, carpet) onto a relatively clean surface (tile or finished wood flooring, paper on floor) such as illustrated between area 3 and area 4 in Figure 1.15. The procedures for using the electrostatic lifter are further addressed in Chapter 5.

Concerning scenes where the perpetrator has tracked through blood, the use of chemical reagents can both detect and enhance latent impressions. On nonporous substrates such as counters or flooring, only after nondestructive methods have been unsuccessful should the application of fingerprint powders to develop impressions be attempted.

Gait Measurements

Gait analysis is the systematic study of human walking. It has traditionally been used to help runners and athletes increase their efficiency, to help diagnose and treat persons recovering from injuries, and for use in the medical management of diseases that affect the locomotor system. The term "forensic gait analyses" is a more recent application and can generally be divided into two categories. One application involves the analysis of surveillance video of a person walking through a crime scene, and involves their visible traits related to their body movements and gait as they walk, including such things as limping, postures, limb and head movements, and the like. With the increased presence of surveillance cameras, research regarding the use and reliability of this information is evolving.[*,†] The second application involves the measurement and use of distances between foot and/or shoe impressions at a crime scene. It is this aspect of the human gait that is being addressed hereafter.

Measurements associated with the human gait include *stride length*, which is the linear distance between two successive steps of the same foot, and *step length*, which is the linear distance that a foot moves in front of the opposite one. The *stride width*, also known as the *walking base*, is the transverse distance between the left and right foot impressions measured perpendicular to the direction traveled. It is measured at the mid-point of the heel. The *foot angle*, also known as the *toe-out* or *toe-in*, is an angular measurement of the midline of the foot in relation to the direction of travel.[‡] These characteristics are not unique to an individual, but are very general measurements that are shared by others. Basic measurements of the human gait are illustrated in Figure 1.17.

[*] Larsen, P., Simonsen, E., and Lynnerup, N., Gait analysis in forensic medicine, http://www.imaging.org/ist/publications/reporter/articles/Rep22_2_EI2007_6491_Larsen.pdf, 2007.
[†] Iwama, H., Muramatsu, D., Makihara, Y., and Yagi, Y., Gait-based person-verification system for forensics, The Institute of Scientific and Industrial Research, Osaka University, Osaka, Japan, 2012.
[‡] Whittle, M. W., *Gait Analysis*, Butterworth-Heinemann, Oxford, England, 1996, pp. 61–62.

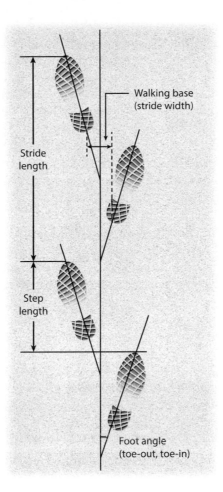

Figure 1.17 Human gait measurements.

Research and medical references have documented the fact that gait measurements also vary considerably within the same individual simply based on speed, substrate condition, and other factors. Studies made regarding the influence of walking speed on the gait pattern have concluded that with increased walking speed, the stride length and stride width increase but the out-toeing angle decreases.[*] Studies have also been made of human locomotion and gait regarding the speed and duration of the walking cycle and the duration of the temporal components of the walking cycle.[†,‡,§] Further, studies regarding the coefficient of friction as it relates to the slip resistance of shoes have been conducted and offer other reasons for gait to vary within the same individual. One such study regarding the coefficient of friction versus top-piece/outsole hardness and walking speed concluded

[*] Murray, M. P., Kory, C., Clarkson, B. H., and Sepic, S. B., Comparison of the free and fast speed walking patterns of normal men, *Am. J. Phys. Med.*, 45(1):8–24, 1966.
[†] Murray, M. P., Drought, A. B., and Kory, R. C., Walking patterns of normal men, *J. Bone & Joint Surg.*, 46-A:335–360, 1964.
[‡] Drillis, R. J., Objective recording and biomechanics of pathological gait, *Ann. New York Acad. Sci.*, 74:86–109, 1958.
[§] Smith, K. W., McDermid, C. D., and Shideman, F. E., Analysis of the temporal components of motion in human gait, *Am. J. Phys. Med.*, 39:142–151, 1960.

that both outsole and top-piece hardness and flexibility of footwear might affect forefoot flexibility, which may in turn affect stride length and gait dynamics.[*] Further, this study concluded that other factors, such as the type and condition of the surface walked upon, caused differences in the kinetics and kinematics of walking, as the subjects in the study adapted to the various aspects of the walkway surfaces. Examples of this are experienced in everyday life as individuals consciously or subconsciously change their gait characteristics as they walk over a slippery icy surface or while at the beach as they walk from firm wet sand onto the softer dry sand. Stride measurements from a crime scene are also influenced by many factors that cause perpetrators to adjust their stride as they walk and maneuver over various substrates and commit various actions within that scene.

It is rare for a crime scene to include successive impressions that represent a sustained "gait" of a perpetrator, but even if this evidence presented itself, there is no reliable or accurate way to know if that individual was walking slowly, walking at a moderate speed, walking fast, and so forth. There is also no way to know if that person was carrying something heavy or was involved in some other activity or distractions that affected their gait. The normal and potentially extreme variations of an individual's gait provide an obstacle to obtaining accurate known gait impressions of any individual for comparative purposes. Further, even if it were arguably possible to provide some level of association between gait characteristics exhibited in a series of crime scene impressions and a set of known gait patterns obtained from a suspect, these measurement characteristics are not individual traits but are shared by many, and thus cannot be used to establish the personal identity of an individual.

Knowledge and observance of gait measurements found on exterior substrates are used in the tracking of individuals by expert trackers.[†,‡] An actual gait measurement is not obtained, but a measuring stick of sorts is used to estimate the position between subsequent signs and/or successive steps. Tracking is an appropriate use of this type of information because the tracker is not relying on any measurement as a means of personal identification but only to assist in the possible location of other signs or impressions in order that they may "track" the individual.

Key Words: wet origin, dry origin, two-dimensional impression, three-dimensional impression, transfer impression, positive impression, negative impression, outsole, oblique lighting.

Key Points

1. Written records of using footwear impression evidence to assist in criminal matters have existed for hundreds of years.
2. Along with fingerprints and DNA, footwear impressions are, by volume, the largest categories of evidence encountered at crime scenes.
3. Footwear impressions are present in a significant percentage of crime scenes but many are latent and must be aggressively and methodically searched for.

[*] Fendly, A. E., and Medoff, H. P., Required coefficient of friction versus top-piece/outsole hardness and walking speed; Significance and correlation, *J. Forensic Sci.*, 41(5):763–769, 1996.
[†] Kearney, J., *Tracking: A Blueprint For Learning How*, Pathways Press, El Cajon, CA, July 1983.
[‡] Speiden, R., *Foundations for Awareness, Signcutting and Tracking*, Natural Awareness Tracking School, Christiansburg, VA, 2009.

4. Footwear evidence provides assistance in including and excluding individuals as the contributors of those impressions; can provide valuable information that can link or associate a person to multiple crime scenes; can reveal the brand and size of footwear the perpetrator was wearing; can often provide information regarding the number of perpetrators; can associate involvement in a crime based on the type, origin and location of impressions; and can confirm or dispute alibis of suspected individuals.

5. Footwear impressions occur in all levels of detail at crime scenes due to the variable substrates and conditions.

6. The preservation and recovery of footwear evidence is directly related to the success of any subsequent examination with the shoe of a suspect.

Photographing Footwear Evidence

2

Photography is used daily for many reasons and by many persons. For most, photography is used to capture memories of family, vacations, weddings, and other events. For others, it is also a commercial venture used for catalogs, magazines, newspapers, and advertisements. Photography is also used as a medium of artistic expression, whether the documentation of cultures or the capture of a sunrise or sunset. For all of these uses, photographers are free to use various qualities of cameras, lenses, lighting, and their own skills and creative methods to achieve their goal. In contrast, the use of photography for the recovery of evidence is different. There is an explicit purpose and responsibility to photograph the evidence in a prescribed way that will ensure a high level of detail and accuracy essential for later use in a forensic examination. This chapter will address established best practices and procedures for the photographic documentation and recovery of footwear impression evidence. It is not intended to be a substitute for basic photographic training or experience or as instruction regarding features of the specific camera you are using.

Cameras of the Past

Cameras in the late 1800s and early 1900s were heavy and cumbersome. The weight and size of those cameras combined with the slow speed of film emulsions mandated long exposure times and the use of a tripod. The camera and tripod combination could easily weigh 50 pounds. Nevertheless, although not as convenient or reliable, these cameras were used to record evidence at scenes of crimes. Over time, these large cameras evolved into smaller cameras, making them more practical for scene documentation of evidence. Although still not small by today's standards, the 4 × 5 inch camera with hand-loaded sheet film and a detachable flash provided for exceptional recording of crime scene evidence. By the 1960s, 2¼ inch and 35 mm format cameras were commonplace in the hands of many crime scene units as well as everyday citizens. Black and white film was normally used, but film continued to improve and eventually color film with acceptable grain quality became an option. Through those years, police departments used a variety of the 4 × 5 inch, 2¼ inch, and 35 mm camera formats and films. On the left of Figure 2.1 is a 4 × 5 inch Speed Graphic camera used by the FBI and most police agencies through the 1970s, and by many departments for years later. Figure 2.2 depicts the use of the Speed Graphic camera and flash while demonstrating the photography of impression evidence. In the center of Figure 2.1 is a medium format Mamiya 645 film camera, and on the right is a 35 mm Canon F-1 camera. In the years before the conversion to digital cameras, more advanced 35 mm cameras were equipped with automatic exposure and motorized film advance capabilities. Exposed rolls of 24 or 36 exposure 35 mm film could be conveniently developed at the police department laboratory or at a local overnight photo service. In casework during those years, it

Figure 2.1 A large format 4 × 5 inch Speed Graphic camera with film holder in foreground. The film holder held two hand-loaded sheets of 4 x 5 inch film. The holder was inserted into a slot on the side of the camera. While in the camera, a thin metal slide covering the film was pulled out before each exposure after which it was replaced to protect the exposed film. The camera shutter had to be manually cocked prior to each exposure. A large flash unit (not shown) with a long coiled cord and a glass flashbulb provided off-camera lighting. In the center is the medium format 2¼ inch Mamiya 645 camera, and on the right the 35 mm Canon F-1.

was not at all unusual to receive evidence that included sets of 35 mm negatives still in the original "one-hour" folder from where that film was commercially processed.

The Digital Camera Emerges

The first experimentations with a digital camera go back many years and include cameras such as Kodak's 100 × 100 pixel sensor digital prototype in 1975. In 1999, the Nikon D1, and in 2000, the Fujifilm Finepix S1 Pro and the Canon D30 were among the first digital single lens reflex (DSLR) cameras to make their way into use for crime scene photography. The lower resolutions of these early digital cameras, around 2.7 megapixels for the D1 and 3.0 megapixels for the D30, were not capable of capturing the higher level of detail that was possible with film. The low resolution of those cameras prevented them from capably photographing a footwear impression that could later be enlarged to its natural size. For that reason, many police departments properly resisted the change to digital cameras or used them in combination with film cameras. Today, the higher quality professional DSLR cameras equal and in many ways surpass the capabilities of film and film cameras. Professional DSLR cameras with digital backs combined with less cumbersome wireless flash units provide an efficient way to photographically document and recover footwear impression

Figure 2.2 A 1960s vintage photograph of a Special Agent at the FBI Academy demonstrating the use of the Speed Graphic camera and flash to recover impression evidence.

evidence. Whereas film and processing were expensive and always limited the number of exposures taken at scenes, digital cameras with inexpensive storage cards and other storage options now allow for an unlimited quantity of exposures. Photographers who used film cameras had little idea of the success of each exposure until the film was later developed. With the digital cameras of today, each exposure can be instantly viewed on the camera's large LCD screen. Even better, the photographer can frame and preview the impression prior to making the exposure with the use of the live view setting, as shown in Figure 2.3.

Figure 2.3 Using the live view option enables the photographer to frame the shoe impression and ruler through the digital display on the back of a DSLR camera prior to the exposure.

Even though the digital age has provided the opportunity to photograph evidence more efficiently, nothing is guaranteed. It is still essential that photographers be well trained, knowledgeable, and experienced with the specific camera they are using, and that they follow the best practices while photographing impression evidence. Stated simply and bluntly, someone who took bad photographs with a film camera is equally able to take bad photographs with a digital camera.

Although crime scene photography is now performed with digital cameras, many cold cases are still being actively investigated, some dating back decades. In many of those cases, the original photographs were taken with film cameras. In addition, for a period of years, there was a transition time between film and digital cameras when it was often the practice of police departments to use various combinations of film and low-resolution digital cameras. It was not uncommon for a roll of film to be processed at a one-hour photo service with the option of digitally converting the film images and placing those images onto a compact disc (CD). These images were usually transferred at high speed with very low resolution, but this low-resolution CD was often then submitted as evidence in lieu of the film. Many did this unknowingly, believing that anything digital was an improvement over film. The significance of this is that investigators working on cold cases today might be provided digital images on a CD and mistakenly believe the original photographs were taken with a digital camera, when in fact the original film negatives containing far better detail may exist. The best evidence for a film camera is the original film negative and for a digital camera the original archived digital files. If you are requested to examine photographs taken with film, the negatives can be scanned at a high resolution and saved as a digital file.

The Camera and Its Resolution

Camera technology continues to change rapidly. In the past, digital cameras were spoken of in two categories: fixed lens "point and shoot" cameras and professional DSLR cameras. The point and shoot cameras have traditionally been more compact, designed for simple operation, less expensive, and used mostly for taking informal photographs. Modern day smart phones, such as the iPhone, are now the most common point-and-shoot cameras. Some point-and-shoot cameras, including smart phones, may have higher megapixel ratings than many DSLR cameras, but they also have lower quality lenses, smaller sensors, and fall way short of having the features needed to capably document evidence. Figure 2.4 shows three photographs of a full impression in soil taken by a smart phone, a traditional point-and-shoot camera, and a professional DSLR camera. The top portion includes an enlarged area of each photograph showing the contrast in the detail. Point and shoot cameras and smart phones should not be used for the photography of crime scene evidence. Professional DSLR cameras have enormous capabilities, including high-quality interchangeable lenses, higher resolution, better focus options, live view, a changeable lens, aperture priority mode, the ability to take RAW images, wireless off-camera flash capability, and full frame sensors. They are the recommended cameras for the recovery of crime scene and impression evidence.

Regardless of the specific DSLR camera used, crime scene and examination quality photography should always be taken using the largest resolution possible. A simple definition of resolution is "the ability to see separate items in the object as separate in the

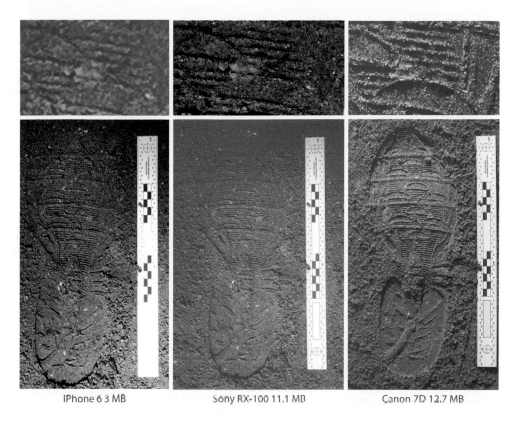

IPhone 6 3 MB   Sony RX-100 11.1 MB   Canon 7D 12.7 MB

Figure 2.4 Three photographs of a full impression taken with an iPhone 6, a Sony RX-100 point and shoot camera, and a Canon 7D DSLR camera. The enlarged area at the top represents about a 1- × 1.5-inch portion of the photograph.

image."* Camera resolution is commonly discussed in a comparative way based on the total number of pixels in the image as calculated by multiplying pixel columns by pixel rows and dividing by one million. However, many other factors besides megapixel ratings influence the final image quality, including the sensor size, pixel qualities, and sharpness of focus and lens quality. A point and shoot camera with an 18-megapixel rating will not be able to produce the same quality image that can be obtained using an 18-megapixel rated full sensor professional DSLR camera.

In 2004–2005, the Institute for Forensic Imaging, funded by the National Institute of Justice, conducted a study to see how well experienced footwear examiners could differentiate detail in photographs of footwear impressions taken with four different camera types. The cameras used included a 120 Pentax 6 × 7 film camera, a 35 mm Canon EOS film camera, a Canon EOS-10D (6.3 megapixels) and a Kodak DCS Pro 14n (13.5 megapixels) digital cameras.† Each camera was used to photograph the same impression evidence in a very standardized way. Experienced footwear examiners were then asked to examine specific areas of photographs taken with each camera. The 120 Pentax camera with film produced slightly better detail, but the examiners were unable to differentiate between detail in

* Blitzer, H., Stein-Ferguson, K., and Huang, J., *Understanding Forensic Digital Imaging*, Academic Press, Amsterdam, 2008, p. 314.
† Blitzer, H., Hammer, R., and Jacobia, J., Effect of photographic technology on quality of examination of footwear impressions, *JFI*, 57(5):641–657, 2007.

photographs made using the 35-mm film camera and the two digital cameras. Thus within the parameters of this specific study, professional DSLR cameras were able to effectively capture detail competitive with that of the 35 mm film camera. It found that images made with the Canon EOS-10D 6-megapixel resolution digital camera, particularly if printed on a high-end printer, were equally suitable for examination, and could not be distinguished from images taken with the other cameras. It should be noted that the cameras used in the study were each equipped with a quality lens and all photographs were taken in focus and with identical lighting. As a matter of interest, later research determined that a top of the line 35 mm film camera and lens using Kodak T-Max 100 film had the equivalent of 13.7 megapixels.[*] Overall, the final recommendation made because of that study was that a DSLR camera with a minimum resolution of 8 megapixels be used.[†] The Scientific Working Group for Imaging Technology made this recommendation as well.[‡] Many years after this now outdated study, professional DSLR cameras will and should far exceed those recommendations.

File Format Choices

In the years since digital cameras were first used for the capture of evidence, much has changed. Storage cards were once low capacity and expensive; thus the Joint Image Photographic Experts Group (JPEG) format with its lossy compression was popular and economical and allowed more images to be stored. However, with the JPEG format, the camera automatically makes adjustments in white balance, color values, contrast, sharpness, and other settings before converting the image to the JPEG file on the storage card. The photographer has no control over this, and this automatic conversion process loses raw data and some image quality that cannot be recovered later. If for some reason you must use the JPEG format for capturing images, the highest quality resolution setting with the least compression should be selected in the JPEG mode of the camera you use. If you decide to later process any JPEG images of impressions using programs such as Adobe Photoshop, you should save that image as a tagged image file format (TIFF) file, and only then continue with any processing.

Because the forensic photography of evidence is critical to capturing the greatest amount of detail, most recommend the use of a raw image format (RAW). The RAW format allows for capture of original unprocessed data just as was done with the film negatives of the past. Today, almost all professional DSLR cameras have the ability to capture and store images in the RAW format.[§] Low prices and high capacity storage makes this both practical and possible. Many cameras are capable of capturing both JPEG and RAW images simultaneously, either on the same storage card or with the use of two separate storage card slots. Camera technology is changing rapidly but the point made here is that when selecting a DSLR camera for evidence photography and when operating that camera, the choice and use of file capture and storage are important to consider.

---

[*] Personal communication with Herb Blitzer, January 29, 2012 and referenced in Chapter 17 of *Understanding Forensic Digital Imaging*, Blitzer, Stein-Ferguson, and Huang, p. 318, Academic Press, 2008.

[†] Blitzer, H., and Jacobia, J., *Effect of Technology on Footwear Photography*, presented at the International Association for Identification International Education Conference, July 2006.

[‡] Scientific Working Group for Imaging Technology, www.swgit.org, General Guidelines for Photographing Footwear and Tire Impressions, Section 9, September 27, 2013.

[§] Nikon's version of a raw image format is the Nikon Electronic Format (NEC).

Storage and Management of Images

As exposures are made during the photographic documentation of a crime scene, all should be maintained. This means if 100 photographs are taken, they should all be saved, regardless of whether they are out of focus, accidental, or less than perfect exposures. This is standard protocol and establishes the integrity and complete record of what was photographed at the scene. Images on the storage card must be archived, normally by downloading them from the storage card to a computer or directly onto a DVD. An archived image should be an exact copy of what the camera recorded onto the storage card. Some refer to this as digital film. The archived images should be stored in a safe manner to ensure they are not lost and to ensure that a copy of those original unaltered files is maintained. Many departments keep two copies of the digital images, with one being in a fire secure location separate from the other. There are many considerations with the security and storage of digital images, and any forensic photographer, laboratory, or police department generating these images should have a good plan in place. There are commercial companies that sell software and specialize in this type of file management if such assistance is needed.

General Crime Scene Photography

General crime scene photography is the process of taking photographs of the overall crime scene from various distances and positions in order to record and document that scene and the items of evidence within it. No linear scale is necessary and in most cases, where ambient light is adequate, exposure times are sufficiently fast to allow the images to be taken while holding the camera. When taking general crime scene photographs, each impression or item of evidence should have an identifier positioned next to it so as to assign each its own specific number (1, 2, 3) or letter (A, B, C). Later, that same identifier can be used in any notes that refer to a particular impression and should also be used on subsequent examination quality photographs, lifts, or casts of the same impression. Figure 2.5 includes three general crime scene photographs of a mock scene that illustrate how this simple technique can be used. The overall long range, medium range, and close range photographs provide a "zoom-in" effect that documents the footwear impression identified as item #8. Written notes taken about that impression will refer to that same number. Later, examination quality photographs taken of that impression will use that same #8 on a label in each photograph. Eventually, the impression will be cast and the label containing the same #8 will be set into the back of the cast. If this were a two-dimensional impression, #8 would be used to identify any lift made of that impression.

Written notes should refer to those specific identifier designations and should be supplemented with descriptions of impressions (i.e., a muddy impression on sidewalk), their direction (i.e., heading up exterior basement stairway, etc.), and any notable weather and substrate conditions (dew on grass, impression in newly fallen snow on front walkway, wet origin tracks just inside forced point of entry on a rainy day, etc.).

It is extremely important to note here that general crime scene photographs such as those in Figure 2.5 are not suitable or adequate for detailed comparisons with known footwear but are taken strictly as part of the documentation process.

Figure 2.5 General crime scene photographs typically include long distance or overall (top), medium distance (center), and close range (bottom) photographs. These are taken with the use of identifiers to document the evidence at the crime scene. These types of photographs are for documenting the scene and are not of value for later detailed forensic comparison with footwear.

Examination Quality Photography

Examination quality photographs such as the one depicted in Figure 2.6 are taken from directly over the top of the impression, specifically for use in a direct physical examination with known footwear. Evidence such as shoe impressions, tire impressions, bare foot impressions, fingerprints, tool marks, blunt force pattern injuries, and bite marks need to be photographed in this prescribed way to ensure the *maximum* amount of detail is recorded with accuracy. Failure to follow the proper procedures will seriously compromise the value of those photographs in any subsequent forensic examination. Even though some footwear examiners' duties don't include the recovery of evidence from crime scenes, they need to

Figure 2.6 An examination quality photograph of the impression alongside identifier #8 in Figure 2.5. Note the label placed on the ruler that reads #8 and associates this photograph with the general crime scene identifier. The same label will be set into the freshly poured cast later made of this impression.

be trained and experienced in the photography of impression evidence in order to properly evaluate photographs submitted for examination, to understand and recognize a photograph's limitations, and to provide guidance and training to crime scene investigators.

A professional DSLR camera should always be used for this type of photography. The use of a standard or normal lens, one that produces an image that roughly matches what the human eye sees (normally around 60 mm), will require you to adjust the height of the camera on the tripod to properly frame the area you are photographing. As an alternative a zoom lens can be used, but in doing so, avoid adjusting the lens to wide angles and try to stay close to the normal focal length.

Figure 2.7 provides a convenient summary of the overall process of taking examination quality photographs. Additional information and instructions about each component of this procedure are discussed hereafter.

EXAMINATION QUALITY PHOTOGRAPHY

1. The Camera. Use a professional DSLR camera set at its highest resolution. Choose Aperture Priority with the appropriate f-stop. Select RAW or the combined RAW/JPEG setting. Select the ISO setting and manual focus. Use the camera's timer along with the wireless remote flash capabilities and remote flash as necessary for your camera to provide off camera oblique light.

2. Prepare Impression. Place an L-shaped or long straight flat ruler alongside the length of the impression. If it is a three-dimensional impression, carefully position the ruler on the same plane (level) as the bottom of the impression. Include a label on the ruler to link this impression to the identifier number used in the general crime scene photographs and notes, as well as in subsequent casts or lifts.

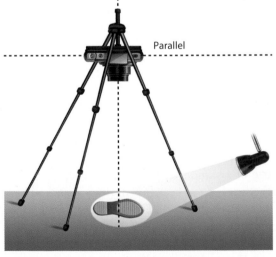

3. Position the Camera. Attach the camera to the tripod and position it directly above the impression. Make sure the sensor (focal) plane of the camera is parallel to the impression being photographed. Use the Live View Mode or viewfinder to assure the impression and ruler fill the image frame.

Figure 2.7 The procedure for taking examination quality photographs. (*Continued*)

4. Focus the camera. Manual focus is recommended and most reliable for sharp focus. Focus on the impression and not the ruler. If the impression is three-dimensional, focus on the bottom of the impression. Always re-focus after each exposure.

5. Use Oblique Lighting. Oblique lighting should be used in most instances for both two-dimensional and three-dimensional impressions, as it provides better contrast. If indoors, darken the room if possible prior to exposure. If outdoors and there is bright ambient sunlight, use a sun shield to allow the flash to become the dominant light source.

6. Photograph. Make the exposure while positioning the flash at least 5 to 6 feet from the impression. This allows the light to evenly illuminate the impression. Aim the flash toward the impression from the appropriate height. Re-check the focus and take the next exposure. Take multiple exposures with the flash positioned from at least three angles (sides) around the impression.

Figure 2.7 (Continued) The procedure for taking examination quality photographs.

Scales

Photographs taken of crime scene impressions require the proper use of a scale so it can later be used to accurately enlarge the impression to its natural size. Figure 2.8 depicts a photograph of a shoe impression taken without a scale. There is no way to know the dimensions of that impression and no information that would enable the enlargement of that photograph to its natural size for examination. To make this point, another photograph of that impression containing a scale is provided at the end of this chapter.

The term "natural size" refers to a photograph that has been enlarged so the impression in the photograph is its actual size in real life.* During the enlargement and printing process, if a 12-inch ruler were used, the enlargement would be made so the image of the ruler in the photographic print was 12 inches. To make this as accurate as possible, the ruler is positioned alongside the length of the impression and, in the case of a three-dimensional impression, on the same plane (level) as the bottom of that impression. Without proper positioning of the scale, it will not be possible to accurately enlarge the image to its natural size and conduct a subsequent dimensional analysis during any examination.

In the past, numerous items have been used as scales. Some were so deficient they restricted the ability to accurately produce a natural size enlargement. Figure 2.9 depicts some scales that were not the best choices available. These included thick yardsticks, sculptured school rulers, retractable metal and cloth tape measures, coins, short 1- and 2-inch scales, and paper laboratory or police department scales. Paper scales are often photocopied, a practice that compromises any assurance of dimensional accuracy.

After years of receiving evidence photographs containing poor scale choices, an effort was undertaken to design a more universal and accurate scale for both crime scene and laboratory use. That effort by four individuals in the FBI Laboratory resulted in the creation of an L-shaped ruler often referred to as the Bureau scale.† This L-shaped ruler,

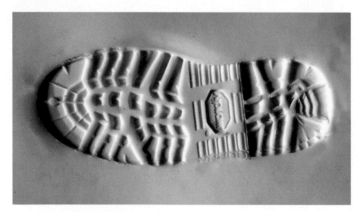

Figure 2.8 The size of a photographed impression cannot be determined when a scale is not used.

* The term "natural size" should not be confused with the original photographic term of "one to one" (1:1). Natural size simply means the photograph was enlarged so the image is its natural size. True 1:1 photographs were possible only when large film format cameras were common and the size of the image on the film negative was equal to the actual life size of the object being photographed. Because full-length footwear impressions are often 10–13 inches, it would be necessary to have a large format film camera with a film negative of that size before it would be possible to take a true 1:1 photograph. Today, it is both common and acceptable to use the terms 1:1 and "natural size" interchangeably.

† This was done collectively in 1988 by four individuals in the FBI Laboratory: Gerald Richards, William Bodziak, Danny Keen, and David Lowe.

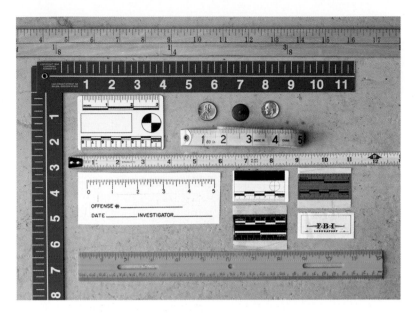

Figure 2.9 Some examples of scales that are not the best choice for use in footwear impression photography. Rulers too thick or beveled, flimsy tape measures, short scales, and coins create problems and limitations in accuracy when enlarging the images.

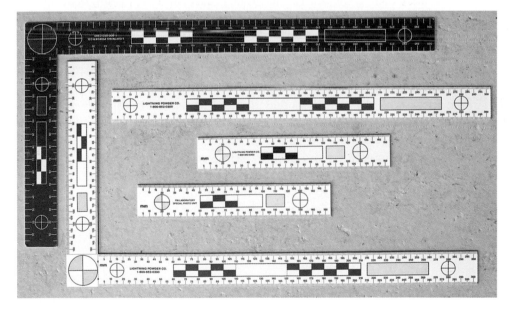

Figure 2.10 The Bureau scale originally sold as a pair of rulers, one being the L-shaped ruler, the other the short 150 mm ruler.

depicted in Figure 2.10, is thin but reasonably rigid and nonreflective. It contains a metric scale in increments of 1 mm. Its total outside length is 13 inches and the ruler's thickness is approximately 1 mm. Features like its 90° L-shape and the inclusion of circles assist in the detection of perspective problems that occur when a camera was not positioned properly over and parallel to the impression. The 90° L-shape, if photographed at an angle, will not reflect a true 90°. When the circles are photographed straight on, they will appear round but if photographed at an angle the circles will appear elliptical. The black side is useful for longer exposures and when photographing dark objects such as black shoe soles or black electrostatic and gelatin lifters. As included in Figure 2.10, the L-shape Bureau scale can be cut into a long and short segment where preferred or necessary. Note the short scale at the bottom contains the original words "FBI Laboratory Special Photo Unit." The Lightning Powder Company was requested by the FBI Laboratory to order the rulers with the FBI designation of "Special Photo Unit," but it was also permitted to make copies with the Lightning Powder name for sale to the general public. The overall purpose was to get as many good scales into circulation as possible.

Other linear scales are also suitable for impression photography but should be of sufficient length, thin, flat, rigid, and nonreflective. Preferably, they will have both white and black sides with a finely divided scale in increments of either millimeters or sixteenths of an inch. They should be at least 12 inches (approximately 300 mm) in length, or in the case of partial impressions, they should be no less than 6 inches or 150 mm.

Another reason for using the full length scale involves the comparative ease and accuracy with which that scale can be used when calibrating a photograph to its natural size. During the enlargement process, a slight amount of inaccuracy might occur when using the hash marks on the scale. If the scale used in the photograph was only 1 inch long, or the person making the calibration is 1/32-inch off when using a small 1-inch scale, that will translate into 12 times that 1/32-inch amount for a 12-inch footwear impression, resulting in a total error of 3/8 inch. If the full 12-inch scale is used, and the person making the calibration is a total of 1/32 inch off, the error would total only 1/32 inch. The same accuracy limitations were true in the past when making enlargements with film in a darkroom. Using a long scale not only assists in the enlargement of accurate natural sized photographs, but it is also much easier to accurately position a longer ruler properly alongside an impression than attempting to do so with a 1- or 2-inch scale.

In conjunction with the identifiers that are used in general crime scene photographs, a label containing the same identifier number or letter and possibly other appropriate data should be included and positioned on top of or adjacent to the ruler, as seen in Figure 2.6. When scales are first purchased and used by crime scene technicians and practitioners, they should be checked for accuracy. There are many sources of scales produced worldwide and on a few occasions, errors can occur during a production run and result in an inaccurate scale. A recent study addressed scale specifications and tolerances.[*]

Positioning the Scale

Equally important to the qualities and length of scale is the manner in which that scale is used. Positioning a thin, flat, rigid ruler alongside the length of a two-dimensional impression on a flat surface usually presents no challenges. Positioning a ruler next to a three-dimensional impression can be more complex. With three-dimensional impressions, because it is the bottom of the impression you are attempting to photographically record with sharp focus and accuracy, the scale must be positioned on the same plane (level) and as evenly as possible with the bottom of the impression. Many three-dimensional impressions are reasonably shallow and flat, requiring only a slight excavation to lower the ruler

---

[*] Massimilliano, F. et al., Dimensional Review of Scales in Forensic Photography, August 2013, NCJRS award 2010-DN-R-7121.

to that level. However, some three-dimensional impressions are deeper and/or uneven and require greater diligence. Some three-dimensional impressions may be sufficiently uneven in depth to make this task impossible, which is one of the many reasons a cast subsequently should be made.

In order to demonstrate the importance of placing the scale at the same level as the bottom of the impression, Figure 2.11 was created. It depicts three identical rulers placed on different levels with 1/4 inch between each level. The rulers were photographed on a copy stand from directly above. In the photograph that was taken, the rulers appear to be different sizes even though they are the same length. The ruler closest to the camera appears larger and the ruler farthest away appears smaller. Figure 2.12 shows the correct and incorrect ruler positions from a different perspective. An easy way to understand this is to think of what you see when you stand in the middle of railroad tracks and look at the tracks both near you and in the distance, as in Figure 2.13. They appear larger (wider)

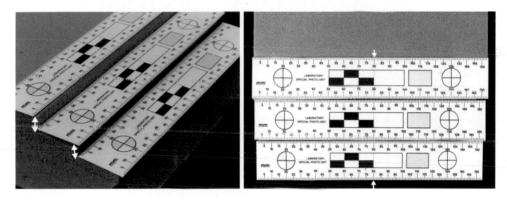

Figure 2.11 On the left, three identical rulers are positioned at three levels, each at ¼ inch difference in height. On the right, a photograph of them taken from above makes it appear the rulers are different in size. This is caused by their different distances from the camera.

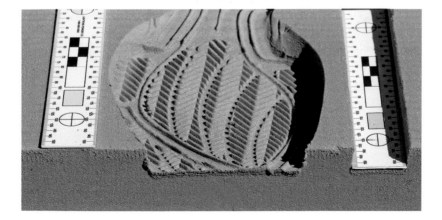

Figure 2.12 A cross-section of a three-dimensional impression demonstrating on the right the correct placement of the ruler at the same depth (level) as the impression's bottom, and on the left, the incorrect placement of the ruler on the substrate's surface, which will cause inaccuracies, as shown in Figure 2.11.

Figure 2.13 The view down railroad tracks demonstrates perspective issues as distances change. The width of the tracks appears to be less in the distance than in the foreground. The same perspective problems occur when photographing three-dimensional impression evidence if the ruler is closer to the camera than the bottom of the impression, as illustrated in Figure 2.11.

when closer to you and smaller (closer together) in the distance. This is not distortion but a simple example of how perspective can change the apparent size of objects both visually and as viewed through a camera. This occurs no differently when placing the scale next to an impression. Failure to place the scale on the same plane as the bottom of a three-dimensional impression will compromise the accuracy of any photographic enlargement of that impression and is an error that will limit any dimensional evaluation.

Another problem occurs when photographs are taken at a slight angle. This most frequently occurs while holding the camera by hand, but can also occur if the camera is not positioned properly on a tripod. Figure 2.14 shows two examples of the perspective problems this creates. In the top example, the camera is viewing the impression from the side by the arrow instead of directly over the top of the impression. The resulting enlarged photographic print will render the distant portion of the scale smaller than the nearer portion. The same perspective issue is seen in the bottom example, only with the camera position from a different side.

Similar scale problems can occur with the use of rulers that have become bent or twisted. This often happens when long or L-shaped rulers are stored in a small camera bag. If the ruler used does not lie flat, as seen in Figure 2.15, the accuracy of the scale of that ruler will be compromised. To illustrate this, I have drawn a red line from the 0–100 mm area and then copied that ruler section and duplicated it next to the end of the ruler. A close examination of the scales shows the measurement between those 100 mm sections is off by at least 3 mm. Photographers of impression evidence should be aware of this and ensure the scale they use lies flat.

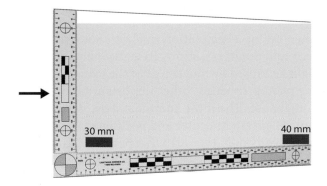

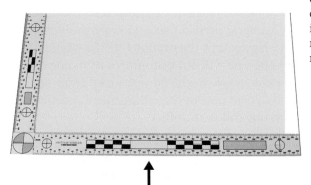

Figure 2.14 If the sensor plane of the camera is not parallel to the impression such as occurs when a camera is not directly over the top of the impression, other perspective issues occur that reduce the accuracy of the scale and any enlargements made.

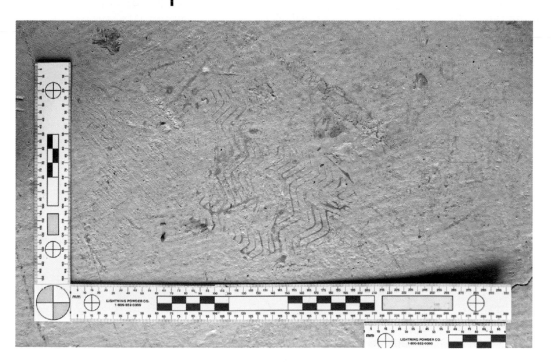

Figure 2.15 Example of a ruler that is not lying flat. The portion of the bent ruler on the right is closer to the camera, and appears larger than the portion of the scale that is flat on the ground. Notice the difference in size of the red-bordered area of the ruler that has been copied and duplicated next to the bent area of the ruler. This reflects an approximate 3-mm difference in that 100-mm portion alone.

Use a Tripod

The use of a good tripod is essential when taking examination quality photographs. It allows the camera to be positioned properly and provides a steady base that helps hold the focus and prevent blur that otherwise might be caused by movement of the camera during exposure. It also frees up the hands of the photographer for other important tasks. There are many excellent tripods from which to choose. The most common style, depicted in Figure 2.16, allows the camera to be mounted beneath its center and positioned so it hangs directly over the impression. Other tripods have a boom type arm that permits the camera to be extended out directly over the impression.

Once the camera is mounted on the tripod, it should be positioned over the impression with the focal plane of the camera parallel to the impression.* With digital cameras, the sensor plane is synonymous with the focal plane. Without a parallel relationship between the impression and sensor plane of the camera, perspective and scale problems will be produced similar to the examples in the Figure 2.14 illustrations. If the camera is tilted just slightly, the scale in the resulting photograph will not be uniform from one end to the other. Although you could enlarge the photograph so the 30 mm scale from one end to the other end on the ruler equaled precisely 300 mm in the enlargement, portions of the scale will be dimensionally different from one end to the other.

Some don't use a tripod and mistakenly believe they can hold a camera steadily in their hands as well as in the proper position to take examination quality photographs. In Figure 2.17, the author demonstrates this poor but all too often encountered practice. Bending over an impression while at the same time trying to hold the camera motionless and in sharp focus, as well as holding the flash far enough away and at the proper angle and height is just not possible. Figure 2.18 is the photograph taken during this demonstration. In this example, the bright ambient sunlight was not shielded from the impression, so the

Figure 2.16 A commonly used tripod that enables the camera to hang beneath the tripod and be positioned directly over the impression. The camera is enabled with a wireless transmitter so no wires need be connected to the flash.

---

* Defined as a plane through a focal point and perpendicular to the axis of a lens, mirror, or other optical system. Thus the focal plane is parallel to the image (impression) and perpendicular to the axis of the lens.

Figure 2.17 The author demonstrates the incorrect method of photographing impression evidence while not using a tripod. Photography without use of a tripod can result in blur, focus, or out-of-perspective problems.

Figure 2.18 The photograph taken by the author in Figure 2.17. Perspective issues, poor lighting and contrast, inaccurate scale, and poor focus are some of the almost assured problems that occur when not using a tripod and the proper photographic procedures.

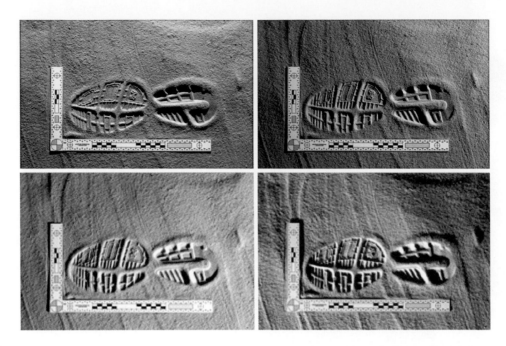

Figure 2.19 Four exposures of the same impression that are framed identically, indicating a tripod was used.

sun was the dominant light source and the flash was unable to provide good contrast. There is also a perspective problem, as the camera was not held parallel to the impression; thus the scale varied along the length of the ruler, limiting any accurate dimensional evaluation. Photographs taken in this manner are more frequently out of focus or blurred due to camera movement. Many think they can take photographs without a tripod and no one will ever know. To the examiner in the laboratory, it is very easy to preview the submitted photographs taken of impressions and determine if a tripod was or was not used. Figure 2.19 represents an example of four sequential exposures taken of an impression when using a tripod. Notice that the precise location and registration of the impression and ruler within the photographic frame are the same, meaning the camera did not move between those exposures. This demonstrates the photographer used a tripod. In the second example in Figure 2.20, the precise location of the impression and ruler is slightly different in each frame, indicating the photographer did not use a tripod and the camera's position changed slightly between each exposure.

Focus

DSLR cameras have high-resolution digital displays that provide a review of each photograph. While a quick glance at the display may appear to confirm what appears to be a well-focused photograph, there is a large difference in what appears to be a focused exposure on the digital display and a photograph that holds sharp focus when that image is considerably enlarged for examination. Failure to take photographs that are in sharp focus is very common. In many cases, the photographer may just be careless about checking the focus or innocently puts too much faith in the camera's autofocus feature. Often the photographer is not fully aware of the various focusing mechanisms on the camera they are using,

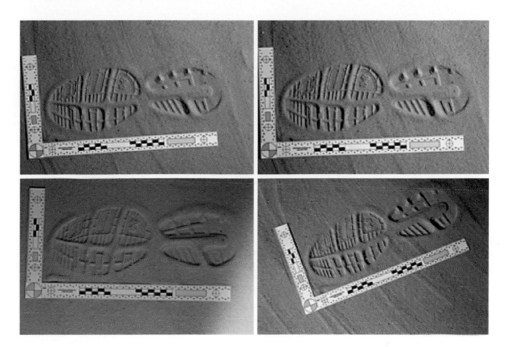

Figure 2.20 Four exposures of the same impression where each exposure was framed differently due to slight changes in the precise position of the hand-held camera. Changes in framing indicate a tripod was not used.

or perhaps they are also not using the aperture priority setting. In other cases, the tripod and/or camera may have been accidently moved or bumped or has simply settled into the soft substrate and the photographer did not take the time to refocus before each exposure. A major reason that enlarged photographs do not reveal the image in sharp focus involves those instances where the photographer uses the autofocus mechanism. Autofocus technology tends to average the focus on multiple spots. There is no way when using autofocus for the photographer to know exactly what the camera is focused on. Producing good photographs that are in sharp focus is not something that just happens but is the result of a conscious and knowledgeable effort of the photographer.

Three-dimensional impressions pose the greatest challenge when focusing. Three photographs were sequentially taken of the same full footwear impression in soil but using different focus choices. The lighting, camera distance, and exposure used were identical. In Figure 2.21, a very small area was enlarged from each photograph. The photograph on the right is sharply focused and was taken with manual focus. Manual focus will always be the most reliable method of focus and is strongly recommended. The center photograph was taken using the regular autofocus selection that brackets numerous points in the photograph. For purposes of convenience and speed, many choose to use this autofocus setting. The results show how the bracketed autofocus choice provided the worst results. The photograph on the left was taken using the spot focus. Spot focus is technically an autofocus function that allows you to aim the focus on a single specific spot. Using a spot focus selection may allow you to focus more successfully on the bottom of the impression but you will not know if it worked for sure until the photographs are later enlarged. It is important to note that each of these photographs was viewed through the LCD display on the back of the camera and all of them initially looked to be in very good focus. The results are no

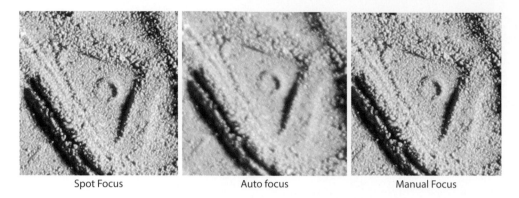

Spot Focus   Auto focus   Manual Focus

Figure 2.21 A greatly enlarged area of an impression using different focus choices. The photograph on the right was taken with manual focus, which is recommended and most reliable; in the center, autofocus was used, which is unpredictable and did not result in sharp focus; and on the left, spot focus, which provides some control but is not as reliable as manual focus. In this example, the spot focus worked well but the results are never known until enlargements are made later.

surprise and actually mimic the photographs routinely received in casework, namely, that at the 4 × 6 inch size they look great, but when they are enlarged for examination, they do not hold sharp focus and therefore restrict the level of detail that can be used in the examination. Every photographer should be familiar with the focus choices on the camera. For close-up detailed photography of footwear impressions, manual focus will always provide the best results. Always refocus before each and every exposure!

Lighting

Lighting plays an important role in the photography of impression evidence. Those who take examination quality photographs by simply pointing the camera and/or using the built-in camera flash will rarely have good results. A built-in or camera-mounted flash results in direct illumination of the impression, often causing a bright reflection known as flash bounce. An example of this is depicted on the right photograph in Figure 2.22. Photographed impressions taken with the existing ambient light may turn out okay but most will have little contrast. The center photograph in Figure 2.22 was taken with the existing interior overhead light (and no flash) and did not provide sufficient contrast to record the faint dust impression. The use of oblique light to illuminate the image from a low angle of incidence will usually provide better contrast. Many also refer to oblique light as "side lighting." The photograph on the left in Figure 2.22 was taken with the overhead lights turned off and the use of a detachable flash that provided an oblique light source.

The failure to use oblique light is one of the most common problems encountered in examining casework photographs. Figure 2.23 illustrates how oblique light works in providing more contrast and detail in the photographic recovery of both two- and three-dimensional evidence. In practice, oblique light should be used when photographing both two-dimensional impressions and three-dimensional impressions in nearly all instances.

Although a separate light source could be used to provide oblique light, detached off-camera flash units are most commonly used. If the flash unit is one that must be attached to the camera with a flash sync cord, that cord will need to be sufficiently long enough for

Figure 2.22 The same area of a wood surface photographed with three different light sources. On the right, the light source was from the built-in camera flash and created flash bounce as well as poor contrast. In the center, only the existing light in the room was used, which still did not visualize or record the impression. On the left, the overhead room lights were turned off and oblique light was used to provide contrast and an excellent photograph of the impression.

the flash to be positioned at the proper height and a minimum distance of 4–6 feet from the impression. Without a long extension cord or a wireless off-camera flash, it will be impossible to position the external flash properly. Both infrared and radio frequency wireless devices are now part of the camera equipment on the market that eliminates the need for a flash sync cord. The camera in Figure 2.16 has a wireless transmitter attached to its flash shoe that activates the flash unit. By using a wireless transmitter combined with the built in timer of the camera and a tripod, the author in Figure 2.16 is able to concentrate on the precise height, position, and direction of the flash during each exposure while at the same time avoiding any camera movement. For those who have camera equipment without this feature, wireless flash triggers and receivers are available that will fit most cameras.

Oblique Light and Two-Dimensional Impressions

For a two-dimensional impression, the flash or other light source must be positioned so the light grazes the surface, allowing the light to reflect off the dust or residue at a 90° angle (Figure 2.23). If the light source is any higher, it will not likely be effective. Hold the flash 4–6 feet away to provide a more even distribution of light over the impression. If the two-dimensional impression is on an interior substrate, the interior lights can be turned down or off to maximize the effect of the oblique light flash and to reduce interference from overhead reflections. The image on the left in Figure 2.22 shows the effective use of oblique lighting to enhance that impression. If the two-dimensional substrate is outside, it may be necessary to block the ambient light as much as possible using a black cloth as a sunscreen, as shown in Figure 2.7.

In some situations involving impressions on two-dimensional surfaces, the impression is only visible when viewed from an angle because of the reflected ambient light. When that

Two-Dimensional Impressions

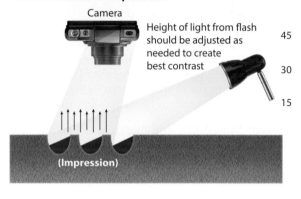

Camera

Light reflected off dust particles into camera

Light from flash held very low to the ground

(Impression)

Oblique light that skims the surface will reflect off the dust or residue at 90 degrees and into the camera lens. The light must be held very low, almost grazing the surface.

Three-Dimensional Impressions

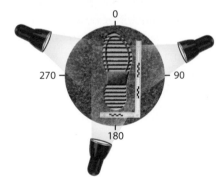

Camera

Height of light from flash should be adjusted as needed to create best contrast

45

30

15

(Impression)

Oblique light creates contrast by shadowing the low areas while illuminating the high areas. The height of the light will be higher with deep impressions and lower with shallow impressions.

0

270

90

180

Holding the light at the proper height, photograph the impression with the light from three different positions around the impression.

Figure 2.23 Using oblique light.

impression is viewed from directly over the top of the impression, the impression becomes either very faint or not visible at all. This may be because the impression is a very thin mark on the surface and thus provides nothing for the oblique light to reflect from. Photographs of impressions of this type often must be taken at the angle from which they are most visible with the reflected ambient light. The impression in Figure 2.24 is a typical one of this type found on a tile floor. The light reflecting off the impression allows for visual detection, but not from directly over the top. In this case, a right-angled ruler is placed around the impression and photographed at the best angle for detail. Other photographic methods and/or subsequent enhancement may provide recovery that is more successful.

Figure 2.24 Impressions that are very thin and do not respond to enhancement with oblique light might only be viewed and photographed at an angle.

Oblique Light and Three-Dimensional Impressions

Figure 2.23 also includes an illustration of how oblique light provides contrast and improved visualization of three-dimensional impressions. The oblique light illuminates the high areas of the impression while creating shadows in the low areas. After exposures are made from the first position exposures should be made from different positions around the impression. As an example, a light source might be positioned at 70°, 180°, and 220° around an impression. The result of doing this is illustrated in Figure 2.25. This technique

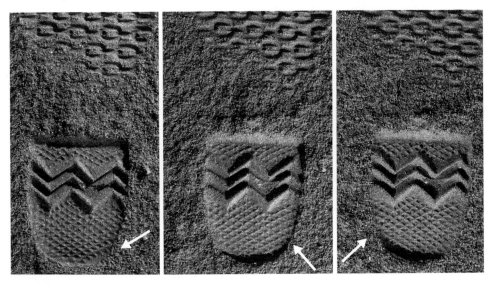

Figure 2.25 Example of how multiple exposures of an impression with oblique light positioned from three different angles (sides) can accumulatively recover more information from the impression than one side alone.

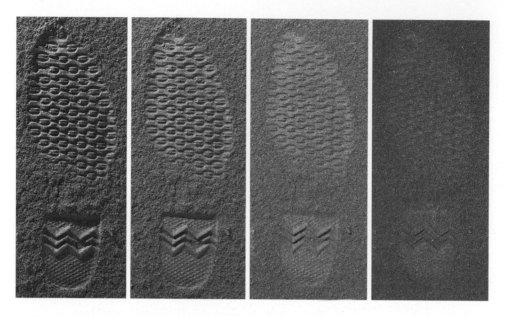

Figure 2.26 Example of oblique lighting used from different heights. Left to right the light was at held at 10°, 25°, 45°, and directly above at 90°.

will collectively capture more detail and information from the impression than photographs with lighting from one position alone.

The optimal height for the oblique light will vary with the depth of each impression. The deeper the impression, the higher the oblique light will need to be positioned or too much shadowing will occur. With shallow impressions, the oblique light must be positioned lower or no shadowing will occur. During daylight hours, the height of the oblique light must be estimated based on experience and the particular impression's depth. After one or two photographs, the results can be viewed on the camera display and adjustments made as needed. The effect of using oblique lights at different heights is shown in Figure 2.26. Photographs of that impression were taken with the height of the oblique light at 10°, 25°, 45°, and 90°.

Blocking Out Sunlight

Crime scene photographs taken of three-dimensional impressions on sunny or bright hazy days require an additional step to obtain the best results. Bright ambient sunlight will be the dominant light source and will reduce or eliminate any effect of the oblique light from a camera flash unit. In order to make the camera flash unit the dominant light source, it is necessary to shield the impression from the sun or bright ambient light. A very efficient way of achieving this is depicted in Figure 2.7. After the camera has been set up on the tripod, a black cloth is draped around the sides of the tripod to make a partial tent.* More efficiently, an assistant can position and hold the cloth. The cloth should extend to the ground. If a black cloth is not available, much of the light can still be shielded using a piece of cardboard or the shadow cast from another individual. Anything that will reduce or block out the

---

* Local fabric stores offer a wide variety of black cloth that can be obtained for this. Make sure that the cloth you use prevents most of the light from coming through.

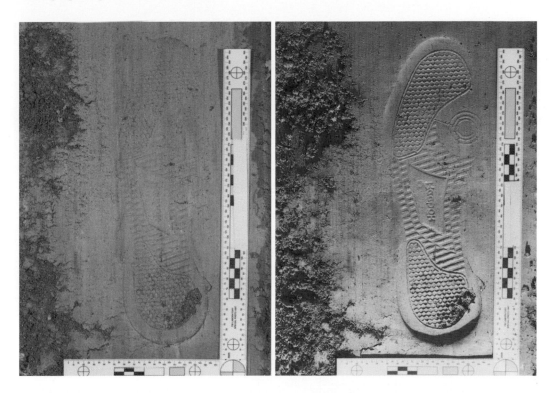

Figure 2.27 The use of a sunscreen is necessary when taking photographs outside in bright light or sunlight. The photograph on the left was taken with oblique light from a flash but without blocking the sun. On the right, the use of a black cloth to block the sun permitted the oblique light of the flash to become the primary light source, creating better contrast and detail.

bright light and thereby allow the off-camera flash to become the dominant light source will improve the resulting photographs. Figure 2.27 depicts two photographs taken on a sunny day. The one on the left was taken using an off-camera flash without a sunscreen, thus allowing the sun to be the dominant light source. The one on the right was taken using an off-camera flash and with the sunlight blocked using a black cloth, thus allowing the oblique light from the flash to be the dominant light source and create contrast.

Inversion Effect

Occasionally, when viewing a photograph of a three-dimensional impression, the actual indented areas of the impression will appear to be raised. In Figure 2.28, the same photographed image was duplicated and rotated 180°. On one side, the impression appears to be depressed into the soil, whereas on the other side it appears raised above the soil. You can take these images and turn them upside down and the opposite will occur. This phenomenon is known as the "inversion effect" and can also be seen in other images of three-dimensional impressions in this book. The inversion effect is routinely encountered in photographs of three-dimensional impressions illuminated with oblique light. People are accustomed to viewing light with the sunlight coming from above so their brains interpret light accordingly. When impressions are photographed with light from different directions, some may provide the illusion of the impression being raised instead of being

Figure 2.28 The inversion effect sometimes encountered with oblique light photography of three-dimensional impressions. One impression appears raised and the same impression, rotated 180°, will appear depressed into the substrate. If you rotate the book 180°, they will appear differently.

depressed. This does not interfere with the examination and interpretation of the detail in a photographed impression and is mentioned here simply for familiarization.

Earlier in this chapter, a photograph of an impression taken without a scale was depicted in Figure 2.8. That same impression is now depicted in Figure 2.29 but is next to a scale and the keychain sized souvenir outsole that produced it. Its dimension is less than 100 mm. This example was provided to show that the absence of a scale in a photograph makes it impossible to determine dimensional information during forensic examination.

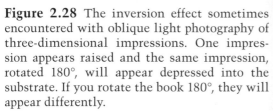

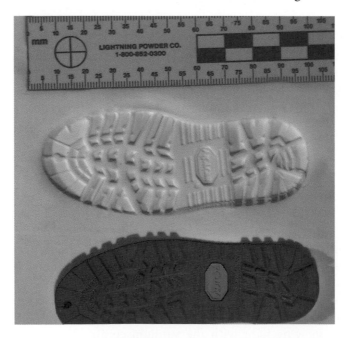

Figure 2.29 To illustrate a point, this keychain rubber sole, less than 100 mm in length, was used to produce the impression in Figure 2.8. Without the scale, an examiner cannot determine or compare the dimensions of an impression.

Key Words: film camera, digital single lens reflex camera, resolution, general crime scene photography examination quality photography, oblique light, inversion effect.

Key Points

1. A professional DSLR camera set at the maximum resolution should be used for all evidence photography.
2. Specific procedures for examination quality photography are necessary to successfully record footwear evidence so it can be accurately enlarged to natural size and be compared with the footwear of suspected individuals.
3. A proper scale should be used in every examination quality photograph. The proper positioning of this scale is also very important.
4. Oblique light is used for photographing both two- and three-dimensional impressions.
5. Manual focus is the only way to ensure a photographed, when enlarged, will remain in sharp focus.
6. Check the focus prior to each exposure.

Casting Three-Dimensional Impressions

3

Three-dimensional impressions occur in exterior soft substrates such as soil, mud, sand, and snow. Most are relatively shallow but some, particularly in snow, can sink much deeper. The practice of casting to recover impression evidence precedes the existence of cameras. Since the invention of the camera, the long-standing protocol for the recovery of three-dimensional footwear impressions has been first to take examination quality photographs, after which a cast should be made of the impression. Over the years, as cameras were invented and evolved, some erroneously believed it was permissible to reduce or altogether discontinue the practice of casting. Examination quality photography can only provide a two-dimensional view of an impression, capturing only what appears with each individual exposure. Even the most diligent and experienced photographer is at a distinct disadvantage because, beyond the apparent outsole design, they are unaware of the specific features of importance the perpetrator's shoe may possess and that may have been replicated in an impression. Casting recovers details not recovered through photography. Making a cast of all three-dimensional impressions should be a regular practice even in those cases where impressions appear to have limited detail. This chapter will cover basic casting information and discuss the materials and methods used for casting impressions in soil and sand. Because of the special nature of casting impressions in snow, the following chapter will address that topic.

Why Make Casts?

Questions about whether a cast is necessary are asked in many ways. The most common include, "If I photograph an impression, do I also need to cast it?" "If there are 10 impressions in soil at the crime scene, do I need to cast all of them?" and "Can casts provide more detail than photographs?" The simple answer to all of these questions is "Yes" and each is addressed further hereafter.

If I Photograph an Impression, Do I Also Need to Cast It?

Whenever there is a three-dimensional impression at a crime scene, it should always be cast! The cast captures the positive representation of the shoe that made it. Once cleaned and turned over, the cast impression can be compared directly alongside the outsole of a suspected shoe. Casts are life-size three-dimensional moldings of impressions that do not involve focus, lighting, scale, or perspective concerns, as is often the case with photographs. Modern casting products, specifically dental stone, have excellent dimensional stability, accurately represent the size of the impression, and consistently provide information that supplements photography.

The experiences of both former and contemporary examiners state how extremely valuable casts are as a means of assuring the maximum amount of detail from an impression has been recovered. In 1930, Hans Müllner wrote, "The greater the number of details which an imprint contains, the more valuable it proves as evidence in court procedure. Those in soft materials, such as dust, flour, fresh snow and mud, exhibit the most numerous and exact markings, but are at the same time, difficult to reproduce."* Müllner recognized the advantage in casting impressions and had developed new methods in the 1920s for casting. In 1945, an article in the *FBI Law Enforcement Bulletin* stated, "Casts are considered superior to photography since they reproduce all three dimensions of the impression and thus permit a more detailed examination than could be made from a photograph." In 1949, in their book, *An Introduction to Criminalistics,* O'Hara and Osterburg state, "By far the best means of studying an impression in mud, snow, or other surfaces is that of the … cast. Quite frequently, a properly made cast will offer much more information to the eye than the impression itself." In 1953, well-known criminalist Paul L. Kirk wrote, "While the photograph of the print is valuable for record, and even for detail comparison, it is less useful than is a good cast of the print."† A similar opinion was expressed by Mansfield, who wrote, "For impressions outside, the … cast provides better evidence than the photograph because of its perspective depth."‡

A Royal Canadian Mounted Police (RCMP) training videotape, narrated by Michael Cassidy, displayed photographs of several impressions in soil.§ In that video, Cassidy pointed out the specific features he could see when comparing the photographs to the shoes that had made them. He then produced the dental stone casts he had made of the same impressions, pointed to the same features, and explained how they were more accurately and clearly represented in the cast. The additional detail he demonstrated in this video was impressive and capably illustrated why three-dimensional impressions should always be cast. In his 1980 book *Footwear Identification*, Cassidy wrote, "The number of accidental characteristics recorded in the three-dimensional impression will surprise you." In 1982, DeHaan stated, "Useful information is more often found in the cast than in the average photograph."¶ And more recently, during a presentation on the casting of snow impressions, an examiner with over 25 years of experience stated, "Almost all of the positive IDs of three-dimensional shoe/tire impression evidence have come from casts, not photos."**

My own experience has been the same. Casts of three-dimensional impressions of footwear evidence will, in the vast majority of cases, allow for a more detailed and accurate examination. Most of the identifications made of three-dimensional impressions were of those recovered through casting.

If There Are 10 Impressions in Soil at the Crime Scene, Do I Need to Cast All of Them?

Personnel, other resources, and circumstances dictate a different emphasis on crime scene priorities from one scene to the next. One scene may involve an attempted burglary with

---

* Müllner, H., and Kaempfer, L. J., The Müllner Moulage method, *Journal of Criminal Law and Criminology* (1931–1951), 23(2):351, Jul–Aug. 1932.
† Kirk, P. L., *Crime Investigation: Physical Evidence and the Police Laboratory,* Interscience Publishers, Inc., New York, 1953, pp. 301–302.
‡ Mansfield, E. R., Footwear impressions at scenes of crimes, *The Police Journal,* 43(2):93–96, 1970.
§ Cassidy, M., Royal Canadian Mounted Police, produced by Identification Services Audio Visual Section (undated).
¶ DeHaan, J. D., Footwear Evidence: An Update, 1982 (unpublished).
** Wolfe, J., Documenting and Collecting Snow Impression Evidence, presented at the International Association of Identification Education Seminar, Milwaukee, WI, August 2011.

no loss of property, while another scene may be a triple homicide. It would be unrealistic to expect that both scenes would be treated with equal resources and time. However, if the question, "Should I cast all impressions?" is asked and answered strictly from an evidential point of view, the answer to this question is a resounding "yes."

When asked this question by novice examiners or crime scene technicians, the response to them is another question: "If you were confronted with 10 latent fingerprints at a homicide scene, which five would you lift and which five would you abandon and leave at the scene?" As no one would even imagine leaving behind latent fingerprints, it should become equally obvious there is no logic in leaving any quantity of any footwear evidence at the scene.

I recently read a pretrial hearing transcript of an examiner in which he boastfully testified how he had sufficient experience to choose three impressions out of eleven at a scene that contained the best detail. He commenced to recover those three impressions photographically, but then failed to cast any of them, even the three impressions he believed were the best. He only included the remaining impressions in general crime scene photographs. I strongly disagree with that examiner's statements and practices. There is no reliable way in which anyone, even an experienced examiner, can accurately predict the evidential value of footwear evidence by simply viewing it at the scene, particularly in the absence of the shoes with which the impressions are to be compared. I am often reminded of this as I reflect on the many proficiency cases I have prepared through the years. After preparing a proficiency case, I would often view the photographs I made of impressions, and then witness exceptionally better detail captured by the casts made of those same impressions. Moreover, in both proficiency case preparation and casework, it was not at all unusual to find a partial impression that when viewed on the ground seemed to have limited detail but actually had retained better information than other more complete impressions at the scene. One of my first experiences with casework involving casts included two dental stone casts made of impressions on a very rocky substrate. In spite of that, the areas between the rocks clearly replicated several randomly acquired characteristics. The photographs of the impressions did not reveal these features, as the rocks shadowed or otherwise obstructed their detail. Fortunately, in that case, the crime scene investigator made casts; one is shown in Figure 3.1. In spite of the many rocks, sufficient detail of many areas of the outsole was replicated in the clay soil and allowed for identification of the impression with the suspect's footwear.

All impressions, whether in soil, sand, or snow, are suitable for casting. Even impressions in very delicate or fragile soil can be cast if the proper procedure is followed. There are no impressions that cannot be cast. With proper preparation, little additional time or effort is involved in casting several impressions than in casting only one or two. Casts should always be made of three-dimensional impressions. Evidence that is left at the crime scene is lost forever!

Can Casts Provide More Detail than Photographs?

Figure 3.2 depicts a photograph of an impression in soil alongside a cast made of the same impression. The shoe that made that impression has a bent nail embedded in the heel. Along the bottom of this photograph are enlarged areas of (1) the portion of the photographed impression that contains the feature of the nail, (2) the portion of the dental stone cast representing the respective portion of that impression, and (3) the bent nail as

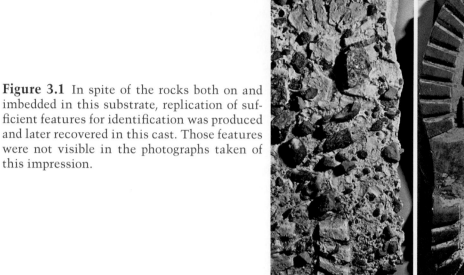

Figure 3.1 In spite of the rocks both on and imbedded in this substrate, replication of sufficient features for identification was produced and later recovered in this cast. Those features were not visible in the photographs taken of this impression.

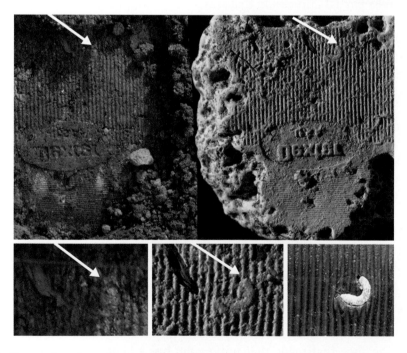

Figure 3.2 Correctly taken photographs of this impression did not provide sufficient detail to clearly distinguish all of the features captured by the cast, including the bent nail embedded in the heel. Remember, the photographer has no way of knowing that features like the bent nail exist when photographically recovering this impression.

it appears in the shoe. Although some possible disturbance can be seen in the area where the metal nail left its mark in the soil, the photograph does not provide sufficient detail to clearly view and evaluate sufficient features of the nail. The cast of that impression recovered those characteristics with far greater detail and accuracy. With only photographs, an examiner would have limited views of the feature. During the examination, unlike the photographs, the cast can be examined in a darkened room while varying the position and height of the light to maximize the ability to evaluate the features of the nail from many different angles and perspectives.

Another example that provides similar comparison between details captured in a photograph versus a cast is represented in Figure 3.3. This impression was made in sandy soil and two enlarged areas of the examination quality photograph are represented on the left. Those areas contain some lettering as well as some representation of randomly acquired cuts. In the center is an enlargement of the same areas captured in the cast. In part A, arrows draw attention to lettering that is clearly seen with greater detail in the cast than in the photograph. In addition, the top arrow in part A points to a cut evident in the cast and shoe, but shadowed out completely in the photograph. In part B, the two indicated cuts appear with far greater detail in the cast than in the photograph. Examples like this occur repeatedly when comparing photographed impressions with casts that were made of the same impressions. There are many possible limitations in photographs when they must be enlarged to this degree, without losing sharp focus and resolution. Casts avoid scale and focus problems, and accurately bring all of the three-dimensional aspects of the impression to the examiner, assisting in the overall comparison and evaluation.

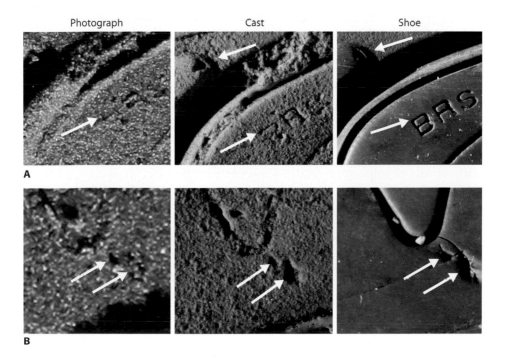

Figure 3.3 Enlargements of two small areas of an impression show how a cast captured better and more complete detail than recovered with the photograph of the same area. This particular photograph was taken with an 18 megapixel DSLR camera. Each area represents approximately one square inch.

Many erroneously believe that casting only works in firm clay soils that are capable of retaining a high level of detail and does not work in sand. One recent study evaluated both photography and casting of impressions in a variety of sandy substrates and concluded that some types of sand are capable of retaining fine detail, often better that that recovered through photography. This study also concluded that when randomly acquired characteristics existed, the casts were better at recovering the fine detail of those features that were often missed through photography.[*,†]

Some substrates might restrict the detail that can be cast, such as a gravel and sand mix like that typically encountered on the shoulder substrate of some roads. Photographs of those types of impressions will be similarly limited. A cast will provide an opportunity to capture the detail that is present and not otherwise obstructed by stones or other debris or lost in the shadows. Even if the impression contains limited detail, the cast of that impression will provide a more accurate capture of the dimensions of the impression.

From Plasters to Stones

Prior to the late 1970s, police forces throughout the world used plaster of Paris for decades to cast footwear impressions. Some published the specific techniques they used, many recommending first sifting some of the plaster powder into the impression to capture better detail.[‡,§,¶,**,††,‡‡] Figure 3.4 depicts the old time-consuming and messy process of making casts with plaster of Paris.

The biggest disadvantage of using plaster of Paris is that it is a soft form of gypsum; thus any attempt to clean and remove soil from a plaster cast using water and a soft brush resulted in destruction of much of its detail. In order to prevent soil from adhering to the soft plaster cast, hairspray, sifted talc or other mixtures needed to be applied to the impression prior to casting to act as a releasing agent. Although release agents were necessary for plasters, applying a spray or powder to the impression always added some risk of damaging it. Figure 3.5 depicts a dental stone cast made in a heavy clay soil. The part of the cast still covered with soil was not treated with any release agent. The portion with a whitish color was treated with a fine sifting of talcum powder. The remaining portion was sprayed with hairspray. If this were a plaster cast, the area beneath the clinging soil would be difficult to clean without loss of important details. However, dental stone products used for casting

[*] Snyder, C., The ability of footwear to produce impressions of good detail in sandy soil substrates, *JFI*, 65(3):2015.

[†] Snyder, C., "The Ability of Footwear Impressions to Retain Good Detail for Footwear Comparisons: A Comparison of Different Sandy Soils and Casts vs. Examination Quality Photographs," IAI 100th Educational Conference, Sacramento, CA 8/7/15.

[‡] Chee, H. W. and Wilson, S. J., A modified method of plaster casting, *The Forensic Science Society Journal*, 83–84, 1963.

[§] Martin, F. W., A simple method of taking footprints, *The Police Journal*, 9:450–452, 1936.

[¶] Samen, C. C., Major crime scene investigation: casting (shoe and tire impressions), *Law and Order Magazine*, 52–57, March, 1972.

[**] Carlsson, K. and Maehly, A. C., New methods for securing impressions of shoes and tyres on different surfaces, *International Criminal Police Review*, 299:158–167, 1976.

[††] Moriarty, C. C., Taking casts of footprints, *Police Journal* (London), 5:229–232, 1932.

[‡‡] Müllner, H., and Kaempfer, L. J., The Müllner moulage method. *J. Crim. Law Crim.*, 23(2):351–355, 1932.

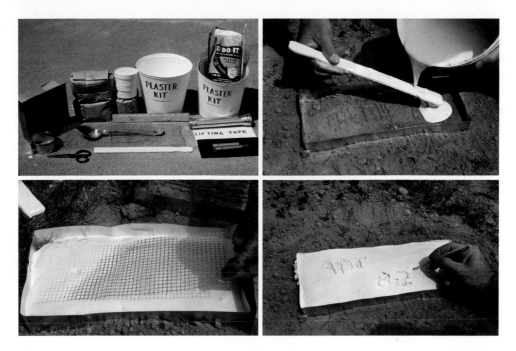

Figure 3.4 Prior to the use of modern dental casting materials, much softer plaster of Paris was used. The procedure required at least 5 pounds of casting material, a form to contain that material over the impression, and metal hardware cloth to place within the cast to prevent it from breaking. The entire process took considerably longer to mix and pour and the process was messy.

Figure 3.5 Examples of using a release agent to prevent soil from sticking to a cast. The part of the cast covered with soil has not been treated with any release agent. The portion with a whitish color was treated with a fine sifting of talcum powder. The remaining portion was sprayed with hair spray. Modern casting materials like dental stone no longer require the use of release agents, as they are sufficiently hard to endure cleaning.

today are much harder. The dental stone cast in Figure 3.5 can be submerged in water to soften the soil, and with the aid of a soft brush, the heavy soil can be removed easily without risk of losing detail. With modern dental stone casting materials, there is no longer a need to prepare an impression with a release agent as was once necessary with plaster of Paris.

As early as 1950, there is a reference to dental stone being preferred over plaster of Paris. Then, FBI Assistant Special Agent-in-Charge E. L. Boyle wrote:

> I have found generally that for this (casting) purpose, plaster of Paris is not too satisfactory and is too fickle a material even for an old expert …. I looked around for some other material and hit upon the commercial product called Castone …. I have found it a much more satisfactory casting material than plaster of Paris. Its detail is 100% better, it is much harder, and for small casts at least, no supporting twigs or other material are necessary.[*]

By the early 1970s, dental stone casting materials were being used throughout the US and in many other countries. In 1986, the FBI Law Enforcement Bulletin stated, "It is now recommended that only dental stone be used for casting impressions." Today, dental stone is used exclusively around the world with great success and has totally replaced plaster of Paris as a casting material for recovering footwear impressions.

Producing Plasters and Dental Stone from Gypsum[†]

The following discussion is provided for both an appreciation and understanding of why dental stone is much better than softer gypsum products such as plaster of Paris. Gypsum is a natural mineral obtained through mining. Chemically, gypsum is known as calcium sulfate dehydrate ($CaSO_4 \times 2\ H_2O$). Gypsum is processed in many different ways, with each providing slightly different properties suitable for various uses. Calcination is the process of heating the gypsum to dehydrate it to form calcium sulphate hemihydrate. Both plasters and stones are products of this process. The specific calcination process determines the strength of the gypsum material. Qualities such as setting time, consistency, fineness, hardness, compressive strength, surface characteristics, and color distinguish the various gypsum products that range from soft plasters to gypsum cements to stones. Commercially, gypsum products are used to cast many objects such as lamp or table bases, art objects, molds, novelties, displays, and teeth, as well as its extensive use in gypsum wallboard for construction. Figure 3.6 shows a simple relationship between all plasters, ranging from the softer molding plasters to the harder dental stones. During the calcination of gypsum, different forms of the hemihydrate are produced depending on the method used. Traditionally, these forms have been designated as alpha hemihydrate (α) and beta hemihydrate (β). Dental stones are the alpha form of calcium sulfate hemihydrate ($CaSO_4 \times 2\ H_2O$). Plasters, including plaster of Paris, are the beta form of calcium sulfate hemihydrate ($CaSO_4 \times \frac{1}{2}\ H_2O$).

[*] FBI Memorandum, Asst. Special Agent-in-Charge E. L. Boyle, January 24, 1950.
[†] Scheller-Sheridan, C., *Basic Guide to Dental Materials*, Wiley-Blackwell, Chichester, UK, 2010, p. 222.

The reaction converting gypsum to plaster or stone with loss of water is reversible, so the addition of water will result once again in gypsum.

$$CaSO_4 \times 2\ H_2O \rightarrow (CaSO_4)_2 \times H_2O \rightarrow CaSO_4 \rightarrow CaSO_4$$

110–130°C	130–200°C	200–1000°C
Gypsum	Plaster	Stone
(Calcium sulfate	(calcium sulfate	(calcium sulfate
dihydrate)	beta-hemihydrate)	alpha-hemihydrate)

There are differences in the amount of water removed during calcination. Production for the α-hemihydrate form (stones) includes heating the gypsum mineral in an autoclave under pressure and in the presence of steam. The powder produced by this method contains particles that are more dense and uniform in shape than the plaster particles. The resulting α-hemihydrate requires much less water when mixing and results in a much stronger and harder cast.

Production for the β-hemihydrate form (plaster) involves heating the gypsum in an open oven at a lower temperature. The resulting product is called beta-calcium sulfate hemihydrate, more commonly known as plaster. The β-hemihydrate requires more water to float its particles for mixing because the crystals are more porous and irregular in shape. The resulting plaster product is softer.

With regard to the casting of footwear impressions, the strength and durability of the α-hemihydrate form (stones) make them superior to the β-hemihydrate form (plasters). The greater compressive strength of the stones and their other qualities preserve detail and require less materials and water than the softer plasters.

The term "dental stone" resulted from the production of a variety of stones specifically for the dental industry. They typically capture better detail and are available in a variety of colors and other qualities.

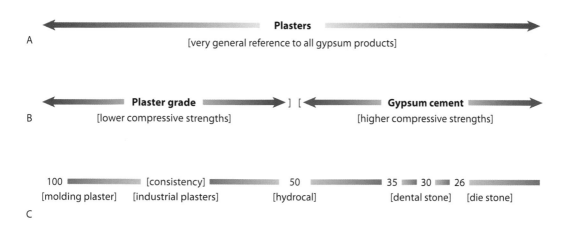

Figure 3.6 Some in the industry refer to all gypsum products as plasters, but there are distinct differences in their qualities particularly compressive strength and hardness, based on the way they are processed.

Water-to-Powder Ratio (W:P)

The ratio of the quantity of water (W) to casting powder (P) is known as the water-to-powder (W:P) ratio. The powder (P) portion of this ratio will always be 100. The water (W) portion of this ratio will vary for different forms of dental stone and plasters and that number is referred to as the "consistency" of the product. A dental stone mixture with a consistency of "30" would mean it should require 30 parts of water to 100 parts of powder and its W:P ratio would be 30:100 or 0.3. The W:P ratio is extremely important, as it directly relates to the density, hardness, strength, and durability of the cast. The more water needed, the longer the setting time, the lower the compressive strength, and the lower the hardness of the cast. Figure 3.7 shows the relation of the wet compressive strengths of Type I through Type V gypsum products one hour after mixing, varying from a W:P ratio of 0.20 to 0.65. Type I includes plaster of Paris (W:P ratio of 0.55 and higher), Type II includes modeling plaster or lab plaster (W:P ratio of 0.40 to 0.55), Type III includes dental stone (W:P ratio of .025 to 0.35), Type IV includes high-strength dental stone (W:P ratio .25 and below), and Type V includes high-strength high-expansion dental stone.[*] Figure 3.7 also illustrates how the strength of the dental stone is inversely proportional to the W:P ratio. Note that the values in this chart represent the wet compressive strengths after 1 hour and not the final compressive strengths that will be much higher.

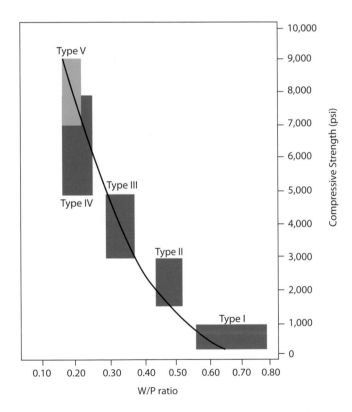

Figure 3.7 Comparison of the wet compressive strengths of Type I–Type V dental stones after 1 hour and their water-to-powder (W:P) ratios.

[*] Anusavice, K., *Phillips Science of Dental Materials,* Elsevier Science, St. Louis, MO, 2003, summarized from p. 260.

Viscosity

Viscosity is a term that describes the thickness of a fluid mixture. Viscosity should not be confused with consistency. Viscosity relates the thickness of the mxture, which in casting relates to how well the mixture will pour and flow throughout the impression. For instance, honey and water have different viscosities. Honey is more viscous and pours and flows very slowly, while water is less viscous and pours and flows quickly. A watery viscosity is not desirable and allows for undesirable penetration of porous substrates. A viscosity that is too high (thick) will inhibit the ability of the dental material to flow freely through the impression. For impressions in sand and soil, a viscosity that could be described as similar to that of thick cream or thin pancake batter is desirable.

Dimensional Stability

Dental stones do not shrink but have a very slight expansion rate. For the various dental stones, the expansion rate normally falls between .08% and .14%. For an expansion rate of .14%, a 12-inch-long cast would expand .0168 inches (.14% of 12 inches = .0014 × 12 − .0168 inches). This extremely minor expansion is not a factor nor can it be detected. For all practical purposes, a dental stone cast is dimensionally accurate.

Obtaining Dental Stone

Police agencies and crime scene units should stock adequate quantities of dental stone, not only for the recovery of footwear impressions, but also for the recovery of larger tire impressions. Any police agency that routinely collects evidence from crime scenes and casts footwear and tire impressions should maintain a minimum of 100–200 pounds of dental stone. Some of this can be divided into bags for footwear impressions while some will be kept in bulk form for casting of wider and longer tire impressions. Responding to a crime scene requiring the use of 100 pounds of dental stone for 10 tire casts can rapidly consume a department's supply. The shelf life of dental stone is reasonable and usually not an issue with departments that regularly make casts at scenes. Dental stone will need to be ordered from dental supply houses or forensic suppliers because it is not available locally in stores. The purchase of bulk quantities of dental stone is less expensive and allows the choice of the precise casting material qualities you require. Any dental stone ordered should have a consistency of 30 or lower and a minimum compressive strength of 8000 psi. This will ensure it will have sufficient hardness to endure the removal of any stubborn soil without compromising the detail captured by the cast. Another consideration is the color of dental stone. White is more difficult to photograph. Other colors like pale blue and pink don't offer much better contrast. One color that is very popular is described as buff or cream colored. It is the color shown in Figures 3.11, 3.12, and 3.13.

Castone is an internationally available dental stone product that I have used since the 1970s.[*] Castone has a consistency of 30 (W:P = 30:100). At the time of writing this book,

---

[*] Available through Dentsply International, York, PA, 800-877-0020. Castone is item #99043, which comes in a cream or buff color in 25-pound cartons. See also www.dentsply.com.

a 25-pound box of bulk Castone dental stone plus delivery charges and an added amount of about \$.10 for a quality 4-mil Ziploc® bag equated to a final cost of less than \$3.00 (US) for a 2-pound bag.* Numerous other dental suppliers offer similar dental stone at similar pricing. Dental stone is usually sold in quantities of 25, 50, or 100 pounds. The 25-pound cartons are easier to handle and are recommended. Whether you purchase dental stone from a dental supplier or from a forensic supplier, you will need to know exactly what you are buying and that it has the qualities that will produce a good cast.

Other Casting Materials

Figure 3.8 shows the aforementioned Castone® dental stone on the top left, Cast-Pro™ on the top right, NuCast 180® on the bottom left, and Traxtone® on the bottom right.† These are casting materials frequently used in the US and other countries. Information about bulk Castone dental stone was the main topic above. Cast-Pro™ is also an excellent dental stone similar if not identical to Castone and is sold in both bulk and preweighed bags. Cast-Pro is also now available premeasured in shakable containers. Traxtone is also a dental stone product that comes in preweighed bags. Traxtone powder contains some colored materials that the directions say can be used to measure the mixing time. It is noted that mixing Traxtone to the point where the colored materials in the powder are consumed

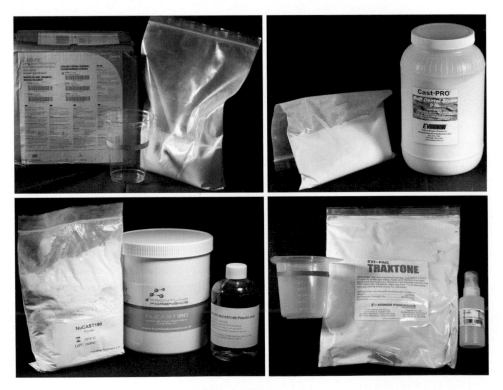

Figure 3.8 Castone, Cast-Pro, NuCast, and Traxtone.

* Based on a 25-pound carton of Castone item #99043 shipped to Florida.
† Castone provided by Dentsply International, Cast-Pro provided by Evident Crime Scene Products, NuCast 180 provided by TriTech Forensics, and Traxtone obtained from Forensics Source.

Casting Product	Powder/Water	Ready to Lift Time
Castone® (bulk)	2 pounds /10 ounces water	17 minutes
Cast-Pro™ (bulk and pre-weighed available)	2 pounds/12 ounces water	17 minutes
Traxtone® (bulk and pre-weighed available)	2 pounds/9 ounces water	25 minutes
NuCast 180® (provided in cast size portions)	1-3/4 pounds/ 9-3/4 ounces of blue liquid provided in bottle	5 minutes

Figure 3.9 Comparison of powder and water quantities and setting times of the casting products in Figure 3.8.

takes less than 1 minute; however, if you use Traxtone, you should always ensure the mixing time is a minimum of 3 minutes, the same as any other dental stone product. Not only is the added time necessary to ensure the powder has soaked up the water, but its final hardness and setting time are a product of the amount of energy that goes into mixing. NuCast 180 is a proprietary powder mixture that behaves like dental stone. It is packaged in a plastic container with the proper measure of powder and a blue liquid in a small bottle. The powder bag is opened and emptied into the container followed by the full contents of the blue liquid. The lid is securely applied, after which the directions say to vigorously shake it for approximately 35 seconds before pouring. NuCast 180 sets quickly, in about 5 minutes. This is a very convenient product to use for casting; however, some disadvantages are its expense and the extra storage room the plastic containers will require. The product works very well in nonsnow substrates but not in snow.

It should be emphasized that each of these products is capable of producing a good cast, but there are advantages and disadvantages of each. A cast was made of impressions in sandy soil using each of these products in the bright sun at 90°F. Some comparative data is set forth in Figure 3.9. All materials worked as promised and allowed for the safe cleaning of the soil from their surface using water and a very soft brush. NuCast set fastest and Traxtone the slowest. This was no surprise, as in previous evaluations, in air temperatures of 60°F Castone took 20 minutes to set while Traxtone took 37 minutes; at a much colder air temperature of 32°F Castone set in 40 minutes while Traxtone took much longer, 91 minutes.[*]

Forensic suppliers sell additional casting materials other than those mentioned above. Before you obtain any supply of casting material, make sure it is dental stone or that you understand specifically what its qualities are, that you know the W:P ratio and compressive strength (psi), and that it meets your requirements. Avoid products that are soft plasters and those with compression strengths below 8000 psi. Avoid any casting products that are alginates, as they have a high shrinkage rate.

There are other casting products available on the market capable of replicating exceptional detail. Some include silicone-based products such as Mikrosil, polyvinylsiloxanes, and liquid silicones. Some are capable of replicating much greater detail than dental stone; however, they do not work satisfactorily for casting in sand, soil, or snow. One assessment compared some of these products against dental stone but failed to point out their incompatibility with use in snow and soil substrates.[†]

---

[*] Bodziak, W., and Hammer, L., An evaluation of dental stone, Traxtone, and Crime-Cast, *JFI*, 56(5):785, 2006.

[†] Yu, A., Knaap, W., Milliken, N., and Bognar, P., Evaluation and comparison of casting materials on detailed three-dimensional impressions, *JFI*, 59(6):626–636, 2009.

Premeasuring Dental Stone in Ziploc® Bags

Most who use dental stone for casting footwear impressions prepares premeasured quantities in Ziploc® bags. A Ziploc® bag measuring approximately 9 × 12 inches can easily hold 2 to 3 pounds of dental stone powder with sufficient room to allow for the addition of water and the mixing process.* The weighing of those portions should be accurate. Once the bags are filled, they can be laid on one side and flattened to remove any excess air and then zipped closed to keep the casting material dry. When the time comes to mix a cast at a crime scene, the premeasured bags of dental stone are ready and convenient and only a premeasured amount of water need be added.

When bulk dental stone is purchased, the W:P ratio should be provided. Some providers list the W:P ratio as P:W. For instance, the previously referenced Castone product has the ratio listed as P:W on the label on the side of its box. Figure 3.10 shows a closeup area of that box that publishes the ratio of 100 g powder to 30 cc water or simply P:W equals 100:30 (consistency = 30). For a 2-pound measure of Castone dental stone powder having a consistency of 30, multiply 30 by .306729, which equals 9.2 ounces of water needed for the mixture.† These amounts are those prescribed for use in the dental applications of this product and thus will be slightly more viscous than desired. Thus, a very slight adjustment should be made to the calculated amount of water so that the mixture creates a viscosity that flows well. Usually, an additional amount of approximately ¾ to 1 ounce of water works well. Therefore, if the calculated amount is 9.2 ounces of water per 2 pounds of dental stone, you should round off that amount to 10 ounces of water. This will provide a mixture that will flow well into and through the impression during pouring. An experienced individual mixing dental stone will normally know within the first 45–60 seconds of mixing if the

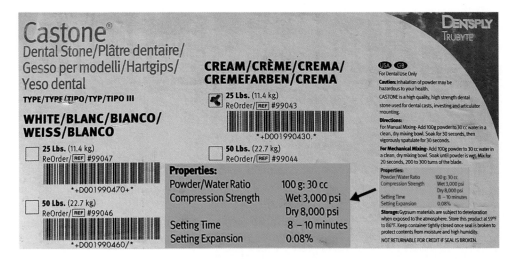

Figure 3.10 The outside of the Castone dental stone box provides important information such as the powder-to-water (P:W) ratio, and the wet and dry compression strengths.

---

* As the average shoe size has increased over the years, some now prefer to measure 2½ to 3 pounds in each bag rather than the traditional 2-pound portion.
† If you are using a 2½- or 3-pound measure of Castone dental stone, you can adjust the amount of water proportionally. Please note this conversion factor from grams and cc to ounces and pounds was calculated only for convenience for this particular P:W ratio and product, and will be different for other products.

mixture is too viscous and whether a very small addition of water should be made. Using an accurate scale to preweigh the dental stone along with a measured cup containing the proper water quantity each time will help make this process more consistent. The above example was calculated for the Castone product only and it is noted that W:P ratios vary slightly from one brand of dental stone to another; thus the premeasured amounts of water to powder must be computed for the specific product you are using. If you are using a product for the first time, regardless of the calculations, you might have to make a very slight adjustment to ensure the viscosity is good for pouring.

The Ziploc® bag method is used worldwide and provides a convenient, efficient, clean, and rapid way of preparing a quality cast. If more than one cast is being prepared, the person in charge of casting can solicit the help of another individual to assist in the mixing portion of this process.

Preparing the Footwear Impression for Casting

Three-dimensional impressions need little or no preparation prior to casting with dental stone casting materials and do not require a form, as was necessary with plaster of Paris. Any stick, stone, leaf, or other debris that was between the shoe and the ground at the time the impression was made has already prevented the replication of any useful detail in those areas. Thus any attempt to remove those items should not be made. If for some reason loose leafs or twigs have fallen or blown into the impression after it was made and are lying freely on top of the impression, they can be removed carefully with tweezers or a sticky cotton-tipped swab.

Fixatives and Release Agents

On many occasions, letters that have accompanied the submission of evidence explained that a cast was not made because the soil was too fragile. On other occasions, some have stated that without the use of a fixative, fragile impressions could not be cast. Older literature is still read by today's crime scene technicians and some have even been trained to use sprays as a release agent or fixative. One reference from an old law enforcement training bulletin, stated, "Spray ordinary white shellac, thinned with wood alcohol, into the print ... Allow the first coat to harden ten to fifteen minutes ... Apply the second coat of shellac ... Allow to harden." In 1951, the FBI Law Enforcement Bulletin recommended, "Impressions in sand, loose soil, and snow must be strengthened with a plastic spray, shellac, or other quick dry fixative ... the spray should be directed over the impression rather than directly at it." More recently, Cassidy advocated, "The impression should now be covered with some form of release agent to allow the dirt to come away from the cast with ease. Various agents from frying pan sprays to oil can be used for this purpose. However, from tests conducted I have found baby powder to be an excellent release agent .... The talc should be drifted over the impression using a small atomizer or aerosol can plus a deflector card."[*]

---

[*] Cassidy, M. J., *Footwear Identification*, Canadian Government Printing Centre, Quebec, Canada, 1980.

More recently, with the use of dental stone instead of soft plaster of Paris, references have stated that release agents or fixatives are of no benefit and may potentially do harm to the impression: "The last item that can and should be eliminated from the casting kit are the fixative and release agents …. Damage to an impression is as likely to occur when the release and fixatives are used as when they are not." The same author also states, "Tests without a fixative and with a clear fixative pointed out that neither … helped produce a better cast."[*][†]

Some believe a fixative is still necessary. My concern is that the application of any aerosol sprayed or any talc powder sifted into a fragile impression invokes a risk of damaging the impression. As long as the casting material is applied with the proper technique, any impression can be safely cast and therefore fixatives are not needed. This includes impressions in silt, very dry and fine soils, and other fragile substrates.

Mixing Dental Stone in Ziploc® Bags

The casting process, simply described, involves the combination of the proper portions of water and casting powder, mixing them together, pouring them into an impression, followed by the setting and drying of the cast. Figure 3.11 shows a sequence of mixing dental stone using the Ziploc® bag method. The process begins with the proper amounts of water and preweighed dental stone. The full quantity of water is added to the bag all at once, which is then closed. The bag can be gently squeezed to facilitate the mixing of the water and powder and to crush any clumps of powder. Usually after the first 60 seconds of mixing the powder will appear to be totally in solution but it is not. After the first 60 seconds, the powder particles are only in suspension and have not had the time to completely absorb the water. It is very important to continue mixing for a minimum of 3 minutes before you pour the casting material. Doing so will ensure a mix that will pour evenly and will produce a stronger cast.

Mixing Dental Stone in a Container

If you do not have preweighed bags of dental stone and are mixing the dental stone in a container, it is less convenient but not a problem. Use a container that has a smooth bottom to make mixing easier. Fill the container with the estimated amount of water you believe will be needed based on the dental stone you are using and the quantity of casting material you anticipate. In our examples, we used 10 ounces of water with 2 pounds of the Castone dental stone. Add the dental stone to the water until it cones up out of the water. Let it sit for about 30 seconds to allow the powder to sink into and absorb the water. Begin stirring the mixture. After the powder is stirred for a short while, you might recognize a need to adjust the mixture slightly by adding more dental stone or more water as needed to achieve the proper viscosity for pouring. Continue mixing for a minimum of 3 minutes.

Some have experimented with the use of plastic containers for mixing and pouring. One study found success with the use of 1.5-liter plastic water bottles. They added

---

[*] Vandiver, J. V., Easier casting and better casts, *Identification News*, 30(5):3–10, 1980.
[†] Vandiver, J. V., Casting materials, *Identification News*, 30(12):3–9, 1980.

Figure 3.11 Mixing preweighed dental stone in a Ziploc® bag. Make sure the mixing continues for at least 3 minutes.

the dental stone to the bottles in advance and added water at the time of casting. They concluded casts produced this way resulted in fewer bubbles in the resulting cast than mixing in a bucket or in a bag.* Others have stated they use old discarded plastic containers with screw lids to mix the powder and water, similar to the NuCast 180 product and the recently introduced CastPro™ shaker product.

Pouring the Mixture

Casting material has sufficient weight and volume to erode and destroy valuable detail if it is carelessly poured directly onto the impression. This is especially critical in the case of impressions in fragile soils. Improper pouring techniques are probably the main reason why details in an impression are destroyed and why many have stated they have not had success casting impressions. Figure 3.12 illustrates a bad habit of holding the bag several inches above the impression while pouring. When pouring dental stone in this manner the

---

* Wiesner, S., Cohen, A., Shor, Y., and Grafit, A., A new method for casting three-dimensional shoe-prints and tire marks using dental stone, Poster presented at the Pattern and Impression Symposium, Clearwater, FL, August 2010.

Figure 3.12 An example of a bad method of pouring a cast where the dental stone is poured directly into the impression from several inches above it, resulting in damage to the resulting cast impression.

force of the dental stone will destroy the detail of the impression. Figure 3.12 also shows the resulting cast and the arrows indicate areas where the force of the dental stone destroyed impression detail. Using an improper pouring method such as this in fragile soils can do even greater damage.

Figure 3.13 depicts a series of photographs illustrating the proper way to pour dental stone into an impression without compromising its detail. This method will allow the most fragile impressions to be recovered without damage. Please note that using watery dental stone mixtures or mixtures that are too viscous will be counterproductive to this method. Photographs 1 and 2 show how the bag holding the dental stone mixture is positioned near ground level and just outside of the impression. The pour is initiated so the dental stone's first flow strikes the ground outside of the impression but is directed to flow into the impression. In photographs 3 and 4, the bag, held only about 1 inch above the impression, is slowly advanced with the dental stone pour continuing to occur behind the leading edge of the dental stone flow. In this way, the newly poured dental stone does not strike the impression directly but simply causes the flow of dental stone to advance. During this phase, the bag should continue to remain approximately 1 inch above the impression and should be positioned best to direct the flow as needed to cover the impression. The speed of the pour should be continuous and reasonably paced, something not possible if the mixture is too viscous. This same process continues in photographs 5 and 6 until the full impression has been covered. The entire impressed area should be filled with casting material to ensure the full impression as well as any detail from the sides of the impression is

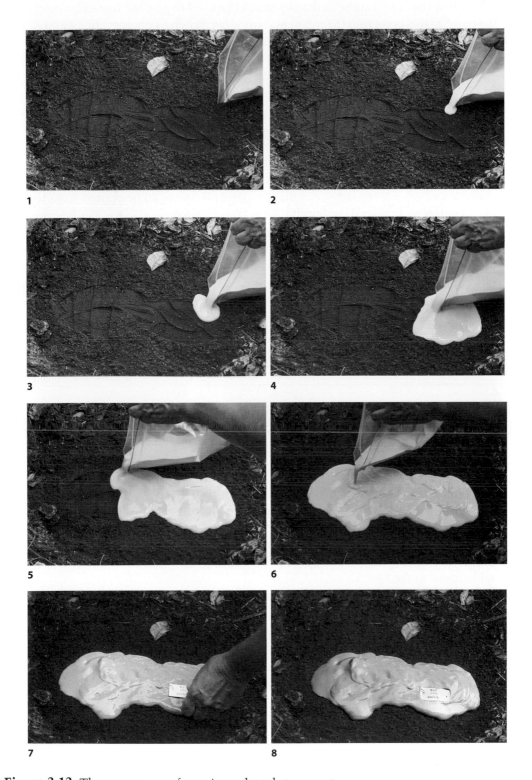

Figure 3.13 The proper way of pouring a dental stone cast.

recovered. All of the dental stone in the bag should be used to give the cast extra thickness. After the pour, a label is set into the wet dental stone, as shown in photographs 7 and 8. This label can be the same one used in the examination quality photographs, containing the identifier number used in those photographs as well as in the general scene photographs. Some prefer to scratch the date, their initials, and other information into the back of the cast after it begins to harden, as was shown in Figure 3.4; however, this requires waiting several minutes until the casts begins to set. The label can be set in the cast immediately, allowing the crime scene technician to go on to the next cast or other tasks. Labels pressed slightly into the dental stone easily survive during the cleaning of the cast and become a permanent part of the cast. Because of the superior hardness and qualities of dental stone that allow for a much smaller quantity of casting material, frames are not necessary. Even if the impression is on a steep slope, it is likely the dental stone can be poured from the bag in a way to control its flow and contain it within the impression.

Some use an alternate method of pouring casting material that involves the use of a very large spoon or flat paint stirrer that is positioned over the impression as was shown in Figure 3.4. The dental stone is poured onto the spoon or stirrer to buffer or deflect the force of the dental stone. Although in practice this could be an effective method, it requires greater coordination and makes it difficult to provide a constant direction of the flow of the mixture.

After You Pour the Cast

The reaction that takes place on combining and mixing water and a gypsum product requires time for completion. During that time, there are a number of stages in the setting process of the cast, which are described by the gypsum industry as follows:

Mixing time: The time from the combination of the powder and water until mixing is complete and the mixture is ready to pour. (For the Ziploc® bag method, this should be a minimum of 3 minutes to ensure all lumps are eliminated.)

Working time: The time available to use the mixture, such as the time after mixing during which the cast may be poured before the mixture begins to set.

Setting time: The time that elapses from the beginning time of mixing until the material hardens to the touch.

Loss of gloss: The point during the reaction at which sufficient excess water is consumed in the reaction so that the mixture's surface loses its gloss.

Ready for use: A subjective amount of time at which the dental stone cast may be safely lifted (normally 30 minutes in moderate temperatures). At this point, the cast is not completely dry and has only achieved its wet compressive strength. It is not ready for cleaning for 24 to 48 hours.

Lifting the Cast

The amount of time you wait will be related to the temperature and the specific casting product you are using. The Castone material used in the illustrations in this book usually sets easily in 30 minutes or less in moderate temperatures, with a longer time required in cold temperatures. Casts can easily be destroyed or damaged if lifted too soon. To be certain a cast is ready to be lifted, scratch the back of the cast with your fingernail. If you are able to easily inflict a scratch mark in the cast, it should be allowed to set longer. If you are unable to scratch it, it can be lifted. Casts poured in dry sand or loose soil should lift relatively easily because air can get beneath them. Casts poured in moist or heavy soils, such as mud or clay, will likely require more careful treatment and sometimes slight excavation to assist their removal without risking breakage. Trying to pry a thin cast out of heavy soil by pulling too hard on its edge can easily cause it to break. Once lifted, although the dental stone will feel hard and dry to the touch, it is neither completely dry nor completely hard.

Air-Drying the Casts

The compressive strength (psi) of the cast is affected, in part, by the amount of energy that goes into mixing and the method with which it is dried. For dental stone having a compressive strength of 8000 psi, perhaps only approximately 50% of that strength (4000 psi) might be realized when mixing by hand and followed by air-drying instead of the strength achieved with industrial mixing and drying. For casting footwear impressions, using dental stone products with a compressive strength of at least 8000 psi will ensure it will still be sufficiently hard to retain all of its detail when cleaned. As was shown in Figure 3.10, information about the W:P ratio, and the wet and dry compressive strengths are furnished on or within the bulk casting material containers. The amount of water required to physically mix the product will always be more than the reaction requires. The extra water is known as "free water" and remains within the cast until it has evaporated. The cast's compressive strength before drying is known as its wet strength. Wet strength is defined as a cast's strength when the water in excess of that required for hydration of the hemihydrate is still in that cast. The information in Figure 3.14 was provided by the U.S. Gypsum

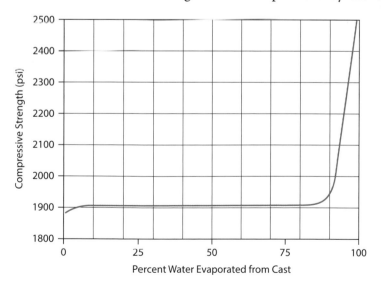

Figure 3.14 The compressive strength of a cast does not increase much until almost all of the water within it has evaporated. This chart, redrawn from information provided by the US Gypsum Corporation, shows that 93% or more of the water must evaporate before the compressive strength increases.

Corporation and illustrates how the total compressive strength of a cast increases very little until almost all (93%) of that extra water has evaporated.[*] For example, a particular dental stone may have a final dry compressive strength of 8000 psi, but may only have a wet compressive strength of 3500 psi 1 hour after setting. This is highly significant because it illustrates the importance of allowing a cast to completely air-dry before attempting to clean it. When the excess free water has evaporated from the cast, normally over a period of 24–48 hours, the cast will have reached its dry compressive strength. To facilitate this, after lifting the cast should be positioned so air can circulate freely around it.

Cleaning the Cast

After lifting, the impression side of casts will often retain a quantity of wet soil or sand. If desired, you can safely remove loose soil with your fingers, as shown in Figure 3.15, to help the drying process. Under no circumstances should soil be removed with a stick or should the cast be cleaned with water and a brush at this point! After drying for 24–48 hours, any remaining soil can be removed by rinsing the cast surface with water assisted by the use of a soft brush. For those casts covered with heavy clay soil that will not rinse away, a method suggested by Brennan works well.[†] This method involves soaking the cast in a saturated solution of potassium sulfate for approximately 1 hour.[‡] During this procedure, you might witness some streams of air bubbles being released from within the cast. This is normal and may assist in loosening clinging soil. After the cast has soaked, a soft brush can be used to help remove that soil from the surface of the cast. Brushing can be done with the cast still submerged in the solution. The cast should then be thoroughly rinsed with water and allowed to drain and air-dry.

Figure 3.15 After lifting a cast, removing excess soil with your fingers is safe and can assist in drying.

---

[*] United States Gypsum Company, Bulletin No. IG502, Chicago, IL, February 1996.
[†] Brennan, J. S., Dental stones for casting depressed shoe marks and tyre marks, *J. Forensic Science Society*, 23:275–286, 1983.
[‡] The potassium sulfate used can be a low-cost fertilizer grade.

Shipping and Storing

Dental stone casts are very durable, but they can still break if not protected during shipping or storage. Casts should never be sealed in plastic bags because there is always a chance they still contain a little moisture inside. After a cast has dried, a loose but open covering of bubble wrap or similar material placed around the cast to allow it to breath, followed by storage in a large paper bag will provide ample protection during storage. When shipping casts, dry packing material of sufficient thickness should be used to provide additional protection from breakage. The container should be marked "fragile."

Key Words: gypsum, cast, dental stone, plaster, water-to-powder ratio, viscosity, consistency, free water

Key Points

1. Casts recover additional information and should always be made of three-dimensional impressions after examination quality photography.
2. A much higher percentage of identifications are achieved when casts are made in addition to photographs.
3. Dental stone is stronger and harder than the softer plaster casting materials used years ago; it is much easier to mix and use and can be cleaned without compromising detail.
4. The "consistency" and the proper water-to-powder ratio of the dental stone used are important.
5. Dental stone should have a viscosity that allows it to flow easily into the impression.
6. The technique used to pour dental stone into an impression is critical to the successful capture of detail.
7. Before casts are cleaned, they should always be allowed to completely air-dry, a process that will take between 24 and 48 hours.

Recovering Impressions in Snow

4

In many areas of the US and the world, snow is on the ground for a substantial number of days during the year. Whether a fresh light dusting, a heavy snowfall, refrozen snow, or melting slush, snow can retain footwear impressions produced at the scene of the crime and provide investigators with excellent information regarding the number of suspects, their shoe designs, the point of entry and exit, and the recovery of that physical evidence that can later be examined with the shoes of the perpetrators. The methods and materials used to photograph and cast impressions in snow are presented in a separate chapter to provide a clear distinction between methods used to cast impressions in soil and sand. Older methods of casting footwear impressions in snow involved tedious procedures with very limited results. References for snow casting would advocate techniques like producing a layer of talcum powder sprinkled over the surface of a snow impression to insulate the snow from the heat of the setting plaster, or dusting multiple layers of talc over the impression, each followed by a layer of shellac or clear lacquer.[*,†] Some recommended dusting three thin layers of dry plaster alternating with a water spray over the original crust.[‡] Despite these inconveniences, investigators and examiners in colder climates realized the value of making casts of snow impressions. One wrote, "Whenever practical, crime scene footwear impressions in snow should be photographed and then cast to preserve their evidentiary value."[§] Now, newer materials and methods provide far easier and more efficient ways to cast snow impressions. Like casts in sand, those in snow add additional information beyond what can be recovered through photography and permit a higher comparative value.

About Snow

Snow is the formation of pieces of frozen water that precipitate and fall to the ground in the form of crystalline flakes. Snow occurs in many forms and under a wide range of temperatures. Once fallen, snow is constantly subject to change and may be categorized with many descriptors such as fresh, refrozen, wet, dry, slushy, compact, loose, and granular. The most significant factor that influences the amount of detail in a snow impression involves the characteristics of the snow itself. One crime scene may have a fresh coating of snow that is moist and cohesive and retains very fine detail while another scene has snow that is dry or granular and retains little or no detail. The type of casting product or method used will not change those facts. If the detail in the snow impression is good, the recommended methods discussed in this chapter are capable of recovering that detail. If the snow is not capable

---

[*] Karlmark, E., Taking of casts in snow, *FBI Law Enforcement Bulletin*, 8, 1939.
[†] Pick up the trail with plaster casts, *FBI Law Enforcement Bulletin*, 20(5):6–10, 1951.
[‡] Samen, C. C., Major crime scene investigation: casting (shoe and tire impressions), *Law and Order Magazine*, 52–57, March 1972.
[§] Nause, L. A., Casting footwear impressions in snow: snowprint-wax vs. prill sulphur, *RCMP Gazette*, 54(12):1–7, 1992.

of retaining good detail, the best of snow casting materials and methods will not improve that. Snow that contains moisture will provide a substrate that will retain better detail then dry snow. It is not the intention of this chapter to discuss the various types of snow. Those who live in colder climates should have some awareness of this but it is best addressed more thoroughly in other sources.[*][†]

Photographing Snow Impressions

Recovery efforts of snow impressions require prompt attention. Snow impressions can be easily trampled or simply filled in by blowing snow or additional snowfall. Snow impressions also melt due to temperatures above freezing or through sublimation. Sublimation is the process where snow passes directly from a solid into a gas without going through the liquid phase; thus no evidence of melting is obvious. Sublimation is accelerated when impressions are exposed to sunlight or bright ambient light.

Making an effort to outline or otherwise mark the location of potentially relevant impressions, such as in Figure 4.1, should be a priority at the crime scene. The poor contrast of impressions in snow makes them more susceptible to being trampled over and often the current or predicted weather, air temperatures, or other factors require they be treated first. Like impressions in soil or sand, those in snow should be documented with general crime scene photographs and placards followed by examination quality photographs. The procedure for taking examination quality photographs for snow impressions is not unlike those in sand or soil, requiring placement of a scale on the same plane as the bottom of the impression, the use of the manual focus setting to ensure the bottom of the impression is in sharp focus, and blocking out ambient light and/or using oblique light for the purpose of creating additional contrast. The main problems regarding the photography of snow impressions are their lack of contrast and translucent nature that often interfere with the quality and detail that can be recovered.

Figure 4.1 The early location and marking of impressions in snow ensures they are protected from accidental trampling and their location is more easily documented.

[*] Adair, T., Tewes, R., Bellinger, T., and Nicholls, T. Characteristics of snow and their influence on casting methods for impression evidence, *JFI*, 57(6):807, 2007.

[†] Colbeck, S., et al., The International Classification for Seasonal Snow on the Ground, prepared by the Working Group on Snow Classification and issued by the International Commission on Snow and Ice of the International Association of Hydrology, and the International Glaciological Society, 1985.

Highlighting and Coating Impressions to Increase Contrast

One easy and successful method that can be used to increase the contrast of snow impressions is to highlight them with the application of colored sprays.[*,†] Snow Print Wax™ and Krylon™ Indoor-Outdoor Gray Primer #51318 work very well for this and do not damage the impression. Colored paint aerosols should never be used, as they contain materials that will chemically melt the snow. Figure 4.2 shows these two products with the original snow impression on top and the respective results of applying them to highlight the impressions directly below. Examination quality photographs of the impressions should be taken prior to and after highlighting. No different than with impressions in soil, the placement of the scale next to and on the same plane as the bottom of the impression is necessary. The scale can be temporarily removed during highlighting with the aerosol spray and then replaced prior to photography of the highlighted impressions. Caution must be used when highlighting an impression. If the snow is powdery, the force of the spray can easily damage the impression. The spray should be applied at a low angle of approximately 10–25°. The can should be initially held around 1.5 feet away from the impression to ensure the force of the spray does not destroy detail. Once the spray is initiated, it can be moved closer and aimed as necessary to carefully and evenly highlight the impression.

When highlighting the impression, note the side that any bright ambient lighting is coming from and apply the highlighting with the direction of the spray going in the opposite direction of that light. Figure 4.3 shows two impressions as they appear in diffused sunlight. The photographs at the bottom show one highlighted with a light spray of Krylon gray primer in the same direction as the diffused sunlight, and the other highlighted in the

Figure 4.2 Snow Print Wax and Krylon Gray Primer #51318 are two products that can successfully and safely be used to highlight snow impressions. Aerosol paint sprays should not be used.

[*] Bodziak, W. J., *Footwear Impression Evidence: Detection, Recovery and Examination*, 2nd Ed., CRC Press, 2000.
[†] Hammer, L., Wolfe, J., Shoe and tire impressions in snow: Photography and casting, *JFI* 53(6):647–655, 2003.

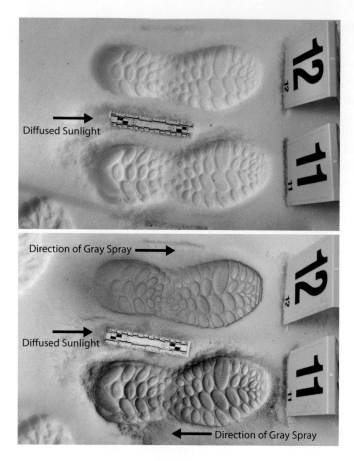

Figure 4.3 Applying the gray primer spray toward the direction of the diffused sunlight provides the best results when highlighting impressions. (Photographs provided courtesy of Jim Wolfe.)

opposite direction. The application of the gray primer provided much better contrast when applied toward the direction of the diffused sunlight.

The purpose of highlighting is to increase contrast by applying some color to the higher portions of the impression without completely painting the impression. The amount of spray used is a judgment that is made with each impression. With some, a very light application of color works well, while other impressions may require slightly more. This technique is a very quick and efficient way to increase the contrast and enhance details that can be easily recovered photographically. It is important to note the use of the highlighting technique and the subsequent coloring of the impression will result in the snow absorbing more energy from the ambient light, instantly making it more prone to melting. Impressions that have been highlighted should be photographed immediately, followed by casting or covered with an inverted box until this can be done.

Coating an impression involves a complete covering of the impression to a solid color. Coating an impression with the Krylon spray is an option in much colder conditions, usually below 20°F. Figure 4.4 includes a series of photographs of the same impression ranging from ambient light to highlighting to complete coating with Krylon gray primer. Figure 4.5 shows the results of coating a slushy impression with Snow Print Wax. Photography of coated impressions works best with oblique light and may be counterproductive without it.

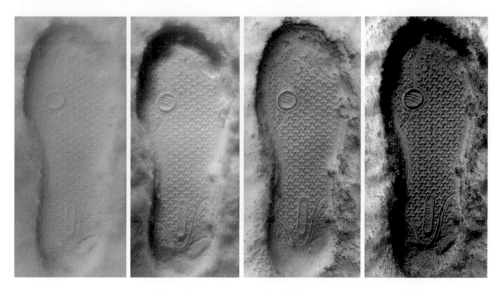

Figure 4.4 A series of sequential photographs of a snow impression. From left to right: the snow impression photographed in ambient light; with oblique light; after highlighting with gray primer; and after coating with gray primer. (Photograph provided by Jim Wolfe, Forensic Scientist, Anchorage, AK, 2014.)

Figure 4.5 A photograph of a slush impression in ambient light and a photograph of that same impression after coating with Snow Print Wax. (Photographs provided courtesy of Jim Wolfe.)

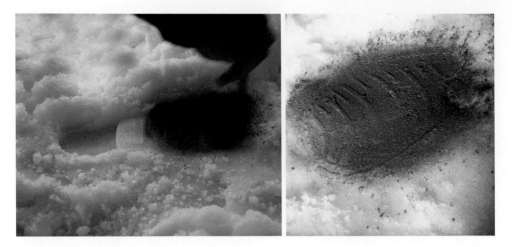

Figure 4.6 Snow Print Powder can be used to increase contrast for frozen snow or heavy slush. It should not be used in fragile or fresh snow.

Snow Print Powder™

Snow Print Powder is a red powder that can be used with a fingerprint brush on wet melting or cold frozen snow or slush to coat the surface, allowing for more contrast during photography.[*] Casting can follow this procedure. It is not recommended for fresh and fragile snow, as the brushing action will destroy the impression. Figure 4.6 shows an impression being highlighted with this technique and the results. It is noted that the same highlighting can be achieved with Snow Print Wax or Krylon Gray Primer as previously discussed.

Casting Methods and Materials

In the prior chapter there was much discussion regarding the additional detail achieved with casts and the fact that casts result in most identifications of three-dimensional impressions. The same is true for impressions in snow. A cast will provide more confirmable dimensional information and typically better detail than photographic recovery alone. Identifications, when made, usually occur because of the details provided by a cast. Many years ago, casts of snow impressions were made with plaster of Paris using modified methods.[†,‡] Newer snow casting products and methods exist and are covered hereafter.

---

[*] Kjell Carlsson Innovations.
[†] Allen, J. W., Making plaster casts in snow, *International Criminal Police Review*, 89:171–174, 1955.
[‡] Soule, R. L., Reproduction of foot and tire tracks by plaster of Paris casting, *Identification News*, 8–12, January 1961.

Snow Print Plaster (Snow Stone™)

Snow Print Plaster, also known as Snow Stone, is a product introduced in 2014.[*] It provides a very quick, easy, and efficient method of casting impressions in snow. It is sold as Snow Stone[†] and as Snow Print Plaster.[‡] Snow Print Plaster can be used without highlighting, or after highlighting or coating with Krylon gray primer. It is the most versatile of all of the snow casting materials, working well in all temperatures and with all snow types. Snow Print Plaster is shown in Figure 4.7 as sold in a plastic tub that contains three 800-gram bags of casting material. Each 800-gram bag is more than sufficient for a full shoe impression. On the tub is a water line that indicates the quantity of water (800 ml) required to mix with the powder in each bag. The procedure, shown in Figure 4.8, begins by sifting a small portion of the plaster powder over the snow impression. Sift a sufficient amount to completely cover the bottom of the impresison, normally about 2–3 mm thick. A kitchen strainer works well for this. Equal volumes of the powder and water are then combined in the provided tub or suitable container. The mixture will be very watery at first. Mixing should be continuous and quickly combine the powder and water with attempts to eliminate any lumps. In as little as 45 seconds, the mixture will begin to thicken. In some cases, this may take a bit longer. The variation of time seems to be a product of several factors, such as the preciseness of mixing equal volumes, water temperature, air temperature, and the aggressiveness of the mixing process. Since the ratio of this product to water is equal by volume, e.g., 800 grams and 800 ml water, for partial impressions you could use a smaller quantity such as 400 grams of the casting powder and combine it with 400 ml of water. As soon as the mixture begins to thicken, it should be poured directly into and spread as necessary over the impression. The mixture will thicken very rapidly and if not promptly poured it will harden rapidly in the mixing container within a matter of seconds. Once the mixture has been poured into the impression, the powder that was sifted over the impression will absorb moisture from it if it has not already done so from the snow. The mixture sets so quickly that any exothermal heat produced occurs after the cast is hard

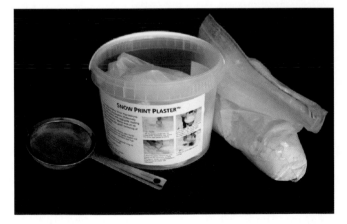

Figure 4.7 Snow Print Plaster, also known as Snow Stone, is the easiest and most versatile method of casting snow impressions in snow.

[*] Snow Print Plaster (Snow Stone) was developed by Kjell Carlsson Innovations in Sweden.
[†] Evident Inc., https://www.shopevident.com/category/casting-footwear/snowstone.
[‡] Arrowhead forensics, http://www.crime-scene.com/store/snow-impressions.shtml.

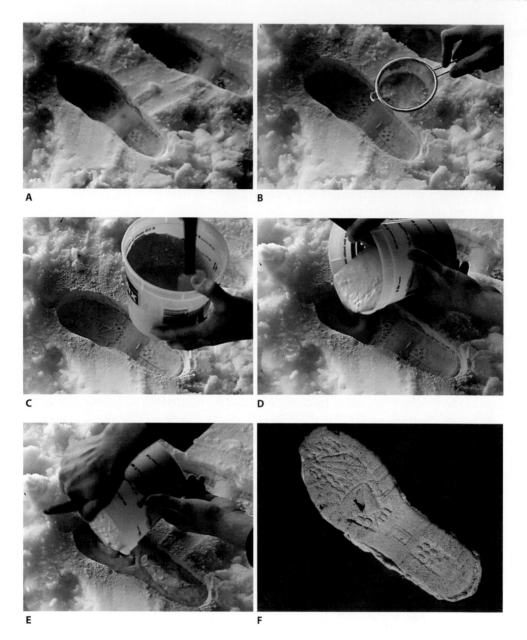

Figure 4.8 Using Snow Print Plaster to cast an impression in snow (A), sifting 2–3 mm of Snow Print Plaster powder over the snow impression (B), mixing equal volumes of Snow Print Plaster and water (C), pouring the mixture directly into the impression as soon as it begins to thicken (D), filling the impression with the mixture (E), the snow cast that results (F).

and is therefore irrelevant. The cast is safe to remove from the snow in 10 minutes. Like any gypsum-based casting material, the full hardness and strength of the cast will not be achieved until it is completely dry in 24 hours. Snow Print Plaster is not a dental stone, but a very soft plaster. Since snow casts do not need to be cleaned, the use of the softer plaster does not present a problem but it makes this product unsuitable for use in soil. A typical snow cast produced with Snow Print Plaster is shown in Figure 4.9. Snow Print Plaster is easy and quick to use, requires no elaborate equipment, and works in all snow.

Figure 4.9 A snow cast made with Snow Print Plaster. The detail in the cast will reflect the detail that has been retained by the snow but will often exceed the detail captured through photography alone. (Cast provided courtesy of Jim Wolfe.)

Snow Print Wax™

Snow Print Wax was introduced in Sweden in 1982 by Kjell Carlsson.[*] It is an aerosol spray wax, bright red in color.[†] In addition to highlighting impressions, it offers a quick and easy method for casting footwear impressions in snow.[‡,§] When it is applied to the impression according to the directions on the can, it produces a wax shell that captures the detail of the snow impression. The soft wax shell is then filled with a thick mixture of dental stone so that it may be lifted from the ground. This progression is shown in Figure 4.10. The snow impression is on the left (1), it is then highlighted and rephotographed (2), after which three coats of snow wax are sprayed into the impression to form a wax shell (3). The three separate layers of Snow Print Wax capture the detail of the impression but also seal the impression so any dental stone poured into the impression will not pass through the bottom or sides of the impression. Dental stone will be added to the coated impression and when it sets, the cast can be turned over (4). Since the function of the dental stone is only to allow the wax shell to be lifted, it should be a thicker mixture. In very cold conditions, a tablespoon of potassium sulfate can be added to the water used to mix the dental stone to reduce its freezing point and to accelerate the setting of the cast. Using a thinner mixture of dental stone increases the chances of the dental stone breaking through any small fissures in the wax shell or through the sides of the impression that might not be totally protected with the wax. Figure 4.11 shows two Snow Print Wax casts. Like other substrates, impressions in snow contain areas where some snow has spilled back into the impression and other areas where the snow did not replicate the shoe very well. The cast on the left reflects many excellent details that would almost certainly not be recovered through photography. The arrows on the left cast, from top to bottom, point to features like specific

[*] Carlsson, K., A new method for securing impressions in snow, *Crime Laboratory Digest*, 1–4, December 1982.
[†] A similar product sold in the US by Sirchie as Snow Impression Wax is more of a reddish brown color.
[‡] Ojena, S. M., A new improved technique for casting impressions in snow, *Journal of Forensic Sciences*, 29(1):322–325, 1984.
[§] Kenny, R. L., Identification of a footwear impression in the snow, presented at the International Symposium on the Forensic Aspects of Footwear and Tire Impression Evidence, FBI Academy, Quantico, VA, June 27–July 1, 1994.

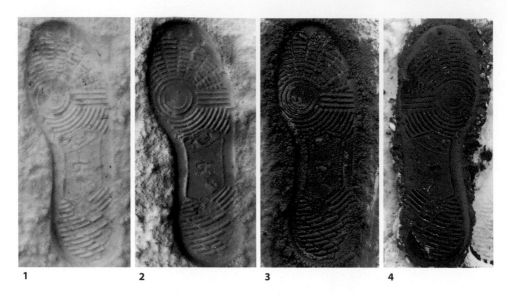

Figure 4.10 The sequence of using Snow Print Wax from the original impression (1), the highlighted impression (2), three layers of Snow Print Wax covering the impression (3), and after filling the wax-covered impression with dental stone, the finished cast turned over (4).

wear, the "Made in Korea" wording across the calendered rubber of the Wellman cut outsole, the hand-attached "size 8" label, and even a piece of string sticking out from beneath the front of the molded heel. The cast on the right was taken of an impression in a different snowfall, but also provides more reliable detail and dimensional information than could be achieved with photography. The cast on the right is provided here to illustrate a situation where sufficient coatings of Snow Print Wax did not completely seal the impression and/or the dental stone mixture was possibly too watery allowing it to pass through the sides of the impression, flowing down and beneath the actual impression, and undercutting some of the detail (see arrow). More careful application of the Snow Print Wax to the sides of the impression and the use of a thicker mixture of dental stone will prevent this from occurring. It is noted that Snow Print Wax on the cast remains soft. The soft wax layer that has captured the detail can be damaged if handled or stored carelessly. For that reason, snow casts should be photographed at the earliest convenience.

Snow Print Wax works well for both highlighting and casting if used properly. The wax spray works best at room temperature, and one disadvantage has been problems with the spray when it has been stored in a vehicle and subjected to extremely cold temperatures. Another disadvantage has been the tendency for the nozzle to clog or not spray evenly, although this was more of a problem years ago and the nozzles on the current product seem to work much better.

Dry Casting with Dental Stone

Dry casting is a method for casting snow impressions in moist snow that involves sifting three layers of dental stone powder over the impression, followed by the normal application

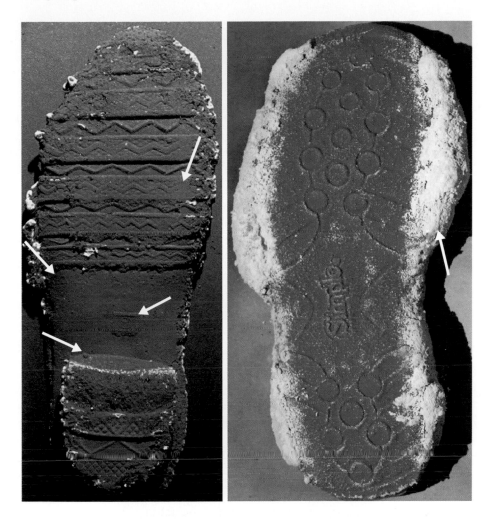

Figure 4.11 Two Snow Print Wax casts. The one on the left contains excellent detail. The cast on the right is provided as an example of undercutting that can occur if the added dental stone seeps through and/or down the sides of the impression, undercutting parts of the bottom.

of mixed dental stone.[*] Many methods mentioned in older literature advocated similar sifting methods to coat or protect the details in an impression prior to the addition of a casting product.[†,‡,§] The sifted layers capture the detail of the impression and protect it from any heat released by the subsequent addition of the dental stone mixture. Figure 4.12 depicts the sequence in the dry casting process. The impression at the top is in fresh moist snow. In the center photograph, three layers, each about 1/8 inch deep, are sifted over the impression. This first layer should be sifted slowly and evenly as opposed to quickly dumping a

---

[*] Adair, T., and Shaw, R., The dry-casting method: a reintroduction to a simple method for casting snow impressions, *JFI*, 57(6):824–831, 2007.

[†] Müllner, H., and Kaempfer, L., The Müllner moulage method, *J. Crim. Law Crim.* 23(2):351–355, 1932.

[‡] Reynard, J. N., Footprints—the practical side of the subject, *The Police Journal*, 30–34, January–March 1948.

[§] Allen, J. W., Making plaster casts in snow, *Int. Crim. Pol. Rev.* 89:171–174, 1955.

Figure 4.12 Dry casting involves sifting three layers of dental stone over the impression. The bottom shows the prepared impression ready to be covered with a dental stone mixture. Dry casting works only in moist snow.

lot of powder into the impression. It is noted that problems can occur with this method if too much powder is added too quickly. Using a kitchen strainer or lightly tapping the side of a flour sifter will provide more control. The light yellow color of the powder will visibly darken as it absorbs the moisture from the snow. A second and third 1/8-inch layer are also applied. If the snow contains sufficient moisture, such as in the case of an impression in slush, the second and third layers will also absorb sufficient moisture to turn dark. If the second or third applications no longer absorb moisture from the snow and remain light in color, a spray bottle can be used to mist water from the top until those layers turn dark. Applying moisture from the top is not detrimental as long as the first layer has successfully absorbed water from the snow, allowing it to protect the details of the impression. After the three layers are applied, a thick mixture of dental stone can be poured into the impression. When temperatures are well below freezing, a tablespoon of potassium sulfate can be added to the water when mixing the dental stone to accelerate the setting and reduce the freezing temperature of the solution. After the cast sets, it can be turned over and lifted. Most snow will contain sufficient moisture to saturate the first layer of sifted powder and allow this method to be used.

This process is similar to the Snow Print Plaster method but it should be emphasized that dry casting only works with impressions in snow that contains moisture. It relies on sufficient moisture in the snow to be absorbed by and wet the first layer of sifted powder. Whereas the Snow Print Plaster is able to absorb moisture both from the snow beneath as well as from the poured mixture above, this is not the case with using dental stone and the dry casting method. If the snow is dry and the only way to apply moisture onto the first sifted layer of dental stone is by spraying water on top of it, the net result will be degradation of detail caused by the disturbances of the water. This is the reason why the dry casting method with dental stone has not been successful for casting impressions in sand or soil.

Yellow Sulfur

Yellow sulfur has been successfully used to cast impression evidence for many years. The use of yellow sulfur powder or yellow prill sulfur has been reported extensively in the literature.[*,†,‡,§] If performed properly, the method is as capable as any method for recovering excellent detail in snow impressions. The melted sulfur, when cooled down to just above its solidification temperature, will harden the instant it is poured into the impression and touches the snow, instantly capturing the detail of the impression. The process of casting with yellow sulfur, once learned, is not that difficult, but for the inexperienced crime scene technician or for those who only occasionally encounter snow impressions, the process can be sufficiently complicated to result in failure. In addition, the sulfur casting method requires more materials and equipment and takes 20–30 minutes to cast each impression.

The materials needed include

1. A quantity of yellow sulfur powder or prill sulfur. The quantity can vary with impression size, but normally about 5 pounds will be needed for the first impression, realizing that some of this will remain on the sides of the container into which it is melted.
2. An electric heating element or hot plate will be needed to melt the sulfur. This may mean that a generator is also needed if in a remote location. Although a propane gas burner could be used, the use of any flame around sulfur is not recommended.
3. A pot to melt the sulfur in is usually in the 2–3 quart size. More important is the quality of this melting pot. Inexpensive pots do not distribute heat well and allow for hot spots that could damage the sulfur. A reasonably thick and better quality pot will make the melting process uniform and efficient.

---

[*] Carlsson, K. and Maehly, A. C., New methods for securing impressions of shoes and tyres on different surfaces, *International Criminal Police Review*, 299:158–167, 1976.
[†] Cassidy, M. J., *Footwear Identification*. Canadian Government Printing Centre, Quebec, Canada, 1980.
[‡] Bodziak, W. J., *Footwear Impression Evidence: Detection*, Elsevier Science Publishing Co, New York, 1990.
[§] Nause, L. A., Casting footwear impressions in snow: snowprint-wax vs. prill sulphur, *RCMP Gazette*, 54(12):1–7, 1992.

4. A long metal or wood spoon to safely stir the sulfur in the pot without your hands being too close. Magnetic stirring rods placed in the bottom of the pot will not work. Stirring must be almost continuous and start as soon as the heat is turned on, even as the sulfur is still in the powder form.

5. An infrared thermometer to determine the temperature of the sulfur at various times during the melting and cooling process will assist those trying this for the first time. Once you are accustomed to this process, you will not need the thermometer.

This process is illustrated in Figure 4.13. A quantity of sulfur is added to the melting pot that is then placed on the electric heating plate. The heat should initially be placed on a low setting and increased gradually. Overheating can occur in the bottom of the pot if not frequently stirred. Even in its powder form, a stirring stick should be used to move the sulfur around the bottom of the pot. Having patience in melting the sulfur is critical. Eventually some of the sulfur will begin to melt and the remaining powder will follow more quickly. Those making sulfur casts on a regular basis will know what temperature setting to begin with on their equipment and how much they can increase the heat as the melting process proceeds. Sulfur melts at around 115°C; however, if the sulfur reaches 170°C, it will change into a syrupy, thick, brown mass. This change is irreversible and will permanently ruin the mixture, which will need to be discarded. There will be a point where the majority of the powder is melted but large clumps of sulfur are still present and this is normal. When most of the sulfur melts, additional yellow sulfur can be added if needed. Even once melted, it is necessary to constantly monitor and stir during this entire process to avoid sulfur on the bottom of the pot from overheating. Once the entire quantity of sulfur has been melted,

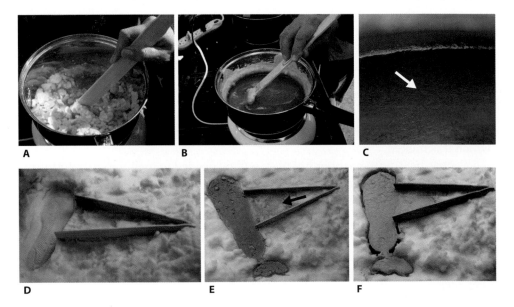

Figure 4.13 Casting with yellow sulfur. Slowly melting the sulfur in a 2–3 quart pot (A); cooling the sulfur back down while continuing to stir (B); crystals forming in the cooling sulfur (C); preparing a channel for pouring the sulfur (D); just after pouring, the sulfur is hardened where it touches the impression beneath, but is still hot on the surface (E); after cooling the sulfur returns to its lighter yellow color (F).

the heat is turned off. Stirring must continue to ensure a uniform temperature remains throughout the liquid sulfur even as it cools. This can be monitored with an infrared thermometer if necessary. When the sulfur gets within a few degrees of 115°C, crystals begin forming in the liquid, giving it a murky appearance. This can be seen in Figure 4.13B and C. Initially, restirring will dissolve these crystals. When the crystals will no longer dissolve on stirring, the sulfur is ready to pour. Prepare a channel that can direct the sulfur into the impression, as shown in Figure 4.13D and E. The sulfur should be poured without hesitation, allowing it to quickly flow and fill the impression. Once poured, the cooled sulfur will turn back to its original light yellow color. The time it takes to completely cool is dependent on the temperature and quantity of sulfur, but as a matter of safety, it is best to leave the cast undisturbed for 20–30 minutes before lifting. Yellow sulfur casts are extremely fragile and even the gentlest attempts to lift them from the snow can result in breakage. Some have advocated using a liquid plastic material to coat the back of the sulfur cast to strengthen it.[*] A quicker way to strengthen the cast is to pour dental stone on the back of the cooled sulfur cast before lifting it. To do this, prepare a thick mixture of dental stone and pour about a ½-inch layer over the back of the sulfur cast, up to about ½ to 1 inch from its edge. Note in Figure 4.13F that a gap has occurred around the perimeter of the cast resulting from the heat of the sulfur. Do not allow the dental stone to flow over the edges of the sulfur cast into this gap. Doing so will result in the dental stone flowing beneath the cast and undercutting it, obstructing part of the detail. An example of undercutting is provided in Figure 4.14.

Sulfur casting is capable of reproducing a high level of detail; however, that detail may also include the texture of the snow. The cast that was produced in the series of photographs in Figure 4.13 is shown in Figure 4.15. The snowfall was moist and retained good detail but had some texture that was also recovered by the sulfur casting and is evident across the surface of the cast.

Figure 4.14 Once the sulfur has cooled, dental stone may be applied to the back of a sulfur cast to keep it from breaking during lifting and storage. A thick mixture should be used. If the dental stone is allowed to flow over edges, it will undercut the detail as shown by the arrows.

---

[*] Adair, T., and Tewes, R., Strengthening sulfur casts with plasti-dip, Information Bulletin for Shoe Print/ Tool Mark Examiners, 12(2), August 2006.

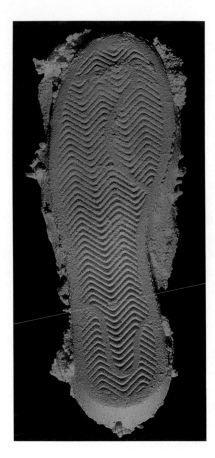

Figure 4.15 A yellow sulfur cast, as poured in Figure 4.13. The grainy surface is a product of the snow characteristics and not the sulfur technique.

Sulfur Cement

The use of sulfur cement for casting impressions in snow was introduced in 2007.[*] Sulfur cement is a product derived from sulfur and sold as Basolit Sulfur Cement.[†] It is less flammable and stronger than yellow sulfur. It is melted in a similar way as just described for yellow sulfur. Figure 4.16 shows the product and the flake form it comes in. It can be melted in an electric hot pot. Once melted it must be cooled down to the point where it begins to crystallize after which it can be poured into the snow impression. The use of an infrared thermometer is of value not only in keeping track of the temperature during cooling but also of the temperature of the poured cast to ensure it is not too hot to lift. It should be left to cool for 20–30 minutes before lifting.

Other Methods

Other methods have been tried but are not recommended. One involves the use of regular dental stone alone that has been mixed with cold water to which a tablespoon of potassium

[*] Wolfe, J. R., Sulfur cement: a new material for casting snow impression evidence, *JFI*, 58(4):485, 2008.
[†] Sauereisen Basolit Sulfur Cement #600, www.sauereisen.com.

Figure 4.16 Casting with sulfur cement.

sulfate has been added to accelerate its setting time. In spite of these modifications, the exothermic reaction and weight of the dental stone directly against the snow is not a very successful or recommended method.

Paraffin wax has also been used in the past but is not recommended. Paraffin wax must be melted slowly over a hot plate like sulfur. Hot paraffin is not compatible with the moisture in snow and that results in popping and air pockets, illustrated in Figure 4.17.*

Figure 4.17 Paraffin wax cast with air pockets that occur when the hot paraffin comes into contact with the cool moist snow.

* Bodziak, W. J., *Footwear Impression Evidence: Detection, Recovery and Examination*, 2nd ed., CRC Press, Boca Raton, FL, 2000, pp. 92–95.

After pouring, the warm paraffin wax remains soft while its warmth melts the surrounding snow, usually causing the cast to sag, twist, or bend. The level of detail it recovers is not good.

Summary

Casting methods for snow impressions have been documented and used for many years. Examiners repeatedly and consistently comment that far better examination results are possible when snow impressions are cast. Casting methods that use either yellow sulfur or sulfur cement can work well but are a drain on resources and time and are not an encouragement to most crime scene investigators. Highlighting impressions to increase contrast for photography is a very quick way to recover greater detail. For casting, Snow Print Plaster provides an efficient, safe, and highly successful way of casting footwear impressions in any type of snow.

Key Words: highlighting, coating, Snow Print Wax, Snow Print Plaster, Snow Stone, Snow Print Powder, sulfur cement, dry casting.

Key Points

1. The amount of detail varies considerably in different types and conditions of snow.
2. Impressions in snow should always be photographed first.
3. Highlighting impressions is an excellent method to enable better contrast recovered through photography. In colder climates, coating the impression is possible.
4. Casts of snow impressions provide additional detail that supplements the photography of snow impressions alone.
5. Snow Print Plaster (Snow Stone) is a safe and easy way to cast snow impressions in any type of snow.

Treatment and Lifting of Two-Dimensional Footwear Impressions

5

Dust, dirt, mud, blood, and other substances acquired on footwear outsoles transfer with each step back to the substrate, replicating features of that outsole in the form of two-dimensional impressions. These include both visible and latent forms on substrates such as tile, linoleum, wood, carpet, asphalt, and concrete, and less commonly on other surfaces such as counters, kicked doors, toilets, paper, broken glass, clothing, and skin. Dust impressions have even been reported on ice.[*] General protocol for the detection and recovery of two-dimensional impressions includes searching with both specialized light sources and the electrostatic lifting apparatus, general crime scene photography, examination quality photography, recovery of the original evidence when prudent and possible, and various other lifting and enhancement techniques. Too often, two-dimensional footwear impressions are photographed without any further attempt to recover additional details of that impression. For many, this involves a misconception that the full details replicated in an impression are completely visible and once photographed and viewed on the back of a digital camera, have been totally recovered. Experienced scene of crime investigators and experts recognize that the practice of making lifts and/or the use of enhancement techniques allows for the recovery of many additional details possibly not captured through conventional photography. Lifts provide a natural size recovery of the impression from the substrate, without any focus, scale, or perspective problems that may occur with photography. It is true there are some risks when attempting to lift an impression and not all lifts will be successful, but for impressions that cannot be removed from the scene, it is better to be equipped with the proper materials and knowledge and attempt a lift or other form of enhancement than to make no attempt at all and leave the impression behind. Leaving an impression behind to be cleaned up without making further efforts to recover detail beyond photography is unjustifiable.

Types of Two-Dimensional Impressions

Positive or Transfer Impressions

Two-dimensional impressions that occur when materials acquired on the raised outsole tread are transferred back to the substrate in subsequent steps are known as positive or transfer impressions. These were discussed in Chapter 1 and illustrated in Figure 1.3A. The majority of two-dimensional impressions fall into this category.

---

[*] Gervais, R., Footwear impression on ice, *Identification Canada*, 144–145, December 2006.

Negative Impressions

Negative impressions were also discussed in Chapter 1 and occur when the raised outsole tread removes material from a substrate and produces what is known as a negative impression. An example of a negative impression was shown in Figure 1.6 where the substrate contained a heavy coating of accumulated dust and the shoe outsole removed that dust where its tread made contact.

Dry Origin Impressions

A *dry origin* impression or mark is produced when both the shoe and the receiving substrate are dry at the time the impression is made. They commonly occur when dry shoes track across a dirty substrate and then onto a dry but relatively cleaner substrate. As an example, shoes could track over an exterior dirty porch, accumulate dirt on their outsoles, and in the first 2–3 steps inside, transfer that dirt to a cleaner substrate. Another example occurs when walking on carpet that contains a fine layer of dust accumulates on the outsole and results in dry origin impressions on papers that had fallen to the floor. In a similar way, a bank robber will often acquire sufficient dust or residue on his shoes from the bank lobby floor that is then transferred onto the teller counter he jumps on. When dry origin impressions are produced, the layer of dry material transferred from the outsole does not bond to the substrate. For that reason, dry origin impressions are easily lifted from nonporous substrates and from many porous substrates as well. These impressions are typically very thin and composed of light colored dust or residue, making them either barely visible or latent. They occur routinely but are easily missed if the crime scene officer is not aware of how they are formed and how and where to search for them.

During the production of dry origin impressions produced under low humidity, a small electrostatic charge is produced that can be demonstrated.[*,†,‡] This small charge dissipates quickly and thus has no crime scene recovery value, but it likely contributes to the substrate's retention of dry dust. More importantly, it demonstrates that some interaction between shoes and substrates is greater than most would realize.

One concern about dry origin impressions is that they can accidently be wiped away and destroyed when large areas of flooring or countertops are treated with fingerprint powder without first thoroughly searching for latent dry origin footwear impressions. When arriving at a crime scene, part of every CSI's protocol should be to look for areas where the conditions are suitable for the production of dry origin impressions. These include areas where the perpetrator may have tracked from a dusty or dirty substrate to a relatively cleaner substrate as well as any paper items on the floor that might have been stepped on.

Understanding the difference between dry origin and wet origin impressions is important when assessing potential methods of recovery. Figure 5.1 depicts two impressions created on a magazine page. The impression on the left was made after walking over a dry

[*] Young, P. A., Electrostatic detection of footprints, *Police Research Bulletin*, 21:11–15, 1973.
[†] Davis, R. J., Footwear training seminar, Michigan State Police Training Academy, Lansing, MI, 1985.
[‡] Bodziak, W. J., *Footwear Impression Evidence: Detection, Recovery and Examination*, 2nd ed., CRC Press, Boca Raton, FL, 2000, pp. 8–9.

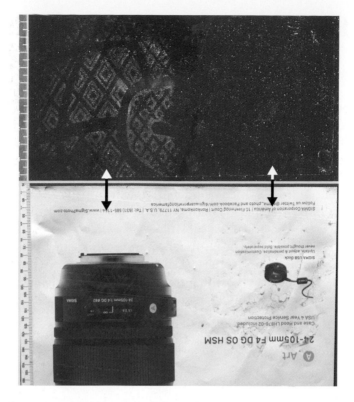

Figure 5.1 The bottom portion depicts a magazine page where two impressions were made. On the left is a dry origin impression and on the right is a wet origin impression. The top portion of this photograph shows the results of the electrostatic lift. The dry origin impression was easily lifted whereas details of the wet origin impression were not.

but dirty exterior surface (dry origin) while the other was made with a muddy shoe (wet origin). An electrostatic lift was made of the entire page. An electrostatic lift of that area resulted in a lift of the dry origin impression but was unsuccessful lifting the wet origin muddy print that bonded more firmly to the paper.

Wet Origin Impressions

A two-dimensional wet origin impression occurs when the shoe outsole and/or the receiving substrate are damp or wet at the time the impression is made. When moisture is present, the impression will have a greater bond to the substrate and often includes some penetration into or absorption by the substrate. Moisture on the shoes of the perpetrator can come from rain, damp grass, melting snow, and other sources. Wet origin impressions vary considerably. Some are produced from soiled or muddy outsoles and include some coloration that makes them more visible. Others are thin and transparent, and more difficult to find. Like the muddy print on the magazine page in Figure 5.1, moisture-laden impressions dry very rapidly and thus these impressions will be dry by the time a crime scene investigator locates them. Some, but not all, wet origin marks will reflect visual features of their origin type and components such as blood or mud.

Why Lifting Can Be Complex

There are many different levels of porosity and texture of substrates. Figure 5.2 is not intended to represent all situations surrounding all impressions but merely to illustrate that there are so many possibilities. The top example in Figure 5.2 depicts three impressions on a nonporous substrate such as a smooth countertop or tile floor. One is a dry origin impression resting loosely on the surface. It has a minimal bond to the substrate and will be easy to lift. Next is a wet origin impression such as might be created by a muddy or dirty wet outsole. This impression would become dry shortly after it was produced and although lying on top of the nonporous substrate, its moisture provides a greater degree of bond to the substrate. Third is a dried blood mark that is initially wet and so also bonds to the substrate. The bottom example in Figure 5.2 shows the same three impressions but now they are on a porous substrate. Porous substrates vary widely. Items like paper could be coated or have sufficient fillers and be minimally porous while other paper items like cardboard may be more porous and absorbent. Fabrics also vary widely, ranging from tightly woven water repellent versions to those that are more coarse, absorbent, and openly woven. Unfinished concrete, raw wood, and many other substrates have wide ranges of porosity.

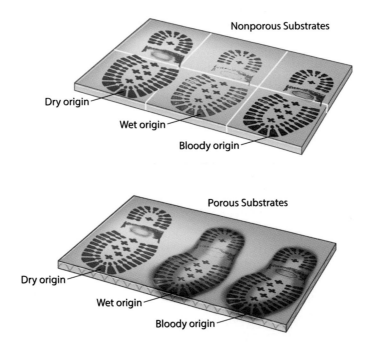

Figure 5.2 Dry origin, wet origin, and bloody impressions on numerous nonporous and porous substrates create many different lifting challenges and require various techniques and materials. No single lifting material will work for all of the different combinations.

Dry origin impressions on porous substrates may still rest loosely on the surface enabling them to be lifted. Wet origin and blood impressions will have some degree of penetration into the porous substrate depending on the amount and type of moisture, the degree of porosity, and possible absorption.

When deciding what methods of lifting should be used, many factors should be considered. Is the substrate nonporous? If porous, to what degree and how much has the impression penetrated? Is it also absorbent? Is the substrate clean or is it dirty and likely to interfere with a lift? Is the impression of wet or dry origin? Is the composition of the transferred material blood, mud, grease, dirt, dry dust or residue, or simply unknown? Is the impression very thin and barely visible? Are there other methods of enhancement that should be considered instead of lifting or in combination with lifting? Is there a sequence of lifting and/or enhancement methods to be considered that would provide a greater chance of success? There is no single step-by-step procedure or list of materials that will always work for every impression. When crime scene investigators have many appropriate lifting materials and enhancement techniques at their disposal and the experience of using them, they will be best equipped to make good choices and have productive results.

Not every impression can be lifted with any one method because they are not all composed of the same materials nor are they on the same type substrate. Many investigators and crime scene technicians are equipped for or experienced with only one type of lifting material. This significantly reduces the chances of success. Not all lifts will be successful but a good percentage of impressions can be lifted in a conventional way, have their detail transferred to a gelatin lift even though the actual impression doesn't lift, or can be chemically enhanced after which the chemical traces can be lifted. More conventional methods of lifting impressions or the details of those impressions are covered in this chapter. Methods that involve gelatin lifting of traces after chemical enhancement of bloody impressions are covered in Chapter 7.

Electrostatic Lifting

History

In May 1965, Tokyo's Yomiuri daily newspaper contained an article, summarized as follows:

> The Metropolitan Police Department (MPD, Japan) has developed a new method for exact reproduction of footmarks, often a vital element in criminal investigations. The new method is the brainchild of a group of three MPD identification experts led by police sergeant Sancyasu Toma who used static electricity to produce this simple yet highly practical device. The new method consists of rubbing the surface of a black celluloid sheet with a piece of woolen cloth to generate static electricity. This sheet is then placed on an object bearing a footprint, after which the celluloid sheet is rubbed once again with the same woolen cloth. The static electricity thus generated attacks dirt sticking to the surface of the object, causing the footmark to emerge distinctly on the sheet.[*]

---

[*] Personal communication from FBI Legal Attache, Tokyo, December 20, 1965.

Figure 5.3 A black celluloid sheet and wool cloth were originally used to create a small static electric charge to make an electrostatic lift of dry origin impressions.

Figure 5.3 shows the above-cited black celluloid sheet and wool cloth sold in Japan in the 1960s. In July 1970, a 41-year-old police officer named Kato Masao of Shikoku, Japan, observed that dust always accumulated around the high-voltage boxes of television sets. With further research and experimentation, he was able to produce the first electrostatic lifting device using a high-voltage source to produce static electricity.[*] This initial machine was large and not very portable, as it needed to be plugged into a main current source. It also utilized a permanent black lifting plate that necessitated that each lifted impression be photographed and then wiped cleaned before making the next lift.

In 1981, Young and Morantz created a prototype portable battery operated electrostatic lifter.[†] In 1983, the Metropolitan Police Forensic Science Laboratory produced battery operated electrostatic lifters specifically for in-house use.[‡,§] Foster and Freeman produced the first commercially available portable high-voltage electrostatic lifting device that operated on rechargeable batteries and utilized disposable lifting film. Figure 5.4 depicts the original Foster and Freeman device that came in a small briefcase.[¶] With this portable lifting device, a piece of disposable black lifting film was placed over the impression, black side down, and the static charge produced by the high-voltage unit would cause the dust or residue particles composing the footwear impression to transfer to the black side of the lifting film. Figure 5.4 also depicts a before-and-after case example of a lift of dry origin impressions from a paper item collected from a bank robbery scene.

---

[*] An electrostatic method for lifting footprints, *International Criminal Police Review*, National Police Agency, 272:287–292, 1973.

[†] Brennan, J. S., The visualization of shoe marks using the electrostatic detection apparatus, *MPFSL Report #10*, Metropolitan Police Forensic Science Laboratory, October 1981.

[‡] Davis, R. J., Footwear training seminar, Michigan State Police Training Academy, Lansing, MI, 1985.

[§] Davis, R. J., The enhancement of two-dimensional footwear impressions using electrostatic lifting, ESDA and gel lifting, presented at the International Symposium on the Forensic Aspects of Footwear and Tire Impression Evidence, FBI Academy, Quantico, VA, June 27–July 1, 1994.

[¶] Obtained in 1983 from Foster and Freeman, Ltd.

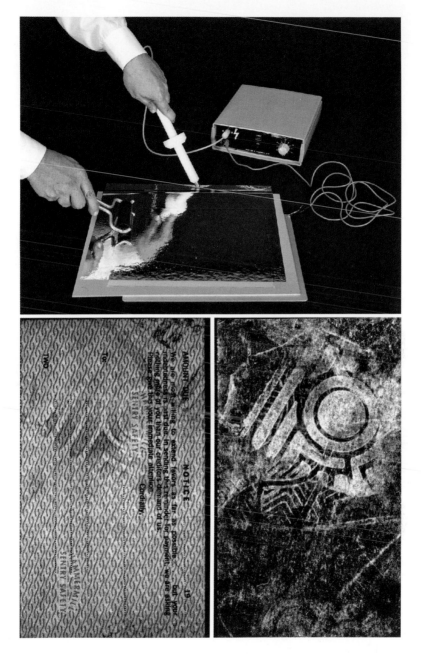

Figure 5.4 The top photograph depicts Foster and Freeman's Dustmark Electrostatic Lifter first sold in 1983. The bottom photographs illustrate a case example of a piece of paper stepped on during a bank robbery and the electrostatic lift of the impressions on that paper.

Choices of Electrostatic Lifters

During electrostatic lifting, thousands of volts are used to create a static electric charge that attracts the dust particles to the lifting film. For many years, the portable electrostatic lifters were housed in briefcases and were comprised of a high-voltage unit, a large aluminum ground plate, a cable for connecting the ground plate to the main unit, and a

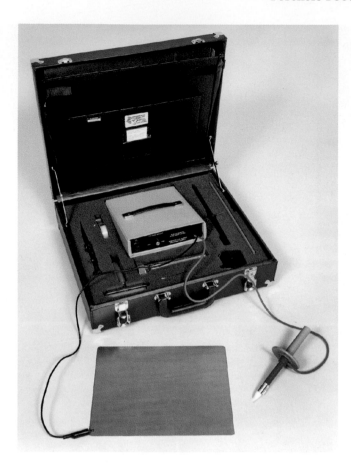

Figure 5.5 For many years electrostatic lifters were sold in a briefcase such as this one introduced in 1985 by the Kinderprint Company.

metal hand-held probe, as shown in Figure 5.5.* In 1995, Robert Milne designed a hand-held portable wireless lifter named the Pathfinder ESL Unit.† Milne actually developed this unit in the 1980s but it was not until the 1990s that it was commercially produced and sold by Crime Scene Investigation Equipment, Ltd.‡ Shown in Figure 5.6 and Figure 5.7, the Pathfinder is approximately 4 × 6 inches yet has the same lifting power as the larger briefcase versions. On its back, when making a lift, the two metal ground poles at one end (see arrows) are positioned on the small aluminum ground plate while the single metal pole for the positive lead (see single arrow) is positioned on the aluminum side of the lifting film. The Pathfinder has proved to be extremely successful and popular and has replaced most briefcase versions. The Pathfinder also has a ground plug that can be connected to the ground portion of a main electrical socket in those situations where extra grounding is necessary. Other hand-held lifters such as the Sirchie Unit, also shown in Figure 5.6, have since been created. Electrostatic lifters utilize high voltage but very low amperage.

---

* Electrostatic Lifting Kit produced in 1985 by Steve Ojena of the Kinderprint Company.
† Milne, R., The development of a wireless electrostatic mark lifting method and its use at crime scenes, *JFS*, 62(2):154, 2012.
‡ Personal communication with Grahame Sandling, Crime Scene Investigation Equipment Ltd., 2015.

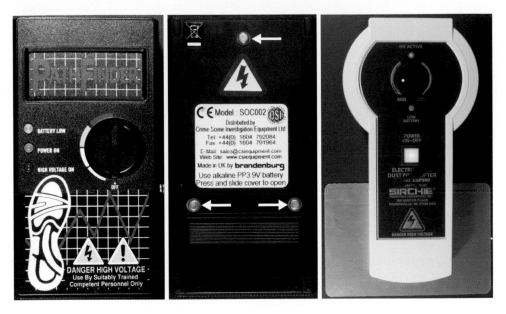

Figure 5.6 On the left and center are the respective front and back views of the Pathfinder ESL Unit. On the right is an electrostatic lifter sold by Sirchie.

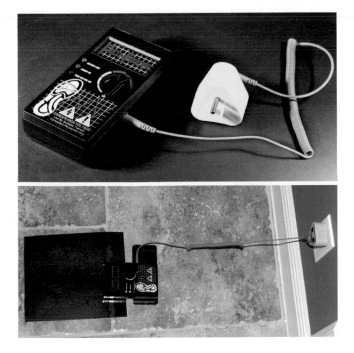

Figure 5.7 The Pathfinder ESL unit shown with an earth-grounding device. On the bottom is a lift in progress with the earth ground cord plugged into the electric wall socket.

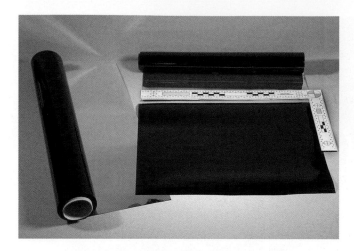

Figure 5.8 Electrostatic lifting film is commercially sold in various forms, including long rolls and precut sheets of various sizes.

The Lifting Film

The disposable lifting film for electrostatic lifting is a polyester film that is coated with a glossy black finish on one side and contains a vacuum deposition of aluminum on the opposite side. The glossy black color provides excellent contrast with the light gray color of dust or other residues that are typically lifted. The aluminum-coated side provides even distribution of the static charge across the film. The film is available in individual sheets as well as long rolls, as shown in Figure 5.8. Individual sheets of 10 × 14 inches offer the convenience of being precut and work well when you only need to lift a single or partial visible impression. Individual sheets of that size are neither of sufficient size nor are practical for searching large surfaces. Long rolls of lifting film also come in 12 to 18 inch widths, are easy to handle and carry, and can be cut to whatever length is necessary when searching large areas for impressions. They are also easily cut into smaller sheet size pieces of film when impressions are partially visible and lifted individually.

Electrostatic Lifting Applications

The texture and color of many substrates combined with thin dust mark impressions result in poor contrast, often preventing their successful detection. The result of the successful case lift shown in Figure 5.4 illustrates an example where a portion of the impression was visible and resulted in an electrostatic lift that provided far greater detail as well as the visualization of a second shoe design.

Although the initial search for footwear dust marks on two-dimensional substrates involves visual means assisted by reflected and oblique light, many detailed dry origin impressions are often present but cannot be located using those methods alone. An additional method of searching for latent impressions involves the use of large sections of lifting film and the electrostatic lifting apparatus (ESLA). This process, sometimes called cold or blind searching, is very successful in detecting and recording previously undetected impressions where the perpetrator has entered the crime scene and tracked from dusty or dirty substrates to cleaner ones.

The potential for lifting dusty shoe impressions from human skin with the electrostatic lifter has been explored and provided some success, particularly on homicide victims prior to being removed from the crime scene.[*] Further research comparing electrostatic lifting, adhesive lifting, and gelatin lifting concluded gelatin lifters were the most successful for recovering dust prints from skin.[†,‡,§]

The Lifting Process

The original briefcase versions, a few of which are still in use, have rechargeable batteries that don't last forever and must be replaced. The newer and smaller electrostatic lifters, such as the Pathfinder, utilize 9V batteries and have low-battery warning lights that tell the user it is time to change the battery.

For those new to electrostatic lifting or with limited experience, attempting lifts of dry origin impressions on a variety of substrates is the best way to gain a good understanding of when and where to use this device at a future crime scene. Many impressions located visually at a scene may appear to represent a portion of the impression but are actually more complete impressions. Thus, using larger pieces of lifting film is recommended. It is not uncommon for shoes to partially step in blood, leaving subsequent partial bloody impressions as shown in Figure 5.9, but the likelihood exists that the non-bloodied portion of the shoe also made contact with the substrate and transferred its latent impression. Prior to any chemical enhancement of partial bloody impressions, consideration should be made to make a lift to recover the remaining possible portion of the shoe impression. In the Figure 5.9 example, the shoe produced an impression partially in blood and partially in dust. The lift has recovered the dust portion but has not prevented the subsequent chemical enhancement of the blood portion. In this demonstration, a gelatin lifter was used, as it also provided some recording of the blood area and was best for this illustration; however, an electrostatic lifter would also have recovered the dry origin portion of the impression and would not have harmed the blood portion. After the lift was made, the blood mark was treated with diaminobenzidine, providing additional enhancement. To illustrate this further, the bottom portion of Figure 5.9 is a typical crime scene photograph where paper items on the ground were stepped on with bloody footwear and lifts of the paper items could potentially visualize latent impressions of the non-blood areas.

Attempting to lift residue footwear impressions from dirty substrates whether they are nonporous or carpeted will often result in the lifting of the background dust as well. For instance, carpet contains considerable dust and if you walk across a carpet, your shoes will pick up and redeposit the same dust back onto the carpet. An electrostatic lift will not distinguish the impression from the background dust but will result in a lift of all of the dust. If the carpet were very clean and a different type of dry material were transferred to the carpet from the shoe, some success using electrostatic lifting could occur. The same would apply if you walked across a dry dusty basement floor where shoes would pick up and redeposit the

[*] Adair, R., and Dobersen, M., Lifting dusty shoe impressions from human skin: a review of experimental research from Colorado, *JFI*, 56(3), 2006.

[†] Tovar, R., The use of electrostatic equipment to retrieve impressions from the human body, *JFI*, 54(5):530–533, 2004.

[‡] Wiesner, S., Cohen, A., Shor, Y., and Weiss, R., A comparative research on recovering dust shoeprints from bodies, presented at the Pattern and Impression Symposium, Clearwater, FL, August 2012.

[§] Shor, Y., Cohen, A., Wiesner, S., and Weiss, R., Recovering dusty shoe prints from skin: comparative research, *The Open Forensic Science Journal*, 7:1–5, 2014.

Figure 5.9 The top left photograph depicts a partial bloody impression; the top right a gelatin lift of the entire area showing that the non-bloody areas of the shoe produced a dust impression of the heel area on the tile; the top center is a diaminobenzidine enhancement of the bloody portion made after the lift. The bottom photograph is an example of evidence found at a crime scene where portions of the impression are in blood but latent portions in dust likely exist on the paper.

same dust back to the floor; however, if the shoe then stepped onto a relatively clean piece of paper or onto a clean counter or any other relatively clean substrate, the acquired dust on the shoe would transfer to that cleaner substrate in the form of a detectable impression.

Since most electrostatic lifters used today are of the smaller, portable variety like the Pathfinder Electrostatic Dustprint Lifter, the following procedures and discussion will utilize that device.*

---

* Provided courtesy of Crime Scene Investigation Equipment Ltd, www.csiequipment.com (Europe).

Position the Pathfinder, Film, and Ground Plate Figure 5.10 illustrates a demonstration of the lifting process with the Pathfinder. When making a lift, place the sheet of lifting film over the impression with the black side down. Since dry origin impressions are fragile, avoid sliding the lifting film over the impression. Position the ground plate about 1 inch from the lifting film. The plate needs to rest flat on the substrate so it makes maximum contact to provide a good electrical ground. The pair of metal ground poles at one end of the Pathfinder should be positioned on the ground plate. The single metal pole at the opposite end represents the positive lead and should be placed so it rests on top of the aluminum side of the lifting film. Once this is done, the Pathfinder can be turned on to initiate the lift. The red light on the Pathfinder will light up when both the ground poles and positive pole are making contact.

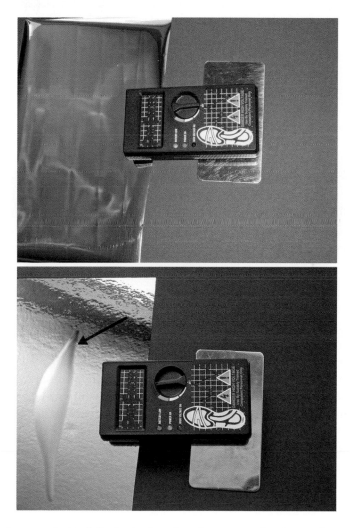

Figure 5.10 At the top, the Pathfinder is placed with its ground poles on the metal ground plate and its positive pole on the lifting film. Notice the film is loose prior to applying the charge. When the power is turned on, the film draws down tightly against the surface. Sometimes an air bubble (see arrow) will be trapped beneath the film and substrate. In most cases, just waiting 15 to 30 seconds will result in that air bubble dissipating. If not, a fingerprint roller can be gently used to move the bubble toward the edge of the film.

Make Sure You Have a Good Ground   A good ground is necessary when making an electrostatic lift. The supplied aluminum metal ground plate works very well in most situations. When the Pathfinder is in contact with both the film and the ground plate, and the power is turned on, the film will "draw down" as if being attracted to the substrate. This is evident in the bottom photograph of Figure 5.10. If this does not occur and the film remains loose, it can be due to a weak battery or for other reasons related to poor grounding. Poor grounding may occur if the surface is uneven or textured and the ground plate is not making complete contact with the substrate. In that case, one alternative would be to take a scrap piece of lifting film and use it in lieu of the ground plate. To do this, fold a scrap piece of lifting film in half like a book so the aluminum-coated side faces outward on both sides and use it in lieu of the ground plate. When the charge is applied, the side facing the substrate will conform to and make better contact with any uneven surface while the other side will stay in contact with the ground poles of the Pathfinder. The Pathfinder also now has what the manufacturer calls an earth bonding kit. This is depicted in Figure 5.7 and includes an optional way to connect the Pathfinder ground to the ground pole of an electric socket, resulting in additional lifting power to the film.

Once the film is drawn down, the lifting process will be complete in a few seconds. If any pockets of air become trapped between the film and the substrate, no lift will take place beneath those areas. An air pocket like that shown with the arrow in Figure 5.10 will usually collapse or migrate to the edge in a few seconds. If not, a fingerprint roller can be gently used to eliminate the air pocket by directing it toward the edges of the film. Only the weight of the roller is needed to achieve this. When the lift is complete, the lifter can be turned off but should remain in contact with the film for 2 seconds. This provides time for the film to discharge and reduces any static shock when the film is lifted. Milne notes that in those cases where the film is not attracted to a surface, it still has a high voltage charge and the use of a roller will cause contact between the dust and film, allowing for a successful lift.[*]

Removing the Lifting Film   After the Pathfinder or other lifting device has been turned off, keep it in contact with the film for a couple of seconds to allow the film to discharge. Ensure you have marked the back of the lifting film and/or made notes regarding the direction of the film and location within the crime scene. This is best done carefully with a soft tipped marker in a corner of the lift to ensure you are not making any indentations that would transfer to the opposite side and interfere with a lifted impression. The film can be removed from the impression by carefully peeling it back from one end to the other. Once removed, the film can be examined carefully with an intense oblique light source grazing its surface to see if any impression was successfully lifted. Many times, lifting film viewed in bright ambient light and/or without a strong oblique light source will initially appear to contain no impressions, only to find later that examination of that film in total darkness with a strong oblique light reveals the presence of faint, but very valuable impressions. If this type of examination is not possible at the crime scene, the lift should be saved until it can be properly examined.

When impressions have been successfully lifted, a snapshot photograph can be taken and provided immediately to the investigation team. The sooner they have this information,

---

[*] Milne, R., The development of a wireless electrostatic mark lifting method and its use at crime scenes, *JFS*, 62(2):163, 2012.

Figure 5.11 A smartphone and oblique light were used to make an informal photograph of an electrostatic lift taken at a scene to provide or send a quick photograph to investigators so they can be aware of what shoe design to be searching for during their investigation. Sharing the design quickly with the investigative team should be a priority. Properly taken examination quality photographs with a scale will be taken later.

the more valuable this evidence will be. Figure 5.11 depicts an example of an informal photograph taken of a lift by using a smart phone and oblique light from a flashlight. This photograph is not for forensic comparison, but taken to provide investigators a quick image of the outsole design that possibly belongs to the perpetrators. Examination quality photographs will be taken later in the laboratory for future comparison with any seized footwear.

Using Rolls of Lifting Film   Rolls of lifting film provide a means of searching large areas such as the floor just inside the point of entry. For this process, larger overlapping lifts are necessary. Figure 5.12 depicts how a roll of film is used to search for latent impressions in a large area where the perpetrator may have tracked across and produced latent dusty footwear impressions.

When using a roll of film to search a large area for latent impressions,

1. First, identify the area of interest to be searched. This will often be a nonporous substrate just inside a point of entry or possible point of entry but can also be other areas throughout the crime scene.
2. Position the roll of film so that, as it rolls out, it will cover the desired area. Unroll the film for the first few inches only.
3. Position the ground plate about 1 inch from the end of the film. Place the Pathfinder in a position so it makes contact with the ground plate and film.
4. Turn the Pathfinder on and increase the charge to maximum. This should charge the film and draw it down against the substrate. With the charge on, use a non-conductive item such as a pencil or plastic ruler to assist in rolling the charged film over the desired area. When this is done with the charge on, few to no air pockets will form. Alternately, if you cut a large sheet of film and laid it on the surface and then charged it, many large pockets of air would be trapped. Normally on ground substrates, there is sufficient grounding to make large lifts of 4–6 feet in length. An example of this is shown in the top portion of Figure 5.12.
5. Turn off the Pathfinder and leave it in contact with the film for a couple of seconds to discharge the film.

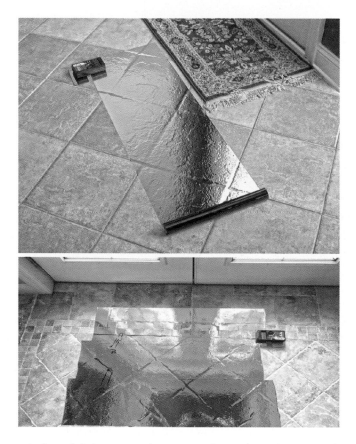

Figure 5.12 A single long lift being made just inside a point of entry. On the bottom, three overlapping lifts were made to cover a larger area.

6. Mark the film as necessary to identity the lift and where the impression was located.
7. Cut the film to separate it from the roll. If making a second or third overlapping lift as shown in the bottom of Figure 5.12, reposition the roll of film and proceed to repeat the above procedure. Use a marker to identify each lift and its relative position.
8. When done, the film can be turned over and examined with a high intensity oblique light. Informal photographs, as shown in Figure 5.11, can be taken to document lifted impressions for the investigation team.

Lifting from Metal Substrates

The occasion to make an electrostatic lift from a metal substrate such as a car hood or metal countertop is rare. Since this would occur only if the impression were visible, the easy solution may be to use a gelatin lifter instead. If there is a need to make the electrostatic lift from a metal substrate, it can be accomplished by placing a piece of clear polyester or Mylar film over the impression followed by placing a slightly smaller piece of the black lifting film over the polyester. The polyester creates a barrier that prevents direct contact between the lifting film and metal substrate.[*] The impression will transfer to the clear polyester whereas the black lifting film was used only to facilitate the lift.

Handling and Storage of the Individual Lifts

Lifted impressions cling to the lifting film because of the slight residual charge; however, lifted impressions are fragile and can easily be wiped away if touched or not stored properly. For smaller lifts, placing them in a folder is a practical and safe way to both preserve and store them. The folder must be clean and large enough to accommodate the lift. Figure 5.13 shows a legal size folder with a lift placed on one side and secured with a small piece of tape to prevent movement. With the tape holding it in place, the folder can be closed and reopened without damage to the lift. Since many lifts are larger than legal size folders, larger sized custom-made folders from local stationary or office supply stores can be acquired for this purpose. Once used, any folder used to store a lift should be dedicated to that lift and not be reused for another case. Dust or residue on the lift can transfer to the folder and, if reused, can transfer back from the folder to the lifting film used in a future crime scene. An example of a partial transfer of a lift to the folder is shown in Figure 5.14.

Another method is to place the lift in the bottom of a clean exhibit box. Storage in boxes requires the lift to be securely taped so it does not roll up on itself or move around freely inside the box when moved. This may be acceptable as a temporary way to transport the film, but over time, the tape will dry out, allowing the film to curl or roll up, particularly if the boxes are stored on their sides in an evidence room. Corrugated boxes and pizza boxes like those shown in Figure 5.15 contain inherent cardboard dust that the residual charge on the film will attract; thus these are not recommended. Lifts or original items that contain dry residue impressions should never be covered in plastic or stored in a plastic bag.

In cases where long lengths of film are used, the film can be rolled up onto itself from one end to another with the metalized side on the outside. It is natural that it does not roll up perfectly straight, and you should not try to correct this by rerolling the film or tapping

Figure 5.13 Large folders are an excellent way to preserve and store electrostatic lifts.

[*] Bodziak, W. J., *Footwear Impression Evidence: Detection, Recovery, and Examination*, 2nd ed., CRC Press, Boca Raton, FL, 2000, p. 108.

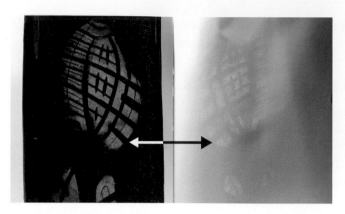

Figure 5.14 When the folder is closed, some of the dust or residue from the lift may transfer to the opposite side of the folder. This is minimal but the folder should be dedicated to this lift and not be used in another case.

Figure 5.15 Corrugated pizza boxes contain cardboard dust and are not a clean choice for storage. The residual charge of the film often attracts the loose dust, obscuring important detail.

its ends, as this will rub and degrade the impressions. Once rolled up, a piece of tape placed on the roll will secure it. The rolled up lift can now be carefully transferred to the laboratory. The film should not be unrolled until it is photographed in the lab. Unrolling and rerolling the film can cause deterioration of lifted impressions. Even if done carefully, some research has concluded that lifts will degrade more quickly if rolled up and/or placed in tubes.[*] As an alternate to rolling the film, the positions and directions of any successfully lifted impressions on long lifts can be documented and then the individual impressions can be cut out and placed in separate clean folders. In either case, lifts will deteriorate over time, thus photography should precede storage of lifts as a manner of preservation of evidence.

Briefly summarized, successful electrostatic lifts should be photographed at the scene to provide important information to the investigators, should then be transported to the laboratory in clean folders or securely taped in clean containers, and they should be photographed as soon as possible in preference to relying on their long-term storage without fading.

---

[*] Bandey, H., Footwear mark recovery, presentation before the Scientific Working Group for Shoe Print and Tire Track Evidence (SWGTREAD), March 2010.

Photographing Electrostatic Lifts

Forensic examination of electrostatic lifts relies on the photographs because the dust marks on the film are fragile and because the photographs often visualize impressions much better than viewing them directly on the film. The black lifting film can be photographed with oblique light in a totally darkened room with a professional DSLR camera. Because the black film is glossy, reflected images of the camera or other objects will become part of the photograph if precautions are not taken to avoid this. The black side of a flat scale with light-colored scale markings should be placed on the opposite side of the lift from which the light will come. A black magic marker can be used to darken the edge of the scale that will be facing the light source. A black cloth can be used to cover any light-colored reflective areas such as walls or nearby equipment that might be present and reflect light into the camera lens. A strong beam of oblique lighting that grazes the surface of the lift is required and should be directed from several feet away so the light is evenly distributed across the film. The lift should be viewed through the camera lens using the live view on the LCD screen to adjust the position of the oblique light for optimal results. It is essential that the camera be directly over the lift being photographed so the sensor is parallel to the lift. Figure 5.16 depicts an electrostatic lift being photographed in a laboratory studio. Certain LED lights such as shown in Figure 1.16 may also be used for photography of electrostatic lifts.

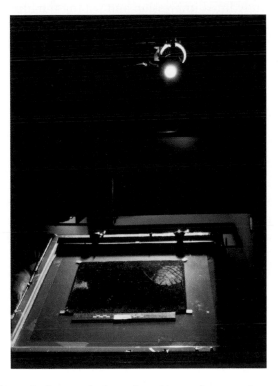

Figure 5.16 Using oblique light in a darkened studio to photograph an electrostatic lift.

Cleaning Dust from Impressions and Lifts

Some lifts not only contain impressions but may also include additional background dust from the substrate. Substrates like raw wood, dirty floors, carpet, and corrugated cardboard boxes typically contain loose particles that are also attracted to the film during lifting and as a result, obscure the impression. One case involved a faint impression on a piece of gypsum board. Gypsum board contains a lot of residual gypsum dust that would also be lifted with an electrostatic lifter and obliterate or interfere with details of the impression. The area of dust beneath the footwear impression has been compacted by the shoe and will usually be more firmly attached to the board than the loose adjacent dust. In the case example, using a strong blast of compressed air to blow away the residual loose gypsum dust cleaned the impression area while the compacted dust beneath the shoe impression remained. That impression was then photographed and lifted. Compressed air has also been used to remove excess residual dust from electrostatic lifting film without harming the lifted shoe impressions. It is noted there is no guarantee these techniques will always work, but because they potentially can provide improved results after the film has first been photographed, they might be considered an additional means of recovering better detail.

Reusing Film

Lifting film that is used at scenes should never be wiped clean with the intention of reusing that film. Many lifts are successful but the lifted impressions can only be seen in a totally dark room with intense oblique light. A cursory look at film under normal ambient lighting may miss a successfully lifted impression and wiping the film clean will destroy that evidence. Even if the lift is photographed in the laboratory, portions of the impression may remain after wiping and remain on that film when used again. This could result in cross-contamination between scenes. There is no justifiable reason to reuse film when recovering actual evidence.

Static Cling Film

Vinyl static cling film (VSCF) is commercially used for signs, decals, and window graphics and has been reported to have success lifting visible dust impressions.[*] The film comes with a white backing that is removed prior to placing the film over the impression. This film does not have a strong static charge, thus once positioned over the impression, a fingerprint roller must be used to assist in the transfer of dust to the film. The film must be secured by hand at all times or it will slide freely over the surface. Figure 5.17 shows a lift of a heavy dry dust impression from a piece of paper, with portions lifted using a black gelatin lifter, an electrostatic lifter, and the static cling film. This example was made to demonstrate that the static cling film can make a successful lift but the film does not provide any advantages over nor does it have the same lifting power as electrostatic or gelatin lifts.

---

[*] LeMay, J., Adams, S., and Stephen, A., Validation of vinyl static cling film for the collection and preservation of dust impressions, *JFI*, 61(4):317–332, 2011.

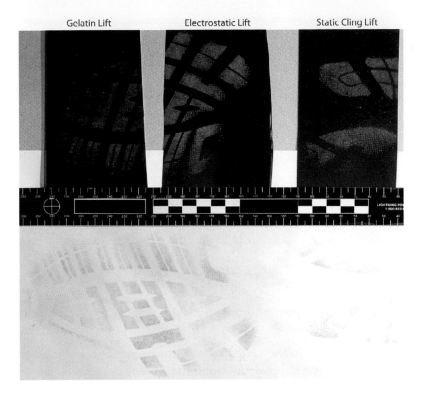

Figure 5.17 Lifts of a single dust impression using a gelatin lifter, an electrostatic lifter, and static cling film adjacent to the original impression.

Gelatin Lifters

The gelatin-coated surfaces found on photographic sheet films were once used to lift impressions, as referenced in older literature. One early account of this described the method of using photographic sheet film that became tacky when moistened and could then be used to lift dust and other impressions from flooring surfaces.[*] Others used similar ways well before the commercial production of gelatin lifters.[†,‡,§] One recommended the use of a neoprene material they described as having sufficient flexibility and tackiness to lift impressions.[¶] Some police forces actually made their own versions of gelatin lifters before they were commercially available.[**]

Commercially sold gelatin lifters, shown in Figure 5.18, are sold in sealed foil pouches that extend their useful life and help protect them against excessive temperatures. As long

[*] A method of reproducing footmarks, etc. from certain objects, *The Police Journal*, 9, 1936, Philip Allan & Co. LTD, London.

[†] Hamilton, D., Traces of footwear, tyres and tools, etc., in criminal investigation, *The Police Journal*, 22:42–49, and 128–137, 1949.

[‡] O'Hara, C. E., and Osterburg, J., *An Introduction to Criminalistics*, The MacMillan Company, New York, 1949, pp. 103–120.

[§] Abbott, J. R., Reproduction of footprints, *RCMP Quarterly*, 9(2):186–193, 1941.

[¶] Watson, J., A method of lifting and photographing for evidence, *J. Criminal Law, Criminology and Police Science*, 49:89–90, 1958.

[**] Davis, R. J., A systematic approach to the enhancement of footwear marks, *Canadian Society Forensic Science Journal*, 21(3):98–105, 1988.

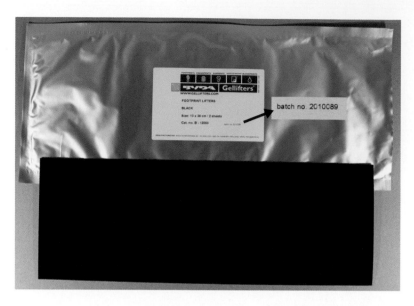

Figure 5.18 The BVDA gelatin lifters come two per foil package. The package contains a number that indicates the year and batch number.

as the gelatin lifters remain in the sealed aluminum pouch at reasonable temperatures, they will be useable for several years, although the manufacturer officially recommends their use within two years because that is the length of the warranty.* The BVDA foil pouch will have a batch number on it. An example of a batch number might be 2015107. In this example, 2015 indicates the year 2015. The 107 in that number is the batch. According to the manufacturer, it is normal to produce on average one batch each day, so batch 107 would be around the twenty-second week of 2015.†

Gelatin lifters are composed of a mixture of water-based gelatin materials supplemented with dyes, anti-fungal agents, and other materials, laid over a linen-reinforced natural rubber backing. Their lifting side is protected with a clear cover sheet that must be removed before use. Gelatin lifters come in white, black, and transparent in a variety of sizes but those for use in lifting footwear impressions are typically 5.2 × 14.4 inches (13 × 36 cm) or 7.2 × 14.4 inches (18 × 36 cm). The gelatin layer is low tact with minimal stickiness, allowing it to lift impressions from almost any surface. Black gelatin lifts are used for dust impressions as well as impressions developed with any color powder. It is noted that the manufacturer recommends the use of black lifters even when lifting black powdered impressions. White gelatin lifters can be used when lifting dark original impressions, impressions powdered with dark powders, or for lifts of chemically treated impressions when the procedure is focused on fluorescence photography, or for dropping complex background coloration or patterns.

Using Gelatin Lifters

The lifting side of a gelatin lifter is protected by a clear cover sheet that requires a good grip on the corner and a reasonable amount of tugging to separate it from the actual gelatin.

---

* Personal communication with Patrick van Vilsteren, BVDA International, March 2015.
† Personal communication with Patrick van Vilsteren, BVDA International, April 2015.

In casework, lifts of impressions of the same shoe design have been received that exhibited minor variations in size. One study explored the possibilities that dimensional changes could be the result of stretching produced when removing the cover sheet, recommending the user let the gelatin lift "rest" for 5 minutes after the cover sheet is removed before applying it to the impression.[*] Another study explored the same potential problem but those efforts proved unsuccessful in changing the dimension of the gelatin lifter regardless of the force used to remove the cover sheet.[†] Neither study addressed the methods of applying the lift at the crime scene. The use of a fingerprint roller to apply a gelatin lift from one end to another over the impression with moderate force can easily result in a 5 mm difference in length. When the gelatin lift is removed from the impression, it will rebound quickly to its original size, and in doing so, shorten the length of the lifted footwear impression. For this reason, it is recommended that fingerprint rollers not be used during the application of gelatin lifts. Instead, the lifts can be applied to the impression by touching the middle of the lift to the center of the impression and lowering the ends, or alternately by securing one end first, allowing the rest of the lift to lie over the impression, as illustrated in Figure 5.19. To ensure good contact with the substrate and to eliminate any trapped air, apply light pressure by rubbing with your fingers. Once applied to the impression, gelatin lifters should not be removed immediately but should be allowed to remain on the impression for a period of time. A representative of the company that produces gelatin lifters advised they could detect a significant difference in the success between a gelatin lift that remained on a faint residue impression for 1 minute over a lift allowed to remain on the impression for 2 minutes, with no further differences noted if the lift remained longer than 5 minutes.[‡] This would seem to suggest that 2 minutes is a good time to minimally let a gelatin lift remain on a dust impression before its removal;

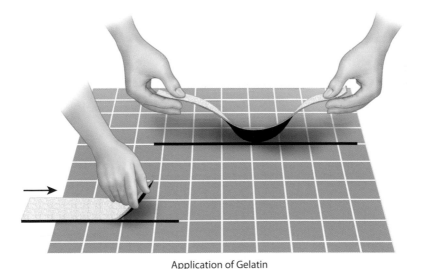

Application of Gelatin

Figure 5.19 Proper methods for applying a gelatin lift to an impression. Fingerprint rollers should not be used forcefully as they can easily stretch the gelatin lift causing inaccurate dimensions of the lifted impression.

[*] McConaghey, D., Resting gelatin lifters prior to use, *JFI*, 63(6):653–659, 2013.
[†] Nordanstig, R., Short observations about stretching of gel lifter, presented at the 11th European Shoe Print/Tool Mark Meeting, Prague, Czech Republic, October 22, 2014.
[‡] Personal communication with Patrick van Vilsteren, BVDA, the Netherlands, March 2012.

however, gelatin lifts are used to lift impressions of many different quantities and qualities and no single test or research will provide the best information for every situation. No information has been presented in the literature that suggests that leaving a gelatin lift on an impression for 5 minutes would compromise the quality of a lift. Thus it would appear that a good practice to follow would be to leave gelatin lifts on dust impressions minimally for 5 minutes before removing them, particularly if it were an original impression more firmly bonded to the substrate. As will be discussed later, the use of gelatin lifters to lift chemically enhanced impressions requires leaving the gelatin lifters on the impression much longer. One presentation suggested 10 minutes and only for impressions that were completely dry.[*] Another recommended leaving the lifter on for 30 to 60 minutes for lifting chemical traces as well as the use of weight placed on top of the gelatin lifter.[†]

Degradation of Impressions Lifted with Gelatin Lifters

Original impressions lifted with gelatin lifters can fade and degrade over time. The amount of degradation is affected by the interaction between the lifted material and the gelatin, the substrate, and whether a cover sheet has been reapplied. Research has determined that recovering the gelatin lifts with a cover sheet accelerates the degradation process whereas storage of uncovered gelatin lifts in a box resulted in far less degradation.[‡,§,¶,**] Gelatin lifts should always remain uncovered after lifting until photographed. If quality photography is not immediately possible, the uncovered lifter can be temporarily taped in a clean box until later scanned or photographed. Photography should take place as soon as possible in order to recover the maximum detail. In many instances, particularly in those cases where gelatin lifters are used to lift chemical traces, degradation can begin occurring rather quickly. Since original impressions will degrade regardless of whether they are covered, examination quality photographs should be made as soon as possible and take precedence over storage.

For gelatin lifts of impressions that have been powdered, research has indicated no loss of detail as long as the cover sheets were not placed back on the gelatin lifters, but showed loss of detail if the cover sheets were replaced.[††]

Photographing and Scanning Gelatin Lifts

Gelatin lifters can be photographed, or they can be scanned using specialized imaging systems such as the GLScan shown in Figure 5.20.[‡‡] The GLScan utilizes a movable vacuum bed to hold the gelatin flat while it passes beneath the line scan camera and high intensity light

---

[*] Johnson, M., Use of gelatin lifters for forensic footwear evidence, presented at the IAI Annual Educational Conference, Spokane, WA, July 2010.

[†] Velders, T., New insight into the chemical improvement of shoeprints and fingerprints placed with blood on non-porous surfaces, *Identification Canada*, 35(3):80–102.

[‡] Bandey, H., and Bleay, S., Fingerprint and Footwear Forensics Newsletter, Home Office Scientific Development Branch, Hertfordshire, UK, February 2010, Publication No. 6/10.

[§] Shor, Y., Wiesner, S., Chaikovsky, A., and Tsach, T., Methods for improving problematic footwear prints, presented at the SPTM Meeting, Stavern, Norway, May 2005.

[¶] Bandey, H., Footwear mark recovery, Fingerprint and Footwear Forensics Program, Home Office Scientific Development Branch, presented to the Scientific Working Group for Shoe Print and Tire Track Evidence, March 2010.

[**] Bleay, W., Bandey, H., Black, M., and Sears, V., The gelatin lifting process: an evaluation of its effectiveness in the recovery of latent fingerprints, *JFI*, 61(6):592–594, 2011.

[††] Bandey, H., Ibid.

[‡‡] Provided courtesy of BVDA www.usa.bvda.com

Figure 5.20 The BVDA GLScan equipment. (Courtesy of BVDA.)

to record the lifted impressions. Black gelatin lifters are glossy and reflect approximately 95% of the light, which significantly differs from the diffusion of light that occurs when it strikes the impression. Because of this difference in reflectance, the GLScan is able to produce very high-resolution scans with excellent detail, even when impressions are dark and/or faint. An example of a black gelatin lift of a dust impression that has been scanned with the GLScan is shown in Figure 5.21. Examination quality photography of a gelatin lifter can also record excellent detail, but not all methods and lighting will provide the same results. Figure 5.22 shows an enlargement of a small portion of one gelatin lift photographed first with 45-degree light on a copy stand, next with oblique light, and then with reflected white light at a high angle. After photography, if a cover sheet is applied or reapplied to the gelatin lift, according to the manufacturer, the cover sheet should be cleaned or a new cover sheet used.*

Gelatin Lifting versus Electrostatic Lifting

The question of whether a gelatin lifter or an electrostatic lifter is best for dry origin impressions does not have a simple answer as the innumerable number of crime scene conditions will never be totally represented under research conditions. Because of their tackiness, gelatin lifters have the ability to lift more of the impression from the substrate than electrostatic lifters; thus gelatin lifters are often the better choice for lifting visible footwear marks, particularly

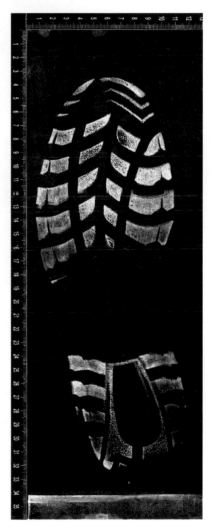

Figure 5.21 A GLScan of a BVDA black gelatin lift. (Courtesy of BVDA.)

* BVDA Gel lifter manual, BVDA International, the Netherlands.

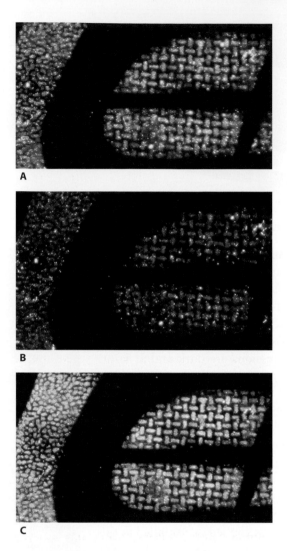

Figure 5.22 Different lighting provides different levels of detail when photographing gelatin lifts. Incandescent light (A), oblique light (B), and reflected white light (C).

when they are faint. Gelatin lifters are the best choice for lifting wet origin impressions because electrostatic lifters have no success when moisture is involved. When searching large areas for latent impressions, the application of long electrostatic lifts to the substrate is far more successful and practical than the use of gelatin lifters. For heavier dry origin impressions that contain excess dust, dirt, or loose materials, some suggest the electrostatic lift be applied to make an initial lift, after which a black gelatin lifter can be applied to make a second lift. The initial electrostatic lift will clean away the excessive dust and the secondary gelatin lift will sometimes result in better detail.

Research on this topic has found that gelatin lifters are superior on most substrates, including substrates that are porous and/or not smooth, and also for wet prints.[*,†] One

[*] Bandey, H., Ibid.
[†] Shor, Y., Belser, C., and Wiesner, S., A comparative study: gelatin lifter vs. electrostatic lifter, presented at the European Meeting for SP/TM examiners, May 2007, Copenhagen, Denmark.

Figure 5.23 The top photograph depicts a section of a concrete driveway. An electrostatic lift of that area recovered not only the suspect's tire impression but also recovered shoe impressions. (Photograph courtesy of Ron Mueller.)

study noted that for large and dusty substrate areas like dusty floors, electrostatic lifting gave better results and in some cases both gelatin and electrostatic lifts performed equally well.[*] Research also noted in some instances the sequence of using the electrostatic lift first, followed by the gelatin lift was often superior.[†,‡]

An unusual case example shown in Figure 5.23 depicts a very successful electrostatic lift of both tire and shoe impressions from a dry concrete driveway.[§] Several gelatin lifts would have been necessary to cover the same area of this substrate and would have also lifted undesirable extraneous background dust and dirt.

Gelatin lifters are also favored where the logistics of uneven or oddly shaped substrates such as a chair seat, make the use of an electrostatic lifter less likely to be successful. One reported technique for lifting impressions from porous items such as fabric, cardboard,

---

[*] Ibid.
[†] Wiesner, S., Tsach, T., Belser, C., and Shor, Y., A comparative research of two lifting methods: electrostatic lifter and gelatin lifter, *JFS*, 56(1), January 2011.
[‡] Shor, Y., Belser, C., and Wiesner, S., A comparative study: gelatin lifter vs. electrostatic lifter, presented at the European Meeting for SP/TM examiners, May 2007, Copenhagen, Denmark.
[§] Presented at the IAI Educational Conference and provided courtesy of Ron Mueller, Charlotte County Sheriff's Office, Punta Gorda, FL.

and drywall recommended placing a black gelatin lifter over the impression area covered with a smooth pad and then placed in a pneumatic press for a few seconds to apply even pressure. It was found that uniform pressure provided better results in many instances. When the gelatin lift is removed, fibers and other contaminates that might have transferred to the lift could be removed by cleaning the gelatin lift with a sheet of adhesive.[*,†]

Both gelatin lifters and the electrostatic lifter are necessary for recovering footwear impressions at the crime scene. Failed attempts to achieve a successful lift with the electrostatic lifter will not compromise the ability to use a gelatin lifter.

Adhesive Lifters

Adhesive lifters have been used more than any other method in the US. This is likely due to the processing of crime scenes by many who were both equipped for and more focused on recovering fingerprints. A large portion of those lifts involved impressions developed with fingerprint powder combined with the use of makeshift adhesive lifters never intended for the recovery of footwear evidence. Among these were included clear adhesive fingerprint hinge lifters, wide clear adhesive tape transferred to a white card stock, and large clear adhesive lifts. The use of clear adhesive to lift both powdered and unpowdered impressions often produces poor results and poor contrast. Three examples of clear adhesive lifts received in actual casework are shown in Figure 5.24. The two on the left of Figure 5.24 are smaller lifting tapes and lifters intended for fingerprint recovery. Their use for lifting much larger footwear impressions required they be spliced together, resulting in seams, overlapping areas, and folds. Adhesive lifters are not recommended for lifting original or powdered impressions, as much better lifting materials and methods exist. Of course, if no other methods or materials are available to a particular crime scene unit, making an adhesive lift of an impression that otherwise would be left at the scene is better than not making any lift at all.

Powdering Impressions

Many who process crime scenes for latent fingerprints also process nonporous substrates with fingerprint powders to search for footwear impressions. Whereas powdering may ultimately develop latent or enhance visible impressions, powdering should never be a first choice for footwear impressions. Substrates that potentially contain impressions should always be searched first using nondestructive methods such as high intensity oblique light, alternate light sources, and electrostatic lifting prior to any application of fingerprint powder that might destroy any latent dry origin impressions. Only in those cases where footwear impressions are visible and/or other methods have been unsuccessful, should powdering impressions for enhancement and subsequent lifting be considered. If an attempt is made to enhance visible impressions with powder, it should be attempted on

[*] Shor, Y., Tsach, T., Vinokurov, A., Glattstein, B., Landau, E., and Levin, N., Lifting shoeprints using gelatin lifters and a hydraulic press, *JFS*, 48(2):368–372, 2003.
[†] Shor, Y., Tsach, T., Wiesner, S., and Meir, G., Removing interfering contaminations from gelatin lifters, *JFS*, 50(6), November 2005.

Figure 5.24 Three makeshift clear adhesive lifters from casework demonstrate their inability to provide the best lift or contrast. The lifts on the left and center were made with overlapping pieces of clear tape and include problems such as seams and overlapping areas. On the right, a one-piece adhesive lift of an original residue impression shows the blotchy nature of adhesive lifts and the lack of contrast achieved.

a very small portion first to see if it is successful. Only if successful should the powdering continue. Impressions such as those produced on a waxed or polished surface, such as the top of a bank counter, or even a smooth tile floor that is mopped daily, often reveal excellent detail when developed with fingerprint powder. If successfully enhanced, the powdered impressions can be lifted with gelatin lifters or Mikrosil.

Figure 5.25 depicts a case example where using black fingerprint powder on a tile floor developed both positive and negative representations of shoe impressions.

Lifting Impressions with Mikrosil

One silicone-based product that is excellent for lifting powdered impressions is Mikrosil™.* Mikrosil comes in white, black, gray, and brown. The white and black colors are typically used for footwear impressions, while the gray and brown for tool marks. White Mikrosil is excellent for lifting impressions that have been developed with black fingerprint powder. Mikrosil lifts the full amount of fingerprint powder whereas gelatin and adhesive lift-

---

* Developed by Kjell Carlsson Innovations, Sweden.

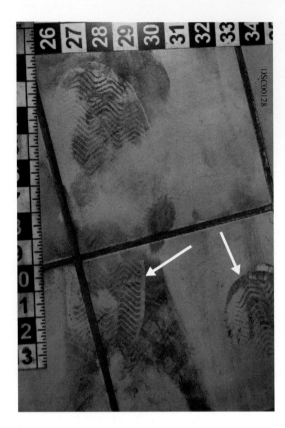

Figure 5.25 A case example where powdering a tile floor resulted in developing both positive and negative impressions.

ers usually leave part of the powdered impression behind. This is very important since many impressions developed with powder are faint, thus lifting them entirely is significant. Mikrosil is also able to lift better when any texture or other irregularities of the substrate are present. Figure 5.26 depicts the white Mikrosil base and the blue hardener and illustrates the steps involved in mixing and applying Mikrosil to a powdered impression. The Mikrosil and hardener are combined and mixed quickly and thoroughly on a disposable surface such as a pad of paper or, in the case of this demonstration, on the substrate adjacent to the impression. Less catalyst will provide longer setting times but more working time to mix and apply, whereas more catalyst provides shorter working time and shorter setting time. Once mixed, apply the Mikrosil over the center of the powdered impression with the spatula, being careful not to scrape the impression. Place a piece of silicone-coated paper that is larger than the impression over the top of the Mikrosil with the silicone side against the Mikrosil. Silicone-coated paper is available as waste from shipping labels, adhesive lifts, adhesive shelf paper, and other sources. If silicone-coated paper is not available, regular paper can be used. Using your fingers, press down on the paper over the center of the Mikrosil to begin directing the Mikrosil outward so it covers the impression. Continue spreading the Mikrosil by holding down one side of the paper while using a fingerprint roller to spread the Mikrosil from the center outward. Do this in whatever direction is necessary to cover the entire impression area. This procedure will flatten and spread the Mikrosil and eliminate any air pockets. The Mikrosil will bond to the paper

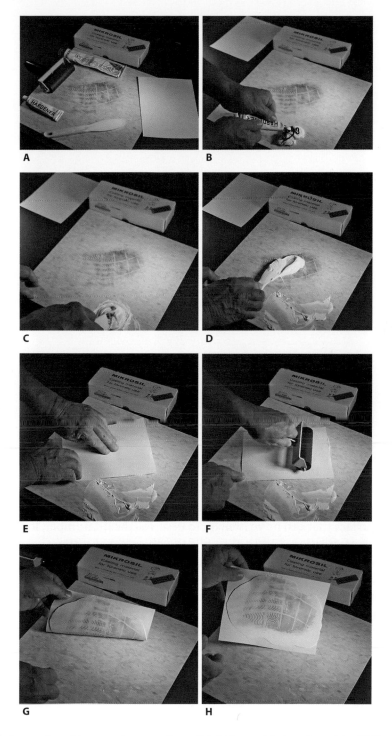

Figure 5.26 A powdered impression on tile to lift (A); combining the white Mikrosil and blue hardener (B), mixing (C), applying the mixed Mikrosil on top of the impression (D), applying paper over the top and pressing down to begin spreading the Mikrosil (E), using a fingerprint roller to spread the Mikrosil further (F), removing Mikrosil after it sets (G), and the successful and complete lift (H).

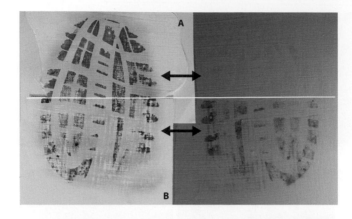

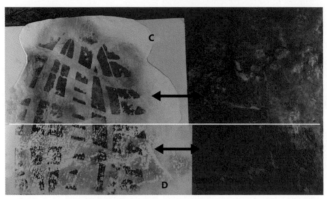

Figure 5.27 A comparison of Mikrosil and gelatin and adhesive lifts of powdered impressions. At the top (A) a Mikrosil lift of the powdered impression on painted wood was complete. Next to it (B) the white gelatin lift left some of the powder behind. Next (C), Mikrosil again lifted the entire powdered impression on textured tile, whereas the adhesive lifter did not make a good or complete lift (D).

and provide a surface that can be written on to describe the lift number, location, date, and other necessary information. Mikrosil fulfills the objective of lifting the entire powdered impression and not just a portion of it. Shown in the final photographs of Figure 5.26, Mikrosil lifts the entire powdered impression. Gelatin lifters and adhesive lifters usually leave some of the powdered impression behind. To illustrate this, the top photograph in Figure 5.27 shows the results of lifting a powdered impression from a piece of painted wood, half with Mikrosil (A) and the other half with a white gelatin lifter (B). The bottom example of Figure 5.27 is a powdered impression on a slightly textured tile floor, half lifted with Mikrosil (C) and half with an adhesive lifter (D). In both cases, the Mikrosil did a much better job of lifting the entire impression. Some powder remained in the areas where the gelatin and adhesive lifts were made.

Mikrosil has also been tried for lifting original impressions on nonporous substrates that may not have responded to photography or to enhancement attempts with powders or other lifting techniques. Figure 5.28 depicts a sequence demonstrated at a recent meeting using black Mikrosil to lift an impression that was difficult to both see and photograph.*

---

* Demonstrated by Kjell Carlsson at the 11th European Meeting for SPTM, Prague, Czech Republic, October 2014.

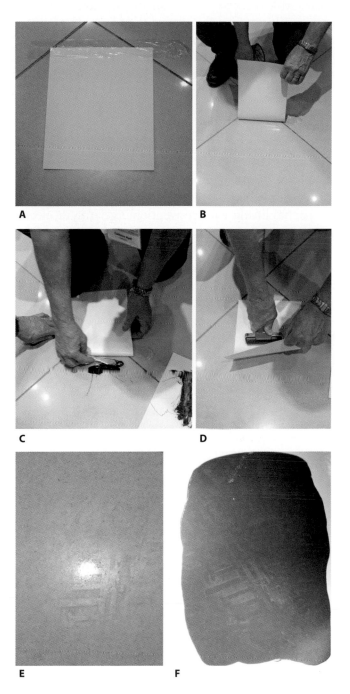

Figure 5.28 The impression (E) is covered with a piece of silicone paper and taped to the substrate at one end (A). The paper is pulled back (B) and mixed black Mikrosil is applied to the substrate (C). A fingerprint roller is used to spread a very thin coating of the Mikrosil over the impression (D). The resulting lift is shown (F).

The impression was on a glossy nonporous floor and at best was seen at an angle with reflected light (E). Black Mikrosil was mixed using about half the normal amount of hardener to allow for more working time. Because of the reduced amount of hardener, the lift was allowed 30 minutes to set before it was lifted. It is noted that during this demonstration the photograph of the successful Mikrosil lift (F) was taken with a point-and-shoot camera from a distance and the actual lift contained much better detail than is shown here.

Lifting with Dental Stone

Dental stone is most commonly used to cast three-dimensional impressions, but it can be used in some instances to lift other impressions.[*][†] These are typically impressions such as dried muddy tracks on a wood or concrete surface that would normally be crushed or would only allow partial lifting with conventional gelatin, or electrostatic or adhesive lifts. One consideration of using dental stone is whether the color of the dental stone used will provide sufficient contrast between the colors of the impression. Figure 5.29 depicts a simple procedure for lifting an exterior partial muddy shoe impression on concrete using dental stone. A highly textured substrate will grip the dental stone and not allow the cast to be released when it sets. To avoid this, duct tape is applied closely around the impression to minimize the contact area between the dental stone and the nonimpression areas. The dental stone mixture is applied over the impression as well as over a good portion of the duct tape. When the dental stone is completely hardened, the tape can be lifted and will normally assist in the release of the cast from the substrate.

Indented Impressions on Paper

In a small percentage of cases where a shoe has left impressions on paper, latent indentations of details of the outsole are recoverable.[‡] Examiners of Questioned Documents routinely develop indentations of handwriting on paper in the same manner. For footwear evidence, an electrostatic lift would first be made of the paper to recover dry origin impressions. This would be nondestructive to any indentations that might be on the paper. The paper could then be processed using one of two devices that are each capable of recovering indentations—the first being the electrostatic detection apparatus (ESDA) and the second being the indentation materializer (IM). The IM is shown in Figure 5.30. Both devices have a perforated vacuum bed that creates suction and pulls the paper being processed flat against the surface. The paper item recovered from the scene is placed on this vacuum bed to hold the paper flat and in place. A very thin piece of Mylar film is stretched across the paper, after which a high-voltage charge is applied by passing a corona bar back and forth over the paper. Once done, a specially charged black toner powder is lightly brushed over the Mylar film. If indentations are present on the paper, the toner will be attracted to those

---

[*] Geller, J., Casting on road surfaces, 73rd Annual Educational Conference, International Association for Identification, July 1988.
[†] Bodziak, W. J., Ibid., pp. 124–125.
[‡] Ibid, p. 112.

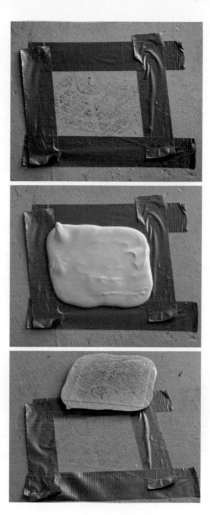

Figure 5.29 A muddy impression on a painted concrete floor is surrounded with duct tape to minimize the area the dental stone will contact and to provide some assistance in lifting the cast. A dental stone mixture is applied to the impression and allowed to extend over the tape. When the cast is fully set, pulling upward on the tape will release the cast from the impression. The cast should be photographed immediately in the event the impression degrades.

areas. A clear adhesive cover sheet can be placed over the Mylar to permanently fix any developed impression so it can be removed and examined. Although only a small percentage of paper items that are stepped on retain indentations, this device offers another possible way of recovering impression evidence. Research in comparing electrostatic lifting in combination with or preferential to using the ESDA or IM to recover indentations reported a preference for electrostatic lifting due to the higher quality results that were obtained.* It is noted that both can be used on paper items in sequence, using the ESLA first for dust marks, then the ESDA or IM for indentations.

---

* Craig, C., Hornsby, B., and Riles, M., Evaluation and comparison of the electrostatic dust print lifter and the electrostatic detection apparatus on the development of footwear impressions on paper, *J. For. Sci.*, 51(4):819–826, July 2006.

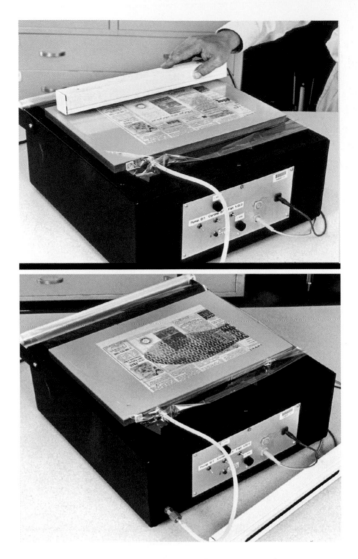

Figure 5.30 An indentation materializer (IM) or electrostatic detection apparatus (ESDA) can be used to develop indentations of footwear on paper items.

Key Words: positive impression, negative impression, transfer impression, dry origin, wet origin, electrostatic lifting, gelatin lifter, adhesive lifter, Mikrosil

Key Points

1. Two-dimensional impressions are composed of varied substances on varied substrates and therefore require a variety of lifting materials and methods. No single method of lifting will work on all impressions.
2. Lifting or other forms of enhancement should be attempted whenever possible to supplement photography, as they provide additional details of the impression.
3. Electrostatic lifting, if unsuccessful, will not destroy impressions or prevent subsequent methods of lifting or enhancement from being attempted.

4. Electrostatic lifting is routinely used at a crime scene to search large areas where no visible impressions are present, but where the circumstances exist for the likely presence of latent dust impressions.

5. Black and white gelatin lifters are more versatile and have more lifting power because of their tacky surface. They can be used in a variety of applications to lift original impressions, powdered impressions, and impressions that have been treated chemically.

6. Adhesive lifters, in particular makeshift adhesive lifters, do not provide the best method of lifting impressions.

7. The use of Mikrosil is an excellent method for making a complete lift of powdered impressions.

Blunt Force Pattern Injuries

6

Injuries to the skin are traditionally divided into two categories: those caused by sharp forces and those caused by blunt forces. Sharp force injuries are those that occur from objects having a sharp edge or point like a knife, axe, or piece of glass that incise or cut into or through the skin. Blunt force injuries are those that occur from blunt objects such as a club, hammer, belt buckle, shoe, or tire. Blunt force injuries often result in a bruise (contusion) on the skin. The skin consists of three layers: the outer layer or epidermis, the middle layer or dermis, and the bottom subcutaneous layer. Bruising occurs when there is sufficient force to rupture small blood vessels in the dermis and subcutaneous layers that results in the escape of blood into the surrounding tissue. Although the surface of the skin often remains intact, the resulting discoloration can be seen through the overlying semi-translucent tissue. If the conditions are right, blunt force trauma produced by patterned objects can result in the replication of certain features of that object. When this occurs, these injuries are referred to as blunt force pattern injuries. Figure 6.1 shows a case example of a blunt force pattern injury on a victim's head. The bruising or discoloration at the onset of these injuries is a reddish color reflecting the color of the blood beneath the skin. In a living individual, over time, depending on the extent of the subcutaneous bleeding and other pathological factors, the coloration of the bruise will change to a darkish purple color, then continue to change over the following days, both dispersing and transitioning to other colors such as brown, green, and eventually yellow before disappearing. In a deceased individual, some coloration changes can also occur.

Abrasions are also caused by blunt force trauma but occur when the force is applied in a scraping or abrasive action that results in removal of part or all of the skin's outer layers. Skinning a knee during a fall is a good example of an abrasion. The abrasion area will be reddened depending on the severity of the injury. In some cases, sufficient layers of the skin may be removed to allow for bleeding. Because this form of injury is a result of lateral abrasive forces, there is much less opportunity for the transfer of any design features of an object or substrate that caused it. An example of an abrasion is shown in Figure 6.2.

Lividity is not a blunt force pattern injury and is only mentioned here to make that distinction. Lividity is the settling of blood into the lowermost blood vessels due to gravitational forces after a victim is deceased and circulation has ceased. The settling of the blood results in a bluish-purplish discoloration of the skin. Some patterns may be found within the lividity area because of the pressure of clothing worn by or objects beneath the victim but these are easily distinguished from a blunt force pattern injury. Figure 6.3 depicts the backside of a deceased victim who was found with her back facing down. The discoloration on her back resulted from lividity. The pressure of the victim's clothing straps was sufficient to keep the blood from settling in those areas, creating some representation of their pattern (arrows).

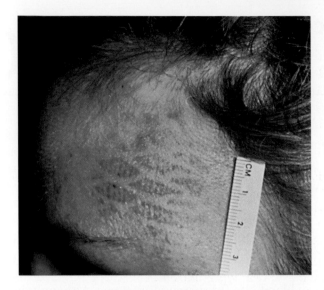

Figure 6.1 An example of a blunt force pattern injury on a victim that was made by a shoe outsole.

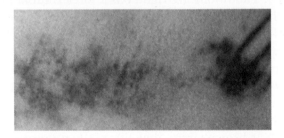

Figure 6.2 An example of an abrasion.

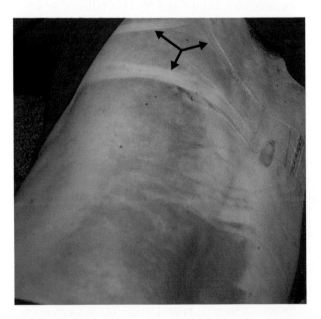

Figure 6.3 An example of lividity.

The Mechanics of Blunt Force Pattern Injuries

A study performed at the Institutes of Legal Medicine in Germany reviewed 36,274 autopsies between 1980 and 1997.[*] Those autopsies included documentation of 152 cases that involved kicking, of which 46, approximately one-third, exhibited shape injuries characteristic of shoe sole patterns. Most of the injuries were localized in the head and neck region. The study also discussed the possibility that kicking can occur without leaving any evidence of the shoe sole, particularly in cases where the skin may have been protected with clothing.

Injuries of this type have been categorized as those that are dynamic loaded (high impact of shoe with victim) and those that are static loaded (standing on a victim). As one study has summarized,

> Skin injuries in dynamic loading result from impact with velocities varying from low to high. High-velocity blunt force trauma may lead to injuries with a pattern or imprint …. The object causing the injury, mostly bruising, is mirrored by the pattern. … The impact caused by the blow with the object will distort and crush the skin and underlying tissues and rupture subcutaneous vessels (venules and capillaries) in contact with the edges of the object. … Injuries caused by low velocity impact loading usually do not show recognizable patterns or shapes.[†]

The above quoted comments are in agreement with blunt force pattern injury case experiences, specifically the observations regarding the speed and force required to produce a blunt force pattern on skin. Static (standing) or even semi-harsh contact between the bottom of a shoe and the skin does not typically result in a blunt force pattern injury. It must be noted that there are many variables that enter into this equation, including the location of the injury, bony versus soft underlying tissue, the pathology of the recipient of the injury, medications the victim may be taking, the depth of the shoe pattern, and others. As a matter of curiosity, I have allowed an adult to stand on my back while exerting their full weight on one shoe and this did not result in any pain or pattern injury. What did occur was a brief compression of the skin beneath the shoe. The raised areas of the outsole that normally touch the ground would press into the skin, while the adjacent grooves and other void areas of the outsole (non-pressure areas) would be filled with skin stretched up into those areas. The temporary depression or mark that was produced disappeared in a few minutes and no hemorrhaging, permanent mark, or injury resulted. This was also demonstrated by firmly pressing a shoe outsole against my forearm. The raised areas of the outsole pressed against the skin forced the blood in the underlying tissue to migrate to areas of less pressure such as the grooves and void areas of the design. Figure 6.4 illustrates the result that was photographed the instant the shoe was removed. Seconds later, there was no evidence of any shoe mark on my arm. Although in this case the resulting replication of the outsole design is temporary and produces no injury, it demonstrates the pattern a particular outsole would produce if the skin were struck by the outsole with sufficient speed and force to rupture the blood vessels and produce a blunt force pattern injury. This exercise is useful for understanding the mechanics of pattern injuries as well as possibly

---

[*] Strauch, H., Wirth, I., Taymoorian, U., and Geserick, G., Kicking to death—forensic and criminological aspects, *Forensic Science International*, 123:165–171, 2001.
[†] Bilo, R. A. C., Oranje, A. P., Shwayder, T., and Hobbs, C. J., *Cutaneous Manifestations of Child Abuse and Their Differential Diagnosis: Blunt Force Trauma*, Springer, Heidelberg, 2013, pp. 41–42.

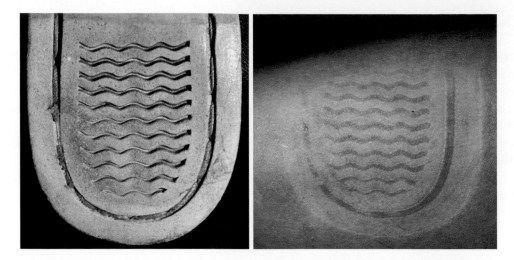

Figure 6.4 The mechanics of a blunt force pattern are demonstrated using a heel that has been pressed hard against a forearm, photographed immediately on removal.

Figure 6.5 In the center is a case example of a blunt force pattern injury. The shoe of the suspect is on the right and a test impression on an arm is on the left.

producing a different type of known impression of a particular shoe. Figure 6.5 illustrates a blunt force pattern trauma from an actual case alongside the shoe and a test impression of the shoe later produced on an arm.

In order for a blunt force trauma injury to occur, a large amount of force must be applied very rapidly, such as in the case of a kicking or stomping action. This causes very rapid tissue compression over a very short period of time. As one medical examiner explains, "this results in tearing and rupturing of small blood vessels in the tissue … It is the subsequent bleeding that is noted as a bruise when the subcutaneous tissue is involved. The hemorrhage is noted through the overlying intact skin as a blue-black-purple discoloration …."[*]

---

[*] Curran, W. J., McGarry, A. L., and Petty, C. S., *Modern Legal Medicine, Psychiatry and Forensic Science*, FA Davis Co, Philadelphia, 1980, p. 367.

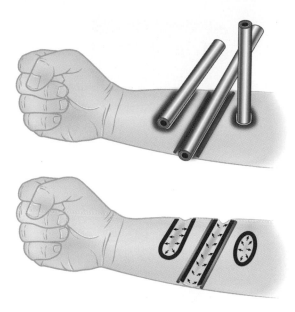

Figure 6.6 An illustration of the basic mechanics of blunt force pattern injuries, using a pipe striking a forearm.

When there is sufficient speed and force to create a blunt force pattern injury, many factors can contribute to its quality and detail, including the depth and details of the shoe design, the degree and speed of impact, the angle of the shoe relative to the skin, the presence of either soft tissue or bony structure beneath the skin, interference of clothing, and any movement of the victim at the time of impact. A shoe design could therefore be replicated well in a blunt force pattern injury if the circumstances supported it or the shoe pattern might not be replicated at all.

To further illustrate the mechanics of blunt force pattern injuries, begin with a simple object, such as a pipe. As illustrated in Figure 6.6, when the pipe strikes the skin with sufficient speed and force, it compresses the skin and forces the blood beneath the skin on each side of the pipe outward, resulting in the rupture of those vessels and the leakage of blood into the adjacent tissue. In conjunction with this, there is also stretching of the skin that contributes to the injury. The resulting representation of the pipe depends on its position and angle during contact. The resultant injury shape or pattern can be seen through the overlying translucent skin.

Figure 6.7 illustrates a similar example but with a more complex pattern. The solid areas of this pattern will press into and compress the skin, forcing the blood to the outer and inner edges (non-pressure areas) of the patterned object. When this occurs with sufficient speed and force, rupturing will occur in the subcutaneous blood vessels, and a resulting replication of the pattern may take place. The normal observer who does not understand the pathology of this event would look at the blunt force trauma injury and reason that the reddened areas were directly representative of the raised pattern of an object; however, it is actually a mirror or negative representation of the patterned object. Figure 6.8 shows a case example of a blunt force pattern injury on the head of a victim that was made by a herringbone-patterned outsole. The raised ridges of the herringbone shoe pattern that made contact with the skin are represented by the light areas. The void

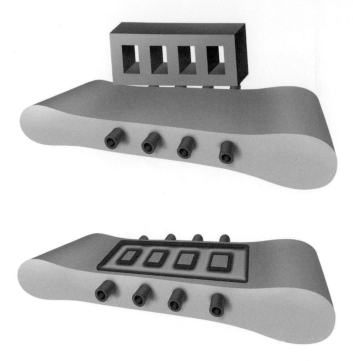

Figure 6.7 The same illustration of mechanics using a more complex pattern. The pattern forces the blood to its edges and void areas.

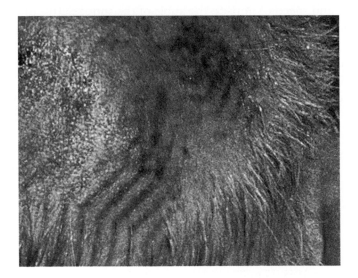

Figure 6.8 A blunt force pattern made by a herringbone outsole pattern. The dark red pattern areas represent the void areas between rows of herringbone lines.

areas of the shoe are represented by the reddened portion of the pattern injury where the blood was forced. Figure 6.9 shows what a slightly more complex pattern might look like. The reddened areas represented the void portions of the outsole to where the blood was forced, whereas the light areas represented the raised portion or pattern of the outsole design that exerted pressure against the skin.

Figure 6.9 A more complex shoe design on skin. The light areas represent the raised areas of the outsole design. The red areas represent the void area of the outsole pattern where the blood has been forced.

Relevance of Blunt Force Pattern Injuries

Impressions made by footwear on skin are typically encountered in violent crimes when the perpetrator kicks or stomps on the victim. They are also encountered when the victim has been hit with another patterned object, or run over by a vehicle.[*] Blunt force pattern injuries produced by footwear afford an opportunity for a forensic comparison with footwear of suspected individuals, when shoes of a similar pattern are seized. If the initial investigation does not produce similarly designed footwear, the blunt force shoe pattern injuries on a victim can be searched through a database to associate them with a specific brand or style of footwear. Information obtained from such an effort that reveals the brand and other information about the footwear can be used by investigators in their search for possible suspects. Also relevant is the fact that considerable force is required to produce a blunt force pattern injury. This fact demonstrates that the perpetrator did not simply stand on or make incidental contact with the victim, but had to direct deliberate and considerable force against the victim in order to produce those injuries.

Replication Limitations and Accuracy

The skin is not the best medium to record detail. In addition, because of the topography of the body, attempts to photograph this evidence are challenging and sometimes problematic. One forensic pathologist stated, "Contusion impression patterns on human skin often

---

[*] Zugibe, F., Costello, J., Identification of the murder weapon by intricate patterned injury measurements, *J. Foren. Sci., JFSCA*, 31(2):773–777, 1986.

do not match test impressions of shoes in every exact way. This may be due to a number of reasons, including photographic problems of both scale and perspective and for physical reasons, due to tissue variations and body movement during impact."[*]

In casework, it is common to receive a series of photographs of a pattern injury only to find that no scale was used in some or all of those photographs, or that the scale was positioned in a way to render it useless. Even when the scale is placed in the best position possible, the injury is often on a curved part of the body of varying depths, restricting the accuracy of any photographic recording. Limitations with the examination of this evidence exist for other reasons as well. Patterned injuries are often irregular in their replication, with some areas providing good detail while immediately adjacent areas don't replicate the pattern at all. In some cases, they are located on the sides or top of the head where hair may obscure and/or interfere with the detail. With regard to injuries in the facial area, the topography in the area of the nose, eyes, and mouth will interfere with the replication of detail. Blunt force pattern injuries are not impressions in the same sense as an impression in soil or residue. Rather, they are a pathological reaction to the force of the outsole. The diffusion of blood into surrounding tissues that are covered with the outer layer of skin does not usually produce a crisp and sharp representation of the object that produced it. Despite this, I have examined impressions where surprisingly good detail was replicated. Some have even provided clear evidence of wear or other features. The top left photograph of Figure 6.10 depicts the appearance of a blunt force pattern injury as recorded at the scene. It is covered partially with smeared blood and difficult to see. The top right photograph, taken a short time later at autopsy, shows a much more evident injury pattern after the dirt and dried blood were cleaned away. The bottom photographs show a reverse photograph of the heel of the accused's boot and a known impression of that heel superimposed over the injury. The arrows point to the worn area in the heel. Recognition and documentation of this pattern and the subsequent recovery of the Hi-Tec boot by investigators were crucial to this particular homicide. The pattern on the victim corresponded in design, size of that design, and general wear with the respective area of the right heel of the recovered boot of the accused. In another case, shown in Figure 6.11, only limited portions of the injury replicated some details like the stitch holes in the curved heel of the worn deck shoe.

Blunt force pattern injuries often lack sufficient detail to allow for any meaningful comparison, leaving no evaluation of the impression possible. However, in those cases where reasonably detailed and clear patterns do exist, my experience has been that the accuracy of the replicated pattern can be very good. When an outsole makes forceful contact with a victim's skin, the raised design of the outsole presses firmly against the skin which is forced up into the void areas of outsole design, locking the shoe firmly in place. In other cases where there was an uneven surface of the body, movement of the victim, and/or movement of the footwear, replication details would suffer and be expressed in any pattern injury that resulted. Each case must be evaluated separately. Other case examples that have been reported also demonstrated value for this form of evidence.[†]

---

[*] Oliver, W. R., The pathology and interpretation of blunt force pattern injuries to the skin, presented at the International Symposium on the Forensic Aspects of Footwear and Tire Impression Evidence, FBI Academy, Quantico, VA, June 27–July 1, 1994.

[†] Chochól, A., Świętek, M., Shoe prints on the human body—An analysis of three cases, Problems of forensic sciences, Institute of Forensic Research, Krakow, Poland, 78:239–247, 2009.

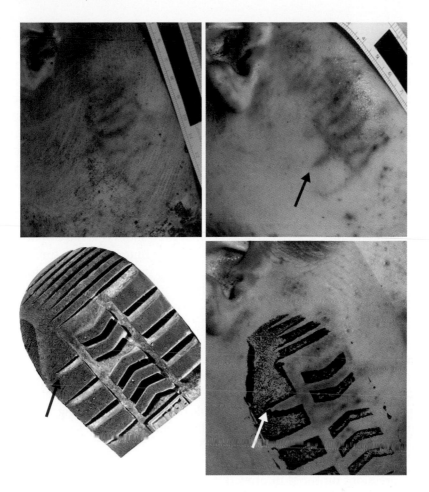

Figure 6.10 A blunt force pattern injury photographed at the scene (top left) and later at autopsy (top right), and the comparative relationship of the boot heel of the accused (bottom). The arrow indicates a shortened groove that corresponds to the general wear of the heel.

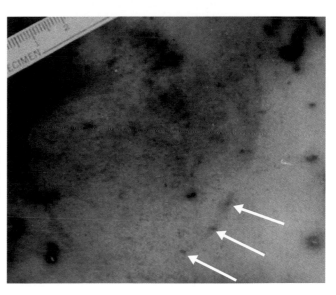

Figure 6.11 Some blunt force pattern injuries have more limited detail, but still may reveal important features. In this case, the curved edge of the heel of the shoe is represented faintly while the arrows refer to three corresponding stitch holes.

Recovering Blunt Force Pattern Evidence

During the commission of violent crimes, blunt force pattern injuries are often made with an outsole that simultaneously transfers blood, soil, or residue to the skin or clothing. In some cases, an impression may look like it was simply produced by the transfer of dirt or blood, and it may not be apparent that an underlying blunt force injury pattern is present. Alternately, the coloration of a blunt force pattern injury may show well, and it may not be apparent that dirt or dust may also be present on the surface of the skin as part of that same impression. The vast majority of cases involving blunt force pattern injuries involve homicides during which the victim has been violently kicked or stomped. The pattern of the outsole is not the only part of the shoe capable of producing these injuries. Pattern injuries can also be produced with other parts of a shoe, such as the toe areas, lace areas, and heel. Consideration should also be given to objects other than shoes that have a pattern and may have been used to strike the victim, resulting in pattern injuries. Many times these objects are still at the scene in the vicinity of the victim. The crime scene investigator should have a mindset regarding all of the causative possibilities of impressions on a victim and the potential of recovery of the object that may have produced them. If non-blood impressions are present on the skin, attempts to make a lift of those from the skin of the victim will not be destructive to any underlying blunt force injury pattern. In one reported case, although no visible impressions were observed on the skin or exterior clothing, laboratory enhancement with an alternate light source and chemical reagents revealed contact of the inner side of the clothing against the skin during a stomping injury was sufficient to transfer skin cells that provided some replication of an outsole design.* Thus clothing that covered areas over the top of any blunt force injuries potentially contains traces of footwear patterns even though they are not immediately visible.

In order to allow for a thorough examination involving blunt force pattern injuries and other impressions on the skin of victims, examination quality photographs must be taken. Examination photography at the scene is important even though it may be limited due to clothing, body position, hair, or other factors. The injuries should be photographed again at the autopsy prior to any cleaning of the body. This will not only record those changes in coloration during that period of time, but will allow for more thorough photographic documentation than may have been possible at the scene. These same injuries should then be photographed after the victim's body has been washed at autopsy. In those cases where dried blood, sweat, dirt, or other interferences may have muted the appearance of any blunt force injury, the cleaned area will likely reveal more information about the blunt force pattern, like the example in Figure 6.10. In cases where the injuries are obscured by hair, the hair should not just be cut short, but should be thoroughly shaved from those areas at autopsy to allow for the best documentation of the pattern injury. For those victims of blunt force trauma who have survived, the coloration and appearance of the injury will change within hours and over the following days and additional documentation may be warranted at various time intervals in those cases. One study reported the greatest success of photographically recovering bruising on skin involved the use of white

---

* Hamer, P. and Price, C., Case report: a transfer from skin to clothing by kicking—the detection and enhancement of shoeprints, *Journal of the Forensic Science Society*, 33(3):169–172, 1993.

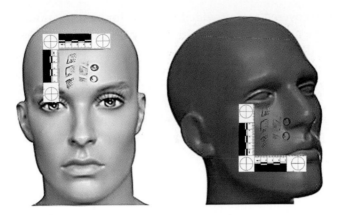

Figure 6.12 Placement of the scale during photography of blunt force pattern injuries can be difficult due to the topography of the skin.

light (400–700 nm) or cross-polarized light, which involves the use of two linearly polarizing filters perpendicular to one another.[*] The same study found that reflected UV and IR light were far less effective.

A scale should be included in every photograph. Although positioning a flat scale on a curved body is problematic, the scale should be positioned on the same plane as the injury as well as possible. If the injury is on a relatively flat portion of the body, such as the temple or forehead, this will be easier and the scale can be positioned immediately adjacent to that injury, as shown on the left in Figure 6.12. If the injury is across portions of the face or other areas of the body involving a more complex and curved topography, such as in the eye socket area, as illustrated on the right of Figure 6.12, it may not be possible to take a photograph that will accurately represent the scale of that full pattern injury. Make the best attempt at placing the scale on the same plane and take multiple photographs. It should be noted that bending or curving a scale to conform to the body does not solve this problem but only complicates the ability to make natural size enlargements. Blunt force pattern injuries cannot be cast or lifted. One innovative method that has been used to recover dimensional information from an injury involves firmly holding some clear film or acetate over the pattern injury while another individual carefully traces the pattern onto the acetate.

Examination

The forensic examination of a blunt force footwear pattern injury with known footwear requires the same knowledge, training, and procedures used in any other footwear comparison. It should be conducted in the same manner, including preparation of natural size enlargements, digital enhancement of images as appropriate, and preparation of known impressions. The forensic examiner should make every attempt to ensure all photographic

[*] Baker, H., Marsh, N., and Quinones, I., Photography of faded or concealed bruises on human skin, *JFI*, 63(1), 2013.

evidence has been recovered and provided to them for examination. In addition to photographs taken at the crime scene or at autopsy by police officials, pathologists routinely make photographic documentation of injuries during autopsy or during hospital visits in those cases when the victim is alive. On occasions when the victim is still alive, even family members may have taken photographs. In reading a recent appeal, it became apparent that the examiner was only provided one set of photographs of the injury, when in fact there were four sets of photographs of the injury taken at four different times by four different persons. In many cases worked over the years, the medical examiner's photographs provided the best detail but were not submitted with the evidence.

Although blunt force pattern injuries are capable of replication of good detail, most fall short of that. Consequently, their partial and often incomplete detail, as well as frequent problems with how accurately they are photographed, may impose some limitations during examination. Comparative conclusions should be based only on reliable and clearly visible components of these injuries. Unfortunately, on some occasions the injury is viewed and documented at autopsy by well-intentioned investigators, pathologists, or coroners who form their own non-expert opinions. It is noted that their conclusions are the product of their informal visual inspection and not a forensic footwear examination. If they believe they recognize the injury as one caused by footwear and they have shoes to which they want it to be compared, they should document the injury as well as possible and then submit the evidence to a laboratory for a full and proper evaluation by a qualified footwear expert. In one reported case, a medical examiner reported her comparison of "discontinuous contused abrasions with a vague circular pattern correspondence of class characteristics" on the right side of the victim's face and "circular and semicircular patterned contusions" on the left side of the victim's scalp, concluding that she noted similar class characteristics with a pair of shoes she was later asked to examine. She also noted in that case skin was a poor receptor for a tool mark, and correctly pointed out, "Identification of a tool mark involves expertise and subsequent court testimony of a tool mark examiner."[*] Her mislabeling of the blunt force footwear pattern as a tool mark, among other statements in her published account, illustrated her limited knowledge of footwear evidence. Pathologists, investigators, and coroners, in some cases, routinely make observations and comments regarding blunt force pattern injuries but do not have the knowledge, training, experience, or resources to conduct a full and fair forensic footwear evaluation of that evidence.

Key Words: blunt force, sharp force, blunt force pattern injury, contusion, abrasion, lividity, subcutaneous hemorrhaging

Key Points

1. Blunt force pattern injuries from footwear occur when sufficient speed and force of a shoe contacts the skin, causing subcutaneous hemorrhaging that leaves some representation of the shoe that produced it.
2. The pattern is a product of a pathological reaction and is not a direct transfer impression.
3. A blunt force pattern usually mirrors the image of the object that produced it.

---

[*] Rao, V. J., Patterned injury and its evidentiary value, *Journal of Forensic Sciences*, 31(2):768–772, April 1986.

4. Detail of a blunt force pattern injury relates to many factors, including the nature of the patterned object, the position on the body, and the resistance of underlying bones or tissue.
5. Detail from blunt force by a pattern object like a shoe varies from case to case.
6. A properly trained footwear examiner should make the forensic comparison between any blunt force patterns and the shoes of the accused.

Enhancement of Footwear Impression Evidence

7

A high percentage of footwear impressions produced at crime scenes are either latent or scarcely visible because of their poor contrast with the substrate. They often go undetected if various methods are not used to search for and increase their visualization. Enhancement methods increase the number of impressions detected at a crime scene as well as increase their detail available for examination. Crime scene investigators and laboratories that do not utilize enhancement methods will almost certainly lose part of the evidence.

To illustrate a typical example representative of so many cases, Figure 7.1 depicts a bloody footwear impression across several bricks. The scene photograph of the impression on the bricks contained minimal detail. Fortunately, these bricks were removed from the scene and brought to the laboratory, where they were enhanced with Amido Black. The results of the enhancement of this evidence are impressive and provided detail far in excess of what the photograph taken at the scene captured. Instead of a conclusion that showed a similar design with insufficient detail, the enhancement provided extensive additional detail that allowed for exclusion of the suspect's shoes. Years later, another suspect was arrested and convicted.[*]

Enhancement of two-dimensional impressions can be divided into methods that utilize (1) alternate light sources, specialized lighting, and forensic photography; (2) physical methods such as powdering and lifting; (3) chemical reagents for bloody and nonblood impressions; and (4) digital enhancement techniques. Although many methods have been in existence for years, new reagents and techniques, newer lasers and alternate light sources, and the increased abilities of digital software have provided additional opportunities to enhance impressions. Because enhancement includes such a broad range of possibilities, other sources will have to be consulted to cover this topic more thoroughly. This chapter will mention many methods briefly but will focus mainly on some of the more successful methods for enhancement of bloody impressions.

Forensic Photography and Specialized Lighting

Photographic methods are nondestructive and thus should always be attempted first. When original evidence can be transported to the laboratory, it allows for access to greater photographic resources and forensic techniques than possible at the crime scene. In general, forensic photographic methods use varied lighting and filter combinations that often enable the visualization and recording of detail beyond that of basic examination quality photography. Forensic photographic methods are often used in conjunction with other physical and chemical enhancement methods. The methods briefly mentioned hereafter are some of the more commonly used. Those who wish to practice various forensic photographic techniques should consult other sources for more in-depth information.

---

[*] Shuler, R., *Small Town Slayings in South Carolina*, History Press, Charleston, SC, 2009, pp. 113–136.

Figure 7.1 Five bricks that contained a faint bloody impression were recovered from a crime scene. On the left is a crime scene photograph of the bricks. The center photograph shows the bricks in the laboratory after treatment with Amido Black. The red color of the bricks was then dropped photographically using a red filter, as shown on the right.

High-Contrast Photography and the Use of Filters

Contrast can refer to the differences between black and white tones or between colors. High-contrast photography is a general term that pertains to a variety of ways in which lighting and filters are used to increase the contrast of the impression against the substrate. The example in Figure 7.1 shows the result of using a red filter to drop the red color and to produce better contrast. Similar contrast adjustments are also commonly used with digital methods.

Specialized Lighting

Light and the way it reflects from, is absorbed by, or penetrates an impression or the substrate can be useful in increasing the visualization of impressions. The term "specialized lighting" simply refers to the use of various forms of light to assist in the visualization and photography of the impression. Not all impressions are readily visible or can best be seen or photographed with the existing ambient light. Everyone has experienced observing a footwear impression on the floor from a distance, but as they walk toward it, it becomes less visible. When further away, the specular reflection of the light allowed you to see that impression because the reflective qualities of the light were bouncing off the impression differently than the substrate beneath the impression. When you stood over the impression and looked straight down, the difference in those reflective qualities was no longer as pronounced and the impression became less visible. An example of this is shown in Figure 7.2, where a section of glossy black floor tile has a blood mark that can hardly be seen from directly over the top of the tile in the existing light, but becomes easily visible when a white light source is directed at the impression and reflects off it at a slightly different angle. At crime scenes, when all other attempts fail, it may be necessary to photograph an impression at a slight angle followed by the digital correction of any perspective problem. One

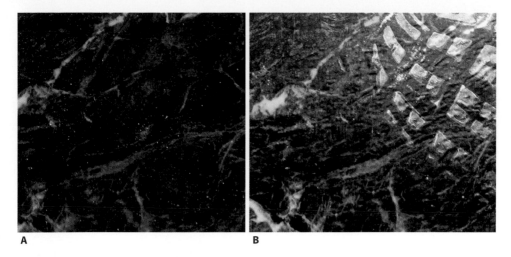

Figure 7.2 A piece of black tile with an impression. The impression is not visible when viewed in normal lighting (A) but is easily visible when intense reflected white light is used at just the proper angle (B).

reported technique uses a perspective control tilt-shift lens that can be offset slightly allowing for the visualization of the impressions without any perspective problem.* Additional specialized types of lighting are discussed hereafter.

Oblique Light

Oblique light is light that is directed across the impression at a low angle of incidence. In some cases, the light may be so low that it is just grazing the surface. Oblique light is also known as side lighting because the light source is held and aimed from the side of the impression. The use of oblique light works differently for two-dimensional and three-dimensional impressions, as explained in Figure 2.23, but provides increased visualization of the impression in most instances. Oblique light is routinely used to photograph impressions in soft substrates, on electrostatic lifting film, and in combination with other techniques. For instance, the piece of glass depicted in Figure 1.12 was photographed with oblique light and a dark field background, both adding considerable contrast to the impression thereon.

Cross-Polarization

Cross-polarizing filters are used to remove reflections from the substrate. When that occurs, the impression's intensity and clarity will often increase. Cross-polarization involves the use of two polarizing filters. One is placed in front of the light source that is illuminating the impression, typically a flash unit or LED light held at an oblique angle. The other is placed in front of or attached to the camera lens and can be rotated until the best image of the impression is achieved. Other cross-polarization filters are mounted directly onto the camera on top of one another and rotated to get the best result.

* Chung, J., Enhancement of difficult to capture two-dimensional footwear impressions using the combined effects of overhead lighting and the perspective control lens, *JFI*, 57(5), 2007.

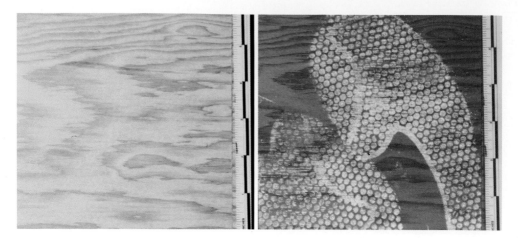

Figure 7.3 A chemically treated impression on raw wood is visualized and recorded with UV photography.

Ultraviolet Light

Ultraviolet light (UV) ranges from 10 to 400 nm on the light spectrum. Long wave or near UV extends from about 300 to 400 nm and short wave UV from about 200 to 300 nm. Although the UV portion of the light is not visible to the naked eye, in the past UV light-sensitive films have been used in combination with an 18A filter that absorbed all visible light except UV light. Figure 7.3 depicts a long wave reflected UV photograph of a chemically treated impression on raw wood. The use of short wave UV with digital cameras is very similar but special equipment is necessary for this type of photography.[*][†]

Infrared Light

The infrared (IR) portion of the light spectrum ranges from 700 nm and above. The portion used when observing and photographing evidence ranges from 700 to 900 nm. Although most of the IR light spectrum is not visible to the naked eye, certain films were used that were sensitive to IR light. When photographing reflected IR light, an IR-sensitive film was used along with a tungsten light, which produced a strong source of IR light. Various filters such as Wratten 18A, 87, 87A, 87B, 87C, and 89D were placed over the camera lens so that all portions of visible light were blocked out but not the IR light. These methods have been documented for years and are part of forensic photography techniques.[‡] Taking true IR photographs using most digital cameras is more complicated, as they often come with mirrors or filters that prevent the IR light from reaching the sensor, requiring an IR conversion kit or alternatively the use of special digital cameras created for IR photography.[§] An example of an infrared reflected photograph of a bloody shoe print on black fabric, taken with a digital camera, is illustrated in Figure 7.4.

---

[*] Richards, A., and Leintz, R., Forensic reflected ultraviolet imaging, *JFI*, 63(1), 2013.
[†] Reflected Ultraviolet Imaging System (RUVIS), www.spexforensics.com.
[‡] Perkins, M., The application of infrared photography in bloodstain pattern documentation on clothing, *JFI*, 55(1):1–9, 2005.
[§] DeBroux., S., McCaul, K., and Shimamoto, S., Infrared photography, http://www.crime-scene-investigator. net/Infrared_Photography_research_paper.pdf, January 2007.

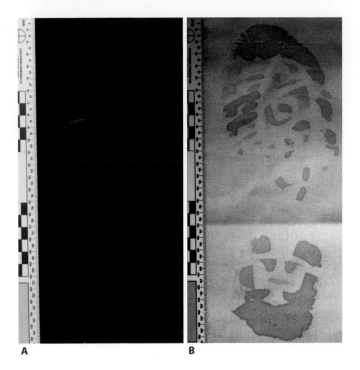

A   **B**

Figure 7.4 A bloody impression on black fabric on the left and the same fabric photographed with reflected infrared photography. (Courtesy of Sheri Shimamoto, Lakewood, CO.)

Alternate Light Sources and Lasers

A number of companies produce alternate light sources (ALS), which can provide a controlled high intensity light source at various wavelengths of light. These light sources, used in combination with special goggles or filters, enable impressions to be viewed and photographed in the visible and UV spectrums. They also have applications at crime scenes concerning searching for and detecting impression evidence. Some of these ALS are stronger and more versatile than others. One example is the CrimeScope®, which utilizes a 500 W lamp and provides a full range of tunable light from 300 to 670 nm.* Lasers are also used for detecting impressions.

Figure 7.5 shows bloody impressions on linoleum and a photograph of that area taken with an ALS.

Physical Methods

Certain forms of enhancement are categorized as physical methods. Examples involve the physical transfer of an impression from one surface to another through lifting, through detection of physical indentations with the use of an electrostatic detection apparatus (ESDA) or indentation materializer (IM), and with the application of fingerprint powder that attaches to either the impression or substrate. These methods have been addressed in Chapter 5. Other methods such as iodine fuming and cyanoacrylate fuming are included in this category.

* www.spexforensics.com.

A   B

Figure 7.5 A piece of flooring with blood marks on the left is enhanced with the CrimeScope ALS at 535 nm with the results as shown on the right.

Iodine

Iodine has long been used to develop fingerprints by reacting with the grease or fat content of the prints. If fatty, oily, and other organic materials are present in a footwear impression, the iodine vapor may be absorbed, resulting in increased visibility as the impression takes on a yellow to brown color. Iodine has been occasionally successful in enhancing footwear impressions of wet origin. Remoisturizing these prints often improves the results. In the case of some materials, especially fabrics, a strong background reaction may occur due to starches or fillers; therefore, it may be desirable to test a small portion of the background material prior to fuming. Enhancement of dust or dry residue impressions and muddy impressions has not been successful using this method. Iodine is viewed as nondestructive because it will eventually evaporate from the stained impression. Iodine is not a commonly used form of enhancement for footwear impressions.

To treat a footwear impression with iodine, it must be fumed in an iodine chamber. A saucer or small tray of steaming water can be placed in the chamber and a smaller saucer or tray that contains iodine crystals can be floated in the tray of steaming water. This will provide high humidity that will moisturize the impression and provide the necessary heat needed to cause the iodine crystals to fume. Any reaction should occur in minutes. Since the iodine reaction will weaken in time, immediately photograph any enhanced impressions. To make the enhanced treatment more permanent and convert the impression to a blue color, it can be treated with benzoflavone.

Cyanoacrylate Fuming (Super Glue)

Whereas cyanoacrylate fuming is well known and practiced for fingerprint development, the same has not followed for footwear impressions although some success has been reported.[*,†] More comprehensive research revealed excellent results for wet origin impressions on most nonporous substrates but also determined the necessity of fuming for longer times in a chamber, sometimes in excess of 30 minutes. In addition, this research found that best results were found when the impressions were refrigerated for 15 minutes followed by fuming, followed by powder or Rhodamine 6G dye.[‡] Obviously, these types of procedures and other factors present logistical problems for processing substrates at the scene of the crime. One individual developed a portable fuming chamber that could be positioned over a large area of a substrate and both humidify and super glue footwear impressions.[§] Very few footwear marks enhanced with this method have been encountered with evidence recovered from crime scenes. It is noted that the cyanoacrylates will cover bloody impressions and prevent subsequent contact with enhancement reagents, preventing enhancement.

Using Chemical Reagents to Detect and/or Enhance Impressions

The application of chemical reagents provides another way to both detect and increase the detail of an impression. Many formulations exist for the chemical enhancement of impressions, some the same or similar to those used to develop latent fingerprints, to detect trace materials and metal ions, or to stain or react with components of blood. In general, nonporous substrates that are smooth, such as flooring, counters, glass, and the like, allow for the replication of higher quality detail and also provide a relatively easy substrate from which lifting and enhancement techniques can be performed. Substrates that are porous do not always allow for the best replication of detail. Factors encountered with porous substrates that complicate the choices of lifting and other enhancement techniques include the condition of the substrate (clean, dirty, wet, dry); the porosity, texture, or absorbability of the substrate; the color of the substrate; the composition of the impression itself (mud, dust, dirt, blood); and whether the technique must be applied at the crime scene or can be applied in the laboratory.

Research and reports on case experiences have provided invaluable insight and recommendations for various enhancement reagents and procedures; however, it should be noted that the scope of these does not always provide guidance applicable or valid for every condition and every crime scene situation.

For crime scene investigators or others who use chemical reagents to detect and/or enhance footwear impressions, both positive and negative controls should be used as appropriate. When a reagent is mixed, there is no guarantee it will work. Thus it should be tested on a known sample. For instance, if a blood enhancement reagent like Luminol is going to be applied on evidence, it should first be tested on a known blood sample (positive control) after it is mixed to ensure the reagent is working. Without utilizing a positive control procedure, it would not be possible to determine if a failure to detect impressions when using that reagent was due to the absence of blood or the failure of the enhancement

---

[*] Llewellyn Jr., P., and Dinkins, L., A new use for an old friend, *JFI*, 45(5):498–503, 1995.
[†] Wilgus, F., Latent shoeprint recovery on human skin, *JFI*, 54(4):428–432, 2004.
[‡] Paine, N., The use of cyanoacrylate fuming and related enhancement techniques to develop shoe impressions on various surfaces, *JFI*, 48(5):585–601, 1998.
[§] Cairnduff, R., Design, development and evaluation of a model portable cyanoacrylate fuming chamber to develop and enhance shoe impressions on immovable surfaces, Specialist Project Report, Diploma of Applied Sciences, Canberra Institute of Technology, New South Wales Police Service, 1997.

reagent. Negative controls are those that test whether the substrate itself will react adversely with a reagent, thus interfering with the reagent's ability to visualize the impression. An easy example would be the application of a dark blue-black colored blood reagent such as Amido Black on an absorbent substrate like a piece of cardboard resulting in absorption of the reagent, and interfering with the visualization of the impression. A negative control test would determine this problem in advance.

Whenever treating evidence with chemical reagents, photographs should be taken at every stage of the process. As a general safety precaution and habit, any method involving the use of chemicals in the laboratory should be conducted under a ventilated hood. Whenever using chemical reagents, gloves, goggles, and protective clothing should be worn to prevent contact of the chemicals with the skin and eyes. Material Safety Data Sheets (MSDS) will provide information about hazards or precautions that need to be considered while using various chemicals or chemical reagents.

Chemical Reagents and Methods for Enhancement of Bloody Impressions

In crimes where blood has been spilled, the perpetrator often tracks through that blood, leaving a succession of impressions. Crimes that involve blood are inherently serious and footwear impressions made in the victim's blood have obvious evidentiary value. Every possible technique should be used to ensure that all of the footwear impressions have been detected, recovered, and fully enhanced. When an individual bleeds, the blood is oxygenated and very red. In time, the blood will darken. Heavily soaked areas of blood such as a pool of blood next to a victim will remain dark but very thin traces of blood, such as faint bloody footwear impressions, will fade over time. Those faded impressions on evidence recovered weeks or months prior are still totally present and can be enhanced just as successfully as if done the day of the crime.

A shoe or naked foot can generally hold sufficient blood to produce approximately 6 to 10 successive impressions before the blood becomes depleted. This will vary depending on the condition and type of outsole, the quantity of the blood initially stepped in, and the substrate. Sock-clad feet will retain larger amounts of blood, and thus will produce larger numbers of impressions before the blood is depleted. Figure 7.6 shows a series of eight successive bloody shoe impressions made on corrugated cardboard both before and after enhancement. The first impressions have larger quantities of blood that actually fill in and/or interfere with the replication of fine detail, as shown in impressions 1 through 3 in Figure 7.6. Subsequent impressions with lesser quantities of blood often reveal exceptional detail, but only after they have been enhanced with chemical reagents. In this example, the last four impressions are still visible on the light-colored cardboard, but had they been produced on other substrates that provided less contrast, they could easily go undetected.

Chemical reagents have different qualities and limitations. Some used to enhance blood provide instantly visible results in ambient light while others can only be viewed in the ultraviolet or infrared spectrum or in total darkness. Others have a greater sensitivity to blood and are therefore preferred for enhancing small traces of blood. Deciding which reagent to use is important and depends on numerous factors, including the substrate's porosity, texture, and color(s); whether the enhancement involves application to a small surface such as a single floor tile, or must be applied to the floor surfaces of a large room; as

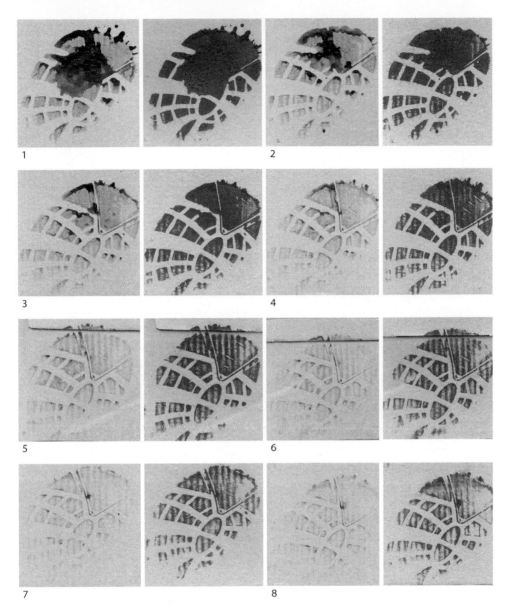

Figure 7.6 A sequence of eight bloody shoe impressions on corrugated cardboard shows the depletion of blood with each successive step. The first two or three impressions often have too much blood to allow for replication of good detail. The use of chemical reagents to enhance subsequent impressions allows for the use of their exceptional detail.

well as the capabilities, experience of, and resources available to the crime scene or laboratory personnel. When bloody footwear impressions are present at a scene and the full capability of chemical enhancement is not available, preference would be to secure the scene until assistance with enhancement of the blood marks can be arranged. Alternatively, consideration can be given to recovering original items bearing the bloody impressions so that they may later be enhanced in a laboratory. This effort may extend to cutting out sections of carpeting or other flooring but runs the risk of missing latent blood marks that cannot be seen prior to enhancement.

Fixing Bloody Impressions with 5-Sulfosalicylic Acid

Blood and blood marks of footwear are soluble in water. Fixing blood marks prior to staining or application of other reagents precipitates the basic proteins, preventing the leaching or diffusion of the blood.[*] When blood is not fixed prior to the application of chemical reagents, part or all of that blood will wash away and the evidence likely destroyed. The use of 5-sulfosalicylic acid has been proven a safe and effective way of fixing blood.[†] To fix the blood at the scene of a crime so that it may be enhanced with a chemical reagent, the blood impression item should be immersed in a 2% weight-to-volume aqueous solution of 5-sulfosalicylic acid (20g/l distilled water) for 5 minutes. If logistics prevent the immersion of the impression area, the 5-sulfosalicylic acid can be sprayed onto the area two or three times over 5 minutes.

In those instances where large areas are being searched for latent bloody impressions, treating the area first with 5-sulfosalicylic acid is not practical. In those cases, using a reagent that includes the fixative will reduce degradation of any impressions. Even so, experience has shown that diffusion of the impressions may still occur, indicating fixation does not occur instantly. The best and safest practice is to apply a fixative in any situation where impressions are initially visible, even if your reagent includes a fixative. It is also noted for those who purchase premixed reagents, the inclusion of a fixative in that reagent is often not stated or known, leaving users with uncertainty of what they are using. This is just another reason to fix any visible blood prior to treatment with a reagent.

Protein Stains and Dyes

Enhancement reagents include stains and dyes that colorize the protein components present in blood. Their application process includes fixing the bloody footwear impression, staining the impression, and then destaining the impression and the background. Enhanced impressions can be photographed and, depending on the reagent used, can possibly be lifted with a white gelatin lifter that can separate the mark from any background pattern and/or colors. With some reagents, the lifted impressions can be successfully photographed with fluorescence.[‡] Stains and dyes increase the contrast of bloody impressions that have already been visually detected but experience and research shows their application often results in the detection of additional latent impressions.[§,¶,**]

Many stains or dyes are dark in color; thus, if absorbed into a porous substrate such as raw wood, paper, or absorbent fabrics, the result will be an undesirable and irreversible background staining that interferes with the enhancement process. An example of this is shown in Figure 7.7, where Amido Black was applied to bloody impressions on raw wood. With some reagents on some substrates, a destaining and thorough rinse process

---

[*] Farrugia, K., Savage, K., Bandey, H., and Nic Daéid, N., Chemical enhancement of footwear impressions in blood on fabric—Part 1: protein stains, *Science and Justice*, 51:99, 2011a.

[†] Hussain, J., and Pounds, C., The enhancement of marks in blood, Central Research Establishment Report, No. 649, February 1988.

[‡] Velders, M. J. M., Fluorescing traces in blood on white gelatin lifters with Hungarian Red, 81st Educational Conference of the International Association of Identification, Greensboro, NC, 1996.

[§] Fischer, J. F., and Trozzi, T. A., Chemical Blood Enhancement Techniques Workshop, handout and presentation at the International Association for Identification Educational Conference, July 19–25, 1998, Little Rock, AR.

[¶] Farrugia, K., et al., 2011a, Ibid.

[**] Velders, T., Brabant South-East Department, Eindhoven, the Netherlands, Research Report 2011–2012.

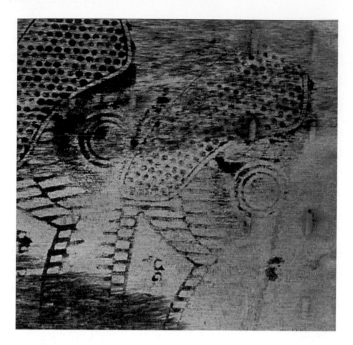

Figure 7.7 The use of colored dyes and stains on porous substrates, such as the use of Amido Black on raw wood in this example, produces background staining that cannot be removed and interferes with the enhancement process.

will remove most or all of the excess stain retained by the substrate; however, this is not predictable and is a good reason to consider use of a negative control. In general, colored stains and dyes are best used for impressions on nonporous substrates where background staining does not occur. Their additional possible use on certain light-colored fabrics and the successful use of Acid Yellow 7 on dark fabrics and nonporous substrates under fluorescence has been reported.[*]

Amido Black (Acid Black 1)[†,‡]

Amido Black is a dye that stains blood proteins a dark blue-black color. Amido Black is best used on substrates that are nonporous and whose background will not absorb the stain. Figure 7.8 shows a case example of Amido Black used on linoleum. The dark blue-black color of Amido Black provided excellent contrast against the lighter nonporous substrate with no background staining. In this particular case, the stain was applied in the laboratory 8 years after the impression was recovered from the crime scene, although it could have been applied at the scene the day of the crime.

The original methanol formulation for Amido Black is prepared by dissolving 2 g of Amido Black in 100 mL of glacial acetic acid and 900 mL of methanol. The rinse solution consists of a mixture of 900 mL of methanol and 100 mL of glacial acetic acid alone.

---

[*] Farrugia, K., et al., 2011a, Ibid.

[†] Sears, V. G., and Prizeman, T. M., Enhancement of fingerprints in blood—Part 1: The optimization of Amido black, *JFI*, 50(5):470–480, 2000.

[‡] Sears, V. G., Butcher, C. P. G., and Prizeman, T. M., Enhancement of fingerprints in blood—Part 2: protein dyes, *JFI*, 51(1):28–38, 2001.

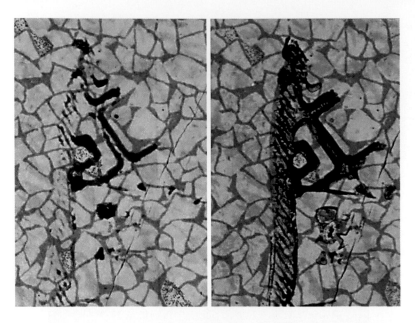

Figure 7.8 A case example of Amido Black applied to a partial bloody impression on linoleum 8 years after the crime. Additional significant detail was developed, which enabled a higher level of association with the suspected footwear.

In general, the use of a methanol-based Amido Black reagent at crime scenes is not recommended, as it is flammable and toxic. Methanol-based Amido Black reagent is usually reserved for use under a laboratory hood. When used, it should be cautioned that the methanol-based reagent can erode certain painted and varnished substrates, resulting in degradation of any impressions.

As an alternative to methanol, various aqueous formulations of Amido Black have been used. One aqueous-based Amido Black formulation has proven very effective, particularly for crime scene applications.* It is prepared by combining and mixing the following ingredients in the order listed: 500 mL distilled water, 20 g 5-sulfosalicylic acid, 3 g Amido Black, 3 g sodium carbonate, 50 mL formic acid, 50 mL glacial acetic acid, and 12.5 mL Kodak Photo Flo 600 solution, and then diluted to 1 L with distilled water. This aqueous-based Amido Black reagent has a long shelf life and provides a safer means of application at the crime scene with no flammability or toxic fumes, nor any adverse affects on painted or varnished surfaces. Although the Amido Black reagent formulations include a fixative, prior fixation with 5-sulphosalicylic acid is recommended.

Regardless of whether the methanol-based or aqueous-based Amido Black reagent is used, the application to the blood-marked area can be achieved with immersion or through a controlled application over small areas of the impression. Although staining often appears immediate, the stain should be allowed to work for 5 minutes, particularly for faint impressions. Destaining and rinsing should be as thorough as possible and the stained impression should be allowed to air dry. Forced air can be used to assist in removing excess solution and droplets from the impression area. Blotting or wiping the stained

---

* Fischer, J. F., and Trozzi, T. A., Chemical Blood Enhancement Techniques Workshop, handout and presentation at the International Association for Identification Educational Conference, July 19–25, 1998, Little Rock, AR.

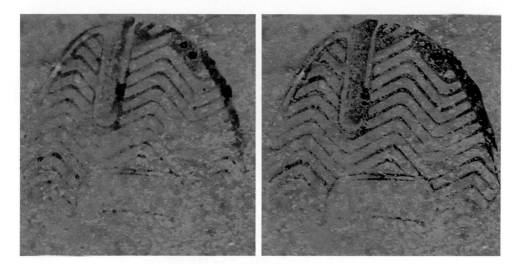

Figure 7.9 A bloody impression on ceramic tile, enhanced with Amido Black, rinsed and then wiped with a soft cloth, creating numerous light spots where the enhanced blood was physically removed.

impression before or after rinsing is not recommended and may result in degradation of the impression. Figure 7.9 depicts a test where a bloody impression was stained with aqueous Amido Black and rinsed, after which it was gently wiped with a soft cotton cloth. Because of the wiping, some areas of the stained bloody impression were removed and resulted in numerous light spots. This example was a simulation but mimics what has been observed in casework when impressions on smooth nonporous substrates are physically wiped or blotted.

Research regarding the sensitivity of Amido Black, and whether it only reacts with blood, has determined that trace amounts of various household substances having a protein component would react as well as other substances without protein but only when larger amounts of those substances were present. The research also concluded that in order to track trace amounts of any substance through a crime scene and to have repeated positive reactions with Amido Black, the outsole of the shoe would have had to come in contact with a high protein substance such as blood.[*]

Amido Black is one of the most commonly used reagents for the enhancement of bloody footwear and fingerprints on nonporous substrates probably due to its long time familiarity, its low cost, and the amount of contrast it can provide. Although often a good choice, Amido Black is not always the best choice and should not be the only enhancement method available. Logistical limitations also apply for application of Amido Black to large surface areas due to the necessity to apply and rinse small areas at a time.

Acid Fuchsin (Acid Violet 19) and Hungarian Red

Acid Fuchsin is a water-soluble dye. It reacts with and stains the protein components in blood a deep magenta color, as shown in Figure 7.10. The magenta color provides another

[*] Harnum, W., and Stanley, G., Amido Black presumptive false-positive tests, Royal Newfoundland Constabulary Forensic Identification Unit, RNC File #2007–3299.

Figure 7.10 Bloody impressions stained with Acid Fuchsin or Hungarian Red turn a deep magenta color.

choice when blood marks are present on substrates that are opposite colors. For instance, a blood impression on a blue substrate could be enhanced with Acid Fuchsin and photographed, after which the blue background substrate color could be digitally dropped.

To prepare Acid Fuchsin, dissolve 20 g of 5-sulfosalicylic acid and 2 g of Acid Fuchsin in 1 L of distilled water. A small area of the substrate being stained should first be tested with the staining solution. If the substrate background retains the stain and it cannot be rinsed away, a different reagent should be used. Stain the impression by immersing the item in the dye solution or spraying the impression area. Some staining occurs quickly but the reagent should be allowed to remain in contact with the impression for 5 minutes. Rinse well with water and air dry.

In 1996, a modified version of Acid Fuchsin called Hungarian Red was introduced with a procedure that recommended the use of a white gelatin lifter to lift traces of the Hungarian Red from nonporous surfaces when necessary to eliminate any background interference or patterns. Once lifted, the impression on the gelatin lifter could also be photographed under fluorescence, allowing detection of trace amounts.[*,†] This particular research used BVDA Hungarian Red and noted that it produced better results than achieved with Acid Fuchsin from other sources.[‡,§] The impression should first be fixed with 5-sulphosalicylic acid for 5 minutes. Hungarian Red is then applied for 5 minutes. The impression is then rinsed with an acetic acid and water mixture and forced air can be used

---

[*] Velders, M. J. M., Fluorescing traces in blood on white gelatin lifters with Hungarian red, presented at the 81st Educational Conference of the International Association for Identification, Greensboro, NC, July 1996.

[†] www.bvda.com, How to use Hungarian Red, 2015.

[‡] Velders, T., New insight into the chemical improvement of shoeprints and fingerprints placed with blood on non-porous surfaces, *Identification Canada*, 35(3):80–102, 2012.

[§] The author notes that using Acid Fuchsin, 5-sulfosalicylic acid, and distilled water on some blood marks on tiles produced no differences between the results achieved with that mixture and Hungarian Red.

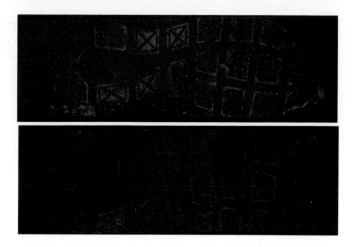

Figure 7.11 Two very faint bloody impressions on tile were treated with Hungarian Red and lifted with white gelatin lifters. They fluoresced at 555 nm.

to assist in drying the impression. The impression can be photographed with white light, followed by fluorescence photography at the appropriate wavelength. After completely dry, a white gelatin lifter can then be applied to the treated blood impressions and allowed to remain in contact for 30 minutes. During this time, pressure should be applied to the lifter by using a 10–20 pound weight over a pad to distribute the weight in order to ensure complete contact is made. When the gelatin lift is removed, it should be photographed within 30 minutes, both in white light and with fluorescence, in the event the lifted impression later diffuses into the gelatin. Figure 7.11 depicts the fluorescence of two faint blood impressions on tile, treated with Hungarian Red, and lifted with white gelatin lifters as described above. The fluorescence of the impressions was viewed at 555 nm using red goggles. The fluorescence was much more pronounced after lifting with the white gelatin lifts. Others have reported results with the fluorescence of Hungarian Red and Acid Fuchsin in the 515–560 nm range.[*]

Acid Yellow 7

Acid Yellow 7 is a dye solution in a water/acetic acid/ethanol mixture.[†] It works well on impressions on nonporous substrates. It is not recommended for use on highly absorbent substrates like paper, cardboard, or carpet, but has been found to work for enhancement of blood marks produced on a variety of fabrics.[‡] The mixture will stain a bloody impression yellow but its main value for recovering detail comes from fluorescent photography. To prepare the reagent, mix 1 g of Acid Yellow 7, 50 mL glacial acetic acid, 250 mL ethanol, and 700 mL distilled water.[§]

After fixing the impression, spray with the Acid Yellow 7 as necessary to allow it to remain in contact with the bloody impression for 5 minutes. This might require repeated

---

[*] Velders, Ibid.

[†] Sears, V. G., Butcher, C. P. G., and Fitzgerald, L. A., Enhancement of fingerprints in blood—Part 3: reactive techniques, acid yellow 7, and process sequences, *JFI*, 55(6):741–763, 2005.

[‡] Farrugia, K. et al., 2011a, Ibid.

[§] www.bvda.com, Product information on Acid Yellow 7, http://www.bvda.com/EN/prdctinf/en_acid_yellow_7.html.

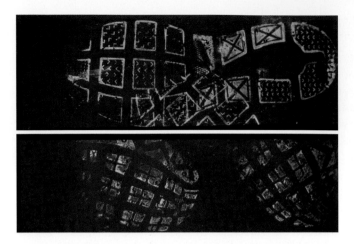

Figure 7.12 Two very faint bloody impressions treated with Acid Yellow 7, lifted with white gelatin lifters, and viewed under fluorescence between 415 and 490 nm.

sprayings. Rinse thoroughly with the same acetic acid solution minus the Acid Yellow 7 until no coloring remains on the substrate except for that on the impression(s). Allow the impression to air dry. The Acid Yellow 7 will provide a strong fluorescence, allowing for separation of the background color of a substrate. Fluorescence is excited in the 400–490 nm range and viewed with an orange or yellow filter. Beyond photographing the Acid Yellow 7 directly, traces of the enhanced blood mark can be lifted with a white gelatin lifter. The gelatin lifter should remain on the impression for 30 minutes under the pressure of a 10–20 pound weight to ensure complete contact as described previously for Hungarian Red. The lifting allows for separation of the impression from background colorations and patterns. Figure 7.12 depicts two white gelatin lifts of faint blood marks from tiled flooring treated with Acid Yellow 7, viewed in the 415–490 nm range.

Ninhydrin

Ninhydrin reacts with amino acids in perspiration and is routinely used for development of latent fingerprints. The Ninhydrin reaction produces a dark color called Ruhemann's Purple. Since amino acids are also present in blood and laboratories have this resource, some have used Ninhydrin to enhance bloody footwear impressions on porous substrates like paper or fabric. The impression is sprayed with Ninhydrin and allowed to evaporate from the substrate. A humidity chamber is used to accelerate the reaction. Alternately, heat and steam can be applied with a steam iron to accelerate the development of the reaction. Because the Ninhydrin spray is flammable, the heat should not be applied until the Ninhydrin has thoroughly dried. Reportedly, Ninhydrin has no effect on subsequent DAB processing.[*] Research on bloody footwear marks with Ninhydrin resulted in good contrast on light colored fabrics but either less or no contrast enhancement on dark colored backgrounds.[†] Ninhydrin is not an enhancement choice for application at crime scenes.

---

[*] Trozzi, T. A., Developing bloody footwear impressions with the use of diaminobenzidine, presented at the International Symposium on the Forensic Aspects of Footwear and Tire Impression Evidence, FBI Academy, Quantico, VA, June 27–July 1, 1994.

[†] Farrugia, K., Nic Daéid, N., Savage, K., and Bandey, H., Chemical enhancement of footwear impressions in blood on fabric—Part 3: amino acid staining, *Science and Justice*, 53:8–13, 2013.

Peroxidase Reagents

Some reagents react with the heme group in hemoglobin that is present in blood. These reagents are colorless dyes that yield color or light (luminescence) through a catalytic action in the presence of an oxidizing agent. Leuco crystal violet (LCV), leuco malachite green (LMG), diaminobenzidine, tetra-methylbenzidine (TMB), fluorescein, and Luminol are examples of peroxidase reagents that have been used to provide enhancement for bloody footwear marks. These reagents can be sprayed onto the impressions with various techniques, either at crime scenes or in the laboratory on the original evidence recovered. At the scene some reagents can be applied with a heavier pump spray unit since it is important to saturate the substrate when searching for impressions and because those reagents have the fixative in them. In other applications, a finer spray should be used. For example, if a reagent such as Luminol is sprayed with a heavier pump spray, although a reaction will still occur if blood is present because no fixative is used, the excess spray can result in considerable diffusion of the mark and degradation of detail. Excellent results have been reported with very fine sprayers such as the Bluestar® Ecospray unit.[*]

Leuco Crystal Violet (LCV)

LCV is the reduced colorless form of crystal violet. When LCV and hydrogen peroxide come into contact with hemoglobin or its derivatives, a violet colored dye (crystal violet) is formed. LCV is easily applied to large surfaces via spraying and the colorless solution turns violet almost instantly on contact with blood. A heavier spray application can be used for this purpose. Thorough rinsing of impressions should be made and the area dried with forced air. The color of LCV's reaction is illustrated in Figure 7.13 on white tile and in Figure 7.6. Its ease of application and the ability to apply it quickly to large areas has resulted in its extensive use at crime scenes. To prepare LCV, first dissolve 10 g of 5-sulfosalicylic acid in 500 mL of 3% hydrogen peroxide. To that add 4.4 g of sodium acetate and 1.1 g of LCV and stir until completely dissolved.[†]

Figure 7.13 A bloody impression on white tile treated with LCV provides both enhancement and a change to the violet color.

---

[*] Farrugia, K., Savage, K., Bandey, H., Ciuksza, T., and Nic Daéid, N., Chemical enhancement of footwear impressions in blood on fabric—Part 2: peroxidase reagents, *Science & Justice*, 51(4):112–114, 2011b.
[†] Formulation from personal communication with John Fischer, July 1, 1998.

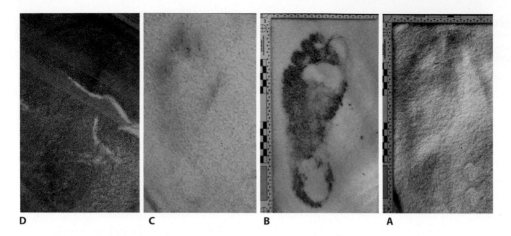

Figure 7.14 A naked footprint made after stepping in very dilute bloody water (A), enhanced with LCV spray (B), that unpredictably degraded after 24 hours (C). A real case piece of LCV-treated evidence that shows how an LCV-treated towel photoionized and turned color over time (D).

Prior research and experience compared numerous blood enhancement methods and concluded that LCV was both a commonly used and excellent technique for the application to bloody footwear impressions at both the crime scene and laboratory.[*,†] Other research concluded that treatment with LCV improved the visibility of random characteristics of both faint and latent bloody impressions on floor surfaces.[‡] Some success has also been reported regarding the ability of impressions treated with LCV to fluoresce and luminesce under a variety of wavelengths in both the UV and IR spectra.[§,¶,**] More recent research has indicated that in certain situations involving visible impressions on nonporous substrates, the best results may not come from the use of LCV but rather the use of more sensitive reagents such as Hungarian Red or Acid Yellow 7 combined with fluorescence photography of those impressions and the use of white gelatin lifters to remove interferences of background colors or patterns.[††] Thus LCV may be useful to apply at a crime scene to initially locate and visualize impressions on nonporous substrates, but enhancement could then extend to cutting out individual impressions for processing with more sensitive reagents and techniques in the laboratory.

One disadvantage of LCV is its tendency to photoionize and/or degrade when it cannot be thoroughly rinsed. Figure 7.14 depicts an example of a barefoot impression (A) made with dilute bloody water on a towel followed with application of LCV (B). This is an

[*] Bodziak, W. J., Use of leuco-crystal violet to enhance shoe prints in blood, *FSI*, 82(1):45–52, 1996.

[†] Theeuwen, A. B. E., and Limborgh, J. C. M., Enhancement of footwear impressions in blood; comparison of chemical methods for the visualization and enhancement of footwear impressions in blood, presented at the European Meeting of Forensic Sciences, Lausanne, Switzerland, September 1997.

[‡] Chabert, S., and Girod, A., LCV enhancement of a shoeprint's sequence, presented at the First European Meeting of Forensic Science, Lausanne, Switzerland, September 1997.

[§] Fischer, J. F., Forensic light sources and their application to tire and shoe examination, presented at the International Symposium on the Forensic Aspects of Footwear and Tire Impression Evidence, FBI Academy, Quantico, VA, June 27–July 1, 1994.

[¶] Lake, S., and Ganas, J., Optical enhancement of leucocrystal violet treated impressions in blood, Victoria Police State Forensic Science Laboratory, Macleod, Australia, 1995.

[**] Bodziak, W. J., Use of leuco-crystal violet to enhance shoe prints in blood, *FSI*, 82(1):45–52, 1996.

[††] Velders, T., New insight into the chemical improvement of shoeprints and fingerprints placed with blood on non-porous surfaces, *Identification Canada*, 35(3):80–102.

example where the impression on the towel could not be rinsed without compromising its dimensions. Within 24 hours, the impression degraded considerably (C). In some cases, the entire background can photoionize. A case example of an LCV treated impression on a towel shows how it photoionized over time and resulted in the entire towel turning violet (D). Because of the distinct possibility that unrinsed impressions will photoionize or degrade, examination quality photographs of those impressions should be taken immediately after the enhancement process.

Diaminobenzidine

Diaminobenzidine (DAB) (3,3′-diaminobenzidine tetrahydrochloride) is converted to a dark brown insoluble product in the presence of hydrogen peroxide as a result of the peroxidase activity of the hemoglobin derivatives in blood. The colorless reagent allows for the use of DAB on both porous and nonporous items. The dark brown color produced makes it useful in combination with digital methods that can be used to drop background colors and patterns. For example, Figure 7.15 depicts some bloody footwear marks on a light green shirt and the result of enhancement of those blood marks with DAB followed by digitally dropping the green color.

To prepare the DAB working solution, mix 100 mL of 1M phosphate buffer (pH 7.4) with 800 mL of distilled water. Now mix 1 g of 3,3′-diaminobenzidine tetrahydrochloride in 100 mL of distilled water to prepare the DAB solution. Combine the buffer solution and DAB solution and mix together. Then add 50 mL of 3% hydrogen peroxide. DAB must be freshly prepared prior to use. Its formulation does not include a fixative, so prior to its application, 5-sulfosalicylic acid must be applied to the impression area for 5 minutes. In

Figure 7.15 DAB treatment of bloody impressions on a green shirt with the green color digitally dropped. The original untreated area is shown above with the final results below.

some cases, it may be possible to immerse impressions in a tray of DAB working solution. For larger substrates, apply by spraying the DAB working solution on the impression sufficiently to soak it and repeat spraying the area every 2 minutes until the enhancement process is complete. Unlike most reagents, the enhancement reaction with DAB does not occur instantly but develops over a period of several minutes. Some change will usually be noticeable within 1 or 2 minutes but the impression must be allowed to remain in the solution or continue to be sprayed with fresh solution for at least 10 minutes. In the case of faint impressions, they may remain in the solution much longer if necessary, as no background staining will occur. When the enhancement is complete, rinse with distilled water. Reportedly, DAB does not react on items previously treated with LCV or Luminol.[*]

Luminol

Luminol is very possibly the oldest chemical method used for the detection and enhancement of latent blood and blood marks. The compound 3-aminophthalhydrazide (5-amino-2,3-dihydro-1,4-phthalazinedione) was first created by Schmitz in 1902.[†] In 1928, a German chemist found that the chemiluminescence of aminophthalic acid hydrazide was enhanced by blood in an alkaline solution of hydrogen peroxide.[‡] In 1934, Huntress called this compound Luminol, which means producer of light.[§] In 1937, it was reported this formulation could be used to locate and recognize traces of blood.[¶]

The Luminol reaction is unique because instead of colorizing the blood, it results in the production of light known as chemiluminescence. To some, this makes the use of Luminol inconvenient because it must be simultaneously applied and photographically recorded in total darkness. In many crime scene applications, this can be a great advantage as the application of Luminol in darkness drops any background colors and/or patterns and also enables the detection of very small traces of blood.[**] One study reported the Luminol reaction to blood in dilutions of 1:100,000 for 1 minute.[††] Another examiner reported the unaided eye could detect blue chemiluminescence in dilutions of 1:10,000 and with the use of night vision goggles could detect traces of blood in dilutions of 1 in 1 million.[‡‡] Others have reported detectable traces as dilute as 1 in 5 million.[§§] Luminol is highly sensitive and that has enabled its use, to not only detect and photograph bloody foot and shoe marks, but

[*] Trozzi, T. A., Developing bloody footwear impressions with the use of diaminobenzidine, presented at the International Symposium on the Forensic Aspects of Footwear and Tire Impression Evidence, FBI Academy, Quantico, VA, June 27–July 1, 1994.

[†] Schmitz, A. Uber das hydrazid der trimensinaure und die hemimellitsaure, Inaug. Dissertation, Heidelberg, 1902, cited in Curtius, T. and Semper, A., Ber. Btsch. Chem. Ges. 46:1162, 1913.

[‡] Albrecht, H., Über die Chemiluminescenz des Aminophthalsäurehydrazids" (On the chemiluminescence of aminophthalic acid hydrazide) Zeitschrift für Physikalische Chemie 136:321–330, 1928.

[§] Huntress, E., Stanley, L., and Parker, A., The preparation of 3 aminophthalhydrazide for use in the demonstration of chemiluminescence, J. Am. Chem. Soc., 56:241–242, 1934.

[¶] Specht, W., Die Chemiluminescenz des Hämins, ein Hilfsmittel zur Auffindung und Erkennung forensisch wichtiger Blutspuren (The chemiluminescence of haemin, an aid to the finding and recognition of forensically significant blood traces), Angewandte Chemie, 50(8):155–157, 1937.

[**] Lytle, L., and Hedgecock, D., Chemiluminescence in the visualization of forensic bloodstains, JFS, 550–562, 1978.

[††] Tobe, S., Watson, N., and Nic Daéid, N., Evaluation of six presumptive tests for blood, their specificity, sensitivity, and effect on high molecular-weight DNA, JFS, 52(1), 2007.

[‡‡] Thornton, J., and Maloney, R., The chemistry of the luminol reaction—where to from here? CAC Newsletter, September 1985, pp. 9–17.

[§§] Kirk, P. L., Crime Investigation, 2nd ed., John Wiley & Sons, New York, 1963, p. 184.

also to process specific areas of crime scenes, vehicles, or washed clothing to successfully locate traces of blood that can be subsequently associated with the victim through DNA analysis. Several reports have documented that Luminol can even be detected under several layers of paint used to cover the blood.[*,†,‡,§,¶,**] One field study concluded sufficient traces of blood were still present for a Luminol reaction after being exposed to the outside elements for 8 years.[††] A comparison of peroxidase reagents regarding enhancement of blood marks on fabric found in general that Luminol (Bluestar Magnum version) was the most efficient for weaker impressions.[‡‡,§§]

My experience in preparing bloody impressions for training demonstrations has indicated that Luminol does not luminesce as well when blood is very fresh, yet old bloody impressions are easily detected years after the date of the crime. Whether this is valid or not, there is definitely no rush to search for or treat bloody marks with Luminol particularly if other priorities at the scene must be addressed first. I have successfully used Luminol to enhance latent bloody shoe marks on carpet over 15 years after the crime.

Because Luminol is usually applied through spraying in a closed environment, precautions should include appropriate protection such as masks, ventilation, protective clothing, gloves, and goggles. One study reported no significant health concerns for Luminol but recommended suitable precautions be taken.[¶¶]

Luminol is a water-based solution and blood is water-soluble. A fixative is not included in the Luminol reagent formulation. It has been reported that 5-sulfosalicylic acid may create a layer on top of the blood mark and the effect of the acidic nature of the fixative results in reduced intensity of the luminescence.[***] My own experiences when applying a fixative prior to Luminol treated also resulted in a diminished reaction. Without a fixative, its application to a bloody footwear impression may dissolve the blood leading to degradation of impression details. Application of Luminol should be made with a very fine spray. This light application enables the detection of impressions with minimal degradation of unfixed blood. The fine spray also allows for photography of any luminescing impressions with greater detail particularly if on nonporous substrates. Latent impressions detected with Luminol on nonporous surfaces should be photographed and then should be fixed with 5-sulfosalicylic acid to preserve remaining traces of blood for possible future enhancement methods.

[*] Adair, T., Experimental detection of blood under painted surfaces. *Int. Assoc. Bloodstain Pattern Analysts*, 12–19, 2006.

[†] Ibid.

[‡] Farrar, A., Porter, G., and Renshaw, A., Detection of latent bloodstains beneath painted surfaces using reflected infrared photography. *J. Forensic Sci.*, 57(5):1190–1198, 2012.

[§] Howard, M., and Nessan, M., Detecting bloodstains under multiple layers of paint. *J. Forensic Ident.* 60(6):682–717, 2010.

[¶] Timmons, K., Ackeren, J., Rushton, C., and Staton, P., Detection and documentation of bloodstains concealed by paint: a practical approach, Marshall University Forensic Science Center, Huntington, WV.

[**] Bily, C., and Maldonado, H., The application of Luminol to bloodstains concealed by multiple layers of paint. *J. Forensic Ident.*, 56(6):896–905, 2006.

[††] Stene, I., Shimamoto, S., Gabel, R., Tewes, R., and Adair, T., Using luminol to detect blood in soil eight years after deposition, *J. Assoc. Crime Scene Reconstruction*, 19(1):1–4, 2013.

[‡‡] Farrugia, K., et al., 2011b, Ibid.

[§§] Bluestar Magnum, Bluestar Forensics, http://www.bluestar-forensic.com/gb/bluestar-magnum.php.

[¶¶] Larkin, T., and Gannicliffe, C., Illuminating the health and safety of Luminol, *Science and Justice*, 48:71–75, 2008.

[***] Farrugia, K., An Evaluation of Enhancement Techniques for Footwear Impressions Made on Fabric, PhD Thesis, University of Strathclyde, 2011, p. 106.

Formulation

The Luminol reagent has a limited useful life and should be mixed just prior to use. To prepare the basic Luminol formulation, dissolve 0.1 g Luminol and 5 g sodium carbonate in 100 mL of water. Just prior to using the mixture, add 0.7 g sodium perborate and mix thoroughly. Luminol can also be purchased premeasured to which only water needs to be added to create a working solution.

Some Luminol products and formulations include a peroxide-based oxidizer that tends to accelerate the reaction and thus provides a greater amount of luminescence in a shorter period of time. Products such as these have been popular with some because the additional luminescence allows for easier photography; however, proper photography in total darkness will yield better contrast.

Using Luminol to search for blood marks at crime scenes: When there are large areas of carpeting or flooring that need to be searched for latent blood and bloody shoe impressions, a concise method must be used. An impression that is latent to begin with does not consist of a large quantity of blood and if treated with a heavy spray for the purposes of detecting that blood might not have sufficient blood remaining to react when attempts are made later to photograph it. A spray device that is capable of providing a fine application of Luminol should be used in lieu of heavier pump type sprayers like those found in a hardware store. The smaller droplet size enables more control, recovery of more detail, and less consumption of the impression. Figure 7.16 depicts a section of carpet that has been screened and marked in preparation for the application of Luminol for photography. The same general procedure can be modified for any substrate.

In the search for bloody impressions on the carpet in Figure 7.16, the room was prepared and totally darkened, including blocking light from beneath doors and other unwanted sources. The Luminol was mixed fresh and a positive control test was performed. After the lights were turned out, 2 to 3 minutes were allowed to lapse prior to beginning the procedure to give the eyes time to adjust to the darkness and thus create an improved ability to detect any luminescence. Night vision goggles, if available, should be considered for at least one observer. On hands and knees in one corner, and crawling backward, the carpet was lightly sprayed with Luminol. As soon as any luminescence was detected, the application of Luminol ceased and that area was marked with a black marker, indicating it as an area for subsequent Luminol treatment while being photographed. The backward crawling continued using the same technique to detect and mark additional areas that provided a luminescent reaction and possibly contained footwear marks. When the end of the carpet was reached, the search shifted about 3 feet over and the search direction was reversed, eventually covering the entire carpet. Areas that had a positive reaction were retreated while being photographed. In the example in Figure 7.16, even though the carpet was light colored, no shoe impressions were visible prior to treatment, but a total of 42 impressions of the suspect's shoes were detected and photographed on three sections of carpet. The chart in Figure 7.16 shows their location throughout the scene in relation to the entry door where the homicide occurred and a back room where the victim was found. The alibi of the suspect was that two unknown individuals had attacked both him and his father; however, only his shoe impressions were found and no unaccounted for bloody impressions of others were found. The accused pled guilty prior to trial.

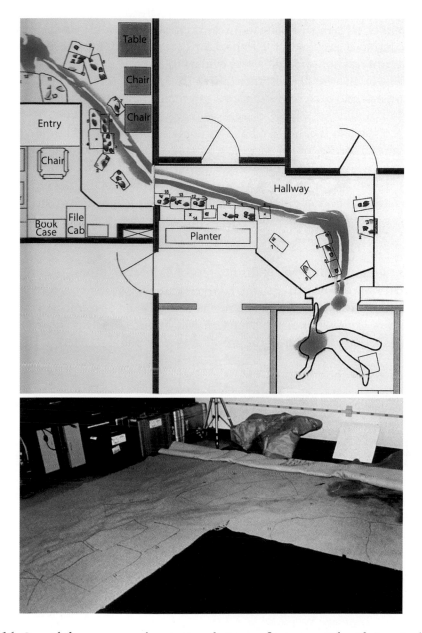

Figure 7.16 One of three rooms of carpeting that were first screened with Luminol for areas containing bloody shoe impressions and marked with black markers. Later, a camera on a tripod was set up over each area and photographed while being treated with Luminol in total darkness. Even though no shoe impressions were visible prior to treatment, 42 impressions of the suspect's shoes were detected and photographed. The chart shows their location throughout the scene in relation to the entry door where the homicide occurred and a back room where the victim was found.

Photography of Luminol

As stated previously, when using Luminol to initially screen general crime scene areas for latent blood marks, spraying to locate footwear impressions should be done with a very fine mist and discontinued as soon as the impressions are detected. For those with good night vision, even a faint reaction should be very evident in a totally darkened room. If available, night vision goggles may be of assistance during this procedure. Once bloody impressions are located and marked, each respective area can then be photographed during additional treatment with Luminol.

Because the reaction is short lived and can only be photographed in total darkness, a special photographic procedure is necessary. Photography of the Luminol reaction should not be performed without prior experience. Figure 7.17 depicts a bloody footwear mark on brown carpet, a photograph of the mark during treatment with Luminol in total darkness, and an attenuated light photograph of the same reaction where a conventional scale has been exchanged for the copper pennies. To photograph a footwear impression that is being enhanced with Luminol, follow the procedure as set forth here:

1. Identify the specific area where the impression is located. Be aware of the fact that the actual impression may occupy a larger area than initially estimated; thus if only the heel area is believed to be present, consider the possibility that there may be an entire impression of the shoe that will luminesce when treated. Place the camera on a stable tripod over the area that is to be photographed.

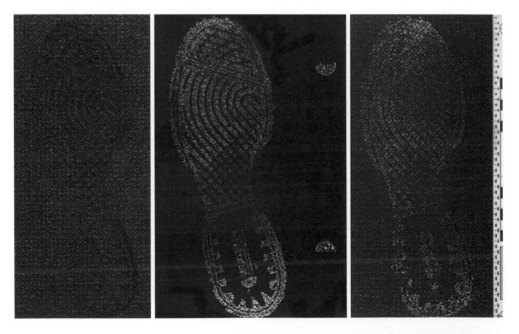

Figure 7.17 A bloody shoe impression on brown carpet (left) is photographed in total darkness as it is treated with Luminol (center), then rephotographed with attenuated light and a conventional scale (right). Note in the center photograph the two copper pennies taped 6 inches apart are used as a scale.

2. Understand the significance of the law of inverse proportions that states that when you double the distance of the camera, four times the amount of light is required to result in the same exposure. Adjust the height of the camera so that the impression and the scale fill the desired area but keep the camera as close as possible to the bloody impression area.

3. Prepare a scale by taping two copper pennies on a piece of thin card stock or on a ruler, with their edges a premeasured distance apart. The tape should cover only half of each penny to allow the other half to react with the Luminol. Place this scale next to the impression. Do not place the scale over an area that may potentially contain additional latent portions of the impression. The copper in the pennies will luminesce when treated with Luminol, as seen in the center photograph of Figure 7.17. The distance between their edges can be used to enlarge the photographic prints to a natural size.

4. Select a professional DSLR camera. Cameras with full size sensors and a high quality lens will record the lower levels of light better. The lens should be one that will focus at a close distance. The camera must be equipped with a shutter cable release that can be locked to hold the shutter open. Set the ISO level as high as needed based on what your experience dictates for the camera you are using.

5. Seal off all ambient light in the room so that the photograph can be made in total darkness. Spray the area of interest with a fine mist of Luminol, adjusting the direction of the spray as necessary to cover the entire blood mark. If the impression's luminescence begins to weaken before the exposure time is over, respray the impression. Avoid overspraying the impression if it continues to luminesce well. Experience will dictate the proper amount of spraying and the time of exposure necessary.

6. Since the impression will still be luminescing, a second photograph can be taken with attenuated or indirect light. It may be necessary to respray the impression with Luminol and, sometime during the exposure, provide a small amount of indirect light to permit a minimal recording of the background, but not so much as to wash out the luminescing impression. One way to provide this light is to fire an electronic flash sometime during the exposure aimed either away from the impression at a corner of the room or at the ceiling. This will allow a minimal exposure of the blood area without completely overpowering the luminescence and will provide evidence of the location of the impression. A regular scale can be used. The best procedure is to first photograph the luminescing impression in total darkness and then, without moving the tripod or camera, make the second exposure with indirect light.

Other Luminol formulations and reactions: Many use Luminol formulations other than the original Luminol formulation cited above. These typically include peroxide components. One individual cited alleged instability of the original formulation using sodium perborate, but did not indicate the source of that information.[*] My own extensive experience with this formulation over the past 30 years have been without any problems. Another

---

[*] Dilbeck, L., Use of Bluestar forensic in lieu of Luminol at crime scenes," *JFI*, 56(5):707, 2006.

advised he used hydrogen peroxide in lieu of sodium perborate.[*] Other Luminol-based products marketed as Bluestar® and Bluestar Magnum® are probably peroxide based so they can provide a greater reaction intensity. Published accounts comparing various Luminol-based products with peroxides usually cite the ability to observe and photograph the luminescence in less than total darkness.[†,‡] In one study using both film and digital cameras, color film instead of black and white film was used and the photographs appeared to be taken at an angle.[§] My overall impression of many of these studies is that they seem to be more concerned with convenience and ease of use photographing the impression rather than the increased detail achieved in total darkness.

It is noted that Luminol will react with some metals, particularly copper. In addition, slight luminescence will occur when applied over some bleaches or strong oxidizing agents and some vegetable matter. With the exception of copper, Luminol reactions with items other than blood are different in their duration and intensity. For instance, application of Luminol to residual traces of bleach or other non-blood products may cause a brief reaction, but the behavior of that reaction is easily distinguished from its reaction with blood. To be more specific, when Luminol reacts with blood, the luminescence is initially greatest and the intensity of that luminescence gradually fades. If additional Luminol is re-applied to the blood, the luminescence increases in intensity again, and again gradually fades. When Luminol is applied to other products such as vegetable matter, bleaches, and the like, those which react do so with a very short-lived reaction that ends abruptly. The luminescence does not gradually fade and if sprayed again, there is no repeated reaction.

Effects of Reagents on DNA

Whenever a sample of blood can be taken prior to the application of any reagent, powder, or other potentially adverse techniques or material, it goes without saying that is the best and safest procedure. This was highly significant many years ago when DNA testing utilized less sensitive RFLP and PCR techniques and most chemical reagents had some adverse effects on their results. Current STR analysis is reportedly not affected adversely by the application of chemical reagents applied to detect and enhance blood. One test evaluated the effect of Luminol, Fluorescein, and Bluestar and found their application did not interfere with STR analysis.[¶] Another concluded "none of the (seven) chemicals they examined had a deleterious effect, on a short-term basis, on the PCR amplification of nine STR systems plus the gender determination marker."[**] In a study that looked at six presumptive tests for blood, including Luminol, Leuchomalachite green, and Bluestar, they found

[*] Velders, T., personal communication, April 11, 2015, uses 2 g Luminol per liter with 3.6 g sodium hydroxide and 10 mL of 30% hydrogen peroxide.

[†] Ibid, p. 713.

[‡] Young, T., A photographic comparison of Luminol, Fluorescein and Bluestar, *JFI*, 56(6):907, 2006.

[§] Ibid, pp. 906–912.

[¶] Jakovich, C., STR analysis following latent blood detection by Luminol, Fluoroescein, and Blue Star, *JFI*, 57(2), 2007.

[**] Fregeau, C., Germain, O., and Fourney, R., Fingerprint enhancement revisited and the effects of blood enhancement chemicals on subsequent *Profiler Plus* fluorescent short tandem repeat DNA analysis of fresh and aged bloody fingerprints, *J. For. Sci.*, 45(2):354–380, 2000.

Luminol had the best specificity and sensitivity, did not destroy DNA, and could be reapplied.[*] It is noted this study found Leuchomalachite green destroyed the DNA although other studies have not reported this. Another study considered a very large number of reagents and chemicals, and found almost all, including Leucomalachite green, did not adversely affect DNA typing.[†] And yet another study found it possible to get DNA profiles after treatment with Acid Black 1 (Amido Black), Acid Violet 17, and Acid Yellow 7.[‡]

Sequencing of Enhancement Techniques for Bloody Impressions

Sequencing refers to the practice of first recording and enhancing impression evidence with the use of nondestructive methods followed by those least likely to degrade the impression, and finally with those that may have success but may prevent or restrict the use of subsequent techniques. It is a simple concept but not possible to recommend a one-sequence-fits-all procedure as the various physical and chemical enhancement methods combined with the reality that footwear impressions are composed of numerous materials occurring on numerous substrates complicates doing so. Obviously, photographic recording and other nondestructive methods using specialized lighting, photography, and electrostatic lifting would always be attempted first. Beyond that, the decision of how to proceed in any specific case must rely on the knowledge, experience, and judgment of the crime scene technician or examiner as well as the resources available to them.

Visible bloody footwear marks on non-porous substrates

The choices for the enhancement of blood impressions on nonporous substrates are numerous. Some methods are more sensitive to blood traces particularly when used with fluorescence photography. An excellent illustration of the sequence of various enhancement methods of a single faint bloody impression on a nonporous substrate is shown in Figure 7.18 as conducted by Velders.[§] One of the significant findings of Velders' research was that multiple blood enhancement reagents could be used in a sequence. Most believed one method of enhancement might reduce or consume all traces of a faint blood impression, reducing or eliminating any chance for subsequent enhancement methods. Velders' research demonstrates this is not the case. In Figure 7.18, the sequence begins with a visual but faint footwear blood mark (A) followed by treatment of that mark with Luminol (B). It is noted here that Velders applied the fixative 5-sulfosalicylic acid to the impression just after the application and photography of Luminol (B), and this would be similarly recommended at a crime scene. Even after treatment with Luminol, sufficient traces of the blood remained for subsequent reaction with LCV (C). Since many crime scene investigators do

---

[*] Tobe, S., Watson, N., and Nic Daéid, N., Evaluation of six presumptive tests for blood, their specificity, sensitivity, and effect on high molecular-weight DNA, *J. For. Sci.*, 52(1), 2007.

[†] Spear, T., Barney, S. Khoshkebari, N., Silva, A. The Impact of Body Fluid Identification and Fingerprint Reagents on PCR-Based Typing Results, presented at the CAC Seminar, May 2002.

[‡] V.G. Sears, C.P.G. Butcher, L.A. Fitzgerald, Enhancement of fingerprints in blood—Part 3: Reactive techniques, Acid Yellow 7, and Process Sequences, *J. Foren. Identif.*, 55(6):758, 2005.

[§] Velders, T., New insight into the chemical improvement of shoeprints and fingerprints placed with blood on non-porous surfaces, *Identification Canada*, 35(3).

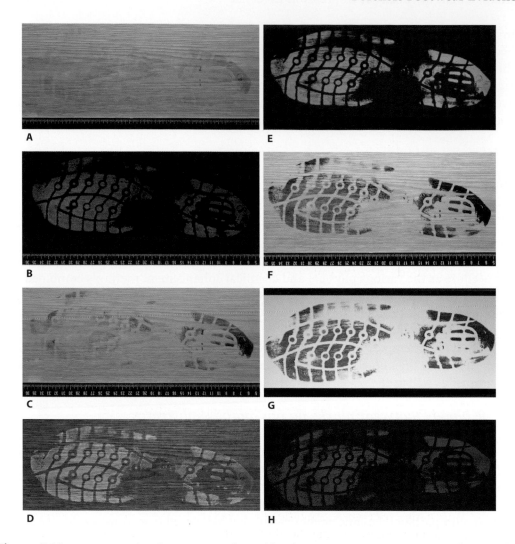

Figure 7.18 Sequence of enhancement of one bloody impression on nonporous flooring (A); photography of Luminol luminescence of that impression (B), then followed by treatment with 5-sulfosalicylic acid; then LCV enhancement (C); Acid Yellow 7 treatment photographed with fluorescence (D); white gelatin lift of Acid Yellow 7 photographed with fluorescence (E); Hungarian Red enhancement (F); white gelatin lift of Hungarian Red (G); and white gelatin lift of Hungarian Red photographed with fluorescence (H). (Photographs courtesy of Theo Velders.)

not use Luminol, the search for latent marks at a scene could also have begun with the detection of impressions as a result of the application of LCV. As can be seen by the results in Figure 7.18C, LCV is not the most sensitive enhancement method. That by itself is very significant because many who process the scene of a crime and who use LCV would likely believe the slight enhancement of the mark as shown in photograph C was a success and they would stop at that point. In those cases where the impression was originally visible at the crime scene and Luminol was not used as a first step, the fixative should be applied before any enhancement begins. Velders continued the sequence after LCV by applying Acid Yellow 7 for 5 minutes followed by a thorough rinsing. The results are shown in a white light photograph of the Acid Yellow 7 (D). Using a white gelatin lifter, Velders lifted the Acid Yellow 7 from the same impression and photographed it in fluorescence (E). The gelatin lift remained on the Acid Yellow 7 treated impression with weight for 30 minutes prior to lifting. Next, the same impression was treated with Hungarian Red and photographed in white light (F) and then similarly lifted with a white gelatin lifter (G) and the gelatin lifter photographed in fluorescence (H).

Velders' research provides an excellent demonstration of the potential for sequencing of bloody impressions on nonporous substrates. It demonstrates impressions composed of very slight trace amounts of blood can provide excellent detail, especially when using methods that involve fluorescence and gelatin lifters that eliminate background interference. It also provides proof that latent impressions located through treatment of nonporous substrates with Luminol, once photographed, should be immediately fixed with 5-sulfosalicylic acid and preserved for further enhancement using fluorescence and performed later in the laboratory, therefore necessitating cutting out the pertinent areas of flooring. Whereas protein stains and LCV worked after Luminol, in another research evaluation, Luminol gave little or no chemiluminescence when applied after Ninhydrin or DFO and also performed poorly after the use of protein stains.[*]

Visible Bloody Footwear Marks on Porous Substrates

Choices for sequencing on porous substrates are more limited due to the inability to rinse some substrates after application of reagents, the possibility of background absorption of the reagent, and the limited retention of fine detail associated with many porous substrates.

Using Alginate Materials to Lift Bloody Impressions

Whereas transferring trace blood marks on nonporous substrates to gelatin lifters is a way to eliminate background patterns and colors, a similar use of casting materials to lift blood marks from porous materials such as fabric has been reported. One study tried different materials and found alginates had more success than attempts with other materials when lifting bloody marks from fabric and other substrates, both before and after chemical treatment.[†] Application involves mixing the alginate and then a spatula application of it to the fabric substrate. Once the alginate sets, it can be removed from the fabric. At this time, traces of the bloody impressions that have transferred to the alginate should be fixed with 5-sulfosalicylic acid as previously described. The impression on the alginate can then be treated with a chemical reagent by immersion.

Research comparing four protein stains on alginate lifted blood marks prepared on black cotton fabric concluded the variables of age and protein stain had significant effects on the results and concluded that optimal enhancement occurred with alginate lifts that were aged for 7 days and then stained with Amido Black.[‡] Part of an alginate lift is illustrated in Figure 7.19. Other research with alginates also found Amido Black (Acid Black 1)

[*] Farrugia, K., Nic Daéid, N., Savage, K, Bandey, H., Chemical enhancement of footwear impressions in blood on fabric—Part 3: Amino acid staining, *Sci. & Justice*, 53:8–13, 2013.

[†] Adair, T., Casting two-dimensional bloody shoe prints from concrete, fabric and human skin, *I.A.B.P.A. News*, March 2005.

[‡] Jurgens, E., Hainey, A., Shaw, L., and Andries, J., Chemical enhancement of footwear impressions in blood recovered from cotton using alginate casts, *JFI*, 65(3), 2015.

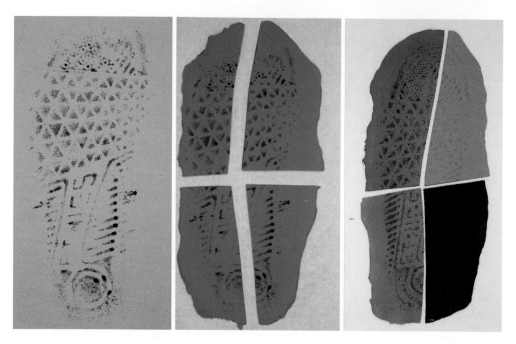

Figure 7.19 A bloody impression on cotton fabric (left), an alginate lift of the blood that has been divided into four segments (center), and the results after application of various reagents to enhance the blood on the alginate (right). (Photograph provided courtesy of Eline Jurgens, Centre for Forensic Science, University of Strathclyde, Glasgow, Scotland.)

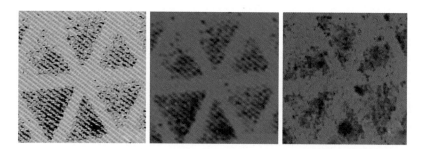

Figure 7.20 Enlarged portions of the fabric (left), alginate lift (center), and enhancement (right) in Figure 7.19. The original impression and unenhanced alginate lift appear the same, but the enhancement of the alginate offers different information.

and LCV provided excellent results.[*][†] The author's experience with alginate lifts from blue jeans in a real case showed dissimilarities between the enhanced alginate lift and the appearance of the original bloody impression on the jeans of the victim. Also of concern is the reduced quality between the enhanced portion of an alginate lift from the prior cited research and the alginate lift itself as shown in Figure 7.20. Future research is underway to explore these methods further.

---

[*] Farrugia, K., Savage, K., Bandey, H., and Nic Daéid, N., Chemical enhancement of footwear impressions in blood deposited on fabric—evaluating the use of alginate casting materials followed by chemical enhancement, *Science and Justice*, 50(4):200–204, 2010.

[†] Wiesner, S., Izraeli, E., Shor, Y., and Domb, A., Lifting bloody footwear impressions using alginate casts followed by chemical enhancement, *J. For. Sci.*, 58(3):782–788, 2013.

It is important to note that alginates shrink as the water used to mix them dries from the cast; thus enhancement with reagents and the subsequent photographic documentation need to be made promptly after the cast is removed from the fabric.

Chemical Reagents and Methods for Enhancement of Non-Blood Impressions

The recovery and enhancement of non-blood impressions on two-dimensional substrates is usually more reliant on lifting methods and materials. The wide variety of components that make up non-blood impressions means that the use of one reagent to enhance any one impression is neither practical nor successful for most others. Following are some methods that have proven to have some success for a small percentage of impressions.

Potassium Thiocyanate

Potassium thiocyanate was first reported in 1963 in Japan as a possible method to enhance impressions by reacting with the iron in soil residue.[*] Figure 7.21 shows the coloration of potassium thiocyanate as it reacts with the iron present in the soil-based impression resulting in a reddish-brown color. Potassium thiocyanate has a long shelf life and may be more convenient to obtain already mixed. It is toxic to inhale and therefore should be applied in a hood or with other precautions. To prepare the reagent, add 120 mL of acetone, 15 mL of water, and 15 g of potassium thiocyanate and mix thoroughly. Then slowly add 10 mL of dilute sulfuric acid to the water/acetone solution. (Note that dilute sulfuric acid may be prepared by adding 1 mL concentrated sulfuric acid to 9 mL of distilled water. Always add the concentrated acid to the distilled water and not the water to the acid.) A milky mixture will result, which, if left standing for several minutes, will separate into two layers. When completely separated, the top clear layer is the potassium thiocyanate reagent solution.

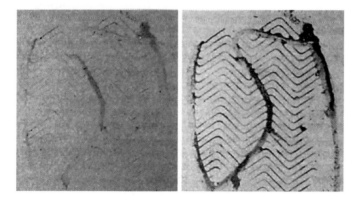

Figure 7.21 Potassium thiocyanate is successful for enhancement of muddy impressions if the soil contains iron. On the left is a muddy impression on cardboard and on the right is a muddy impression after treatment with potassium thiocyanate.

---

[*] Someha, S., Chemical techniques for the enhancement of footwear and tire impressions in Japan, presented at the International Symposium on the Forensic Aspects of Footwear and Tire Impression Evidence, FBI Academy, Quantico, VA, June 27–July 1, 1994.

It can be decanted into a dark glass bottle and stored for months. The procedure works well for soiled-based impressions on all substrates as long as the soil contains iron ions. The application of potassium thiocyanate might be a good choice if the impression has sufficient thickness that might degrade during lifting, if the impression is on a porous substrate, and if the reddish color provides additional contrast that could be photographed. It could also be applied to any portion of the impression that remains after lifting attempts.

Physical Developer

Physical developer (PD) was introduced as an additional method to develop fingerprints.[*] The formulations of PD have been previously reported.[†,‡] Due to the complexities of mixing PD, its use is usually restricted to large laboratories where it demonstrated an increase in the quality and number of fingerprints developed after Ninhydrin.[§] The initial use of PD found it most useful for development of fingerprints on items that had been wet or subjected to high humidity. The development of footwear impressions on recovered paper items occurred occasionally in conjunction with processing paper items for fingerprints.[¶] In cases where paper items are recovered from the floor surfaces of crime scenes and may contain latent impressions of footwear, PD is a process that may be considered after electrostatic lifts have been made to recover any dry origin impressions. Figure 7.22 depicts a piece of paper stepped on with the heel of a shoe. Only the right half of the paper was processed with PD.

Bromophenol Blue

Bromophenol blue is a pH indicator that is yellow at around pH 3.0 and blue at around pH 4.6 and above. The potential of using Bromophenol blue to enhance residue impressions was first reported as a potential means of enhancing two-dimensional impressions, citing the fact that calcium ions are very abundant in exterior soil and dust.[**,††] Additional research led to the use of Bromophenol blue as a method of enhancing dusty or muddy two-dimensional footwear marks by lifting them with low tack adhesive lifters that could later be treated with Bromophenol blue in a laboratory environment.[‡‡,§§] A 1% solution of Bromophenol blue is prepared by adding 1 g of Bromophenol blue to 95 mL methanol and 5 mL distilled water. It is necessary to use a very fine misting device to spray the

---

[*] Hardwick, S. A., User guide to physical developer—a reagent for detecting latent fingerprints, Home Office, Sci. Research and Development Branch, Sandridge, December 1981.

[†] Bodziak, W. J., *Footwear Impression Evidence: Detection, Recovery and Examination*, 2nd ed., CRC Press, Boca Raton, FL, 2000, pp. 147–149.

[‡] Cantu, A., Silver physical developers for the visualization of latent prints on paper, *For. Sci. Rev.*, 13(1):29–64, 2001.

[§] de Puit, M., Koomen, L., Bouwmeester, M., Gijt, M., Rodriquez, C., Wouw, J., and de Haan, F., Use of physical developer for the visualization of latent fingerprints, *JFI*, 61(20), 2011.

[¶] Bodziak, W. J., Ibid., 2000, pp. 147–149.

[**] Glattstein, B., Shor, Y., Levin, N., and Zeichner, A., Improved chemical reagents for the enhancement of footwear marks, presented at the International Symposium on the Forensic Aspects of Footwear and Tire Impression Evidence, FBI Academy, Quantico, VA, June 27–July 1, 1994.

[††] Glattstein, B., Shor, Y., Levin, N. Zeichner, A., pH Indicators as chemical reagents for the enhancement of footwear marks, *JFS*, 41(1):23–26, 1986.

[‡‡] Shor, Y., Vinokurov, A., and Glattstein, B., The use of an adhesive lifter and pH indicator for the removal and enhancement of shoeprints in dust, *J. Forensic Science*, 43(1):182–184, 1998.

[§§] Ibid.

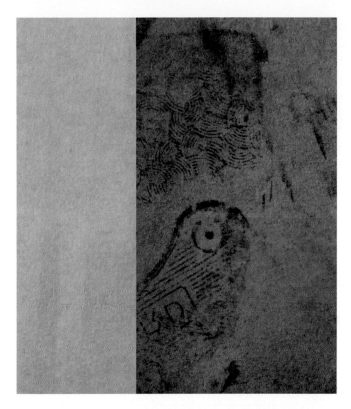

Figure 7.22 Physical developer will occasionally develop latent footwear impressions on paper items. A heel mark was produced on paper that was cut into two halves. Only the right half was processed with physical developer.

Bromophenol solution onto the lift of the impression. In the presence of small amounts of humidity, calcium carbonate reacts with the Bromophenol blue, causing the impression to turn blue. In drier climates, the reaction turns yellow. The blue color is desired as it provides better contrast; thus, if during the application, the impression turns yellow, the addition of water vapor will be required to turn the impression blue. In some regions of the world, calcium carbonate ($CaCO_3$) is a large trace component of dust and therefore part of the residue that shoes routinely transfer to the substrate. The success of Bromophenol is related to the presence and quantity of calcium ions in any particular geographical area. A recent study involving the assessment of using this method in a Canadian province found it effective on many items and provided better contrast than potassium thiocyanate.[*] The success of the use of both bromophenol and potassium thiocyanate is dependent on the presence of either calcium or iron components in the residue in a certain geographical location. It is also noted that a very fine spray must be used, particularly on nonporous substrates.

Other Non-Blood Methods
Shoe marks involve the transfer of a wide variety of non-blood materials. These can be dry residues and dusts of various components and minerals, or can be marks made with moist or liquid sources that dry on the substrate. As a consequence, not all marks react

[*] McNeil, K., and Knaap, W., Bromophenol blue as a chemical enhancement technique for shoeprints, *JFI*, 62(2):143–153, 2012.

with chemical reagents for the purpose of enhancement and of those that do, not all react with the same ones. There is a volume of research concerning methods that have been tried to enhance non-blood impressions using a variety of reagents. One study assessed the use of chemical enhancement of soil-based marks on various substrates followed by gelatin lifting for the recovery of those marks. This research pointed out the use of gelatin lifting can be successful in recovering and transferring soil-based marks and, in some cases, chemical enhancement can provide additional enhancement. The study noted the quality of the lifted mark depended on the substrate from which the lift was made. It also noted that certain chemical enhancements were dependent on the mineral contents of the soil as well.[*] Another success was reported using a gelatin lifter to lift muddy impressions followed by treatment with 1,8-diazafluoren-9-one (DFO).[†] Other research found the chemical enhancement of soils in mud on fabric and clothing possible but not highly successful and highly dependent on the soil composition and morphology of the fabric.[‡]

Digital Enhancement

The use of computers and graphic arts software has been used extensively for the enhancement of physical evidence. Programs such as Adobe Photoshop are used routinely to digitally enhance impression evidence, a very integral part of the overall enhancement process. Photographic images of impression evidence can be enhanced in a variety of ways, some including the adjustment of images taken in the RAW mode; the increase of contrast, brightness, and saturation; dropping background colors and patterns; using the black and white adjustment option;[§] and using Lab Color Mode to split channels.[¶]

Key Words: forensic photography, specialized lighting, digital enhancement, protein stains, peroxidase reagents, sequencing, chemical reagents

Key Points

1. Enhancement is a way to increase the visualization of impression evidence. The improved visualization not only increases the number of impressions detected at a crime scene but also improves the detail available for examination.
2. Enhancement can be achieved through forensic photographic techniques, through physical methods such as lifting techniques, through chemical reagents, and through digital software.
3. A number of chemical reagents are highly successful for the detection and enhancement of bloody footwear impressions, many of which can be used in sequence.

---

[*] Hammell, L., Deacon, P., and Farrugia, K., Chemical enhancement of soil-based marks on nonporous surfaces followed by gelatin lifting, *JFI*, 64(6):583–608, 2014.
[†] Velders, M. J. M., Mud prints on paper activated for DFO with black gelatin lifters, presented at the 82nd Educational Conference of the International Association for Identification, Danvers, MA, July 1997.
[‡] Farrugia, K., Bandey, H., Dawson, L., Nic Daéid, N., Chemical enhancement of soil based footwear impressions on fabric, *Forensic Science International*, 219:12–28, 2012.
[§] Osborn, S., and Wilson, K., Digital enhancement of latent prints using Adobe Photoshop black and white adjustments, *JFI*, 59(4):373–385, 2009.
[¶] Smith, J., Computer fingerprint enhancement: the joy of lab color, *JFI*, 62(5):464–475, 2012.

4. Efforts to recover and enhance impression evidence should always be sequenced to use nondestructive methods first, then other methods in an order to maximize the chances of recovering additional detail.

5. Positive controls should be used to ensure a reagent has been properly mixed, and negative controls should be used to avoid unwanted background reactions with and/or without absorption of reagents.

Sizing Feet and Footwear

8

The words *size*, *shoe size*, and *outsole size* come up repeatedly in this book and in discussions of footwear evidence. To the nonexpert, the terms *size* and *shoe size* both refer to the size designation the manufacturer places on the shoe or shoebox, such as size 8, 9, or 10. To the forensic expert, size also refers to the outsole and its components as they consider if it is or is not capable of having produced the same dimensional features present in a crime scene impression.

Questions are often asked about shoe sizing, including, "How do you determine what size shoe a person wears?" "Can the accused wear a particular shoe size?" and "Can you determine what size shoe made the crime scene impression?"

Measuring a person's foot size is one way to estimate the shoe size they will wear, but as explained herein, there is a loose relationship between the dimensions of a person's feet and the dimensions of the outsoles of various types and brands of footwear. This chapter will provide general information about how the foot is measured (foot size), the origin of shoe sizing, various shoe sizing systems, what is involved in determining the shoe size of a particular person, and some of the reasons for variations in a manufacturer's shoe size designations. The information in this chapter also serves as background information helpful with discussions in later chapters regarding the size of crime scene impressions and the design/size relationship of footwear.

Origins of Shoe Sizing

Very early man as well as the indigenous Indians and settlers in America wore moccasins. Moccasins were a slipper type of shoe usually made of soft leather such as deerskin, but also utilized other components such as woven grass, bark, and fur. Although some were crude foot coverings, they allowed traversing over rough terrains and the ability to tolerate various climates. Neither moccasins nor other forms of footwear were mass-produced but rather were custom made, often by a shoemaker. Although the indigenous people of America made their own moccasins for hundreds of years prior, Thomas Beard, who arrived on the Mayflower in 1629, is generally credited as being America's first well-documented shoemaker.[*][†]

The role of the shoemaker was to make shoes while a cobbler's job was to repair shoes. Until the late 1800s, a shoemaker would hand-last the shoe, a process where they had to stretch and tack the upper of the shoe over a wooden foot form known as a last. Lasting the upper was a laborious and time-consuming task. Figure 8.1 shows a wooden last next to a modern synthetic last. In 1883, Jan Ernst Matzeliger invented the first lasting machine,

---

[*] Guernsey, J., Shoe Retailing, 1930 US Census.
[†] Hislop, D., Shoe making is an old profession, notes from the Paynesville Historical Society, Paynesville, MN (undated).

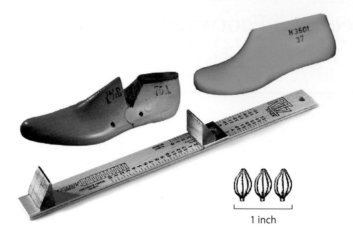

Figure 8.1 Photographs of an old wooden last, a modern synthetic last, a Ritz stick, and a sketch of three barleycorns.

an invention that enabled much faster production.[*] Another significant invention, this one by Lyman Blake in 1858, was a sewing machine that was designed specifically to attach the soles of the shoe to the upper.[†] The discovery made by Charles Goodyear involving the process that enabled the vulcanization of rubber, also made it possible to produce footwear with rubber soles.[‡] These inventions and others contributed significantly to the increased mechanization of shoe making and reduction of the cost of shoes and resulted in the formation of hundreds of shoe factories in Massachusetts alone by the late 1800s. With mass production and competition came the opportunity for the average person to purchase more affordable footwear. Along with this was an increased need for a more detailed and standardized shoe-sizing system.

Barleycorns, a drawing of which is included in Figure 8.1, are often mentioned when discussing the origins of shoe sizing measurements. A barleycorn was the smallest Anglo-Saxon unit of length, and was defined as 1/3 inch. The barleycorn unit was the base unit from which the inch was defined, as described in historical references on measurements, an example of which follows:

> It is remembered that the Iron Ulna of our Lord the King (Edward I) contains three feet and no more; and the foot must contain twelve inches, measured by the correct measure of this kind of ulna; that is to say, one thirty-sixth part [of] the said ulna makes one inch, neither more nor less ... It is ordained that three grains of barley (barley corns), dry and round make an inch, twelve inches make a foot; three feet make an ulna; five and a half ulna makes a perch (*rod*); and forty perches in length and four perches in breadth make an acre. The perch or rod, as it was also known, was a traditional Saxon land measure and survives in the twentieth century. It had originally been defined as the total length of the left feet of the first sixteen men to leave church on Sunday morning.[§]

[*] Karwatka, D., Against all odds, *American Heritage of Invention & Technology*, 6(3):50–55, Winter 1991.
[†] Schachter, R. J., *The Art and Science of Footwear Manufacturing*, Footwear Industry of America, 1983, p. 5.
[‡] Korman, R., *The Goodyear Story: An Inventor's Obsession and the Struggle for a Rubber Monopoly*, Encounter Books, San Francisco, CA, 2002.
[§] http://www.npl.co.uk/educate-explore/posters/history-of-length-measurement/.

A full shoe size is one barleycorn or 1/3 inch (8.46 mm). Half of that, or 1/6 inch (4.23 mm), is a half size. The standard length of a corn of barley was determined in relation to a particular rod of metal, typically a yard-bar, and thus 1/108 yard, 1/36 feet, or 1/3 inch.[*,†]

Shoe Sizing Systems

The first recorded shoe sizing system was reportedly introduced in 1688 in England by Randle Holme and was based on a ¼-inch system. The next recorded description of a shoe sizing system was not until 1856 by Robert Gardiner in England and used a scale where each full size was 1/3 inch longer, taken from the barleycorn system.[‡] The first shoe sizing system in America is credited to Edwin B. Simpson of New York. Simpson prepared the first chart of standardized measurements that included detailed proportional measurements for both lasts and shoes. Simpson also introduced a system of half sizes, measured in 1/6-inch increments, and also shoe widths, measured in 1/4-inch increments.[§,¶] Simpson's system was later adopted by the American and British footwear industries around 1888. The barleycorn system and Gardiner and Simpson's work are still the basis for UK and US shoe sizes. Manufacturers today will typically allow for 8.46 mm difference in length of an outsole for each full size, and 4.23 mm difference for each half size.

The European system was originally based on a measurement of 2/3 cm, known as a French Paris point. Each size is 2/3 cm longer than the previous size. Shoes measured in the European system are not further divided into half sizes. The centimeter system, used predominantly in Asia, simply uses a size increment of 1 cm for each size. Mondopoint is another shoe sizing system that was intended to be a way of internationally standardizing shoe sizing.[**] The Mondopoint system has never gained wide acceptance and is not commonly used. Mondopoint defines the size of a shoe from metric measurements of the length and width of the actual foot. If a person's foot is 280 mm long and 110 mm wide, then the shoe size most appropriate in Mondopoint is 280/110. It is often found on ski boots and reportedly is still used in South Africa and some eastern European countries.[††]

Although various sizing systems provide some standards in the footwear manufacturing industry, each manufacturer remains free to interpret them differently during the design and production of their footwear. To say it another way, there are standards in shoe sizing, but there is not standardization between manufacturers. As a result, the precise fit of a shoe can vary between manufacturers.

[*] Zupko, R. E., *British Weights and Measures: A History from Antiquity to the Seventeen Century*, University of Wisconsin Press, 1977, p. 21.
[†] The author notes a large number of references show these measurements or very similar ones were used in ancient Egyptian, Greek, and Roman cultures, although not specifically with regard to the application in shoe sizing.
[‡] *The True Story of Shoe Sizes*, Sterling Last Corporation, Long Island City, NY (undated).
[§] *The True Story of Shoe Sizes*, Sterling Last Corporation, Long Island City, NY (undated).
[¶] Rossi, W. A., How shoe sizes grew, *Footwear News Magazine*, March 1988, p. 34.
[**] ISO 9407:1991 Shoe sizes – Mondopoint system of sizing and marking.
[††] Andersson, B., Foot last shoe: recommendation to suppliers and manufacturers of orthopedic footwear concerning sizes of shoes and lasts, a report from The Swedish Handicap Institute, Sweden, 2004.

Shoe Size Conversion Charts

The relationship between sizing systems is often displayed on what is known as a size conversion chart such as the Brannock conversion chart provided in Figure 8.2.* The red line placed on this chart illustrates how a US men's size 10.5 falls between sizes 44 and 45 in the European system, corresponds to size 10 in the UK system, and falls between sizes 27 and 28 in the centimeter system. Any shoe can only be manufactured using one sizing system; thus these conversions from one size to another represent the closest equivalent size. Because of the worldwide distribution of footwear and the need to list sizes for people accustomed to different sizing systems, shoe size labels and shoeboxes often have more than one size printed on them. Figure 8.3 depicts the ends of four shoeboxes and labels from two shoes to illustrate how manufacturers provide this conversion information as a convenience for buyers.

It is very important to note that not all size conversion charts are the same. For instance, Figure 8.4 depicts a chart that has been around for many years.† In contrast with the Brannock conversion scale in Figure 8.2, the inch scale on the chart in Figure 8.4 is positioned differently as related to the adjacent sizing systems. On the Brannock conversion chart, the US men's size 10.5 aligns close to the 10⅞-inch mark on the inch scale. On the conversion scale in Figure 8.4, the US men's size 10.5 aligns close to the 11¾-inch mark. The relative positions of the inch scale on conversion charts from different sources are often found to differ. Many believe they can simply measure a shoe impression from heel to toe and look at any conversion chart to determine the size of the shoe that produced it. This is not an accurate or proper method. It is unknown why the inch scale is included on the conversion charts, but perhaps one reason is to show the relationship between dimensions in inches in the US and UK shoe sizes, namely, that 1 inch equals three shoe sizes (three Barley corns). That can be seen best on the Brannock chart where the inch scale at the 5-, 8-, 11-, and 14-inch marks aligns perfectly. The Brannock Device and similar devices measure feet and are not intended to measure impressions of shoes or calculate shoe size. You cannot use the inch scale on conversion charts to measure a shoe impression at a crime scene and convert the number of inches to one of the shoe sizes on various conversion charts. To say it another way, using the Brannock Device or other similar devices to convert a heel-to-toe measurement of a shoe impression that is 11¾ inches long and conclude it means that the shoe that made it is a US men's size 13 to 13½ is not accurate. On more than one occasion, cases have been submitted with information that investigators have taken heel-to-toe length measurements of crime scene impressions and used size conversion charts for the purpose of estimating a shoe size. Size conversion charts are provided to depict a general relationship between the various sizing systems in the world. Their purpose is not for determining shoe size from impressions but to assist consumers when purchasing footwear.

US Women's Sizes

The Brannock Device scale in Figure 8.2 shows US women's sizes as 1 size larger than US men's sizes; thus a size 11.5 women's shoe is equal to a size 10.5 men's shoe. This is not consistent among manufacturers. Nike has always used a one and a half size difference

---

* Provided with consent of The Brannock Device Co. Inc., Liverpool, NY.
† Taken from *The True Story of Shoe Sizes*, Sterling Last Corporation, Long Island City, NY, p. 8 (undated).

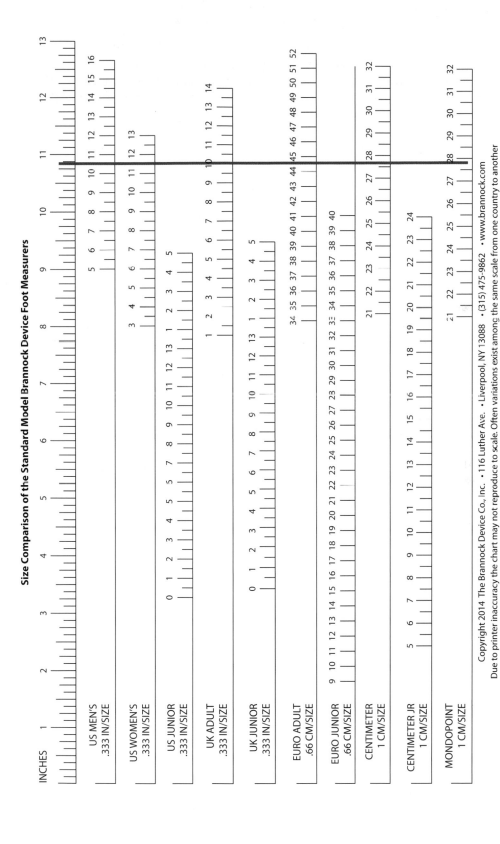

Figure 8.2 A Brannock Device Company conversion chart shows the relationship of different sizing systems used in the world.

Figure 8.3 The ends of four shoeboxes and labels from two shoes demonstrate how manufacturers provide conversions to other sizing systems as a convenience to the buyer. If you examine the conversions on these boxes and labels carefully you will note that they are not all identical.

between men's and women's sizes. Thus, for a Nike shoe, a size 11.5 women's shoe is the equivalent of a size 10 men's shoe.[*] Many other manufacturers also use the 1.5 size difference. If this is a significant item in an investigation, the specific manufacturer should be contacted regarding its conversion values for a particular shoe style.

Mismated Feet

Most individuals have left and right foot dimensions that are not exactly the same size. A foot-measurement survey of 4000 females and 2800 males, conducted by the Prescription Footwear Association, concluded that it was "most likely all individuals in society have mismated feet; that is, the two feet of probably no individuals are exactly alike in size, shape, or proportions."[†]

While most have minor differences between the length of one foot and the other, some have feet that are more severely mismated. This may be due to injuries, polio, clubfoot, problems related to diabetes, genetics, or any number of other reasons. Persons with significant differences must either pay more to purchase shoes of two different sizes or deal with wearing ill-fitting shoes on at least one foot. If someone has a discrepancy in their shoe sizes of at least one full size, a few shoe stores, such as Nordstrom's, will split two different-sized pairs to make the pair needed for that individual and charge for only one pair.[‡] Some websites also assist individuals with this problem by allowing site users to list their single shoes or mismatched pairs of shoes for sale and to search for other single shoes or mismatched pairs of shoes for sale in their sizes.[§] Although I have never encountered

---

[*] Personal communication with Mr. Herb Hedges, Nike, Inc., on May 13, 2014.
[†] Rossi, W., The high incidence of mis-mated feet in the population, *Foot and Ankle*, American Orthopaedic Foot and Ankle Society, Inc., 4(2), 1983.
[‡] http://www.post-polio.org/net/what5.html.
[§] http://www.oddshoefinder.com/links.

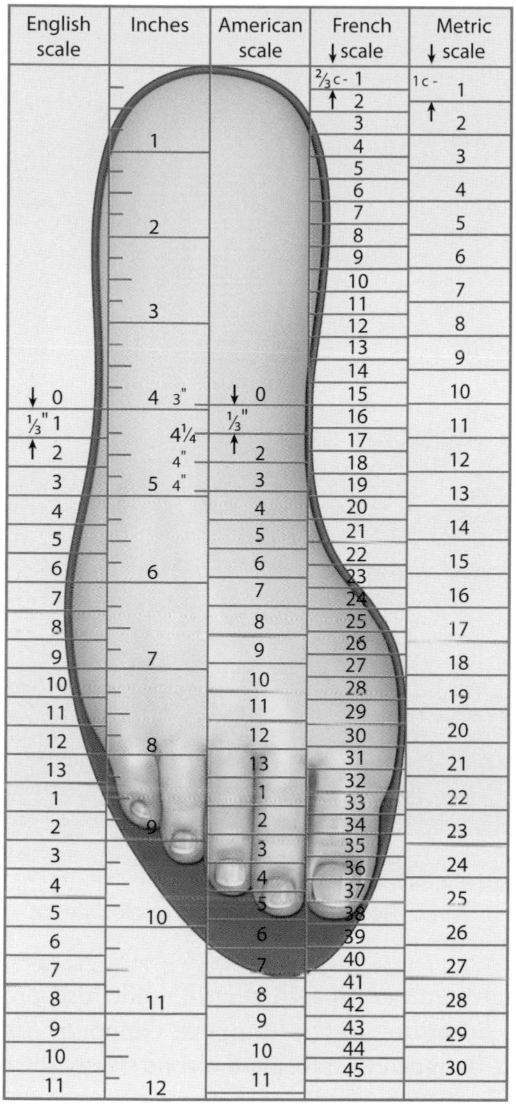

English scale	Inches	American scale	French ↓ scale	Metric ↓ scale
			⅔ c - 1	1 c - 1
			↑ 2	↑ 2
			3	
	1		4	3
			5	
			6	4
			7	5
	2		8	
			9	6
			10	7
			11	
	3		12	8
			13	9
			14	
↓ 0	4 3"	↓ 0	15	10
⅓" 1		⅓"	16	11
↑ 2	4¼	↑ 2	17	
3	4"	3	18	12
4	5 4"		19	13
5		4	20	
6		5	21	14
7	6	6	22	15
8		7	23	16
9		8	24	17
10	7	9	25	
11		10	26	18
12		11	27	
13	8	12	28	19
1		13	29	20
2	9	1	30	
3		2	31	21
4		3	32	22
5	10	4	33	23
6		5	34	24
7		6	35	25
8	11	7	36	26
9		8	37	27
10		9	38	28
11	12	10	39	29
		11	40	30

Figure 8.4 An old conversion chart. This chart and others like it cannot be used to predict shoe size from an impression.

this in casework, the remote possibility exists that different sized left and right shoe prints at a crime scene belong to a single perpetrator, or that you may be provided shoes of a single suspect for examination consisting of different left and right sizes.

Measuring a Person's Feet to Determine Shoe Size

Measuring a person's feet to determine shoe size is typically done with the aid of a foot-measuring device, the most common in the US being the Brannock Device.* This device, pictured in Figure 8.5, has been in existence since 1927. It can measure overall foot length

* The Brannock Device Company Inc., Liverpool, NY, www.brannock.com.

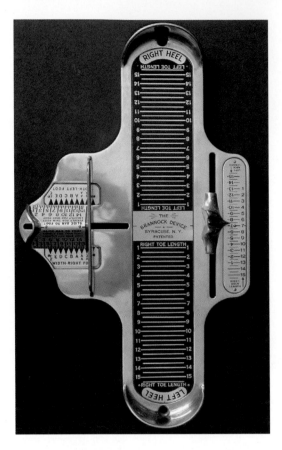

Figure 8.5 The Men's Brannock Device. Similar models are made for women, children, sports, and for large men's sizes. In some cases, a specific Brannock Device will be made for the specs of a particular shoe manufacturer.

both as a heel-to-toe length and as an arch length, while also providing an approximate measurement of width.[*] According to the Brannock Company, the device, while called a foot-measuring device, is designed to indicate the shoe size while also including a built-in additional ½- to ¾-inches of room within the shoe for the space between the longest toe and inner tip of the shoe.[†] Others recommend ⅜ to ½ inches of room between the longest toe and the tip.[‡] There are numerous versions of the Brannock Device, including standard models for men, women, and children's feet as well as a Pro Series for men's large US sizes 10 through 25. When using this device, the proper method for measuring feet is to have people stand with their weight equally on each foot. The individual should place the heel of one foot firmly against the properly designated left or right end of the Brannock Device. An example of this foot position is depicted in Figure 8.6. The slide on the medial side of the foot should be adjusted so the concavity of that slide is positioned around the bulge at the first metatarsal-phalangeal joint. Some persons will have a very prominent bulge while that

---

[*] The author notes in his experience, he has observed that the vast majority of shoe sales personnel have little to no training in shoe fitting and rarely are aware of the arch length measurement.

[†] Personal communication with Timothy Follett, Brannock Device Company, Liverpool, NY, May 9, 2014.

[‡] "When the Shoe Fits: The Basics of Professional Shoe Fitting," a course manual created and produced by the American Orthopaedic Foot and Ankle Society, The National Shoe Retailers Association, and the Pedorthic Footwear Association (1997).

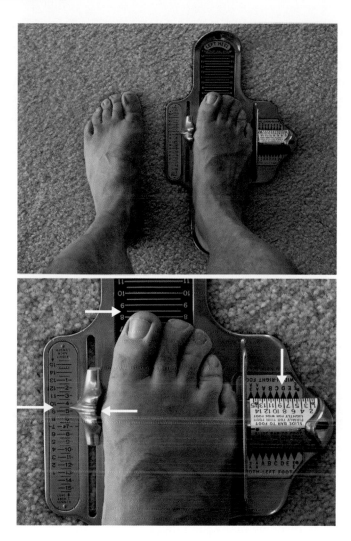

Figure 8.6 Measuring feet with the Brannock Device requires the individual to stand with their weight evenly distributed between both feet and with one foot in the device. The slide is aligned with the bulge of the first metatarsal phalangeal joint (arrows). In this example, the respective heel-to-toe and arch length readings provide two shoe sizes—one size 8.5 and the other size 9.5. Depending on where the foot flexes, one of these will be more reliable than the other. The width is computed based on the heel to toe length.

feature in others might be very minimal. At this point, there will be two length measurements that can be read. The first measurement is read looking directly down over the foot at a 90-degree angle and noting the measurement at the tip of the longest toe. This is known as the heel-to-toe length, which is size 8.5 in the example shown in Figure 8.6. The second length measurement is the arch length, which measures size 9.5. This is the measurement pointed to by the slide that was positioned around the first metatarsal-phalangeal joint. The heel-to-toe length and arch length measurements, as in this example, are often not the same because some feet have proportionally longer toes while others have shorter toes. For some, the arch length may be a better gauge of fit. With the foot still positioned in the Brannock device, the width bar is moved against the lateral side of the foot and the width measurement is deduced from the scale based on the previously determined heel-to-toe size. In our example, the width bar indicates a D width for the heel-to-toe size of 8.5. It is important to note the ideal width designation for a person's foot is a product of more than one dimension that is not possible to determine with the Brannock Device alone. For comfort of fit, persons with a high instep or large foot volume may require a greater size width than the Brannock device might indicate. The position of the Brannock device is then reversed and the process repeated for the opposite foot. Other devices similar to the Brannock device are also found in the US and other countries.

The Ritz Stick, also included in Figure 8.1, was once a well-known and common foot-measuring device in the United States.* The Ritz Stick was developed under a government grant in order to standardize foot sizing for the US Army. It is no longer commonly found in shoe stores.

The use of scanners or cameras that permit a quick measurement of a customer's feet as well as 3D foot measurement devices are becoming increasingly common in shoe stores.† One of these is shown in Figure 8.7, as a young man stands on the foot bed and can see instant results on the screen above.

Measuring devices can assist in finding a shoe that fits but there is no such thing as a perfect fit. Too many factors enter into the equation of shoe fitting for any one size to always be the best. Dimensional variations between left and right feet, variations between a shoe manufacturer's application of shoe sizing to different styles, and the personal preferences of how people want their shoes to fit are just a few of the reasons why the shoes in your closet will likely not all be the same size.

Footwear measuring devices measure feet and only provide an approximation of what shoe size a person wears. They were not created nor are they intended to contain information that could be used to make an accurate determination of a shoe size based on the impression a shoe leaves at the scene of a crime.

Variations in the Physical Dimensions of Identically Sized Shoes

The fact that shoes are made by many manufacturers in many countries combined with different sizing systems and conversion scales to produce different styles of footwear such as work, athletic shoes, dress and casual shoes, means any one individual will likely see a lot of variance in both the outsole dimensions and the manufacturer's shoe sizes among the footwear they own. Different types of footwear have different shapes that relate to their style and function. A heavy work boot with a steel toe will likely be square-toed and bulky, while a western boot will usually have a pointed toe and a raised heel. An athletic cross-trainer will be heavier and wider than a lightweight running shoe. Likewise, one manufacturer may produce size 9 athletic shoes that fit an individual well, whereas that same individual may require a size 10 from another manufacturer for the same general type of shoe. The dimensions of the outsole and the internal dimensions of footwear of a single size will vary, even between similar types of footwear. Figure 8.8 lists the results of a study that documented variations of length measurements taken from 450 outsoles of five brands of basketball and tennis court shoes. Comparing the lengths for US size 10.5, one Adidas shoe measured 308 mm, a Converse Chuck Taylor All Star measured 310.6 mm,

---

* Invented in 1913 by Oliver C. Ritz-Woller.
† Blain, L., 3D foot measurement devices roll out in the USA, *Gizmag*, June 25, 2007.

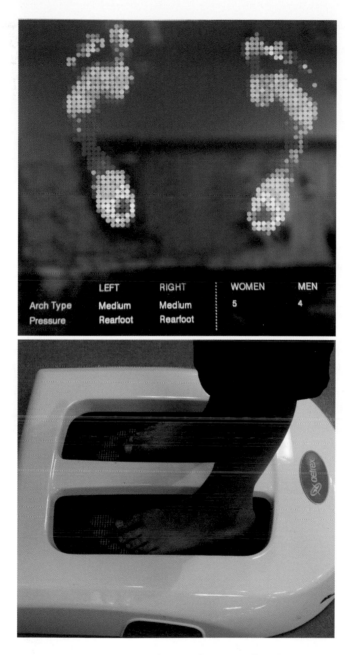

	LEFT	RIGHT	WOMEN	MEN
Arch Type	Medium	Medium	5	4
Pressure	Rearfoot	Rearfoot		

Figure 8.7 A pressure sensitive scanning device that provides the suggested shoe size of the person standing on it.

a Converse standard athletic shoe was 304 mm, a Nike was 300.9 mm, and a Puma was 310.2 mm.[*] Also note that in those instances where more than one shoe of the same style and size was in the store, a deviation between their measurements was recorded as well. Although performed in 1985, the type and extent of the variations provided in this study are just as prevalent today. Personal choice is also a factor, as some individuals prefer their

[*] Van Hoven, H., A correlation between shoeprint measurements and actual sneaker size, *JFS*, 30(4):1233–1237, 1985.

Average Length Measurements and Standard Deviations of Five Major Brands of Sneakers

Size	ADIDAS mm.	ADIDAS std. dev.	CONVERSE ALL STAR mm.	CONVERSE ALL STAR std. dev.	CONVERSE STD. PATTERN mm.	CONVERSE STD. PATTERN std. dev.	NIKE mm.	NIKE std. dev.	PUMA mm.	PUMA std. dev.
6	--	--	273.5	1.08	267	--	--	--	271.5	0.58
6 1/2	272	0	277.5	0.93	271	--	267.6	1.82	274.8	0.96
7	277.8	0.79	282.2	1.48	275	--	271.9	2.33	278.9	1.36
7 1/2	281.4	1.35	286.0	1.15	279	--	275.2	0.75	283.2	1.99
8	284.9	0.99	290.1	0.88	283	--	283.3	1.03	289.5	0.71
8 1/2	289.6	1.51	294.7	1.16	287	--	285.4	1.06	293.2	0.92
9	293.9	1.10	298.6	0.84	291	--	288.3	1.37	297.3	1.06
9 1/2	297.9	1.25	301.8	1.40	295	--	290.2	0.44	302.1	0.57
10	303.3	0.89	306.1	1.29	300	--	294.8	2.66	305.5	0.53
10 1/2	308	0	310.6	1.51	304	--	300.9	2.18	310.2	0.79
11	310	1.10	315.0	0.82	308	--	302.9	1.29	313.8	1.17
11 1/2	--	--	318.6	1.17	313	--	--	--	320.5	2.38
12	320.8	0.71	322.8	0.96	317	--	311.7	1.64	322.4	0.84

Figure 8.8 A comparison of actual dimensions of five different athletic shoe styles showing how their heel to toe size varies both brand to brand and within one brand and style.

shoes to fit loose while others may prefer them to fit tight. Even the same individual may choose to select a tighter fit in an athletic shoe than a casual shoe.

Because of the many possible variables, persons who own numerous pairs of shoes will likely notice the shoes in their closet are not all the same shoe size. Figure 8.9 lists the brands,

Shoes Owned by One Person

Shoe Brand	US Men's Size	Length	Widest Part
Nike jogging	10.5	300	112
Under Armour	10	300	105
Nike trainer	10.5	305	118
Nike running	10	300	110
New Balance	10 4E	310	121
Merrill	9.5	280	97
Skechers running	10	305	109
New Balance	10 2E	310	121
Gender boots	10.5	307	115
Bass casual	9.5M	300	113
Bass dress shoes	9.5M	305	111
Bass dress shoes	9	300	106
K-Swiss	10.5	295	106
Skechers casual	10	303	119
Wal-Mart starter	10	314	115
Sperry deck shoe	9M	295	105

Figure 8.9 The shoes of one person will vary in dimension as well as shoe size. Few if any will wear the same shoe size for every brand and type of shoe. The survey of this individual's shoes shows a range of 1½ shoe sizes.

sizes, and dimensions of the shoes of one person. The shoe sizes range from size 9 to size 10.5. The lengths range from 280 to 314 mm and maximum widths range from 97 to 121 mm.

Even socioeconomic factors occasionally influence shoe sizes. Certain individuals might not have the choice of the exact size they would prefer because their shoes may be handed down from siblings, donated, or traded or because a particular pair of shoes they were able to purchase at a reduced price was not exactly the best fitting size but was more affordable.

Determining What Size Shoe a Person Wears

In some investigations, shoes similar in outsole design to footwear impressions recovered from the crime scene were never obtained from the accused for comparison. On occasion, it may be requested to determine the size of the footwear that produced the crime scene impressions, a topic that will be addressed in Chapter 12. The relevant question may also be asked, "What size shoe does the accused wear?" Because of the variations previously discussed and the fact that an individual likely owns and wears more than one size of shoe, there is no simple answer to that question. The only alternative is to collect as much sizing data about that person's feet and shoes as possible. In Figure 8.10, an example of data collected from the feet of one individual is provided.* In that example, you can see the left and right feet have slightly different measured sizes, which is normal. The heel-to-toe and arch length measurements are not the same. The Biofoam impressions and tracings provide a secondary way of measuring the heel-to-toe measurement. The shoes suspects were wearing when arrested and, when applicable, other shoes seized, which the suspects admit are theirs, also provide important corroborating shoe size information. The data in Figure 8.10 provides more data than one simple measurement alone. The data is not sufficient to conclude the precise size Mr. Jones would wear for every specific shoe style or brand but provides useful information about the size range for each foot.

Sizing Data Source	Left Foot	Right Foot
Brannock heel to toe measurement	12	11.5
Brannock arch length measurement	13	12.5
Biofoam impression length/equivalent shoe size	288 mm/Size 12	290 mm/Size 12.25
Tracing measurement length/equivalent shoe size	290 mm/Size 12.25	295 mm/Size 12.75
Shoes worn by Mr. Jones when arrested	Size 12 Nike Shox	Size 12 Nike Shox

Figure 8.10 Data collected from the feet of one individual as well as shoes they are known to have worn provides information about their range of shoe size for each foot.

---

* The data provided here is an example of measurements obtained during an actual case.

Can a Person Wear an Extremely Different Size Shoe?

In some cases, crime scene impressions may have been determined to be a specific size of a brand and style, such as Nike Air Force 1, size 8. At the same time, information or data may also be presented that the feet of the accused are considerably different, such as size 12. The question is then asked, "Could the accused, a size 12, wear size 8 shoes?" There is no easy answer to this question. Obviously, in the example stated, wearing shoes that are four sizes smaller, if possible, would be very uncomfortable. Shoes like knee- or calf-high slip-over boots or cowboy boots can be difficult if not impossible to wear if they are as little as two sizes smaller than an individual's actual measured foot size. However, low-top athletic footwear that can be loose or open-laced can often accommodate a much larger foot if the person is willing to wear the shoes in discomfort. Even in an opposite scenario, where the accused has a shoe size of 8 and the impressions at the scene were determined to be size 12, it makes little common sense that they would be committing a crime in shoes of such different size. In these cases, the forensic examiner can assist in sizing the crime scene impressions and in helping provide information about the foot size of the accused, but should not reach definitive conclusions whether an individual did or did not wear shoes that were extremely different from their normal size.

Determining Shoe Size Based on Only Heel-to-Toe Measurements?

To illustrate some of the problems in attempting to size impressions when only a heel-to-toe measurement is possible and no brand information or samples from a manufacturer are used, look at the two shoes represented in Figure 8.11. Both are size 9 shoes, but one, a K-Swiss athletic shoe, is not nearly as large as the size 9 Brahma boot. Heel-to-toe measurements of the impressions these shoes leave would not be the same.

Another reason the heel-to-toe length data alone is often unreliable is illustrated in Figure 8.12. On top, a size 8.5 Sperry deck shoe has a flat profile outsole, and below it, a size 10.5 Wal-Mart Starter athletic shoe has an outsole that curves up in the toe area. Shoes with flatter profile outsoles such as the Sperry shoe will make more dimensionally consistent impressions on both two- and three-dimensional surfaces. Shoes like the Wal-Mart Starter athletic shoe that have an extended curved outsole in the toe area will produce a wider variety of heel-to-toe dimensions in the impressions they produce. For instance, if the wearer of the Wal-Mart shoe is simply standing on a flat and firm substrate, much of the toe portion of the outsole may not make contact with the substrate and thus not leave its full impression. However, if the person walks in such a way that they roll their foot forward, the extended outsole in the toe area can be recorded and leave a much longer impression. As an exercise, full heel-to-toe impressions of these two shoes were provided to 27 persons in a class. Each class attendee was asked to independently provide their best estimate of the shoe size of each impression. They were not aware of the brand or profiles of each shoe, nor had access to manufacturers' information during this exercise and thus were restricted to making their best assessment of the exact size based on only the heel-to-toe measurements of each impression. For the Sperry impression, only 7 out of 27 persons arrived at the correct answer of size 8.5. Their choices ranged from size 8 through size 11. Even more dramatic were the results for the Wal-Mart athletic shoe. None of the 27

Figure 8.11 Different shoe types are naturally larger or smaller, even though their shoe size may be the same. These are both size 9 shoes, but the Brahma boot is much larger.

Figure 8.12 Some shoes, like the Sperry deck shoe on top, have a rather flat outsole profile while others, like the athletic shoe below, have a more curved profile. The heel-to-toe dimensions of impressions of the curved profile athletic shoe will vary in different impressions.

selected size 10.5, the correct answer. The answers were scattered and ranged from size 10 through size 15, with the majority of them being much larger than the actual size. This was because the impression in this exercise included some of the extended outsole that curved up in the toe. The purpose of the exercise was to impress on the class that it is not possible to use the heel-to-toe dimensions alone of a shoe impression to accurately estimate the size of a shoe. If they were able to determine the brand of the shoe design and obtain standards of that design, from either stores or manufacturers, the results would be extremely different and far more accurate.

Grading Sizes during Shoe Design

During the design phase of a shoe, normally a model or prototype will be produced and tested. For some manufacturers, they may always make their prototypes in size 7, whereas another manufacturer may use size 9 or some other size. Prototype models will usually be worn and tested. Once approved, a computer will produce dimensional information used to produce each size of shoe of that design. Manufacturers call this process grading. With regard to the outsole lengths for each US and UK size, outsole dimensions for each half size will typically differ by 4.23 mm, thus 8.46 mm per full size.

Bell Curves and Size Distributions

Another common question often asked is, "What is the most common shoe size?" Although this question sounds easy to answer, it is more complex. There are sources, both general and specific, that provide information about the percentage of shoes sold across the range of sizes. A summary of a survey conducted by Footwear Market Insights involving 316,215,000 pairs of men's athletic shoes sold in 1998 indicated the most common men's shoe size was size 10, representing 13.7% of all shoes.[*] Not only have average sizes increased since then, but other factors come into play. Figure 8.13 is a table showing sizing information for three categories of Nike footwear based on recent orders.[†] Note that the most common sizes are not the same for each category. For basketball shoes, size 11 was the

Category	5	5.5	6	6.5	7	7.5	8	8.5	9	9.5
Basketball	–	–	0.024	0.097	1.593	3.079	6.294	7.051	9.015	10.002
Running	0.161	0.294	1.914	2.758	4.914	6.672	9.752	10.147	10.539	9.335
Training	0.02	0.037	0.45	0.545	0.977	1.614	4.603	5.943	8.337	9.998
Category	10	10.5	11	11.5	12	12.5	13	13.5	14	15
Basketball	11.591	11.718	11.808	6.178	10.368	0.322	7.592	0.021	2.398	0.83
Running	10.489	7.69	8.814	4.07	6.392	0.223	4.359	1.121	0.356	–
Training	11.811	13.488	12.832	6.669	11.026	0.561	7.974	–	2.196	0.884

Figure 8.13 A table showing how different categories of Nike footwear have different size distributions based on their category of use.

---

[*] Bodziak, W. J., *Footwear Impression Evidence*, 2nd ed., CRC Press, Boca Raton, FL, 2000, p. 191.
[†] Hedges, H., Nike Inc., personal communication, January 2014.

most common size (11.80%); for running shoes, size 9 was the most common (10.53%); and for training shoes, size 10.5 was the most common (13.48%). This reflects certain facts such as basketball players are taller on average and have larger feet, while joggers are not as tall and thus on average have smaller feet. To be even more accurate regarding size distribution, the specific size breakdown known as a bell curve for the sales figures for a specific brand and style would be more informative. This type of information may not have any relevance in a case if it is a common and widely produced brand, style, and size that could be worn by a significant percentage of the population. Only impressions on the extreme ends of the bell curves of shoe sizes may provide some limited investigative significance.

Shoe Size and Stature

Another question occasionally asked by investigators is, "Can you calculate the height of the perpetrator based on the dimensions of the crime scene impressions?" The answer is no, not with sufficient accuracy to be reliable.

On average, the size of an individual's feet and shoe size increases in relation to height. Taller individuals would therefore tend to have longer feet and larger shoes sizes than those who are shorter. This conventional wisdom is supported by data in the footwear industry, such as the example in this chapter in Figure 8.13. However, the relationship of foot or shoe size to height is not a strict one. A study that required the collection of barefoot impressions of 500 individuals, 399 of whom were males, included the collection of the shoe sizes and heights of each contributor.[*] This data is displayed in the chart in Figure 8.14. The data illustrates the correlation between the height of each individual and the size of the shoes they were wearing. Although a correlation exists, the relationship of height and shoe size is very loose. Using the data in Figure 8.14, the height of a person wearing size 10½ shoes could range from 68 to 76 inches, with the majority of persons in the survey being from 70 to 74 inches in height. This type of result offers no helpful investigative assistance and using this type of information to reach any accurate conclusion is simply not possible.

An anthropolgist's study based on large US Army databases of foot dimensions provided further insight and analysis of the relationship of bare foot and shoe size to stature. The study, as summarized by the authors, concluded that "… Scientifically estimating height in humans by means of some component of their bodies, whether femur length, finger length, or foot length, can never provide exact results nor be properly discussed except in statistical terms."[†]

Determining Shoe Sizes of Worn or Degraded Footwear

In some cases, it may be necessary to determine the size of a particular shoe or pair of shoes when the conventional size markings are no longer present or are indecipherable.

[*] Bodziak, W. J., Discrimination of individuals based on their barefoot impressions, presentations at the International Association of Forensic Sciences meeting, Vancouver, BC, August 1987 and American Academy of Forensic Sciences, Las Vegas, NV, February 1989.

[†] Giles, E., and Vallandigham, P. H., Height estimation from foot and shoeprint length, *Journal of Forensic Sciences*, 36(4):1134–1151, July 1991.

Survey of 399 Males Shoe Sizes

Height	Shoe Size															
	6	6.5	7	7.5	8	8.5	9	9.5	10	10.5	11	11.5	12	12.5	13	14
63				1												
64																
65	1	1		4	1		1									
66		1			2	1		2								
67				2	2		3		2							
68		1	1		4	9	7	7		1	1					
69				1	3	8	14	10	8	3	2					
70			1		3	4	13	15	15	18	3	1				
71			1		3	3	7	5	14	9	7		2			
72							7	11	11	21	11	4	3			
73						2	1	2	4	11	8	1	7		1	
74							1	1	7	8	5	3	4		1	1
75									1	2	3	2	5	1	2	
76								1	1	1		1	3		1	1
77													4		3	
78																
79																1
80															1	
81																
82															1	
Totals	1	3	3	8	18	27	54	54	63	74	40	12	28	1	10	3

Figure 8.14 A table showing the loose correlation between height and shoe size as reflected in a group of 399 males.

Examples could include a partially decomposed shoe recovered containing bones of human remains, the discovery of abandoned shoes that relate to a crime and are purported to be the shoes of a suspect or victim, or simply shoes in normal casework with the conventional markings faded or worn away. If the shoes still contain a logo or other evidence of their brand, a cooperative manufacturer could provide information of value regarding the shoe size. They would also possibly be able to confirm it was one of their shoes as opposed to a counterfeit, and also provide the years that shoes using that particular outsole were produced. In other cases, the rubber sole or heel parts may be all that survived. Those parts may contain some information of value. In the case of most molded soles and heels, their back may have mold numbers, size codes, or even a brand or company name. Figure 8.15 depicts examples of the information that might be present on various shoe components, such as mold numbers, mold sizes, date coding, mold factory codes, and size code notches. The presence of these may provide important information to either the footwear examiner or investigator. The examples on the top left and center left in Figure 8.15 are cases where the inner sole was removed to reveal mold numbers that allowed for identification of the specific mold used. On the heel of one is the original size 9, but contains a hand written "8T," which stands for 8½. In another example, human remains with shoe parts were uncovered at a new construction site. The marks on the rubber heel and soles provided the information that identified the shoe company, and because the heel also contained date coding, it was possible to establish that the shoe parts were over 40 years old.

Figure 8.15 Areas on the back of molded shoe outsoles and heels often contain mold and size numbers. Inner liners and upper components may also contain size codes.

Size Code Schedule

In addition to the outsole and midsole, numerous upper components are used to create a shoe. To keep track of the size of these components during their assembly, a size code schedule is used. The size code schedule in Figure 8.16 depicts various combinations of "V" and "U" notches for identifying the various sized components. The right side of Figure 8.16 depicts an example of those notches on an upper shoe component. Matching a component of a shoe having one of these notch patterns to a particular shoe size should only be done with the assistance of that particular manufacturer. The bottom left photograph in Figure 8.15 depicts another image of size codes in the inner liner components.

Size Code Schedule

1	U		5 1/2	V	v	10	VV	
1 1/2	U	v	6	VU		10 1/2	VV	v
2	UU		6 1/2	VU	v	11	VVU	
2 1/2	UU	v	7	VUU		11 1/2	VVU	v
3	U		7 1/2	VUU	v	12	VVUU	
3 1/2	U	v	8	VU		12 1/2	VVUU	v
4	UU		8 1/2	VU	v	13	VVU	
4 1/2	UU	v	9	VUU		13 1/2	VVU	v
5	V		9 1/2	VUU	v			

Figure 8.16 A size code schedule. This or similar size code schedules are used to correctly join together various components of a specific size shoe during manufacturing.

Key Words: Brannock device, design/size relationship, foot size, last, shoe size

Key Points

1. There are many shoe sizing systems in the world and shoe size conversion charts show their relationship.
2. The Brannock Device and other shoe sizing devices measure a person's feet and are not intended for use in determining shoe size from crime scene impressions.
3. Shoe sizing is a measure of a person's feet, but only provides an estimate of what shoe size they may require and are not specific for a particular brand or style of footwear.
4. The left and right feet of most individuals are not the exact same size.
5. It is normal for persons to own shoes of more than one size.
6. The most accurate way to determine the percentage of the population wearing any particular size is to have the manufacturer's bell curve for a particular brand and style of shoes.
7. Heel-to-toe measurements of a crime scene impression alone can be misleading when attempting to estimate shoe size. Samples of outsoles of the same brand and style footwear will enable this to be more accurate.

Manufacturing
Producing and Texturing Molds

9

Through the mid-1980s, there were still many shoe production factories in the US and they were staffed with knowledgeable persons, many who had worked there for 20–35 years. What I learned from them at the approximately 40 factories I visited was valuable information relevant to the examination of footwear evidence. The design and the physical dimensions of the outsole originate during manufacture in many different ways. Understanding some basic information about the origin of those features assists during the examination and interpretation of manufactured class characteristics as well as the possible variations that occur with some processes. As an example, not all molded shoes of a particular brand, style, and shoe size are produced in one mold. Popular styles produced in large numbers require that the manufacturer produce more than one mold in each size to meet production times. Variations between some molds of the same size and style will exist depending on how they were made, or because of the addition of texture separately to each individual mold. Variations also may occur in some cases if those outsoles require subsequent cutting or trimming in the finishing steps of the manufacturing process, with the addition of foxing strips or other rubber components by hand, as a result of siping and/or stitching, and due to the expansion of certain soling compounds. When questions arise, footwear manufacturers are generally accommodating in assisting law enforcement, but many responding to those requests are legal representatives or customer service personnel who have little or no knowledge of the actual manufacturing process. Further, with the modern footwear industry spread throughout the world, the persons you need to talk to are not always easily accessible. As an expert, you understand the forensic problem or question faced in certain examinations better than anyone does; thus when making an inquiry in a particular case, you should provide a clear set of questions, preferably accompanied by some photographs. What you get out of those inquiries for assistance will be heavily dependent on having some foundation of knowledge about manufacturing, how you articulate your questions, and your confirmation of the answers provided.

This chapter will concentrate primarily on the production of molds in which individual outsoles known as unit outsoles are formed. This and the following two chapters will address production of outsoles using those molds, how outsoles may be modified after they are molded, the process of cutting outsoles from sheet and calendered stock, and how other production variables that occur may be relevant in a forensic examination.

The World Footwear Market

The footwear industry today is truly a world industry. Approximately 99% of the footwear sold in the US are not produced in the US, but are produced in numerous other countries. Consideration of the specific methods and materials used to produce an outsole is driven by the technology on hand, the local labor costs, the projected market cost of the particular shoe being made, and other factors. The end result is an economically competitive world marketplace that provides shoes and outsoles produced using a mixture of both old and new methods. Outsoles composed of synthetic rubber compounds are found on the majority of shoes produced, especially athletic footwear. Most forensic case examinations involve athletic shoes, but boots, dress shoes, and other footwear with synthetic outsoles are also received in casework.

Producing Outsole Molds

Several methods are used in the production of outsole molds. Some methods have been in use for decades while newer ones are the product of constantly evolving technology and the competitive nature of the world footwear market. Older techniques are still used if warranted and if they make economic sense. Newer technology and designs usually begin with top end athletic shoe companies and move to smaller producers over time. The demands of the consumer and the competitive nature of this industry create a constant stream of new upper and outsole designs. In some cases, outsole molds are used for one production cycle and then destroyed. Molds that are more popular may be used for several years, and may be stored for future additional use or in anticipation of a future "retro" release of that design. Following are brief descriptions of four primary ways in which molds have been and still are produced.

Hand Milling

Prior to the 1990s, hand milling was the most common method of mold making in the world. Although the vast majority of outsole molds are now made using computer aided equipment and/or mold-casting methods, outsoles molded in hand-milled molds are still encountered in casework. In some cases, molds that were hand milled years ago are still used to produce some designs, and some manufacturing venues in the world still have sufficiently low labor costs to economically warrant new hand-milled mold production in those areas.

During the hand-milling process, a template containing a portion or all of the outsole design is used with a pantograph to transfer and mill the design into the metal outsole mold. Figure 9.1 shows a person milling part of a design into a mold using a pantograph. The pantograph is simply a set of mechanical linkages or arms that reproduces a shape or pattern in the template to a second location, normally at increased or decreased size. The adjustments of the pantograph allow for the use of one template throughout the size range. For more complex outsole designs, multiple templates are necessary. Figure 9.2 illustrates a simplified example of this. The first template would be used to create the herringbone pattern, after which two other templates would be used to create the curved designs in the sole and heel. When multiple molds of the same design and size are milled, the operator must change the templates on the pantograph. This results in slight variance of their relative positions, meaning several hand-milled molds of the same sizes will have distinguishable differences most noticeable where their design components intersect. In Figure 9.2, the precise position of the herringbone pattern in relation to the perimeter varies between the two molds of the same size. In addition, when the two curved designs are added, they intersect each herringbone pattern differently, examples of which are indicated by the arrows. To further compound this, mold sets will often be made in more than one factory to meet production

Figure 9.1 The pantograph is used to hand mill designs into metal to create the mold. The operator is using his right hand to trace the cutout design in the plastic template. The arms of the pantograph transfer that design at the scale desired to the milling device.

Hand-Milled Mold Making

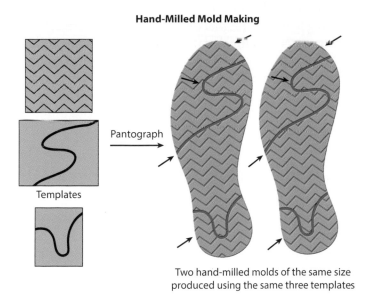

Templates

Pantograph

Two hand-milled molds of the same size
produced using the same three templates

Figure 9.2 A drawing showing the use of multiple templates to hand mill an outsole design.

requirements, resulting in even greater variation. In the example in Figure 9.2, the angles of the herringbone pattern, the segment length of each part of the herringbone pattern, the number of rows of design per inch, and other features could vary on the different templates used in different factories. All of these variables are acceptable and occur rather normally as a product of hand-milled mold making. In addition to the aforementioned reasons for variation, each time a new mold is milled, the metal mold block is likely positioned a little

Figure 9.3 Adidas outsoles of the same style and size obtained from different Adidas factories. Different hand-milled molds resulted in wide variations of outsole characteristics even though they are the same size.

differently as well, creating even another reason for variation. In Figure 9.3, two outsoles that are the same style, manufacturer, and size came from two hand-milled molds in different factories and illustrate the degree of variations that can occur. In some cases, more than one mold maker is used, either because they are in different cities or for other reasons. Although they may have used the same blueprint design, their specific interpretation and application of producing templates for that design can result in even greater variations. The arrows point to just three of the many variations, some obvious and others more subtle. In this example, even the logo box size and position varied. Figure 9.4 provides another case example of variables between molds of the same size as a product of hand-milled mold making. Variations between molds like these were commonplace until computer-based design and mold-manufacturing methods began replacing hand milling in the late 1980s to early 1990s.

Computer-Aided Design–Computer-Aided Manufacture (CAD–CAM)

In the mid to late 1980s, computer-aided design and computer-aided manufacture (CAD–CAM) were gradually developed for the design and production of outsole molds. In the CAD–CAM process, the design is generated and stored in a computer. Figure 9.5 shows a CAD screen of an operator who is in the process of designing a shoe, and part of a computer-generated drawing that would be part of a CAD–CAM-generated outsole design. Changes and improvements in the design can be made without having to start from scratch and computer algorithms can be used to grade the dimensional changes between one size and the next. After the design is generated (CAD), the computer program directs the engraving machine to mill that design into a metal mold blank (CAM). The use of a CAD–CAM system means different mold makers can produce molds of the same design in different factories in different locations that could theoretically be indistinguishable except for any texture added later. Today almost all mold manufacturers use CAD–CAM systems to design outsoles and to produce molds and/or mold models for casting.

Figure 9.4 Converse All Star outsoles of the same size and design from different hand-milled molds from the same factory. They reflect more subtle but still distinguishable variations.

Electrical Discharge Machines (EDM)

EDM is a process where a desired shape or design is created as it removes metal from a mold blank through the production of a rapid series of repetitive electrical discharges. These discharges are passed between an electrode in the shape of the outsole design and the metal being machined. The electrode produced in the size and shape of the outsole design can be formed using a CAD–CAM process. The top of Figure 9.6 depicts an outsole design carbon electrode model. The bottom photograph shows that model mounted above a mold being manufactured with the EDM process. As the carbon model is repeatedly lowered onto the mold, the EDM process slowly burns or erodes the metal design into the metal through a repetitive up and down motion. This up and down motion produces only the flat portion of the outsole. After the basic design is created in this manner, finishing work will still be required to complete the mold. Some mold makers once used this to produce a good portion of their molds but it was a slow process and required touch-up work. EDM machines are still used but mainly for logos and other smaller design applications.

Cast Molds

The cast method involves the production of a casting master model created either by hand or with the CAD–CAM process. Through a series of casting steps, the model can be used

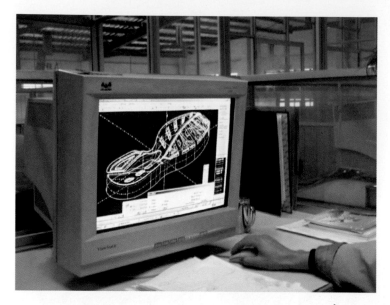

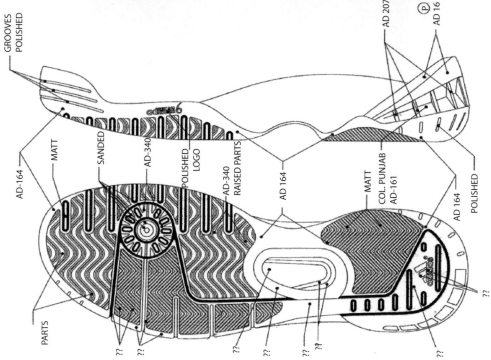

Figure 9.5 An outsole designed on the computer is known as computer-aided design (CAD).

to produce multiple molds sharing the same class design features. Figure 9.7 shows a hand-made wooden model from the 1970s on the left, and a hard wax CAD–CAM-generated model on the right from the 1990s. Figure 9.8 shows an example of one of many steps in a more modern casting process to produce a mold. In any casting process, multiple molds made from the same model in the same size should be indistinguishable until texture is later added to their surfaces.

Figure 9.6 A carbon model of a shoe design (top) is used to burn its design into a mold blank using the electrical discharge machine (EDM).

Figure 9.7 A handmade wooden model (circa 1970s) and a CAD–CAM-generated wax model (circa 1990s), both capable of being used as a master design from which more than one cast mold can originate.

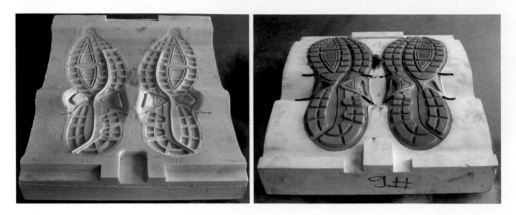

Figure 9.8 One of the steps in a more modern casting process where a CAD–CAM-generated outsole design has been used to create a model that is then cast and capable of producing multiple molds.

Industry Open and Proprietary Molds

Most brand-named athletic footwear designs are proprietary and come from molds produced by that company. The only exception to that would be in the case of counterfeiting. But there are many companies that produce only outsoles and do not manufacture footwear. The term *industry open mold* describes outsole molds that can be used to produce outsoles sold to more than one manufacturer. A good portion of industry open molds are made for boots and other non-athletic footwear. Figure 9.9 depicts an example of an industry open mold. This outsole molding company had two different logos that could be changed on the same mold. One was used to produce an outsole with the Bruno Magli logo and the other to produce an outsole with the Lord logo.[*] Figure 9.10 illustrates how

Figure 9.9 An industry open mold that utilized two different logo names, easily interchangeable, as shown in Figure 9.10.

---

[*] Bodziak, W., *Footwear Impression Evidence: Detection, Recovery and Examination*, 2nd ed., CRC Press, 2000, pp. 445–446.

Figure 9.10 The oval-shaped logo can be punched out of the mold and the oval containing a different logo can be inserted quickly.

this logo name was changed. In this example, only two logos existed for producing outsoles in this mold design. In other examples, a third-party manufacturer may produce outsoles in the same molds using a blank logo area or using many different names, giving access to outsoles produced in the same molds to many manufacturers. Industry open molds will usually have a round, oval, or rectangular shaped logo area that allows for the insertion of a different logo or a blank logo plate. The presence of this defined area, in itself, does not mean the mold is an industry open mold, but merely suggests the possibility. The significance of this is that it creates a situation where impressions at crime scenes that do not include replication of a name in the actual crime scene impression could potentially have been produced by any outsole coming from the same molds that had been sold to many manufacturers.

The Addition of Texture to Mold Surfaces

Texture is a general word to describe a shallow pattern added to some mold surfaces after the basic mold design has been created. When added to the mold, this texture pattern becomes part of the outsole design of every outsole formed in that mold. A large percentage of athletic shoes and other synthetic rubber outsole designs contain some texture. The edges or sides of outsoles and midsoles may also contain texture. Texture on outsoles is commonly replicated in two-dimensional impressions but can also be replicated in highly detailed three-dimensional impressions. Texture is mainly used on footwear for aesthetic reasons but in some cases texture can have a limited functional purpose. Information about the origin and features of texture is highly significant to the footwear examiner. The ways in which texture is added to the mold surface have such variability that the texture on any mold will be easily distinguishable from the texture of other molds, both of the same size and different sizes. There are two predominant ways to produce texture on a mold surface; one is a mechanical method known as hand stippling or hand-struck stippling, and the other is a process known as acid etching.

Hand Stippling or Hand-Struck Stippling

Hand stippling involves the physical production of texture with the use of a steel die whose tip contains a pattern. Figure 9.11 shows the tip of a steel die containing pattern #1030. The example pictured in front of the tip of the die illustrates the more complex texture pattern that can be produced with multiple strikes of that die. Figure 9.12 shows a manufacturer's sample sheet containing some of that manufacturer's choices of hand-stippled patterns. The pattern on the tip of the die is featured on the left of each pattern, along with examples of multiple strikes of that die. Additional samples of hand-struck stippling are shown in Figure 9.13 where the areas representing the patterns on the tips of the steel dies are indicated by the arrows. Figure 9.14 shows how an artisan places the tip of the die against the mold surface and forcefully strikes the die with a hammer. During this process, the die on the mold surface is typically repositioned before the next strike of the hammer. If the pattern is one where the artisan is attempting to create rows of a geometrical design such as stars, they will proceed more slowly to carefully position the die for each strike. However, most texture patterns like those shown in Figures 9.12 and 9.13 are the result of numerous successive and overlapping strikes of the die. As each overlapping strike is made, it will obliterate and/or alter portions of the previous strike. The rotation of the die and overlap of multiple die strikes as well as variations in the force and angle of each strike result in a texture pattern that quickly becomes unique to each mold. Figure 9.13 represents only about 2 cm of pattern width. The small pattern on the die tip has been used to create a unique pattern in just a portion of that small area. If you carefully study the stippling examples in each figure, you will find partial portions of the die tip design, but will not be able to find larger duplicate areas. Only a small area of a texture pattern of an outsole is needed to establish that a crime scene impression shared a common mold source.

Figure 9.11 Steel die pattern #1030 rests just above the larger pattern it produces with multiple overlapping strikes. The die is hand struck with a hammer to press the pattern into the mold surface.

Figure 9.12 A portion of one sample sheet showing a few of many choices of hand-struck stippling offered by one manufacturer. On the left of each is a single strike of the steel die and to the right of that is an example of multiple strikes of that die.

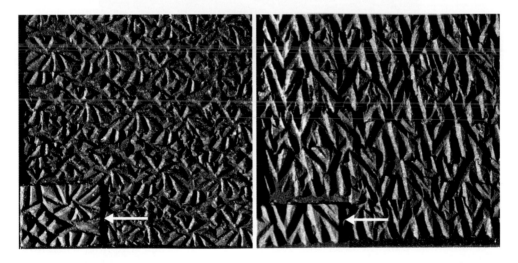

Figure 9.13 Two additional examples of hand-struck stippling showing the size and content of the tip of the die for each pattern at the bottom left (arrows), and the pattern that results from multiple overlapping strikes of that die.

Hand-struck stippling has its own characteristic features. The depth of each strike of the die will vary because of the varied amount of force and the angle that is used to strike the die. This can be observed under magnification by viewing a new or unworn area of an outsole. Figure 9.15 shows a small area of a new outsole design that contains texture stemming from both hand-struck and acid-etch processes. The top two arrows point to

Figure 9.14 An artisan hand strikes a steel die with a hammer to transfer that design into the metal mold surface.

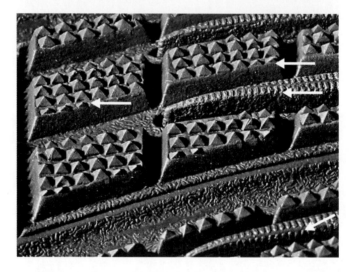

Figure 9.15 A view from the side of a portion of an outsole with texture resulting from both hand-struck stippling (top two arrows) and acid-etch methods (bottom two arrows).

the pyramid-shaped hand-struck stippling. Note the variation in their depth, which is a product of how hard the die is struck. Also note the hand-struck stippling, when unworn, is considerably deeper than the adjacent acid-etched texture indicated by the two bottom arrows. The inflexible tip of the steel die cannot strike its design on the sides of mold contours or design elements. This is why there is no hand-struck stippling on the sides below the pyramid-shaped texture. To the contrary, acid-etch texture is transferred to the mold surface from paper and thus can be bent and positioned on both the bottom and the sides of mold design areas if desired. Note how the acid-etch texture extends around curved areas and the sides of the design elements, as seen by the bottom arrows. Both the depth and positioning of texture are distinguishing features between hand-struck and acid-etch

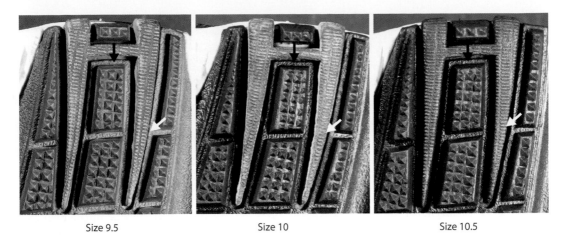

| Size 9.5 | Size 10 | Size 10.5 |

Figure 9.16 The same respective areas of outsoles from three adjacent sized molds show differences in the precise hand-stippled and acid-etch texture patterns.

Figure 9.17 A tool operated by air pressure that creates reciprocating strikes against a mold surface to create a very shallow and random design.

texture applications. Figure 9.16 shows the same area of three outsoles of this same design and the many variations of the texture.

In addition to using a hammer to hand strike a steel die's pattern into a mold surface, I have seen on one occasion a pneumatically operated tool as depicted in Figure 9.17. The air pressure forces the pointed tip to reciprocate and rapidly strike the mold surface. This form of texture, unlike the hand-struck variety, is very shallow and produces more of a disturbance in the surface rather than any defined pattern features. Any texture it does produce is also highly random and mold specific.

There is only one instance when the texture pattern on multiple molds is the same. This involves the toe and heel star texture areas of the Nike Air Force 1 design and possibly very similar Nike designs that have the same toe and heel design. This area originally was textured with a deep hand-struck stippled star design. Due to the large number of molds produced of this design, an insert with the hand-stippled pattern was produced and copied for each half size and is placed in the cast model before the metal is poured around it, as shown in Figure 9.18. This results in multiple molds of the same size possessing the same star pattern texture in the heel and toe areas. The acid-etch texture that covers the remainder of the mold's surface is applied separately to each mold and is unique to that mold.[*]

---

[*] Personal communication with Herb Hedges, Nike, Inc. on April 22, 2010 and January 30, 2014.

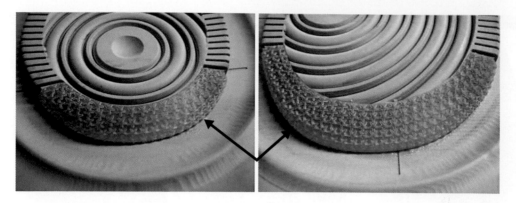

Figure 9.18 Inserts with premade star-shaped texture for each size are placed in the heel and toe areas of the cast model of Nike Air Force 1 designs, meaning that area will have identical texture in multiple molds of the same size. The other texture areas of the Air Force One are unique to each mold.

Acid Etching

Acid etching involves the transfer of a pattern composed of a soft gooey acid-resistant substance on paper that is cut into small pieces to fit into areas of the mold's surface. When the mold is later submerged in an acid bath, the gooey substance protects the metal beneath the pattern areas from the acid. The general use of acid etching to create texture on surfaces is very common in the footwear industry as well as in many other industrial applications. The source of the selected texture pattern may originate from a thin metal sieve having a pattern prestamped through it, as shown in Figure 9.19. The gooey acid-resistant substance is forced into and fills the void areas of that sieve pattern. Paper is then placed over the sieve and a hydraulic press will force the gooey substance from the void areas of the sieve onto the paper. More modern methods use a computer to create a pattern from which a silkscreen is made. In that case, the gooey acid-resistant substance is transferred through the silkscreen

Figure 9.19 An older method that uses a thin metal sieve containing a pattern that is filled with a black gooey substance. That substance will first be transferred to paper, then from the paper to the mold surface after it is cut and fit into the mold design.

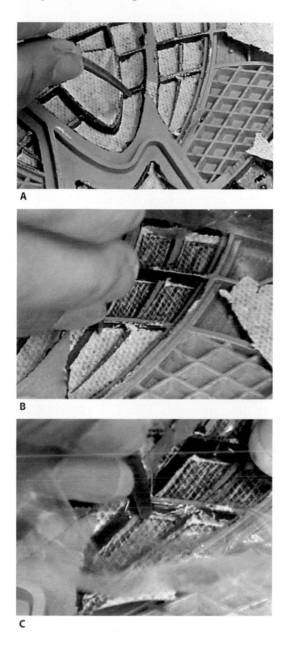

Figure 9.20 An artisan cuts small pieces of paper containing a pattern composed of a gooey substance and fits them into each design area of the mold (A and B); the paper is then rubbed with a tool to transfer the gooey pattern to the mold's surface (C).

pattern onto paper. With either method, once the gooey substance is transferred to paper, the paper is cut by hand into pieces to fit into the various shapes on the mold. The top photograph of Figure 9.20 shows an artisan using tweezers to fit small randomly cut pieces of paper into specific areas of the mold. The gooey acid-resistant substance on the paper is positioned down against the mold surface. With a piece of thin clear plastic on top, a tool is used to firmly rub and transfer the gooey pattern from the paper to the mold surface. Before it is placed in an acid bath, any other portions of the metal mold, including the sides and backs of the mold itself, must be coated with a substance that will protect those areas from the acid. Once this is done, the entire mold is placed in the acid bath. In the areas where the gooey substance is touching the metal, it will protect the metal from the acid. The acid will erode and remove the metal in areas that are not protected. In doing so, a version of the texture pattern is permanently acid etched into the mold surface, providing a three-dimensional version of that pattern. The paper will dissolve in the acid bath.

Significant variations are caused in the acid-etch process due to (1) variations in the specific texture pattern used, (2) the random cutting and hand-fitting of the many small pieces of paper containing the pattern into the areas of each mold, (3) the pressing of the pattern to transfer the gooey substance to the mold surface, a process that further alters the pattern, and (4) variations in the actions of the acid bath related to its concentration and the duration of that process.

One feature of acid-etched texturing is its uniform and shallow depth in contrast to hand-struck stippled patterns. Acid etching is further characterized by designs that are uniform and separated by space on all sides of the tiny texture pattern elements, as depicted in Figure 9.21. Because the texture pattern is transferred from pieces of flexible paper, the paper can easily be placed around the sides of the design elements, allowing texture in those areas as shown below the arrows in Figure 9.15 and Figure 9.16. Figure 9.22 shows additional samples of acid-etch patterns from one manufacturer's sample sheet. It should be noted that the completed acid-etch pattern on any shoe mold will be distinctly modified from any manufacturer's samples due to the variables involved. An example of this is provided in Figure 9.23, which shows enlarged portions of the same area of four new outsoles of the same size, but from different molds. Note how varied the acid-etch pattern is, even though it was intended to be the same pattern. An excellent case example of a worn outsole is shown in Figure 9.24. The top arrow points to texture that extends around the side of the design and the bottom arrow points to the seam created where two separate pieces of paper containing the texture pattern were positioned against one another on the mold surface. Both are clear evidence of the acid-etch texture process.

Whether hand-struck stippling or acid-etch texturing is used, the texture pattern on any outsole mold surface is distinctly unique to one mold to the degree that even very small

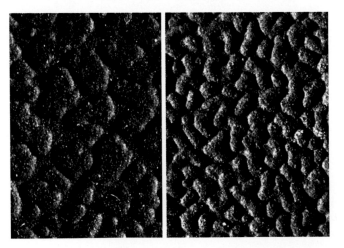

Figure 9.21 Two samples of acid-etch patterns on outsoles show how they are uniform in depth and have separations between the small design shapes.

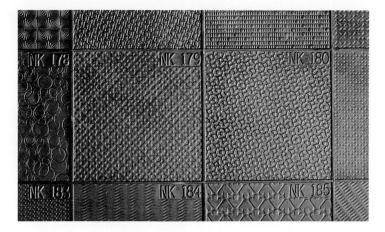

Figure 9.22 Samples of acid-etch patterns offered by a mold maker.

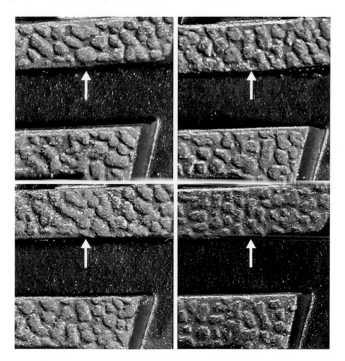

Figure 9.23 Enlargements of the same area of four outsoles of the same style and size, but from different molds, showing the easily distinguishable differences in acid-etch texture. These were chosen from the same pattern but look completely different after the acid-etch process.

areas of any texture may be distinguished from the respective areas of other molds. This is even further compounded when the texture's specific features are considered in relation to their position to the general design features of the outsole. By this I mean texture characteristics such as those next to the bottom arrow in Figure 9.24 have even greater value because of their specific location on the outsole, further reducing any chances of duplication on another mold.

Over the years, the question has often been asked if and when new technology might allow for computerized or automated ways to apply duplicate texture to the surface of

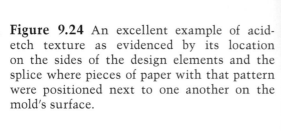

Figure 9.24 An excellent example of acid-etch texture as evidenced by its location on the sides of the design elements and the splice where pieces of paper with that pattern were positioned next to one another on the mold's surface.

multiple molds. Years ago, one industry representative advised they were using the wax transfer method with the metal sieve for chemical etching and there was no effort to duplicate etching on different molds.[*] Another advised that they were using a silkscreen of the texture design and that each factory made its own formula of a gooey substance they silk-screened onto paper and transferred to the mold's surface.[†] Presently the same two processes of hand-struck stippling and acid-etch texture, described above, continue to be used throughout the footwear outsole mold making industry. The only exception to this practice was mentioned above and involves the use of an insert of the star pattern design in the heel and toe areas of the Nike Air Force 1 and a few other Nike designs sharing the same toe area design. Some of the reasons are likely the inability of molding bits to create the same level of fine and sharp detail that is achieved with conventional texture methods, as well as the expense and time that might be involved doing this with machinery.

Forensic Applications of Texture

The presence of texture in forensic examinations is valuable for many reasons. Finding texture in a crime scene impression that corresponds to a molded shoe outsole establishes they both originated from the same mold or mold source. That is more specific than

[*] Personal communication with Mike Chase, Quabaug Rubber Company, March 3, 1997.
[†] Personal communication with Dan Potter, Nike, Inc. on March 17, 1997.

Figure 9.25 General wear shows up well where the texture has been worn away.

concluding general correspondence of design and dimensional features because it links them through their unique mold characteristics. Finding texture in a crime scene impression that corresponds to a shoe cut from a premolded or calendered sheet may require a different valuation because it is associated with a mold or process used to produce a sheet of outsole design and not an individually made mold of a specific size. Texture is also of use to exclude shoes as the source of an impression as well as helping to distinguish footwear in those cases where the accused person or persons owns more than one pair of shoes of the same design. If no shoes have been seized, and proper outsole samples can be obtained, the association of texture in a crime scene impression with an outsole from a particular mold is usually the most accurate way to determine the size of the shoe that produced the impression. Texture is also an excellent indicator of the degree and position of general wear because it is shallow and is therefore worn from the outsole surface more quickly. The shoe in Figure 9.25 is a good example of how texture is easily worn away, producing a distinct reflection of the general wear on that outsole. A clear impression of this shoe will replicate the positions and degree of general wear more distinctly than a shoe without texture, as clearly defined by the erosion of specific portions of the shallow texture.

An occasional concern of novice examiners regards the ability to distinguish hand-struck from acid-etched stippling. Much of that has been addressed above and should be evident to an experienced examiner. However, because both the hand-struck and acid-etch methods of texturing result in texture unique to a specific mold or mold source, it is not essential to establish which method was used.

A case example where texture was of importance in a homicide case involved multiple bloody shoe impressions on the tiled kitchen floor next to the victim. A portion of one of those impressions is represented at the top left of Figure 9.26. On the top right is a known impression of the respective area of the shoe of the suspect. For demonstrative purposes, the color of a portion of the known impression was changed to red and superimposed over the respective area of the crime scene impression. That portion, slightly enlarged, is provided in the circular area of Figure 9.26, offset slightly to assist in comparing the two. The random hand-struck stippled texture pattern, where it was present in areas of the bloody impressions, corresponded with that on the shoe and allowed for the conclusion that the suspect's shoe originated from the same mold as the shoe that produced the crime scene impression.

Figure 9.26 A case example where bloody impressions contained texture that corresponded with that of the accused's shoes, indicating they originated from a common mold.

An Unusual Case Application Regarding Texture

Not all footwear is seized in the hours immediately after the crime. In one case examined, the shoe of the perpetrator of a homicide produced a very partial impression on a piece of plastic broken from a stereo component during a violent struggle. The impression on the plastic was very clear but only about 2 inches long and 1 inch wide. Although photographs of that case are not available, a simulated partial impression shown in Figure 9.27B represents the crime scene impression in that case, specifically the texture (arrows). It clearly depicted a Puma logo with surrounding design and clearly replicated texture. The shoes of the suspect were not obtained until his arrest many months later. The texture in the corresponding area of his shoes was now worn away, as shown in Figure 9.27A, and prevented comparison with the texture impression on the stereo component. His shoe had a compression-molded cup outsole that typically has mold numbers and size information in the recessed areas of the honeycomb pattern on its topside like the example shown in

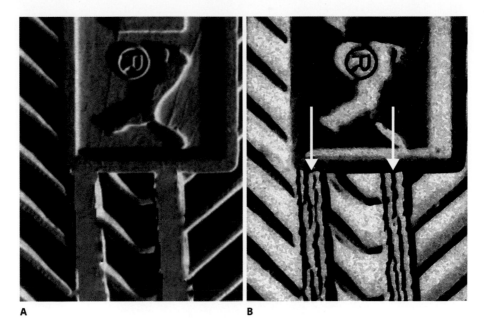

A   B

Figure 9.27 A simulation of a case where texture wore away prior to the arrest of the accused but the ability to compare that texture was restored by obtaining a new sample of the molded sole.

Figure 9.28. By removing the inner sole liner, the mold number was identified and used to obtain a new outsole from Puma produced in the same exact mold as the suspect's shoe. Since that new outsole possessed the full design and texture pattern, it was now possible to compare the texture associated with that mold with the crime scene impression.

Assistance from Manufacturers and Other Sources

Footwear manufacturers that produce popular athletic footwear sold in the US will usually have a US office address and contact number for assistance available on the Internet. With most examinations, it will not be necessary for an examiner to contact a manufacturer. Contacting a manufacturer to determine how many shoes of a particular style and/or size were sold is not recommended. Shoes are sold in very large numbers and manufacturers cannot determine how many shoes of a particular design and size have made their way to or still exist in a particular town. Not only do manufacturers' records rarely reflect anything regarding specific distribution; today, any distribution information would not take into consideration Internet sales. Regarding more pertinent questions that relate to the examination or interpretation of evidence, or on issues requesting the need for outsole samples, it is important to consider several things. If the shoe is still being manufactured and sold, first attempt to simply examine samples at a local store. In many cases, simply searching the Internet for the style number of the shoe will provide information regarding whether that shoe style is still sold and, if so, how to purchase it. If the need for manufacturer's assistance remains, initial contact should identify the person at that company that might be the most knowledgeable person with whom to communicate. A formal request to that individual via email will make it easier for him or her to understand your request, and if

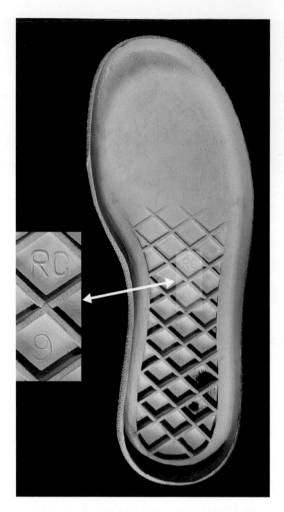

Figure 9.28 The top of many molded outsoles contain mold and size information in recessed areas.

necessary, pass that request to someone else in the company. In most cases, your request should include photographs and information as needed to clearly identify yourself and explain why you are making the request and the information you are seeking. Figure 9.29 is a diagram provided to Nike in a case where Nike was requested to provide samples of outsoles for the purpose of sizing a bloody crime scene impression. The scene impression is on the right and on the left an Internet photograph of the shoe design. Arrows, numbers, and words were included to make the written request easier to understand. This diagram was submitted along with dimensional information that would make it both easier and more accurate for Nike to narrow down the range of what sole sample sizes were needed.

Often, by the time shoes are sold, worn, and leave their impressions at a crime scene and you receive that evidence, that particular design is no longer sold. In those cases, particularly when assistance from a manufacturer is not possible or a manufacturer has advised it has destroyed the molds, Internet sources including www.ebay.com may be of some assistance in locating reference shoes. Many discontinued shoes are still being sold on the Internet as well as collector shoes and used shoes. Searching eBay for shoes of a specific brand name and style has occasionally provided adequate samples for sizing, for

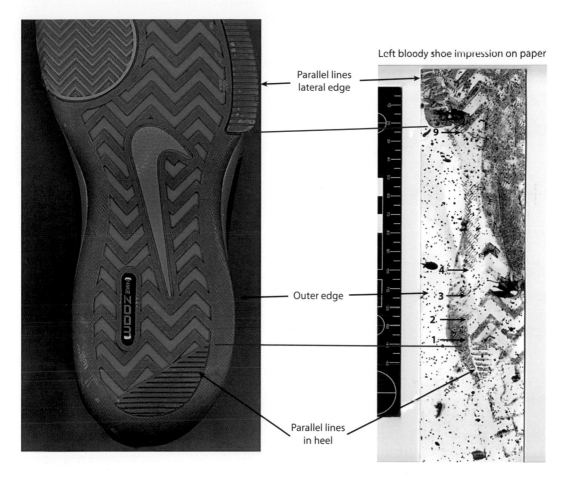

Figure 9.29 A prepared illustration sent to Nike to request sole samples for sizing.

investigative assistance, and for other reasons that might contribute to the evaluation of footwear evidence. When shoes from the Internet are used as a sizing standard, caution must be used to ensure they are not counterfeit.

Key Words: acid etch, CAD–CAM, compression molding, EDM, industry open mold, mold characteristics, mold dams, mold defect, outsole, pressed sole, retro design, specific sole design, stippling, texture.

Key Points

1. Understanding how molds are made assists an examiner in the evaluation of manufactured class characteristics.
2. Industry open molds are often used to produce outsoles that are used to produce more than one brand and design, making it impossible to know how many shoes of that outsole design have been sold. This is more common with boots and non-athletic footwear.
3. The addition of texture to a mold surface makes shoes produced in that mold distinguishable from others of the same design that originated from other molds.
4. Texture is useful in a number of ways in both the examination and sizing of footwear.

Manufacturing
Molding Processes and
Modification of Outsoles

10

Once molds are manufactured they can be used to produce thousands of outsoles. The majority of outsoles formed in molds will not be cut or trimmed or otherwise changed and will therefore be indistinguishable from others produced in the same mold. However, some molded outsoles will be produced in an oversized configuration, or for other reasons, will be cut, trimmed, or ground to properly fit the midsole and/or upper to which it is attached. These modifications often have significance that becomes part of the forensic examination of footwear evidence. This chapter briefly describes three common molding processes used for the production of molded outsoles: compression molding, injection molding, and open pour molding. It also provides some examples of how some molded outsoles are trimmed or cut, and how those and other factors might result in variations between footwear outsoles of the same brand, size, and design. The examples will also assist in recognizing certain characteristics that might indicate changes have been made to an outsole since it left the mold, and the significance those changes may have in a forensic examination. The examples provided do not represent all footwear produced and could always be subject to a change in manufacturing methods in the future.

The Compression-Molding Process

Compression molding is an "open-mold" process, meaning the mold is open at the time the preweighed soling material, sometimes referred to as a biscuit of rubber or preform, is placed into the mold cavity. Compression molding can be likened to making waffles, where the batter is placed on the bottom waffle iron after which the top half of the waffle iron is closed, with any excess batter leaking from the sides. Nike's famous waffle sole and the fact that the founders of Nike used an actual waffle iron to experiment with the potential of sole designs is noteworthy of that relationship.[*] Compression molding uses a wide variety of soling compounds consisting of custom blends of natural rubber and synthetic rubber polymers combined with accelerators, homogenizers, waxes, oils, carbon black, fillers, various coloring agents, recycled materials, and numerous other possible components. These components are mixed in a large two-story blender known as a Banbury mixer, illustrated in Figure 10.1. Some of these blends provide very dense outsole compounds while others provide microcellular compounds for lightweight soles. In the industry, compression-molded outsoles are often referred to as "pressed" soles.

A compression mold has a bottom sole plate that contains the outsole design and a top plate that will eventually close over and cover the bottom plate. The top may be smooth, but in many molds it contains a honeycomb or grid pattern to reduce the amount of soling compound needed as well as to reduce the weight of the outsole. Compression molds

---

[*] Bill Bowerman, co-owner of Blue-Ribbon sports, later known as Nike, used waffle irons around 1971 to produce lightweight soles for running shoes.

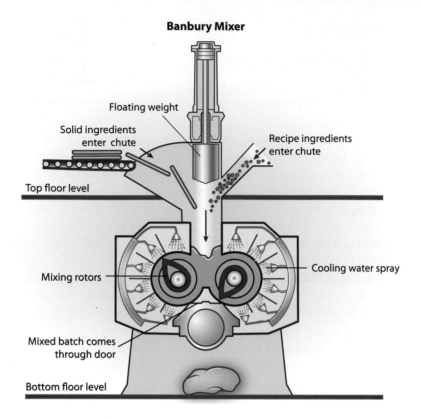

Figure 10.1 A Banbury mixer uses natural rubber and other solid synthetic rubbers with the addition of chemical ingredients that are mixed and blended into a specific soling compound.

are sometimes hinged like those shown sitting on an old style compression-molding press in Figure 10.2. The biscuits of rubber are placed on the bottom plate of those molds. The molds are inserted into the press where heat and pressure force them closed and the compound takes on the details of the mold design. The time the molds remain closed varies with the compound, the press, and other factors. Some old style compression molds are not hinged, but have the top and bottom portions permanently mounted on the respective tops and bottoms of the compression-molding press. A more modern press is shown in Figure 10.3 where the outsole plate with the outsole design is mounted on the bottom and the top plate of the mold is mounted on the top. After the preformed biscuits of rubber compound are set in place, the top and bottom sections close together as they withdraw into the press. Preformed biscuits of rubber intentionally include more soling compound than needed. Consequently, as the mold is pressed closed, excess compound escapes where the two halves of the mold meet. This excess material is referred to as flash. Some examples of flash are shown in Figure 10.4. The flash can be torn away or trimmed in a number of ways.

Many outsoles are produced using one color, but compression molds are often designed to allow for the production of multiple colored outsoles. Many molds have thin metal dams that separate design sections. This allows for the hand placement of different colored soling compounds in those areas. When the rubber melts during molding, the dams restrict the color to their respective areas. A simple example of a dammed area can be seen around the Vibram logo area in Figure 10.5. In this example, the manufacturer places precut yellow

Figure 10.2 An old style compression-molding press. The operator has just placed biscuits of soling rubber into the hinged molds. The arrow points to a mold that has been placed into the press. During this process, heat and pressure will close the mold, melting and pressing the biscuit of rubber into the style and shape of the outsole mold cavity.

Figure 10.3 A more modern compression-molding press.

rubber inserts into the dammed area. A black biscuit of rubber is then placed over the top. As the outsole is molded the dam keeps the yellow color within that area. When the outsole is molded, the Vibram name appears in yellow within the black outsole. Figure 10.6 is another example but with the added yellow rubber on each side of the logo. The manufacturer can also choose to leave the entire outsole black. In some factories, hinged molds with multiple components are used to allow different color combinations of both the outsole and the midsole. Figure 10.7 depicts a four-piece compression mold. The bottom sole plate will have dammed areas as necessary to contain one or more colors hand placed in various

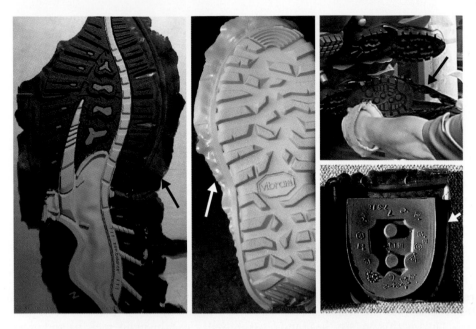

Figure 10.4 Examples of flash. Flash is the excess rubber compound that is squeezed out between the halves of the mold. It can be removed in a number of ways.

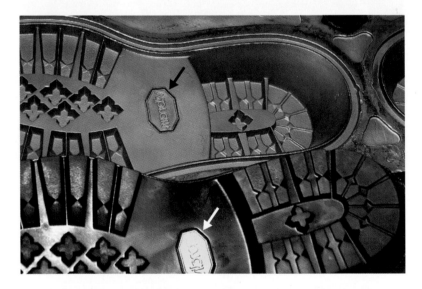

Figure 10.5 A compression outsole mold (top) has a small raised metal perimeter known as a dam (black arrow) that confines the yellow color to within that area of the outsole (bottom).

portions of the outsole design. Once the colored compounds are placed in those areas, the separator plate is lowered and the mold is briefly placed in the compression mold to melt those portions. The separator plate is then removed, the side rings of the mold are lowered, and a biscuit of rubber or preform that will comprise the midsole color will be placed over the top of the existing materials. The top plate of the mold is then lowered and the mold is placed back in the compression mold press to complete the molding process and bond all of the rubber components together. In compression molding where multiple colors are used,

Figure 10.6 Another example of a compression mold using dammed areas to confine different colors within that space.

Four Piece Mold for Multi-Color Process

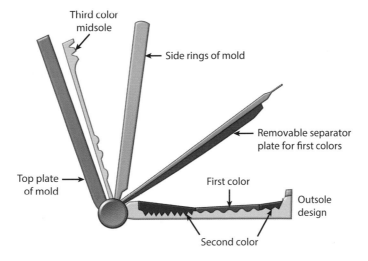

Figure 10.7 A four-piece mold used in compression molding that allows for different colors in the outsole and midsole areas.

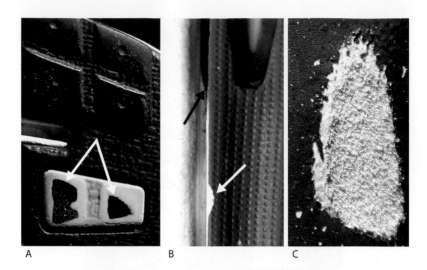

Figure 10.8 (A) An area where the thin yellow-colored outsole material has worn away and exposed the underlying black outsole material of the same density; (B) a new shoe outsole where the blue and white colors have bled into one another during molding; (C) a worn outsole where the underlying white microcellular midsole has been exposed through the surrounding solid black rubber outsole.

there may be areas on the finished outsole where one color has bled or worn into another. This may be noticed when a shoe is new or become more obvious after considerable wear. Figure 10.8 shows a worn area of a compression-molded shoe where the yellow color has worn away enough to reveal the black color beneath it (A). In the center, a new compression-molded shoe on the right has the white and blue colors bleeding into each other (B). In those instances, if the density of the rubber compound used is the same for both colors there will be no interface or physical difference from one color to the other and no replication of this will occur in an impression. In the case where an outsole wears down far enough to expose the midsole or another layer of a different compound and density, e.g., solid rubber wearing away to expose a microcellular midsole layer, there can be sufficient physical differences that allow for replication of that in detailed two-dimensional impressions. An example of this is provided in the third example on the right of Figure 10.8 (C).

The versatility of the compression molding process allows for a wide variety of footwear outsoles and styles, be it a flat sole deck shoe, a deep cup-sole sneaker, the thin outsole of a running shoe, heavy boots, walking shoes, or rubber heels for leather shoes. Most forensic footwear examinations involve athletic shoes and most athletic shoes have compression-molded outsoles. Figure 10.9 shows a small sampling of compression-molded outsoles to illustrate the diversity and flexibility of styles made with this process. Some are molded with sculptured midsoles; some have flat outsoles bonded to a midsole; some have a raised heel; and one is even the five-toe variety of shoe. Hinged two-pieced molds like that pictured in Figure 10.2 typically produce flat soles. Molds similar to those in Figure 10.3 typically produce more complex designs and shapes with greater depth. The versatility of compression molding not only extends to the countless styles and shapes of outsoles, but to the wide variety of compounds possible from the Banbury mixer and the ability to integrate them with various midsole shapes and materials.

Figure 10.9 A few of the countless examples of footwear made using compression-molded outsoles demonstrate the versatility of the process.

Mold Warp

To reduce molding time, compression-molding operations often remove solid rubber outsoles from the mold slightly early. The outsoles will be very hot and will continue to "cook" for a short period of time. In some operations, immediately after removal from the molds several outsoles are stacked on top of one another, a practice that places them in a non-flat and/or warped position. As they cool, they may retain some of that unevenness, often referred to as "mold warp." Although the outsole may appear flat and even, the effect of the mold warp may prevent small areas of the outsole from evenly contacting a flat substrate, resulting in some nonprinting areas in the impression. This only happens during the first days or weeks of use until general wear eliminates those minor irregularities. Figure 10.10 shows a new compression molded shoe alongside a test impression made while wearing that shoe on a firm surface. The parts of the impression that do not print are due to very minor irregularities in surface topography caused by mold warp. Note that although there

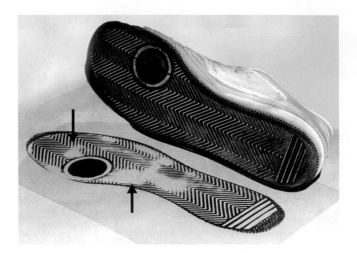

Figure 10.10 An example of a new shoe with a compression-molded outsole that contains some mold warp that results in small nonprinting areas. These minor irregularities will disappear during the early stages of wear.

is some randomness to mold warp, the features are short lived and will vary considerably based on the pressure and substrate involved during the impression process. If this is encountered in crime scene impressions, it may or may not contribute to the examination depending on the clarity and characteristics involved, whether multiple impressions at the crime scene reflect the same features repetitively, how soon the shoes are obtained for examination, and how similarly known impressions reflect the same irregularities.

Solid Compression-Molded Outsoles

The following represent a few examples of solid rubber compression-molded shoes.

Converse Chuck Taylor All Star Shoes

The Converse Chuck Taylor All Star (CCTAS) basketball shoe is one of the oldest, most popular, and widely recognized basketball shoes made.[*,†,‡,§] First introduced in 1917, its design consisted of a canvas upper and a brown vulcanized rubber sole. In 1932, the name "Chuck Taylor," a basketball player and salesman for Converse, was added to the shoe.[¶] For the first several decades, several generations of hand-milled compression molds were made as needed to accommodate increased demand and production. Through the early 1990s, the variety of hand-milled molds that Converse had accumulated over the years varied considerably. In some cases when finished shoes were paired up on the assembly line, the left and right outsoles would be noticeably different. Figure 10.11 provides an example of

---

[*] Bodziak, W. J., *Footwear Impression Evidence*, Elsevier, 1990.
[†] Bodziak, W. J., *Footwear Impression Evidence: Detection, Recovery and Examination*, CRC Press, Boca Raton, FL, 2000.
[‡] Bodziak, W. J., 1986.
[§] Hamm, E., 1989.
[¶] Peterson, H., Chucks! The Phenomenon of Converse Chuck Taylor All Stars.

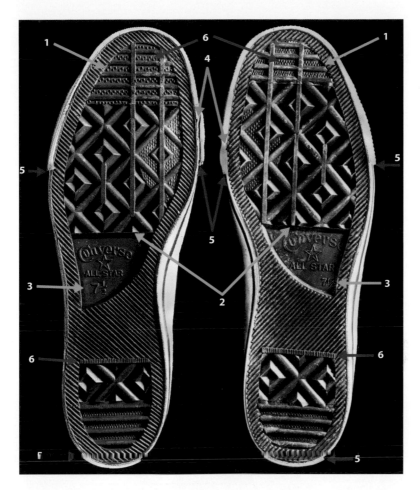

Figure 10.11 Converse Chuck Taylor All Star shoes purchased in the 1980s and prior years would very often not have mirrored outsoles due to the way they were assembled that allowed for many variables.

this seen in a pair of CCTAS purchased in the 1980s. Although sold as a pair of size 7.5 shoes, the many different hand-milled molds used varied considerably, including the differing number of transverse bars in the toe area (#1), differences where the diamond/square pattern intersects the logo area (#2), and the style and size of lettering and numbers within that logo area (#3). During the combination of the outsole with the uppers, two foxing strips were wrapped around the perimeter of the shoe after which a toe bumper guard and heel label were added. The arrows in Figure 10.11 point to additional variations including the typical triangular void area formed by the overlap of the foxing strip (#4), the toe bumper guard and heel label that were added by hand that also varied in position from shoe to shoe (#5), the hand-struck stippling that was specific to each mold including the stippling in between the parallel line rows in the toe and heel, the ball area, and the hand-struck stippled rows of parallel lines in the front of the heel area (#6). The many varied features of outsoles from different hand-milled molds of both the same and different sizes combined with the variables of the added toe bumper guards, heel label, and foxing strips provided much valuable information during examination of crime scene impressions made by this shoe design.

Figure 10.12 A pair of Converse Chuck Taylor All Star shoes produced in the late 1990s with CAD–CAM mold-making methods.

In the early 1990s, Converse had new molds produced using a CAD–CAM process. The new sets of computer-generated molds in each half-size were indistinguishable, except for the hand-struck stippling that was applied after the molds were made. The variations between the left and right outsole pairs that were so common with the mixture of hand-milled molds used in prior years were eliminated. Other variables in the assembly process remained the same, including the application and overlapping of the foxing strip and the variations of the exact position of the toe guard and heel label. Figure 10.12 depicts the outsoles of a pair of CCTAS produced in the late 1990s with the CAD–CAM mold-making methods.

In July 2003, Nike purchased Converse.* Nike remade the molds and made slight changes in the assembly of the shoes. Figure 10.13 depicts two left outsoles of CCTAS shoes

---

* Wayne, L., Nike purchasing Converse, a legend on the blacktop, NYTimes.com, July 10, 2003.

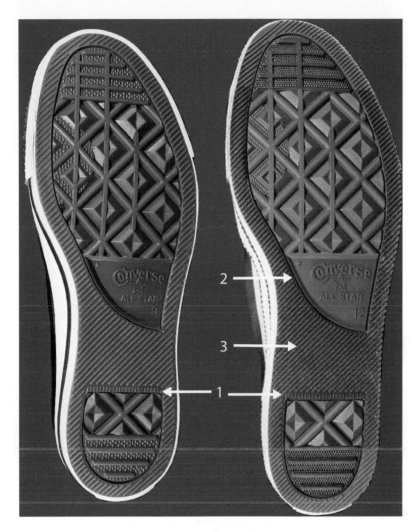

Figure 10.13 Two left Converse Chuck Taylor All Star shoes purchased in 2014. The one on the right has been molded with the incorporation of a thin layer of fabric (#3) that shows up darker on this shoe.

purchased in 2014. One noticeable change in this version of the CCTAS shoes involves the short parallel lines in front of the heel that were once a product of hand-struck stippling but are now simply part of the computer-generated design (#1). The lines are very shallow and no longer different on each mold. Other stippling on the outsole in the heel, toe, and ball regions is still the product of genuine hand-struck stippling. Another change involved the use of a butt joint (end against end) of the foxing strip rather than the overlap of the foxing strip that previously resulted in the triangular gap as shown in Figure 10.11 (#4). Some evidence of this butt joint can still be seen in some shoes. Toe guards and heel labels continue to be added by hand but appear to be more consistent in their positions, although variables still exist. In addition, a groove runs around the heel and sole surrounding the diamond/square and transverse line patterns (#2). This is the result of a raised metal dam that has been added to help contain fabric that is placed in the molds for the CCTAS shoes sold in the US market. The shoe on the left in Figure 10.13 does not include the fabric like the one on the right. When used, the thin layer of fabric covers a good portion but not all

Figure 10.14 A pair of Converse Chuck Taylor All Star shoes made in 2013 showing the changes in the fabric that occur as the shoe is worn.

of the outsole (#3). The fabric is imbedded in the rubber during the compression-molding process. Because the fabric is very thin, it wears off quickly and often serves as a good indicator of the position and degree of general wear. Figure 10.14 shows a pair of worn CCTAS, made in 2013, with portions of the fabric worn completely away. In the areas where the fabric covers the hand-stippled texture, the features of that texture usually do not replicate well. This is likely due to the embedding of the fabric in the rubber; thus, the stippling and fabric are worn away simultaneously. The placement of fabric on outsoles was created for the US market due to a loophole in the tariff structure that has made this a money-saving incentive for various manufacturers. The fabric reclassifies the footwear, allowing manufacturers to reduce the tariffs they pay on the import of those shoes.[*][†] In 2013, the US Customs Agency published additional criteria for the abrasion resistance testing of

---

[*] 1989 Harmonized Tariff Schedule of the United States (HTSUS) Chapter 64.
[†] Cole, G., Your sneaker is a slipper—wacky tax, Wednesday, March 25, 2015, http://www.avalara.com/blog/2015/03/25/your-sneaker-is-a-slipper-wacky-tax-wednesday

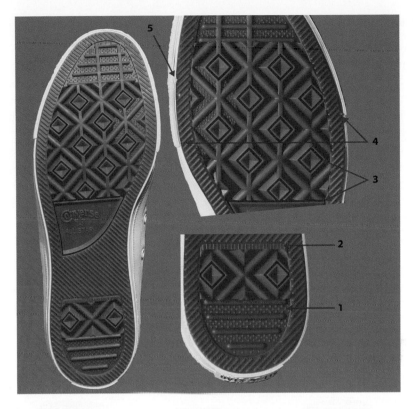

Figure 10.15 The Converse Chuck Taylor All Star 2 shoes, introduced in July 2015. Recessed areas in the heel and toe are still hand-stippled (1); but the area in front of the heel is imitation molded stippling (2); new grooves run around the logo area and each small square/diamond design (3); two small stipples appear to indicate the desired beginning and ending location for a toe bumper guard (4); and the foxing strips are butt joints (5).

footwear to determine if it meets the intentions of the original tariff classification.* How these new criteria will affect the future production of fabric embedded soles is unknown at this time. In 2015, there was a mixture of outsoles with and without the fabric embedded in the US marketplace and it is not uncommon to find this on outsoles of shoes of other brands. Even though this modification is beneficial only in the US market, CCTAS shoes with this fabric have also been found in European markets.

In July 2015 Converse released a new version called the Chuck Taylor All Star 2, which looks very similar but has more modern inner liners. The outsole of this shoe, shown in Figure 10.15, no longer reflects the grooves that fully surrounded the square/diamond designs in the sole and heel for the purpose of adding fabric as shown in Figure 10.13, but it now includes grooves around the logo area and the small square/diamond design elements. Small raised areas in the form of a single stipple seem to be located in positions to gauge where to begin and end the hand-wrapped toe cap.

The CCTAS shoes provide a great example of flat compression-molded soles that contain additional features such as the fabric, toe bumper guard, heel label, and foxing strips. Many shoes of other brands in the marketplace have similar construction and components that, if replicated in a scene impression, may play a role in a forensic examination.

* US Customs ISO 20871, Footwear—Test Methods for Abrasion Resistance, November 15, 2013.

Vibram Lug-Soled Boots

In 1935, the death of six men in an alpine mountain climbing expedition inspired an Italian named Vitale Bramani to develop an all-purpose boot sole that would provide both traction and protection from the extreme elements. Working with the tire manufacturer Pirelli, Bramani obtained a patent in 1937 and began producing a boot he called "Vibram," a combination of his first (Vitale) and last (Bramani) name. This boot was produced in Italy for many years, but in 1965, the Quabaug Rubber Company of North Brookfield, Massachusetts was granted the exclusive license for manufacturing the Vibram outsoles in North America.* Figure 10.16 depicts some of Vibram's original boot outsole designs still made today. The basic solid rubber compression-molded Vibram design, consisting of what many call stars and lugs, is likely the most copied outsole design as numerous other manufacturers have produced innumerable look-a-like versions modified and scaled to fit a broad range of footwear that includes not only boots, but also other types of footwear.

Most compression-molded outsoles produced in-house by shoe manufacturers are molded in the exact size needed to fit a specifically sized shoe. However, hundreds of outsole producers in the world, such as Vibram and Quabaug Rubber, do not manufacture shoes, only the outsoles. Some designs are proprietary for a certain brand, and some are industry open mold designs. The Vibram boot designs like those shown in Figure 10.16 are produced in an oversized configuration to accommodate the various brands and styles of footwear of the manufacturers they will be sold to, thus those manufacturers will need to cut and trim them to their various styles and sizes. Oversized compression-molded

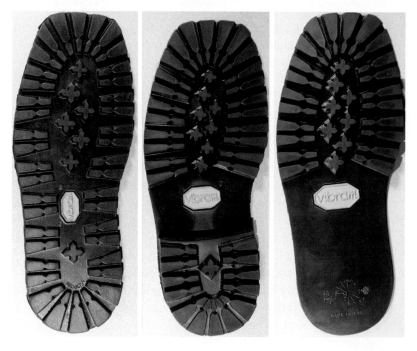

Figure 10.16 Three original Vibram boot outsole designs made in an oversized configuration for various shoe manufacturers. The outsole on the left has a one-piece flat profile, in the center is a one-piece raised heel profile, and on the right an outsole that can accommodate a separately added raised heel.

---

* www.vibram.com

unit soles made with high-density solid rubber compounds are too thick and tough to die cut and must be trimmed to size in another way. Although each manufacturer may vary slightly in how they do this, it is important to have a general understanding that (1) these modifications only occur in some footwear, typically boots, and (2) they account for some variations between outsoles, even on footwear of the same size. Figure 10.17 illustrates an example of how an oversized solid rubber outsole of this type is trimmed during construction. Starting at the top left, the bottom of the upper of the boot is coated with special contact cement (A). An oversized outsole is then positioned by hand onto the upper in a

Figure 10.17 The assembly of oversized boot outsoles during construction of a boot and how variations occur during trimming of excess portions of the outsole.

process known as "spotting" (B). Spotting is critical because it must be done so the perimeter of the upper falls within the perimeter of the outsole. At the instant the outsole makes contact with the upper, the contact cement will bond and prevent the spotted position from being changed. Some manufacturers will use oversized boot outsoles in every other size (e.g., size 8, 10, 12), while others may choose to use each full size (e.g., 8, 9, 10, 11, 12). Those using every other size will have a larger margin when spotting but will also have more room for variations between the precise positioning of the outsoles within any specific size. The excess amount of outsole size once spotted is most apparent at the outsole's edges where the trimming takes place, shown with the arrow (C). That excess must be trimmed away using a Rough Rounder machine (D). Once the majority of the excess is removed, a grinding wheel is used to grind the edges smooth (E). Finally, for this particular boot, a few stitches are placed in the toe area to provide extra reinforcement (F). On completion, any finished shoe of a particular size will have an outsole whose overall length and width are the same, but due to the variations of the spotting, trimming, and grinding, specific portions of the pattern may be shorter or longer at various points around the perimeter. These variations enable an outsole to be distinguished from many other outsoles of the same size and design. Figure 10.18 shows a case example of same size right boot soles made utilizing this process. Although all six are the same size (10½), brand and style variations occurred in various dimensions of their outsole design elements. These variations are most noticeable in the lug sizes around the perimeter due to the various ways they were spotted and trimmed, but also result in some length and width variations. A few of those variations are summarized in the chart in Figure 10.19. Although some of these variations only measured 1 or 2 millimeters, some were much greater. For instance, shoe #1 had a 6 mm difference in the length of its toe lug from shoe #6 even though they are the same size. Although texture was not part of the outsole design of those boots, other designs might include texture. If texture were part of an oversized outsole design, the texture could be used to link an impression to a mold source, but depending on what sizes of oversized soles a particular manufacturer used, that texture might not be limited to just one size of footwear. For example, a size 14 oversized outsole might be cut down to produce size 11.5, 12, and 13 boots. For that reason, if attempting to size partial impressions of boots made in this way, limitations may exist based on construction methods and choices.

Microcellular Outsoles

The term microcellular applies to a wide variety of lightweight soling materials. Compression-molded microcellular outsoles and midsoles are used on a variety of footwear, ranging from dress shoes to boots to athletic shoes. Most microcellular outsoles remain true to their mold cavity size on demolding. Other microcellular outsoles contain blowing agents that cause the expansion of the outsole to a size greater than their mold cavity. This expansion occurs instantly when the mold opens. Some microcellular outsoles are intentionally produced larger than usual to provide a flexible size margin for those companies that will die cut or trim them accordingly as they combine them with the uppers to produce the finished shoe.

For outsoles made of expanded (blown) microcellular materials, they will always be oversized because their amount of expansion cannot be accurately predicted and varies

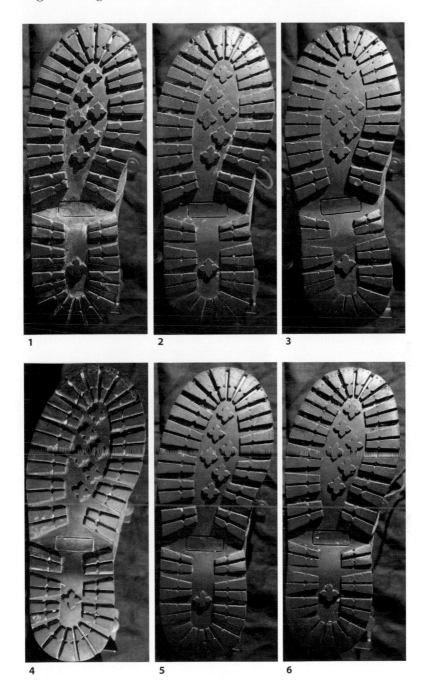

Figure 10.18 Six compression-molded right boot outsoles of the same size, style number, and brand contain variations in the lug sizes around their perimeters due to variations in the spotting and trimming during construction.

slightly each time an outsole is molded. The specific amount of the expansion is related to the compound mixture and other factors. Figure 10.20 depicts a close-up view of expanded microcellular compression-molded outsoles. As the mold opens, the outsoles instantly burst to a larger size than the mold cavity. In the example in Figure 10.20, the two black lines placed at each end of the mold cavity define the size of the mold cavity in contrast with

Shoe	Heel to Toe	Inner Lug Heel to Toe	Toe Lug Length	Heel Lug Length	Maximum Width
1	326 mm	244 mm	46 mm	36 mm	118 mm
2	326 mm	246 mm	43 mm	37 mm	115 mm
3	324 mm	246 mm	42 mm	36 mm	115 mm
4	322 mm	243 mm	44 mm	35 mm	117 mm
5	328 mm	245 mm	45 mm	38 mm	117 mm
6	322 mm	244 mm	40 mm	38 mm	117 mm

Figure 10.19 A few of the dimensions of the boots in Figure 10.18 illustrate the resulting variables between those outsoles.

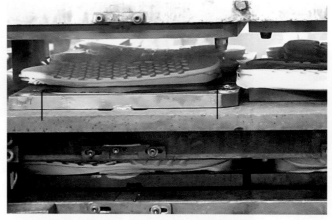

Figure 10.20 An example of outsoles that are compression molded with blown rubber that causes them to burst from their molds and expand to a larger size.

Figure 10.21 Microcellular outsoles can be die cut to a particular shape and size as needed.

the size of the expanded outsole. Oversized microcellular outsoles are softer and therefore can be die cut to size, as shown in Figure 10.21. The extra size of the outsole allows for some variance in the position of the die from one outsole to the next. Figure 10.22 depicts two expanded outsoles taken from the same mold cavity 15 minutes apart. The differences in the size due to expansion variables are minor in this example but the varied positions of the dies when they were cut create more obvious variations between the two, most noticeable in the toe areas.

Figure 10.22 Two expanded microcellular blown rubber outsoles from the same mold. They were both die cut to the same dimensions but because of the slightly different position of the die and some slight expansion variables, differences can be noted, most noticeably in the toe area.

Many athletic shoes have very light microcellular outsoles that do not use expanded compounds and come out of the mold at their specific size. A typical example is provided in the Skechers brand athletic shoe in Figure 10.23. Since there is no expansion and no cutting or grinding, there are no variations between multiple soles from the same mold.

An athletic shoe exception to this is the classic Nike Cortez, first released by Nike in 1972 and shown in Figure 10.24. The Cortez is produced with an expanded rubber outsole and is offered here as an example of variations encountered with expanded microcellular outsoles. The oversized Cortez outsoles are combined with colored wedge and midsole components into a blocker unit that is then die cut to its specific size. The edges are then ground to provide a smooth transition between the midsole and outsole components. Figure 10.25 shows the Cortez outsoles after the compression mold has opened. The microcellular sole has expanded slightly larger than the mold cavity. On the right, a die is positioned over a Cortez outsole that is already glued to the midsole components. Different positioning of the die will allow for additional variations between soles of the same size. Because of the slight amount of expansion, the oversized outsole, and the various positions of the die cutting process, not all Nike Cortez in one size will have the same number of rows of the outsole's herringbone pattern. This is illustrated in a pair of Nike size 10 Cortez shoes shown in Figure 10.26. The rows between the logo area and the toes number 24 on one shoe and 26 on the other as indicated in the photograph.

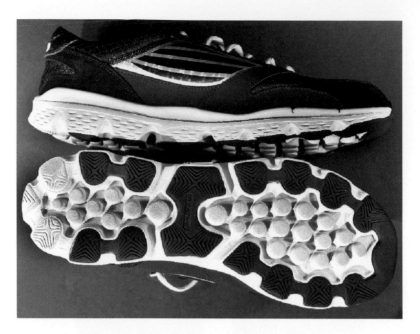

Figure 10.23 Athletic shoes use microcellular compounds to produce lightweight outsoles. These are not expanded and therefore their dimensions do not vary from one outsole to the next. The molded design along the outsole edge shows it has not been cut or ground.

Figure 10.24 Unlike the vast majority of athletic shoes, the Nike Cortez, produced since 1972 and still sold, uses blown expanded microcellular rubber for its outsole that is glued together with the wedge-shaped midsole components and die cut to size, after which its edges are ground smooth.

Figure 10.25 Nike Cortez outsoles expand about 5% when the molds open and are oversized. The expansion and subsequent die cutting result in further variations between the same size Cortez shoes.

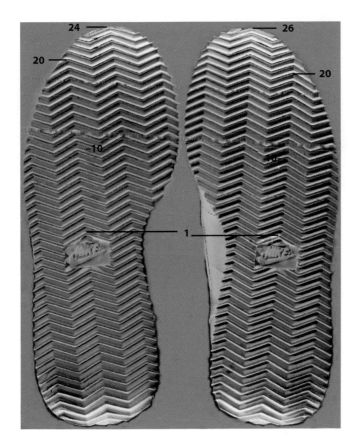

Figure 10.26 A pair of Nike Cortez has a different number of rows due to the expansion of the outsole rubber, and the variables associated with die cutting them to the proper size.

Injection Molding

Injection molding is a closed molding process. Soling compounds such as polyvinyl chloride (PVC), polyurethane (PU), ethylene vinyl acetate (EVA), and thermoplastic rubber (TPR) are mixed or melted outside of the mold and injected into the closed mold through an injection port. The most basic form of injection mold produces individual unit soles that must be glued and/or stitched to the upper. This type of injection mold has a sole plate (bottom) and top plate like the injection mold in Figure 10.27. The soling compound is injected into the closed mold through an injection port that directs the compound through narrow channels that lead to the sole design plate. Once assembled on a shoe, an injection-molded unit sole may be difficult to distinguish from a compression-molded unit sole.

Another form of injection molding is called direct-attach injection molding. The mechanics of this process require a mold assembly that can open and close around the upper of the shoe. Figure 10.28 includes a drawing and photograph of a one-step and one-color direct-attach injection process (A). The points where the left and right mold side rings come together in the toe and/or heel area (see arrow in B) will leave a visible seam as a result of the seepage of some soling compound in that area (C and D). The presence of this seam in either the heel and/or toe area is evidence of direct-attach injection molding. In some designs, the seam on the edge of the outsole may be intentionally removed with

Figure 10.27 An injection mold that produces individual unit outsoles. The injection channels are colored red in this illustration to show how the outsole compound enters the closed mold.

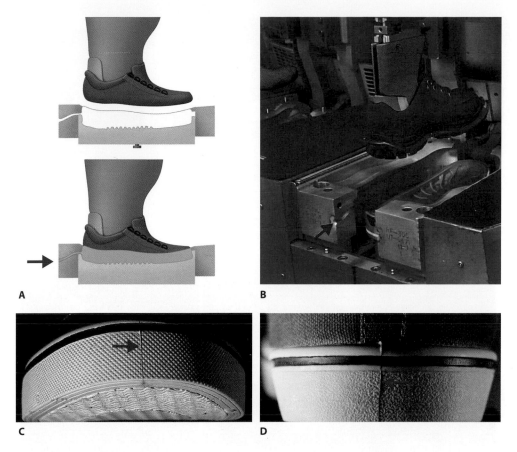

A   **B**

C   **D**

Figure 10.28 A one-step direct-attach injection-molded system involves a mold that closes around the shoe upper. The soling compound is injected around the upper. In many cases, a seam will be evident in the toe and/or heel area of the finished shoes. It is noted that in this particular example, the dark stripe around the foxing strip is hand painted.

a grinding wheel. In other instances, the direct attached applications do not result in this seam on the outsole as they are using premolded unit outsoles that are placed into a special mold where the midsole portion is injected over them. Direct-attach injection molding is versatile and the equipment varies considerably, ranging from machines that produce one-color soles to those with multiple stations that allow for multiple outsole compounds and colors.

Some direct-attach injection-mold systems are known as dual density injection systems because the outsole and midsole materials can include both different colors and different compounds. A drawing of this process is shown in Figure 10.29. At the top, a thin outsole is first injected using a dummy plate in place of a shoe upper. The dummy plate covers the sole design plate while the side rings close, after which the outsole compound is injected. In the middle photograph, the injected thin outsole remains in place and the shoe upper is lowered until it rests on top of it. At the bottom, the side rings of the mold assembly close again and a different microcellular compound is injected through the second injection port to create the midsole, bonding the previously injected outsole to the shoe upper. Figure 10.30 illustrates a factory sequence of this same process. The top left photograph shows the dummy plate and sole design plate and the side-rings that are in the open position. The bottom arrow points to

Figure 10.29 Drawings of a dual density direct-attach injection process.

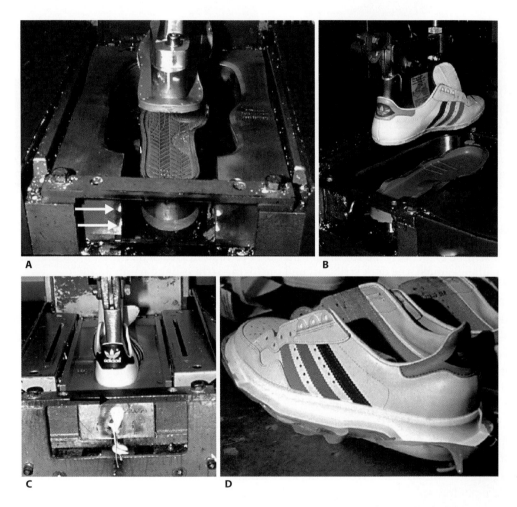

Figure 10.30 A factory example of the dual density direct-attach injection molding process. The dummy plate is lowered onto the sole plate, the side rings come together, and the thin outsole is injected through the bottom port (A); the lasted upper of the shoe is then lowered onto the injected outsole (B); the side rings close again and the white midsole is injected through the upper port, bonding the gray outsole to the upper (D). The flash between the midsole and outsole as well as in the heel seam will be trimmed away.

Figure 10.31 An injected polyurethane (PU) outsole produced in the 1990s on athletic shoes often contained numerous air bubbles.

the bottom injection port where the thin outsole will be injected between the dummy plate and sole plate. The top arrow points to the top injection port where the white midsole will be injected (Figure 10.30A). In Figure 10.30B, the shoe upper is lowered onto the previously injected outsole. Figure 10.30C is after injection of the midsole and Figure 10.30D after the shoe is removed from the mold. The shoe still has flash between the outsole and midsole as well as in the heel and toe area where the side rings meet. This flash will be trimmed off but some evidence of the seams will remain. This direct-attach process can also be used with premolded compression- or injection-molded unit soles that are placed by hand in the mold and attached to the upper with injection-molded midsoles.

PU was once commonly used on athletic outsoles in the direct-attach injection-molding process.[*,†,‡,§] PU outsoles in the past often contained large numbers of air bubbles. The bubbles would tend to collect in the same locations in the pattern with remarkable similarity, and in some cases would even appear in the texture, as shown in a PU outsole from the 1990s in Figure 10.31. PU is commonly used today for midsole materials, although the use of PU on athletic shoe outsoles is no longer common. In those cases where outsoles are produced on other footwear, the PU is usually more dense and derived from different PU compounds, resulting in fewer or no air bubbles.

Open Pour Molding

Pouring PU into an open mold is known as open pour molding. Many applications of open pour molding involve using PU to join the shoe upper to a premolded outsole of a more solid density. This is illustrated in Figure 10.32, where previously made compression-molded outsoles have been placed in the bottom of a mold. The PU is poured into the mold

* Bodziak, W. J., Ibid., 2000, pp. 230–237.
† Music, D., and Bodziak, W. J., A forensic evaluation of the air bubbles present in polyurethane shoe out-soles as applicable in footwear impression comparisons, *Journal of Forensic Science*, 33(5), September 1988.
‡ Katterwe, H., Forensic-physical investigations of polyurethane treads, *Archiv für Kriminologie*, 174:89–95, September/October 1984.
§ Keijzer, J., Identification value of imperfections in shoes with polyurethane soles in comparative shoe-print examination, *Journal of Forensic Identification*, 40(4):217–223, 1990.

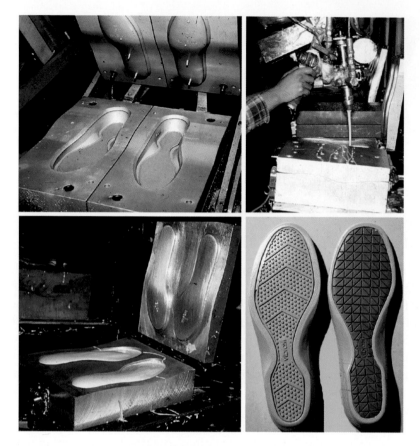

Figure 10.32 Solid compression-molded outsoles are positioned into a specially fit mold, after which PU is poured. The mold is closed as the PU expands. The result provides a solid rubber outsole with a lighter weight PU midsole.

and expands. The top of the mold is closed and locked. The finished result is an outsole of a rubber compound combined with a lighter microcellular PU midsole material. Various applications of this process exist in the industry ranging from individually poured outsoles to those that involve larger semiautomatic direct-attach systems.

Siped Outsoles

Siping is the process of placing thin cuts in a rubber outsole to improve traction. The process was invented and patented by John Sipe in 1923.* In the footwear industry, sipes are typically used on boat and deck shoes. The outsoles of those shoes are first compression molded, after which they are siped. This process is shown in Figure 10.33 where a pair of compression-molded outsoles, void of any design, are being fed through a siping machine (10.33A). A sipe blade (10.33B) mounted in the machine, and with a hacking action cuts one row of sipes at a time as the outsole is advanced through the machine (10.33C). True sipes are tightly closed (10.33D) and only open when the outsole is flexed (10.33B). Figure 10.34 illustrates how slight variations in the outsole position will affect the precise location and

---

* April 17, 1923, patent 1,452,099.

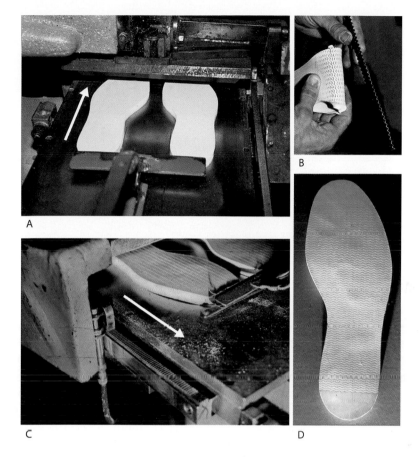

Figure 10.33 The process of siping outsoles.

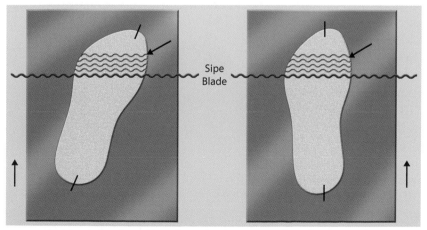

Slight variations in position of outsole when passing through siping machine

Figure 10.34 Variations can occur due to the positioning of the outsoles on the siping platform.

Restricting Sipe Blade to Specific Areas

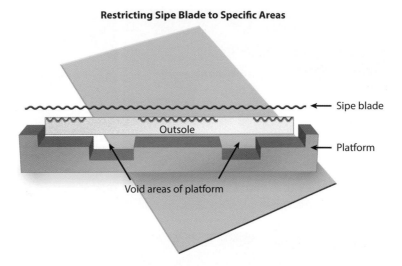

Figure 10.35 When a sipe blade strikes the outsole, it will not cut into it if there is not firm resistance such as a platform behind it. Special platforms can be made that have void areas where siping will not occur and other areas with firm backing where siping is desired.

angle of the cut row of sipes as it passes through the siping machine. True sipes cut into the outsole after molding will have slight variations for many reasons, including their precise direction and the completeness or incompleteness of each sipe cut.

A few siped shoe styles contain siping in different directions on the same outsole or are restricted within small areas. This can be achieved with multiple passes through the siping machine and/or the use of a form that restricts siping to certain locations. Siping platforms can be made to sipe specific portions of an outsole design. Figure 10.35 is a diagram to illustrate that an outsole, when struck by the sipe blade, will not be cut unless a firm backing provides resistance. Instead, the blade will simply push the rubber aside. In the diagram, the outsole is resting on a platform that has two void areas. When the sipe blade strikes the outsole, it will only cut a sipe in the areas that have a solid backing. In the areas that are void, the outsole will just be pushed away and remain unsiped.

True sipes cut into the outsole should not be confused with narrow molded grooves that imitate sipes and are part of the molded design of some shoes. Figure 10.36 depicts two shoes that have imitation sipes in contrast to the outsole shown in Figure 10.33. Imitation sipes result from thin blades of metal that are part of the mold design and will be reproduced identically on every outsole produced in a mold. It is easy to recognize the differences because molded imitation sipes remain open, while a true cut sipe stays closed unless the shoe is flexed.

Figure 10.36 Examples of imitation molded sipes that remain open.

Stitching

Some shoe construction involves the use of stitching to further secure the outsole to the upper. Stitching can pass directly through the outsole as shown in Figure 10.17 or within a pre-molded groove such as typically found in deck shoes. Figure 10.37 shows a stitching machine operator directing the stitching in a groove of a deck shoe. Operators control this process as they rotate and position the shoe. The speed of the stitching process slows down in the curved toe and heel as the operator strives to keep the stitching in the groove. The spacing between the stitches varies and their positional relationship to the molded design of a heel or

Figure 10.37 An operator guides the stitching needle along a molded groove in the shoe outsole while stitching it to the upper.

sole provides another variable. When stitching is very close together, variations are more difficult to notice, but when the stitching is farther apart, the variations are more noticeable. As shoes are excessively worn, particularly in the heel, the thread of the stitching can wear away but the holes where the stitches passed through the outsole remain. Figure 10.38 depicts the heels of a worn pair of shoes that demonstrates how the stitches are spaced differently. The forensic significance of this is the additional contribution it may make regarding the inclusion or exclusion of footwear when evidence of stitching is present in a crime scene impression.

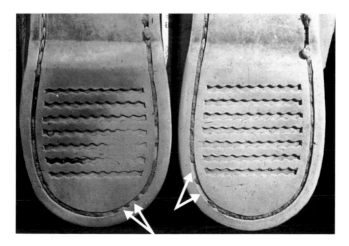

Figure 10.38 A pair of deck shoes with stitching in the perimeter grooves shows variations in the precise position and spacing of the stitches.

Key Words: Banbury mixer, die cut, cold cement process, expanded soling compound, injection molded, compression molded, open pour molding, rough rounder machine, spotting, sipes, microcellular soling compound, biscuit of rubber, preform

Key Points

1. A Banbury mixer is used to prepare formulations of various rubber compounds that can be solid or microcellular rubber. These are further milled prior to compression molding.
2. Compression molding is an open molding system, is used to produce the outsoles on the majority of athletic shoes, and is very versatile and used to produce all types and shapes of outsoles.
3. Injection molding is a closed molding system and can be used to make unit soles as well as directly attached molded outsoles to shoe uppers.
4. Some companies make only outsoles that they then sell to shoe manufacturers. These are often intentionally oversized and will require cutting or trimming when assembled to the uppers, resulting in variations between components of outsoles of the same size.
5. Most microcellular outsoles for athletic shoes are made in a specifically sized mold and do not vary from one molding to the next.
6. Siping and stitching are additional processes that can add variable features to an outsole.

Manufacturing Cutting Outsoles from Sheet Stock

11

The vast majority of shoes encountered in forensic examination are those formed in a mold cavity although, as covered in the prior chapter, some may be subjected to additional trimming or grinding after leaving the mold. For most, shoes with outsoles cut from sheet stock are only occasionally encountered in casework. When they are involved in an examination, it is necessary to recognize outsoles that are cut from sheet stock as well as to understand the impact that process may have on a forensic comparison. Outsoles are cut using two methods. One is known as die cutting and involves the use of a sharpened steel die that can cut through thin soling stock much like a cookie cutter. Much of this soling stock is molded in large sheets, approximately 30 × 40 inches in size, but the die can also cut freshly milled unvulcanized soling material known as calendered rubber. The second cutting method involves the Wellman outsole cutting machine that utilizes a knife blade that can only cut through soft freshly milled unvulcanized calendered rubber and not through the harder premolded sheets. Each of these cutting processes and the outsoles made using these processes involve their own sets of variables. This chapter will illustrate these two cutting methods and explain some of the manufacturing variables of each that can be significant in a forensic examination.

Die Cutting from Sheet Stock

A wide variety of outsole designs are typically produced and sold by separate companies in the form of premolded sheets. This is evident when you view the countless number of designs found on cut sole flip-flops and beach shoes. A considerable percentage of footwear sold under various casual brand names are fitted with die cut outsoles from sheet stock.[*] Die cutting from thin molded sheets of outsole materials employs the use of a hardened steel die, as shown in Figure 11.1. During the die cutting operation, the die, which has a sharpened edge, is positioned on the sheet of soling material. Using a hydraulic press, known in the industry as a "clicker" machine and shown in Figure 11.2, the die is forced through the material in a cookie-cutter fashion. Dies for left and right outsoles are made in each size and shape to accommodate the different styles of footwear a manufacturer produces. With many considerations including time needed to meet production quotas, the direction of the cut required, and attempts to get as many cuts out of a sheet as possible, the operator quickly cuts many outsoles. When die cutting thousands of outsoles, the exact position of the die cut will eventually be duplicated many times, simply because there is a limit to the number of different ways the die can be positioned over any particular pattern. The extent of the differences between outsoles depends on the repetitive nature of the design of the outsole material, how many times the pattern repeats on any particular sheet

---

[*] See casual footwear websites that include many flip flops and other footwear with cut outsoles, such as www.flipflopshops.com, www.quiksilver.com, www.reef.com, and www.sanuk.com.

Figure 11.1 A steel die positioned on a premolded 30 × 40 inch sheet of herringbone outsole material.

Figure 11.2 A steel die is positioned on a slab of calendered outsole material as the operator prepares to die cut an outsole using a hydraulic clicker machine.

of outsole material, and whether the specific design requires that the die be lined up in a certain direction. Cutting a herringbone or wave pattern would likely require that pattern run across the outsole, whereas cutting a random sheet of textured material would allow for cuts with the die positioned in any direction. An example of die cutting is illustrated in Figure 11.3 and shows how the slightest shifting of the die results in a change of the cut pattern, most noticeable where the design meets a reference point like the perimeter. Dies that have a reference mark on them, such as the die on the right of Figure 11.3, may indicate a factory process is being used to help orient the die with a specific part of a design. This would reduce variations between cuts and could result in close to mirrored pairs of outsoles. Each factory has its standards and protocol and may or may not use a procedure like this. When left and right shoe outsoles do not contain a pattern that mirrors each other, it is a significant indicator they may have been cut. Figure 11.4 illustrates an example on the left of a pair of sandals die cut from a sheet of wave pattern alongside a second left shoe of

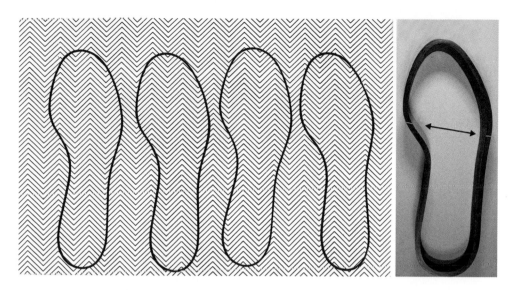

Figure 11.3 Drawing representing four identically sized dies over herringbone outsole sheet stock demonstrating how the cuts vary by changes in the die position. On the right is a steel die that has marks on its left and right sides (see arrow) that might be used to assist in the position of a cut by lining up those marks with a specific point on the outsole pattern.

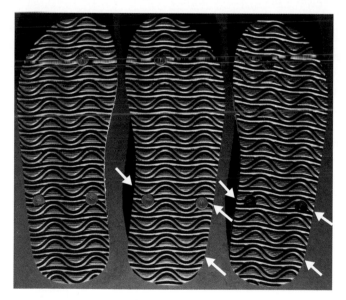

Figure 11.4 A pair of sandals on the left that were die cut from sheet stock and do not have mirrored left and right outsoles. On the right, a second left outsole of the same brand, style, and size shows how it varies from the left outsole of the pair. These variations are normal in outsoles die cut from outsole sheet stock.

the same brand and size. The pair of die cut sandals are clearly not a mirror image of one another. The left sandal of the pair (in the center) and the additional left sandal of the same size and brand (at the right) have clearly different cut features. The arrows indicate just a few of the clear distinctions. These variations are a product of the many possible positions of the die when cutting outsoles from premolded sheet stock. Similarities or dissimilarities in the position of the cut are useful in the inclusion or exclusion of shoes in a forensic

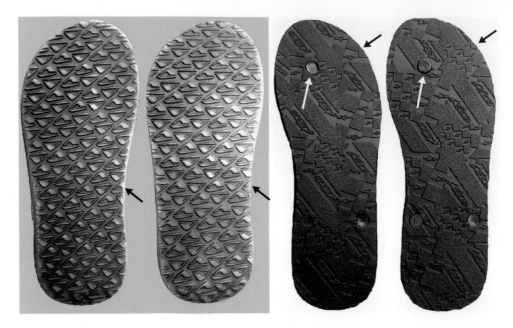

Figure 11.5 Two right size 10 and two left size 11 outsoles of different patterns, demonstrating the variations typically encountered in outsoles die cut from sheet stock. The more complex the pattern of the sheet stock, the easier it is to distinguish one outsole from others. One pair includes the addition of three plugs that penetrate the pattern (white arrows).

examination. If a crime scene impression corresponds with a portion or all of the outsole perimeter of a suspect shoe, that correspondence would be significant, as the majority of other shoes of that style would have different edge cut characteristics. It should be emphasized that the extent of that significance would be greater when the majority of the outsole is represented in contrast with a small partial or fragmented impression.

On the left side of Figure 11.5 are two right sandals of the same size and design. To the right is a pair of sandals of the same size and design with the addition of plugs that penetrate the outsole, as with the sandals in Figure 11.4. The plugs provide additional reference points and variations that occur in this type of construction. Countless sheet outsole patterns are produced for sandals. While it is true that pricier sandals typically have molded outsoles, there is also a good selection of high priced sandals with die cut outsoles. The cut sandals in Figure 11.4 were only a few dollars while those in Figure 11.5 were far more costly.

In one case study of this process, it was determined that 77 of the 78 Adidas sole units that were die cut from a calendered herringbone material were clearly distinguishable from each other. Only one was close to being duplicated but was still not a perfect match. The differences were mainly attributable to the precise position of the cut of each unit and the resulting change in the position and direction of the design around the perimeter.[*]

In another case study involving the comparison of 100 pairs of one size (size 10) Locals brand die cut flip-flops, no two outsoles shared identical features.[†]

---

[*] Birkett, J., Variations in Adidas "Kick" and related soles, MPFSL Report #34, Metropolitan Police Forensic Science Laboratory, June 1983.
[†] Kainuma, A., Manufacturing variations in a die-cut footwear model, *JFI*, 55(4):503–517, 2005.

The process of forcing a die through outsole material creates certain characteristic features. These include (1) left and right outsole pairs that are not mirror images, (2) a 90-degree cut edge that possibly may still contain some tool marks from the die; (3) or evidence of a grinding wheel used to smooth the outsole edges. In Figure 11.6, photograph #4 depicts the edge of an inexpensive sandal that still shows some striations (tool marks) caused by the die passing through that material. Normally the striations are ground away, as in the case of the edges of the two die cut sandals shown in photographs #1 and #2, each now reflecting the characteristics of the grinding wheel. When a microcellular material

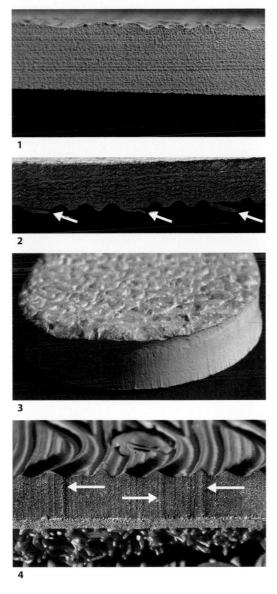

Figure 11.6 #1 and #2 show characteristic grind marks resulting from a grinding wheel used to smooth the edges. #2 also shows slight tears (arrows) that also accompany this process. #3 shows striations that evidence the passing of a die through soft calendered rubber that will be covered later. #4 shows the edge of a die cut sandal from calendered rubber stock that did not have its edges ground but still contains some evidence of striations caused by the die (arrows).

like that used in #1 and #2 is molded in a sheet, the portion that touches the mold forms an integral skin and that skin often does not grind away the same as the rest of the microcellular material. This is why little pieces of the skin are still attached as shown by the arrows in Figure 11.6 #2. Photograph #2 also shows evidence of slight tearing of the outsole because of buffing its edges with the grinding wheel. Photograph #3 in Figure 11.6 depicts striations from top to bottom on the edge of an outsole die cut from calendered material. Since the calendered outsole is soft, the edges cannot be ground to eliminate those features but these features will be covered later with a foxing strip and not visible on a finished shoe.

Although the edges of die cut outsoles often reflect evidence of striations of the grinding wheel as illustrated in Figure 11.6, this, in itself, does not prove an outsole was cut from sheet material. Many oversized microcellular molded outsoles and even some specifically sized direct-attach molded outsoles may have their edges ground either to smooth the midsole/outsole interface or simply for aesthetic reasons.

Although outsoles die cut from sheet goods provide plenty of basis for discriminating their precise design and dimension from the majority of other outsoles cut from that same design, there are cautions that an examiner should be aware of. First would be the mistake of misevaluating a shoe as being die cut from sheet goods when it was actually molded. When the left and right outsoles mirror each other, even if they only correspond very closely, it is highly likely they are molded, even though their edges may be covered with a foxing strip or ground smooth. When there is any doubt, contact with the manufacturer or locating other shoes of the same brand and style in the marketplace can provide additional information regarding the process being used.

Figure 11.7 illustrates die cuts made by two dies of different sizes and, although easily distinguishable around the majority of their perimeter, the arrow shows how they could still share a small area that is indistinguishable. This is of concern in cases where the crime scene impression is only partial. The examination of fragmented or very partial impressions may further limit conclusions in cases where the perimeter or some other reference point is not clearly represented in the crime scene impression. To illustrate this, the Figure 11.8 impression was made by one of the shoes in Figure 11.4 but it is so limited in size, it could have been made by virtually any outsole cut from a sheet of the same pattern.

Calendered Material

The calendering process was rather common at one time. It is mainly used in conjunction with the manufacture of waterproof boots, hunting boots, knee high and hip waders, industrial boots, firefighters' boots, and similar applications but can also be used to produce other outsoles. The process utilizes freshly made soling compound produced onsite in a Banbury mixer. The calendered rubber process and the accompanying shoe production processes involve many persons and are labor intensive. For this reason, this process is no longer used in factories in the US or in other countries where labor costs are high. In some countries with lower labor costs, this process is still used to produce certain types of boots and footwear that are then exported to other countries. The calendered process is summarized in Figures 11.9 and 11.10. The raw ingredients of the soling compound are mixed in a Banbury mixer, then fed into the back of the calendering machine. There a series of several smooth calender rollers will form the material into a continuous sheet of uniform thickness. The

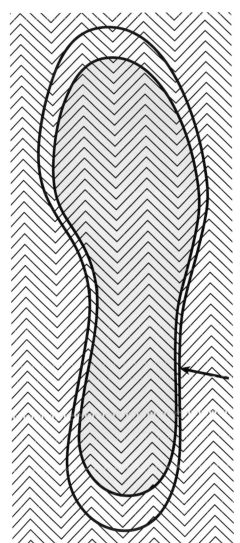

Figure 11.7 A drawing that demonstrates the possibility that a partial representation of a design could be duplicated, even when cut by dies of different sizes.

Figure 11.8 A fragment of an impression that contains no reference to other portions of the shoe that produced it and thus could possibly have originated from any sheet stock with the pattern like in Figure 11.4.

final calender roller contains an outsole design that is pressed into the warm and softened unvulcanized rubber. Design rollers are interchangeable so factories using this process will have many design choices and can produce a variety of outsole stock. Some rollers include those with a design in both the heel and sole areas, used to produce flat profile footwear. Other calender rollers will have a design in the sole area but only a smooth area in the heel.

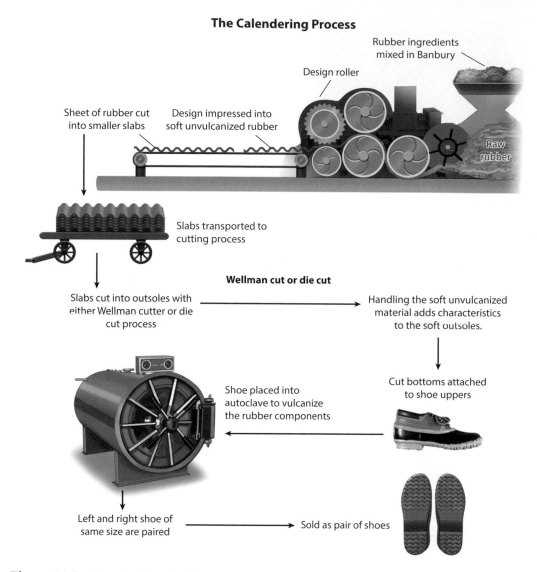

Figure 11.9 The calendered rubber process.

This smooth area is the location where a heel is later added. Because the design is pressed into the rubber as it passes beneath the rotating calender roller, outsoles cut from calendered stock will have a design direction that runs across the width of the outsole. This left to right orientation of the design is shown in the final image in Figure 11.9. Almost all calender roller designs also have some division between the heel and sole areas. This division often includes a strip of design that reads, "Made in USA," "Made in China," or similar wording as shown in Figure 11.10 and Figure 11.11. The lettering on the calender rollers is hand struck and will not be uniform in spacing and position. The newly formed outsole material exits the machine on a conveyer belt and is cut into workable slabs approximately 5 feet long. The unvulcanized calendered outsole stock is then taken to the cutting area.

Variations occur to outsole material produced with the calendering process. Many are very subtle and of little or no significance, but others are more obvious and are shown in Figure 11.11.

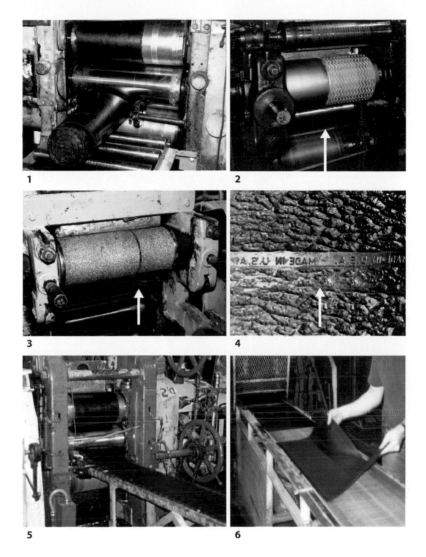

Figure 11.10 Photographs of the calendered rubber process: (1) Newly mixed rubber compound being fed in the back of the calendering machine. The stack of several steel calender rollers will produce a warm sheet of rubber of uniform thickness. (2 and 3) The final calender roller is the design roller. Some have no design in the heel area (#2), providing a place for a raised heel to be added later. Some have a design in both the heel and sole areas (#3). (4) Most calender rollers also have a narrow band of writing with the words "MADE IN USA" or "MADE IN CHINA," which will become part of the outsole design. (5) The newly pressed calender sheet stock exits the machine on a conveyer belt. (6) The stock is soft, warm, tacky, and unvulcanized and must be cut into slabs around 5 feet in length.

Variations in the calendering process include

- Variations in the rubber compound.
- Variations in the heating of the rubber before being pressed by the calender roller will affect the ability to impress the design. If not sufficiently soft and warm, the calender roller may not transfer complete design details.
- Stretching and distortions of the slabs of the warm and soft unvulcanized outsole material as it is handled coming off the conveyer belt.

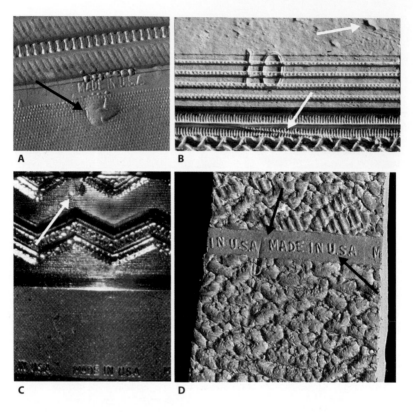

Figure 11.11 Damage on the calendered roller as shown in C will result in raised rubber as shown in A. Both B and D show examples of damage that occurs to the soft calendered rubber as it is handled or comes into contact with other objects. The bottom of photo C and the "Made in USA" lettering in D show the randomly stamped lettering typically found on a calendered roller.

- Indentation, scratches, or other damage to the actual design roller that will be transferred to the outsole material. Even though flaws in the design roller will repeat every 2½ to 3 feet with each rotation, they can appear on outsoles subsequently cut from this material in many different positions.
- Flaws or damage to the outsole material. Since the warm unvulcanized calender material is so soft, fingers, fingernails, or any object that touches it can inflict cuts and other random characteristics in the material.
- Any texture in the sole or calendered heel of a calendered outsole is directly from the textured design on the roller, although the position of that texture will vary on cut outsoles.

The Wellman Outsole Cutting Process

Another method of cutting outsoles is achieved with the Wellman outsole cutting machine, patented in 1931 by the Wellman Company of Medford, Massachusetts.* The Wellman outsole machine represents old technology. It cannot be used to cut premolded

---

* US Patent Office, patent 1,794,979, March 3, 1931.

Figure 11.12 The Wellman outsole cutting machine. The operator places a slab of calendered rubber on a sliding base. As he moves the slab across the table he uses a pedal to make the cuts of each outsole that occur when the table rises and the slab is pressed into a knife blade that travels around a template (A); a close view of the template and the knife blade (B); a template and a Wellman cut outsole of that size and shape (C).

sheet materials or premolded outsoles because those materials are already vulcanized and hardened. It is only used to cut soft, unvulcanized calendered rubber. Since the Wellman cut process can only be used with the unvulcanized calendered outsole material, any shoe made with this process will also include the variations associated with calendered rubber. The Wellman process is still used in some countries that have low labor costs and is usually reserved for specialized applications such as waterproof boots, hip boot waders, firefighters' boots, and boots used in cold and snowy environments. Although most boots are now made using molding processes, it is not uncommon to find boots made in this way in hunting and fishing specialty stores. Photographs of the Wellman outsole machine, knife blade, and template are provided in Figure 11.12. During use, the operator advances the slab of outsole material by hand along the table and with each cut uses a foot pedal to cause the table to rise up. The upward movement of the table presses the calendered material against the template, holding it firmly in place while the knife blade punctures the outsole material and rapidly travels around the template, cutting the outsole. An experienced operator can quickly guide and move a slab of calendered outsole material through the machine, cutting 6 to 10 outsoles in seconds. The end result of the methods and procedures used in this process is similar to those that occur in the die cutting method resulting in variations of the precise position of the cut. Any cut outsole will be distinguishable from most others. The templates dictate the shape and size of each outsole.

Figure 11.13 depicts a slab of calendered material where seven outsoles were cut using the Wellman outsole machine. The unvulcanized material is sticky; thus, after cutting the outsoles they must be pulled from the slab by hand. This particular slab passed beneath

Figure 11.13 A slab of calendered material after the Wellman machine cut seven outsoles. On the bottom are enlarged portions of the first and last outsoles. The "10" was pressed into each outsole during the cutting process. Because the slab passed beneath the cutting head of the Wellman machine at a slight angle, the position of the "10" on each outsole shifted position slightly.

the cutting head at a slight angle evidenced by the shift in the position of the numeral 10 size designation on the first outsole cut, in contrast with the numeral 10 in the last outsole cut. The numeral 10 was pressed into the soft outsole material by the template at the time of each cut. Passing the slab at different angles affects the precise pattern of the outsole cut concerning its features more noticeable around its perimeter.

Assembling the Wellman Cut Calendered Outsoles

Some calender rollers are designed to produce outsole material thicker in the heel area providing a slightly raised heel, while others produce material with a flat profile of the same design for the entire outsole. And some are plain with no design in the heel area providing space to add a heel. Heels of the same design can be die cut from calendered material sheet stock or a molded heel from another source can be used. Figure 11.14 depicts four Wellman boots with calendered outsoles. The top two boots have heels that were die cut from solid calendered stock. The other two have molded heels evidenced by their straight edges. Usually if a heel is molded, it will reflect a mold number. One boot has a small piece of string protruding from the front of the molded heel. Because molded heels often have air cavities on their reverse side, the air within that cavity will expand when the assembled shoe is placed in an autoclave, increasing the pressure and causing the heel to separate from the outsole. The string, which is laid across the heel area before the heel is pressed into position, prevents this by equalizing the air pressure. Figure 11.15 depicts a bottom view of Wellman boots with heels that were die cut from solid calendered stock and thus are not mirror images of one another as a pair of molded heels would be. Figure 11.16 shows

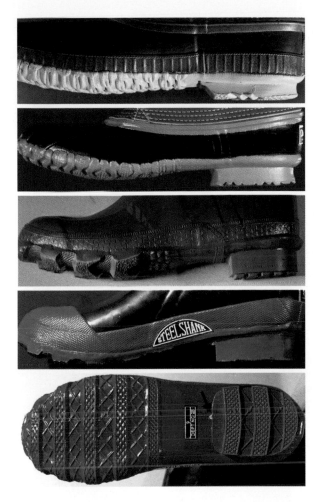

Figure 11.14 Four boots with Wellman cut outsoles. The top two have die cut heels from calender stock. The bottom two boots have molded heels that have very straight sides and edges. Note that at the very bottom string (arrows) is sometimes used with molded heels to equalize pressure created in the air pockets of the back of the molded heel when the boot is placed in the autoclave.

an enlarged area of the lettering on these boots. Note the characteristic irregularity of the position of the repeating words "MADE IN USA" that cross this area. The irregular position of the lettering is due to the fact that a calender roller has these words hand stamped repeatedly many times around its circumference, and when an outsole is randomly cut, the positions of these letters vary considerably from one outsole to the next. If a shoe has lettering that appears like the drawn example on the bottom of Figure 11.16, with only one repetition of the words neatly positioned in the center of the outsole, it would not be a calendered outsole but a molded outsole that was mimicking the calendered method.

A worn pair of Wellman boots shown in Figure 11.17 illustrates variations in the differences in the precise cut of the left and right calendered outsoles: the repeating words "MADE IN CHINA," as shown with the top arrows, the hand-cut and hand-positioned labels with the size, the positions of the string beneath each molded heel (bottom arrows), and the varied positions of the molded heel. It is noted that a string is not necessary on heels that are solid rubber.

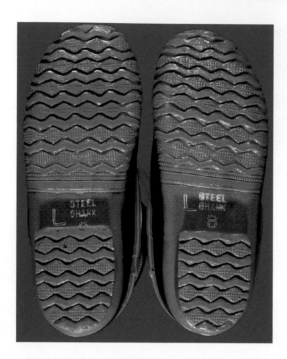

Figure 11.15 A pair of Wellman cut boots with calendered outsoles, and with heels that were die cut from the same calendered stock. The die cut calendered heels are not mirror images of each other and are easily distinguished from a molded heel. Note also the variance in the relation of the heel/outsole positioning between left and right boots.

Figure 11.16 Enlargements of the portion of the boots from Figure 11.15 show the random repeating words "MADE IN USA," which are typical of outsoles cut from calendered stock. Molded imitations of the process also occasionally include similar words, but they would be a singular repetition of the words centered in the middle of the outsole (bottom example).

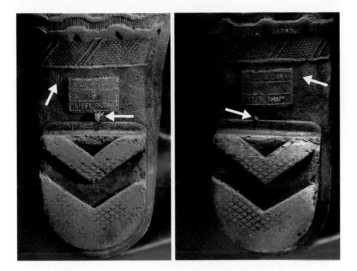

Figure 11.17 A pair of worn Wellman cut boots showing the random words "MADE IN CHINA," the pieces of string beneath the molded heels, and the hand-placed rubber size indicator. Also, note the random cuts of the outsole pattern do not mirror one another.

Once the Wellman outsoles are cut from the calendered material, they are combined with upper components. The various unvulcanized upper components are sticky and will adhere to one another. To further secure the components together until they are bonded during vulcanization, some factories will use a stitching wheel, shown in the top left picture in Figure 11.18. The stitching wheel has raised ribs that create linear indentations that press the soft rubber components together. Evidence of these marks is often found in boots where a stitching wheel was used, as shown by the arrows in Figure 11.18. Later this boot will be placed in an autoclave, where under heat and pressure, the various rubber components of the boot will be vulcanized and permanently bonded together. There are many boot designs in the marketplace that in one way or another imitate features of the Wellman cut calendered boot design. Figure 11.19 shows a molded boot outsole that imitates the transverse sole design typical of calendered rubber but clearly does not contain any of the characteristics of the Wellman cut or calendered outsole process.

Variations in Wellman Cut Outsoles

Many variables can occur during the Wellman cut outsole process as noted here:

- Since Wellman cut outsoles must be cut from the calendered outsole material, some or all of the calendered rubber variables may also apply.
- Variations in the precise cut of the outsole. These would include the position of the cut, which is eventually repeated but differs from most other cut outsoles. These are influenced by the random starting position with each slab that is cut, the size and shape of the template, and the position and angle of the slab as it passes beneath the cutting head.

Figure 11.18 A stitching wheel helps press together the soft unvulcanized rubber components while at the same time producing evidence of its linear indentations, as seen on a finished shoe indicated by the arrows.

Figure 11.19 A molded boot outsole with an outsole design that appears similar to a calendered rubber design.

- The choice of heels that are used. If heels are die cut from calendered material, their precise cut features will be varied from one cut heel to the next. If the heels used are molded, there will be variations in mold source and possible texture differences on the heel and variations in the position of the string, if used.
- The position and angle of any heel, calendered or molded, will vary because it is positioned there by hand.
- With some manufacturers, a rubber label or stamp will be added to denote the size. This will be done by hand and thus its position on the outsole will vary.

Someone very familiar with the Wellman outsole process and calendered rubber can easily recognize footwear made in this way as distinguished from molded outsoles. For those not as familiar, refer to Figures 11.14 through 11.18 and note the following characteristics that are good indicators of this process:

- Calendered Wellman cut boots will have the outsole design either wrapped around the edge or beveled edges. The specific edge contours on the left and right shoes will not be identical. In contrast, a molded boot sole will have straight edges, complex molded edges, or edges that have been ground. You cannot grind the edges of calendered rubber outsoles.
- Many Wellman cut outsole boots will have heels that were added to blank areas of calendered sheet stock. Some heels may be die cut from calendered material and some may be molded. If a molded heel is used, its edges will be straight and it may have a mold number on it. A string may be present but not always. If the heel was die cut from calendered material, it will be irregular and will not have straight edges like those produced in a mold cavity. The edge of the heel's perimeter that touches the ground will not be a square edge but will reflect some irregular features that result as the die passes through the soft calendered material.
- The left and right boot outsoles will not be mirror images if cut from calendered material. If there are words across the outsole just forward of the heel area, they will be random and in different positions on the left and right outsoles.
- Other components such as rubber size labels, and foxing strips, if added, will be irregularly placed.
- Linear marks may be present on rubber components from the stitching wheel. The location of these marks will be irregular and different between the left and right boots.

Determining Whether a Shoe Outsole Is Molded or Cut

It should be noted that determining whether an outsole is cut or molded is not always necessary and is case dependent. In cases where that information is of possible relevance in the forensic examination, the manufacturer may be the best source to confirm the method of construction. Just be cautious when receiving this information, ask many questions, and perhaps request a sample or find some way you can confirm their information. While it may be important in some examinations to recognize the manufacturing method, it is equally important not to misinterpret one process for another and consequently overvalue the manufacturing characteristics of the shoe being examined. Since the great majority of shoe outsoles in the marketplace are molded and identical to thousands of others, it is easier to approach this process presuming the pair of shoes is molded, and then look to find evidence it is not.

In addition to the characteristic features of the die cut and Wellman cut processes and calendered material discussed previously, the following discussion is provided to assist in identifying features that will indicate if outsoles on any footwear are from sheet goods, are molded in a specific size, or are molded in an oversized configuration and then cut or ground.

Characteristics of molded shoe outsoles that you would not find in cut outsole sheet goods nor in calendered rubber include detailed molded logos or logo areas, varying and complex depths in the outsole design, multiple colored outsoles, continuous molded borders, and asymmetrical outsole designs. Sheet goods are normally plain, symmetrical, not very thick, and usually absent of any lettered information unless it is the type that repetitively repeats as part of the outsole pattern.

The Outsoles

When looking at outsoles, first examine the pair to see if they are mirror images of one another. Molded outsoles are designed on a computer; thus the left and right outsoles will be exactly the same except for their orientation, unless they have been cut or modified in some way. If they are mirror images of each other, that is almost certain proof they are molded. If they are molded outsoles that have been cut or modified slightly, and/or if their edges have been ground, they will still be almost mirror images of each other. On the other hand, outsoles cut from sheet stock will have variations in the position and angle of the cut and usually will not mirror each other in multiple ways.

Look at the Edges of the Outsole

If the edges of an outsole have molded features, they have remained unchanged and will be the same as others from the mold. In order for any variations to exist, their edges would have to reflect evidence of cutting and/or grinding, unless covered with a foxing strip that prevents viewing this. Figure 11.20 depicts the edges of a dozen shoes. Numbers 9 and 11 show evidence of cut and/or ground edges. In addition, their outsoles are not mirror images of each other, and they were die cut from sheet goods. Number 10 has a foxing strip covering its edges but the shiny edge of a portion of the molded sole was evident and the left and right outsoles were the same; thus the outsoles were molded. All of the other shoes in Figure 11.20 have molded edges and are not cut outsoles.

In Chapter 10, a photograph of a Nike Cortez was provided in Figure 10.24 with a commonly encountered wedge-shaped profile. As explained in Chapter 10, the Nike Cortez outsole was combined with midsole components, then die cut to a specific size, followed by the grinding of the edge to make the three parts uniform and to create the wedge-shaped profile. In many instances, as the edges of molded outsoles are ground, very small portions are missed and therefore still retain their sheen from the mold. The ground edge of the wedge-shaped outsole in Figure 11.21 reveals small portions of the original shiny untouched skin from the molded outsole that were missed by the grinding wheel, showing that this outsole was molded and not cut from a sheet or oversized blocker.

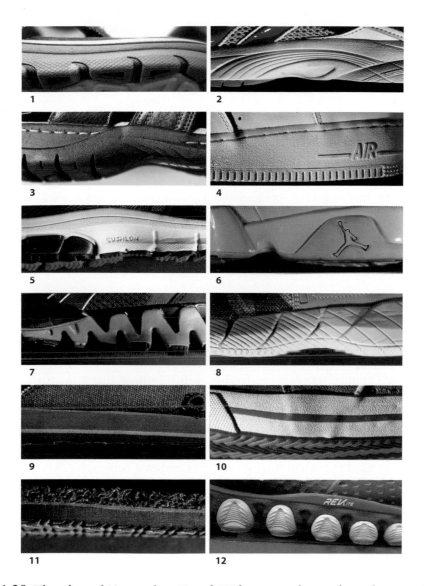

Figure 11.20 The edges of 12 outsoles. #9 and #11 have outsoles cut from sheet goods and the edges have been ground. #10 has an outsole wrapped with a foxing strip but small portions of the edges of the matched molded outsoles are still partially visible. All of the other examples show molded edges that represent the tremendous variety of molded outsoles that come from a mold cavity and are unchanged.

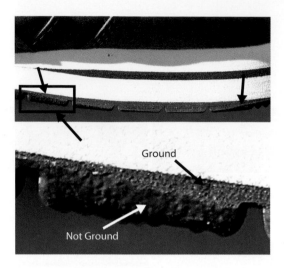

Figure 11.21 An outsole midsole combination that has been ground to make the edges uniform. A few tiny areas, one shown by the arrow, were untouched by the grinding wheel and still evidence the glossy edge of the molded outsole and prove the outsole was molded.

Key Words: calendering process, Wellman outsole cutting machine, die cut, stitching wheel

Key Points

1. Die cutting is a method where outsoles can be cut from premolded sheets of outsole material or from unvulcanized calendered rubber.
2. Calendered rubber results from freshly milled rubber that runs through a calendered stack of rollers, the final roller containing the outsole design. It remains soft and easily stretched and thus may easily acquire random damage until finally vulcanized as a finished boot or shoe.
3. Wellman outsole cutting is achieved on the Wellman outsole cutting machine and can only be used to cut soft unvulcanized calendered rubber.
4. Shoes that possess cut soles potentially possess many variables from the cutting process, the assembly of the components, and the qualities and variability of the outsole materials used.
5. The majority of athletic footwear is molded and unchanged after it leaves the mold; however, examiners should be familiar with characteristics that indicate an outsole was made using a cut process because of the potential significance in examinations that involve cut outsoles.

Outsole Design and Dimension 12

Author's Note: In this and other chapters, several examples are provided regarding outsole designs and how they may or may not change in dimension in various sizes, as well as information about other features that may be significant during a forensic examination. It should be noted that there are thousands of designs in the marketplace and these change constantly. Many designs closely resemble examples provided in this book, but in fact may be counterfeit, look-a-likes, or different brands produced with different manufacturing methods. Over time, a manufacturer may even reintroduce an older design and change the molds or methods used to produce it. The examples provided in this book do not represent all footwear outsoles that are produced, but are provided as illustrations to help understand the information you may need to know or investigate about the shoes you are examining.

Examination between crime scene impressions and footwear should always begin with comparison of the design and physical size of that design that stem from the numerous methods and materials used by manufacturers to produce outsoles. It is the natural order in which an examination of this type should proceed and there are inherent dangers for an examiner to hastily look for characteristics of wear or randomly acquired features prior to properly going through the evaluation of design and dimension. Correspondence of the outsole design and physical dimensions alone does not provide a basis for identification; however, because of the thousands of outsole designs in the public marketplace, it greatly reduces the remaining population of footwear that could have produced an impression. Likewise, confirmed differences in the class characteristics of an outsole design and/or dimension provide a basis for exclusion.

Outsole Design

The footwear industry defines the bottom unit of a shoe as its outsole. Athletic and other synthetic footwear outsoles almost always include some design or pattern for purposes such as aesthetics, function, and/or traction. Outsole design can be defined as "a specific pattern or arrangement of design elements on an outsole typically associated with a manufacturer and having a name and/or style number."* For purposes of discussion of outsole designs in this chapter, a reference to a particular outsole design will include both its basic design as well as any texture that may be replicated in a crime scene impression and would therefore be part of the forensic examination.

---

* Terminology used in the forensic examination of footwear evidence, Scientific Working Group for Shoe Print and Tire Track Evidence, 2013.

There are many thousands of different outsole designs in the public marketplace and new designs are constantly being purchased while older ones are discontinued. Although most of those designs are distinguishable, some are remarkably similar to others, particularly with the frequent use of basic design components such as parallel lines, wave, or herringbone patterns and lug-type shapes found on shoes produced by different manufacturers.

Design and dimensional characteristics of any outsole are so intertwined they are almost always compared simultaneously. Those cases where no scale is present in the photograph, where detail is limited, and where impressions are very fragmented or partial, can severely restrict the examination and the resulting level of association or disassociation between a crime scene impression and shoe.

Physical Size of the Design

The physical size and shape of the design should not be confused with the manufacturer's label shoe size, but refers to the dimensions, shapes, spacing, and relative positions of design elements on the outsole. Shapes and dimensions of specific design elements on an outsole may or may not vary throughout the size range. When a shoe size gets larger, there must either be more of the design to fill the larger size or the dimensions of that design must increase.

Design–Size Relationship

The design–size relationship is the relationship between the outsole design and physical dimensions of that design as a shoe outsole progresses from smaller sizes to larger sizes. Although it may not be possible in every case to know the way a shoe's content changes from one size to the next without contacting the manufacturer, it is essential for an examiner to understand the concept of the design–size relationship. Shoe outsoles of any one design must change in some way as they get bigger or smaller, e.g., size 12 outsoles cannot have the same total design and dimensional content as size 10 outsoles. How this changes from one size to another is not the same for all shoe designs. Examples 1 through 4 show how an outsole design varies as it is graded by the manufacturer throughout its size range. Examples 5 and 6 describe ways an outsole design may vary in its dimensions based on additional events that occur during the manufacturing processes.

Example 1: Proportional Grading

Some shoe outsoles are simply graded proportionally throughout the size range like photographic enlargements in that their content remains the same and only the dimensions of that content change with each increase in half size. Figure 12.1 depicts two examples of this, one showing two Nike Air Jordan 9 Retro outsoles of different sizes and the other showing two Skechers outsoles of different sizes. Impressions of an outsole produced by shoes graded in this way can be distinguished only by their physical size differences and not changes in the content of the design. The heel-to-toe difference in one half size is approximately 4.23 millimeters. For this type of design–size relationship, the ability to accurately distinguish different sizes becomes increasingly difficult when an impression

Figure 12.1 Examples of two outsole designs that are graded proportionally. They each contain the same content in all sizes.

is partial or is only represented through inaccurately scaled photographs. In those cases, it may not be possible to distinguish an impression as having been made by a particular size versus an adjacent size of the same design. One case example involved a photographed impression of a Nike Air Jordan 9 Retro shoe impression on a counter with an L-shaped scale. The scale did not reflect a 90-degree angle but was off by 3–4 degrees. The impression in that photograph did not conform well to the shoe being examined. Fortunately, a lift was made and represented the impression accurately. The known impression and shoe corresponded precisely with the lift.

Example 2: Outsole Design Element Sizes Remain the Same and Thus Larger Sizes Include More of Those Design Elements

Some molded outsoles have design elements that remain the same size throughout the entire size range. This may be because a single template was used when making molds for every size or because during the computer design of the outsole, it was decided to keep the design element size constant for all sizes. As the size of the shoe is graded to smaller to larger sizes, more of those design elements will be needed to fill the additional space within the shoe's perimeter. An example of this exists in the Bruno Magli design in Figure 12.2 where one template was used to hand-mill the design elements on each mold throughout the entire size range. As a consequence, each mold size is easily distinguished. Variations are most apparent at the point where the design elements intersect the perimeter border of the sole and heel. Even partial impressions of adjacent sized heels of this design reveal obvious visual differences. Figure 12.3 illustrates differences between a European size 45 heel print on the left and the slightly larger European size 46 heel print on the right. In any outsole where the design element size remains the same throughout the size range, it provides very useful information in the comparison process. In this specific example that was a product of hand-milled mold making, the directional shape of the design elements and other variables prevent the left and right outsole designs from being mirror images, even though they were made in mold pairs.

In outsoles cut from identical premolded sheets of outsole stock where the design is usually basic and remains the same, the same net result occurs, meaning larger outsoles will

Figure 12.2 An example of two Bruno Magli compression-molded outsoles that contain a design element that originated from one template and therefore remains the same dimension throughout the entire shoe size range. The result is that smaller sizes of this shoe will have fewer design elements, with larger sizes requiring more, resulting in a different interfacing of those elements most noticeably around the border.

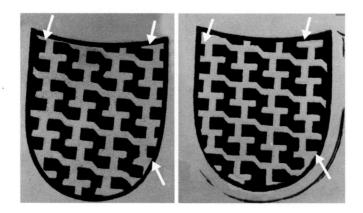

Figure 12.3 Two adjacent sized heels of the shoe design in Figure 12.2, showing how easily their impressions can be differentiated.

require more of that pattern than smaller outsoles. Variations in the positions of the die cuts, as discussed in Chapter 11, further complicate shoes cut from sheet stock. Fragmented or partial impressions may be indistinguishable from other sizes. This was illustrated in Figures 11.7 and 11.8. It is also possible that not all sheet stock of a particular design is exactly the same. Two die cut sandals of the same size and Locals brand in Figure 12.4 originated from very similar sheet stock but the square pattern of one is slightly larger than the other, thus the number of squares in one is different than in the other. Further examples of outsoles cut from sheet stock are seen in two right die cut Skechers outsoles in Figure 12.5. In this example, variations in these two right outsoles of the same brand and size include those that occur along the left and right perimeter borders, and in the varied quantities of

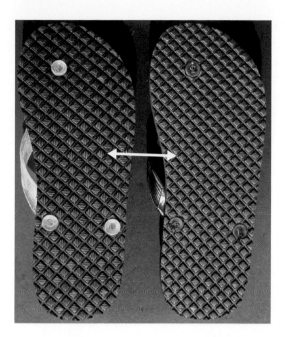

Figure 12.4 Outsoles of the same size cut from sheet stock often originate from the same or indistinguishable molded sheets. In this example, the die cut outsoles originated from sheets of a similar pattern, but one having a square design slightly larger than the other.

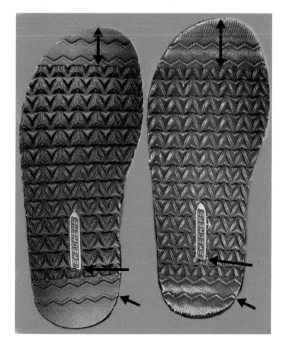

Figure 12.5 Outsoles of the same style and size die cut from sheet stock contain many variations.

design in the toe and heel. Thus variables are not only because the shoe sizes are different but resulted from different positions of the die as each outsole was cut. Imagine the mistake that could be made if a crime scene impression represented the forward half of the outsole on the right, and an investigator or examiner compared the length of the toe area (arrow) with shoes in a store to estimate size. In addition, in this example, a Skechers logo has been added, providing another reference point, but its position does not seem to be associated with any change in size.

Example 3: Some Molded Designs Involve a Portion That Remains Constant in Size While Others Portions Change in Size

The classic K-Swiss Luxury Edition outsoles shown in Figure 12.6 consist of sizes 10 and 11.5. This style includes their "brick" design, two flex grooves across the ball area, and the K-Swiss logo. As the outsole sizes increase, the size of the bricks remains constant; thus, a larger size shoe will include more of the bricks than the smaller sizes, similar to the previous Bruno Magli example. But in this example, the size of and the distance between the flex grooves increase as sizes get larger. As a consequence, the brick design intersects differently with the flex grooves as well as the logo and perimeter border with each size. A logo such as the K-Swiss shield might remain constant in size or be gradually increased like the flex grooves. If the crime scene impression includes the brick design and parts of the other design elements and border, it becomes easy to distinguish one size from another. Even if many molds were made for a particular size of this design, if produced using CAD–CAM, these features would be the same for all molds of that size. Only any texture added later would distinguish them, whereas a combination of these features provides great assistance in examination and sizing. Dealing with fragmented impressions that only include the brick pattern would mean that any size shoe of this design could

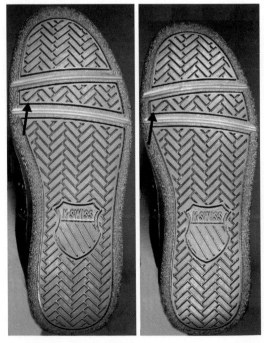

Figure 12.6 Two outsoles of different sizes where the basic brick-shaped design element stays constant throughout the entire size range but the flex grooves are graded to increase in size and distance apart with each additional shoe size. The exact way in which the bricks intersect both the border and the flex grooves and logo area will differ in each size.

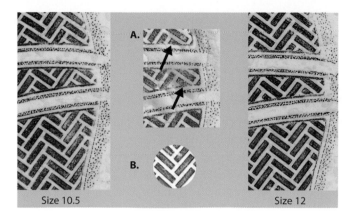

Figure 12.7 A sample case application of a shoe like that in Figure 12.6. Impression "A" can be excluded from the size 10.5 and 12 examples based on differences in the brick design intersections, and impression "B" could have come from any shoe size of this design.

have produced it. To illustrate this, two simulated crime scene examples of this design are provided in Figure 12.7. Impression A includes part of the border and two flex grooves and the constant sized brick design. This allows for easy exclusion of both the size 10.5 and 12 K-Swiss shoes. But since the brick sizes are the same throughout the size range, the fragmented impression B could have originated from the size 10.5 or size 12 shoes as well as any other size with that brick design. In an actual case, a comparison that involved impression B and this brick design of the K-Swiss shoe, a conclusion that impression B corresponded in design and physical size might be technically correct, but would be misleading and therefore other possible sources must be qualified as potentially coming from any K-Swiss shoe of that design.

Another example of this is found in the Converse Chuck Taylor All Star (CCTAS) design discussed in Chapter 10. The dimensions of the diamond/square design shown in Figure 12.8 are constant through the adult size range. Locations where that design intersects other design components around its perimeter, including the logo area, the parallel

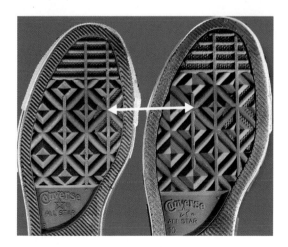

Figure 12.8 The Converse Chuck Taylor All Star square/diamonds are the same size throughout the adult size range, but as shoe sizes change, the number of those square/diamonds and how they intersect other design areas of the outsole will differ.

bars in the toe area and the perimeter border, offer good comparative information relating to the specific size or mold origin. Impressions that only contain the diamond/square pattern are much more limited.

Example 4: The Nike Air Force 1

The popular Nike Air Force 1 offers an example of a more complex outsole design. Shown in Figure 12.9, the compression-molded outsole design consists of a variety of design element shapes, including concentric circles in the heel and ball (C), a logo box area, curved toe and heels containing the stippled star pattern (A), and small rectangular shapes on the medial and lateral borders (B). Figure 12.10 includes a sample of Nike Air Force 1 soles sized 8 through 14. All sizes include 41 rectangular blocks along the medial border and 45 blocks along the lateral border. The size of these blocks will be smaller in smaller sizes and larger in larger sizes but detecting subtle differences between adjacent sizes would be difficult if not impossible. The new molds of this design were produced using an insert for the heel and toe areas of the mold, meaning that the stippled star pattern in all molds of a single

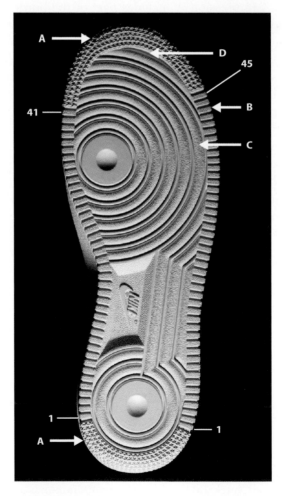

Figure 12.9 The Nike Air Force 1 outsole has separate areas that increase proportionally through the size range but in doing so, the different areas intersect differently.

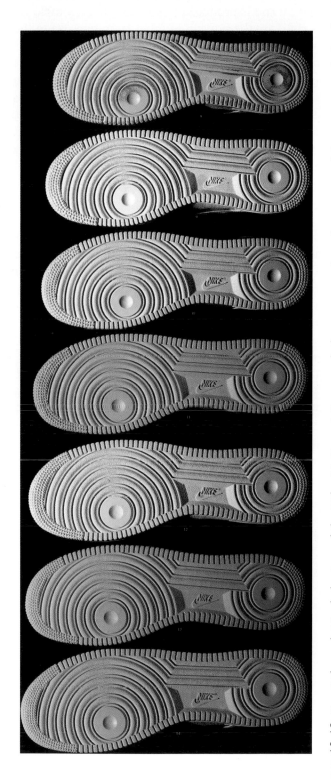

Figure 12.10 Size 3 through 14 whole sizes of the Nike Air Force 1. In general, they appear to be enlargements of the same exact design, but the individual design elements are enlarged separately and thus intersect each other slightly differently. This allows for some distinction between sizes although the differences are very subtle.

size will be identical. Acid-etch texturing covers the remaining areas of design like those labeled B and C in Figure 12.9 and is produced separately for each mold and thus unique to each mold. The curved rings are the same in number from one size to the next with the exception of minor variations where they intersect a different curvature of other components. An example would be at area D where some minor differences can be noted between sizes because the radius of the curvature of the toe is different from the radius of curvature of the concentric circles that intersect it. Other very subtle variations between sizes will occur at other junctures such as the intersection of the thin concentric circle ring at the top of the logo area as it intersects the curvature of the rectangular boxes on the medial side. Because the Nike Air Force 1 is very popular, there are extensive counterfeit versions— some that may not have the precise design–size relationships as the genuine Nike shoes.

Example 5: Oversized Solid Rubber Outsoles

Sometimes two identically sized and molded outsoles can undergo changes in the manufacturing process that modify portions of their original dimensional features. Chapter 10 discussed the process of using a rough rounder to cut excess outsole materials from the perimeter of oversized molded solid rubber boot soles, such as those in Figures 10.16 and 10.17. Variations in hand spotting of oversized outsoles followed by trimming away excess rubber around the outsole perimeter results in dimensional variations of the size of lug design elements around the perimeter. Six boots, all of the same brand, size, and design and made with that process, were depicted in Figure 10.18. The six pairs had varied dimensions of their peripheral lug sizes. Figure 10.19 listed various dimensional differences in the lugs of those boots. Examples from casework that clearly show dimensional differences in the toe lugs of two identically sized boots made using that same process are depicted in Figures 12.11 and 12.12. This type of variation, if represented in a partial print at the scene, could be very misleading regarding the size of the shoe that made it. Outsoles modified (cut) in this way may limit or prevent the use of dimensions of peripheral design elements of their outsoles as an accurate indicator of shoe size as a smaller outsole manufactured in

Figure 12.11 After being produced in a mold, outsoles were trimmed, resulting in significant altering of their perimeter design element sizes. The toe areas shown here are from a case example of two boots of the same brand, style, design, and size.

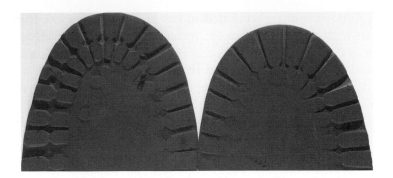

Figure 12.12 A case example of a pair of left and right boots where cutting or trimming likely resulted in different lug sizes in the toe.

this way could have larger peripheral design components than respective ones on footwear of a larger size. In addition, many boot outsoles of this type are not totally flat but rise up slightly around the perimeter, often not making full contact with the substrate and thus not leaving a full representation of the full dimensions of their lugs.

Example 6: Expanded Microcellular Materials (Blown Rubber)

Expanded or blown outsoles involve a type of microcellular compound that creates rigid air cells. Blown outsoles will expand as the compression mold is opened. The amount of expansion varies; thus, outsoles with expanded microcellular compounds must be die cut to their specific size to fit a shoe upper. Because of the varied expansion and because they are die cut after molding, specific outsole features and dimensions within the same size will vary. An example of expanded outsoles was discussed and illustrated in Chapter 10 regarding the Nike Cortez outsole. As part of that discussion, Figure 10.26 illustrated how the number of rows in one pair varied between the left and right shoes due in part to differences in expansion. Variations in the specific outsole design were also due to shifts in the position of the die cutting of each outsole. Thus, attempting to size this particular style based only on the number of rows of design would not be accurate. Although that example involved an athletic shoe, blown expanded microcellular outsoles are more commonly found in lightweight boot and dress shoe outsoles and rarely in athletic footwear.

The aforementioned six examples do not address every style of footwear or every aspect of the design/size relationship of outsoles, but are only intended to provide examples to create awareness that not all shoes change in one simple way as they are graded through the size range. Examinations that only include partial or fragmented impressions may be severely limited when considering conclusions of correspondence or noncorrespondence of design and dimension; however, in some cases, knowledge of how the design–size relationship works on a particular outsole design may enable a stronger conclusion even with partial impressions, such as was shown in Figure 12.7A.

Texture on Outsoles in Relation to Design and Physical Size

When attempting to associate a crime scene impression with a particular mold, texture is the most specific and reliable design feature because each mold has its own individually applied texture. Texture is often replicated in two-dimensional scene impressions. This level of detail has tremendous value in the inclusion or exclusion of footwear. The case example previously discussed and provided in Figure 9.26 enabled the conclusion that the suspect's shoe and the shoe that produced the crime scene impression originated from the same mold. Had the texture been different, it would have enabled the exclusion of the suspect's shoe.

In another case, a pair of size 9 shoes was seized during a search warrant more than a year after the crime. The shoes appeared unworn but were submitted for examination for comparison with an impression lifted from a counter at the crime scene. The lifted impression appeared to have been made by a shoe of much greater general wear but also had two small areas of texture that replicated themselves clearly in the impression. Comparison of the seized shoes confirmed the texture was completely different from that of the lifted impression, allowing for exclusion of the shoes. Later comparison of the texture in the crime scene impression with samples from another size 9 mold provided by the manufacturer enabled confirmation the impression was produced by size 9 shoes, but not the pair originally submitted. Another application of using texture was previously addressed in Chapter 9 and in Figures 9.27 and 9.28.

Additional Design Aspects of Interest

Additional design features discussed in prior chapters included variations in the stitching on the bottom of the outsole, irregularly applied foxing strips, fabric imbedded in the molded outsole, and the hand positioning of heel labels and toe guards. All of these features, once added, become part of the outsole design that produces an impression, and thus can be used to support inclusion or exclusion in forensic examinations.

What You Can Conclude from the Pair of Shoes You Are Examining

Most footwear outsoles are produced in molds and remain unchanged during their attachment to the upper. A small percentage of shoes do undergo some cutting, trimming, and/or grinding to adjust them to the size and outline of the uppers. Details of the edges of the outsoles combined with whether the specific design of the left and right outsoles are mirror images can provide considerable information regarding whether their outsoles were molded and unchanged, were molded and modified in some way, or were cut from sheet stock.

Shoes that have finished molded edges are evidence an outsole is a solid, nonexpanding material that has not been changed since it left the mold. This would also extend to athletic shoes where molded specific size outsole and midsole components were assembled in a cold adhesive process without any need for modification. Figure 12.13 shows a very small portion of an athletic shoe assembled using specific sized midsole and outsole components, requiring no cutting or ground edges or other type of modification. Evident in that illustration is the sheen of the edge of the black outsole showing it had not been cut or ground (1), traces of the flash from the black molded outsole that did not get fully trimmed before being glued to the red midsole (2), and traces of adhesive between the outsole and

Figure 12.13 An enlargement of the edge of a shoe with a specific sized molded outsole attached to a specific size molded midsole with the cold adhesive method. The original sheen of the molded outsole indicates it was not ground (1), a trace of flash corroborates it was molded (2), and traces of adhesive between the outsole and midsole (3) are evident.

midsole (3). Outsoles of shoes of the same size in both of these examples will, for all practical purposes, be identical except for any texture that might distinguish one mold source from another. The vast majority of synthetic soled shoes fit into this category. Microscopic examination of the edge characteristics of shoes reveal a variety of features useful in assessing the production methods and include characteristics such as contoured and complex molded edge geometry, molded logos and/or lettering, varied finishes and sheens that indicate original molded soles versus cut and ground soles, traces of flashing from molded soles, molded texture patterns, adhesives, and stitch marks. Shoes that have cut or ground edges combined with left and right outsoles that do not mirror each other indicate they have been produced from cut sheet stock, which can have class characteristic significance provided those respective features are clearly evidenced in the crime scene impression. It is important to repeat that the presence of ground edges alone does not mean the manufacturing process involved significant variations as some boots and shoes will have their edges ground simply for style reasons. Also be reminded that outsoles covered with foxing strips may be molded pairs or may be randomly cut. If part of the edge of the outsole can be seen, it may still be possible to determine if it was from sheet stock or was molded. Wellman made boot outsoles cut from calendered material have their own set of features that were covered in Chapter 11.

Forensic Significance of Design and Size

In the everyday examination of footwear impression evidence, a large percentage of comparisons are limited to levels of association that only include the design and/or physical size of that design. The number of different shoe outsole designs in the marketplace at any one time is extremely large. After attending many shoe trade shows and discussing this topic with individuals in the footwear industry, it became apparent that no one can provide any specific number of how many different designs actually exist at any time. It is safe to conclude that the number of shoe outsole designs in the marketplace easily exceeds 10,000 and is very likely a much greater number. A 1986 publication of the Footwear Industry of America contained approximately 10,000 brand and trade names.[*] Common sense would dictate that most if not all of those brands produced more than one outsole design. One visit was made by the author to a New York City shoe fair that hosted over 1600 vendors that each designed and manufactured many different styles of shoes and outsoles. Current popular Internet sites for shoe sellers contain many thousands of footwear outsole designs.[†] For competitive and marketing reasons, all footwear producers are constantly adding new designs as old ones are discontinued, a practice that is very evident to consumers who routinely shop for their own footwear. It is noted that the number of designs would significantly increase if each mold with its own distinct texture was categorized as a separate design.

It was recently reported that 2.31 billion pairs of shoes were sold in the US, and that, on average, every American spent $234 on their purchase of 7.5 pairs of shoes in 2013.[‡] US imports accounted for approximately 98.6% of the US footwear market, with China providing 8 out of 10 pairs sold. Equally important, at any one time, many individuals keep at least some of their shoes for more than one year; thus, the number of footwear for any general population will be quite a bit larger than the number of shoes sold during one year alone. Someone who owns numerous pairs of shoes may not wear each pair equally, however; on average, they will not wear out any one pair of their shoes as quickly as someone who only owns one or two pairs. How long a person keeps any particular pair of shoes will depend on other factors as well such as their activities, how often they wear specific shoes, and the substrates over which they walk. The large number of shoes sold per year combined with shoes purchased in prior years equates to many billions of shoes in the US.

The significance of this relates to how common a particular design and dimension of footwear are in the public venue. One study involved the collection of 1607 shoe prints from random persons visiting various motor vehicle license offices across Texas in 2004 and 2005.[§] The fact that virtually every driver from all walks of life must visit these facilities to renew his or her license provided a good adult population sampling of footwear for this study. Impressions of the right shoe of each contributor were compared with the others collected in the study. Most were of distinctly different designs, but when the design was similar, other features like the variations in the precise pattern of die cut sandals or differences in the texture pattern of molded shoes were used to determine if any two were totally identical in design and size. Out of the 1607 shoe prints collected, there were only a few that were similar in both design and physical size. Of those, general wear could be used to differentiate between them.

In 2006, a collection in Alaska of the shoe impressions of 353 persons was made at the local motor vehicle department over a period of six weeks.[¶] Only two pair had outsoles of the same design and size.

[*] The International Directory of Footwear Brand and Trade Names, Footwear Industries of America, Arlington, VA, 1986.
[†] Including but not limited to www.zappos.com, www.dsw.com, www.famousfootwear.com, and www.shoebuy.com.
[‡] American Apparel and Footwear Association, Shoe Stats Report, 2014.
[§] Parent, S., The significance of class associations in footwear comparisons, Pattern and Impression Symposium, Clearwater, FL, August 2010.
[¶] Hammer, L., and Amick, J., personal communication, 2006.

In 2012, a study involved the review of 402 known footwear impressions produced by footwear submitted for examination in a state laboratory. They were compared to determine if they could be distinguished based on only design and size. Only two were found to be the same specific design and size, but those were easily distinguished by their general condition of wear.[*]

Another study involved the shoes of 1276 persons at a scientific exhibition, including the design, style, and size of the shoes as well as noting the wearer's age.[†] The study concluded the most common outsole pattern was present in only 1% of the population studied. Several patterns were found more than once, but the published paper did not report if any of those patterns were of the same or different size or could otherwise be distinguished. The collection from this group at the scientific exhibition was obviously not as random as the collection of footwear sampling in the cited Parent study. Of additional interest in the Hannigan study was a breakdown of the brand name information such as the fact that the Nike brand was extremely weighted in the 16–25 age group, while the Ecco and Clark brands were most weighted in the over-35 age group. This observation indicates that favoritism of brands or types of shoe styles by certain demographic groups and ages may play some role in the choice of footwear that individuals wear.

The above information and studies support the significance of conclusions of correspondence between the design and dimension alone of a scene impression and shoe. The large number of footwear designs in the marketplace combined with the variety of outsole sizes means only a small fraction of 1 percent of those in the general population will own a pair of shoes of any particular design and dimension. When the comparison involves the additional design feature of texture or other mold features, that percentage is even smaller. Cases involving shoe designs that are not major brands and thus are less common and/or those shoe designs that have not been sold for many years may have even more significance. Exceptions to this might be possible in those cases involving very popular designs among certain groups or individuals. These may include gangs, or simply the popularity of certain designs by location (e.g., beach sandals at a particular Florida high school). Examples of shoes that have been popular and owned more frequently include long-standing popular styles like the Converse Chuck Taylor All Star, Nike Air Force 1, or various Nike Air Jordan shoes. Even then, most if not all of their footwear would still likely be distinguishable due to different sizes and other variables.

A more recent study involving 1511 shoeprints taken from students at universities in New Zealand and Australia categorized them in pattern groups. The study concluded that pattern frequencies vary from location to location, e.g., a sole pattern common in one location may not be as frequent in another location.[‡] The conclusion in this study mischaracterized Bodziak as advocating for an assessment of sales figures. What this author clearly has stated is that correspondence of design and physical dimension of a suspect's shoe outsole with a crime scene impression significantly reduces the remaining population of shoes that could have produced it; however, sales or distribution figures, nor percentages

[*] Gross, S., Jeppesen, D., and Neumann, C., The variability and significance of class characteristics in footwear impressions, *JFI*, 63(3):332–351, 2013.

[†] Hannigan, T. J., Fleuey, L. M., Reilly, R. B., O'Mullane, B. A., and deChazal, P., Survey of 1276 shoeprint impressions and development of an automatic shoeprint pattern matching facility, *Sci. Justice*, 46(2):79–89, 2006.

[‡] Benedict, I., Corke, E., Smith, R., Maynard, P., Curran, J., Buckleton, J., and Roux, C., Geographical variation of shoeprint comparison class correspondences, *Sci. Justice*, 554(2):335–337, 2014.

of designs in police databases have any significance at all in the physical comparison or in the final weight of that comparison.[*]

What Do "Design and Size" Mean to the Defense and Prosecution?

When the evidence does not permit exclusion or identification but does demonstrate some level of association exists between a scene impression and shoe, it often leaves both the prosecution and defense with different opinions of what this might mean to their case. To the prosecution, there is a high degree of significance in the conclusion that the accused's footwear is capable of having produced the crime scene impression, considering the fact that thousands of shoe outsole designs are available in the full range of sizes. In other words, of all the shoes the accused could have been wearing, they had a pair of shoes that corresponded in design and/or physical size with the impressions recovered from the scene. Not surprisingly, jurors are usually impressed by this conclusion as it can be visually shared with and explained to them. On the other hand, the defense attorney may rebut this argument, pointing out the fact that this could merely be a coincidence as thousands of shoes were sold with that particular design and size and any of those could have produced the impression at the scene. This is true and in any written or stated opinions of the examiner, they should clearly point this out and state they are not identifying the shoe, and other shoes of that design and size cannot be excluded as a possible source.

There have been occasions where conclusions of a lower level of association are misstated. One example would include those very limited examinations of fragmented or small partial impressions, particularly those of commonly used designs such as herringbone or parallel lines, or those where all sizes of a shoe design could have produced a particular partial impression. Most egregious of those examples would be the case where a mark or impression lacked sufficient detail to conduct any meaningful comparison, or might even be so insufficient as to determine the mark was even produced by footwear, yet experts might be asked in court if they could exclude the accused's shoes. Of course, the question is not a fair one, as under those circumstances, the examiner could not exclude those shoes or the shoes of anyone else, but nevertheless the inference to the jury might suggest the shoes of the accused made the impression.

Are Any Shoes "One of a Kind" When New?

Although not common, there are manufacturing processes that result in outsoles that are "one of a kind." So the answer to this question is technically yes, but very few footwear or processes fall into this category. Outsoles made from raw, naturally coagulated rubber, known as crepe rubber soles, are considered one of a kind due to the random crinkled texture that occurs during the coagulation process. A natural crepe rubber sole and an enlarged area of that sole are provided in Figure 12.14. Once much more common, true natural crepe soles are now sold in very limited numbers, are expensive, not used on athletic footwear, and not typically encountered in casework. Much more common is an

---

[*] Bodziak, W. J., *Footwear Impression Evidence: Detection, Recovery and Examination*, 2nd ed., CRC Press, Boca Raton, FL, 2000, p. 370.

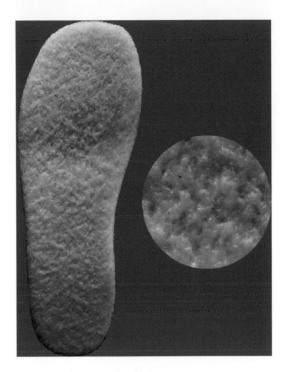

Figure 12.14 A natural crepe rubber outsole will result in a unique pattern due to random coagulation of the rubber.

imitation crepe sole, which is simply a molded sole whose features simulate the appearance of natural crepe rubber. Imitation crepe soles are not one of a kind, but instead are identical to others produced in the same mold.

Sandals made with scraps of worn tire tread rubber were popular many years ago and, although not mass produced, still exist today. Any handmade shoe that is randomly cut from different portions of worn tires of different tread designs will have a unique design that will make them unlike any other shoe outsole. It is extremely unlikely to encounter these in casework. There are videos over the Internet that provide instructions on how to make these. Some small businesses in poor countries produce these on a small scale but market them on the Internet. Other sandals with tire designs found on the Internet are actually molded imitations; thus, they would have the same class characteristics as any other molded outsole.

Shoes made using soft unvulcanized calendered rubber, from which soles are either die cut or Wellman cut, are often found to contain random marks or dings from the handling of those soft soles during their manufacture that could establish an outsole as one of a kind even before it was worn. Some of these random marks were previously discussed and depicted in Figure 11.11 in Chapter 11.

Classic Designs and Retro Designs

A great portion of outsole designs only last for months and are never used again. The molds for those designs are destroyed. The molds of more popular outsoles may be saved and reused years later with different uppers and a different name and style number. A few designs have proven to be so popular they have remained in the marketplace for many years. A manufacturer may refer to these as "classic designs." Examples include the Nike Cortez (1972–present), the Nike Air Force I (1982–present), the Chuck Taylor All Star (1917–present), the original Vibram boot outsole (1937–present). In addition to classic designs, many shoe styles were discontinued and later reintroduced using the same outsole molds. These are typically referred to as "retro designs." An example of a retro design is the Nike Air Jordan 9 Retro. This shoe was originally released in 1993 and has had several subsequent release dates as a retro design, such as the "9 Retro Wolf Grey" released in April 2014.

Counterfeits, Knockoffs, and Look-a-Likes

In the footwear industry, the term *counterfeit* is a legal term used when a shoe company's trademark and/or patent rights have been violated. Examples include the unauthorized use of a Nike swoosh or Adidas trefoil used on a shoe upper or shoe sole, as well as the unauthorized use of outsoles whose specific design is covered under the patent rights of a certain company. Counterfeiting popular athletic shoes has occurred for decades and continues to be a concern of major manufacturers. The more popular a design becomes, the more susceptible it is to being counterfeited. Counterfeit shoes were once sold mainly at outdoor markets or by street vendors, but the Internet has made them widely available not only to the individual consumer but to resellers who purchase them by the thousands.[*] One particular accounting details the various ways in which a counterfeit Nike shoe can be detected by the manufacturer, including the quality and colors of the upper, insole, and outsole; the size label; and specific mold features of the outsole.[†]

The term *knock-offs* or *look-a-likes* apply to shoes that are technically not counterfeit as they do not legally infringe on patents or trademarks, but are very close to copying the design of the shoe and its outsole. Some manufacturers simply produce an outsole that resembles the more popular brand. Figure 12.15 depicts a shoe purchased in a national chain store. Although not the exact design of the Nike Air Force 1, it reflects a similar design theme and would be considered a look-a-like. Depending on the quantity and quality of a crime scene impression, it may or may not be distinguishable from a true Nike Air Force 1 design.

Similar Designs

Not necessarily qualifying as a look-a-like, many general design elements are simply popular and are made under various brands. They are not copies of any particular brand or style of outsole, but have been used on many shoe brands and styles over the years. Figure 12.16 shows three variations of a common athletic shoe outsole design that at times have been used by many manufacturers.

---

[*] Schmidle, N., Inside the knockoff tennis shoe factory, *NY Times*, August 19, 2010.
[†] Wisbey, D., Counterfeit Nike sneakers, *JFI*, 60(3):337–351, 2010.

Figure 12.15 A look-a-like outsole that has some resemblance to the Nike Air Force 1 design.

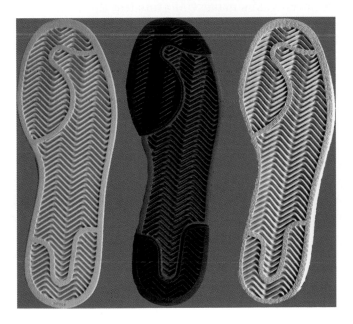

Figure 12.16 Some shoes are produced by more than one manufacturer that have outsoles that are "similar" and have been used by various manufacturers for many styles over many years.

Are the Shoes You Are Examining Counterfeits?

If you are examining a shoe and it corresponds with the design and size features of the crime scene impression, determining if that shoe is counterfeit may have little or no relevance to the comparative conclusion. Proof of counterfeiting extends to the entire shoe, not just the outsole. When it becomes important to determine if a shoe is counterfeit, the manufacturer's cooperation will be necessary to do this. It can recognize features that are subtle but proof that the shoe is counterfeit. For instance, a pair of counterfeit shoes of a particular popular design being sold on EBay or by a street vendor may have a sole or upper color that the legitimate manufacturer has never offered. Other components including the label information and format, the shoelace style, or other minor features may provide information obvious to the manufacturer that the shoe is counterfeit. One example was reported where a counterfeit Nike Air Force 1 outsole, although extremely similar, contained confirmable variations from a genuine Nike Air Force 1 outsole.[*] When considering issues of size, it is noted that counterfeit shoes often have outsoles that are not dimensionally the same as their legitimate counterparts. When considering issues of the production date of the shoe, any date information contained on a counterfeit shoe may not be accurate.

Determining Shoe Size from Impressions When No Shoes Are Recovered

In some investigations involving footwear impressions, the shoes of the accused are never recovered and a request may be made to determine the manufacturer's size of the shoe that made the crime scene impression. Estimating shoe size based on the heel-to-toe length is the most common effort investigators make. Unfortunately, this is not an accurate method to determine shoe size. The results from using this method can be wrong by 2–3 sizes or more for reasons discussed in Chapter 8. Determining a shoe size from crime scene impressions is most accurately done when the brand can be determined and samples of various sizes of outsoles are made available either through the marketplace or provided by the manufacturer. The accuracy of the result will depend on the samples obtained, whether texture is present in the crime scene impression, the completeness of the crime scene impression, and the design/size relationship of the outsole of that particular shoe. Things that might restrict these efforts include cases where the brand and source of the shoe cannot be determined, cases where the impression involves older shoes no longer being produced thus preventing standards from being obtained, outsole manufacturers who are overseas and unable to be contacted, and, on rare occasions, the lack of cooperation of a manufacturer.

If samples are obtained and a specific sample has identical texture, this provides a highly accurate way of relating the crime scene impression to a specific mold source and the conclusions of shoe size that can be derived from that. In most cases, the mold will be specific to a size, but as previously discussed, an exception would occur when outsoles from that mold were used on more than one size shoe. If no texture is present in the crime scene impression, either due to limitations in replication or because the shoe design does

---

[*] Lee, T., The Case of the Counterfeit Nike, presented at the 2010 Impression and Pattern Symposium, Clearwater, FL, August 2010.

not include texture, samples of various outsole sizes can still be of value. One of the most well-known examples of this application was the sizing of the Bruno Magli shoe soles in the OJ Simpson case.[*] These shoes were costly casual shoes but had limited production. Only 10 molds were produced to cover the entire production schedule and size range. One mold was specifically used to produce US size 12 shoes. Even though no texture was part of that design, the different arrangement of the design elements and where they intersected the perimeter border of the shoe were distinctly different in each mold. An example of that is provided in Figure 12.3.

When working with partial impressions that have no texture or reference to a border, logo, flex groove, or other reference feature, an accurate determination of size will not be possible. Likewise, if no brand information is known and/or no samples can be obtained for size reference, the possibility of making any accurate determination of the shoe size that produced an impression is reduced.

Key Words: class characteristic, classic design, counterfeit shoes, design element, design/size relationship, flex grooves, grading, retro design, texture

Key Points

1. An association of a crime scene impression with the manufactured class characteristics of design and physical size of that design with suspect footwear is significant due to the many thousands of distinguishable footwear designs and sizes in the overall shoe population that could have otherwise produced that impression.
2. Outsoles are designed in different ways and have different design/size relationships on different styles of shoes. As shoe outsoles increase in size, either more design must fill the outsole or that design must be larger.
3. Texture from hand-stippling or the acid-etch process is part of the design of an outsole and link it to a specific mold source.
4. The edge details of the outsole and whether a pair of shoes has a mirrored design each provides important information regarding whether they are cut or molded construction.
5. In order to most accurately determine shoe size based on features and dimensions of a crime scene impression, samples of that shoe design from the marketplace or the manufacturer are necessary.

[*] Bodziak, W. J., 2000, Ibid.

Evaluation of General Wear 13

The topic of general wear in a forensic examination has been the least addressed in the literature. As simple as the concept of general wear of an outsole might seem, many things can complicate its evaluation. Shoes that are in various stages of general wear produce crime scene impressions. Some are produced by outsoles in newer condition where any changes due to general wear may be minimally detectable. Other outsoles have acquired more visible and detectable wear and some involve footwear in a condition of extreme wear. Further, regardless of their condition, general wear on the outsole may not always be represented well or accurately in a crime scene impression. This may be due to various ways the shoe contacted the substrate, or to limitations imposed on its replication due to substrate conditions or other reasons. The evaluation of general wear may also be limited if the full details of scene impressions are not properly recovered. This is particularly true of photographs that are limited by issues of poor focus, low resolution, or poor lighting. Another complication is that general wear is a changing feature; thus the general wear on an outsole can differ if the shoe is not obtained until weeks or months after the crime. General wear, when clearly represented, can be significant in an examination, serving to further reduce the number of possible shoes of a particular design and size that could have produced an impression. In some cases, it can also be used for exclusion. This chapter provides basic information regarding factors that should be understood and considered during evaluation of general wear in a forensic footwear examination.

Basic Principles Regarding Evaluation of General Wear

Some basic considerations and information that surround the evaluation of general wear in a forensic footwear examination should be stated up front. Those include

1. If replication of detail in a crime scene impression is sufficient, features of general wear can serve to further discriminate one shoe from others in that population.
2. Different individuals in the general population share general wear on their shoes sufficiently similar in position and degree that impressions of their shoes cannot be distinguished.
3. General wear is caused by erosion of the outsole compound due to both horizontal and vertical forces. The horizontal forces are more related to activities the shoes are used for. An individual may have wear characteristics that vary in positions and degrees on different pairs of their shoes due to differences in the type and extent of usage.
4. General wear on shoes changes as the shoes continue to be worn.
5. The more wear on a shoe outsole, the less chance that wear will appear similar to wear on other shoes.

6. Forensic evaluation of general wear will be limited when features in the crime scene impression are not clearly replicated and/or not recovered properly.

7. Due to the possibility an impression may not always accurately represent the condition of general wear, examinations must rely only on clear replication of detail.

8. Identification of footwear should never be based on general wear alone.

9. The wearing of shoes results in the production of features that are not characterized as general wear in an examination. Those include the Schallamach abrasion pattern (feathering) and damage such as holes or tears that can occur in extremely worn outsoles. These features are not included as general wear features, but due to the random events surrounding those features, are treated as randomly acquired characteristics. These are discussed further in Chapter 14.

From New Soles to Worn Soles: Factors That Influence Outsole Wear

When shoes are worn, frictional forces occur during repeated contact with the substrate, resulting in a gradual erosion of the outsole compound. The product of this erosive action is visually evident on both the outsole and in impressions that outsole produces, and is referred to as general wear. Areas of the outsole that do not receive as much friction are affected less and undergo less change than areas that are affected more harshly. Outsoles that are new or that have minimal wear are easily categorized as such. Most wear on newer or less worn outsoles is first noticeable on the outer and rear portions of the heels. Heels may reflect visible wear, even after a short period of use; thus, most shoes, even if in newer condition, will have some trace of general wear in the heel area. Shoes with minimal wear have fewer features that would enable them to be distinguished from other shoes of minimal wear. Even so, when minimal wear is evident in a crime scene impression and corresponds with the suspect shoe being examined, other shoes of that same design and dimension having distinctly more advanced conditions of wear can be excluded as the possible source. Thus the absence of general wear on a shoe does not eliminate the value of this category of examination.

As the shoe continues to be worn, the wear in the heel increases and additional portions of the outsoles will receive sufficient wear to the extent they become more visibly noticeable. How soon wear gets to a visibly moderate level and specifically how that is defined for a particular outsole will depend on factors such as the tread depth, outsole composition, the presence and location of any texture on the outsole, and the ability of the substrate to retain those details. If the owner continues to wear the shoes long enough, the general wear on some areas of the outsole will become extreme to the point where portions of the design are severely eroded and possibly bald. Figure 13.1 shows three shoes of the same design, one that is new, one that was worn for 35 days, and one that was worn for 102 days.

The erosive actions on a shoe outsole during its life are complex and the cumulative result of many factors. In a forensic footwear examination, it is not possible or necessary to know the degree of influence each had on the wear of that shoe. Rather, the examination concerns itself with similarities or differences of general wear as it pertains to the ability or inability of the shoe to have produced those features in the crime scene impression. Nevertheless, to provide some appreciation for the complexity of factors that contribute to general wear and why wear varies between individuals, a few factors are listed hereafter.

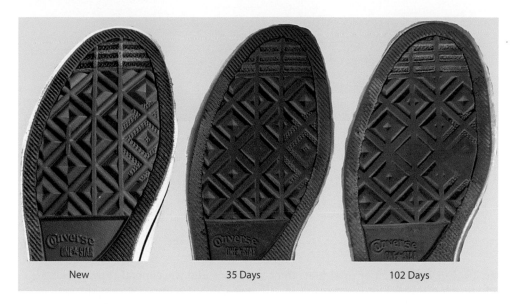

| New | 35 Days | 102 Days |

Figure 13.1 Three shoes with wear ranging from new to 35 days to 102 days. (Courtesy of Sarah Walbridge-Jones.)

Biomechanics and Personal Features of the Wearer

The personal features and biomechanics of individuals include but are not limited to attributes such as genetics; body weight; foot and lower limb flexibility; the effects of injuries, pathologies, or disease, and differences in left and right foot size and morphology. During the walking cycle, the foot can move in four directions by pointing the toes downward (plantar-flexion), pointing the toes upward (dorsi-flexion), turning the foot inward (inversion), and turning the foot outward (eversion). The ability of the foot to perform the four basic motions is essential for normal function. When the ability to perform any of these motions is reduced, the foot will be unable to function normally. In the walking cycle, upon contact with the substrate, a normal foot will sense the surface and pronate. During pronation, the joints in the foot become loose, allowing the foot to be flexible and to adapt to the substrate on which it is stepping. During the pronating motion, the forefoot rolls inward, flattening out the arch, and distributing the weight throughout the foot. At the point where the weight of the body is centered over the foot and when the ball of the foot has contacted the ground, the foot will begin to supinate. During supination, the foot will become more of a rigid lever, allowing the feet to more efficiently push off from the supporting surface.[*] This is a simple description of what is supposed to happen, but the precise degree and manner to which this occurs in each individual vary.

Many individuals have flexible and normally functioning feet that adapt well to the substrate during the normal gait cycle. Some have rigid feet that remain more supinated and others have feet that pronate excessively during foot strike. Two extreme foot types and a normal foot are illustrated in the foot models in Figure 13.2 along with examples of the related contact areas those foot types make in their impression. These attributes

[*] Dr. Irving Miller, Technical Conference on Footwear and Tire Evidence, FBI Academy, 1983.

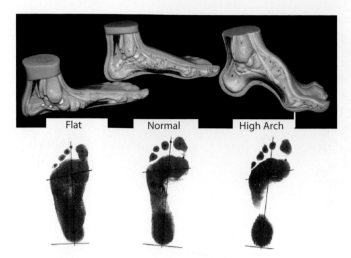

Figure 13.2 A flat foot, a normal foot, and a rigid foot and the general type of footprint they will produce. Different foot types result in different transmission of weight through footwear, affecting the degree and position of wear.

contribute to the way shoe outsoles interact with the substrate and how weight is distributed from an individual's body and feet through the bottom of a shoe. In addition, different individuals stand or walk with their feet toed out to different degrees as illustrated in Figure 13.3, and some strike their heel hard with each step while some land on their forefoot when walking fast or running. Different individuals have a wide range of foot types and functions for these reasons and others.

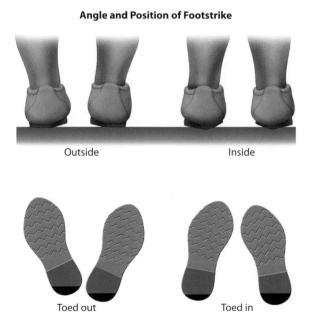

Figure 13.3 Both the amount of toe out or toe in as well as the position of the foot at heel strike affects the position of general wear.

Types of Forces Involved

Biomechanics specialists divide the wear forces that act on a shoe into two categories. One involves the vertical forces, i.e., those transmitted downward through the foot and shoe such as caused by the weight of the wearer. The other involves horizontal forces, i.e., those that result from the relevant movement between the outsole and substrate. Horizontal forces create most of the friction and therefore have a greater effect on the position and degree of outsole wear.[*] General wear caused by horizontal forces is more a product of athletic and other activities than of the biomechanics and personal traits of the individual. Activities such as walking, running, basketball, tennis, and others will result in horizontal forces related to those activities. A shoe worn for daily mixed usage will not have the same horizontal forces that a shoe used specifically for tennis or jogging may have. Shoes of the same individual can have general wear located in different positions and to different relative degrees on different shoes as a product of different horizontal forces from different activities. For example, "tennis shoes will have much more wear in the medial and lateral regions as well as wear in the 'toe drag' area. The walking shoe will have mostly linear wear along the length of the shoe as a result of the repetitive motions of walking."[†] Thus, the same person could have different areas of general wear on different shoes based on the specific activities for which those shoes are used.

Occupation and Activities of the Wearer

The occupation and/or habits of the wearer can also have an impact on the quantity and quality of general wear. Certain occupations or activities cause greater contact or movement of the shoe than others. For instance, delivery people will often pivot on one foot as they exit and enter their vehicle hundreds of times each week. Some motorcyclists use their foot to change gears hundreds of times causing a higher percentage of wear on specific areas of one shoe. Many persons wear their shoes in a carpeted office each day and will not wear shoes out nearly as fast as others who work on their feet all day or who have lifestyles that are more active. Different individuals wearing the same design footwear over different substrates for different activities will acquire different degrees of wear over the same period of time. There is no consistent rate of wear that can be predicted. For instance, one individual may weigh 175 pounds, play basketball daily on an outdoor rough concrete surface, and wear those shoes all day every day. Another individual may weigh 150 pounds and may divide wear among several pair of shoes in an office where the floors are entirely carpeted and where the person enjoys a sedentary job. Obviously, the outsoles of these two individuals will wear both differently and at different rates. One study involving 25 individuals wearing athletic shoes of the same design found wear began at the outside edges of the heel and along the lateral side of the shoe and that the wear on the shoes varied among the 25 individuals in location and intensity.[‡]

---

[*] Personal communication with Gordan Valiant, Biomechanics Specialist, Nike, March 13, 2012.

[†] Hayes, A. J., Factors that influence wear on shoes, presented at the International Symposium on the Forensic Aspects of Footwear and Tire Impression Evidence, FBI Academy, Quantico, VA, June 27–July 1, 1994.

[‡] Tart, M. S., Adams, J., and Ohene, A., Wear patterns: location and rate of advancement, The Forensic Science Service, Birmingham, UK, Report No. RR801, June 1999.

Manufacturing and Design

Soling compounds and outsole design can also influence the resulting general wear of an outsole. Microcellular soling materials, although lightweight and good for shock absorption, wear more rapidly than dense outsole materials. Shallow tread outsole designs permit better visual representation of general wear than deeper tread outsoles. The last a shoe is built on can also influence wear. The same foot positioned inside of a shoe built on a curved last will be positioned slightly different than within a shoe with a straight last design. Outsole designs combined with extra rubber, reinforcements, stabilizers, and cushioned inner liners can also affect the transmittal of wear forces in shoes. Figure 13.4 shows both Nike and Under Armour heels designed with more rubber beneath the inner or medial side of the heel area. Some manufacturers are now incorporating this in running shoes to affect the transmittal of forces during the heel to forefoot transition.*

Many molded outsoles have honeycomb or grid designs on their topsides. The walls of these grids transmit the majority of weight resulting in greater wear directly beneath the walls. In shoes with extreme wear like those in Figure 13.5, the grid pattern becomes evident. Also included in Figure 13.5 is a superimposition of the grid pattern on the top of a new outsole over its bottom showing where the grid pattern would transmit its weight.

In siped outsoles, the peaks and valleys of the sipes protrude as the shoe flexes. Sipes can be gradually worn down, as is happening in the shoes in Figure 13.6. The two arrows on the left show how peaks of the siped design have worn away. Areas of specific wear may occur as portions of sipes of uneven depth wear completely away as in the area indicated by the right arrow in Figure 13.6.

Foxing strips, when not applied evenly with the outsole, can prevent parts of the outsoles of newer shoes from contacting the surface. Figure 13.7 shows a portion of a Converse Chuck Taylor All Star shoe and an impression of that shoe. The arrows to the right show an

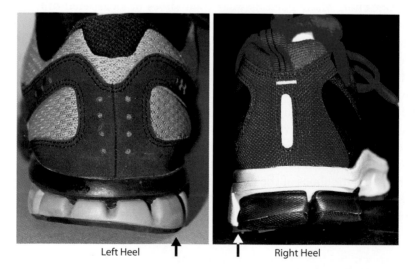

Left Heel ⬆   ⬆ Right Heel

Figure 13.4 Athletic shoe manufacturers will design heels in a way to affect the transmittal of wear forces.

* Personal communication with Herb Hedges, Nike Inc., September 2, 2014.

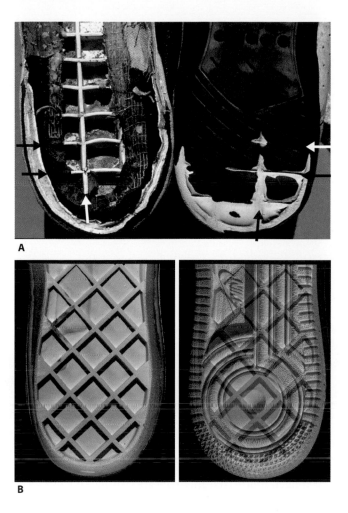

Figure 13.5 A shoe (A) viewed from the top and bottom after removal of the inner liner shows the effect the grid pattern has on wear. Below are photographs of the top of a new molded outsole and a superimposition of it over the bottom of that same outsole showing where the grid pattern would transmit weight (B).

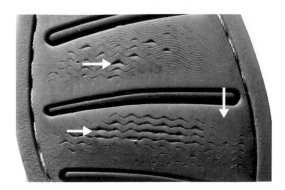

Figure 13.6 The arrows on the left show two true sipes where the leading and trailing edges are eroding away. The arrow on the right shows how the combined effect of uneven sipe depth and wear leaves only portions of the sipes.

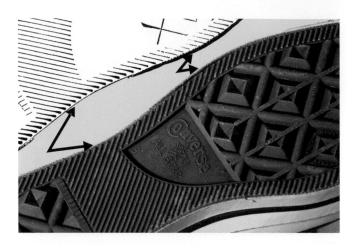

Figure 13.7 A new Converse Chuck Taylor All Star shoe with part of its foxing strip low and part of it high affects the impression it leaves. After sufficient wear the foxing strip and outsole will become even.

area where the foxing strip extends below the outsole level, interfering with the replication of detail just inside the corresponding perimeter of the impression. The arrows on the left show an area where the foxing strip is above the outsole level; thus, the edge of the molded sole prints clearly while no evidence of the foxing strip appears. As this shoe is worn, these uneven areas will eventually be worn to the same level.

Figure 13.8 depicts an athletic shoe with a relatively flat profile alongside a Wellman boot that has considerable curvature to its outsole. This curved Wellman outsole will not contact the substrate on its lateral and medial edges or in the toe area in the same way as this flat profile athletic shoe, consequently influencing the areas that receive wear.

Outsoles have even been made that incorporate simulated wear as part of their outsole design, as shown in the new unworn shoe in Figure 13.9.

Figure 13.8 Some outsoles are flat profiled and some have curvature. This will have some effect on the position of general wear.

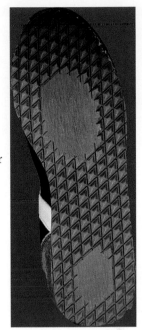

Figure 13.9 A new shoe outsole designed to appear as if it is worn.

Differences in Wear between an Individual's Shoes

A person's left and right foot are not matched perfectly in size, shape, and function and as a result, the general wear of the left and right shoes will not be exactly the same. The extent of these differences can be very minor, or in other cases very pronounced. In lesser-worn outsoles, the differences will be difficult to see but for outsoles that have advanced wear like the pair shown in Figure 13.10A, it is more easily observed. Having impressions at a scene that correspond with varied wear in respective left and right shoes may be of additional discriminating value. The degree of significance will depend on the clarity of the wear features and how much the left and right outsoles differ.

Different shoes of one individual can vary significantly due to the types and uses and degrees of wear as shown in Figure 13.10B.

Factors Affecting the Replication of General Wear Features

Many two- and three-dimensional impressions are clear and replicate accurate details about the condition of outsole wear; however, this is not always the case. Simple events may either mask or interfere with replication and, in some cases, may provide misleading details. One example would include outsoles whose tread design was packed with soil. Figure 13.11 is a classic example of soil clinging to a shoe. The detail relating to the condition of wear in the impression just produced, and the subsequent impression(s) are both affected. The same occurs frequently in snow. This type of interaction between substrate and outsole results in less accurate and potentially misleading information. Impressions

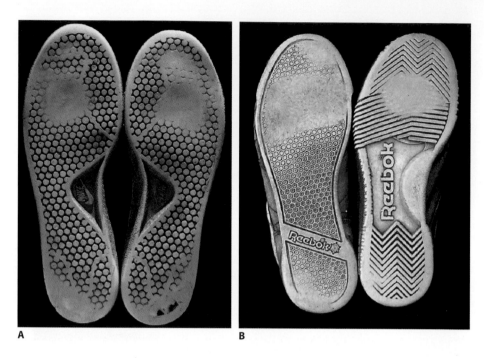

Figure 13.10 A left and right shoe of an individual will not wear exactly the same (A). Right shoes of the same individual showing variations in the position and degree of general wear (B).

Figure 13.11 Soil or snow that sticks in an outsole will affect the replication of general wear and other features.

may present the appearance of a worn shoe because the soil or snow pack prevents accurate replication of the design. Later, when the shoe is seized and that soil and snow is no longer present in the outsole, the shoe could be misinterpreted as one in newer condition than suggested by the filled-in crime scene impressions. Although this typically occurs in three-dimensional impressions, it can also occur in two-dimensional impressions. Examples include the aforementioned scenario where the mud- or snow-packed outsole tracks across a two-dimensional substrate. Similar misrepresentation of general wear can also occur when excessive blood is squeezed beneath an outsole, forced into and filling unworn areas of the

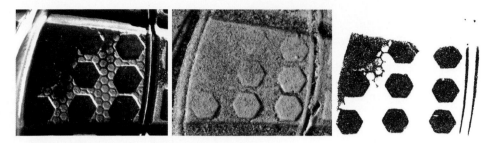

Figure 13.12 A small area of a shoe with some texture pattern worn to the same level of the outsole in the top left corner. In the center is a cast of an impression made by that shoe that shows the general wear in that same area, but did not replicate the worn texture. A known impression of that area shows more detail. The ability to compare general wear is limited by substrate and replication of detail.

design. Other factors such as slippage, twisting, or other movement between the shoe and substrate, back filling of loose sand, soil, or snow into an impression, and firm substrates that do not allow full recording of the depth of an outsole design can all mislead, mask, or misrepresent information about the condition of general wear on an outsole.

Even when shoe outsoles are clean, it is normal for the quality of replication of detail to vary under different conditions and in some cases limit or prevent accurate interpretation of general wear. Figure 13.12 shows the respective areas of a very small portion of a shoe, the respective area of a cast of its impression in sandy soil, and a known impression made by that shoe. The impression in sand that was cast was detailed but did not replicate the very shallow texture pattern. An impression on a nonporous surface would provide a better evaluation of the specific degree of wear in that area.

Examination of the Position and Degree of General Wear

General wear is clearly an acquired feature separate and apart from the manufactured design and dimension of the outsole. The position of wear refers to its location(s) on an outsole as evidenced by the erosion of rubber in those areas, typically changing the appearance of the outsole design. In some cases, worn areas are very indistinct and spread out. In other cases, the position is more specific. Examples of position of wear include wear on the edge of a heel, under the ball of the foot, or at locations where texture or sipes are visibly worn. When clearly represented in an impression, any definable position of wear can be compared with the respective areas of the shoe being examined. The degree of wear refers to the extent of the wear in each position. As shoes are increasingly worn, the degree of wear will increase as well. Figure 13.13 shows a small area of the heel of a shoe that illustrates how the degree of general wear spreads. In forensic comparisons, the position and degree of general wear are used to reduce the general population of footwear capable of having produced a crime scene impression. Correspondence of general wear will support the hypothesis the shoe produced the impression. In some cases, clear differences in the position and/or degree of general wear may allow for exclusion. Many factors need to be taken into account. The examination should consider only features clearly replicated in scene impressions. Less detailed impressions often restrict the degree to which general wear can be compared and may prevent a comparison of wear in a particular examination.

Figure 13.13 Wear on the edge of a heel (left) gradually expands as the shoe continues to be worn, as seen on the right.

Wear Patterns

One term occasionally used when describing the position and degree of wear is *wear pattern*. Some forensic reports will state, "The wear pattern in the crime scene impression and the wear pattern on a shoe correspond." Defining any condition of general wear on an outsole as a wear pattern is misleading and overstates its value in an examination. Its improper use may infer each person's shoes have his or her own unique wear pattern and this misconception can easily mislead the investigator or jury to equate this terminology to believing the conclusion is one of identification. There is no empirical or experience-based data that defines or supports the use of the term *wear pattern* or its use in the forensic evaluation of general wear. The term *wear pattern* was not included on the SWGTREAD Standard for Terminology Used for Forensic Footwear and Tire Impression Evidence.

Exclusions Based on General Wear

Many impressions can be excluded when a crime scene impression reflects general wear characteristics that are well defined and clearly different from those in the shoe being examined. The differences would need to establish the shoe, in its current condition of general wear, was not capable of producing the scene impression. The examination must always take into account cases where impressions may be made under circumstances that might not result in a true replication of the condition of wear of the outsole. The date the crime scene impressions were produced and the date the shoes were obtained should always be considered.

Different Positions and Degree of Wear

Exclusion is possible in cases where the scene impression contains distinct and clear wear in different positions and/or different degrees than the shoe being examined. This would normally apply to shoes that were obtained relatively close to the date of the crime, essentially eliminating any possibility that the general wear of those shoes could have changed significantly.

Crime Scene Impression Has More Advanced General Wear than Shoe

Exclusion is possible in cases where the general wear in the scene impression is clearly defined and is more advanced than on the respective areas of the shoe. The exclusion would

Figure 13.14 An example of an impression that was created by a shoe with greater wear than the suspect shoe shown on the right.

be based on evidence that the shoes could not have produced characteristics of general wear they do not possess. Figure 13.14 depicts a very partial impression in clay soil but the shoe being compared is in almost new condition and still contains texture, wider grooves between the heel circles, and the circles in the shoe still have a round contour.

Wear Is Less in Impression than on Shoe

Exclusion is possible in cases where the general wear in the scene impression is distinctly less than on the respective areas of the shoe. The exclusion would be based on clear evidence that the shoe was more worn than the shoe that produced the impression. This conclusion would only be possible if the shoes were seized on or close to the date of the crime so they did not have an opportunity to receive additional wear of any significance. Shoes that could have received sufficient additional wear between the date of the crime and the date they were seized would not be excludable. Figure 13.15 shows an example of a cast impression where the rectangular boxes on each side of the design are clearly present in the

Figure 13.15 Example of cast impression on the right that clearly shows rectangular design boxes on both the lateral and medial sides of the impression. Those boxes are completely worn away on the shoe that was acquired the day after the crime; thus, that shoe did not produce the impression.

impression. The rectangles on the shoe are completely worn away; thus, the shoe could not have produced the cast impression.

Is General Wear a Basis for Identification?

General wear is not a single event but an accumulation of events over time. The collective causes of general wear on a person's shoes are the sum of all influencing factors of every step up to the time it produces a crime scene impression. If a person were to buy two identical pairs of shoes and were to wear them equally, the wear on those two pairs, although likely to be extremely similar, would never be exactly the same. As part of some research, several examiners were asked to distinguish and compare the general wear on multiple pairs of shoes used by a professional runner.[*] The runner had saved numerous pairs of the same brand and size shoes she had used for her training runs. She ran over the same areas and would change shoes every 500 miles. Detailed known impressions were made of the shoe being used for the questioned impression as well as several other shoes that had received similar wear. All of the examiners were able to distinguish which shoe had produced the questioned impression. This was possible because there were very slight variations between the general wear of each of the shoes; however, it is noted that without the highly detailed powdered impressions it would clearly not have been possible to differentiate one from another.

This is not in any way to imply that wear expresses itself in a crime scene impression with sufficient quantity and quality to form a basis for identification, or to conclude that different persons could not have shoes of the same design with indistinguishable wear. The reality is that given the limitations of detail replicated, retained, and recovered in questioned impressions, the general wear in impressions made by many shoes of the same design and size is indistinguishable. This is particularly so in those cases where shoes are relatively new and contain minimal wear.

Some have proposed that general wear is unique to each outsole.[†] Obviously at an extremely high level of detail, all shoes could be theoretically differentiated from others. The hypothesis could also be proposed that thousands of new shoes of the same size and design could also be distinguished from one another if magnified at microscopic levels sufficient to detect every possible feature. Forensic footwear comparisons do not involve comparisons between shoes, but involve comparison between shoes and crime scene impressions, and those comparisons would never allow for that level of macroscopic examination because they are always limited by the detail produced and recovered in the crime scene impressions.

Using general wear as the sole basis for identifying shoes as the source of impressions is not one that is practiced or one that has a sound basis. Any inclination or migration of examiners toward using wear as a sole basis for identification would not only be unjustifiable but would be highly detrimental to the discipline as it would involve highly subjective evaluations of evidence and inevitably lead to incorrect evaluations. Another potential danger is that over time the practice of any examiners that might do so could evolve to

---

[*] Personal communication with Brad Putnam.
[†] Vanderkolk, J., Presentation at the International Association for Identification, Providence, RI, August 2013.

a lower expectation with future casework evaluations requiring increasingly less general wear features to opine identifications.

Opinions should be based only on features that are clear and can be confirmed in an impression. The weight of a forensic examination, if capably evaluated and transparently expressed in a written report and/or testimony, can convey the significance of any general wear characteristics in context with the rest of the examination without having to risk its overvaluation.

Some very bad experiences involving the misuse of general wear involved cases worked in the 1970s and 1980s by Dr. Louise Robbins. Dr. Robbins was a physical anthropologist who had conducted research regarding fossilized footprints in caves and eventually worked on fossilized footprints in Tanzania with the famous anthropologist Dr. Mary Leakey. During the mid-1970s, Dr. Robbins, without any forensic training or experience, began acting as an expert witness in cases involving both barefoot evidence and shoe prints. In one of her early forensic publications, she outlined her views on the individuality of the human foot.[*] She advised much of the basis for her forensic work was a product of more recent research involving approximately 1000 impressions she had taken from university students, but no physical evidence of this research was ever made available even when personally requested.[†] Eventually, Dr. Robbins published a book that states, on its cover, "Through the measurements and shape expressions developed from a footprint, bare, socked, on shoe insole or reflected in wear on the shoe tread, it is possible to identify one individual ...."[‡] Dr. Robbins claimed she could find uniqueness in the bare foot impressions she examined as well as see the unique features of the feet transferred through the wear on shoe outsoles. This view or practice was clearly not shared in the forensic community of footwear examiners or in that of other anthropologists.[§] Many footwear examiners, including this author, opposed Dr. Robbin's opinions in court, including one case that remains one of the most infamous wrongful convictions. A full accounting has been written of this unusual case.[¶] The crime occurred in 1983, when the accused, Stephen Buckley, and two others were charged with the homicide of a young girl. The only physical evidence against Buckley was a shoe print on the kicked-in front door of the victim's residence. After other examiners had excluded Buckley's shoes, the prosecutor retained Robbins, who concluded the impression was made by Buckley even though the precise outsole pattern of his seized shoes was different. She asserted her identification was based on the pattern of wear on the shoe print on the door that was unique to the pattern of wear on Buckley's shoes. The jury was hung and subsequently the FBI examined the impression and excluded it.[**] Eventually another individual named Dugan, whose shoes Robbins had eliminated through a similar comparison of the wear pattern on his footwear, confessed to this crime. His confession was later corroborated with DNA analysis. Dr. Robbins died in 1987, but not before she had testified in court in over 20 cases that centered around her claims, including some of those stating that she could relate the wear on the shoes of an

---

[*] Robbins, L. M., The individuality of human footprints, *Journal of Forensic Sciences*, 23(4):775–778, 1978.
[†] Personal communication with Dr. Louise L. Robbins at UNC, Greensboro, NC, 1982.
[‡] Robbins, L., *Footprints: Collection, Analysis, and Interpretation*, Charles C Thomas, Springfield, IL, 1985.
[§] Personal communication with Dr. Owen Lovejoy, Kent State University, April 1984.
[¶] Frisbie, T., and Garrett, R., *Victims of Justice Revisited*, Northwestern University Press, Evanston, IL, 2005.
[**] Bodziak, W. J., *Footwear Impression Evidence: Detection, Recovery and Examination*, 2nd ed., CRC Press, Boca Raton, FL, 2000, pp. 422–425.

individual through the wear pattern on other shoes they owned or based on their feet, a method that was neither practiced nor accepted in the scientific community. One accounting of Robbins casework in general points out "… Robbins was alone in claiming that she could tell whether a person made a particular print by examining other shoes belonging to that individual."[*]

Extreme Wear Can Produce Randomly Acquired Characteristics

When shoes are worn to extremes that result in sufficient degradation of the outsole's compound and integrity, this eventually results in ruptures, holes, random tearing, and other random features that are appropriately defined as randomly acquired characteristics (RACs). This includes the Schallamach abrasion patterns that are accumulations of random tearing events on the outsole. These characteristics are covered in the next chapter.

Are Shoes of Value for Comparison Months after the Crime?

There is always a chance the perpetrator of a crime will still possess the shoes many months later. In most cases, shoes not recovered until weeks or months after the crime contain general wear advanced beyond the condition they possessed on the day of the crime. Much of this depends on the number of shoes the individual owns and wears, the condition of the shoes at the time of the crime, and whether the perpetrator is transient or maintains a permanent residence that might serve as a long time repository for their footwear. Some individuals wear the same shoes every day and wear them out rapidly. Others use multiple pairs of footwear, dividing the wear among them. Newer shoes will likely remain around longer than ones that were almost worn out the day of the crime. Many cases have involved shoes obtained even months or years after the crime. One fugitive from crime conveniently stored his belongings and shoes in a storage locker prior to leaving town to evade the police. The shoes were recovered over two years after the crime. In many other cases, shoes recovered at much later dates had not received additional wear and still retained their RACs. Investigators should never give up the possibility they will find footwear. Shoes are very personal items of clothing and many persons hold onto them longer than one might expect.

Does General Wear Have Any Value When No Shoes Are Recovered?

There are occasions where distinctive wear is reflected in crime scene impressions yet no shoes of that design are recovered from the accused. Some have maintained it is possible to associate the general wear of other shoes belonging to the accused with the general wear present in the crime scene impressions, even using shoes of different designs that belong to the suspect. This is bad advice and not a valid comparison and is not based on any research, data, or knowledge obtained through experience within this discipline.

---

[*] Hansen, M., Believe it or not, *ABA Journal*, 79:64, June 1993.

Figure 13.16 In some cases, the general image of a foot is reflected in the general wear on a shoe outsole, referred to by some as an anatomical wear pattern. Research has shown this is not reliable for association with an individual.

One of the most notorious cases involving an erroneous evaluation of general wear was cited above involving Dr. Robbins who claimed she was able to identify an impression based on the wear on other shoes of an individual.* She also eliminated the wear on the real perpetrator's shoes as the source of the impression to buttress her identification of the first suspect. She was wrong both times.

Occasionally, some scene impressions will reflect what appear to be reasonably good representations of the heel, ball, and toes of the foot reflected on the worn outsole. Some refer to this as an anatomical wear pattern as shown in Figure 13.16. Although the position of wear seems to represent the foot within the shoe well, the pressure exerted by the foot and vertical forces passed through the shoe are muted and spread out due to the thickness of the insole, midsole, and outsole.

One study addressed general wear by making known the impressions of worn shoes of seven individuals (shoes sizes 8–11) to document the areas of wear on those shoes. Impressions taken of each shoe were compared to see if the wear could be distinguished. In spite of the small sample group, "several shoes were found to coincide sufficiently well to suggest a common origin." In the same study, 33 pairs of shoe impressions that bore textured (crepe) or patterned tread were compared using overlays in order to achieve a "best fit" of the worn areas. The degree of fit was categorized as "good" where length, width contour, and the wear margins coincided; "fair" where most features agreed but some discrepancy existed; or "none" where major differences existed. The results showed about the

* Bodziak, W. J., *Footwear Impression Evidence: Detection, Recovery and Examination*, 2nd ed., CRC Press, Boca Raton, FL, 2000, pp. 422–425.

same number of combined good and fair agreements as those that contained none. The large number of good fits between shoes of different individuals suggests "single wear patterns for the most part are not unique."[*]

Studies Concerning Wear

Several forensic studies have addressed the topic of wear on shoes. The aforementioned DeHaan study included 650 pairs of used men's footwear in all. Part of the study used transparent grids superimposed over the heels of these shoes as a means of measuring the position of wear. The shoes were in various stages of wear, ranging from almost new to well worn, and included all varieties of dress shoes, boots, and athletic shoes. The study concluded that the majority of shoes had wear that fell somewhere within a 60° arc on the outside of the heel. This same study concluded that wear in other areas of the heel or in multiple areas of the heel were less common. This finding is consistent with the fact that the feet of most persons are slightly supinated and/or toed out during the heel strike phase of the walking cycle, causing the outer portion of the heel to make contact with the substrate first.

In another study of general wear, 97 separate shoes and test impressions taken from those shoes were compared. The shoes were of police recruits and were restricted to two designs. The shoes were worn for identical periods of time within a very confined geographical area. Some conclusions of this study were (1) the chances of general wear being accurately duplicated decreased in proportion to the length of time shoes were worn. Seventy-four percent of the shoes worn two months had similar wear compared with 18% of shoes worn for five months. (2) The value of wear becomes more significant as the shoe becomes more worn. (3) Identification of footwear should not be based on general wear alone. (4) Minor disagreements of wear should not constitute a bar toward identification.[†]

Research was also conducted on shoe wear patterns and how they relate to the distribution of pressure under the feet as transmitted through shoes.[‡] This research used computer technology and pedobarograph images to attempt to associate the position and contour features of wear patterns on a shoe with patterns generated through an individual's foot. According to the research, variations in shoe designs and types, some of which do not reflect these wear patterns equally, as well as the varying degrees of wear that could be encountered in any shoe, made the endeavor difficult. This research suggests that shoe type and construction have an effect on the way in which vertical forces are transmitted by the foot through the shoe and the degree that general wear reveals itself in impressions.

Another study was undertaken to determine the discrimination value of wear in the comparison of two-dimensional impressions with shoes.[§] The study included size 10 right military combat boots that had a Vibram Kletterlift outsole, and were worn by Marines

---

[*] DeHaan, J. D., Wear characteristics of men's footwear, presented at the International Association of Forensic Science meeting, Vancouver, BC, Canada, 1987.

[†] Cassidy, M. J., *Footwear Identification*. Canadian Government Printing Centre, Quebec, Canada, 1980, p. 99.

[‡] Facey, O. E., Hannah, I. D., and Rosen, D., Shoe wear patterns and pressure distribution under feet and shoes, determined by image analysis, *Journal of Forensic Science Society*, 32, 1992.

[§] Fruchtenicht, T., Herzig, W., and Blackledge, R., The discrimination of two-dimensional military boot impressions based wear patterns, *Science and Justice*, 42:97–104, 2002.

for five weeks during training. The study involved 127 right boot known impressions. The images of the impressions were scanned and dimensional data was measured using an image marker measurement system. The study concluded that general wear has discrimination value. It should be noted that this study included the comparison of ink quality known impressions and was not a test of the lesser detail retained in two- and three-dimensional crime scene impressions.

In 2012, an informal survey was conducted among 13 European laboratories to determine if their evaluation of general wear was similar to each other and to that of US examiners.[*] Included in that survey were four casework examples accompanied by specific questions as to how each examiner would value the wear characteristics. The survey found that European and US laboratories were consistent in their practices in that all agreed that general wear is insufficient in its degree of uniqueness to be used as a sole basis for identification. They also agreed that irregularities in holes or tears in outsoles that result from extreme wear included features that reflected a degree of randomness, allowing those features to be categorized as randomly acquired characteristics and did not fall under the category of general wear.

Key Words: wear, general wear, wear characteristics, degree of wear, position of wear, vertical forces, horizontal forces

Key Points

1. General wear on footwear gradually changes the appearance of the outsole. Wear characteristics are replicated in crime scene impressions and if sufficiently clear, may contribute to the forensic examination.
2. Many factors influence the degree and position of general wear on an outsole.
3. Minor wear such as on relatively new shoes is of lesser value and has less power of discrimination than wear that is more advanced.
4. Some individuals in the general population wear their shoes sufficiently similar to result in characteristics of general wear indistinguishable from shoes of others.
5. The same individual can produce different positions of wear on different shoes based on the specifics of their use and the resulting differences in horizontal forces.
6. Sufficient details of the specific condition of general wear is often not replicated in poorly detailed impressions and/or may also be lost in the recovery process, preventing its use in an examination.
7. Evaluations of general wear between a crime scene impression and shoe must be conservative and any conclusions should be based only on clearly replicated features.
8. General wear as limited by the details in crime scene impressions and other factors is insufficient in its degree of uniqueness to be used as a basis for identification.

[*] Bodziak, W., Hammer, L., Johnson, G., and Schenck, R., Determining the significance of outsole wear characteristics during the forensic examination of footwear impression evidence, *JFI*, 62(3):254, 2012.

Randomly Acquired Characteristics 14

Simply defined, the word *random* means unplanned and by chance. Randomly acquired characteristics (RACs) occur on shoe outsoles as they repeatedly contact various substrates that contain objects like glass, sharp rocks, and other damage-inflicting objects, or that contain debris or small stones that become imbedded in or attached to the outsole. RACs range from the smallest feature to those with larger and more distinct shapes. RACs of shoe outsoles serve to further distinguish them from other shoes of the same class characteristics. When replicated in a crime scene impression, they contribute toward and are essential in establishing a specific shoe was the source of that impression. This chapter will discuss RACs and the various considerations surrounding them.

Random and Randomly Acquired Characteristics

In the past, the terms *randomly acquired characteristics, accidental characteristics, identifying characteristics, individual characteristics, individualizing characteristics,* and others have been used freely when referring to the random events that occur on shoe outsoles. Some believed calling a characteristic individual infers that it alone is unique and therefore not the best descriptive word to use; rather, they preferred to use the term *individualizing* characteristic. When discussing how examiners have traditionally identified an impression, one examiner drew the distinction between the terms *identify* and *individualize,* explaining the term *identify* simply refers to describing an object such as a shoeprint or fingerprint, whereas the term *individualize* refers to the process of establishing the uniqueness of a shoe or impression.[*]

In a peer-reviewed decision concerning appropriate and recommended terminology, the Scientific Working Group for Shoeprint and Tire Tread Evidence (SWGTREAD) selected the term *randomly acquired characteristic* as a more appropriate term as it provides a simple and general description of any random event on the shoe. SWGTREAD defined *randomly acquired characteristic* in its terminology standard issued in March 2013 as, "A feature on a footwear outsole or tire tread resulting from random events including, but not limited to: cuts, scratches, tears, holes, stone holds, abrasions and the acquisition of debris. The position, orientation, size, and shape of these characteristics contribute to the uniqueness of a footwear outsole or tire tread. Randomly acquired characteristics are essential for an identification of a particular item of footwear or tire as the source of an impression."[†] The term *randomly acquired characteristic* makes no assumption of the uniqueness or the weight of that characteristic in the comparison process but simply states the characteristic was acquired on the shoe outsole in a random manner.

---

[*] Tuthill, H., and Graeme, G., *Individualization: Principles and Procedures in Criminalistics,* 2nd ed., Lightning Powder Company, Jacksonville, FL, 2002.
[†] Scientific Working Group for Shoeprint and Tire Tread Evidence Standard for Terminology Used in Forensic Footwear and Tire Impression Evidence, www.swgtread.com (updated August 2013).

Examples of Randomly Acquired Characteristics (RACs)

In the examination of footwear impression evidence, RACs include features that have been randomly removed from the outsole of the shoe as well as those randomly added to the outsole of the shoe. Examples where outsole material has been taken away are provided in Figure 14.1 and include cuts, scratches, tears, holes, punctures, abrasions, and air bubbles. The examples in Figure 14.1 also include RACs that have been added to the outsole such as stones that become wedged in the outsole design (stone holds), gum, tar, running shoe patch materials, nails, and any other debris that might adhere to, penetrate, or get stuck in the outsole. Some of these forms of RACs are described further.

Cuts, Scratches, and Punctures

As a shoe outsole traverses over varied substrates, it can make contact with sharp objects that penetrate or otherwise cause removal of portions of soling material, resulting in cuts, nicks, scratches, abrasions, and punctures. Some are very shallow while others are much deeper. The random location and the random manner in which the outsole rubber is removed results in almost countless shapes and sizes of RACs. Small and featureless cuts, punctures, or nicks contribute less toward identification. As an RAC becomes more complex, it means that in order to duplicate that on another outsole, a larger number of factors must be the same. RACs that are larger and/or more complex and contain more features are less likely to be duplicated or found on another outsole, thus they carry greater weight toward identification. Figure 14.1, numbers 1, 2, 4, and 5, depict examples of cuts, punctures, and scratches.

Tears and Rough Edges around Holes

Outsoles worn excessively can incur tears or breaks completely through the outsole materials that result in randomly formed irregular and ragged edges. Figure 14.1, numbers 6, 8, and 10 show examples.

Demarcations between Outsole Compounds

When the outsole of a shoe wears into a midsole material composed of a different compound and density, their differences can result in irregularly shaped and sized borders that contain demarcations that may be physically reproduced in two-dimensional impressions. Figure 14.1, number 17, is an example of this where the solid black rubber outsole has worn into the microcellular midsole.

Abrasions

The Schallamach abrasion pattern is present on the worn footwear of many individuals. The wavelike ridge pattern is randomly formed as smooth rubber of the outsole slides over a smooth rigid surface. Due to its shallow nature, it is only replicated on two-dimensional smooth substrates that can retain high quality impressions. Its examination requires magnification. This pattern is named after an engineer, Adolf Schallamach (1905–1997),

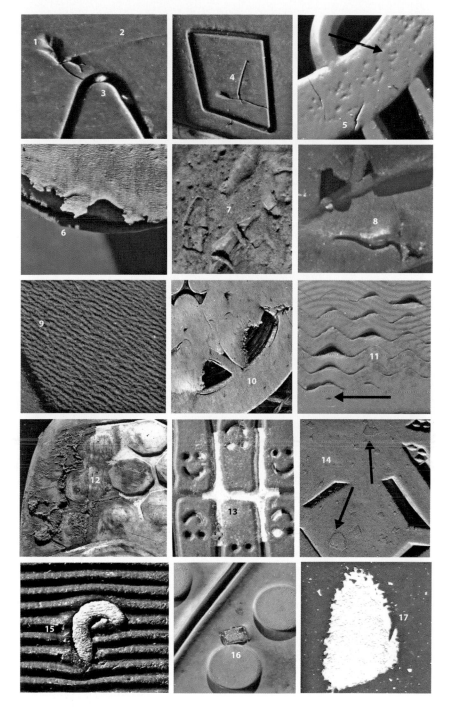

Figure 14.1 A variety of randomly acquired characteristics on shoe outsoles. #1, a puncture; #2, a fine scratch; #3, a stone hold; #4, a complex cut; #5, a small irregular cut; #6, tears of the outsole in heel area; #7, burns on shoes of a steel worker; #8, tears of a degraded outsole; #9, a Schallamach abrasion pattern feathering; #10, tears along edges of holes in heel; #11, tearing along edges of sipes; #12, tar stuck on outsole; #13, glue and remnants of label stuck in outsole; #14, irregular chunks of unmixed soling compound; #15, bent nail in heel; #16, glass embedded in outsole; #17, black outsole worn through to microcellular midsole resulting in random edge line.

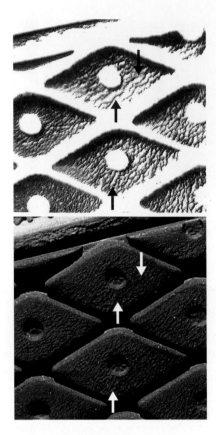

Figure 14.2 Enlargement of a Schallamach abrasion pattern on a shoe and its impression.

who conducted extensive research on rubber abrasion.[*,†,‡,§,¶,**] The Schallamach pattern is also referred to as feathering.[††] Figure 14.1, number 9 depicts an enlarged portion of the Schallamach pattern on an outsole. Figure 14.2 illustrates an example of the Schallamach pattern on a small area of a shoe and how that pattern appears in the impression it makes. Figure 14.3 illustrates how the Schallamach pattern is created as the outsole scuffs the substrate between steps. The red-colored wedge represents the abrasive frictional forces of the substrate that grab hold of the outsole rubber as it scuffs the substrate and stretches portions into ridges or waves perpendicular to the relative direction the outsole is moving. In some instances, the rubber is simply stretched and in other instances it is stretched enough to cause tears in the rubber. The process is ongoing with each step and the cumulative stretching and tearing resulting from the abrasive action quickly create a series of joining ridges or waves. The resulting pattern appears similar to the friction ridge pattern on

[*] Schallamach, A., *Friction and Abrasion of Rubber*, The British Rubber Producers' Research Association, Vol. 1, 384, 1957–1958.

[†] Schallamach, A., Abrasion, fatigue and smearing of rubber, *Journal of Polymer Science*, 12:281, 1968.

[‡] Schallamach, A., Abrasion of rubber by a needle, *Journal of Polymer Science*, 9(5):385, 1952.

[§] Schallamach, A., How does rubber slide? *Wear*, 17:301, 1971.

[¶] Schallamach, A., A theory of dynamic rubber friction, *Wear*, 6:375, 1963.

[**] Schallamach, A., The adhesion and friction of smooth rubber surfaces, *Wear*, 33:45, 1975.

[††] Tart, M. S., Downey, A. J., Goodyear, J. G., and Adams, J., The appearance and duration of feathering as a feature of wear, *Forensic Science Society Report No. RR 786*, August 1996.

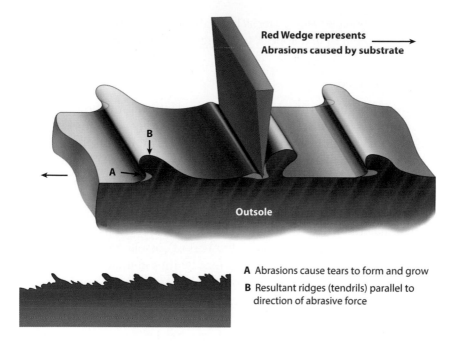

Red Wedge represents Abrasions caused by substrate

B

A

Outsole

A Abrasions cause tears to form and grow
B Resultant ridges (tendrils) parallel to direction of abrasive force

Figure 14.3 Diagram showing how the Schallamach abrasion pattern is formed. The red wedge represents the substrate causing abrasion as the outsole scuffs across it, causing ridges (tendrils) to be cumulatively formed in a random way. These ridges connect to form the overall pattern.

skin. The Schallamach pattern does not occur across the entire outsole but only on smooth areas that are repeatedly scuffed. On the shoes of some persons, the formation may be restricted to small isolated areas such as the edge of a heel or small area of the sole where they unknowingly scuff their feet between steps. Some individuals will not walk in a way that causes the formation of this pattern on their outsoles. Others may scuff or drag their feet more heavily in a way that results in larger areas of the outsole acquiring this pattern. Because the abrasion pattern is acquired only on the smooth solid rubber surface of outsoles, areas that are originally textured must first be worn smooth before the Schallamach pattern can occur. Abrasions do occur on microcellular outsoles, but the microcellular materials usually do not replicate and hold the pattern very well. Dense polyurethane outsoles usually do not retain this pattern at all.

After the Schallamach pattern is replicated in a crime scene impression, the pattern on the outsole will continue to change with additional usage of the shoe. If the shoe is worn minimally and/or over less abrasive substrates, it is possible the pattern will remain unchanged for a longer period. If the shoe is worn considerably and over abrasive substrates, the pattern can change quickly. Some research on its uniqueness and how it can change concluded that the pattern develops in as little as 9 hours of wear and changes sufficiently to appear different after an additional 6 to 16 hours of wear. In comparisons between many pairs of shoes, individual heel units, and outsole test strips, the Schallamach patterns were completely different. They were so diverse that it was determined that only a small area of a few square millimeters will represent an identifiable pattern, unique to that shoe alone.[*]

[*] Davis, R. J., and Keeley, A., Feathering of footwear, *Science & Justice* 40:273–276, 2000.

Other references to abrasive wear patterns have also indicated their potential importance, the time it takes for them to first appear, to change, and their transient nature.[*,†]

Manufacturing Source

A number of things occur during the various manufacturing methods that have varying degrees of randomness. Some are more significant than others. Processes that utilize poly-urethane outsoles may result in entrapment of air bubbles in the outsole and although these are technically random, pattern-related air bubbles routinely repeat in the same or similar areas of the outsole, significantly minimizing their value.[‡] On rare occasions, outsole compound fillers may not blend properly, leaving random pieces across the outsole, as shown in Figure 14.1, number 14.[§] Outsoles that are randomly die cut from sheet goods or Wellman cut from calendered material will be distinguishable in some way from the majority of others of that style and size; however, due to the large numbers of outsoles made, others that are indistinguishable will also be produced. In outsoles made with soft unvulcanized calendered outsole material random accidental cuts and other random features can be inflicted during handling and assembly. Many other variables also occur during the use of calendered rubber. Some shoes utilize foxing strips that are added by hand and are assembled in a way that results in a wide range of variables. Recently, fabric has been placed in the mold for some molded footwear that can vary in its exact position from one molding to the next. Many of these aforementioned events and others in the manufacturing process involve some degree of randomness and can be used to various degrees to discriminate one shoe from others.

Stone Holds

Stone holds occur when a small stone or pebble gets wedged in the grooves or spaces between the design elements of an outsole. In some cases, they may only remain in the shoe for a few steps but in other cases they may get sufficiently wedged in the outsole to remain for long durations. Because stones are usually deeply entrenched, they may not leave any evidence of their presence in two-dimensional impressions. Figure 14.4 illustrates a stone hold and the distortion of the tread design it may create. If the stone is retained for a period of time, that distortion of the tread pattern could be retained even after the stone breaks apart or is ejected. Figure 14.1, number 3 depicts a smaller stone wedged deeply in the outsole.

Gum, Tar, and Shoe Patch

Although not as common, there are occasions where gum, tar, or other forms of sticky materials become attached or stuck on or in the outsole design. In addition, commercially

---

[*] Tart, M. S., Downey, A. J., Goodyear, J. G., and Adams, J., The appearance and duration of feathering as a feature of wear, *Forensic Science Society Report No. RR 786*, August 1996.

[†] Tart, M. S., Adams, J., Downey, A. J., Goodyear, J. G., and Ohene, A., Feathering, transient wear features and wear pattern analysis: A study of the progressive wear of training shoe outsoles, *Information Bulletin for Shoeprint/Tool Mark Examiners*, 4(1):51–68, 1998.

[‡] Music, D., and Bodziak, W. J., A forensic evaluation of the air bubbles present in polyurethane shoe outsoles as applicable in footwear impression comparisons, *Journal of Forensic Science*, 33(5), September 1988.

[§] LeMay, J., Accidental characteristics in a footwear outsole caused by incomplete blending of fillers in the outsole rubber, *JFI*, 63(5), 2013.

Figure 14.4 A stone wedged in an outsole pattern known as a stone hold. In time the stone will permanently distort that area of the outsole design.

sold shoe patches such as Shoe Goo are intentionally applied to outsoles for repair or to provide additional material to the outsole in worn areas. These substances may be applied over only a small area but, like the example of roof tar in Figure 14.1, number 12, can also extend over a larger portion of the outsole.

Nails or Other Objects Embedded in Tread

Small nails, staples, tacks, metal shavings, glass, and other objects can both pierce and remain embedded in the outsoles and heels of shoes. Although not common, when present, their varied sources and shapes include many unusual features and their durability may allow them to be embedded in the outsole for a long time. Figure 14.1 shows examples of an embedded bent nail (number 15) and piece of glass (number 16).

Labels and Other Debris

Paper or plastic stick-on labels that are placed on outsoles to indicate sizes or brands or prices are often attached with glue or high-tack adhesives. If the owner does not remove them, they or their remnants will often remain on the outsole for a considerable time. Not only does the hand-applied position of a label vary slightly from shoe to shoe, its paper and glue components will break up or degrade randomly. Figure 14.1, number 13 depicts the remnants of glue and fiber from a label that was attached to the outsole.

The Weight or Value of Randomly Acquired Characteristics

Each RAC involves the position at which it randomly occurs on the outsole, its size and shape features, and its direction or orientation on the outsole. Position, size, shape, and orientation are independent of one another. The ability to distinguish RACs is minimal with regard to very tiny nondescript features, such as a pin tip might produce, but rapidly increases when the characteristics increase in complexity. The ability to distinguish RACs also relates to their clarity as it is represented in the crime scene impression. Characteristics with more complex shapes that replicate with clarity allow for greater correspondence with the respective features on the outsole that produced them.

Position

Random characteristics can occur anywhere on the outsole of a shoe. Even recessed areas can hold stones, imbedded items, or sticky substances. When two shoes of the same size and design each acquires a single RAC on their outsole, they will almost certainly be in different positions simply because of the many possible locations. Figure 14.5 depicts a metric grid over a shoe sole and an enlarged area containing a small RAC (A). The specific location of this RAC on the outsole is easily observed and documented. The outsole in this example

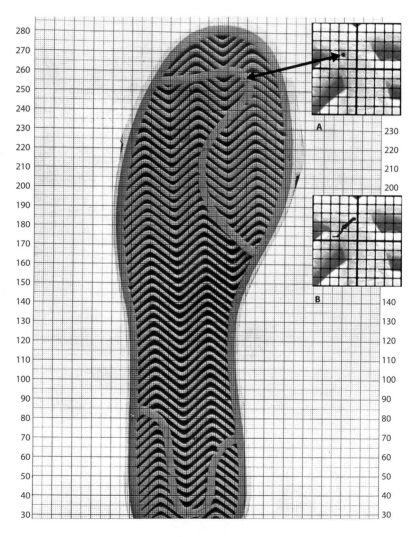

Figure 14.5 A metric grid superimposed over a shoe outsole demonstrates the large number of distinguishable positions at which a RAC could occur. Although the small nondescript cut at Figure 14.5A has little size or shape, its position alone is still significant. When size, shape, and orientation are added, such as with the cut in Figure 14.5B, the weight of a single characteristic increases exponentially.

contains approximately 16,000 square mm of area. Should the RAC's position differ by 1 mm or more in any direction, its position would be distinguishable. The use of physical or computer-generated overlays allows for the position of a RAC in a scene impression to be compared accurately with a characteristic on an outsole. In the Figure 14.5A example, the characteristic's position has no relationship to and is independent of its features of size, shape, or orientation, and the example is only provided to consider its location on the shoe outsole. Even if a RAC is only a mere nick or pinhole-sized cut, if confirmed present in both the shoe and scene impression, it is a relevant feature because the likelihood another shoe of this size and design will contain a similar RAC in that precise position is small. When more than one RAC is present on an outsole, the chance that RACs on other outsoles would be in the same respective positions becomes increasingly unlikely.[*]

Size and Shape

The size and shape features of RACs range from a small, minimally detectable cut or blemish to complex features such as the tar, burns, long scratches or complex cuts and tears illustrated in Figure 14.1. Size and shape features are independent of one another as are their position and orientation on the shoe. Figure 14.6 depicts a small portion of one outsole that contains numerous RACs. Number 7 is similar to the example provided in Figure 14.5 in that it is very small and nondescript. Its value is more for its position, and its shape features, size, or orientation are of minimal value. Numbers 1 and 6 are similar in length but oriented differently. Number 6 is also deeper, wider, and has more shape features. Size and shape features that are more complex will be less likely to occur on another shoe outsole and therefore carry more weight in an examination than small nondescript features. Equally important, the degree to which each RAC's size and shape features are valued strongly relates to the completeness and clarity of its replication in the crime scene impression and the subsequent degree of comparative association that can be made with corresponding features in the impression. In Figure 14.5B, a second RAC was drawn to provide an illustration of the addition of size, shape, and orientation in addition to position alone.

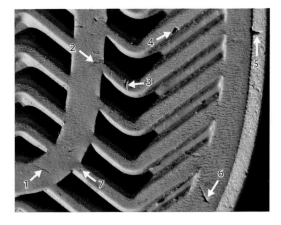

Figure 14.6 A shoe sole with several RACs of different sizes and shapes.

[*] Stone, R. S., Footwear examinations: mathematical probabilities of theoretical characteristics, *JFI*, 56(4):577–599, 2006.

Orientation

Orientation refers to the rotational axis of any RAC. The orientation of the cut in Figure 14.5B would be easily distinguishable from a similarly shaped and sized cut oriented differently. On the other hand, the orientation of a very small and round cut such as in Figure 14.5A would likely not be possible to distinguish. The orientation of RACs is independent of their position, size, and shape.

Quantitative versus Qualitative Aspects

RACs occur in varying quantities and qualities. In one examination, there may be only one clear RAC while another may have eight or more. There must be sufficient clarity to find some cause-and-effect relationship between the characteristic in the scene impression and the respective characteristic on the shoe. Sufficient clarity means the examiner can relate details of the characteristic in the crime scene impression with the respective RAC on the outsole. A characteristic in the scene impression that is clear and correlates well with the known shoe will carry far more value in the examination as that clarity allows for its specific edge details and features to be more closely examined. Clarity problems occur routinely for a variety of reasons. Some substrates are simply not conducive to good replication. An example would be impressions made in coarse soils or rocky and sandy mixtures that are not capable of replicating fine details. Another example would be impressions made in a wet or fluid substance such as blood that may be squeezed into a characteristic, masking portions of or all of its features. Clarity can also be limited in impressions recovered improperly due to shortcomings in photography or other recovery methods. When random characteristics are not sufficiently clear to correlate well with respective features in the shoe, their weight in the examination is reduced accordingly. Characteristics that are of such limited clarity that they only appear as a possible disturbance in the questioned impression, even if they are in the same position, may possibly be of no value in the examination. The examiner must be as objective as possible in associating RACs on an outsole with characteristics in the questioned impression. Some examiners claim they have a "trained eye," stating they can see features better than the average person. This is not correct. Although an examiner's training will enable him or her to find features more efficiently and understand their significance far better than an untrained person, any characteristics they find should be observable by everyone.

Confirmation as Random

What appear to be RACs on an outsole should not automatically be presumed to be random. In most cases, it is easy to confirm that a particular feature was not part of the manufactured outsole and is a RAC. Foreign matter such as rocks, gum, nails, and debris is easily recognized and verified as such and is obviously not part of the original outsole. Larger RACs that are a result of the loss of part of the outsole (large cuts, scratches, gouges, etc.) are equally easy to recognize as random, but smaller ones should be examined under magnification as necessary to confirm they represent an area where part of the outsole was randomly damaged and not a surviving remnant of molded texture or design. Surviving

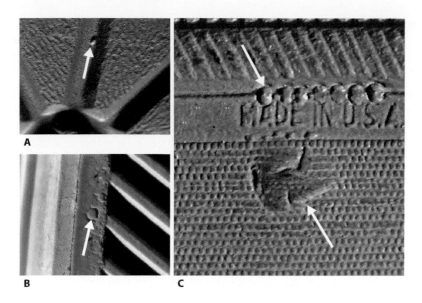

Figure 14.7 Outsoles showing air release ports that are manufactured mold characteristics (A and B), and an outsole showing date code marks (C); and a large area of rubber that filled in random damage to a calender roller (C).

bits of a groove or texture in a worn area of the outsole can easily be mistaken for a cut. The arrow in Figure 14.1 (#11) points to a small remnant of a sipe that could be accidentally mistaken for a random cut. The arrow in Figure 14.1 (above #5) points to one of many remnants of worn texture that appear across this area of the shoe and are not RACs.

During examination, the distinction between certain characteristics of a mold and RACs that are random damage should be clearly understood. For instance, areas representing coded manufacturer's marks, dings or scratches in metal molds or calender rollers are depressed and therefore fill with rubber compound during molding, appearing on the shoe outsole as raised areas of rubber. Mold damage is not commonly encountered, as manufacturers tend to repair those quickly, but air release ports, date coding marks, and other features will occasionally be seen on outsoles and should be distinguished from random damage (RACs) that occurs after the outsole is made. Figure 14.7 shows some examples of outsoles with raised areas of rubber that resulted from intentional marks on a mold and damage to the calender roller. Because these will be repetitively produced on many outsoles, they represent class characteristics. This is clearly different from RACs such as cuts or scratches where rubber is randomly removed from a single outsole resulting in a void area on the outsole. The only exception to this will be the vary rare occasion where something like unmixed soling compound may randomly appear on the surface of a specific molded outsole, such as shown in Figure 14.1 (#14).

Footwear Compared to "Points" on Fingerprints

Fingerprints and shoe impressions have some common association, but their similarities lie mainly in ways they are detected, recovered, and enhanced at crime scenes. The evaluation of their features is quite different. During embryological development, the ridge patterns of fingerprints are randomly formed on the skin's surface. Any single ridge feature like an ending ridge, bifurcation, or island, in the strictest definition, is a class characteristic as each can be found on more than one individual. These ridge features are permanent and remain the same throughout an individual's entire life. The presence of many of these features and their relative positions on a finger, palm, or foot provide the basis for an examiner to reach an opinion that a latent crime scene print originated from a specific individual. Unlike fingerprints, shoes come in many designs and sizes. Most people do not have the same or even similar outsole designs; rather, thousands of choices exist when purchasing footwear and most own many pairs of shoes. Shoes, unlike fingerprints, are constantly changing throughout their usable life due to the erosion of the outsole and randomly acquired features. Although an individual may be arrested with the shoes on his or her feet, technically speaking, shoe marks and impressions are not identified with a person but with his or her shoes.

A misunderstanding between fingerprints and shoe prints concerns an often-asked question, "How many points do you need in a footwear impression to make an identification?" This question has arisen from the public's familiarity with the term *point* or *point of identification*, as has been used in the field of fingerprint identification for decades. Even though this term is no longer used in fingerprint examination, the term still lingers as well as the incorrect presumption that it is also applicable to footwear evidence. The term *point* originated as reference to a specific area of minutiae of a fingerprint. There are literally thousands of designs of shoes, each coming in a large variety of sizes, any of which could be distinguished from one another. How many points would there be for any particular design? How many points would there be for a particular size? How many points would there be for general wear or more extreme wear or for RACs? How would the points vary for RACs of different sizes and shapes and clarity?

A point system has never been used in forensic footwear examination because of the mixed valuation of class, wear, and RACs that collectively forms that basis for opinion.

Replication or Lack of Replication of Randomly Acquired Characteristics

In order for any feature on an outsole to be replicated in a mark or impression, many things must be just right. For a two-dimensional impression, there is usually a transfer of a substance from the shoe to the substrate. The quantity and nature of the substance on the outsole, the features of the substrate, and other factors involved will affect whether an impression is produced and the degree to which its replication is successful. For a three-dimensional impression, the conditions must be sufficient to be reproduced in that medium. For example, a shallow cut or scratch, or a shallow acid-etch texture may be replicated in a crime scene impression on a smooth substrate but would not be expected to replicate itself in an impression in most soil or snow.

For both two- and three-dimensional impressions, conditions for replication are often poor. Many factors interfere with, restrict, or prevent impressions or portions of impressions from being formed. A few of those include variations in the quantity and quality of substances on the outsole; contaminates and other factors that diminish a substrate's ability to replicate and/or hold detail; irregularities in the content and/or moisture of sand, soil, and snow; movement of the shoe during the impression process; and the weight or forces exerted. Even when conditions are ideal, the production of an impression at a crime scene by an item of footwear is not a perfect process and will vary from one step to the next. There should be no expectation that every feature of a shoe will be perfectly represented in an impression it leaves or even that it will be represented at all. This is normal and demonstrable, and the absence of evidence of a RAC in an impression does not constitute a basis for exclusion.

Changes in Randomly Acquired Characteristics after Additional Wear

Once a random characteristic is acquired on a shoe outsole, it is subject to changes as the shoe continues to be worn. Some may completely disappear in a matter of a few steps, such as a stone hold being released from the tread. Others may last a long time but gradually become altered as the outsole gradually erodes away. Casework experience has demonstrated the potential of RACs surviving for long periods of time for various reasons. If the wearer owns many pair of shoes, it is possible the shoes will not be worn again for weeks or months if ever at all. Even when the shoe is worn, many RACs can survive for long periods of time. Because of the many variables possible, there is no way to calculate how long a RAC will or should last. Cases where RACs were still present many months later are not rare. One study explored the rate of disappearance of artificially applied cuts to various parts of a shoe sole.[*] It concluded that the characteristics such as cuts easily survived the seven-week period of their study and thus concluded RACs could be of value weeks after the date of the crime. Another study followed the changes in general wear and the randomly acquired characteristics of 26 laboratory employees for two months and found many of the RACs survived, some disappeared, and new ones were acquired.[†] Cassidy published his study of new heels over a period of 68 days and kept track of when RACs first appeared and when they disappeared. Of the 36 RACs he tracked, he stated, "I was surprised to find a number of characteristics lasting for 59–68 days. This number represents 33% of the characteristics examined …. Possibilities do exist for identification more than 21 days after an offence."[‡]

Another study examined the number, location, and duration of RACs and how long it took them to wear away. It concluded, "Features appeared on all sections of the outsole at approximately the same rate and lasted roughly the same duration. There appeared to be a large number of very short lived features (100–200 hours) with longer lived features becoming progressively rarer." They also concluded "… a shoe worn for approximately 150 hours after an offence could be expected to lose over 50% of the features observed in the original impression."[§]

---

[*] Sheets, D. H., Gross, S., Langenburg, G., Bush, P., and Bush. M., Shape measurement tools in footwear analysis: A statistical investigation of accidental characteristics over time, *Forensic Science International*, 232:84–91, 2013.

[†] Wyatt, J., Duncan, K., and Trimpe, M., Aging of shoes and its effect on shoeprint impressions, *JFI*, 55(2):181–188, 2005.

[‡] Cassidy, M. J., *Footwear Identification*. Canadian Government Printing Centre, Quebec, Canada, 1980.

[§] Tart, M. S., and Adams, J., Transient wear features, The Forensic Science Service, Birmingham, UK, Report No. TN824, October 1997.

As RACs begin to erode and wear away, they will eventually only include portions of features they originally had. Even then, if a portion of their shape or orientation survives, it may still be possible to associate them with the crime scene impression. With additional use, shoes can also acquire new RACs that were not part of the outsole at the time of the crime.

Chances of Another Shoe Having the Same Randomly Acquired Characteristic

The unlikely chance of the features and position of any RAC being duplicated on another shoe are what make RACs so important in forensic footwear examinations. Through the experiences of examiners over time, there is agreement the possibility of finding two indistinguishable RACs in the same position on two shoe outsoles of the same design and size is inconceivable. Studies conducted to test these experience-based observations have either been limited in scope (number of footwear) for logistical reasons, or alternately predicted as mathematical calculations. One mathematical calculation involved the outsole shown in Figure 14.5. The 1 mm square size of the grid was used as it is realistic and easy to distinguish the position of any RAC by changes of 1 mm.[*] The surface area of the model shoe was estimated as 16,000 square mm; thus the chances of another shoe (of any design) having a RAC in the same position was calculated at 1 in 16,000. This calculation was made based on a very small and featureless cut, and for purposes of this study did not attempt to take into consideration additional features of that cut such as its size, shape, and orientation. Further, the equation did not take into consideration the number of shoes sold with that outsole design, or other features of that shoe outsole. Using this model, the chances of a shoe having two consecutive characteristics produced in the same two sectors was calculated at 1 in 127,992,000, three characteristics at 1 in 683 billion, four characteristics at 1 in 2.7 quadrillion, and five characteristics at 1 in 8.7 quintillion.[†] To be clear, these calculations only applied to the positions of the RACs and excluded consideration of the size, shape, and orientation of those RACs as well as the outsole design and general wear of the shoe used. The mathematical model used in these examples provides appreciation of the importance and strength of RACs based on their position alone and was not intended to represent the precise statistics or circumstances that might surround a specific case with specific RAC features. An updated version of this study considered some basic RAC features such as their size, shape, and orientation, demonstrating how quickly they decreased the chances of a second shoe duplicating those combined events.[‡]

Another study used facial recognition techniques to study the quantitative aspects of RACs on five pairs of shoes of the same design worn by the same individual. It concluded,

[*] Stone, R. S., Mathematical probabilities in footwear comparisons, presented at the FBI Technical Conference on Footwear and Tire Impression Evidence, Quantico, VA, April 1984.

[†] Ibid.

[‡] Stone, R., Footwear examinations: mathematical probabilities of theoretical individual characteristics, *JFI*, 4(56):577–599, 2006.

"... the ability to still easily distinguish between such shoes with minimal detailed data strongly supports the claims of the great discrimination power of footwear impressions."[*]

A more practical study of the formation of RACs involved six pairs of the same style of new Hi-Tec boots worn by both men and women during an approximate 7-mile round trip hike up a summit in Colorado and six additional new pairs of the same style worn on the return hike down the summit. This study was a little different from others in that it involved randomly acquired damage to new boots worn by six individuals over the same substrate for the same distance for only part of one day. The hiking trail substrate was composed of a soil and rock mix. Numerous RACs occurred on all of the boots. None of the boots acquired RACs in the same positions and none of the RACs shared identical size or shape features.[†]

A small study involved only two co-workers who wore Nike athletic shoes of the same design on similar surfaces and for similar distances over a period of months. This study also documented that none of the RACs acquired on the two pairs of shoes repeated.[‡]

Another study involved 39 pairs of Adidas Supernova Classic men's size 12 shoes that were worn by the same runner. The runner ran over the same three primary locations and logged the distances that were run in each pair. The distances averaged about 341 miles for each pair. The shoes the runner saved represented a period of several years.[§] This study only counted RACs that replicated in the test impressions made on a two-dimensional substrate. The stone holds and Schallamach patterns on each shoe were not included. The study documented 39 areas of each outsole, noting great variance in the positions and features of the RACs.

A much larger study of RACs in actual footwear was in progress at West Virginia University (WVU) at the time this book went to press. The WVU study, entitled "A Quantitative Assessment of Shoe Print Accidental Patterns with Implications Regarding Similarity, Frequency and Chance Association of Features" involves over 1000 pairs of shoes of varied sizes and brands. The long-term goal of this project is to determine the chance of random duplication of RACs as a function of location and shape. All outsoles selected for inclusion in this study will create a "RAC map" of at least three features (with some outsoles having more than 100 RACs). Each RAC comprising the map will be classified (i.e., as lines, curves, etc.) and compared with regard to position and geometry. When this is repeated for isolated RACs (as well as combinations of RACs such as pairs, triplets, etc.), the dataset can yield estimates concerning the frequency of chance association between features present on known nonmatch outsoles.[¶]

[*] Petraco, N., Gambino, C., Kubic, T., and Olivio, D., Statistical discrimination of footwear: a method for the comparison of accidentals on shoe outsoles inspired by facial recognition techniques, *J. Forensic Sci.*, 55(1), January 2010.

[†] Adair, T., LeMay, J., McDonald, A., Shaw, R., and Tewes, R., The Mount Bierstadt Study: an experiment in unique damage formation in footwear, *JFI*, 2(57), 2007.

[‡] Hamburg, C., and Banks, R., Evaluation of the random nature of acquired marks on footwear outsoles, presented at the Impression and Pattern Evidence Symposium, August 2010, Clearwater, FL.

[§] Wilson, H., Comparison of the individual characteristics in the outsoles of thirty-nine pairs of Adidas Supernova Classic shoes, *JFI*, 62(3), 2012.

[¶] Speir, J., A quantitative assessment of shoe print accidental patterns with implications regarding similarity, frequency and chance association of features, West Virginia University (2014–2016), NIJ Award No. 2013-DN-BX-K043.

How Many RACs Are Necessary for Identification?

As additional empirical data and statistical studies are completed, they continue to confirm the tremendous weight RACs contribute toward the individualization of shoe outsoles. Any random event that occurs to a shoe outsole becomes increasingly less likely to be duplicated as the dimensional and shape complexity of that characteristic increases. Research cited previously has provided quantitative information regarding the chance duplication of the position, orientation, size, and shape of RACs on other outsoles. The number of RACs needed for identification relates strongly to their complexity and quality (clarity) of replication, and examiner assessment of this is an extremely important factor. A RAC cannot be used at all if it is not replicated in the crime scene impression with at least minimal quality. The examiner must be convinced he or she is seeing a characteristic in the scene impression that can be related to a RAC on the respective position of the outsole. Sufficient edge detail is required to establish this relationship and not just the mere fact they are in the same position. RACs that contain and therefore can be examined by virtue of their corresponding edge detail and features can be evaluated more objectively.

Examiners have occasionally commented on the number of RACs required to make an identification of a shoe. One examiner explained, "A scientist would attach much greater significance to a large characteristic than to a small one ... One good 'characteristic', taken with other factors like pattern, etc. can be sufficient to identify a shoe conclusively."[*] Another examiner stated, "A number of factors enter in the number of accidental characteristics required before a positive identification can be established, the most important of which are the examiner's experience, the impression's clarity and the uniqueness or significance of the characteristic."[†] Others have also addressed this question, stating, "The answer depends upon the uniqueness and individuality of the characteristics themselves and the number felt necessary in the examiner's judgment."[‡]

Reaching a conclusion of identification based on only one random event is theoretically possible but only if that RAC included sufficient complex features combined with sufficient clarity. It is noted after 44 years' experience, the author has never opined identification with just one RAC although I cannot exclude this possibility should the proper evidence exist. A reason for this stems from the necessity for the impression to have a complex RAC that has been replicated with sufficient edge detail and clarity to make this possible. In cases where this occurs, the impression usually has retained multiple RACs. Another reason is the desire to make the examination as objective as possible; thus, one RAC, even if complex and replicated with good clarity, might still fall short of what an examiner requires before opining a shoe is the source of an impression.

Key Words: random, randomly acquired characteristics (RAC), position, size, shape, orientation

---

[*] Davis, R., Michigan State Police class on Footwear Evidence, East Lansing, MI, 1985.
[†] Cassidy, M. J., *Footwear Identification*. Canadian Government Printing Centre, Quebec, Canada, 1980, p. 96.
[‡] Zmuda, C., and Brodie, T., Limitations in the identification of foot and shoe impressions, Miami, FL (undated).

Key Points

1. A randomly acquired characteristic (RAC) is a feature on a shoe outsole resulting from random events including, but not limited to, cuts, scratches, tears, holes, stone holds, abrasions, and the acquisition of debris.
2. The position, size and shape, and orientation of RACs contribute to the uniqueness of a footwear outsole and are essential to opining a shoe as the source of a crime scene impression.
3. There is no set number of RACs necessary to identify a shoe as the source of an impression.
4. The complexity of size and shape features of RACs combined with the level of clarity in the crime scene impression determines the weight or value of that characteristic in the examination.
5. Randomly acquired characteristics are not replicated in every impression. Their absence in an impression is not a basis for exclusion. Additional RACs could occur on footwear of a suspect between the date of the crime and the date the shoes were seized.
6. Research has demonstrated that RACs occur on shoe outsoles in a highly random manner, and the chance duplication of even one characteristic's position, orientation, shape, and size on another shoe of the same size and design would be rare.

Known Footwear and Known Impression Standards 15

Shoes seized from suspects, be they voluntarily provided, obtained incident to arrest, or the result of a search warrant, are usually associated with a known individual and therefore referred to as known footwear. Impressions of those shoes produced during a forensic examination are described with varied terminology, including the terms *known impressions*, *known test impressions*, *known impression standards*, *known exemplars*, *test prints*, and *test impressions*. Known impressions are important during a forensic examination as they demonstrate how outsoles replicate their class and individual features. Known impressions produced on transparent media or an opaque material later converted to a transparent form provide an important comparison tool that can be superimposed over a crime scene impression. In addition to the examination, known impressions can be used in notes and reports and, later, for demonstrative purposes in court. Creating known impressions of shoes as part of the examination of crime scene marks or impressions is an essential part of the comparative process. This chapter covers the examiner's considerations and treatment of known footwear and provides several methods for producing known impressions.

Elimination Impressions or Photographs

Many crime scenes reveal footwear impressions but it is not always evident whether those impressions belong to the perpetrator, are impressions produced prior to and thus unrelated to the crime, or were produced by first responders, medical personnel, or investigators. In many instances, it is important to keep a record of the footwear outsole design of every individual known to have entered the scene so their footwear can be distinguished from those worn by the perpetrator(s). Traditionally, records of footwear for elimination purposes were made by producing known impressions and were referred to as "elimination impressions." Since these are for exclusionary purposes and only need to record the shoe design, the digital camera is now usually used to produce this elimination record. The purpose of the photograph of the outsole is not to provide a known exemplar for a full forensic examination, but to allow for documentation and subsequent exclusion of the footwear of innocent persons based on their different outsole designs. An example of an elimination photograph is provided in Figure 15.1. The photograph does not require a scale but should include some identifier or record of whose shoe is in the photograph. Creating this elimination record of footwear is very important for evidentiary reasons, and allows crime scene personnel to focus on the recovery of impressions that cannot be accounted for and are likely the impressions of the perpetrator(s).

Figure 15.1 Digital photographs of shoes of first responders and others who may have walked through the crime scene should be made for elimination purposes so focus can be directed to impressions likely to be those of the perpetrator. A case example of this process was discussed in connection with Figure 1.2.

Examination Requires the Actual Shoes

When investigators have seized a suspect's shoes for comparison, both shoes should be submitted to the examiner. Providing only test impressions or photographs will not be sufficient to allow a proper examination. The forensic footwear examiner should be the one who makes test impressions, and will need the shoes to evaluate them at their highest detail level. Occasionally, circumstances sometimes present themselves where the shoes were simply not seized and are no longer available and only photographs of their outsoles were retained. Without the shoes, the scope of the examination will be limited; however, some evaluation may still be possible.

Obtaining Known Shoes from a Suspect

There are many reasons why individuals who commit a serious crime do not discard their footwear. Impressions produced during the crime are often produced in low ambient light and/or are latent, meaning the perpetrator will not be aware he or she produced them. Even when highly visible impressions like those in blood are produced, factors relating to the conditions of the perpetrator such as their mental condition, their use of alcohol or drugs, or simply ignorance of the potential evidential value of the impressions may cause or contribute to a lack of awareness or concern regarding that evidence. In addition, factors surrounding the commission of a crime often require a hasty exit from the scene with little opportunity to clean up evidence. Of course, there are also those who are just not smart, as well as those who simply won't part with a favorite pair of athletic shoes.

Many suspects are interviewed and/or arrested within minutes to hours of the crime, leaving them little or no time to change their footwear. In other investigations, days or weeks may pass before suspects are interviewed or arrested. In those cases, investigators should be cautious and discreet when asking about footwear or mentioning footwear impressions until they are in a position to seize all of the suspect's shoes. In addition, no public statements should be released to the press regarding footwear evidence, as the release of this information to the public will only educate and provide opportunity for the perpetrators to discard their shoes. There have been many occasions when news commentators have announced the existence of footwear evidence in major unsolved homicide cases prior to the development of a suspect or the seizure of their footwear. This grossly irresponsible practice can result in loss of evidence. When crime scenes are being processed for footwear evidence in the public view, such as making casts or photographs of exterior impressions, these events may be witnessed and filmed by TV news crews. Should this be apparent, the news personnel should be requested not to publish that video, as it will also act as a signal to the perpetrator to discard the footwear.

Sometimes the single pair of shoes a suspect is wearing is seized and it turns out those shoes were actually responsible for producing the crime scene impressions; however, the investigator seizing those shoes has no way of knowing that at the time. They could have been the wrong shoes that just coincidentally had a similar looking outsole design as it is not uncommon at all to find individuals owning more than one pair of either the same design or similar designs. If the shoes seized were not those used during the crime, the perpetrator will likely, at his or her first convenience, discard the relevant and incriminating pair. Investigators should be aware of this when addressing the extent of their search for footwear. Searches and search warrants should extend to all footwear of an individual. Figure 15.2 shows four pairs of shoes seized in a serial homicide case. The suspect was wearing the top left pair at the time of his arrest. The top right pair was of the same design, color, and brand and seized from his mother's house where he resided along with the other similar looking pairs. The top right pair was identified with impressions from the crime scene. If the shoes this individual was wearing at the time of his arrest were the only shoes seized, the forensic examination would have excluded those shoes and the shoes that made the crime scene impressions would likely never have been recovered. Fortunately, his arrest was conducted along with a search warrant for all shoes.

Shoes of Additional Perpetrators

It is not rare for partners in crime to wear footwear of the same or similar design. This could be for coincidental reasons but might also be a situation where both were wearing the same design because those shoes were trendy, were the accepted footwear of a particular group or gang, or for other reasons. One case example of this occurred in a homicide on a small island. The seized shoes one suspect was wearing were visibly similar to the casts of

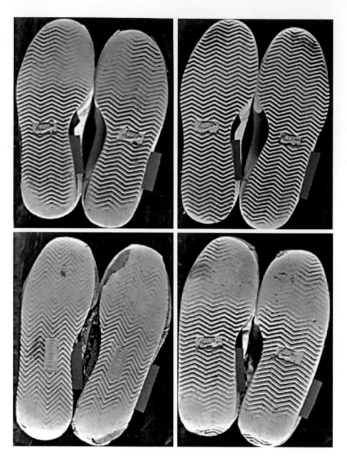

Figure 15.2 Four pairs of shoes seized from one individual incident to arrest and a search warrant. One of the pairs he was not wearing at the time of arrest was identified with the homicide scene.

footwear impressions in mud next to the victim. When the investigator seized the shoes of the first suspect, she recognized the similar design and believed they were the shoes that had made the impressions, and thus made no further attempt to obtain a search warrant or pursue looking for the shoes of the second suspect. When submitted for examination, it turned out the shoes were the same design but a much larger size with different mold characteristics and they were easily excluded as the source of the impressions. By the time this was known the shoes of the second suspect were gone.

Another case example involved two pieces of paper stepped on during a safe burglary and theft of $35,000. Seven partial impressions across both pieces of paper appeared generally similar to the herringbone and circle design of the first suspect's shoes. Upon examination in the laboratory, the first suspect's shoes were identified with one of those impressions but his shoes were clearly excluded as the possible source of the other six impressions. In this case, the investigators were more fortunate. Weeks after the forensic footwear report revealed there was a second pair of shoes of the same design involved, they seized those from a second suspect who later confessed to his participation in the crime.

Shoeboxes, Receipts, Photographs, and Other Options

Many case investigations never result in obtaining footwear that corresponds with the design of the crime scene impressions. That doesn't mean all is lost. Searches for shoeboxes, receipts of footwear purchases, and photographs of the suspect wearing the shoes occasionally result in the discovery of evidence relating to the shoes of interest. Some individuals discard their shoeboxes but others save them for various uses. One memorable case was a homicide where several bloody marks were produced by the perpetrator on pieces of paper lying next to the victim. The impressions were produced by Adidas Ilie Nastase size 8.5 tennis shoes. Although these shoes were never recovered, the perpetrator saved the shoebox for use as a temporary mailbox while his front porch was being repaired. This case is discussed in Chapter 19.

In some cases, proof of a suspect's purchase of footwear of the same brand and size shoe as the shoes that produced the impressions at the scene has been productive. This may involve physical receipts still in the suspect's residence or evidence of the purchase of footwear discovered through a search of credit card transactions. In one small-town homicide, the receipt found in the home of the suspect was actually handwritten by a local shoe salesman who was able to provide additional valuable evidence.

The OJ Simpson civil case is undoubtedly the most famous case involving a photograph of the accused wearing the same brand and style footwear.[*] However, finding photographs or video that shows the suspect wearing shoes of the design and brand that produced the crime scene impressions can come from many sources. Digital camera storage cards of the accused or his or her friends, including their smart phones, as well as surveillance videos recovered near the scene might also reveal a suspect wearing the shoes used in the commission of the crime.

Finally, searching the crime scene impressions through a database to determine their brand often provides investigative leads. Photographs of the shoe design can be obtained from that source or from online sources and can be shown to witnesses and friends of the accused for recognition as shoes they may recognize the accused once owned. In one case, an informant provided information that a homicide was committed by a certain group. Bloody impressions of two shoe designs were associated with two specific brands as well as the description of those shoe uppers. Surveillance identified individuals in that group wearing those designs, which led to a warrant and seizure of their footwear and subsequent identification.

Treatment of Seized Footwear

Any shoes that are wet or bloody should be thoroughly air dried before being placed in an evidence bag. It is not recommended that shoes be sealed in plastic as any residual moisture they contain could contribute to the growth of mold or the degradation of other evidence. The date shoes were seized should always be provided on the evidence container. Shoes not only leave their evidence in the form of impressions but also can acquire blood, hair, fibers,

---

[*] Bodziak, W. J., *Footwear Impression Evidence: Detection, Recovery and Examination*, 2nd ed., CRC Press, Boca Raton, FL, 2000.

glass, soil, and other evidence that might later be determined relevant in the proof of facts. For that reason, any footwear seized from a suspect should be treated with the maximum precautions to preserve that evidence. Footwear impression comparisons should take place only after all other evidence concerns are met. If in doubt, a footwear examiner should ensure that all blood and trace comparison work is completed and that it is permissible to make known impressions for comparison.

Documentation of Seized Footwear

Before conducting an examination, photographs of the shoes and outsoles should be taken to document their general condition and appearance as received. Seized shoes often contain mud, possible RACs of a temporary nature, or materials that may interfere with or prevent the production of known impressions. They should be photographed first to make a record of those features and then cleaned to enable the production of known impression standards. Examination quality photographs of the outsoles should be taken with emphasis on documenting the design, general wear, and any randomly acquired characteristics. Figure 15.3 shows a top and side view of a shoe being photographed on a copy stand. Although shoe holders or shoetrees will help keep footwear reasonably straight, the outsole will still likely have some curvature as can be seen in the heel and toe areas of the photograph. Photographs are necessary for documentation but they are not true to scale or dimensionally accurate. Photographs alone should not be used for direct physical comparison in lieu of known impressions.

Examiner notes should contain a general description of the shoes, including brand, color, size, and a photograph of the label and/or size information area. If the date on which

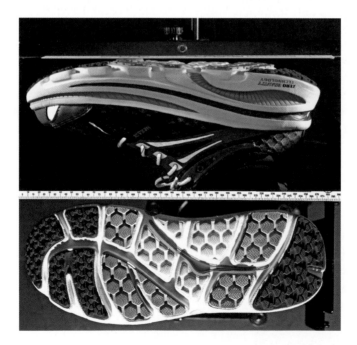

Figure 15.3 Copy stand photographs of known shoes are made to document and record details; however, the curvature of the footwear outsole reduces the dimensional accuracy.

the shoes were seized has not been provided, that date should be obtained from investigators. In consideration of the chain of custody, the evidence should be initialed or an identification card attached.

Basic Information about Known Impressions

Figure 15.4 is a reversed photograph of a well-worn heel alongside a two-dimensional known impression of that heel. It is a good example of how difficult it is to just look at a shoe outsole and visualize what its impression would look like because of how an impression is influenced by very subtle variations in sole depth and pressure.

Known impressions provide an excellent comparison tool, whether examining two- or three-dimensional impressions in the form of photographs, casts, or lifts. They provide natural size known impressions of the outsole in its impression form. Transparent forms of a known impression in the form of an overlay can be superimposed over the crime scene impression, allowing for simultaneous comparison of multiple design and dimensional characteristics.

Not every impression made of a shoe will reflect every detail; thus, more than one known test impression of the shoe should be made to provide a more complete evaluation of how that shoe leaves its impression.[*] One examiner points out "…one test impression doesn't ensure that we have the most representative print…the forensic procedure for making test impressions must include a requirement for creating several test impressions of the shoe, possibly under different conditions."[†]

Figure 15.5 illustrates variations between two known impressions made by the same shoe, one right after the other. Variations are normal and occur for various reasons, including minor differences in pressure, weight shift, substrate, the amount of ink, powder, residue, or blood on the shoe, and other factors. The purpose of producing known impressions is not to expect they will provide an exact duplicate of the crime scene impression, but rather to produce information on how that shoe repetitively replicates its features as well

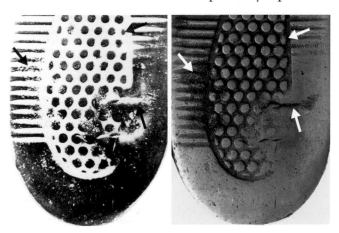

Figure 15.4 A heel and its impression show how it is difficult to predict how a shoe outsole will be replicated in an impression.

---

[*] Bodziak, W. J., *Footwear Impression Evidence: Detection, Recovery, and Examination*, 2nd ed., CRC Press, Boca Raton, FL, 2000, p. 287.

[†] Shor, Y., and Weisner, S., "Why should we make several test impressions" presented at The 11th European Shoeprint/Toolmark Meeting, Prague, Czech Republic, October 21–23, 2014.

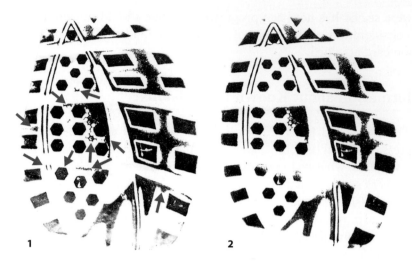

Figure 15.5 When making known impressions of a shoe, there will always be some variation between them. This is normal. The arrows point to a few areas that vary slightly from the second impression.

as to provide a tool that will assist in the physical comparison process with those impressions produced at the crime scene. During the examination, any relevant features can be simultaneously compared between the crime scene impression and the actual shoe outsole.

Known impression methods should strive to obtain a high level of detail. It is neither possible nor necessary to duplicate the precise conditions and impression as formed at the scene; however, some examinations may warrant attempts to make known impressions under similar conditions to those estimated to have existed at the crime scene.

Methods of Producing Known Impressions

Known impressions should be produced in ways that provide accurate and highly detailed recordings of the shoe outsole. They can be made using a firm smooth surface as a background or while using a soft pad or other material as a background substrate. Not every detail will be present in every known impression. Having the experience and materials to make test impressions in a number of ways is essential. In this chapter, several ways to produce known impressions are described. They are divided into two-dimensional and three-dimensional methods. Some techniques involve wearing the shoes while others do not. Slight dimensional variations sometimes occur between impressions produced when the shoe is worn in contrast to those impressions produced by pressing the shoe against a recording medium or transferring powders or inks from the outsole to adhesive lifts.

There are many other acceptable methods of producing known impressions as well as slight adaptations of those described next. The following methods are more popular and provide good detail.

Two-Dimensional Known Impressions

In the vast majority of cases, two-dimensional known impressions are sufficient for comparison with both two- and three-dimensional crime scene impressions. A two-dimensional known impression in a transparent form is an excellent comparative tool whether comparing it to an impression on a tile floor, a photograph of a three-dimensional impression in soil, or to an impression that has been cast. When superimposed over the crime scene impression, transparent overlays allow for simultaneous comparison of multiple design components, dimensions, wear, and RACs. Some methods involve producing the actual impressions on transparent films that enable their immediate use as a comparison overlay. Others produce impressions on opaque materials that require a copy machine, printer, or other process to convert them to a transparent overlay. Copying processes may create slight dimensional changes; thus, a long flat ruler should always be included in any copy or scan of a known impression standard. The dimensional change usually involves no more than 1 mm from heel to toe and in some cases may not exist at all. Some prefer to scan test impressions into a computer graphic program such as Adobe Photoshop or to use a laboratory imaging system where they make the comparison on the computer.[*] Computer methods are commonly used to supplement the physical comparison traditionally made between the actual impression and shoe, although a few examiners are now using laboratory imaging systems to conduct the majority of the examination process. Following are descriptions of several ways to produce two-dimensional impressions. These are not provided in any order of superiority or preference.

Identicator® Pad and Paper

The Identicator® system produces an inkless impression used for shoe print applications. The LE-25 shoe print inkless pad contains a chemical solution that upon contact with chemically treated paper instantly turns black. Figure 15.6 depicts the Identicator yellow pad and an impression made with this method by first stepping on the yellow pad and then onto the paper. The reaction is instant and results in a detailed deep black permanent

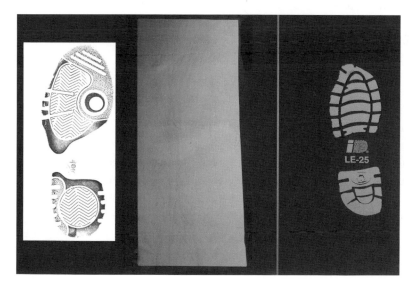

Figure 15.6 The LE-25 Identicator inkless impression pad. An impression is produced by stepping on the yellow pad then onto the chemically treated paper.

[*] Trasoscan Laboratory Imaging (LIM) is one such example; www.forensic.cz.

impression. This product produces excellent detail, easily recording texture and abrasion patterns. The method is very quick and convenient and thus serves well for many examiners as an initial method for making known impressions or as a quick record of excluded footwear. The yellow pad is removable, so as one side becomes soiled after some use, it can be turned over to a clean opposite side. In some cases when new, the pad may be oversaturated with solution and will result in impressions that are not satisfactory. If this is the case, it may be necessary to first step on a blank piece of paper and then onto the treated paper. As the pad is used, it will consume the excess solution and this will remedy itself.

Fingerprint Powder and White or Transparent Adhesive

This is a common method that can be used in a variety of applications. It involves either a high-quality white adhesive or clear adhesive sheets to capture the transfer of black fingerprint powder from the shoe outsole. A Handiprint 9 × 12.5 inch white adhesive lifter and cover sheet are used in Figure 15.7 to demonstrate this process.[*] The method works best with very fine black fingerprint powder and a fiberglass fingerprint brush. First, several very light coatings of black powder are slowly painted across the outsole. This is best done by placing a small quantity of fine black fingerprint powder on a paper towel and picking up small amounts of that powder with a fingerprint brush that has been cut to half its length (A). Spread the powder slowly and evenly over the entire outsole, repeating this procedure four to six times until the outsole is sufficiently and evenly powdered (B). Note that the brush is best used to paint the powder onto the outsole rather than spinning the brush as if you were dusting for fingerprints. The amount of powder on the outsole should be applied evenly in small amounts and does not need to be heavy to produce a good impression using the white adhesive. Tap the shoe on its side to remove any loose powder. Remove the protective layer from the adhesive sheet and lay the adhesive sheet on a smooth counter with the sticky side up, letting 1 inch extend over the counter's edge. Place the shoe against the adhesive sheet with the heel toward the counter's edge and hold in place (C). Grab the edge of the adhesive sheet extending off the counter with the opposite hand while continuing to hold the shoe firmly against the adhesive. Pull the edge of the adhesive upward to secure it against the rear of the heel (D). Rub the tips of your fingers back and forth underneath the adhesive to secure the adhesive firmly against the bottom of the heel. While slowly advancing the shoe toward you, continue to rub your fingers back and forth to secure the adhesive firmly against the outsole (E). When you have done this for the full outsole, turn the shoe with the adhesive sheet still sticking to it upside down. With a soft cloth or paper towel, rub the entire surface of the adhesive sheet against the outsole, ensuring the full perimeter edges, logo areas, and other details of the outsole are recorded on the adhesive (F). Beginning at one end, pull the adhesive sheet away from the outsole and place it adhesive side up on the counter (G). The cover sheet can be applied from one end using a fingerprint roller to avoid trapping air bubbles (H). When this same method is used with clear adhesive sheets, it provides a first generation transparent known impression. The

[*] Handiprint is a product of CSI Forensic Supply (formerly Kinderprint) and is a white adhesive sheet that comes in a 9.5 × 12.5 inch size for footwear impressions. Clear adhesive sheets of a 9.5 × 13.5 inch size are also available. Matching clear cover sheets are either included or can be purchased at the same time.

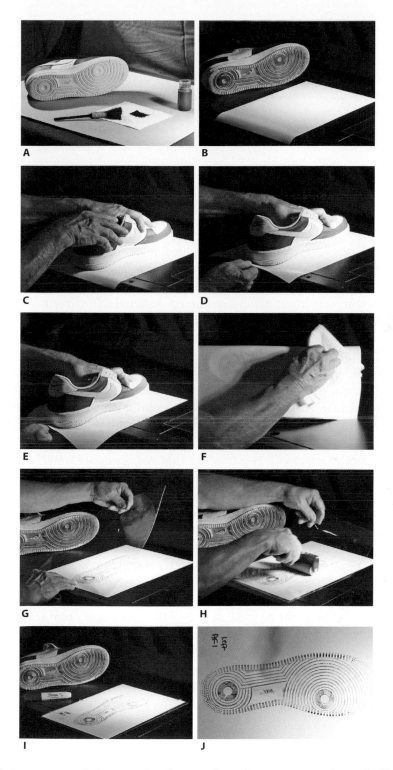

Figure 15.7 A sequence of photographs showing how fingerprint powder and adhesive sheets are used to prepare known impressions.

clear adhesive sheet requires a slightly heavier application of black powder in order to provide sufficient contrast. Whether white or clear adhesive is used, a marker should be used to indicate the identity of the shoe and whether it is the right or left shoe as soon as each impression is completed (J). Many times clear transparencies need to be reversed or clear copies of white known impressions are copied in transparency form, so having the left and right descriptor written on each impression is a good habit. As a variation of this method, you can powder the outsole and then step on the adhesive sheet while wearing the shoe, turning the shoe and adhesive over, and rubbing the surface with a soft cloth, to complete the contact between both. Some use colored fingerprint powders with this method if they provide better contrast with the dark areas of many photographed impressions or lifts.

Roller Transport Film

This method utilizes fingerprint powder applied to a shoe outsole to produce highly detailed impressions on a Kodak product known as roller transport cleanup film.[*] This Kodak product has been used for years for making known impressions but the film is no longer available and existing supplies are almost depleted. No current source of a comparable film is known at this time.[†] The description of the process is provided here for those who still have a supply of the film but also to encourage the discovery of a similar gelatin-coated film that might serve as a substitute. The film contains a thin gelatinous coating on each side. When moistened, the gelatin coating becomes soft for a minute or two, allowing the fine black fingerprint powder transferred from the outsole to become embedded in its surface. Although the use of this technique relies on a future replacement or substitution of this or a similar product, the results achieved with this product were a first generation transparent impression that was as good as or more detailed than most others were. Figure 15.8 shows this procedure that requires only water, a sponge, a piece of roller transport film, a good squeegee, and a powdered shoe. A generous coating of fine black fingerprint powder is first applied to the outsole of the shoe using a short zephyr or similar fiberglass brush. The shoe will need to be tapped firmly on its edge to knock off any excess powder. A piece of roller transport film cut to approximately 8 × 13 inches should be wet by lightly passing a dripping wet sponge across its surface. No rubbing is necessary, as this is merely a way of ensuring the entire surface of the film has been touched by water for the purpose of softening the gelatin. A clean squeegee is then passed once across the film at a slight angle to remove any excess water from that side of the film. Squeegees that are old or damaged should not be used, as they will leave streaks that will be reproduced in the impression. The film should then be placed on a clean smooth floor surface. The impression needs to be made within a minute to two. To produce the powdered impression, wear the shoe and step on the softened transport film. The fingerprint powder will transfer to and become embedded in the softened gelatin coating and the impression will become permanent when the gelatin coating hardens minutes later. The result is a highly detailed

---

[*] Petraco, N., A rapid method for the preparation of transparent footwear test prints, *Journal of Forensic Sciences*, 27(4):935–937, 1982.
[†] Carestream Dental sells Roller Transport cleanup film, believed to be the identical Kodak product, but this has not been confirmed. See https://www.pattersondental.com/Supplies/ProductFamilyDetails/10267

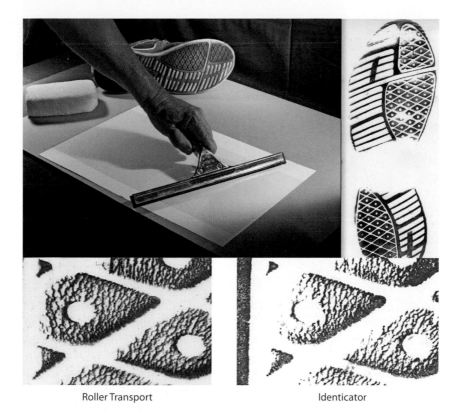

Roller Transport   Identicator

Figure 15.8 Roller transport film is first wet with a sponge and then wiped with one firm pass of a squeegee. The shoe with fingerprint powder on its sole will imbed the powder into the soft gelatin coating on the transport film, leaving a very highly detailed impression. A portion of the impression made with this method is compared with the highly detailed Identicator method.

impression on a very clear transparent film. Figure 15.8 also shows a highly enlarged section of the roller transport impression alongside an Identicator impression. Although both produce a high level of detail, the soft gelatin coating of the roller transport film picked up a more complete representation of the Schallamach pattern.

Black Gelatin Lift and GLScan

The GLScan or similar line scanners can be used to record excellent known impressions on black gelatin lifters. The shoe outsole needs to be washed clean and allowed to air dry. Any lint, dust, or dirt on the shoe will interfere with or contaminate the impression. An even impression can be made by stepping with the clean shoe on the black gelatin lifter. The GLScan is then used to scan the lifter. Figure 15.9 shows an enlarged area of the GLScan of the impression next to a photograph of the shoe. This form of impression is easy to make and highly detailed. As more people acquire the GLScan and other line scanners and increasingly make portions of their examination on a computer, this method could become more commonly used.

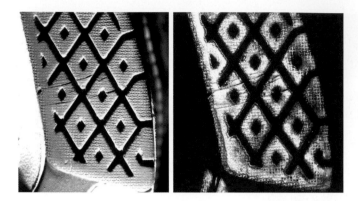

Figure 15.9 An impression made by a clean shoe on a black gelatin lifter and scanned on the GLScan, shown on the right, in contrast to the same area of the shoe, shown on the left.

Oily Substances and Fingerprint Powder on Paper

Coating an outsole with a thin layer of petroleum jelly, WD-40, or countless other materials to produce an oily print on paper is an old but adequate method used by many to produce detailed known impressions. Some prefer using the silicone-coated applicators for shining shoes to rub a thin coat of the silicone across the outsole; some use various oils on a soft cotton rag; while others prefer to use their fingers to spread a very sparse and even coating of petroleum jelly onto the outsole. Once the outsole is coated, wear the shoe to step on a piece of legal size paper. The oily material will be transferred to the paper, after which it can be developed with black magnetic fingerprint powder resulting in a detailed impression. Figure 15.10 shows an impression made by wiping a Kiwi shoeshine sponge across the outsole, stepping on white paper with the shoe, and then developing the impression with black magnetic fingerprint powder. The quality of the paper and the type and quantity of the oily material might be something you need to experiment with before you find the best combinations.

Figure 15.10 Silicone applicators for shining shoes or other oily materials can be used to coat an outsole, after which an impression is made on paper. The impression is developed with fingerprint powder.

Inks

Certain oil-based inks can be used to prepare impressions on both opaque and transparent wet media film when producing known tire impressions.[*] Some oil-based inks like fingerprint ink are formulated to dry instantly. These may not produce the darkest impressions and require reinking if making multiple impressions. Other oil-based inks allow for multiple impressions but may take hours to dry. Speedball oil-based block printing ink is universally available on the Internet and dries within hours, depending on the surface it is applied to. In general, inks tend to be messier and oil-based inks cannot be completely cleaned from the outsole. Although black and other colored oil-based inks can provide excellent contrast and come in many colors, the degree of detail does not exceed and often does not equal other methods that use fine powders. Figure 15.11 illustrates one method that involves spreading the ink on a firm and smooth surface with a fingerprint roller in order to create a uniform and thin coating of ink on the roller. The ink is then rolled across the outsole. An adhesive lift is then made of the outsole. An alternate method is to use the fingerprint roller to spread a light coating of ink across a larger smooth surface such as a piece of solid chart board. While wearing the shoe, the inked surface is stepped on and subsequent impressions are made on paper or wet media film. Any impressions made using this method with block oil-based inks will usually need to dry overnight before use. Oil-based inks come in many colors and work well on clear wet media film to produce impressions. Water-based inks are used by some, dry faster, and although easier to clean, don't replicate the detail as well as the oil-based versions and for that reason are not recommended.

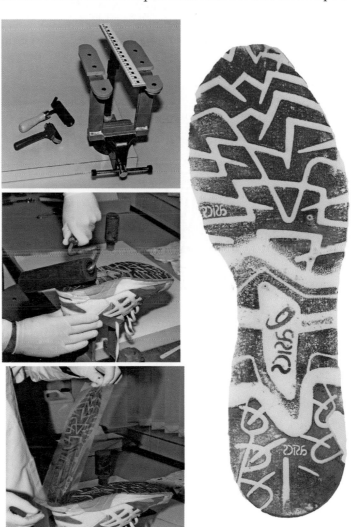

Figure 15.11 Ink can be applied to the shoe outsole to make an adhesive lift as shown at the bottom, or by wearing the shoe and producing an impression by stepping on wet media film or paper.

[*] Bodziak, W. J., *Tire Tread and Tire Track Evidence*, CRC Press, Boca Raton, FL, 2008.

Three-Dimensional Known Impressions

Two-dimensional known impressions in transparent form are normally sufficient as a comparative tool but there are occasions where three-dimensional known impressions are preferred or necessary. Three-dimensional known impressions are also prepared for demonstrative aids in notes, reports, and court. Figure 15.12A shows the heel of a shoe next to both two- (B) and three-dimensional (C) impressions of that heel. In the last picture (D), the two-dimensional impression is superimposed over the three-dimensional impression. Some of the areas of the heel not represented in the two-dimensional impression but replicated in the sand impression are colored green. A number of methods and materials to make three-dimensional impressions are routinely used. The one chosen may depend on whether a full or partial impression is needed, whether the shoes need to be worn, and other case-specific reasons. Some methods of producing three-dimensional known impressions are described hereafter. They are not in any order of preference or level of detail.

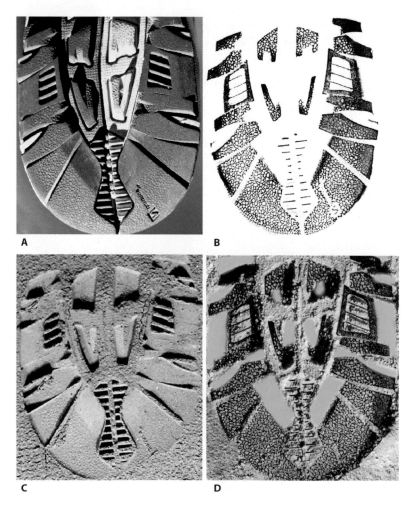

Figure 15.12 Two- and three-dimensional known impressions of the same heel show the variations in how each represents the heel of the shoe.

Polyvinylsiloxane

Dental casting materials known as polyvinylsiloxane (PVS) or polysiloxane provide a quick and convenient way to produce three-dimensional representations of an outsole. Polyvinylsiloxanes are available through dental suppliers in various forms and colors. These products are made for use in the mouth and so are safe to handle. The degree of detail is very good and the PVS impression hardens so it can be retained. No release agent is necessary. Figure 15.13 shows two examples of PVS. The Elite HD Plus consists of both soft base and catalyst putties.* These are normally mixed in 50/50 proportions. The other example is Zetaplus, which consists of a putty base and a gel catalyst in a tube. Polyvinylsiloxanes are very easy to use. Figure 15.14 provides a sequence of the use of the Elite HD putty to create a cast of a heel. Equal parts of the two soft putty components are mixed and kneaded with the bare hands (A and B). The warmth of the hands softens the product and is the recommended way to mix the materials. The components must be combined very quickly by folding them into one another and kneading them together until they are one color (C). The

Figure 15.13 Polyvinylsiloxane products are used in the dental industry and are useful for producing three-dimensional impressions of outsoles.

* Elite HD plus and Zetaplus are Zhermack polyvinylsiloxane products and are available from dental suppliers.

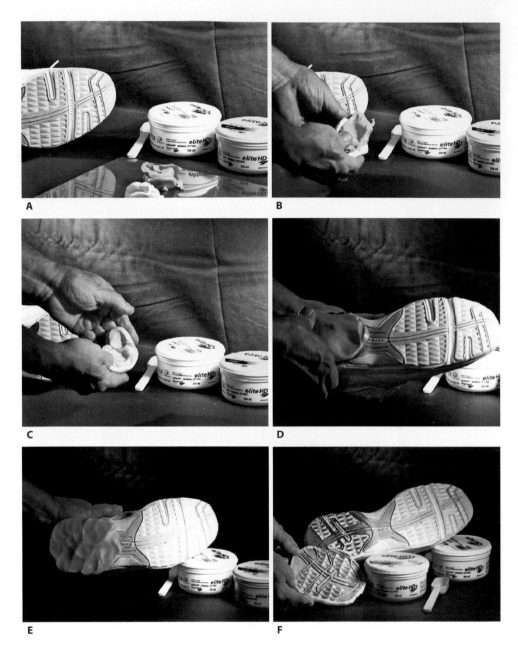

Figure 15.14 Using polyvinylsiloxane putty to produce a three-dimensional impression of a heel.

mixed putty is then spread over the relevant area of the inverted shoe (D). During this process, the soft putty is very pliable and easily spread with the hands and should be pressed into the outsole design to avoid air pockets (E). Placing the PVS on a substrate and pressing the shoe into it does not work and results in incomplete impressions and air entrapment. The entire mixing and pressing process must be performed in just 3–4 minutes. The PVS hardens quickly and is easily removed from the outsole in 10–15 minutes (F).

The other PVS product shown in Figure 15.13 is Zetaplus. It comes in a putty form with the Indurent gel catalyst provided in a tube.* Zetaplus and the catalyst, once combined, should be quickly mixed together in your bare hands. Mixing the putty and gel in the hands is messier than mixing two putty components, but more efficient than using gloves. The mixed Zetaplus can be applied to an inverted shoe outsole in the same way as described for the PVS. The Zetaplus will harden and can be removed from the outsole in 10 minutes. Other forms of PVS products are also sold through dental suppliers and come in different setting times, different colors, and varying degrees of hardness. One form that is commonly used for fingerprints and tool marks involves an extruder gun with replaceable 50-ml cartridges that allow for simultaneous injection of small quantities of liquid base and liquid catalyst. This form of PVS may be of use for smaller fingerprints, but is neither practical nor cost effective for use with footwear evidence.

Mikrosil®

The same product described for lifting powdered impressions in Chapter 5 can also be used to create a three-dimensional replication of a powdered outsole. Mikrosil is much softer than polyvinylsiloxane and Zetalabor, so is best mixed and spread with a thin pliable spatula. The spatula can then be used to spread the Mikrosil over and into the outsole design. Sufficient quantities of Mikrosil are necessary for this and care needs to be taken to completely cover the desired areas of the outsole in a way to avoid trapping air. Figure 15.15 shows how this product is used. A light coating of fingerprint powder is applied to the area

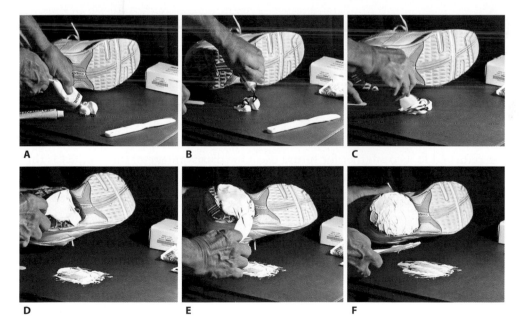

Figure 15.15 Using Mikrosil to produce a three-dimensional impression of a heel.

---

* Note that the Indurent gel catalyst can be used as a substitute for the blue catalyst gel furnished with Mikrosil.

Figure 15.16 From left to right, the ZetaPlus, Elite HD Putty, and Mikrosil casts. Each provided excellent replication of detail.

of the outsole that is to be cast to provide some contrast against the white Mikrosil. The estimated quantity of Mikrosil is squeezed from the tube and the blue catalyst is squeezed over the top (A and B). The two are mixed with the spatula (C). When the blue catalyst is completely mixed with the white base, use the spatula to scoop the Mikrosil onto the shoe, spreading it over and into all of the design areas and grooves (D and E). When done, allow the Mikrosil about 10–15 minutes to harden (F). The Mikrosil can be peeled away from the outsole. Figure 15.16 shows impressions made of the same heel with the previously described three silicone-based products.

MikroTrack™

MikroTrack™ is a reusable product for producing three-dimensional shoe impressions.[*] The soft light-colored material comes in a container as shown in Figure 15.17. Once removed from the container, it can be spread in a way to create a flat and smooth surface. The shoe outsole is then pressed by hand into the MikroTrack product. MikroTrack allows for the reproduction of excellent detail and is capable of providing a very complete and detailed impression of a shoe sole. The impression must be photographed, after which the product can be returned to its container for future use. One disadvantage of the product is the tendency for it to break apart or crack during the impression making process. This is something that can be overcome with the user's technique and after some experience using the product.

Bubber

Bubber is a children's modeling compound produced by Delta of Sweden.[†] It has been used and recommended for the production of three-dimensional known shoe impressions, producing detail exceeding that of sand and Biofoam®.[‡] The product does not harden and can be reused. Because it does not harden, its use is primarily to produce known impressions that need to be photographed. Figure 15.18 depicts a close-up view of a portion of an outsole and a known impression of that area using Bubber.[§]

---

[*] MikroTrack™ is a product of Kjell Carlsson Innovations and is sold through various forensic suppliers.
[†] http://www.deltaofsweden.com
[‡] LeMay, J., Making three-dimensional footwear test impressions with Bubber, *JFI*, 60(4):439–448, 2010.
[§] Provided courtesy of Jan Lemay, Northern Colorado Regional Forensic Laboratory, Greeley, CO, 2015.

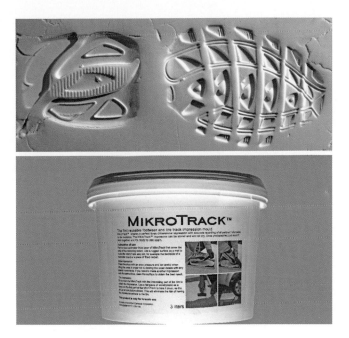

Figure 15.17 MikroTrack™ is a reusable footwear impression material that replicates exccllent detail.

Figure 15.18 A modeling compound called Bubber retains a reasonable amount of detail but does not permanently harden.

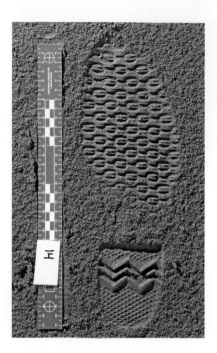

Figure 15.19 A known impression made in moist sand sifted onto the ground.

Homogeneous Sand and Soil

The use of sand or sandy soil is a practical way to produce three-dimensional impressions but the sand or soil should be sifted to remove debris and assure the grain size is sufficiently small and homogeneous. Some moisture should be incorporated into the sand to assist in retention of detail. There is a limit to the detail that can be achieved with this method related to the grain size of the sand. Impressions can be made while wearing the shoe or by pressing the shoe into the sand. Brown or sifted indigenous sand may be preferred over white sand for the additional contrast. Figure 15.19 depicts a photograph of an impression made in sifted dark Florida sand. In order to get the moisture even, add water to the sand and stir while in a bucket, after which a fine layer of the moist sand is sifted through a strainer onto the ground just prior to making the impression. Once made, the impression will need to be photographed immediately as the surface of the sand impression will begin to dry. This method is low in cost and can provide an impression that can be produced and photographed with depth and lighting similar to three-dimensional crime scene impressions.

Biofoam®

Biofoam is collapsible foam normally used to take anatomical impressions of the plantar surface of feet.* Some find it convenient for use in taking three-dimensional impressions of footwear. The detail will provide reasonably good reproduction of class and general wear features, but does not adequately reproduce finer details such as texture and smaller cuts or

---

* Biofoam is a product of Smithers Bio-Medical Systems, Inc. but is available through forensic suppliers; www.biofoamimpression.com, https://www.shopevident.com.

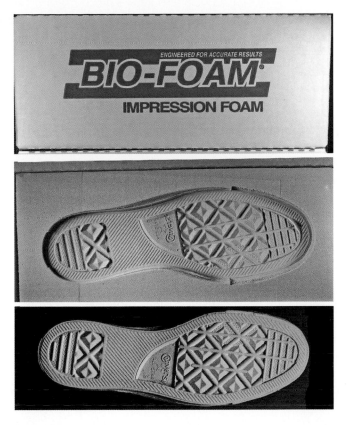

Figure 15.20 Biofoam will produce limited detail for shoes. It is most commonly used for anatomical impressions of bare feet.

scratches. Because Biofoam is easily deformable, only a few pounds of downward pressure need be applied to produce an impression. You can make the impression while wearing the shoe and applying very light pressure, but to have more control, most prefer to press the shoe into the foam by hand. Occasionally, pieces of Biofoam will stick in portions of deeper tread design, interfering with the replication of detail in those areas. Figure 15.20 shows a Biofoam impression and a dental stone cast made from that impression.

Methods Not Recommended

I have reviewed cases where the examiner placed the shoe on a copying machine to produce both opaque and transparent copies of a shoe sole to produce a known standard. This is neither a good method for capturing detail nor one that will be dimensionally accurate, and should not be used. Another method not recommended involves the casting of three-dimensional known impressions made of an outsole for comparison with a crime scene cast as shown in Figure 15.20. Best evidence rules dictate that you should stay close to the original evidence during physical comparisons. Thus, taking a shoe, making an impression of that shoe, and then making a cast of that impression is two steps removed from the best evidence, namely, the shoe. The shoe should simply be compared directly to the crime scene cast.

Key Words: known impressions, Biofoam®, elimination impressions, elimination photographs, Handiprint, Identicator®, MikroTrack™, Mikrosil, polyvinylsiloxane, roller transport film

Key Points

1. A full forensic examination between shoes and an impression requires the actual shoes.
2. Always know the date of the crime and the date any shoes were seized from a suspect to assure the shoes were not made after the date of the crime.
3. Known test impressions are made to demonstrate that certain features are capable of being replicated by a shoe, as a tool to assist in the examination between the shoe and impression, and for record and demonstration purposes.
4. All shoes of suspected individuals that resemble the crime scene impression should be obtained because many persons have multiple pairs of the same or similar design.
5. If shoes of a suspect are not located, consider shoeboxes, receipts for the purchase of footwear, and photographs or video that may show them wearing a similar pair.
6. There are many methods of making two- and three-dimensional known impressions suitable for use in a forensic examination.

Examination of Crime Scene Impressions with Known Footwear

16

Many relate the topic of identity to that involving an eyewitness's identification of the perpetrator. This type of identification relies on the memory, chance observations, eyesight, distances, judgment, and many other limitations of that witness. Many instances have long existed in the literature that establish the fact that few eyewitnesses of a crime are capable of providing accurate information.[*] In a forensic footwear exam, the request made is to determine if a shoe was or was not the source of an impression. The examination is far more complex than just a simple recognition of a shoe design but one that undergoes far greater scrutiny. Unlike eye witness accounting, it is not just a visual glance at the evidence but a structured and methodical evaluation of many things related to the outsole design, the physical dimensions of that design, and the additional presence of any general wear and/or randomly acquired characteristics. The examination process cannot be competently performed by a jury or even a well-meaning investigator. Examinations are often more complex, including those that involve poorly replicated impressions, those with limitations imposed as a product of improper recovery, and those that require enhancement. These require examination by a properly trained and experienced examiner whose conclusions should be as objective as possible and rely only on features possessing sufficient clarity. The purpose of this chapter is to discuss considerations that arise during the comparison and evaluation of footwear evidence.

Basis for Comparison

The recovery and interpretation of physical evidence such as footwear and tire impressions, fingerprints, firearms, and tool marks play an important role in the proof of facts used in both solving crimes and in the legal process that follows. The forensic examination of footwear evidence has been practiced worldwide with references in records dating back hundreds of years. Modern day footwear is mass-produced in thousands of distinguishable outsole designs and dimensions. Thus, any specific outsole design and dimension, even though produced by the thousands, is merely a fragment of a percentage of the billions of shoes owned by the general population. Forensic examinations that find relevant differences in design and dimension allow for the exclusion of shoes as the source of an impression. When shoes are examined and found to contain similar design and dimension as the crime scene impression, they are included as a possible source of that impression, subject to additional examination regarding general wear and possible presence of randomly acquired characteristics.

If there is good correspondence of general wear, it may justify a higher level of association. If the general wear is clearly different, it may be used to exclude the shoe as the source

[*] Kirk, Paul L., *Crime Investigation*, 2nd ed., New York, NY: John Wiley and Sons, 1963.

365

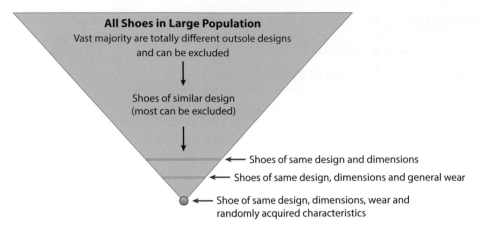

Figure 16.1 The examination process is one that excludes or includes footwear through the initial examination of design and dimension. If included, the process continues to reduce possible sources through the examination of general wear and randomly acquired characteristics.

of the impression. Randomly acquired characteristics (RACs) such as scratches, cuts, stone holds, and other random events also may be present on the outsole and may leave their trace in the impression. Figure 16.1 depicts a simple diagram that illustrates how any impression at a crime scene could potentially originate from a very large population of footwear composed of thousands of outsole designs and dimensions. Those of different outsole designs and/or sizes can be easily excluded as the source of the impression. When the examination is able to associate a more specific design and dimensions of the outsole and possibly general wear and/or RACs, the level of association becomes increasingly greater and the remaining population of footwear that could have produced the crime scene impression is rapidly reduced. Eventually, if sufficient detail and RACs are present, a shoe may be identified as the source of that impression. This process is a simple one that collectively uses the features of a shoe's outsole to exclude portions of the footwear population that do not share those combined features evident in an impression and therefore can be excluded as the possible source. Along the way, the shoe being examined could be excluded as well.

Fundamental Information

Some fundamental information applying to the evaluation and physical examination of footwear outsoles is set forth as follows.

Best Evidence

The term *best evidence* refers to the original scene impression or, if that no longer exists, the closest evidence to that original impression. As an example, the original bloody impression on a tile floor constitutes the best evidence, the original digital image (or the film negative) of that impression is one step removed, a photographic print of that image is two steps removed, and so forth. As you move further away from the best evidence there will be less information to work with and examine. If the original impression was not recovered and no longer exists, then the original digital image (or film negative) now becomes the "best evidence" for examination. Concerning footwear, the shoes are the best evidence, a photograph or known impression of those shoes is one step removed, and a cast or other copy of that known impression is two steps removed. The examiner should have access to and use the best evidence whenever possible.

Variations and Distortion

Repetitive shoe impressions will have slight distinctions between them. These are known as "variations" and they are both normal and unavoidable. No two impressions are exactly alike in every respect. This is true of both known test impressions as well as those occurring at the scene of the crime. Variations occur because the precise set of circumstances of any one impression will not be the duplicate of another. Figure 15.5 in Chapter 15 provides an example of normal variations between known impressions. Figure 1.8 in Chapter 1 provides examples of variations between two impressions on the same tile floor of the same shoe.

Some basic factors contributing to variations include but are not limited to

- The features of the substrate including any unevenness, moisture, debris, and texture and the ability of that substrate to replicate and retain details of the outsole.
- The way the shoe strikes the substrate, including its initial point of contact, its angle, and the weight and the type of and amount of force transmitted through the shoe.
- The quantity and makeup of materials being transferred from the shoe to a substrate, such as the quantity of blood, soil, ink, and moisture.

Distortion is simply a more extreme form of variation, and can be defined as "an unclear or inaccurate representation of the shoe outsole in the impression due to anything that prevents or interferes with a true recording or retention of characteristics during the impression-making process."[*] Distortion may exist in part or all of an impression. When distortion is a limiting factor in an impression, it usually is extensive enough that it is visually pronounced and obvious. Some examples include movement such as excessive slippage, twisting or rotation of the footwear on loose or slippery substrates as well as other factors that interfere with the recording of the impression, excessive moisture or blood that does not retain crisp details, and the collapse or change of the substrate during the impression process, such as would occur in an impression made on a bed sheet over a soft mattress. Distortion applies to deficiencies or actions that occur during the formation of the impression. Photographs that are out of focus or out of perspective, poor quality lifts or casts, and other limitations that result from the recovery process are not distortions of the impressions, but simply a product of the recovery process. For instance, a photograph taken at an angle is not distorted, but is what the camera and the person looking through the viewfinder actually see. A cast that fails to recover clear detail in the impression is simply a bad cast, not distortion. Figure 16.2 illustrates two examples of distorted crime scene impressions.

Research was conducted to determine what effects distortion would have on the shape of the shoe pattern and its RACs. In that study, attempts were made to create distortion in

---

[*] Bodziak, W.J., *Footwear Impression Evidence: Detection, Recovery and Examination*, 2nd Ed., CRC Press, 2000, p. 362.

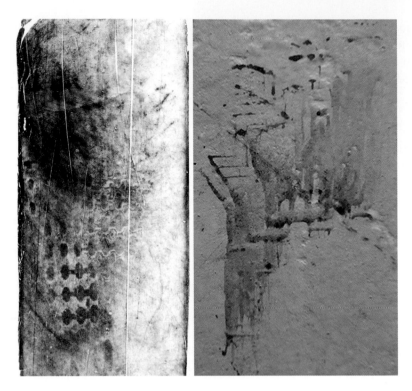

Figure 16.2 Two examples of distorted crime scene impressions. In some cases, portions of distorted impressions are still suitable for examination.

the form of slippage, bending, and twisting of the outsole as the result of applied force. The study utilized different styles of shoe soles to which a number of random damage features of various sizes had been added. The shoes were then used to make impressions by stepping, jumping, and twisting with sufficient force to create a distorted impression. The study concluded that some evidence of distortion will normally be evident in a truly distorted impression and although the distortion may slightly alter the exact position or shape of characteristics like cuts ands scratches, the changes were usually not sufficient to prevent some examination.[*]

Reproducibility and Repeatability

Reproducibility is the ability to reproduce something over and over again. Repeatability is the degree of agreement between those reproductions. Although minor variations always occur, outsole designs are reproducible in a variety of ways and can produce both two- and three-dimensional impressions in a highly repetitive way. Reproducibility and repeatability are basic principles associated with the scientific method. The fact that you can demonstrate that shoes reproduce their class and random features in impressions and do so repetitively over and over again provides validity to the ability for forensic comparison of crime scene footwear impressions to the footwear of individuals.

---

[*] Graham, G. D. Sr., Distortion in two-dimensional shoe impressions: a tool for inclusion, exclusion and identification, National University, Master of Forensic Science Thesis, 1997.

Damage to Molds in Contrast with Damage to Outsoles

The distinction between mold damage and outsole damage should be clearly understood. Scratches or dings in a metal mold or to a calender roller become filled with the outsole compound during molding and result in raised areas on outsole or outsole material. Figure 14.7 in Chapter 14 provides some examples of this. These examples are distinctly different from randomly acquired damage to an outsole such as cuts, scratches, tears, and abrasions that have caused the removal of outsole material and result in depressed areas, as shown in Figure 14.1, numbers 1, 2, 4, 5.

Understand What You Are Examining

Impressions are recovered and submitted for examination in many forms. Dental stone casts, Mikrosil lifts, gelatin lifts, and electrostatic lifts must be turned over to view and examine them. Photographs of impressions in soil or transparent tape lifts of impressions transferred to white card stock can be viewed without turning them over but represent a reversed view of a shoe outsole. Known impressions of left and right shoes that are made or converted to transparent forms, if not properly labeled, can easily be mixed up. The point being made here is to always examine the actual lifts, casts, and any original impressions, and if you are using photographs or scans, or transparencies, be certain of what you are examining to avoid mixing up left and right impressions or shoes.

Reversing Photographs

During preparation for examination, and also for demonstrable exhibits, many examiners make reverse prints of photographs of the shoes to allow for easier side-by-side comparison and documentation of their observations. When film was used, the film negative would simply be turned over and a "reversed" photographic print made. With digital photographs in a computer, the image can be "horizontally flipped" to produce the same reversed image. When this is done, the reversed images should be marked as such, either directly or by a new computer file description.

Full and Partial Impressions

From a strictly technical point of view, no mark or impression made by a shoe is totally representative of the entirety of the outsole that produced it; however, impressions that represent the majority of the outsole are typically referred to as "full impressions." Alternately, the majority of footwear impressions recovered from a crime scene represent far less than the shoe's full outsole and are typically referred to as "partial impressions." These definitions are used loosely in the footwear discipline for general descriptive purposes. Whether full or partial, the same examination applies and the ability to make a relevant and meaningful comparison remains the same for each.

Fragmented Impressions

Fragmented impressions are small portions of a pattern, typically isolated and/or disconnected from other design information of an outsole. Because fragmented impressions are

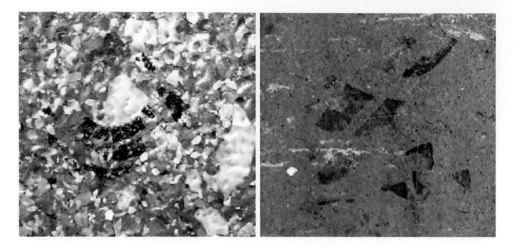

Figure 16.3 Two examples of fragmented impressions.

small and detached, they may or may not be recognizable as part of an outsole pattern. If made by footwear, technically speaking, they are also a partial impression, but the distinction is their smaller size and/or limited detail that places additional restrictions on the examination process. Two examples of fragmented impressions are shown in Figure 16.3. If these patterns corresponded with a suspect's shoes, some limited examination would be possible; however, if no footwear designs could be associated with these patterns, it might not be possible to say with certainty they were produced by a shoe outsole. For instance, is the fragmented pattern on the left side of Figure 16.3 from a shoe or the rubber tip of a crutch or cane?

Equipment and Comparison Techniques

Examination between impressions and footwear is assisted by magnification, dividers, and the use of transparent overlays of known impressions. Comparison made with a crime scene impression positioned alongside the shoe is referred to as a side-by-side technique. Side-by-side comparisons focus on one feature or dimension at a time. Alternatively, comparison made using transparent forms of known impressions superimposed over the crime scene impression is referred to as a superimposition technique. The advantage of superimposition is that it allows for multiple aspects of an impression and its relational dimensions to be simultaneously evaluated in relation to one another. The superimposition technique is the primary manner in which physical comparisons between impressions and outsoles are made. Traditionally they have been performed with physical overlays over hard copy photographic enlargements, but increasingly these are performed or supplemented on a computer.

Known impressions prepared with black ink or powder do not allow for the best contrast with the darker areas of photographed crime scene impressions. Using a light box as shown in Figure 16.4 is helpful. Some also prefer the use of colored inks or powders when producing known impression transparencies as the differences in color provide more contrast. Alternately, black inked or powdered impressions can be scanned into a computer and with programs like Adobe Photoshop, the color and opacity of that impression can be changed to achieve the same objective. Figure 16.5 depicts an impression on the left that

Figure 16.4 The author using a light box while superimposing a known impression over a scaled crime scene photograph during an examination.

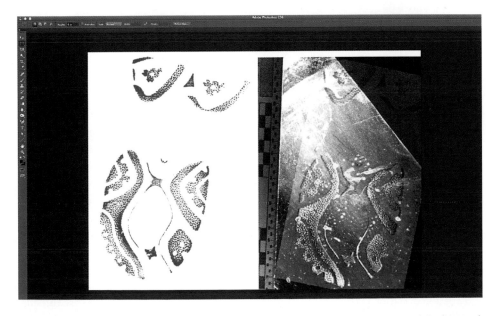

Figure 16.5 Adobe Photoshop is used by many examiners to supplement the physical comparison. The software permits enhancements, scaling, enlargements, and superimposition.

was originally a black powdered impression of a shoe but was converted to a red color on the computer. On the right, the same known impression in red has been reduced in opacity and superimposed over a photograph of a scene impression. Computer comparative software provides an excellent tool for texture and other fine detail best examined at larger magnification. Computer software programs, such as Adobe Photoshop, are also used for enhancements of impression evidence as well as for the preparation of demonstrable items for reports and court displays.

Some systems are designed to enable examiners to conduct the majority of the examination on a computer system. One such laboratory imaging system designed specifically for shoeprints, fingerprints, documents, and other flat surfaces is shown in Figure 16.6. This system uses resolutions of scanned evidence, such as gelatin lifters or known impressions at 1000 ppi. The system contains a vacuum table to hold these items flat while they are scanned. The entire system is set up for high-resolution comparison work and preparation of displays for report and court. It is noted that examinations using these systems should still involve the real impression evidence as well as the footwear in the overall examination process.

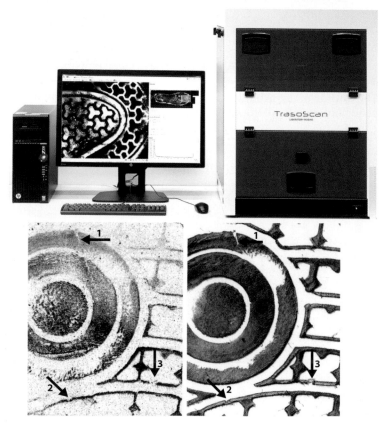

Figure 16.6 A computer system and scanner designed from the ground up to scan, scale, and compare footwear evidence. It can also produce comparison charts for reports or court, an enlarged portion of which is illustrated. (Photographs provided courtesy of Trasoscan Laboratory Imaging, Prague, Czech Republic, www.forensic.cz.)

General Scientific Method

The scientific method is a structure used across various branches of science to investigate a theory and gather knowledge. The use of the scientific method distinguishes science from other forms of inquiry because of its requirement of systematic experimentation. The scientific method is intended to minimize the influence of a scientist's bias on the outcome of an experiment or examination. Although there are varied descriptions of the scientific method and, more specifically, a scientific approach to physical comparisons, the most basic fundamentals involve identifying the problem or a question, forming a hypothesis or theory, conducting experiments and/or tests to test the hypothesis, and deriving some conclusion or altered theory from the observations and test results. As applied in the examination of footwear evidence, these areas might be characterized as follows:

Problem or Question. In the case of an examination between a crime scene impression and shoe, the problem asked of the examiner would simply be stated as, "Did the shoe make the impression?"

Hypotheses (Theory). Physical comparisons of footwear impressions should include dual hypotheses. One hypothesis would be, "The shoe made the impression." The alternate hypothesis would be, "The shoe did not make the impression."

Testing the Hypotheses. This would include all information available such as photographs, casts, lifts; enhancements to attempt to increase data about the crime scene impression; making known test impressions to assist in evaluating if the shoe was or was not capable of replicating the specific design and dimensional features, general wear, and randomly acquired characteristics; observations documented from the physical comparison of the evidence; and possible other applicable information regarding manufacturing variables.

Conclusion. This would include observations that supported correspondence or noncorrespondence of the shoe with the crime scene impression. If sufficient data and details did not permit a conclusion, reasons and limitations would be stated. In forensic comparison, the expression of a conclusion is often derived from the observations and test results and is provided by the examiner's report and/or in court in the form of an opinion.

Subjective or Objective

Objective statements are those based on measurable or verifiable facts and are completely unbiased. Subjective statements refer to personal opinions, assumptions, and beliefs of an individual that have not been verified by facts. In forensics, adversaries often argue that opinions regarding physical examinations are subjective. As experts our purpose in the judicial system is to provide opinion. By definition, opinions are subjective. The important question is: Is the opinion/subjective statement based on a substantial body of knowledge and education, or is it the opinion of essentially "lay experience." Unfortunately the difference between these two is not always clear, and not always differentiated by the court when experts are admitted. For example, an investigator who simply views a crime scene impression and, without any training or experience, makes a statement that the suspect's shoe appears to be the same, is making a "layman's value" subjective statement. On the other hand, if a trained and knowledgeable footwear examiner conducts an examination based on structured and accepted methods and states the crime scene impression corresponds in specific footwear characteristics, and bases that on verifiable facts observed and produced by that examiner as a result of that comparison, this statement becomes much more reliable and credible—an opinion based on substantial objective information. The degree of subjectivity is reduced and the degree of objectivity increased with the collection of facts and verifiable proof that support a statement or opinion.

Method of Comparison

Methods of comparison in a forensic examination involve adherence to guidelines devised by the scientific community to assure results are obtained in the most objective and reliable manner. Part of an effort to be as objective as possible includes considering alternate possibilities and ignoring any predisposed views or bias. In a comparison between footwear and impressions, any predisposed view that the shoe(s) made the crime scene impression(s) simply because they appear similar should be abandoned. Examples have already been given in this book of cases that involved similar designed footwear that turned out was not responsible for producing the crime scene impression. In order to avoid incorrect conclusions, a method of comparison is highly valuable as it instructs the examination process to consider numerous facts or circumstances relevant to the comparison process. Guidelines for examination and method of comparison procedures for an individual examiner are usually part of federal, state, or local laboratory protocols. Scientific working groups may also outline protocols involving the comparison between a scene impression and a shoe. Note taking and documentation should be used as necessary during the examination process. Notes and/or photographic records should support observations that support the basis for any opinion. Some agencies provide forms or templates as a checklist of an examiner's observations. These are fine but examinations require notes and images beyond checklists that are sufficient to permit another examiner to fully understand the basis for any opinion formed.

The following considerations, procedures, and observations apply during physical comparison between crime scene impressions and known footwear. Although it may be routine information for well-experienced footwear examiners, its intent is to provide those with less experience with a reminder of the many issues that potentially crop up in case examinations, and thus should always be considered. Every case comparison involves different evidence, so some of the listed steps or considerations may not be applicable in every comparison. It should be noted that no book, list, or set of protocols should be a substitute for training by a competent examiner and sufficient casework experience.

General Considerations:
- Be aware of what has been submitted to you for examination and the nature of the examination request.
- Ensure you have the best evidence that exists, including all photographs, full size original digital image files, casts, lifts, shoes, and any original footwear impression evidence.

- Consider evidence recovered by multiple responders or at multiple scenes and therefore evidence that may not have been provided by the particular contributor making the request, but may be relevant to your examination. A good example of this would be autopsy photographs of blunt force pattern injuries that were taken by a medical examiner at autopsy, but were not included in the submission of evidence by a specific police department. Contact the contributor as necessary.
- Ensure you know the date of the crime and the date any submitted shoes were taken into evidence. A case where the footwear was not seized until weeks or months after the crime involves the potential that the footwear acquired additional wear. In those cases, use date information on the sizing label when possible to ensure the footwear you are examining was manufactured prior to the date of the crime.
- If applicable to the request, determine if there were any elimination photographs or prints of footwear of first responders, the victim, or others who may have passed through the crime scene and potentially left their shoe impressions.
- Consider scene photographs when needed to help evaluate conditions or limitations that may relate to the questions concerning the footwear evidence or the recovery process or to address questions that are part of the request.

Preparation:
- Photograph any original evidence submitted.
- Clean and photograph casts as necessary.
- Photograph or scan lifts to record and possibly enhance the impression.
- Print images of evidence at natural size as necessary for examination.
- Conduct any enhancement methods. This applies to enhancement of digital photographs, forensic photography of original evidence, chemical enhancement, and physical methods of enhancement or original evidence.
- Prepare a worksheet that adequately describes and accounts for all evidence. The worksheet description of evidence should be the same as on the final report.

Make Known Impressions:
- Known impressions, particularly those prepared as transparencies are an important tool that assists in the comparison between the shoe and impression. They also are used in notes, reports, and testimony to support and demonstrate observations and the basis for opinions.
- Known impressions should be made as needed. For exclusion of outsoles of distinctly different designs, digital photographs or a known impression are usually sufficient. In the case of outsoles that have designs that cannot be excluded without more detailed examination, multiple known impressions, normally made with more than one method, should be produced.
- Photographs should document the outsoles of the shoes as received. If the outsoles must be cleaned, additional photographs should follow. Photographs should be high quality and taken with proper lighting to document both class and random features of the outsole.
- Photographs should also be taken of shoe labels or any other printed or molded information that pertains to size, origin, style number, or date manufactured.

Evaluation of Design and Physical Size of Design

The manufactured class characteristics of the outsole design and the physical size (dimension) of that outsole design should always be evaluated first. This is not an area that should be taken for granted or compared too hastily or lackadaisically. In many crime scene impressions, either the newer condition of the perpetrator's shoes or the lack of replication and/or recovery of detail limit any examination of general wear or RACs; thus, many examination conclusions rest heavily on the examination of design and physical size. The examination is one between the crime scene impression and the shoe; however, the use of known impression standards and superimposition techniques provides an excellent tool for that comparison. The use of the superimposition technique allows for a vectored comparison in all directions of the entire impression with the respective areas of the footwear. In some cases, additional magnification and/or digital imaging software on a computer should be used for more detailed examination, particularly when fine detail such as mold texture and Schallamach abrasion patterns are involved.

- Each crime scene impression should be independently compared with the shoe, even when multiple impressions appear to be in a sequence or in close proximity to one another. Any comparative conclusion should be based on only the features present in each impression.
- Photographs, casts, or lifts of a single impression can be collectively examined if it can be established they all represent the same impression. Thus 10 photographs of a single impression that was later cast can be examined collectively also using the cast, and the accumulative detail can be used during that comparison.
- Examinations are between the actual shoe and the impression. Known test impressions, transparencies, computer overlays, enlargements, dividers, magnification, and other techniques and equipment facilitate the examination.
- Always have a clear understanding of what you are examining, particularly misperceptions of right and left footwear or impressions that may be confused due to the need to turn over shoes or to reverse images of evidence.
- Conduct initial examination of the design evident in the crime scene impression. During this evaluation, establish, when possible, if a right or left shoe produced the crime scene impression. When possible, exclude the opposite shoe with that impression and proceed with examination of the proper right or left shoe. When impressions are so partial or otherwise limited that they cannot be associated with a right or left shoe, indicate this and compare with both shoes.
- If the shoe clearly contains a different outsole design, document differences that form a basis for exclusion and discontinue further examination between that shoe and impression.
- If the impression has a general design similar to the shoe outsole design, proceed with a more detailed examination, to include the specific size and shape of the design elements to determine if the shoe design and dimension is capable of producing the crime scene impression. This should include areas where design elements interface with the perimeter or other design elements where the design/size relationship is easier to distinguish. The purpose here is to ensure both the scene impression and outsole are the same specific design.

- Design evaluation of the footwear should also include any relevant observations with regard to mismatched left and right outsole designs, such as occur when the cutting of shoe outsoles results in a left and right outsole pair that are not mirror images. When present, these same features may be evidenced in the crime scene impression(s) and may have relevance in the examination.
- If texture (hand-struck stippling or acid-etch texture) is part of the design, is that texture replicated in the crime scene impression with sufficient detail to find agreement or disagreement between the respective portions of the shoe?
- If texture is dissimilar, are the differences in sufficient quantity and quality to determine exclusion as a result of a shoe from a different outsole mold source? If so, document the basis for exclusion and discontinue examination.
- If texture is similar, is the texture sufficiently present in quantity and quality to conclude the shoe that produced the impression and the shoe being examined share a common mold source? Document and continue examination.
- When the shoe design has features similar to the scene impressions but is of such limited quantity/quality to prohibit a detailed examination, and to prohibit confirmed and demonstrable correspondence with the specific design of the shoe, a lesser level of association of "similar" is necessary unless characteristics of wear and RACs are present and add to the comparison.
- When examining a generically common design such as herringbone or parallel line patterns, particularly if in a very partial or fragmented form, determine if it is so limited that it could have been produced by many different shoe styles, brands, and sizes that may contain those common design elements, and note and weigh limitations accordingly.
- Negligible variations in dimension attributed to limitations of the scale, perspective issues, or minor variations in known impressions should be distinguished from substantive and confirmable differences in dimension. If the design is similar but significant differences in the outsole dimensions are both confirmable and sufficient to establish the scene impression was produced by an outsole of a different size and origin, note and document this as a basis for exclusion and discontinue further examination.
- Three-dimensional impressions or casts of an impression can have minor variances from the shoe or a known impression of the shoe for many reasons. As an example, superimposing a transparency of a known impression of a shoe over a cast impression may result in correspondence of the design and dimension except for a very slight offset in the toe area. This is very common due to various normal motions of the foot during the push off phase of walking. These include the moment when the toe area of the foot is the last part contacting a soft and giving substrate, slippage of the toe as it loses contact with the substrate, twisting of the foot and substrate movement and/or uneven substrates. Two-dimensional impressions can have similar variations.
- Some obstacles prevent the comparison of specific design and dimension including improper recovery due to incorrect placement of scale; poor focus, low resolution, perspective issues related to photography; creases or other imperfections in

lifts; distortion; poor detail in the crime scene impression; folds in fabric impressions; and so forth.

- In general, adequate notes and, when necessary, known impressions and/or photographs, should document and support the basis for any conclusions of correspondence or noncorrespondence of design and the physical size of design features as well as any limitations imposed by impression quality and/or the recovery of that evidence.

Evaluation of General Wear

General wear results in erosion of rubber from the outsole, eventually resulting in visible changes that distinguish it from outsoles in a newer or unworn condition. General wear ranges from new or relatively unworn outsoles (absence of detectable wear), to outsoles with more visible evidence of the erosive effects of wear, to outsoles with extensive wear. This area of the comparison attempts to establish agreement or disagreement of two factors: (1) the position(s) of the wear on the outsole and (2) the extent or degree of the wear at that position. Not all examinations are able to include general wear because many impressions do not contain sufficient detail to make any accurate evaluation. This may be due to poor or inaccurate replication or because there are limitations to the detail as a limitation of the evidence recovery. When sufficient detail does exist and correspondence of general wear between a crime scene impression and outsole can be established, it serves to further reduce the number of shoes that could have made the impression. General wear, if confirmed to be different, can also be used to exclude footwear as the possible source of an impression.

When comparing general wear in an examination, the following should be considered.

- Establish the period of time that has elapsed between the date of the crime and the date the shoes were seized. This provides for consideration of additional wear, if it did occur on those shoes since the crime scene impressions were produced. The examination is a comparative one of the current condition of the shoe and should involve no expectation of whether that shoe had or had not received additional wear over that period of time. Short time differences such as hours or a few days are normally insignificant, but in cases where shoes were not seized until weeks, months, or even a year or two later, the evaluation of general wear may be limited.
- The presence of additional wear should not constitute a basis for exclusion if the circumstances and time differences could have allowed for this.
- The absence of additional wear, even with considerable time between the date of the crime and seizure of the shoes, is not a basis for exclusion.
- Consider limitations such as poor replication of detail, poor recovery of evidence such as out of focus photographs, and other photographic limitations that either interfere with or otherwise limit the comparison of general wear.
- Consider other detail limitations that might relate to the dynamics of the impression process or other factors that may affect or disguise the reproduction of general wear features.
- Do not confuse general wear with areas in the crime scene impression that simply lack detail. The lack of retention of outsole design detail does not permit evaluation

of the condition of general wear nor does it reliably indicate the design of the outsole has worn away.

- Examine all areas of general wear that are sufficiently detailed and confirmable in the scene impression.
- Document general wear characteristics that agree or that are dissimilar.
- Do not reach any conclusion about general wear without sufficient detail to clearly support that conclusion.

Evaluation of Randomly Acquired Characteristics

Randomly acquired characteristics (RACs) include acquired cuts, scratches, tears, holes, and other void areas as well as stone holds, gum, tar, nails, or other debris embedded in the outsole. Many of these are very small and/or shallow and will only replicate themselves under the best of conditions. The process of replication of every RAC occurs only when the sole and substrate conditions are optimal in that specific location; thus the absence of RACs in an impression is rarely a basis for exclusion. For instance, an RAC on a shoe may replicate because the substrate and conditions were favorable, but within the same impression, another RAC might not replicate because at the specific point, the conditions were not favorable. When RACs are replicated, the quality of that replication can vary from a mere disturbance or nondetailed void area to a very detailed representation of that characteristic. Evaluation of RACs during examination relates directly to both quantity and quality. Correspondences of RACs are weighted according to their agreement in (1) position on the outsole, (2) size and shape features, (3) orientation, and (4) quality issues such as the degree to which those aforementioned features in the scene impressions can be related to the outsole. Further, over time, RACs wear away or can undergo changes while new ones may be acquired.

- Use the original shoes and known impressions of those shoes during the comparison. Any examination conducted without the original shoes will be limited and should be noted and the results qualified as such in both the notes and written opinion.
- Any RACs on an outsole that are relevant to the examination should be confirmed as a random event using magnification and proper lighting. Most RACs, by virtue of their type and content, are easily confirmable as random and instantly recognized as nonmanufactured features simply because of what they are, e.g., stone holds, debris stuck to or lodged in the sole, holes, large tears, jagged cuts, or long randomly shaped scratches. Occasionally a RAC may be harder to establish it is a random event, particularly those that are very small. Examination must ensure that the remnants of hand-struck stippling, acid-etch texture, or a shallow design groove that is almost worn away are not mistaken for a RAC.
- Use magnification and superimposition comparison techniques to compare RACs.
- For each RAC present in both the crime scene impression and known outsole, evaluate the similarity or dissimilarity of its position, size and shape, and orientation. Note any limitations such as poor replication or focus.

- RACs should be evaluated based on a cause and effect relationship, i.e., a zigzag shape in the crime scene impression can be directly related to the size, position, shape, and orientation of a zigzag scratch in the outsole. If there is a zigzag scratch on the outsole, but only a general disturbance visible in the respective area of the crime scene impression, there can be no cause and effect relationship established. Areas in the crime scene impression that contain low levels of replication and/or clarity and may only appear as a disturbance should be weighted less for obvious reasons and possibly considered unreliable and unusable in the comparison.
- Any RAC used should be of sufficient clarity so that it is objectively demonstrable.
- All corresponding RACs should be documented in notes and/or photographs.
- Weight applied to each RAC stems from their collective clarity and confirmability, the degree of their association to the corresponding feature on the outsole, and their size and shape uniqueness.
- It is normal for RACs to not always be replicated in every impression. In addition, the recovery process of every RAC cannot be assured. Further, additional RACs can occur on the outsole between the time of the crime and the time the shoes were seized. Consequently, RACs on a shoe are not evidenced in an impression and vice versa. This rarely would constitute a basis for exclusion.
- When a Schallamach pattern is replicated and recovered from a scene impression and compared with a suspect's shoe, different possibilities exist, such as the pattern can correspond, the pattern can be different, there may be a Schallamach pattern but not in the same precise location, or there may be no pattern at all on the shoe. If a Schallamach pattern is in the same location on the shoe, but its precise pattern does not correspond, this may be because the pattern has had time to change with additional use. Therefore, using differences as a basis for exclusion would be incorrect unless it could be determined that the shoes were obtained in very short time after the crime.

One laboratory system utilizes guidelines for assessing the value of each RAC based on its size and shape components. The greater complexity and size of each RAC lead to a higher value. Numerous examples of RACs are provided to assist different examiners in applying the same value to RACs they encounter in case examinations. The total sum of the value of the RACs will provide guidance for the final conclusion.[*]

Range of Conclusions Scales

In recent years, some have offered criticism of laboratory conclusions and the reporting of those conclusions due to the lack of standardization of terminology and conclusion scales, and thus the lack of transparency and consistency of results from one laboratory or examiner to the next. The suggested need for improved transparency and clarity and a universal conclusion scale to increase the consistency in examination results has been made by

[*] Keereweer, I., Guidelines for Drawing Conclusions Regarding Shoeprint Examinations, Information Bulletin for Shoeprint/Toolmark Examiners, 6(1), 2000.

the Scientific Working Group for Shoe Print and Tire Tread Evidence (SWGTREAD), and the 2009 National Academy of Sciences report, and is also echoed by attorneys and investigators who often do not fully understand forensic reports.

Although most range of conclusion scales used throughout the world have some general similarity and purpose, sufficient variations exist due to the influence of other types of evidence the examiners may work with (e.g. fingerprints, tool marks, questioned documents), laboratory policies, and differences in languages. Minor variations between conclusions scales like shown in Figure 16.7 simply reflect additional choices that describe the strength of the conclusion. One laboratory uses 7 choices while others believe 8 or 9 may be better. If laboratory protocol has not strictly defined the criteria associated with each of those choices, it would be difficult to assure different examiners would use those choices equally. Figure 16.8 depicts the Range of Conclusions Scale recommended by SWGTREAD in 2013[*]; a version of a scale similar to that used by some practitioners the UK[†]; and the European

Minor Variances of Three Range of Conclusions Scales

Example #1	Example #2	Example #3
Exclusion	Exclusion	Exclusion
Probably did not make	Probably did not make	Highly probable did not make
Possibly did not make	Possibly did not make	Probably did not make
Non-conclusive	Non-conclusive	Possibly did not make
Could have	Could have	Non-conclusive
Probably made	Probably made	Could have
Identification	Highly probable made	Probably made
	Identification	Highly probable made
		Identification

Figure 16.7 Minor differences in range of conclusion scales, showing 7, 8 and 9 descriptions of levels of association.

SWGTREAD (US)	Similar to That Used in *R v T*	Harmonized ENFSI WG
Lacks sufficient detail	Inconclusive	Inconclusive
Exclusion	Exclusion	Exclusion
Indications of non-association	Limited through very strong support did not make	Likely not
Limited association of class chars	Weak/limited support	
Association of class characteristics	Moderate support	
	Moderately strong support	Probably
	Strong support	
High degree of association	Very strong support	Very probably
	Extremely strong support	
Identification	Identification	Identification

Figure 16.8 Range of conclusions scales in different countries.

---

[*] The Scientific Working Group for Shoe Print and Tire Tread Evidence (SWGTREAD) Range of Conclusions Standard for Footwear and Tire Impression Examinations, March 2013, www.swgtread.org.
[†] *R v T* Judgment, Case No: 2007/03644/D2 Royal Courts of Justice, Strand, London, 2010, paragraph 31.

ENFSI working group Harmonized Scale.[*,†] These are offered simply to illustrate the types of variations that have existed. The SWGTREAD Range of Conclusions Scale provides different levels of association between a scene impression and shoe based on specified criteria necessary for each level. Other scales used in laboratories around the world may have adopted criteria associated with each level on the scale they use, but those would be the internal policy or practice of individual laboratories and not part of a more universal range of conclusions scale. In any laboratory environment, an examiner may be comfortable and familiar with their particular scale and associated criteria, but for those in other laboratories, the precise meaning may not be clearly conveyed or known.

A study in Europe conducted in 1995 included 34 different forensic laboratories that represented 16 different countries, providing them with photographs of mock crime scene impressions and the outsoles of footwear.[‡] The photographs had arrows that identified randomly acquired characteristics (RACs). The participating laboratories provided their results of each case at their own discretion and using their own choice of wording. The results revealed different opinions in the conclusions rather than the same conclusion for every examiner. A second survey was conducted and resulted in participation of 34 laboratories in 26 European countries.[§] The second survey also used photographs of mock crime scene impressions but added a scale of conclusions using the categories of (1) inconclusive, (2) possible (3) probable, (4) very probable, and (5) identification. The results of the second survey also contained opinions that varied between some different examiners, but the study explored some of the reasons. For instance, some of the laboratories simply, as matter of policy, did not use the category of "probable" or "very probably," while others believed the category of "inconclusive" and "possible" were overlapping. Thus many did not use or agree with some of the terminology. Since these surveys had already marked the relevant characteristics to be weighed, the varying scale of conclusions would appear to be the primary reason for variances and not differing examination opinions.

In 1999, a similar study by Shor and Wiesner tested the consistency of forensic footwear conclusions and involved a total of 20 examiners from nine participating laboratories in Europe and the US.[¶] In this study, two real cases were used instead of mock cases. By their own description, both of the real cases "were ambiguous and controversial due to the nature of the vague imprint at the crime scene and the difficulties in finding the obscure individual characteristics (if they exist at all)."[**] The results of this study noted that some laboratories consistently gave highly conclusive results while others reached lower levels of association and also noted that different examiners within the same laboratory system provided varied results. The authors suggested the variances could be reduced with a set of

[*] Information Bulletin for Shoeprint/Tool Mark Examiners, 10(1):14, June 2004.

[†] ENSFI Expert Marking Group, Conclusion Scale for Shoeprint and Tool Marks Examination, *JFI*, 56(2), 2006.

[‡] Majamaa, H., and Ytti, A., Survey of the conclusions drawn of similar footwear cases in various crime laboratories, *Forensic Science International*, 82(1):109–120, 1996.

[§] Ytti, A., Majamaa, H., and Virtanen, J., Survey of the conclusions drawn of similar shoeprint cases, Part II, Information Bulletin for Shoeprint/Toolmark Examiners, 4(10):157–169, 1998.

[¶] Shor, Y., and Wiesner, S., A survey on the conclusions drawn on the same footwear marks obtained in actual cases by several experts throughout the world, *J. Fors. Sci.*, 44(2):380–384, 1999.

[**] It is noted the participating laboratories were provided photographs and not the original evidence and were allowed to use their own words in accordance to the terminology used in their own countries. Thus they were using their own scales of conclusion in their own languages.

guidelines that would assist the expert and lead to a proper conclusion.[*] Some explanation for variances included possible differences in the experience or training of the examiners. They also noted the limitations of detail in the crime scene impressions used in this study.

A study conducted by Hammer, Duffy and others in 2013 utilized six mock cases sent to examiners in the US and Canada that were certified by the International Association of Identification (IAI). The characteristics in each were clearly identified and the conclusions each examiner rendered were based on the range of conclusion scale of the Scientific Working Group on Footwear and Tire Track Evidence (SWGTREAD).[†] This study demonstrated the use of the standardized SWGTREAD terminology significantly decreased conclusion variations as seen within the prior aforementioned studies.

Others have advocated the use of a Bayesian framework to statistically evaluate forensic evidence, after which the numerical values they have calculated is translated into a verbal scale under their belief that this is more scientific.[‡,§] One serious problem with using statistics in this way lies in the fact that the necessary data is simply not available in cases involving evidence such as footwear. Not only is this a simple reality but in the now famous *R v T* in the UK case ruled on by the High Court of Justice Court of Appeal, the absence of data was a significant reason for the court's rejection of the use of the Bayesian approach for evaluating footwear evidence. In that particular case, the examiner simply approximated what he believed various data might be. For instance, data such as the number or percentage of footwear of a specific size or design in the population of other footwear; how many of that design would have similar general wear; and how many footwear of that design may have an indistinguishable RACs are simply not known. As an example, the only way for an examiner to use a numerical value for the number of shoes of a particular design that have similar position and degree of general wear was to guess what those values might be. To date, no study has been conducted that supports the notion that a Bayesian approach to the examination of footwear results in more 'correct' answers in casework samples when compared to the current practice of reporting opinions based on the results of a traditional examination.

A dual study by the Shoe and Tyre Scientific Working Group (SWG) of Australia and New Zealand were conducted to determine how they should standardize terminology and conclusions. The first study allowed each respective jurisdiction to use their own 'status quo scales of conclusion,' while the second required them to use the SWGTREAD range of conclusion scale. As a result of these two studies, the SWGTREAD range of conclusion scale was implemented. The research group also noted a Bayesian approach scale was not recommended, as there was not sufficient data for footwear evidence to justify such an approach.

From these studies it is apparent that a range of conclusion scale such as produced by SWGTREAD greatly improved the clarity of the results as well as the comparability of conclusions among examiners.

---

[*] Perhaps like the guidelines set forth by SWGTREAD later in 2013.

[†] Hammer, L., Duffy, K., Fraser, J., and Nic Daéid, N., A study of the variability in footwear impression comparison conclusions, *JFI*, 63(2), 2013.

[‡] Taroni, F., and Aitken, C., Correspondence: Interpretation of scientific evidence, *Science & Justice*, 37(1):64–65, 1997.

[§] Evett, I. W., Lambert, J. A., Buckleton, J. S., A Bayesian approach to interpreting footwear marks in forensic casework, 38:241–247, 1998.

The SWGTREAD Range of Conclusions Standard

In 2013, the Scientific Working Group for Shoe Print and Tire Tread Evidence (SWGTREAD) published a Range of Conclusions Standard for Footwear and Tire Impression Examinations.* It was a two-year effort that was peer-reviewed twice before resulting in the final document. The portion of the SWGTREAD standard regarding conclusion levels is included in Figure 16.9. Conclusions such as "Exclusion," "Identification," and "Lacks Sufficient Detail"

4. Opinions and Conclusions	The following descriptions are meant to provide context to the levels of opinions reached in footwear and tire impression comparisons. Each level may not include every variable in every case. This applies to both partial and full impressions.
4.1 Lacks sufficient detail	4.1.1 No comparison was conducted: the examiner determined there were no discernible questioned footwear/tire impressions or features present. This opinion applies when there is insufficient detail to conduct any comparison. In the opinion of the examiner, an impression was either not present or the impression lacked sufficient detail for any comparison. 4.1.2 A comparison was conducted: the examiner determined that there was insufficient detail in the questioned impression for a meaningful conclusion. This opinion only applies to the known footwear or tire that was examined and does not necessarily preclude future examinations with other known footwear or tires. In the opinion of the examiner, the impression lacked sufficient detail for a meaningful conclusion regarding the particular known footwear outsole or tire tread.
4.2 Exclusion	This is the highest degree of non-association expressed in footwear and tire impression examinations. Sufficient differences were noted in the comparison of class and/or randomly acquired characteristics between the questioned impression and the known footwear or tire. In the opinion of the examiner, the particular known footwear or tire was not the source of, and did not make, the impression.
4.3 Indications of non-association	The questioned impression exhibits dissimilarities when compared to the known footwear or tires; however, the details or features were not sufficiently clear to permit exclusion. In the opinion of the examiner, dissimilarities between the questioned impression and the known footwear or tires indicated non-association; however, the details or features were not sufficient to permit exclusion.
4.4 Limited association of class characteristics	Some similar class characteristics were present; however, there were significant limiting factors in the questioned impression that did not permit a stronger association between the questioned impression and the known footwear or tire. These factors may include but were not limited to: insufficient detail, lack of scale, improper position of scale, improper photographic techniques, distortion, or significant lengths of time between the date of the occurrence and when the footwear or tires were recovered that could account for a different degree of general wear. No confirmable differences were observed that could exclude the footwear or tire. In the opinion of the examiner, factors (such as those listed above) have limited the conclusion to a general association of some class characteristics. Other footwear or tires with the same class characteristics observed in the impression are included in the population of possible sources.

Figure 16.9 Section four of the SWGTREAD range of conclusions scale. (*Continued*)

---

* The Scientific Working Group for Shoe Print and Tire Tread Evidence (SWGTREAD) range of conclusions standard for footwear and tire impression examinations, March 2013, www.swgtread.org.

4.5 Association of class characteristics	The class characteristics of both design and physical size must correspond between the questioned impression and the known footwear or tire. Correspondence of general wear may also be present. In the opinion of the examiner, the known footwear or tire is a possible source of the questioned impression and therefore could have produced the impression. Other footwear or tires with the same class characteristics observed in the impression are included in the population of possible sources.
4.6 High degree of association	The questioned impression and known footwear or tire must correspond in the class characteristics of design, physical size, and general wear. For this degree of association there must also exist: (1) wear that, by virtue of its specific location, degree and orientation make it unusual and/or (2) one or more randomly acquired characteristics. In the opinion of the examiner, the characteristics observed exhibit strong associations between the questioned impression and known footwear or tire; however, the quality and/or quantity were insufficient for an identification. Other footwear or tires with the same class characteristics observed in the impression are included in the population of possible sources only if they display the same wear and/or randomly acquired characteristics observed in the questioned impression.
4.7 Identification	This is the highest degree of association expressed by a footwear and tire impression examiner. The questioned impression and the known footwear or tire share agreement of class and randomly acquired characteristics of sufficient quality and quantity. In the opinion of the examiner, the particular known footwear or tire was the source of, and made, the questioned impression. Another item of footwear or tire being the source of the impression is considered a practical impossibility.

Figure 16.9 (Continued) Section four of the SWGTREAD range of conclusions scale.

are very similar to those respective categories on most other scales. The range of other conclusions in footwear examinations extends from a very minimal and limited but similar design feature all the way to those falling just short of identification. The main purpose of this standard was to provide minimum criteria for the various conclusion levels, in order to allow for greater uniformity among examiners and laboratories. It is not intended to be a continuum and include and define every possible level of association or account for every variable or issue that is possible in a forensic footwear examination, but it does provide a more transparent context to the various levels of associations between a shoe and impression. Referring to Figure 16.9, some elaboration on each level is set forth with additional discussion in Chapter 17.

Lacks Sufficient Detail

This category applies to those instances where impressions lack sufficient detail for any meaningful conclusion with the submitted footwear. The category is divided into two parts: 4.1.1 applies to those items of evidence that do not contain any discernable mark or footwear impression, while 4.1.2 applies to those items of evidence that reflect some limited pattern or mark of unknown origin, and although that pattern or mark lacks sufficient detail for meaningful comparison or association with the footwear presently submitted, the possibility that some limited association could be made with additional footwear submitted in a future request cannot be eliminated.

Exclusion

This category applies to examination conclusions that have conclusively excluded footwear as the possible source of the scene impression. The vast majority of exclusions are because of differences in the manufactured class characteristics of design and/or dimension. Although less common, exclusions can also be made based on differences in general wear. The ability to make exclusions based on differences in randomly acquired characteristics are rare and only applicable in specific situations.

Indications of Non-Association

Normally, if differences are found during a comparison, exclusions are made. In some instances, dissimilarities are noted between an impression and shoe, but fall short of sufficient detail to confirm those dissimilarities as a difference that would allow for exclusion.

Limited Association of Class Characteristics

This applies to a wide variety of situations. One example would include impressions that contain limited design information, particularly if the design is commonly found in the general population of footwear, such as a herringbone pattern, or rows of parallel lines. Another example would be when the recovery of the impression was limited, such as would be the case if only general crime scene photographs were taken and did not contain any reference of scale, or were not in good focus. Examinations in these examples and many others are restricted to observations that the design is generally similar, but have limited detail and/or no reference to dimension or other features of value.

Association of Class Characteristics

This applies to those examinations where good correspondence of the specific design and the dimension exists. In addition, some examinations may also include correspondence of general wear but do not reflect any specific wear or randomly acquired characteristics. If both the specific design and the physical size of that design cannot be concluded to correspond, the conclusion must remain at a lower level.

High Degree of Association

This applies to those examinations where there is correspondence of the specific design and physical size of that design as well as correspondence of specific points of wear and/or one or more RACs. This level is intended to be a distinctly higher degree of association than just finding correspondence of design and size. In many examinations, this level may closely approach one of identification.

Identification

This applies to those examinations where correspondences of design, physical size of that design, wear, and RACs are of sufficient quantity and quality to allow for the opinion the shoe was the source of the impression.

Identifications Involving Footwear

Discussions in recent years have involved the topic of the "identification" of a shoe as the source of an impression. One argument is that it cannot be proven something is unique unless all items in that class of items are examined. So to factually state or conclude that a shoe made a specific impression can be done only if every shoe of that design has been examined, obviously an impossible task. Most examiners agree with this to the extent that they should not write a report that states a shoe made the impression "to the exclusion of all others" simply because the technicality of that wording implies they examined "all other shoes." Another argument made is that nothing can be concluded to be unique. Discussions advocating that line of logic conveniently choose categories involving items with extremely large numbers (examples: all the grass in the world, or all of the snowflakes that have ever fallen) that no one would or could dispute their reasoning. But what if the relevant population is a much more manageable and realistic number, such as 40,000 right shoes, size 11, of a particular style and brand of athletic shoe. The effects of wear, abrasions, and RACs acquired by that population of shoes over time would make each of those 40,000 right shoes distinguishable from each other. The only question to be resolved by the examiner is whether the particular impression and shoe being examined clearly contain and share enough of these features to reach that conclusion. In the absence of being able to examine all shoes, at what point is it scientifically sound to opine there are sufficient features to say they are unique? This is often the question an examiner must resolve when conducing an examination: are there sufficient class and random features in common between the shoe and impression that it is no longer reasonable to believe another shoe would share those same combined features? More importantly, most critics fail to realize that this is an opinion the courts allow and expect the expert to offer to assist the trier of fact (judge or jury) in their interpretation of this evidence!

Contacting a Manufacturer for Sales and Distribution Information

Manufacturers are normally not contacted in relation to everyday footwear examinations. When it is necessary, it is usually for reasons such as the need for outsole samples involving examinations relating to sizing and texture, or for confirmation of manufacturing characteristics that might vary and be relevant in a particular examination. Occasionally contacts with a manufacturer are made for determining sales and distribution information for shoes having a specific outsole design.[*,†] More commonly, it is a prosecutor or defense attorney and not the footwear examiner who requests sales and distribution information for a particular shoe style. In a typical response, a manufacturer may report it produced 300,000 shoes of that outsole design and style in a particular size range during certain dates. In most cases, it will have little or no distribution information beyond the initial distributions to a warehouse. For instance, a manufacturer may indicate it shipped 50,000 pairs to a specific athletic chain store's warehouse, but will have no information about distribution from there on.

---

[*] Black, J. P., An interesting case involving footwear distribution information, *JFI*, 55(4), 2005.
[†] LeMay, J., If the shoe fits: An illustration of the relevance of footwear impression evidence and comparisons, *JFI*, 60(3), 2010.

Determining how many shoes of a particular shoe outsole design potentially exist involves additional considerations. Footwear impressions at a crime scene do not provide evidence of the style or color of their upper, nor in most cases, the brand of the shoe that produced them. Many manufacturers use the same outsole design on more than one style over a period of several years. Others purchase their outsoles from a separate outsole manufacturer, including outsoles produced in "open industry" molds. This means other manufacturers may also have access to purchasing the same outsole design for use on their brand of footwear. Thus, without fully investigating the possibilities of the full use of an outsole design on other styles or even the use of the same outsole on other brands, information about the numbers of shoes produced in a specific style could be misleading or inaccurate. This number will be further complicated by Internet sales and, if a highly popular athletic shoe design, by the sale of counterfeit versions of those shoes. Requests for sale and distribution are cumbersome for a manufacturer to research and usually mean very little to a case investigation. Only in cases where it is believed the footwear design is rare or only exists in very limited numbers may this information have relevance to an investigation. In either instance, this is something that is neither part of nor should be factored into the actual physical comparison between footwear and the crime scene impression.

Exclusion and Inclusion

Often an expert is asked to comment on whether he or she can exclude or include a shoe as the source of an impression. This question can be asked in the context of when sufficient detail permits examination, as well as in the context of when an impression or mark lacks the detail necessary to permit examination.

When Sufficient Detail Exists

When sufficient detail exists to support an impression corresponds in design or at a higher level of association with a shoe, there is affirmative information that supports the inclusion of that shoe as a possible source. For example, "the design of the impression is similar to the design of the shoe outsole and is included as a possible source of that impression."

When Sufficient Detail for Comparison Does Not Exist

When an impression or mark is so limited in detail as to prevent any meaningful examination, particularly when that impression or mark may not even contain sufficient detail to be attributable to footwear, the question of exclusion or inclusion is also sometimes asked. In this context, the inability to exclude a shoe in the absence of detail necessary for examination should not be used to support any statement that the shoe should be included as the possible source of the impression. When detail is too limited to allow for an examination or is not sufficient to offer direct evidence a mark was caused by a shoe outsole, stating you cannot exclude that footwear is inappropriate, unscientific, misleading, and biased. The absence of the ability to exclude a shoe should not automatically result in its implied inclusion.

Key Words: range of conclusions scale, best evidence, reproducibility, repeatability

Key Points

1. Footwear produce both class and acquired features that, when replicated with sufficient detail, can be compared to items of suspected footwear.
2. Conclusions of examinations between crime scene impressions and shoes range from exclusions to identification.
3. Poor retention of detail in the crime scene impression and/or poor or incomplete recovery methods directly affect the examination.
4. The examination involves a methodical physical comparison between the crime scene impression and a suspected shoe, beginning with the specific design and dimension to determine whether the item of footwear being compared can be included or excluded as the possible source of the impression.
5. If the footwear is included as the possible source, comparative examination of general and specific wear and randomly acquired characteristics may provide additional information supporting levels of association or exclusion.

Written Reports and Court Testimony

17

In 2009, the National Academy of Sciences (NAS) commission issued its report on forensic science and offered both criticism and recommendations to strengthen the practice of forensic science in the United States.[*] The NAS report's comments regarding forensic footwear examination clearly reflected its lack of understanding of footwear evidence as well as the practices of the forensic footwear community and the NAS could be properly criticized for not including even one certified footwear practitioner. The Scientific Working Group of Footwear and Tire Track Examiners (SWGTREAD) provided several responses to the NAS report, citing some of the misunderstandings and the report's inaccuracies on the discipline.[†] However, most importantly, both the NAS commission and SWGTREAD agreed on and support the need for standards, additional research, and the transparent reporting of examination results. The suggestions provided in this chapter that pertain to report writing are those of the author but address the same goal of providing more transparent reports that clearly convey the findings and opinions of the forensic footwear examiner. Many laboratories have already moved in this direction.

Purpose of Reports

In the US, the Federal Rules of Criminal Procedure requires a written summary of expert testimony the government intends to use during its case-in-chief at trial. This summary must describe the witness's opinions, the basis and reasons for those opinions, and the witness's qualifications.[‡] Because of this rule and comparable ones in state courts, written reports of prosecution experts must be prepared in every case where evidence is examined and/or an expert opinion is offered, regardless of the results. In addition to fulfilling this requirement, a forensic report should clearly convey examination results and opinions to the person or agency that requested the examination such as an investigator, attorney, or police agency. These reports should be transparent and understandable to anyone who reads them. There is a distinct difference between what the reader needs in a report to fully understand the examination and conclusions and what has been minimally included in reports provided by many examiners in the past. Even now, many laboratories only include minimal information instead of attempting to make the report an informative and transparent product of the examination service they provided.

---

[*] Strengthening Forensic Science in the United States: A Path Forward. National Academy of Sciences (NAS) August 2009. http://www.nap.edu/catalog/12589.html.
[†] http://www.swgtread.org/nas-response.
[‡] Fed. R. Crim. P. 16(a)(1)(G), December 1, 2013.

Report Writing Practices

Not every country has the same report writing practices or legal requirements. Many produce more detailed and extensive reports than are routinely written in the US. This is particularly true in countries without jury systems where experts rarely testify in court and thus do not have an opportunity to elaborate or provide additional information on their examinations. In those instances, the judge or a panel of judges relies heavily on the written report, meaning it must include photographs and information that contain every aspect of the footwear comparison and the basis for any opinion. Should the report fail to do this, it might not be considered useful or relevant.

In parts of the UK, a streamlined reporting policy has led to the issuance of brief initial reports for the investigators and/or prosecutors to give them a quicker turnaround and information for their investigation. This could include the results of exclusions or those instances where there is insufficient detail, but would also include a brief statement of any examination having some level of correspondence. Should the court or defense require additional information, a more complete examination and report would be produced.

In the US, written forensic reports have varied considerably over the years, including their format, the extent to which evidence is described, the terminology used, and the degree to which they conveyed the results. Some provide reasonably well-detailed and descriptive reports but others do not provide what is necessary for a reader to have much understanding of the evidence examined or the opinions reached. Many reports leave the reader with more questions than answers.

Examiners in laboratories prepare reports in accordance with their laboratory policy, and most probably believe their reports are more easily understood than they realize. This is understandable because they have significant familiarity with the evidence, have conducted the examinations and recorded their observations, and knew what they meant by their written words. They do not realize that many who read their reports are not familiar with the specific items of evidence nor are they familiar with certain terminology or the scale of conclusions used. A typical report often provides an item number with a minimal description of evidence. A sample of a minimal description might be "Item #7—CD with 84 images of footwear impressions." Likewise, a pair of shoes may be described as "Item #9—One pair of brown athletic shoes," leaving the reader with no further information as to the brand, size, or source of those shoes. Many reports also provide conclusions that, combined with minimal descriptions, are simply unclear. For example, results that state, "Three footwear impressions on the item #7 compact disc correspond in size and design with the left shoe in Item 9" don't allow the reader to know which specific images and impressions they are referring to, nor does it explain anything about the basis for that opinion.

Equipped with computers, scanners, digital cameras, and software, a forensic examiner today is technically capable of producing virtually any type of report format and content. Although most laboratories will have some guidelines or restrictions that limit report writing, many have sufficient flexibility to make improvements. Reports that contain clear evidence descriptions, supporting photographs, and more detailed statements of conclusions, offer a much better product to present the results of a forensic examination in a transparent and informative way.

Report Contents

Reports should provide full disclosure of what was examined and what conclusions were reached. The report should stand on its own and should not require the reader to have prior or special knowledge or familiarity with the evidence. Figure 17.1 provides a general format for a variety of information that should be considered when preparing a report on a forensic footwear examination. It includes

1. The name and address the report is addressed to. This is usually the same agency and/or person who made the request.
2. The date the report was issued.
3. A reference to the communication that requested the examination.
4. The title of the case, often including the name of the suspect and the violation.
5. Applicable case ID numbers and/or laboratory numbers.
6. Detailed descriptions of the physical evidence, including, as appropriate, imbedded photographs when needed to supplement the written description. Each report should stand on its own, so reference to evidence that was described in another case but was part of the requested examination should be described as well. Descriptions of digital images that are submitted on CDs should clearly indicate image numbers and content.
7. Any remarks or a statement of any procedures that were conducted with the evidence such as the production of known impressions or enhancement of the impressions. This might also include comments regarding any additional reference items that were obtained such as outsole samples or photographs of outsoles from manufacturers or retail stores.
8. A summary of the examination requested.
9. A general comparison method statement about footwear examination.
10. Examination results and opinions should use verbiage that complies with the Scientific Working Group for Shoe Print and Tire Tread Evidence's Standard for Range of Conclusions for Footwear and Tire Impression Examination (or other appropriate Scientific Working Group) as well as sufficient additional verbiage that further explains observations and the basis for opinions for each specific examination. Results should also include any limitations of the evidence, as well as comments regarding other possible sources. Photographs should be included in this section as applicable and necessary to assist the reader to understand the opinion.
11. The full range of conclusions scale that was used can be helpful to provide better understanding and context to conclusions, and should be attached to the report or provided as an addendum.
12. Terminology, when necessary to assist the reader.
13. Additional attachments or addendums if necessary.
14. Disposition of evidence.
15. The name and signature of the examiner who conducted the forensic examination and prepared the written report should be provided at the end of the report. It is noted that in some jurisdictions, this is set forth at the beginning of the report. This area may also include examiner verifications.

Forensic Footwear Evidence Report

To: Assistant US Attorney John Jones
        Address

Date: July 1, 2015

Re: Communication dated June 15, 2015

Title: US v PETER SMITH
        FIRST TRUST BANK
        Bank Robbery

Case ID: 15-2341-LA
Laboratory#: 150134

Detailed Description of Evidence and When Received
Remarks or Procedures
Summary of the Examination Requested
General Footwear Comparison Method
Examination Results and Opinion
Full Range of Conclusions Scale
Terminology
Attachments
Disposition of Evidence

For questions about this report, please feel free to contact this examiner at 800-000-0000.

Signature

Figure 17.1 A general list of contents for a forensic report.

Report Example

To provide an example, a mock case involving two pairs of shoes, one cast impression, a piece of tile with a bloody impression, and a compact disc with 6 images was created and a report of that examination is provided in Figure 17.2. The report contains the basic information at the top. The description of evidence has sufficient photographs provided to assure the reader understands what each item represents. It is noted that most case examinations do not involve a large quantity of physical evidence. If any photographs need to be provided in a larger format to later show more detail or the basis for an examination result, they can be provided later in the report or as an attachment. The remarks section advises the reader that the cast was cleaned and photographed, that the bloody mark on the tile was enhanced with an Amido Black reagent and then photographed again, and that known impressions of both pairs of shoes were prepared. A brief statement of the method of comparison provides a reader unfamiliar with footwear impression comparisons some information as to what this type of examination involves. The examination results provide the observations and opinions of the examiner. A range of conclusion scale is attached to the report to allow the reader to understand a broader range of conclusions that are typically possible, and thus provide context for the conclusion stated in the report. In this example, terminology is also provided for three words to assure the reader understands

Forensic Footwear Evidence Report

To: Assistant State Attorney Joy Smith   Date: July 24, 2015
        Main Street
        Sunset, Oregon

Re: Letter requesting examination dated June 22, 2015

Title: PAUL JOHNSON: Suspect
        MIKE PENGRASS: Suspect   Case ID: 15-0645-OR
        HOMICIDE   Laboratory #: 150622012

Items received on June 23, 2015

Q1   Cast of questioned footwear impression of right shoe
        made from impression below front window,
        bearing number 16 on back.

Q2   One piece of tile bearing bloody footwear marks

Q3   CD containing 6 images of the impression in soil
        below the front window, bearing image numbers
        IMG_0906 through IMG_0911

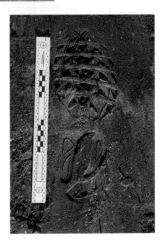

Figure 17.2 A report example. (*Continued*)

K1-2   Left and right US size 10 Wal Mart Starter
        shoes, white with gray and blue trim,
        belonging to PAUL JOHNSON

K3-4   Left and right gray Adidas shoes, belonging
        to MIKE PENGRASS. No size is present.

Remarks

The Q1 cast was received in a clean condition and was photographed. The Q1 cast represents the same impression depicted in the six images on the Q3 CD.

The footwear marks on the Q2 tile were photographed, followed by treatment with Amido Black for enhancement of those marks, after which they were re-photographed.

Known impressions were made of the K1 through K4 shoes.

Examination Requested

The above-described Q1-3 items contain footwear impressions recovered from the crime scene and were submitted for comparison with the K1-2 shoes of PAUL JOHNSON and the K3-4 shoes of MIKE PENGRASS.

Method of Comparison

The physical comparison between footwear impressions recovered from a crime scene and the outsoles of shoes of a known individual include evaluation of the design features of the outsole; the physical size of that design; general wear; and the presence of any randomly acquired characteristics such as cuts, scratches, stone holds, and abrasions. The examination involves a direct comparison between the shoes and crime scene impression. Known test impressions of the shoes are made and superimposed over the crime scene impression to assist in that comparison. If differences in the design and/or dimensions are found, those differences can support the exclusion of the shoes. If the design and physical dimensions of that outsole design correspond, that shoe is capable of having produced those respective characteristics in the crime scene impression, as are other shoes of the same design and outsole dimensions.

Further correspondence of general wear and/or randomly acquired characteristics, if present, can serve to elevate the level of association between the shoe and crime scene impression.

Figure 17.2 (Continued) A report example. (*Continued*)

Examination Results

The impression represented by the Q1 cast and Q3 images exhibits a high level of association with the K2 right Starter shoe. This is based on correspondence in design, physical size of that design, and general wear as well as two void areas in the cast that correspond with the position and specific random features on respective areas of the K2 right outsole. Limited quantity and quality of general wear and randomly acquired features prevented a more conclusive examination. Other left shoes could only be included as a possible source if they displayed all of the aforementioned features. A photograph of the Q1 cast with a known test impression of the K2 right Starter shoe superimposed over it is provided to the right.

The bloody footwear mark on the Q2 tile corresponds with the design and physical dimension of the toe area of the K4 right Adidas shoe. In addition, some general wear is evident in the Q2 impression that corresponds with the K4 right Adidas shoe. The correspondence of these features indicates the K4 right Adidas shoe could have produced the Q2 impression. Other footwear with the same outsole characteristics of design and dimension and similar general wear are included as the possible source of the Q2 impression. The limited quantity and quality of detail in that impression precluded further examination. Below is a photograph of the Q2 tile impression on the left after it was treated with the Amido Black reagent. On the right is a known impression of the toe area of the K4 right Adidas shoe, colored in red, and superimposed over the Q2 tile impression.

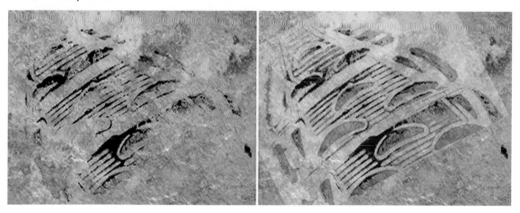

Figure 17.2 (Continued) A report example. (*Continued*)

those terms as they apply to the examination. A statement of any attachments as well as the disposition of evidence is included at the end of the report.

Figure 17.3 illustrates the first page of a mock report from the UK that includes a required witness statement and signature to be placed at the beginning of the report. It also requires some general information about their qualifications, the case, and evidence. Other countries also have similar report requirements that require a signed statement at the beginning and some also require curriculum vitae of the examiner to be attached to the report.

Range of Conclusions Scale

The full range of conclusions scale is attached to this report for reference purposes.

Terminology

The definitions of certain terms used in this report are provided below:
Amido Black - A dark blue/black protein stain used to turn the protein in blood a darker color, providing greater contrast with the substrate.
Known Impression - A test impression made of the shoe to provide samples of how that shoe leaves its impression including its class, wear and randomly acquired features. Known impressions are used to assist in the comparison between the shoe and the crime scene impression.

Correspondence - Agreement between features in the crime scene impression and shoe outsole to the extent that shoe outsole could have produced those respective features in the impression.

Attachments

A CD containing images of (1) the Q1 cast, (2) the Q2 tile before and after enhancement, and (3) the K1-2 and K3-4 shoes of PAUL JOHNSON are attached to this report.

Disposition of Evidence

The above-described evidence was returned under separate cover via Federal Express on July 24, 2015.

For questions about this report, please feel free to contact this examiner at 1-800-000-0000.

Sincerely,

Frank McDonald

Figure 17.2 (Continued) A report example.

Written Conclusions

Conclusions in the form of observations and opinions are provided in written form to (1) formally convey examination results and (2) to provide a record of the examination. Two voiced criticisms of written opinions are that different laboratories do not use a universal range of conclusions scale, and the inability of the reader to fully understand the terminology or conclusions they contain. In 2013, the Scientific Working Group for Shoe Print and Tire Tread Evidence (SWGTREAD) published a Range of Conclusions standard, a portion of which was presented in Chapter 16.[*] Its purpose was to provide examiners a standard or guideline for various levels of associations that could result from examinations between impressions and footwear as well as to include some criteria to further define each level. The criteria for each level provide examiners a general description of features required but, as stated in the scope of this standard, are not intended to address every variable in every examination. The standard clearly recommends that wording used for expressing conclusions should be constructed for each specific examination result in each case. Some of the levels defined will obviously provide some essential core words for some conclusions but are not intended to be a substitute for the totality of what needs to be expressed for a

---

[*] Scientific Working Group for Shoe Print and Tire Tread Evidence, "Range of Conclusions Standard for Footwear and Tire Impression Examinations," March 2013, http://swgtread.org/images/documents/standards/published/swgtread_10_conclusions_range_201303.pdf

---

WITNESS STATEMENT

Statement of	John P. Smithers, BSc., MSc.
Age of Witness	34
Occupation	Forensic Scientist
Address	Impression Forensics Oxford, England

This statement, consisting of 4 pages, is true to the best of my knowledge and belief. Dated the 12th day of September 2015

Signed ___*John P. Smithers*___

Qualifications and Experience

I have a Bachelor of Science degree in Biology and a Masters of Science degree in Forensic Science. I have been a forensic scientist since September 2009 and have made examinations of the type described in this report.

Laboratory Reference # 43-R-005-2015

Circumstances of Case

I have been told that a sexual assault occurred in an East Liverpool neighborhood on August 23, 2015 from which footwear marks were recovered from a piece of broken glass. A pair of Nike trainers were recovered from DENNIS BARROWS.

Items Received

HR 1   Piece of broken glass recovered from the floor just inside broken door window at forced point of entry.

GR/045   Pair of Adidas trainers size 11 (UK) White with blue trim

Purpose of Examination

A request has been made to examine the footwear mark on the recovered piece of glass from 23 N. Broadway Close, East Liverpool, to determine if that mark could have been produced by the shoes of DENNIS BARROWS.

Figure 17.3 The first page of a mock report based on a real report in the UK.

specific examination result. The standard was not intended nor could it possibly include wording that properly applied to all conclusions for every case. Two hypothetical examples based on each of the different levels of association in the SWGTREAD Range of Conclusion scale are provided (Figure 16.9). For simplicity and brevity, the samples will use the designations of Q and K to represent the questioned impression (Q) and known footwear (K). It is noted that in most cases, the use of photographs and additional comments would be recommended to further explain and/or support a greater understanding of the results and in doing so, the written report would include references to those photographs.

4.1 Lacks Sufficient Detail: This level includes those cases where either there is no discernable footwear impression in the submitted evidence to allow for any comparison (4.1.1), or there is some mark or impression present, but it contains insufficient detail to enable any meaningful comparison with the footwear that was submitted (4.1.2).

Sample wording:

- The Q3–6 photographs did not depict any evidence of a footwear impression. Inasmuch as no footwear impressions are clearly discernible, no comparison was made with the K1–2 footwear. (4.1.1)
- The patterns in blood on the Q14 shirt cannot be attributed to or excluded as having been caused by footwear; however, those marks lack sufficient detail to enable any association with the submitted K9–10 footwear. (4.1.2)

4.2 Exclusion: This level includes those examinations where the conclusion is sufficient to determine the shoe did not and could not have prepared the crime scene impression.

Sample wording:

- "The K1–2 footwear outsoles are a different design and therefore were not the source of the footwear impressions depicted in photographs Q5–27."
- "Although the bloody footwear marks on the Q45–46 tiles share some similarity in design, the specific design features of the K11–12 shoes are distinctly different in spacing and arrangement and therefore did not produce those marks."

4.3 Indications of non-association: This level includes those examinations where one or more dissimilarities exist between the crime scene impression and the footwear, but those dissimilarities are not sufficiently clear and confirmable to exclude the footwear.

Sample wording:

- "The parallel line pattern evident in the lifted footwear impression from Q19 reflects some dissimilarities when compared with the K3–4 footwear. Based on those dissimilarities, the K3 or K4 footwear is possibly not the source of that impression. Due to the fragmented nature and limited detail in the Q19 impression, the K3/K4 footwear could not be excluded."
- "The Q1 photographed impression consists of a lug sole design but the specific features and proportion of those design elements appear dissimilar to those of the K6–7 boots. Those dissimilarities indicate the Q1 impression may not have been produced by the K6–7 boots; however, the improper placement of the scale and limited detail in the Q1 photograph prevented a more conclusive examination."

4.4 Limited association of class characteristics: This level includes those examinations where some similar class characteristics were present but limiting factors prevented a stronger association between the crime scene impression and the footwear. Numerous commonly encountered reasons for the limited examination in this category include factors such as the improper positioning of the scale, photographs that are out of focus, and very partial or fragmented impressions.

Sample wording:

- "The photographed impressions on Q24–32 were produced by footwear that contains a design similar to the outsoles of the K21–22 boots. Due to the lack of any reference of scale in those photographs, further examination was not made. No confirmable differences were noted that would allow for exclusion of the K21–22 boots. Other footwear with the same or similar outsole design characteristics are included as the possible source of those impressions."
- "The Q9 impression lifted from the kicked-in door is similar in general design to portions of the K9 left shoe; however, due to distortion in the Q9 impression, a more detailed comparison was not made. Other footwear with the same or similar outsole design characteristics are included as the possible source of that impression. No confirmable differences were noted that would allow for exclusion of the K9 shoe."

4.5 Association of class characteristics: This level includes those examinations where both the design and physical dimension of that design, and possible general wear, correspond with the footwear.

Sample wording:

- "The Q3 and Q9 impressions correspond with the design, physical size of that design, and general wear of the K5 left shoe. The K5 left shoe is the possible source of the Q3 and Q9 impressions as are other left shoes of the same design, dimension, and general wear."
- "The K9 right shoe corresponds with the design and physical size of the design present in the Q2 tile impression and therefore could have produced that impression. No confirmable differences were noted that would allow for exclusion of the K9 right shoe. General wear and/or randomly acquired characteristics that would have enabled a more detailed association or disassociation with this impression were not present. Other footwear with the same outsole class characteristics of design and dimension are included among the possible sources of that impression."

4.6 High degree of association: This level includes those examinations where the design and physical size of that design correspond, as well as additional specific wear features and/or one or more randomly acquired characteristics.

Sample wording:

- "The Q3 blood mark corresponds with the class characteristics of design and physical size of that design with the K5 right shoe and also shares specific positions and degree of wear in the heel and ball areas. In addition, two small void areas in the Q3 mark share general shape, size, and position features with respective randomly acquired cuts on the K5 right shoe. Based on these shared class, general wear, and randomly acquired features, the K5 right shoe exhibits a high level of association with the Q3 mark. Other right shoes could only be included as a possible source if they possess all of the same features."

- "The impression represented in the Q81–88 photographs is a left footwear impression that corresponds with the design and physical size of design as well as the mold texture of the K9 left boot. In addition, an irregularly shaped void feature in that impression corresponds with the shape and position of a scratch in the K9 left boot. Based on these shared design, size, mold texture, and randomly acquired features, the K9 left boot exhibits a high level of association with the Q81–88 impression. Other left shoes could only be included as a possible source if they display the same features."

4.7 Identification: This level includes those examinations where the examiner has opined there is sufficient correspondence of class and random features to permit a conclusion the footwear was the source of the impression.

Sample wording:

- "The K4 right shoe was determined to be the source of the Q7 impression. This opinion is based on the correspondence of design, the physical size of that design, and general wear on the K4 shoe when compared with those respective features present in the Q7 impression as well as the correspondence of five randomly acquired characteristics."
- "It was determined that the K9 left shoe corresponds in design, dimension, and general wear with the Q31 lifted impression. In addition, numerous void areas present in the Q31 lift correspond with the size, shape, and position of randomly acquired damage present on the K9 left shoe. Based on the correspondence of these features, it is the opinion of this examiner the K9 left shoe was the source of the Q31 impression."

Additional Information or Statements Regarding Conclusions

The aforementioned examples only include core information about an opinion. In many instances, reports can and should include a lot more information to the reader that helps address limitations of a particular examination or to further explain the scope of other possible footwear sources. When appropriate, include informative statements such as in the following two examples. Statements like these assist the reader in the further understanding of certain important information relating to the basis for a specific conclusion:

1. The Q2–4 photographs of the footwear impressions did not include a scale such as a ruler, nor were they taken with the use of a tripod. The absence of a scale in those photographs as well as indications the camera was positioned incorrectly prevented accurate enlargement of those photographs to their actual real-life size. This limitation restricted forensic comparison to the visual aspects of the design of the photographed impressions, and prevented examination with regard to the physical dimensions of those impressions. Without accurate dimensional

information, shoes of that design in many sizes must be included as the possible source of those impressions.

2. The Q5 impression in mud was limited in detail due to slippage and distortion. Although the general design of the Q5 impression reflects similar general design features with the submitted K7–8 Vibram boots, it is noted that this particular design is copied by many manufacturers and is widely available in many variations. Without specific details and dimensions in a crime scene impression and because of the commonality of the Vibram design and similar designs, the significance of the similar general design features is limited.

The Footwear Examiner in Court

The US Federal Rules of Evidence, Article 7, Rule 702 describes "testimony by experts" and states, "If scientific, technical, or other specialized knowledge will assist the trier of fact to understand the evidence or to determine a fact in issue, a witness qualified as an expert by knowledge, skill, experience, training, or education, may testify thereto in the form of any opinion or otherwise, if (1) the testimony is based upon sufficient facts or data, (2) the testimony is the product of reliable principles and methods, and (3) the witness has applied the principles and methods reliably to the facts of the case." In the US and many countries, the duties of a forensic expert include being called to court to testify at a trial or hearing. This happens when the prosecution or defense attorney wishes to offer the expert's opinion to the judge or jury in support of their case. Examiners should be aware that almost all jurors have no idea what is involved in most forensic comparisons, including the comparison between shoes and crime scene impressions; thus, the approach to court testimony should be informative and always consider the use of demonstrable exhibits. Like the examination and written report, testimony should be neutral and transparent, including the strong points of any observations but also including any limitations or weaknesses when they exist.

Pretrial Meetings

When called to testify, it is a prudent practice to have a pretrial meeting or telephonic discussion with the attorney in advance of your testimony. This is to assure the attorney fully understands the meaning of your report and your opinion, and to discuss the best way to present your findings including the use of demonstrative aids. Topics of a pretrial discussion would include

- The specific opinion the attorney is interested in having you testify about. Although in cases involving just one impression and one pair of footwear this may be obvious, some cases involve multiple reports, larger quantities of evidence, and shoes of multiple suspects. In some cases, the attorney may only be interested in your testimony regarding part of those findings.
- Discussion of any areas that might not be fully understood, such as an opportunity to discuss various levels of association, and what, if any, limitations might be part

of your final opinion. Many attorneys are not completely aware of the differences of an opinion of identification versus other levels of association.

- What technology is present in the courtroom, specifically whether there is a screen or monitors or some way to project slides or photographs that will help present your findings to the judge and jury. If not, it may be necessary to prepare multiple hard copies of any demonstrable exhibits.
- Your qualifications as a forensic footwear examiner so the attorney can properly present them to the court and qualify you as an expert in the area of footwear impression evidence.

Last Minute Examinations

Requesting an expert to look at additional evidence just minutes prior to testimony occasionally happens. This may involve additional evidence never submitted for examination or may only consist of an additional question the attorney has about a previously submitted piece of evidence. Many of these requests are simple and easily answered, involving exclusions or explanations of examinations already conducted. In cases where the request requires a full examination of new evidence, experts should hesitate to comply without being provided the necessary time and resources. Unfortunately, these requests sometimes occur while on the witness stand, such as when the expert is presented a new photograph or shoe. Common sense should apply to how these requests are handled. If the request is simple and the expert can comply and answer the question, he or she should. An example would be a defense attorney who hands you a shoe with a sole design that is very different from the design of the crime scene impression, and asks if you can exclude it. Obviously you could answer that question. If the request is more complex and requires more time and resources to make a proper evaluation, a hasty examination should not be attempted. Rather, the request should be declined with a response explaining that to make a full examination of additional evidence just now being provided is not possible without access to the proper equipment and time to do so. To simply glance at this evidence and make any statement about it contradicts the use of the proper methodology necessary in order to conduct a fair and thorough examination.

The Use of Demonstrable Aids

Footwear evidence is often referred to as demonstrable evidence because it is usually easy to visually demonstrate important features of that evidence to others. Fingerprints, tire tread impressions, tool marks, bullet and cartridge case comparisons, and handwriting are a few other examples of demonstrable evidence. Forensic comparisons involving evidence of this type should not only consider the use of visual aids in written reports but their use in court as a way to convey examination observations and opinions.[*][†]

---

[*] Bodziak, W. J., *Footwear Impression Evidence: Detection, Recovery and Examination*, 2nd Ed., CRC Press, Boca Raton, FL, 2000, p. 378.
[†] Izraeli, E., Wiesner, S., and Shor, Y., Computer-aided courtroom presentation of shoeprint comparison, *JFI*, 61(6):549–559, 2011.

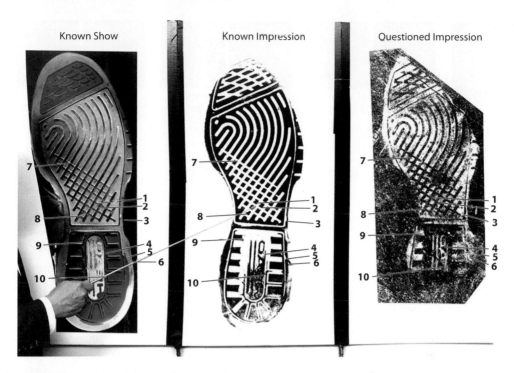

Figure 17.4 An examiner stands next to enlarged photographs pointing to important characteristics that formed the basis for his opinion.

Visual presentations can be provided in a variety of ways. Some of those include hardcopy materials as a separate exhibit prepared for court. These are typically enlarged to their natural size and often with an attached transparent overlay of a known impression of the shoe. They are convenient for both in-court demonstration and for use as a court exhibit that can be reviewed later by the jury during deliberation without the need for special equipment. The same exhibit can also be used in combination with a visual presenter such as an Elmo that projects the images onto a monitor or screen in the courtroom. Years ago, prior to the introduction of newer technology, enlarged photographs were used extensively and are still very useful if preferred. Figure 17.4 depicts an examiner standing in court alongside enlarged photographs explaining to a jury the features that helped form the basis of his opinion. The same presentation could be made standing in front of a projection screen with a laser pointer.

Power Point or Keynote presentations and even Adobe Photoshop presentations permit more photographs and the sharing of more complex cases as well as enlargements of certain areas that provide greater detail. Figure 17.5 depicts a portion of a much larger and more comprehensive slide presentation using Power Point. They are best presented with a projector and movie screen because they provide higher levels of detail in the courtroom when necessary. It is noted that many courtrooms include TV monitors and do not have larger projection screens. If the court is restricted to monitors, any Power Point presentation should be adjusted to assure the necessary detail could still be adequately viewed.

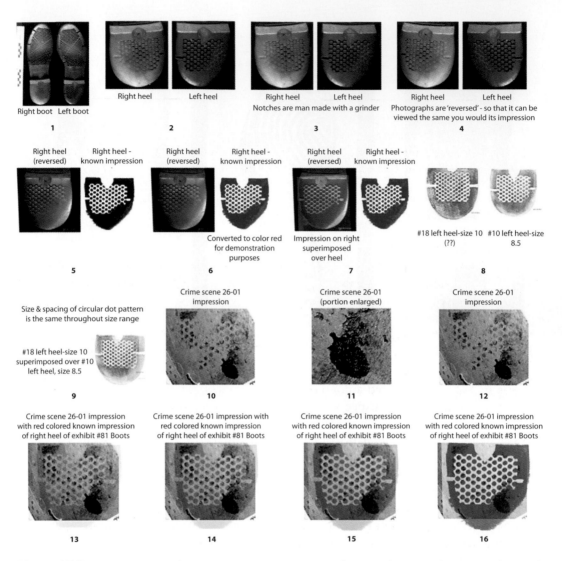

Figure 17.5 Power Point and Keynote presentations are often used to provide a more thorough and detailed explanation of the examination to the jury.

Key Words: reports, transparency, scale of range of conclusions, demonstrable evidence

Key Points

1. Written reports should be transparent, should include good descriptions of each item of evidence, should include all procedures undertaken during the examination, should clearly convey the opinion of the examiner, and should use photographs as necessary.
2. Reports should include a copy of the range of conclusions scale used to provide context and better understanding.
3. The use of demonstrable aids to assist the judge or jury in understanding opinions is encouraged with footwear evidence.

Impressions of the Foot

18

"Qui ne voit tout de suite le parti que l'instruction peut tirer de ce fait, que là, où git aussi un cadavre, est la représentation exacte, fidèle, du pied du meurtier?"[*]

"Who doesn't immediately see the advantage the inquiry could draw from the fact that there, where also lies a corpse, is the exact representation of the foot of the killer?" (Translated from French)

The above quotation comes from Dr. Sév. Caussé's account of barefoot evidence published in 1854. As part of that account, Dr. Caussé also wrote, "Which eyewitness is worth that much: silent, severe, incorruptible? Let science prove that the bloody print is the signature of the foot of the criminal."[†] His words reflect the obvious value of this form of physical evidence. He gives accounts of two cases, one in 1846 involving four bloody footprints on the floor next to the victim. The initial comparison resulted in the exclusion of an arrested suspect. A second arrested suspect committed suicide, so no comparison was made. The other case was in 1847 and involved a double homicide with multiple bloody impressions of a right foot on the floor. Eight suspects were arrested. Exclusion of several suspects was made and based on measurement; one suspect could not be excluded. As his record reflects, "The accused made no objection to tread with her left foot in a thin layer of bullock's blood and then step on a plank of wood ... two impressions were obtained which corresponded with a marvelous degree of accuracy with the marks taken from the house."

Another published account was of a homicide case on July 4, 1862 in Glasgow, Scotland where crucial evidence consisted of three bloody naked left footprints on the floor of the victim's bedroom.[‡] The foot of the deceased contained no blood and her foot was traced and excluded. An older person, present near the scene when the crime occurred, was excluded based on distinct differences. A third person was suspected and the production of known impressions of her feet in blood reflected significant details and dimensions that corresponded with the crime scene impressions. Many years later, this case was reported in a true crime accounting.[§]

In a shod society, there is a low frequency of shoeless impressions produced at scenes of crimes. Many are not familiar with nor have been involved in an investigation where a form of barefoot evidence was present. Impressions produced at the scene of a crime by a perpetrator's naked or sock-clad feet are just as relevant and important as those left by footwear. Like the impressions of footwear, impressions produced by the foot are evidence of a person's presence and are capable of being compared with their known foot exemplars.

---

[*] Caussé, S., *Annals of Public Health and Forensic Medicine*, Series 2, Vol. 1, 1854.
[†] Caussé, S., Ibid., pp. 175–189.
[‡] Taylor, A., *Principles and Practice of Medical Jurisprudence*, 2nd ed., Vol. 1, Henry C. Lea, Philadelphia, 1873.
[§] Brand, C., *Heaven Knows Who*, Charles Scribner's Sons, New York, 1960.

References to the use of this evidence exist throughout the world for tracking, crime scene reconstruction, and comparative evaluation.[*,†,‡,§,¶]

Forensic barefoot evidence occurs in four forms. One includes impressions produced by a naked foot where the circumstances have allowed for replication of the skin's friction ridges and/or flexion creases. A latent fingerprint examiner would examine this form.[**,††] Another form includes two- and three-dimensional impressions produced by a naked foot, but without sufficient replication of friction ridge detail to allow a comparison to be conducted with the skin. A third form includes impressions produced while the perpetrator is wearing socks. A fourth involves situations where an item of footwear is linked to a crime and an attempt is made to associate that footwear with a particular individual through an examination of traces of the feet that may exist on the inner liner of the shoes. An example of each form is included in Figure 18.1. This chapter provides an overview and awareness of this type of evidence.

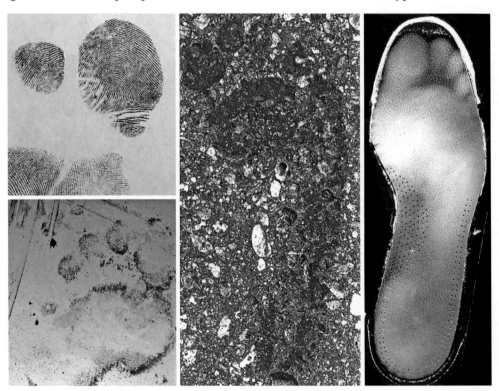

Figure 18.1 Four forms of barefoot evidence include friction ridge detail (top left), a naked footprint without replication of friction ridge detail (center), a sock-clad footprint (bottom left), and the impressions the wearer's foot leaves in his or her shoes (right).

[*] Gayer, G. W., *Foot Prints; An Aid to the Detection of Crime for the Police and Magistracy*, Nagpur, India, 1909.

[†] Adam, J., and Adam, J. C., *Criminal Investigation: A Practical Handbook for Magistrates, Police Officers, and Lawyers*, Sweet & Maxwell, Ltd., London, 1924, pp. 483–552.

[‡] Sharma, B. R., *Footprints, Tracks and Trails in Criminal Investigation and Trials*, Central Law Agency, Allahabad, India, 1980.

[§] Belkin, R., and Korukhov, Yu., *Fundamentals of Criminalistics*, USSR, English Translation by Progress Publishers 1986, pp. 65–66.

[¶] Weiser, W., Analysis of shoe prints, *Kriminalistik*, November 1979, pp. 494–499 (translation from German).

[**] Salmons, R., Identification by flexion creases, *R.C.M.P. Gazette*, 48(11), 1986.

[††] Massey, S. L., Persistence of creases of the foot and their value for forensic identification purposes. *JFI*, 54(3):296–315, 2004.

Forensic Research

As with any physical evidence, questions relating to the value and reliability of that evidence arise. Is the human foot sufficiently different from other feet in the general population to permit the ability to discriminate the feet of one individual from others? Does the foot replicate its features in a way to enable a reliable comparison? Do the various size and shape features of the adult human foot change over short or long periods of time? Are partial foot impressions of value for comparison?

Research and studies involving the individuality of the human foot and the impressions it produces have provided answers to these questions. Some involved studies of a large number of foot impressions such as the research by Qamra involving 725 individuals.[*] Others were smaller studies or were performed to substantiate casework procedures or results.[†,‡,§,¶,**,††,‡‡]

In 1986 and 1987, research at the FBI Academy involved the collection of inked prints of the left and right feet of 500 persons (399 males and 101 females).[§§,¶¶] To provide a way of comparing a large number of impressions to one another, a metric grid was positioned over each impression as shown in Figure 18.2. The horizontal X-axis baseline of the grid would graze the rearmost portion of the heel while the vertical Y-axis would pass through the optical centers of the heel and second toe. The second toe was selected based on observation and experience that its position was least affected by the constriction of socks or narrow toed footwear. Optical centers for the other toes, the center of the toe stem of the great toe where it touches the anterior border of the footpad (metatarsal ridge) as well as the extreme medial and lateral bulges in the ball area of the foot were also marked. Once these reference points were established, a tablet was used to trace and enter information from each impression into a computer and a summary of the data for each pair of feet was provided in a printout such as shown in Figure 18.3. Included among this data were the numerous reference points, length measurements, relative toe positions, the length of the metatarsal ridge, surface areas of the footpad, and toe stem printing information. In addition to the dimensional features, recorded data included other features of the feet that have significant discrimination value such as arch types, the shape of the anterior border of the

[*] Qamra, S., Sharma, B., and Kaila, P., Naked foot marks—A preliminary study of identification factors, *Forensic Science International*, 16:145–152, 1980.

[†] Koehler, J. R. G., Footwear evidence, *RCMP Gazette*, 48(9), 1986.

[‡] Knecht, W., The shoes only fit the murderer, *Kriminalistik*, 673–681, December 1987 (translated from German).

[§] Lucock, L. J., Identifying the wearer of worn footwear, *Journal of the Forensic Science Society*, 7(2):62–70, 1967.

[¶] Laskowski, G. E., and Kyle, V. L., Barefoot impressions—a preliminary study of identification characteristics and population frequency of their morphological features, *Journal of Forensic Sciences*, 33(2):378–388, 1988.

[**] Hammer, L., Nic Daćid, N., Kennedy, R., and Yamashita, A., Preliminary study of the comparison of inked barefoot impressions with impressions from shoe insoles using a controlled population, *JFI*, 62(6):603–622, 2012.

[††] Kennedy, R., Yamashita, A., Barefoot morphology comparisons: A summary, *JFI* 57(3):383–413, 2007.

[‡‡] Borkowski, K., Kryminalistyczna Identyfikacja Śladów Stóp, Centralnego Laboratorium Kryminalistycznego Policji, Warzawa, 2013.

[§§] Bodziak, W., and Monson, K., Discrimination of individuals based on their barefoot impressions, presentations at the International Association of Forensic Sciences meeting, Vancouver, B.C., August 1987 and American Academy of Forensic Sciences, Las Vegas, NV, February 1989.

[¶¶] Bodziak, W. J., *Footwear Impression Evidence: Detection, Recovery and Examination*, 2nd ed., CRC Press, Boca Raton, FL, 2000, pp. 386–390.

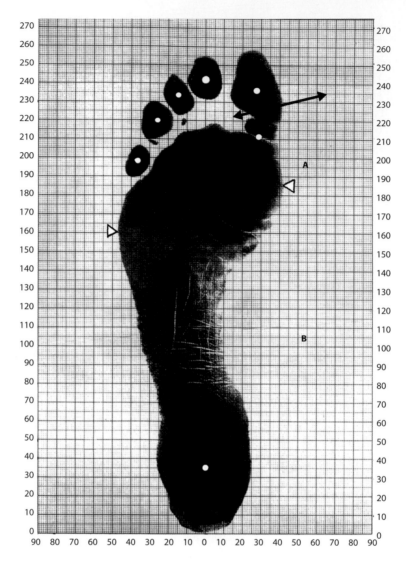

Figure 18.2 Reference points were created using a metric grid to prepare hundreds of bare footprints prior to their entry in a database.

footpad, sometimes called the metatarsal ridge, the X–Y axis relationship of the toes, and surface area proportions. Using the computer's search capability, it was possible to test the ability of these features to discriminate one foot from others. For example, using inked prints of unknown origin provided by the research team in the form of blind tests, searches were performed for learning how reliably an unknown print could be included among, or excluded from, those in the database of 500. This proved to be an easy task that only required three to four general measurements entered with a gracious search parameter of ±5 mm for each measurement. Although a database of only 500 is not a large population, the fact that only minimal basic measurements such as the maximum heel to toe length and ball width, expanded by ±5 mm, were required to demonstrate how easily the feet of one individual could be discriminated from others was significant. As seen in three impressions in Figure 18.4, many other features are present in impressions of the foot that could

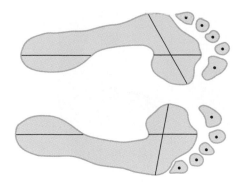

Measurements for Footprint No. 413

Size: 8.0   Age: 26   Ht: 65   Wt: 138   Sex: Female
Toe stem printing (T1-T5) :   Left: Y N Y N N   Right: Y Y Y N N

Foot Areas:	Left	10141	1968	6917		77	5685	63
	Right	10132	2474	6405		72	5824	65

Toe Areas:	Left	487		191	164		195	219
	Right	405	237		190	200	221	

Ant. perimeter: Left 123   Right 133

Left toe X coords:	21	0	−14	−29	−39
Left toe Y coords:	211	220	209	199	182
Right toe X coords:	−24	0	15	28	37
Right toe Y coords:	212	219	207	196	178

LT1-LT5:	Left	224	228	217	207	189
	Right	223	227	216	204	186

MFL:	Left 228	Right 127	MFW:	Left 92	Right 89
LMT-1:	Left 181	Right 171	LMT-5:	Left 157	Right 152
HW:	Left 46	Right 45	T1-MT-1:	Left 144	Right 159

Figure 18.3 A data sheet (top) and the tracing tablet (bottom) used in the FBI research in 1986–1987 that compared numerous features and measurements of the barefoot impressions of 500 individuals.

have been used but were not necessary to search the smaller database. Even when similarly sized impressions with similar arch types were compared as shown in Figure 18.5, other features of the feet can easily discriminate one from another. These six impressions may have a similar appearance at first glance, but features such as the metatarsal ridge (traced in green on the left), the relative positions of the toes, the size and shapes of the toes, the shape and volume of the ball area of the foot, and other features easily distinguish these feet from each other. The differences are even more pronounced when any one impression is superimposed over any of the other impressions. Feet in the general population include

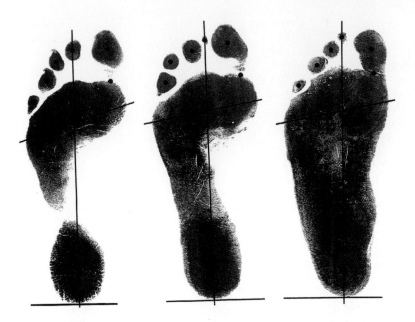

Figure 18.4 Impressions of the left feet of three persons have the same length, but many other features are different.

a far greater range and variety of obvious and significant differences than in the previous example of six feet, selected for their visual similarity. The research concluded that the impression the foot leaves has many features that can discriminate it from the feet of others in the general population; thus crime scene impressions produced by the human foot are highly valuable for forensic comparison with the known impressions of individuals. Forensic comparison can exclude individuals as well as include individuals. As multiple combined similarities of multiple foot features of an individual are increasingly present in the crime scene impression(s), it rapidly reduces the number of others in the general population as the possible source.

Research conducted by Laskowski and Kyle compared shallow three-dimensional impressions of the feet of 107 adult males, also with results indicating a high discriminatory value based on the combined features.[*]

The Swedish National Police College and the Swedish police initiated a joint project in 1994 for the matching of scene-of-crime prints from naked and stocking feet. This project was conducted to determine the degree of individuality that may be left by stocking clad feet at a crime scene and involved preparation of several cases that were then distributed to a number of friends at laboratories in various countries. Three of these laboratories had experience in conducting these examinations while others had minimal or no experience at all. The results demonstrated a high degree of success.[†]

Starting around 1994, extensive research involving much larger numbers of inked prints of feet of adults was conducted by the Royal Canadian Mounted Police (RCMP) and

---

[*] Laskowski, G., and Kyle, V., 1988, Ibid.
[†] Personal communication with Bengt Aspegren, Swedish National Police College, and Kjell Carlsson, Stockholm Police, June 1997.

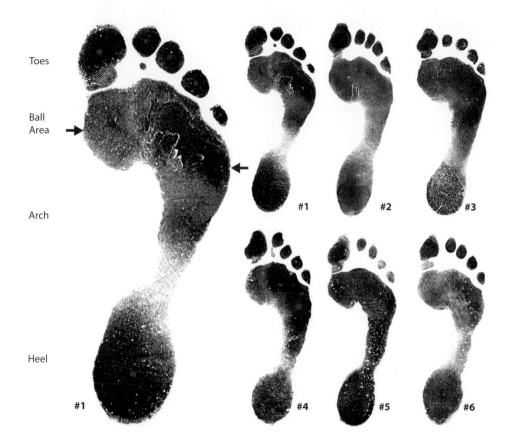

Figure 18.5 Six right foot impressions selected for their general visual similarity. The six impressions still contain numerous features that allow them to be easily distinguished from the others.

Carleton University in Ottawa, Canada.[*,†,‡] The research eventually accumulated a population of 5755 individuals composed of 53% males and 47% females of which 12% were non-Caucasian. The group contributing the impressions was comprised of persons from various venues in Canada and the US. Its focus was to address the underlying question of uniqueness or rarity of the morphological (size and shape) features of the impression of the human foot, for example, how likely it would be for the footprint of a second unrelated person to match the forensic evidence from the crime scene. The study concluded for the general population of the data it had collected, the odds of a chance match were 1 in 1.27 billion. It is noted that these calculations were made based on ink quality impressions that would normally exceed what is encountered in most barefoot evidence recovered from the scene of a crime. Some conclusions and observations of that research note the high degree of individuality of the foot's impression as well as provide an overview of barefoot morphology comparisons. It also notes that monozygotic twins in the study produced different

---

[*] Kennedy, R., Uniqueness of bare feet and its use as a possible means of identification, *Forensic Science International*, 82(1):81–87, 1996.

[†] Kennedy, R. B., Pressman, I. S., Sanping, C., Petersen, P. H., and Pressman, A. E., Statistical analysis of barefoot impressions, *Journal of Forensic Science*, 48(1):55–63, 2003.

[‡] Kennedy, R., Chen, S., Pressman, I., Yamashita, A., and Pressman, A., A large-scale statistical analysis of barefoot impressions, *Journal of Forensic Sciences*, 50 (5):1071–1080, 2005.

foot impressions, and that foot impressions taken from various individuals several years apart were essentially unchanged.[*]

In 1998, examiners from the FBI laboratory hosted persons representing nine countries, including an anthropologist and podiatrists, to discuss the various aspects surrounding this evidence.[†]

Validation of a forensic examiner's ability to reliably distinguish impressions of different individuals in a physical comparison was tested in another study where numerous questioned barefoot impressions along with numerous inked known impressions were sent to 15 examiners in different laboratories, resulting in a total of 1350 comparisons. The examiners were asked to include or exclude the known impressions, which they did without any false associations.[‡]

Another study concentrated on the impressions retained on the inner liner of footwear compared with the respective inked known barefoot impressions of the footwear's owners. Comparisons were also made between insole impressions on the same items of footwear between other shoes of the same persons. The study concluded that comparing inked impressions of a shoe's owner to the insole impressions of their shoes corresponds more closely than with inked impressions of different persons. It also notes that some adjustments and a more conservative approach were required due to the constrictive nature of footwear and the lack of comparability between inked and insole prints. It further concluded that like-versus-like comparisons, for example, insole impressions compared to other insole impressions of the same individual, demonstrated better correspondence.[§,¶]

All of the cited forensic research conducted has repeatedly shown the ability to discriminate the features of the feet of different individuals.

Nonforensic Research

References to the individuality of bare feet also exist in a wide variety of nonforensic literature. The most significant of these was an extensive study conducted in 1946 by the US Army involving the measurement of 27 different foot dimensions of over 6000 soldiers.[**] The survey of these measurements was intended to result in beneficial information that would lead to better fitting boots for soldiers. Instead, the study concluded

> "… the most important observations in this study have been the wide diversity of foot measurements and a lack of a pattern in their interrelationships. Thus, a given foot length may be associated with a great range of ball lengths, a given foot width with a great range of ball girths and heel widths, and either have high, low or intermediate arch lengths, a wide variety of flare

[*] Kennedy, R., and Yamashita, A., Barefoot morphology comparisons: a summary, *JFI*, 57(3):383–413, 2007.

[†] International Seminar on Barefoot Impression Evidence, FBI Academy, Quantico, VA 2/17-20/1998

[‡] Maltais, L., and Yamashita, A., A validation study of barefoot morphology comparison, *JFS*, 60(3):362, 2010.

[§] Hammer, L., Nic Daéid, N., Kennedy, R., and Yamashita, A., Preliminary study of the comparison of inked barefoot impressions with impressions from shoe insoles using a controlled population, *JFI*, 62(6):603–622, 2012.

[¶] Hammer, L., A study of the comparison of inked barefoot impressions to barefoot impressions inside the shoe, Master's Thesis, University of Strathclyde, Glasgow, Scotland, 2007.

[**] Freedman, A., Huntington, E., Davis, G., Magee, R., Milstead, V., and Kirkpatrick, C., *Foot Dimensions of Soldiers: A Survey of Foot Measurements and the Proper Fit of Army Shoes*, U.S. Armored Medical Research Laboratory, Ft. Knox, KY, March 1946.

characteristics, and a wide variety of measurements of all other dimensions. This scatter of measurements makes every foot an individual type …."

Although this study was not a forensic study, its conclusions have distinct forensic implications concerning both research and casework. The Army survey conclusion that the various dimensions of the feet are not inter-related, e.g., the length, width, toe proportions, arch type, heel size, instep, and other measurements are independent of one another, means those features and dimensions are of extreme value in discriminating an individual's feet from a larger general population. Some examples of the measurement observations from this study are summarized and quoted here:

- Ball Length—This measurement was made from the rear of the heel to the bulge at the medial ball. The conclusion of the study states, "The ball length correlates only moderately well with foot length and poorly, if at all, with breadth. There is such a pronounced scatter of the measurements, a given foot length may be associated with a wide variety of ball lengths."
- Toe Length—This measurement was made from the bulge at the medial ball to the tip of the first toe. The conclusion of the study states, "Toe length correlates only moderately well with foot length and poorly, if at all, with breadth. There is a pronounced scatter of the measurements, such that a given foot length may be associated with a wide variety of toe lengths."
- Breadth of Toes 1 through 3—This measurement was made across the width of the first three toes. The conclusion of the study states, "The breadth of the three forward toes correlates poorly, if at all, with foot breadth and with foot length."
- Toe Curve—This was a curve drawn along the tips of the toes that reflects the anterior curvature and orientation of the toes. The conclusion of the study states, "The toe curves and their orientation correlate poorly, if at all, with foot length and breadth. There is such a pronounced scatter of shapes such as that a given foot length and/or breadth may be associated with a wide variety of curvatures."
- Foot Breadth—This is the angular measurement made across the ball area of the foot between the first and fifth metatarsal joints. The study noted that this was difficult to compare because the "angular relationship between the 1st and 5th metatarsal joints differs from individual to individual." This in itself is significant because it again demonstrates the many possible features that vary between feet and how they are independent of the other features.

Similar nonforensic studies have occurred in the footwear industry where research on the shape, function, and biomechanics of the human foot has been conducted in order to develop better footwear.[*,†,‡,§] Examples of the products of this research are reflected in

---

[*] Litchfield, P., Reebok manufacturing techniques, International Symposium of the Forensic Aspects of Footwear and Tire Impression Evidence, FBI Academy, Quantico, VA, 1994.

[†] Potter, D. R., Two types of outsole manufacturing techniques and their influence on footwear impression variations, presented at the International Symposium on the Forensic Aspects of Footwear and Tire Impression Evidence, FBI Academy, Quantico, VA, June 27–July 1, 1994.

[‡] Robert, L., Converse manufacturing techniques, Converse Rubber Company Inc., North Reading, MA, International Symposium of the Forensic Aspects of Footwear and Tire Impression Evidence, FBI Academy, Quantico, VA, 1994.

[§] Adult foot structure, *Sport Research Review*, August/November, 1990, Nike, Inc., Beaverton, OR.

everyday ads that promote specific shoe styles for runners who pronate or supinate, have a hard heel strike, or who require straight lasted footwear or curved lasted footwear.

In 1983, the Prescription Footwear Association, for purposes related to shoe fitting, reported their results of a large survey involving 6800 adults (4000 females, 2800 males). This survey concluded, "Based on our foot-measurement survey findings it is extremely rare in the U.S. population (and presumably anywhere in the world) to find a pair of feet of the same person in which the two feet are exactly alike in size, shape or proportions …."[*] This is useful information for forensic examiners when considering issues relating to sizing as well as reasons for mismated general wear in footwear. It also illustrates how feet evolve slightly differently due to the results and sum of one's life experiences.

Anthropological studies have largely related to the identification of human remains and how the various long bones, including those of the feet, differ among various ethnic and racial groups.[†,‡,§,¶]

Miscellaneous studies in the field of sports research, medicine, biomechanics, and biometrics, although more removed from the sizing and features of the foot, occasionally allude to the variations between the feet of individuals. These studies demonstrate the awareness of individuality issues and further confirm, in a way independent from forensic studies, the individual nature of the human foot and its function.[**,††,‡‡,§§,¶¶]

The Human Foot[***,†††]

The human foot is a complex structure that acts as the interface between the body and the ground. Figure 18.6 depicts two views of a foot and its 26 bones. Included are the talus (anklebone), the calcaneus (heel bone), the 5 tarsal bones (cuboid, navicular, and 3 cuneiforms), 5 metatarsals, and 14 bones of the toes called phalanges. Each foot also has over 100 muscles, tendons, and ligaments and two primary arches—the longitudinal arch between the heel and forefoot and the transverse arch, which runs across the ball of the foot. The foot can move in four directions known as plantar-flexion, dorsi-flexion, inversion, and eversion. Biomechanical descriptions of foot function are complex and vary when walking versus running but a very basic accounting of the gait cycle involves the

---

[*] Rossi, W. A., The high incidence of mismated feet in the population, *Foot & Ankle*, 4:2, American Orthopaedic Foot and Ankle Society, Inc., 1983.

[†] Musgrave, J. H., and Hareja, N. K., The estimation of adult stature from metacarpal bone length, *American Journal of Physical Anthropology*, 48:113, 1978.

[‡] Trotter, M., and Gleser, G. C., A re-evaluation of estimation of stature based on measurements of stature taken during life and of long bones after death, *American Journal of Physical Anthropology*, 16, 1958.

[§] Xiang-Qing, S., Estimation of stature from intact long bones of Chinese males, *Canadian Society Journal of Forensic Science*, 22:2, 1989.

[¶] Stature Estimation, Scientific Working Group for Forensic Anthropology, August 2, 2012.

[**] Nubar, G. W., Biomechanics of the foot and ankle during gait, *Foot and Ankle Injuries: Clinics in Sports Medicine*, 7:1, 1988.

[††] Adelaar, R. S., The practical biomechanics of running, *The American Journal of Sport Medicine*, 14:6, 1986.

[‡‡] White, J., Footwear Research Group, Bend, OR, personal communication, 1985.

[§§] Weise, E., Body may be key to a foolproof ID, *USA Today*, April 8, 1998.

[¶¶] Chan, C. W., and Rudins, A., Foot biomechanics during walking and running, *Mayo Clinic Proc*, 69:448, 1994.

[***] Valmassy, R., *Clinical Biomechanics of the Lower Extremities*, Mosby, St. Louis, MO, 1996, p. 2.

[†††] Miller, I., presentation at the Technical Conference on Footwear and Tire Tread Impression Evidence, April 1984.

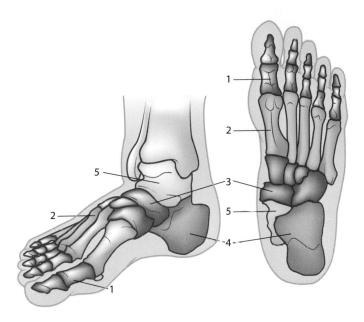

Figure 18.6 The human foot includes 26 bones: the phalanges (1); the metatarsals (2); the cuboid, navicular, and (3) cuneiforms; the calcaneus (4); and the talus (5).

foot relaxing (pronation) as it first makes contact with the substrate, then moving forward, distributing its weight from the heel area through the forefoot, and, finally, becoming rigid (supination) allowing the foot to more efficiently push off and propel itself. This sequence of events and how it is carried out is not precisely the same in each individual. Not all individuals' feet function in a perfect or "normal" way. The mixed morphology and function of individuals' feet provide reasons for variance in the features it leaves in its barefoot impression. In addition to shape features, feet may also have other noticeable pathologies. A few of these are blisters produced by a shoe repeatedly rubbing the skin, corns on toes, calluses on the bottom of the feet that result from a thickening of the skin where shoes repeatedly press, plantar warts, and hammertoes where the end joints of a toe bend downward. When present, these and other characteristics may be reflected in a barefoot impression or transferred to the inner liner of a shoe.

Recovery of Barefoot Evidence

Two- or three-dimensional barefoot impressions are recovered using the same methods, materials, and procedures used for footwear impressions. The majority of naked or sock-clad foot impressions are found on interior surfaces. Of those a great many are in blood; thus, every consideration should be made regarding recovery of the original impressions as well as the utilization of enhancement methods at the scene or in the laboratory. Impressions produced in blood with a naked foot will typically last for only a few steps before the blood has been consumed. Socks are able to absorb and hold a larger quantity of blood than the naked foot and consequently scenes involving bloody sock-clad feet usually include a greater number of impressions. Scenes involving blood-soaked sock-clad impressions of both left and right feet could easily include dozens of impressions. Figure 18.7 depicts what happens after a blood-soaked sock has produced several prior impressions. The pressure of

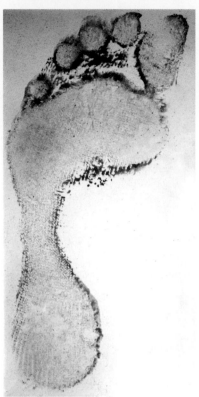

Figure 18.7 Blood-soaked sock-clad impressions can hold much blood and produce many impressions at a crime scene. With each impression, blood is forced toward the perimeter of the foot and toes as well as deposited on the substrate. This impression shows the sock fabric, evidence of blood forced toward the perimeter, and lighter quantities of blood remaining in the pressure areas.

each prior impression has forced some of the blood to the outer perimeter whereas much of the blood beneath the feet and toes has been consumed. The result is an impression with a lighter interior and darker borders in some areas. Areas of the sock that have acquired blood but are not under the pressure of the foot will also result in some sporadic deposition of blood as seen in Figure 18.7 where the bloody sock makes contact between the toes and metatarsal ridge. Depending on the substrate and the thickness of the sock, the weave pattern produced on a sock-clad impression can range from very obvious to nondetectable. Figure 18.8 depicts one of several bloody sock-clad impressions from 14 tiles recovered and submitted for examination. Very good correspondence existed between the left and right feet of a suspect. Because the investigators recovered the actual tiles, subsequent laboratory chemical enhancement also developed small patches of latent skin ridge patterns that were produced after the perpetrator removed his socks before departing the scene. The latent ridge patterns were identified with the suspect's feet by a latent fingerprint examiner.

A significant potential piece of evidence that is often not considered is the footwear of a person suspected of leaving naked or sock-clad bloody impressions. If the perpetrator had accumulated blood on his or her feet or socks and then placed the shoes back on their feet as a person typically would when departing the scene, the inner surfaces of the shoes would likely contain detectable traces of human blood with the victim's DNA profile. Thus the inner surfaces of footwear of a suspect believed to have left bloody sock or naked foot impressions during the commission of a homicide may be harboring valuable evidence that could link him or her to the victim's DNA.

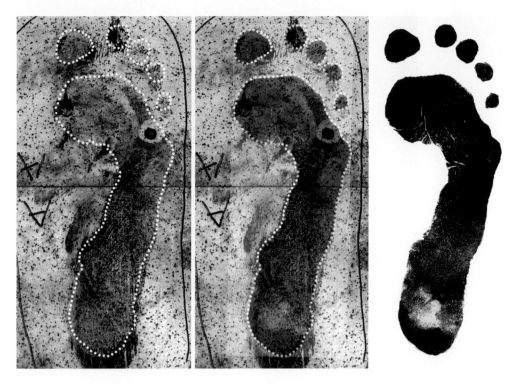

Figure 18.8 A case example of a sock-clad impression and corresponding features of the suspect's known right foot.

At any homicide scene involving bloody footprints, the feet of the victim should also be documented to determine if they were shod, naked, or sock-clad and if any of the bloody impressions at the scene could be theirs. If their feet contain a weight-bearing pattern of blood, this indicates they may have produced impressions. Since deceased victims cannot provide known weight-bearing standards of their feet, the shoes of the victim should be seized as they may contain useful inner sole impressions that could be used as known standards. Figure 18.9 depicts a victim's foot on the left that has walked through blood as evidenced by the blood staining on the weight-bearing areas of the foot. The foot on the right contains blood that spilled onto the victim's foot and flowed around the side of the ankle into some of the flexion creases, but that blood was not acquired because of the victim walking through the blood.

In some instances, recovered footwear may be linked to the crime scene impressions or the presence of the victim's blood on or in the shoes, but when those shoes were recovered they were not being worn by the accused. The discovery of the shoes may be a product of a search warrant or because the footwear were discarded by the perpetrator and later discovered because of information provided by an informant. In some cases, when the accused is confronted with the shoes, he or she will admit ownership. If ownership is denied, the person should not be allowed to handle or wear those shoes as these actions can only interfere with subsequent examination. Shoes of an unknown wearer should be preserved for DNA evidence that may link the person to the owner and/or victim's blood.

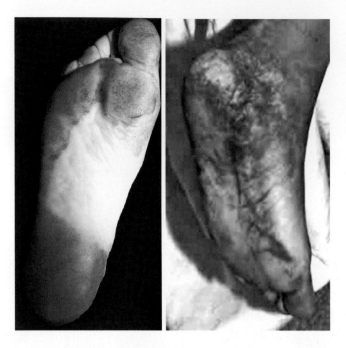

Figure 18.9 A weight-bearing blood pattern on the foot on the left resulted from walking in blood, as distinguished from the foot on the right, which has some blood that has flowed down around the ankle and onto the foot.

Obtaining Known Standards

Before any physical comparisons are conducted, known standards of the feet of the suspected person or persons must be obtained. Depending on the facts of a case, in addition to those of the primary suspect(s), obtaining exemplars of feet may extend to others for purposes of exclusion. Known standards for impressions on firm substrates like tile or wood floors require weight-bearing inked impressions of the feet. Crime scene impressions in soft substrates like soil or sand require the addition of three-dimensional impressions in similar soft substrates and/or Biofoam. For those examinations that involve the question of who was the primary wearer of the shoes, in addition to weight-bearing inked impressions, other shoes the suspect has worn, preferably of a similar type, may provide good known standards. Depending on the features found within the questioned footwear, casts of the forefoot region of the suspect's feet may also be necessary. In all cases, photographs of the feet of the suspect should be obtained as well as shoe sizing information obtained by measuring their feet. Not every exemplar is necessary for every barefoot examination, but when multiple ones are taken, they should be taken with the least messy methods first and the messiest methods last. Following are some instructions for collecting or obtaining known barefoot exemplars.

Video

A video recording of the entire process of obtaining inked impressions of feet should be made of suspects beginning with their entry into the room. This documents the procedure, assures the examiner how the impressions were taken, and provides a record in any instance where it is believed the suspect may have attempted to disguise his or her impressions or otherwise was not being cooperative.

Photographs of the Feet

The feet of the individual should be photographed with good resolution, focus, and proper lighting to allow for the recording of fine detail. Foot photographs should be taken with a proper long scale placed at the correct plane of the portion of the foot being photographed. Some examples are included in Figure 18.10. The various areas that should be photographed are listed here:

- Front, rear, and views from each side with the individuals standing and their weight evenly distributed. These should be taken with the camera near ground level. Pants legs should be rolled up to the knees so as not to interfere.
- Photographs of the bottom of the feet.
- Photographs of the top of the toe region of the feet.
- Sufficient photographs should be assured of capturing the details of any notable features like pronounced bunions, corns, warts, and other features.

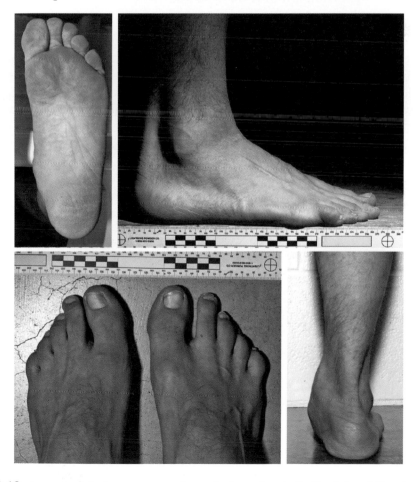

Figure 18.10 As part of the known exemplars, the feet of an individual should be photographed from front and back, from each side, and from the top and bottom.

Sizing Information

The feet of the individual should be measured using a Brannock Device as discussed in Chapter 8, and should include both heel-to-toe and arch length measurements. In addition, any information about the size of the shoes the suspect was wearing when arrested as well as other footwear he or she owns should be documented and included. It is noted that shoes issued to an individual in jail are not a reliable standard of shoe size.

Footwear of Suspect

Any footwear worn by a suspect when arrested or other footwear the suspect admits he wears and belongs to him should be seized in cases where comparisons need to be made with the inner soles of the shoes in question. Figure 18.11 shows an example of this type of exemplar when it is available. As mentioned, in cases where naked or bloody sock-clad impressions were produced at the crime scene, all footwear of suspects should be seized for DNA testing of the inner surfaces for traces of the blood of the victim.

Biofoam and Impressions in Soft Substrates

If the crime scene impression is in a soft substrate, it may be necessary to obtain impressions of the feet using Biofoam (mentioned in Chapter 15) or in a similar substrate such as sifted wet sand. Biofoam is a fragile collapsible foam product and the full weight of the person cannot be used to obtain an impression. The person taking the exemplars should be experienced with this product to get the best results. Direct the person to place his or her foot in the center of the Biofoam and gradually apply light and even pressure until the foot begins penetrating the surface. It may be necessary to assist in pressing the toes into the Biofoam. Depending on the depth of the crime scene impressions, you may wish to obtain

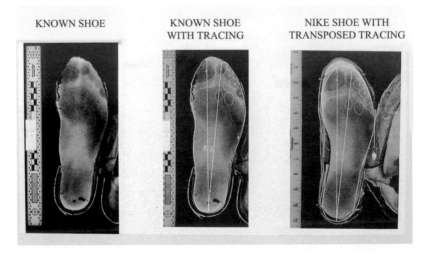

Figure 18.11 Similar known footwear of a suspect provides a good standard for comparison of insole impressions. On the left is the Reebok shoe the suspect was wearing while arrested, in the center are some tracings of features of the impression in the shoe, and on the right is the insole of the Nike shoe lost when fleeing the crime scene, but also sharing almost duplicate features as found in the Reebok shoe.

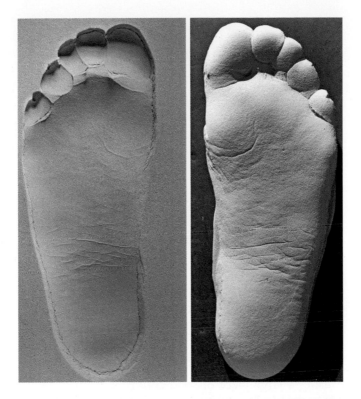

Figure 18.12 Biofoam impressions of a foot and a cast made from that impression.

shallow impressions in one case and deeper ones in another. Figure 18.12 depicts a Biofoam impression of a left foot and a cast made later from that impression.

Walking Inked Naked Foot Impressions

Walking inked impressions of an individual provide repetitive weight-bearing impressions of their left and right feet. Most are taken with the naked foot, but in those cases where sock-clad impressions are being examined, inked impressions while wearing socks should also be considered. Many investigators obtaining inked impressions will use fingerprint ink because of its availability; however, fingerprint ink is designed to dry instantly and the impressions of the feet obtained from it will be lighter and will not produce a good sequence of several dark impressions with good contrast. Instead, oil-based block printing ink should be used. Oil-based block printing ink (do not use water-based inks) can be obtained at graphic arts stores but is also widely available through the Internet. One example is Speedball black oil-based block printing ink #3550.* This ink will enable several impressions with good contrast to be produced. The ink will require a few hours or overnight for complete drying before the exemplars can be rolled up.

Figure 18.13 illustrates the setup for obtaining a series of weight-bearing inked impressions. A sufficiently large area is necessary that includes a smooth floor. An inked surface

---

* Speedball oil-based block printing ink #3550, Speedball Art Products, 2301 Speedball Road, Statesville, NC, 800-898-7224 (www.speedballart.com).

Figure 18.13 Obtaining weight-bearing walking inked impressions.

must be prepared using a large piece of solid core (not foam core) mounting board.* A quantity of black oil-based block printing ink should be spread onto and across the surface of this board using a heavy-duty fingerprint roller. The thickness of the ink should not be heavy but should be adequate to cover any white color of the board and to sufficiently ink the feet. The inked board should be placed at the beginning of a 20-foot-long piece of rolled out white butcher paper that is 3 feet wide. White butcher paper is preferred as it offers better contrast, particularly should the lighter impressions be later used in a friction ridge comparison. If white butcher paper is not available, brown wrapping paper can be used. The paper should be taped to the floor completely across each end and periodically along each side as needed. The tape will hold the paper against the floor and reduce the tendency for the paper to cling to the inked feet. Heavier paper requires less taping than thinner fragile paper. At the distant end of the length of paper, position a scrap piece of mounting board onto which the contributor can step. A chair should also be placed there. To begin the process, the contributor should remove their footwear and socks. The feet should be cleaned as necessary, normally by wiping with a damp towel or alcohol swabs. Once the feet are dry, the contributor should step onto the inked pad and walk around on it, including rising up on the toes and rolling the heels backward to assure the feet are fully inked in any area that could potentially produce part of a footprint. It is noted that any part of the foot that would normally leave its impression, if not inked, will not be included in the inked impressions. The contributor should then be directed to walk down the full length of paper. During this process, the person should walk normally and look forward. Depending on the stride length and the precise length of the paper, each exemplar will typically collect from seven to ten impressions. After the first set of impressions is complete, the contributor should sit on the chair with his or her feet resting on the scrap mounting board. The inked

---

* An example would be a Crescent mounting board, 32 × 40 inches.

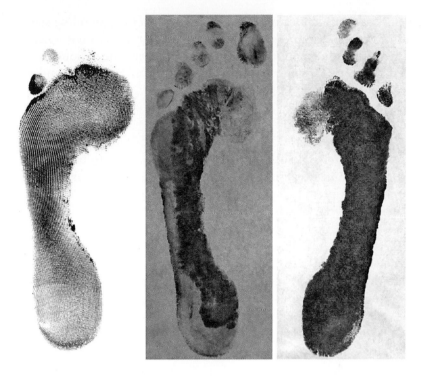

Figure 18.14 Inked impressions taken improperly and with inadequate detail.

impressions can then be removed to an area where they will be safe to dry. A new length of paper should then be taped to the floor and the ink board and scrap piece of mounting board interchanged. The contributor then stands on the ink board to reink his or her feet, and again walks down the new piece of paper, stepping onto the scrap mounting board before sitting down. This can be repeated as necessary until 3 or 4 sets of inked impressions are obtained. In the end, it will be necessary to provide a means of cleaning the oil-based ink from the contributor's feet.

In many cases, it is not the examiner who is obtaining the inked impressions but someone on the investigative team. If the above procedures are not known, impressions will usually be obtained incorrectly often with poor or inadequate detail. One common example is the collection of a known inked exemplar by inking the foot with a fingerprint roller and then pressing paper against the foot or having the individual roll the foot over a cylindrical object in the same way as might be used for a skin ridge examination. Impressions obtained in this way are not weight-bearing impressions and are not comparable with the weight-bearing impressions produced at the crime scene. In other cases, the type of ink or the manner in which the foot was inked resulted in erratic and poor detail. Figure 18.14 depicts some actual case examples of poor exemplars of no value for comparison.

Static Inked Naked Foot Impressions

Static inked impressions are those made when standing as opposed to walking. They can be made with ink and paper in conjunction with the walking impressions, or they can also be obtained prior to inking the foot by using the inkless Identicator product. The contributor should stand with their weight divided evenly between the feet, collecting ink with one foot from the ink pad or Identicator pad, and then producing a standing static impression. Some individuals produce impressions of slightly smaller dimensions when standing versus walking. Since it is often not known in what precise way the various scene impressions were produced, having both static and walking impressions is recommended.

Sock-Clad Inked Impressions

The same procedure that is used to obtain walking and static inked impressions can be used to obtain impressions of sock-clad feet. These only need to be taken in those cases involving sock-clad crime scene impressions. It has been my experience that the naked inked foot impressions provide the best detail and are adequate for comparison with any sock-clad crime scene impressions. Inasmuch as it is rarely known what socks were worn by the perpetrator, selecting socks to use for known impressions is always questionable. Even if the precise brand and type of socks are known, socks change after being worn and washed. Further, socks can be worn loose or pulled up tightly over the feet. These issues raise many questions about how best to make known sock-clad impressions. Each case must be assessed in these regards. Socks that are sufficiently tight can potentially pull toes inward such as in the case of narrow toed shoes. They can also mask the features of an individual's foot. Figure 18.15 depicts a tracing of the naked impression of a foot on top of a known

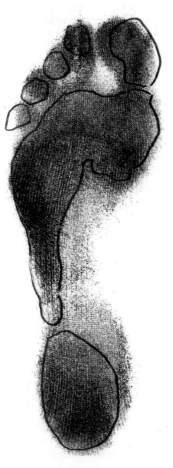

Figure 18.15 Variations that occurred between known sock-clad and naked foot inked impression of the left foot of the same contributor.

sock-clad impression of the same contributor. It illustrates the effect the sock can potentially have on a crime scene impression. Note how the naked foot impression has a bridged arch whereas the inked fabric of the sock is stretched between the heel and ball area and makes the arch appear quite different. Also note how the sock pulls some toes inward and the fabric stretched between the ball area and toes makes it appear as if the toe stems are printing.

Casts of the Feet

Slipper casts of the feet are routinely made by podiatrists and orthopedic specialists within their practices to replicate a patient's forefoot-to-hind foot alignment that would occur during the mid-stance phase of the walking cycle.[*,†] These are obtained with a plaster splint material that is wetted and wrapped around the foot. During this process, the foot is intentionally held in the neutral position until the slipper cast hardens, which means someone's hands are interfering with the toe areas of the foot. In order to take a plaster splint cast that provides good skin detail replication of the forefoot area including the upper areas of the toes, this method must be modified to hold the foot at another location and additional layers of plaster splint material should be used to provide a sufficient amount of plaster to be pressed through to the skin to replicate the skin's detail.[‡]

Other methods exist to make casts of the toe region of the foot that can also capture the features of the side and upper forefoot region. Polyvinylsiloxane and condensation silicone products provide a good method for casting the top of the toe region of the foot. Figure 18.16 depicts an impression made of the toe region using a product called Zetalabor and a dental stone cast form that provides a positive model of the features of the foot suitable for direct physical comparison with the shoes in question.[§]

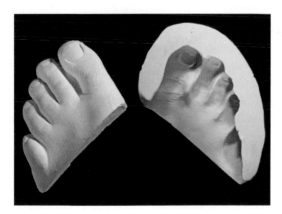

Figure 18.16 A Zetalabor cast of the toe area of the foot (right) and a dental stone cast made from that to provide a positive image of the contributor's foot (left). (Courtesy of Shelly Massey, RCMP.)

[*] Burns, M., Non-weightbearing cast impressions for the construction of orthotic devices, *J Am Podiatry Assoc*, 67:790–795, 1977.
[†] McPoll, T., Schuit, D., and Knecht, H., Comparison of three methods used to obtain a neutral plaster foot impression, *Physical Therapy*, 69(6), June 1989.
[‡] Personal communication with Dr. Irving Miller, April 1984.
[§] http://en.zhermack.com/Technical/Silicones/Masks/C400791.kl

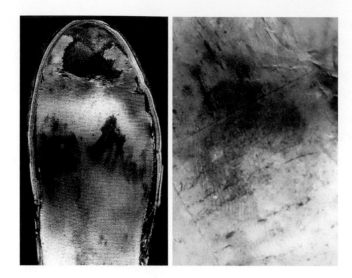

Figure 18.17 Insole and sock-clad impressions that lack sufficient detail for comparison.

Examination Considerations

The human foot is relatively rigid and consistent in the way it leaves its impression. This, combined with the varied morphology of the feet of different individuals in the general population, allows for meaningful comparisons between barefoot evidence recovered from the scene and the known standards of the feet of individuals. When similar features are present that include the individual as a possible contributor, the level of association depends on the quantity and quality of those combined features. Although other persons in the general population possess singular similar characteristics, such as overall foot length, the shape of the arch, or the position of a particular toe, the combination of numerous size and shape features provides a means to discriminate a particular foot from the majority of other feet in that population. As the quantity and quality of multiple corresponding features increase, the remaining portion of the general population sharing those combined features is rapidly reduced. Those same features are also routinely used to exclude individuals.

As with any examination, preparation and preliminary assessment of evidence is made for purposes of describing the evidence, producing and possibly enhancing scaled photographs for examination, and assessing known exemplars that were obtained. Figure 18.17 depicts two examples, one a shoe insole, the other a poorly detailed partial sock-clad impression, each with insufficient detail for meaningful comparisons with the feet of the suspected individuals. Often this level of detail will not even be sufficient for the purpose of exclusion. Conversely, the sock-clad impression shown in Figure 18.8 and the innersole impressions in Figure 18.18 provide excellent detail for a meaningful comparison.

Examination of Naked or Sock-Clad Impressions

The comparison of naked and sock-clad barefoot evidence with known exemplars of individuals involves the size and shape features produced by the weight-bearing areas of the

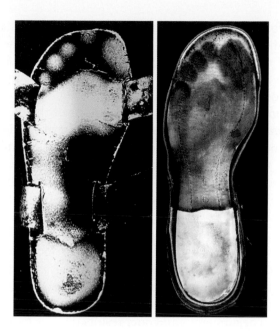

Figure 18.18 Two insole impressions that contain excellent detail for comparison.

feet in both two- and three-dimensional impressions. The examination, referred to as a barefoot morphology examination or a forensic barefoot examination, is divided into four regions: the toe region composed of the five toes, the ball region that includes the metatarsal area and the metatarsal ridge (anterior border of the foot pad), the arch region, and the heel. The toe areas contain the most information, including toe sizes and toe shapes; relative positions of the toes to one another as well as to the footpad; and whether those toes have toe stems that leave their impressions on a two-dimensional substrate. When toes are constricted by socks their movement will be directly inward as was seen in Figure 18.15. The ball area of the foot includes the overall shape of that area, defined by the metatarsal ridge, and the lateral and medial contours as well as its maximum width. The maximum ball width is an angular line drawn between the most extreme edges of the lateral and medial borders of that area as was shown by the white triangles in Figure 18.2. The space between the metatarsal ridge and the toes will have a void area whose shape is defined by the shape of the metatarsal ridge and the positions of the five toes, and can be used to visually discriminate one footprint from most others. The arch area is most valuable when multiple two-dimensional impressions result in repetitive dimensions and contours. Well-defined longitudinal arches on firm substrates can reflect important discriminating features concerning the specific size and shape information of the arch contours. Impressions in three-dimensional substrates and on the insole of footwear often do not provide sufficient or reliable information for comparison in the arch area as the insoles or soft substrates interfere. The heel area involves the size and shape of the heel, again most valuable on firm substrates but not as specifically defined in three-dimensional impressions or shoe insoles.

Comparisons rely on the quantity and quality of detail present in the crime scene impression. Those containing sufficiently clear and confirmable features can provide a good level of association or disassociation with an individual's foot. However, even in some cases with minimal detail, the examination can provide invaluable results. One example of this involved a double homicide involving two suspects. The first suspect confessed and claimed he killed both victims. Investigators believed his girlfriend, the second suspect, actually killed one of the victims. The physical comparison of a single bloody footprint next to that victim in another part of the house, although not containing a high level of detail, was adequate to exclude his feet and include her feet.

Because the relationship of the shapes and positions of the numerous features of the foot is significant, examination includes superimposition of overlays of known impressions over the questioned impressions. In some cases, impressions may be partial and only represent a portion of the foot. If that portion includes only the heel or side of a foot, the partial impression may be insufficient for a meaningful comparison. Partial impressions that only represent the toe and ball regions usually contain sufficient quantity and quality of detail for comparison.[*,†]

It is noted that in cases where insufficient detail is present to allow for exclusion of an individual, this in no way infers any affirmative basis for inclusion. Inclusion should be based on characteristics in the crime scene impression that are sufficient for comparison and show some physical relationship to the feet of the suspect. In some of those cases, the relationship will be limited, but nevertheless present. In other cases, the quantity and quality of characteristics will be numerous and offer results that are more significant and result in a higher level of association. Figure 18.19 depicts a Luminol developed sock-clad crime scene impression on carpet. The impression on the left corresponds well with numerous features of a suspect's right foot. On the right, a second suspect's right foot was easily excluded as it is much larger and contains numerous different size and shape features.

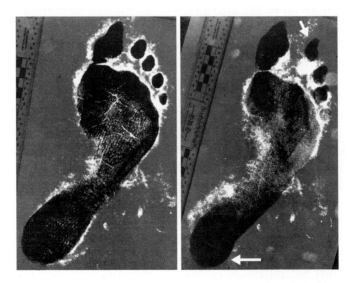

Figure 18.19 A luminol-developed impression on carpet that corresponds well with the right foot impression of one suspect, and that reflects many differences with and can be excluded as originating from a second suspect.

---

[*] Winkelmann, W., The evaluation of human footprints, especially the ball and toes, for identification in forensic medicine, *Z Rechtsmed* 99:121–128, 1987 (translated from German).
[†] Smerecki, C. J., and Lovejoy, C. O., Identification via pedal morphology, *International Criminal Police Review*, 186–190, August 1985.

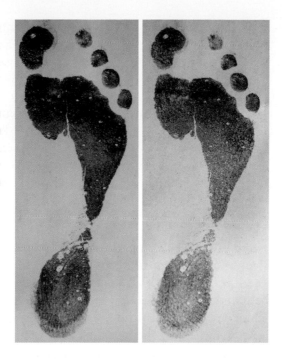

Figure 18.20 Variations between two inked footprints of the same person.

Just like impressions made by footwear, impressions made by naked and sock-clad feet include normal variations. Normal variations also occur between known standards as shown in Figure 18.20. In the case of sock-clad impressions, the sock may cause some inward constriction of the outer toes. Comparisons of this type rely on the quantity and quality of detail present in the crime scene impression.

Association of Footwear with Feet

Insoles, also known as inner soles or inner liners, are either of the removable type or of the type cemented inside the shoe. For athletic shoes, they are typically constructed of a soft material with a textile covering, but dress shoes or boots may use leather or other more rigid materials. Insoles are in direct contact with the naked and/or sock-clad feet of the person who wears the shoes. Over time, the insole of each shoe forms to the foot and acquires a footprint such as shown in Figure 18.18. The time and degree to which this occurs relate to the extent the shoe is worn as well as other contributing factors such as sweat, dirt, pressure, and type of usage. The insole and the inner surfaces of shoes in the toe box area often contain good quality representations of the feet that can be compared to known exemplars of suspected wearers.* If the sides or top of the wearer's feet rub firmly against the inner surfaces of the shoe in some areas, stains or abrasions reflecting that contact can result. An example of this is shown in Figure 18.21 where the medial side of a right shoe upper has both stains and abrasions indicating the locations where the bunion and edge of the first toe pressed against the side of the shoe. In other cases, other features of the feet as well as

---

* Bodziak, W. J., 2000, Ibid., pp. 401–411.

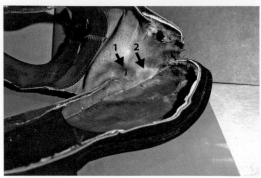

Figure 18.21 The bunion (1) and side of the first toe (2) produced stains and indentations inside this shoe.

occasional features such as corns, warts, or uncut toenails can also produce similar evidence of their presence.

Experience and research note when comparing inked impressions to insole impressions, the constrictive effect of some shoes in the toe area tended to move the positions of some toes toward the centerline of the foot.[*,†] This is familiar to examiners who receive and compare both known shoes and known inked impressions of one individual. Figure 18.18 illustrates an open toe sandal on the left where no constriction of the toes occurred, and on the right a shoe with an enclosed toe box where possible constriction of the toes occurred. Both case experience and research have shown that whenever possible, known footwear of the suspected wearer, when available, should be included as part of the forensic comparison in addition to inked exemplars.[‡,§]

Examination between known standards of feet and impressions on the insoles and other inner surfaces of the shoe is conducted to determine if an association can be made with the purported wearer of the shoe. If a person is arrested in those shoes or admits he or she has worn those shoes, this examination is unnecessary. The need for this form of examination arises in cases where shoes have been identified with the crime scene and there is no admitted owner, as the shoes were discovered during a search and not as they were being worn. The need also arises in those cases where an informant has advised investigators that a suspected individual has abandoned or discarded shoes that are later recovered based on their information and can be linked to the crime. Examinations of this type have been the topic of many case accounts.[¶,**,††,‡‡,§§,¶¶] Like examinations conducted between naked and sock-clad impressions, the focus is first on inclusion or exclusion. Figure 18.22

---

[*] Bodziak, W. J., 2000, Ibid., p. 405.

[†] Hammer, L., Nic Daéid, N., Kennedy, R., and Yamashita, A., Preliminary study of the comparison of inked barefoot impressions with impressions from shoe insoles using a controlled population, *JFI*, 62(6):603–622, 2012.

[‡] Ibid.

[§] Keereweer, I. The Nike project—results barefoot identification, *Information Bulletin for Shoeprint/ Toolmark Examiners*, 4(1):129–138, 1998.

[¶] Leishman, S., If the shoe fits, *RCMP Gazette*, 53(9), 1991.

[**] Hofstede, J. C., and Verzijden, D. J., The relation of foot to shoe as a means of identification, Leiden, the Netherlands (undated) (translated from Dutch).

[††] Castle, D., Cinderella analysis—or does the shoe fit? Metropolitan Police Laboratory, London, England, *Contact Magazine*, No. 23, October 1, 1995.

[‡‡] McCafferty, J. D., The shoe fits, *The Police Journal*, 28:135–139, 1955, London, England.

[§§] Tripathi, R. S., and Jogulamma, M. R., Individualization from footwear—a case report, *Medicine, Science & Law*, 22(2):115–118, 1982.

[¶¶] Nayar, P. S., and DasGupta, S. K., Personal identification based on footprints, *International Criminal Police Review*, 326:83–87, 1976.

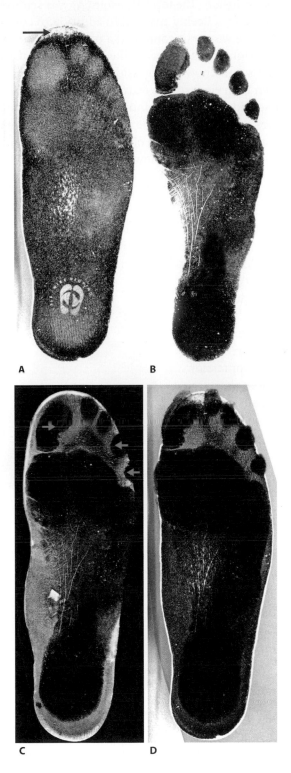

Figure 18.22 An example of an exclusion based on significant differences in morphology.

depicts a case example of exclusion. The top left insole (A) was removed from a questioned shoe abandoned at the scene by a fleeing suspect. In addition to containing size and shape information of the foot of the wearer, it contained a patch of very fragile lint accumulated in the toe area. On the top right (B) is a known inked impression of a suspected wearer. On the bottom left (C) is that same known impression superimposed over the shoes that the suspect was wearing when interviewed. The features of his feet correspond with his shoes, particularly the metatarsal ridge. When this individual wears his shoes, the position of the first, fourth, and fifth toes as positioned in the inked impression are pulled inward by the constrictive effect of the narrow toe box area of the shoe as indicated with the arrows. The same known impression of this suspect is now superimposed over the insole of the questioned shoe, shown at the bottom right (D). The metatarsal ridge does not fit and the foot and toes are considerably longer, extending way beyond the respective toe impressions on the questioned insole. In addition, had this suspect worn the questioned shoe, his larger foot would have easily dislodged the fragile lint in the toe area.

In some examinations, exclusion is not possible for a number of reasons. The amount of detail may be limited, known impressions may be inadequate, or the level of agreement or disagreement between the known exemplars and the questioned item may be conflicting. One such example is shown in the questioned insole impression in Figure 18.23. The length of the known impression appears slightly shorter than the overall insole area but the insole contains no clear reference of a heel or a metatarsal ridge to further compare the foot's length and position. The insole of the shoe reflects some detail of the toes but does not correspond well with the known inked impression. If the suspect were the wearer of these shoes, his third, fourth, and fifth toes would have had to be constricted substantially by this shoe in order to have been moved to those positions. Without more detail and replication of the metatarsal ridge, a good comparison of those features is not possible. Although this individual's foot could not be excluded, there was also insufficient detail to provide any affirmative support for inclusion.

In cases where a foot is included as the possible source, the extent and weight of that inclusion rests with the quantity and quality of features

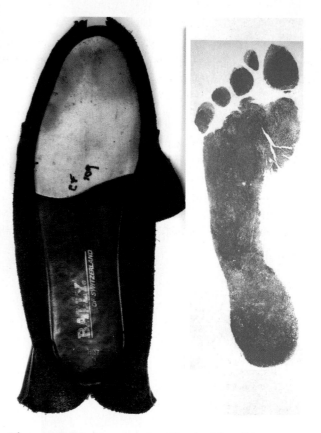

Figure 18.23 An example of limited detail in a questioned insole. Note this shoe upper was cut down the center of the toe and heel with each side laid open as opposed to the shoe in Figure 18.21 where the entire upper except for a small portion was cut around the perimeter and folded over.

that correspond. Some insole comparisons reflect numerous features that have been replicated very well, while others have minimal features or none at all. Those that have distinct and numerous corresponding features carry far more weight than those having less.
Figure 18.11 illustrates the insole of a known shoe a suspect was arrested in and used as
part of the known standards of his feet. On the far right is the insole of the bloody right
Nike shoe lost fleeing the homicide scene. The visible features of the right foot, shown in
this court chart with white tracings, not only includes him as the possible wearer, but demonstrates numerous independent features in common between the crime scene shoe and
the shoes he was arrested in.

During examinations of the inner surfaces of a shoe, and prior to any removal of the
upper, the inner sole and inner areas of the toe box should be inspected using illumination, magnification, macroscopic devices, small mirrors, or any other useful device. This
inspection is to determine if an impression is present on the insole and any locations the
wearer's foot has abraded or produced marks against the inner surfaces of the toe box
area. If no important details of the feet are present on the inner liner of the toe box area of
the shoe and the insoles are removable, they can be removed for further examination. In
those cases where the insole is glued in the shoe or where the examination includes marks
on the inside of the uppers in the toe area, the upper of the shoe will need to be carefully
cut away to expose the inner surfaces. It is critical that the upper is cut in a way that will
not destroy any details that would be part of this examination. One method of cutting
away the upper of a shoe is to cut around the perimeter with the exception of a small area
as shown in Figure 18.21. In that case, a portion of the shoe was left attached so as not to
destroy the marks at that location. Another option is to cut the upper down the middle of
the toe and heel and fold back each side as shown in Figure 18.23. During the process of
cutting open and exposing the inner surfaces of the shoe, consideration should be given to
the collection of any hair or fiber evidence that might have potential evidentiary value in a
particular investigation.

When a barefoot examination involves impressions on the inner soles and liners of
footwear, collection of DNA samples should be made prior to handling the shoes. Case
experience has revealed that the DNA of not only the wearer, but many other individuals,
may be present on the inner liners of footwear because as a person puts his or her shoes
on, epithelial skin cells of other individuals containing their DNA profiles are transferred
from the floor to the inner surfaces of the shoe via the feet or socks. Research has also
shown that mixed DNA profiles are typically contained on the inner surfaces of some
footwear, and noted the wearer's profile was not present in a good percentage of the tests.[*,†]
Testing should also include areas of the shoes a wearer would routinely touch, such as the
heel, tongue, and shoelaces, as these areas may yield better results. Consequently, when
it is important to link shoes to a person, although DNA preservation is important, the
comparison of impressions or marks on the inner liner of the footwear with the suspected
individual's feet is often requested.

[*] Bright, J., Petricevic, S., Recovery of trace DNA and its application to DNA profiling of shoe insoles, *Forensic Science International*, 145:7–12, 2004.
[†] Hillier, E., Dixon, P., Stewart, P., Yamashita, B., Lama, D., Recovery of DNA from shoes, *Can. Soc. Forensic Science Journal*, 38(3):143–150, 2005.

Estimating Height Based on Dimensions of Barefoot or Footwear Impressions

In general, men or women who are taller tend to have longer feet and larger shoes sizes; consequently, the general question many investigators often ask is whether height can be calculated from shoe impressions. Research has shown there is not a strict relationship between a person's height and shoe size due to the many variables involved. Any question that relates to estimates of height from a foot or shoe print at a crime scene must consider the degree of accuracy that can be relied on. Cassidy pointed out that one of the limitations of attempting to do this occurs when first converting the crime scene impression to a shoe size as is necessary before relating any shoe size to a height.[*] Various external dimensions of shoes of the same manufacturer's size but of different categories have been noted previously in this book. Other limitations would include the variance in footwear dimensions between footwear from different manufacturers, as well as limitations with the accuracy of recovered impressions that may occur concerning scale or perspective. Cassidy also noted the fact that most impressions do not represent a full and/or accurate representation of the full length of the shoe or foot that produced them. He published a height calculation table that reflects a variance of height of 4 inches with adult shoe sizes and even then only indicates an accuracy level of 80%.[†]

An FBI study of the collection of barefoot impressions of 399 adult males as well as their recorded height and shoe size is expressed in a scattergram of that data in Figure 18.24. The scattergram illustrates that although a loose relationship between shoe sizes and height exists, it is not sufficient to provide accurate estimation of shoe size from height or height from shoe size.

Survey of 399 Males Shoe Sized and Height

Height	Shoe Size															
	6	6½	7	7½	8	8½	9	9½	10	10½	11	11½	12	12½	13	14
63				1												
64																
65	1	1		4	1		1									
66		1			2	1		2								
67				2	2		3		2							
68		1	1		4	9	7	7		1	1					
69				1	3	8	14	10	8	3	2					
70			1		3	4	13	15	15	18	3	1				
71			1		3	3	7	5	14	9	7		2			
72							7	11	11	21	11	4	3			
73						2	1	2	4	11	8	1	7		1	
74							1	1	7	8	5	3	4		1	1
75									1	2	3	2	5	1	2	
76								1	1	1		1	3		1	1
77													4		3	
78																
79																1
80															1	
81																
82															1	
Totals	1	3	3	8	18	27	54	54	63	74	40	12	28	1	10	3

Figure 18.24 A scattergram of the relationship of height and shoe size of 399 males.

[*] Cassidy, M. J., *Footwear Identification*. Canadian Government Printing Centre, Quebec, Canada, 1980.
[†] Ibid, p. 115.

Some anthropological studies have attempted to develop ratios or equations that could be used to deduct height from barefoot and/or shoeprint length. One concluded, "The correlation between foot length and height underlies estimating height from shoeprint length, but complications arise from variations in shoe style, fit, and the relationship of shoe size to shoeprint length."[*] Another concludes whereas numerous methods have been used for estimation of stature from foot and shoe measurements, the individual error is quite large.[†] And a third concluded research models reflect a strong relationship between foot/boot length and stature, but individual 95% prediction limits for even the best models equate to a plus/minus range of 3.4 inches.[‡]

These studies collectively demonstrate the degree of accuracy is sufficiently low to prohibit the reliable use of foot or shoeprint length for purposes of predicting height. This should not be confused with the possibility of determining shoe size based on mold characteristics and/or texture as discussed in Chapter 12, which in some instances can be very precise.

Those Who Conduct Barefoot Examinations

Early literature reflects the use of medical practitioners to provide assistance to investigations in matters that pertain to the human body. Forensic laboratories and a formalized forensic practitioner did not exist then, thus the migration toward medical practitioners or orthopedic specialists to opine on matters involving the feet is not surprising. Over the years, the evolution of modern day forensic science has led to specialization, research, empirical data, examination experience, and the formation of specialized forensic disciplines. Full-time forensic footwear examiners with formalized training and experience in the field of forensic physical match comparisons, including barefoot evidence, are the appropriate examiners of this type of evidence.

Key Words: barefoot impression, barefoot evidence, metatarsal ridge, sock-clad, weight-bearing impressions

Key Points

1. Barefoot evidence can be present at crime scenes in the form of a naked foot impression containing skin ridge detail, a naked foot impression without the retention of skin ridge detail, a sock-clad impression, and on the innersoles of abandoned footwear.
2. Barefoot impressions are recovered in the same way as footwear impressions. Abandoned footwear should be handled to preserve possible DNA.
3. Both forensic and nonforensic research demonstrate the individuality of the human foot and the lack of an interrelationship of its various size and shape features.
4. The correlation of shoe size, foot size, and height are too loose to enable any accurate height estimates.

[*] Giles, E., and Vallandigham, P., Height estimation from foot and shoeprint length, *Journal of Forensic Sciences*, 36(4):1134–1151, 1991.

[†] Jasuja, O., Jasvir, S., and Jain, M., Estimation of stature from foot and shoe measurements by multiplication factors: a revised attempt, *Forensic Science International*, 50:203–215, 1991.

[‡] Gordon, C., and Buikstra, J., Linear models for the prediction of stature from foot and boot dimensions, *Journal of Forensic Science*, 37(3):771–782, 1992.

Some Case Examples

19

Following are some photographs and brief information about six cases that involved footwear evidence. The examinations in three were performed for the prosecution and in the other three for the defense.

A West Coast Homicide (Requested by the Prosecution)

A fatal stabbing homicide on the West Coast involved several bloody shoe impressions including some clearly visible on several pieces of paper strewn across the floor. Figure 19.1 depicts the victim's shoes without any sole pattern and some of the bloody shoe prints, one of which included the Adidas name and Trefoil logo. Adidas shoes were never recovered from the suspect but an Adidas shoebox for a size 8½ pair of shoes was found at the suspect's residence where he was using it as a temporary mailbox, as shown in Figure 19.2. Printed on the shoebox was the brand, style, and size information that read Adidas Ilie Nastase Super, size 8½. The suspect admitted he was the owner of the shoes that went with that box, volunteered he had purchased them in Europe, but stated he had worn them out and had since discarded them. Contact with representatives of Adidas determined this specific style was only sold in Europe. The relevant question now was whether the bloody shoe prints at the crime scene were produced by a size 8½ of this particular style of Adidas shoe. Adidas advised that these shoes were produced using a direct-attach injection-molding process in three factories in Germany and France and Adidas provided outsole samples produced in each mold in sizes 8, 8½, and 9 from each factory. The injection-molding process is very size specific and involves no trimming nor is it possible to inject an outsole of a different size onto the upper of the shoe. The molds that produced the outsoles were hand-milled; thus, variations existed between each mold, even those of the same size. Figure 19.3 shows two of the outsole samples provided by Adidas that illustrate a few of the many typical variables due to the hand-milled mold process. Notice how the Adidas name is tilted on the outsole sample (B) as well as many other variations including the Trefoil logo size and positions, the different size "8½" symbols, and many other distinguishing specific design features when contrasted against outsole sample (A) and the other samples provided. In addition, each mold had texture added that further distinguishes each mold. Figure 19.3 also includes one of the bloody prints (C) and a test impression (D) produced by the size 8½ outsole shown in (B). This outsole corresponded with the specific design features evident in the crime scene impressions, including the angled Adidas logo as well as the texture pattern. Thus, it was concluded that the bloody scene prints were from a size 8½ shoe. The other outsole sizes, due to their many mold differences, were easily excluded. Also found on some of the recovered papers were dust impressions of another pair of shoes that were identified as the Pro-Wing shoes the suspect was wearing when arrested. Figure 19.4 depicts one of the Pro-Wing shoes and a portion of one of the papers, containing both the

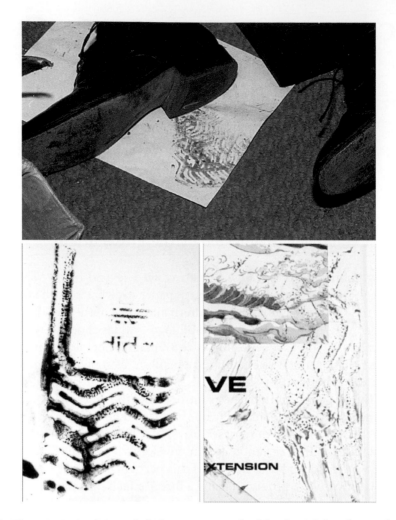

Figure 19.1 The victim's plain soled shoes next to the bloody Adidas design (top); and two laboratory photographs of the blood marks on paper showing portions of the Adidas name and trefoil logo (bottom).

Figure 19.2 The Illie Nastase Adidas shoebox being used by the suspect as a temporary mailbox.

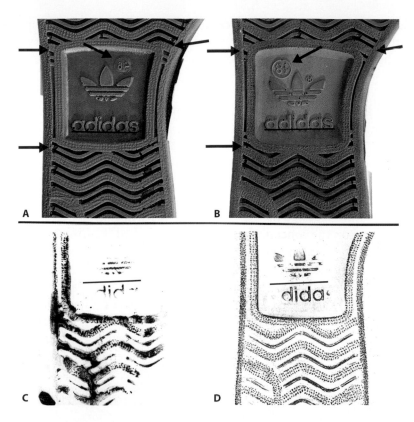

Figure 19.3 Two size 8.5 outsoles provided by Adidas from two hand-milled molds showing how many variables exist between them (A,B), one of the bloody scene marks (C), and a known impression of the corresponding outsole (D).

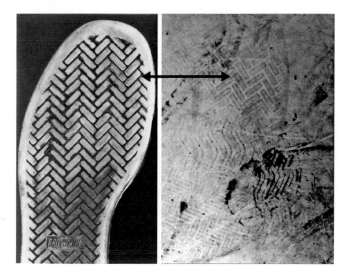

Figure 19.4 One of the shoes the suspect was wearing that had produced dust impressions on the same paper on the ground at the scene as the bloody impressions.

Pro-Wing design and the bloody Adidas design. Some of the Pro-Wing impressions were identified with the suspect's shoes. Testimony was provided in a preliminary hearing, and, prior to the scheduled trial, the suspect entered a plea of guilty.

A Controlled Population Class Characteristic Case (Requested by the Defense)

Controlled population cases are those where the possible number of persons who could have committed the crime is limited. This case involved a homicide that occurred in a prison environment in the victim's cell during an open cellblock period. Approximately 63 prisoners could have accessed the cell to commit this crime. In the victim's cell, a bloody heel print was found on the concrete floor and photographed. Figure 19.5 shows the blood mark (E), a reverse photograph of one of the heels of one suspect's shoes (F), and known impressions of two suspects' shoes (A–D). The bloody heel impression was incomplete and had limited detail. Unfortunately, no chemical enhancement was made of this impression. All of the prisoners were assigned this same shoe design as standard prison issue. The boots were produced from a very old set of hand-milled molds. The heels of this design (F) consisted of rows of small circular dots surrounded by a solid border. The original mold maker was contacted and confirmed that only one template was used to produce the dot patterns on all of the molds. Thus, the size and spacing of the dots were the same for all mold sizes.

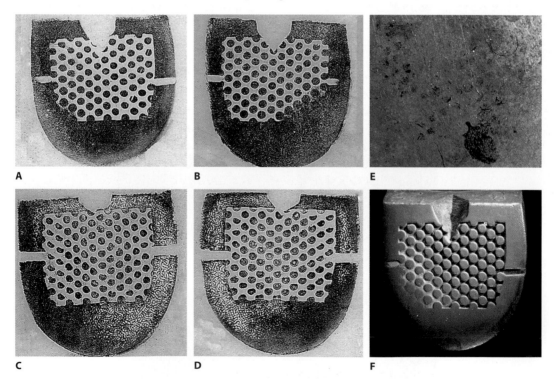

Figure 19.5 Left and right known impressions of heels of two suspects (A,B and C,D), the bloody mark on concrete in the cell of the victim (E), and one of the heels examined showing the individually cut notch in the front (F).

In addition, the manufacturer was requested by this prison system to cut notches in the heel of each molded boot as shown in Figure 19.5(F). The notch was made while holding the heel and using a grinding wheel, resulting in considerable variations of the size and features of each notch as well as how the notch's borders intersected the circular dot design. If sufficient detail of a heel containing these notches existed in an impression, those characteristics could be used to exclude most and possibly all of the heels of shoes worn by the 63 prisoners, except for one of the shoes of the perpetrator. Unfortunately, in the case of impression (E), the detail was not complete enough nor included any reference to the notch, but only a large undefined void space in that general area. Further, there was no inner or outer heel edge replication that allowed for a precise reference to the leading edges or corners of the heel or even the medial and lateral edges. During the examination of the heels of two suspects as well as heel samples from the manufacturer throughout the entire size range, it became even more apparent as to how limited the blood mark was. All of the heel samples had similar circular dot patterns. A few of the very small sizes did not include a sufficient number of dots compared to those present in the blood mark, allowing for their exclusion. However, the majority of heel sizes could not be excluded, including the heels of both suspects.

This case example is being offered for more than one reason. In includes limited class characteristics of footwear and is a good example of how an examiner, when faced with these limitations, should not jump to a conclusion of correspondence of design and size, simply based on a limited design component such as the position and spacing, in this case, of a dot pattern identical in size and spacing on all sizes. Any conclusion that the blood mark corresponded in design and size would be true for the heels of most of the prisoners. In this case, the prosecution examiner initially concluded the blood mark (E) corresponded in size, design, and shape with the heel area on the right boot (B) and although not identifying the blood mark, further opined that any heel that produced this impression must include a missing or nonrecording area at the front and contain a similar amount of wear. Later, his report was amended to include both the right and left heels of (A), (B), (C), and (D) as possible sources, and no longer included the statement about the missing or nonrecording area or the wear. This examiner eventually conceded that heels of most other sizes were also included in the possible source of this blood mark.

With the knowledge that this shoe design was shared by a limited population of prisoners, all of the footwear of the prisoners who had access to the victim should have been seized. Further, the blood mark should have been enhanced with a chemical reagent that very likely would have developed much greater detail that could have been used to more accurately include or exclude any boots examined.

A Wellman Calendered Outsole Case (Requested by the Prosecution)

This case involved multiple burglaries over a period of two months during 1999, some involving the theft of very expensive jewelry. The evidence consisted of both electrostatic lifts and adhesive lifts from three of those burglaries. The suspect was identified in an interesting way. One of the victims, while returning to her home as the burglary was in progress, noticed an older car in her driveway. The burglar heard her enter the house and exited through a rear window. As he drove away, the victim got a quick look at him and

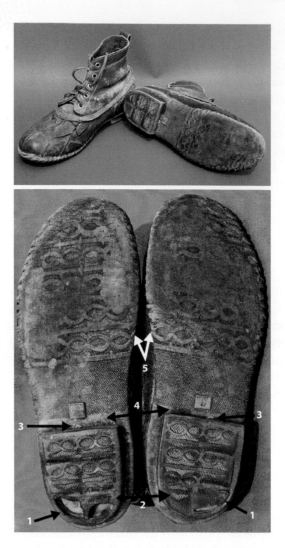

Figure 19.6 An overall view of the well-worn Wellman made boots. The excess wear had resulted in intrusion into the hollow molded heel cavities (1) and specific general wear in other areas (2). The pieces of string often found in this process (3) did not print in the two-dimensional impressions. The relative positions of the calenderer outsole and heels can be seen to vary significantly between left and right boots (4) as well as the varied cut of the outsole using the Wellman process (5).

his car, but not his license tag. Days later as she drove into her community, she recognized him and his car pass her. While calling the police on her cell phone she made an abrupt U-turn and pursued him. While being still pursued, he was stopped and arrested a few miles away wearing a pair of size 9 Eddie Bauer boots as shown in Figure 19.6. The boots had Wellman cut outsoles, cut from unvulcanized calendered outsole material with the addition of molded heels. This process of manufacturing was covered in Chapter 11.

Figures 19.6 and 19.7 show many of the important features of these boots. The random manner in which the outsoles are cut on the Wellman machine results in left and right outsoles that are not mirror images. Figure 19.6 (#4 and #5) point to two areas where this

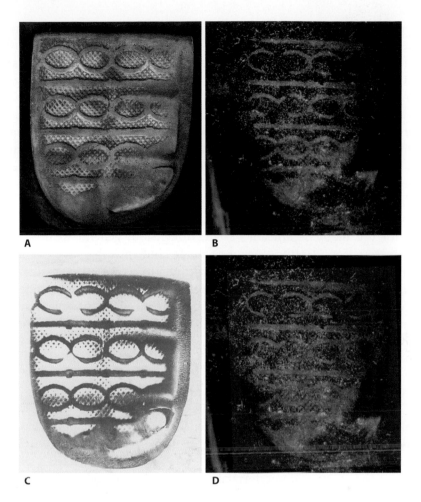

Figure 19.7 A close up of one heel (A), an electrostatic lift from the scene (B), a known impression of the heel (C), and an overlay of the known impression over the lift (D).

is noticeable. However, this is prevalent in many areas when comparing both outsoles. The molded heels (#2) are worn excessively and unevenly including portions where the erosion of the rubber has resulted in the intrusion into the hollow heel cavity and random tearing associated with those events (#1). Both the impressions recovered and these outsoles and heels shared many class, wear, and randomly acquired characteristics. As a result, identification was made between an impression and the left boot and two other impressions and the right boot. Testimony of these identifications was offered at trial.

Although not part of the physical comparison, it is interesting to note these specific boots were offered for sale in the Eddie Bauer catalogue from 1994 through 1996. According to the company, approximately 11,000 pairs were sold but only through the company's Internet sales and not in their retail stores. According to Eddie Bauer, Inc., the boots were not sold after 1996 and the boots were manufactured exclusively for their company. Approximately 20% were size 9. To some, this information may imply that only a small total number of boots were ever produced in size 9 (approximately 2200), that no other boots would have had the same outsole capable of producing the impressions, and very few would likely still be in existence since a few years had passed since they were last sold. But that is almost certainly not the case with this particular outsole, regardless of the information produced by the Eddie Bauer company. The outsoles on these shoes were made using a calender roller and a Wellman cutting operation. Calender rollers are expensive to produce, have a lifetime of many years, and are used in factories that mix the raw rubber ingredients and cut large numbers of outsoles. The outsole design combined with the Eddie Bauer upper and label on the shoes may have been produced specifically for that company during that time period and bear that style number, but the company that manufactured those boots for Eddie Bauer would also have produced thousands of outsoles cut from material pressed by the same calender roller design and used to produce boots for many other brands.

In this particular case, with the abundance of crime scene lifts, many with good detail, combined with the many significant design, dimension, general wear, and randomly acquired characteristics, identifications were made, and thus the issue of the number of shoes of this design that were made was insignificant. This is a good example why information provided by a manufacturer or retail company regarding the sales numbers and availability could easily be misunderstood or misused. The number they sold may be accurate but their perception that no other shoes would have outsoles of the same design was simply misunderstood.

Bloody Heel Mark (Requested by the Defense)

Examination of a bloody heel mark was requested in a case where an individual was accused of a homicide. The heel mark, shown in Figure 19.8, had a very mottled appearance. During the investigation, a pair of boots of the accused was seized and reflected a similar design. A laboratory for the prosecution performed a forensic examination and concluded a high level of association existed between the heel of the right boot and the impression. I was requested to review the evidence and examination results on behalf of the defense.

Features of interest noted during examination of the impression and right heel are illustrated in Figure 19.8. The areas numbered 1 and 2 are cuts visibly present in both the lifted impression and heel, also replicated in the known impression. Area number 3 in the lift is a very small cut extending from area 2. Other than its approximate position, the small cut of area 3 did not have sufficient detail to attribute it to the corresponding feature on the heel versus a coincidental linear mottling of that area that is present elsewhere throughout the impression. Area number 4 in the lift depicts a lateral line going against the direction of most mottling in that impression and corresponds with the approximate position of a scratch in the same area of the heel; however, the precise shape and features were limited. Some specific areas of general wear were also noted as indicated at areas 5 and 6.

This is another example of when enhancement of the impression may have produced additional detail. Further, the general crime photographs of this scene revealed additional heel impressions that were not recovered with examination-quality photography or other means. The 12-inch square tiles at the scene could have easily been removed, allowing for better photography and enhancement later in a laboratory facility. These additional steps would have almost certainly resulted in a stronger conclusion.

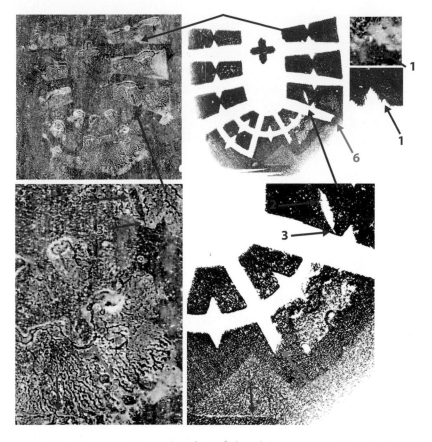

Figure 19.8 A wet origin two-dimensional mark (top left) corresponds in design and physical size with the heel, a known impression (top right). Random damage includes the jagged cut (1), a gouge with a small fingerlike end (2,3), a lateral scratch (4), and two specific areas of general wear (5,6).

Linoleum Latent Blood Mark (Requested by the Prosecution)

Shoe marks composed of very thin layers of blood against substrates that have poor contrast are often overlooked or thought to be of no value. The use of chemical enhancement reagents to detect and enhance blood marks such as those cannot be overemphasized. For crime scene technicians or investigators unable or unequipped to perform chemical enhancement, the alternate choice is to remove the flooring so this procedure can be performed later in the laboratory.

In this homicide case, one heavily bloodied athletic shoe mark was noticed adjacent to the victim next to the rear door and the probable point of exit. A second mark in blood crossed the first but was very difficult to see, and had it not been for the presence of the first impression, may easily have been left at the scene. Fortunately, the section of linoleum floor was cut out and submitted to the laboratory along with a pair of athletic footwear. To enhance the bloody marks on the linoleum, they were treated with Amido Black. The heavier left shoe mark, as often is the case, had excess blood that filled in the fine cuts and details.

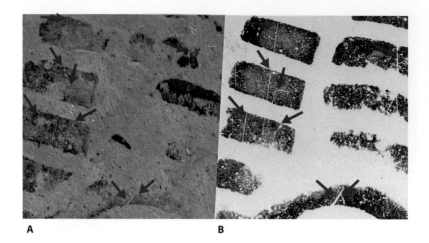

A   B

Figure 19.9 An enlarged portion of a blood mark on linoleum showing a number of very small but distinct randomly acquired characteristics, made visible as a result of chemical enhancement.

The enhancement of the very faint right shoe mark was highly successful and provided excellent details far superior to the heavier one. Figure 19.9 depicts a very small portion of the light mark after enhancement, positioned alongside the respective area of a known impression of the athletic shoe. The portion of the blood mark in this photograph was not visible prior to the enhancement procedure. The full mark contained numerous randomly acquired characteristics, some shown in Figure 19.9, allowing for identification of the right athletic shoe. This case illustrates how important the utilization of blood reagents is for the detection and enhancement of bloody footwear evidence. Chapter 7 addressed some of the chemical enhancement methods that are typically used to develop faint or latent bloody marks.

Random Cut or Something Else? (Requested by the Defense)

As in many cases, the charges of robbery against the defendant were accompanied by much peripheral information about motive, opportunity, and who may have been the perpetrator of the crime. This type of information, except as necessary to understand the reason for the examination being requested, or the items of evidence involved, should never be allowed to influence any forensic examination. The impression in question in this case was not one recovered from the primary robbery scene, but rather from a secondary location near where one of the stolen items was found. The footwear evidence had been examined by another examiner and a high level association had been made between a heel impression in snow and the heel of a boot of the accused. Although not an identification, the examiner's report made specific reference to a mark found in the center of the crime scene heel impression and its correspondence to a cut in the center of the heel. When reviewing opinions of other examiners, or conducting independent examinations for the defense, access to the original footwear, and in this case, the film negatives that recorded the boot prints in snow, did not become accessible until I traveled to the trial. Copies of the evidence were provided in advance and called into question the alleged random cut. In Figure 19.10(A) is the scene photograph of the heel impression in snow. (C) is the heel of the boot of the accused and (B)

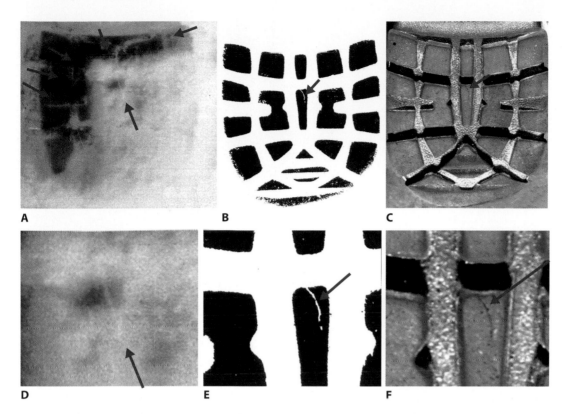

Figure 19.10 The photograph of the crime scene impression (A), known impression of heel (B), reverse photograph of heel (C), enlargements of the center areas of crime scene impression (D), inked impression (E), and heel (F).

is a known impression of the heel. (D), (E), and (F) are enlargements of the center portion of the scene impression, known impression, and heel. The cut in the heel that was referenced by the examiner is indicated in each photograph with an arrow.

My opinion stated that the impression in the snow shared some similar design characteristics with the heel but limited contrast and some scale issues prevented additional examination. Additionally the cut in the center of the heel (E,F) is curved and does not correspond with the straighter linear mark in the photograph of the snow impression (D). Further examination of the negative and print (A) revealed numerous other cuts or scratches passing through different parts of the photographed impression. Some of these are indicated with additional arrows, including the one that passes through the area that was reported to correspond with the cut in the heel. These were all a result of scratches in the film negative that showed up in the printed photograph of the snow impression. They had no connection to any damage in the heel.

This case illustrates the importance of having access to the best evidence, and the need for association of shape features of RACs in an impression and outsole before concluding they are related.

Topics Regarding Prosecution and the Defense

20

Most forensic examiners' exposure to the judicial system is through their jobs at state or federal laboratories. Very few have had an opportunity to read transcripts of other examiners' testimony, to review cases during appeal, to review the notes and conclusions of an examiner with whom they have never worked, or to experience the discovery process from both sides. The experiences of both prosecution and defense attorneys are limited, including their understanding of forensic footwear evidence and forensic reports, what should be required before someone is qualified as a footwear expert, and how various conclusions may affect the facts of the case they are handling. This chapter is intended to address some of these topics and provide other useful information not covered elsewhere in this book.

Admissibility of Footwear Evidence in Court

The use of footwear evidence in the US as well as in courts around the world has been long established. Each jurisdiction and court in the US will have some variance in their admissibility criteria related to the evidence itself and how an expert is qualified. The US Federal Rules of Evidence as well as various federal and state cases provide guidelines and rules regarding expert testimony. Affecting those decisions are certain cases such as *Frye v United States*, 293 F. 1013 (DC Cir 1923); *Daubert v Merrell Dow Pharmaceuticals*, 590 US 579 (1993); *General Electric v Joiner*, 522 US 136 (1997); and *Kumho Tire v Carmichael*, 526 US 137 (1999), as well as numerous state court decisions. Generally speaking, in the US, if a witness is qualified by knowledge, experience, training or education, if that person based their opinion on sufficient facts, data, and principles, if they used acceptable and reliable examination methods, and if that information helps the trier of fact in the understanding of the evidence, then they will be allowed to testify as an expert and provide their opinion. In each court in the US, the judge rules on the admissibility of an expert.

Qualifications of the Footwear Expert

Like any area of forensic science, a footwear expert should have some training and experience before being permitted to examine evidence and provide his or her opinion. It is typical in most laboratories to have footwear evidence experts whose workload and time are dedicated in part to evidence other than footwear evidence and who may only work a small percentage of footwear cases. Although they may have received additional training and experience in footwear examination, in some instances they have not. The Scientific Working Group for Shoe Print and Tire Tread Evidence (SWGTREAD), in their Guide for Minimum Qualifications and Training for a Forensic Footwear and/or Tire

451

Tread Examiner, has made recommendations for minimum qualifications.[*] Another suggested training syllabus is set forth in the International Association for Identification's *Recommended Course of Study for Footwear and Tire Track Examiners.*[†] Both recommend training be under the supervision of a certified or otherwise qualified principal trainer. Since SWGTREAD ceased to be funded in late 2013 and has been replaced by one of the Organization for Scientific Area Committees (OSAC) under the National Institute of Standards and Technology (NIST), it is likely in the future they will create standards for recommended minimal training and qualifications as well.[‡]

In a judicial proceeding, counsel for the opposing side may request an expert's curriculum vitae, which sets forth that expert's qualifications. They may decide to question the expert in further detail regarding those qualifications or absence of qualifications. Whether retaining a footwear examiner or challenging an examiner's qualifications in court, both sides should have an interest in ensuring any forensic footwear examiner meets a minimal standard in this regard. In some cases, the experience and training of an expert may actually be insufficient, yet, due to the loose definition of what constitutes an expert, a judge may still declare them an expert in that field, allow the person to testify, and instruct the jury to weigh their opinion accordingly. Objections by the opposing counsel are rarely successful in preventing a proffered expert from testifying and the best opposing counsel can do is to expose their concerns and the lack of the witness's experience to the jury if they believe it is deficient. It is important to note there are often individuals who are nonexperts in this field who may be allowed to provide an opinion or statement regarding footwear evidence. Some examples of nonexperts include medical examiners, podiatrists, shoe salespeople, and investigators who may have some connection with feet or shoes or the recovery of the evidence, but do not have sufficient training and experience in forensic examination to make comparisons or opine whether a shoe made the crime scene impression.

Concerning the examination of footwear evidence, the following should be considered when evaluating the expertise of an individual.

- *Their Specific Area(s) of Expertise*: Many persons are not limited to examining evidence in just one area. For instance, a footwear expert might also be a fingerprint examiner, a document examiner, a trace analyst, and so forth. They may also share other responsibilities such as crime scene work or supervisory duties. This is not always a problem, as long as they have received proper training, and their work involves regular casework and experience in this field. They should be scrutinized regarding how much training they specifically received in the area of footwear examination. Simply stating they underwent a general training program that included footwear evidence or their training was part of their general police training is inadequate and often simply a way of avoiding the question. Most police training, at best, only includes some reference to collection of the evidence and not its examination. Did they have a specific training syllabus they followed over a certain period of time concerning footwear evidence? Did they work under the direct

---

[*] www.swgtread.org, Guide for Minimum Qualifications and Training for a Forensic Footwear and/or Tire Tread Examiner, March 2006.
[†] Recommended Course of Study for Footwear and Tire Track Examiners, IAI Footwear and Tire Track Subcommittee, International Association for Identification (revised 2006).
[‡] http://www.nist.gov/forensics/osac.cfm

supervision of a certified footwear examiner? Did they take any tests or complete a written program of requirements to complete their training? Are they certified in the area of footwear impression evidence examination? If so, who certified them? If not, do they meet the minimum qualifications to apply for certification? Do they participate in and/or attend forensic conferences or meetings for continuing education regarding footwear evidence? Have they ever conducted any research? Are they published in this field? These questions and their answers will tell a lot.

- *Their Case Experience*: Experience means different things to different people. One examiner may only conduct a few footwear examinations each year. Does an examiner who has worked 5 case examinations per year for 20 years have more experience than an examiner who has actively worked 40 case examinations per year for the past 4 years? It is important to have some idea of the percentage of time an expert spends specifically involving the examination of footwear evidence, as well as an approximate number of actual cases where they examine footwear evidence and provide a written comparative opinion.

- *Certification:* Ideally, a footwear expert should be certified. It is recognized that younger examiners cannot apply for certification until they attain minimum qualifications. Although an examiner can be competent without being certified, certification by an independent organization adds credibility to their qualifications as it ensures they have met an acceptable standard of training and experience in a forensic field, and also the assurance they have been formally involved in the examination of this form of evidence over time. Laboratory accreditation should not be confused with the certification of an examiner by an independent organization.

- *Proficiency Testing:* Does the examiner receive proficiency testing? If so, have they passed those tests? Proficiency testing is another way to assure an examiner has or is maintaining a minimal ability to conduct independent forensic evaluation of footwear evidence. These tests, both internal and external, are best applied as a blind test but are often made known to the examiner prior to taking the test.

Unqualified Opinions of Nonexperts

Investigators routinely testify to their recovery of footwear impressions and their seizure of the footwear of the accused. This is part of their normal duties. This type of involvement with footwear evidence does not provide them with the expertise to conduct comparative forensic examinations or to offer an opinion regarding whether certain shoes were the source of the crime scene impressions. Investigators should not extend their testimony about footwear evidence nor provide the equivalent of a comparative opinion. This often occurs in cases where there is very little detail in the impression(s) and/or instances when that evidence was never provided to a forensic laboratory for a formal examination and a qualified expert opinion.

Unlike other forensic disciplines, commentary and nonexpert opinions about footwear evidence are sometimes tolerated more loosely and courts often permit comments regarding footwear evidence by investigators or medical examiners who are not trained nor qualified to make them. One example of this would be an investigator who advised that he took possession of a pair of sneakers and compared them to a photograph of an impression and stated that they appeared to match. Courts should not allow this type of nonexpert testimony, including statements such as "the shoes look like the impression" or "the shoes matched the impression." This type of general commentary or testimony would never occur with fingerprints, tool marks, firearms examinations, or other areas of forensics. Perhaps since everyone owns shoes, judges occasionally permit nonexpert opinions to be rendered by investigators and medical examiners but there are serious problems with this form of testimony as nonexperts can be wrong for many reasons. Equally dangerous is the fact that members of the jury place tremendous faith in certain witnesses and do not believe they would make statements they were not certain of or qualified to give. Unfortunately, when this happens, the only thing the defense can do is to show, through cross-examination, the witness did not actually make a formal comparison and does not have any specialized training that would enable him or her to reach any reliable conclusion. Although forensic science organizations can provide standards, only the courts can prevent or properly restrict testimony by unqualified nonexperts who do not meet these standards.

Is a Qualified Expert Needed?

Because everyone wears and shops for shoes and has some level of ability to distinguish patterns, a defense attorney may object to the use of an expert to testify to a forensic footwear examination. The argument has been made many times in court, explaining that the jury members all wear shoes and therefore they are fully capable of making their own comparison of a shoe and shoe impression. To infer that we all wear shoes and thus we don't need an expert to examine footwear evidence makes no more sense than saying we all have fingers and therefore we don't need fingerprint examiners. Nonexperts have no training and experience in conducting a physical comparison between footwear and a crime scene impression. They are unaware of subtle differences between similar designs or between different size shoes of the same brand and design. They are unaware of manufacturing variables and significant manufactured characteristics that can be used to both include and exclude footwear as the source of an impression. A jury asked to make a comparison would likely only be supplied with small unscaled photographs of the impression in question and would not have any test impressions of the accused's shoes. They would rely on the general appearance of the evidence and not rely on any structured or detailed examination. There is much information about footwear evidence in this book, including how shoes of the same size may vary slightly, the limitations of partial impressions, and other complexities, which the lay juror is unaware of and not capable of considering during an examination. Finding a design in a crime scene impression that is similar to the accused's footwear might hastily result in a temptation to conclude the shoe made the impression when a methodical and detailed examination may prove it actually did not. Alternately, slight variations that are normal might erroneously lead an untrained individual to think the shoe did not make the impression, when it actually did.

One study examined conclusions of certified footwear examiners.[*] This study was structured in a similar way to a previous study in 1996 in that it involved six cases with

---

[*] Duffy, K., Hammer, L., Fraser, J., and Daéid, N., A study of the variability in footwear impression comparison conclusions, *JFI*, 63(2), 2013.

premarked features. The previous European study reflected considerable variability between conclusions of footwear examiners; however, that study involved the use of different scales of conclusions used in different laboratories in many different countries with obvious translations required.[*,†] The new study concluded: "little variation in the conclusions of certified footwear examiners (in the US) when based on the same features and using the same range of conclusions scale. This study found significant agreement among trained footwear examiners regarding the level of associative value of corresponding characteristics and that a standard range of conclusions scale contributes to the expression of consistent opinions."[‡] The study also found that well-educated nonexperts had a very wide range of conclusions.

Experts not only make comparisons between a shoe and crime scene impression but also perform many other duties that nonexperts would be unable to perform or understand. Some of those include detection and collection of evidence at the scene of the crime; evaluation of the accuracy of photographed evidence; physical, chemical, photographic, and digital enhancements of impressions; preparation of test impressions for comparison; exclusion of footwear; comparison of scene-to-scene impressions; searches for footwear brand; and the sizing of impressions.

Relevance of Footwear Evidence

Like any evidence in a criminal proceeding, footwear evidence may or may not prove relevant to a crime. Impressions that track through the victim's blood, impressions on papers knocked to the ground during the crime, impressions in fresh snow that fell in a certain time frame, impressions on bank counters, and certain others are easily established to be relevant. Other impressions such as a dust mark or wet origin mark on an interior floor might be days or weeks old and thus more difficult to associate with a crime. The burden of proving relevance falls on the prosecution but the defense also needs to consider this in their evaluation of this evidence.

Scientific Conclusions and Opinions

For general research in science, drawing conclusions is the final and most critical part. Conclusions result after using a scientific method that tests a hypothesis through the collection of data and testing. Conclusions are critical to any research regardless of whether they turn out to be weak or strong or whether they support or disprove a hypothesis. What is most important in science is that any conclusion should be based on sound knowledge and test results.

Conducting physical examinations of evidence as a forensic expert using a general scientific method also results in conclusions. Conclusions concerning footwear evidence

---

[*] Majamaa, H., and Ytti, A., A survey of the conclusions drawn of similar footwear cases in various crime laboratories, *FSI*, 82(1):109–120, 1996.
[†] The 1996 study was cited in the 2009 NAS report.
[‡] Duffy, K. et al., Ibid., 2013, p. 213.

support various levels of association or disassociation between a shoe and a crime scene impression based on the collected data resulting from examination. The legal rules of procedure allow an expert witness to express his or her observations and/or conclusions about an examination in the form of an opinion. An opinion is not a fact but is the expert's expression of what he or she learned about the evidence as a product of the examination. That opinion should provide a clear accounting of the observations of relevant similar or dissimilar features and how those features prove or disprove the hypothesis of whether the shoe did or did not produce an impression. Their opinion, like the product of any scientific test or research, should be unbiased and transparent.

Discovery and the Need for Independent Examination

The US justice system allows the defense to utilize experts. The defense is entitled to have any evidence examined that has been recovered from a crime scene, the victim, or the accused. The discovery process for that evidence includes reports, statements, depositions, records, or other documents, including those relating to laboratory examinations and physical evidence, regardless of whether that evidence will be used in proceedings. The discovery process varies somewhat in different jurisdictions. In the US, some states, such as Florida, have more liberal discovery policies than others. Florida allows for a full discovery including the ability to depose witnesses under oath prior to trial.

When two experts examine impression evidence, it is important they have access to and examine the same items. For instance, a state laboratory examiner will have access to the actual footwear, the actual bloody impressions on recovered tile, and other supporting photographs, and needs those items in order to perform a responsibly conducted examination. When two experts do not have access to the same evidence, this alone could cause discrepancies between their comparative results.

The existence of discovery requirements alone does not assure the prosecution has fully complied. Often during this process, the materials provided may include only poor quality photocopies of these items, and prevent any proper or responsible examination by a defense expert. Further, it is not uncommon to find a prosecuting attorney providing only part of the evidence in response to a discovery request because they are honestly not aware of all of the physical evidence that was recovered in that case.

The investigation of a crime can be very complex and often involves the work of multiple persons who recovered evidence from the crime scene. These events may have taken place months or even years prior. There may be photographs taken at secondary scenes, at an autopsy, during a search warrant for shoes, or during subsequent crimes that may be related. Investigative or laboratory work such as footwear impression examinations will also produce discoverable materials. Defense attorneys making discovery requests are doing so because they need to be aware of all of the evidence that has been documented and collected. Their experts need to have access to the same quantity and quality of evidence the prosecution expert used to make the examination. For the sake of clarity and efficiency, when making discovery requests in cases involving footwear evidence, it is best to request any item that exists or may potentially exist. Following is a list of some items that should be requested during the discovery process for footwear evidence because they are routinely recovered from crime scenes or are a product of the subsequent investigation or laboratory analysis:

- The original impression(s) (if recovered) (e.g., the actual impressions on paper, flooring, clothing of victim, etc., that contain the actual footwear impressions).
- If pictures were taken with a digital camera, the original full digital files on a CD of all photographs taken should be requested. Ensure these are not copies with reduced resolution but are the original unaltered digital files that were downloaded from the camera to the police computer. Do not accept emailed images. The discovery request should include all autopsy photographs of any impression evidence on the body of a victim when applicable.
- Some cold cases and old appeals still involve film. If photographs were taken with a film camera, then the original negatives of all photographs should be requested. If the prosecution will not release the original negatives, then a high-resolution digital scan of those negatives should be requested and those images placed on a CD. These should be 3000 to 4000 pixels per inch (ppi) scans.
- Original lifts (electrostatic, adhesive, gelatin, dental stone, Mikrosil) of all footwear impressions from the crime scene.
- Any casts of footwear impressions from the crime scene.
- All original footwear that is to be part of the examination.
- Any photographs of footwear taken during the investigation.
- Any shoeboxes.
- All footwear samples or outsole samples provided by manufacturers or purchased in connection with the footwear evidence and/or investigation.
- All notes, reports, emails, or letters from contacts with any footwear manufacturer.
- All notes, conclusions, or reports of any laboratory examiner who examined the footwear evidence. Reports and notes will establish the identity of the items that have been examined. It is important to note and include in any discovery request the work product of a forensic examiner that extends to and includes any known impressions and photographs of the footwear they have produced as well as possible enhancements and other information maintained on their laboratory computer.
- Copies of known test impressions of footwear made by laboratory personnel must always include a scale (ruler) whether they are scanned images or copied on a legal size photocopier.
- All notes, conclusions, and reports of the crime scene personnel who recovered footwear evidence from the crime scene, including photographic logs or investigative reports pertaining to the recovery and photographs of that evidence.
- Any photographs or impressions taken of elimination footwear of first responders, medical personnel, the victim(s), or others.
- Any results, notes, or reports relating to any attempts to search a footwear database or of any investigative efforts made to locate shoes matching the design of the crime scene impression(s).
- Any information that may exist in the form of notes, photographs, reports, or information relating to the sizing and manufacture of the footwear, including copies of data or photographs received or produced in connection with the same.

Completeness and Integrity of Provided Photographic Images

Protocol requires all exposures taken at a crime scene to be saved. Thus, 125 images taken using one camera at a crime scene should have consecutive and complete image numbers, as an example, IMG_1001 through IMG_1125. When initially viewing photographic image files submitted in discovery, they should appear in their original file sequence and format depending on the brand and model camera. Examples would appear such as DSC_0345, DSC_0346, DSC_0347, or IMG_0755, IMG_0756, IMG_0757, and so forth. If there is not a continuous numerical sequence, then an exposure was deleted or the discovery information was not complete or someone has already selected photographs that apply to certain evidence. Files that are labeled or renamed with titles such as "5-13-716-OF_Foot Impressions of Suspect_13.jpg" are not the original file names assigned by the camera and therefore there is no guarantee they are the complete original files. Without the original files as downloaded from the camera, there is no way to ensure a complete set of scene photographs was provided in discovery; that the files were not changed, tampered with, lost, or selectively screened; what the original file size and content of those files were; nor can their sequence, frame numbers, and other information of potential value be scrutinized. Not having the full original files could also adversely affect the ability to both examine and enhance those images.

When original images are downloaded from a camera, they contain metadata about those images. Metadata includes standardized information about each image file, such as the camera used and lens type, resolution, exposure settings, date the image was taken, file size, file format, etc. This information can be easily accessed on PCs by selecting an image and going to FILE>PROPERTIES. On Apple computers, right clicking on an image and selecting GET INFO does the same. Note that if the camera used to take the image did not have the date and time set properly, that portion of the information will not be correct. Images from scans of prints and images that are copied and resaved with a new file name will not contain original metadata.

Inadequately Recovered Evidence

Footwear impressions occur in various forms at the scene of the crime. Finding and recovering them is critical and has a direct impact on the opportunity and ability to compare them to known footwear and reach the most accurate conclusion. When footwear evidence is not recovered at all or is recovered inadequately, it will interfere with any attempt to associate that evidence with the shoes of the accused as well as potentially prevent the defense from using this evidence to its fullest extent, including the possibility that evidence was exculpatory. As an example, if two impressions in soil are observed and photographed at a crime scene but later are determined to be out of focus and of no value, and no casts were made of those impressions, their inadequate recovery would prevent or limit both the use of this evidence that might favor the prosecution as well as the potential for the defense to use that evidence to exclude those impressions if they were in fact not produced by the shoes of the accused.

Reasons to Retain an Expert

There are many reasons why a defense attorney may need to consult with an experienced footwear evidence expert. Many have never been involved in a case involving this form of evidence and therefore have little knowledge about this field of forensic evidence. In many cases, a state or federal prosecution expert will have already conducted a physical examination of footwear evidence and will have produced a written report and opinion. These reports may be unclear for a number of reasons, including the lack of specific descriptions of the evidence, lack of clarity in the way the written opinion or conclusion is presented, and the ultimate impact any opinion(s) expressed in that report will have on the case against the accused. In some cases, the reports are written in such a way that it is not even possible for another expert to fully understand the results short of examining the evidence themselves or reviewing the notes and work product of the prosecution examiner.

Defense experts can conduct an independent examination of the evidence to see if their observations and opinions are in agreement with those of the prosecution expert, particularly in those cases where some degree of association with the defendant's footwear has been reported. In other cases, footwear evidence exists but the prosecution has not requested the evidence be submitted to a qualified expert for examination, or it is anticipated that they are planning to use an investigator to offer this evidence in court instead of an expert. Under these circumstances, the defense has little or no idea of what opinions or statements might arise during proceedings; thus the use of their own expert to evaluate and review this evidence in advance may be necessary. In cases where the evidence has not been examined, there is always the possibility that evidence might prove to be exculpatory. A defense expert can also provide considerable assistance during preparation for trial. In some cases, they may offer the attorney assistance in the preparation of questions or photographs for a witness that will assist in providing insight into certain facts, to identify potential weaknesses or limitations of the other expert's opinion, or simply to assure they restrict the opinion to what is stated and not anything stronger.

In 2009, John Collins and Jay Jarvis published their study of 200 overturned convictions that, in their estimation, revealed that 13% of those potential causes leading to erroneous convictions were attributable to forensic science misconduct; however, almost all of which were from a small group of charlatans working in nonaccredited laboratories.[*] In 2013, Dr. Jon Gould at American University published what is perhaps the most comprehensive and authoritative social science study on the causes of erroneous convictions.[†] With funding from the National Institute of Justice, Gould and his colleagues studied a large number of cases in which factually innocent defendants were either convicted or nearly convicted. Gould's research found it was not forensic evidence that led to wrongful convictions, but rather it was improper testimony about the forensic evidence that ended up leading to a wrongful conviction. His research also found that risks associated with faulty forensic evidence were worthy of attention but not nearly as serious as other risks he

[*] Collins, J., and Jarvis, J., The wrongful conviction of forensic science, *Forensic Science Policy & Management*, 2009.
[†] Gould, J. et al, Predicting erroneous convictions: a social science approach to miscarriages of justice, February 2013, NIJ award 2009-IJ-CX-4110 (see http://nij.ncjrs.gov/multimedia/video-gould.htm).

reported. "While forensic fraud was a serious issue in a few of our cases, it is not endemic in the system …. If there's one big finding from the statistical evidence here, it is that there are three variables that work in concert to create systemic error. Those three errors are the strength of the prosecution's evidence, the quality of the defense, and whether the prosecution turned over exculpatory evidence."[*] All three of these errors relate to the performance of the attorneys; thus boosting the effectiveness of both prosecution and defense practices can prevent erroneous convictions.

Working with the Defense

The vast majority of forensic experts are employed by state, county, or federal agencies or by a police department. In almost all cases, due to legislative authority and funding restrictions, these examiners can only conduct examinations for the police and prosecution and are not permitted to conduct examinations on behalf of the accused.

Conducting examinations and consulting with defense counsel is not only part of our adversarial system of justice but provides any examiner a more rounded exposure to that discipline's use in our legal system. Many perceive a defense attorney as someone who is simply trying to get the charges against the client dropped, regardless of the facts. Experience has shown most defense attorneys are sincere, honest, and straightforward and while many believe their clients either are or may be innocent, after consultation with their own expert they better understand the examination conclusions, whatever they may be. They are part of a system that is designed to assure the accused has the representation the constitution entitles them to.

Regardless of the side they are retained by, qualified and experienced footwear experts should make the same analysis of evidence in any particular case and should arrive at the same conclusions. Over a period of the past 15 years, my review of cases involving footwear evidence previously examined by a qualified and experienced prosecution expert disclosed very few significant deficiencies. When they did exist, they were either the product of individuals with little or no training and experience, or opinions rendered by those I have characterized in this chapter as nonexperts.

[*] Ibid.

Resources

21

This chapter provides general information about resources relating to footwear, footwear databases, forensic organizations that provide workshops or a forum for forensic presentations and journals, and sources of materials and supplies.

Forensic Organizations and Meetings

There are a large number of international, national, and local organizations that provide meetings, symposiums, and other forums for the exchange of forensic information in the form of continuing education. Some have memberships and membership requirements while others have none. Some meet annually while others meet every two or three years. The following list includes larger international and national organizations and does not extend to state or local forensic organizations.

International Association for Identification (IAI)

The IAI is the oldest and largest forensic science organization in the United States.[*] Founded in 1914, it celebrated its 100th anniversary in 2015. Each year the IAI holds an annual Educational Conference that includes a week of forensic presentations and workshops including many on footwear and tire impression evidence. The IAI has membership requirements but is open for attendance by anyone. Members receive the *Journal of Forensic Identification (JFI),* the official publication of the IAI. The IAI consists of approximately 16 subcommittees covering a variety of forensic disciplines including one on footwear and tire track examination. It offers a Certification Program for Footwear Examiners (CFWE) that requires minimum requirements of training and experience, passing an administered written test, a practical test, and periodic recertification exams. Although not individually listed here, the IAI has many state and international divisions listed on its main web page, some that also have regular meetings and presentations regarding footwear and tire evidence.

European Meeting for Shoe Print and Tool Marks

In 1995, the National Bureau of Investigation (NBI) in Helsinki, Finland, hosted the first European Meeting for Shoe Print and Tool Mark evidence (EMSPTM). This is now organized by the Expert Working Group Marks of the European Network of Forensic Science Institutes (ENFSI). Invitations to their meetings are usually extended to those from non-member countries should someone wish to attend and present a paper. They meet on average every two years in varied locations in Europe, where, on average, approximately

[*] www.theiai.org

100 examiners from 25–30 countries present and exchange information. This is an extremely valuable meeting for footwear examiners in Europe as well as anyone else who is fortunate enough to attend.

American Academy of Forensic Sciences (AAFS)

The American Academy of Forensic Sciences was founded in 1948 and is the second largest forensic science organization in the United States.[*] Its website describes itself as "… a multi-disciplinary professional organization that provides leadership to advance science and its application to the legal system." It meets at varied locations in the United States once each year in February. Composed of numerous sections representing many forensic disciplines, the Criminalistics and General Sections occasionally include a presentation on footwear evidence but, for the most part, the AAFS annual meeting does not attract presentations in the fields of forensic footwear evidence or others that involve physical comparisons such as firearms, tool marks, fingerprints, and tire tread evidence.

International Association of Forensic Sciences (IAFS)

The International Association of Forensic Sciences (IAFS) is a worldwide forensic science organization inaugurated in 1957 to bring professionals together and exchange scientific and technical information together in the various forensic disciplines. The IAFS meets every three years in a different location throughout the world. It met during 2014 in Seoul, Korea under the broader name of the World Forensic Festival. The program varies from meeting to meeting and may or may not include presentations on impression evidence, depending on the decisions of the organizers. Current information about upcoming meetings is published on the Internet about one year prior to the meetings.

Chartered Society of Forensic Sciences

Originally known as the Forensic Science Society, it was founded in 1959.[†] Under this new name, it has over 3000 members representing over 60 countries. It includes the topic of Forensic Mark Comparisons and issues a Certificate of Professional Competence for Forensic Footwear Mark Comparison. The Society is involved in the annual Forensics Europe Expo.[‡]

Australian and New Zealand Forensic Science Society

The Australian Forensic Science Society was formed in 1971. In 1988, the name was changed to the Australian and New Zealand Forensic Science Society (ANZFSS).[§] The society holds an international symposium every two years.

---

[*] www.aafs.org
[†] http://www.forensic-science-society.org.uk/home
[‡] http://www.forensicseuropeexpo.com
[§] http://anzfss.org

Working Groups for Shoe Print and Tire Tread Evidence

In September 2004, the Scientific Working Group for Shoe Print and Tire Tread Evidence (SWGTREAD) was formed.* As cited on its web page, its mission was to provide a professional forum where forensic shoeprint and tire tread examiners share knowledge, evaluate practices, develop standards, identify research needs, and disseminate information. The working group was initially funded by the FBI and later by the National Institute of Justice (NIJ). The working group created and shared many resources through its web page including an examiner's forum and published peer-reviewed guidelines and standards. The working group stopped meeting when funding ceased in 2013. In 2014, it was replaced by a new initiative by the National Institute for Standards and Technology (NIST), which established the Organization of Scientific Area Committees (OSAC).† The OSAC is composed of 24 committees including one on Footwear and Tire Evidence that first met in January 2015.

In Europe, the European Network of Forensic Science Institutes (ENFSI) currently includes 17 expert working groups including the Expert Working Group Marks (WGM). It is open to examiners employed by ENFSI organizations but also can include guests outside of ENFSI. It organizes the website for Expert Working Group Marks, organizes the European Meeting for Shoe Print and Tool Mark examiners, and compiles the Information Bulletin for Shoeprint/Tool Mark Examiners.

Publications and Forensic Journals

There are many peer-reviewed forensic journals and periodical publications. Subscriptions to many of these are included with memberships in forensic science organizations while others are subscription based only.

Journal of Forensic Identification (JFI)

This is a publication of the International Association for Identification and is included as part of its membership benefits, or can be subscribed to separately. The *JFI* routinely publishes articles and information about footwear and tire impression evidence and research (www.theiai.org).

Journal of Forensic Science (JFS)

This is the official journal of the American Academy of Forensic Sciences (AAFS). The *JFS* is included with AAFS membership, or can be subscribed to separately. Although an occasional article about footwear or tire evidence may be published, the topics largely cover other forensic areas (www.aafs.org).

---

* SWGTREAD, www.swgtread.org
† Organization of Scientific Area Committees (OSAC), www.nist.gov/forensics/osac

Forensic Science International (FSI)

Forensic Science International is a peer-reviewed journal that covers most forensic disciplines including occasional articles on footwear and tire evidence and related research. Additional information is available on their web page.[*]

Science and Justice and CSEye

Science and Justice is the journal of the Chartered Society of Forensic Sciences and is available to members of that organization. It is also available through online journal services per information on their web page.[†] CSEye is a more recent free electronic magazine that publishes research articles, case studies and technical notes.[‡]

Symposiums

There have been four symposiums in the United States that covered footwear and tire evidence extensively.

FBI International Symposium on Footwear and Tire Evidence

In 1994, the FBI hosted the first International Symposium on Footwear and Tire Evidence at the FBI Academy, Quantico, VA. Two hundred and thirty practitioners representing approximately 30 countries attended the symposium. Beyond abstracts, the full proceedings of the symposium were never published.

2010 and 2012 Pattern and Impression Symposiums

In August 2010 and August 2012, the National Institute of Justice sponsored two Pattern and Impression Evidence Symposiums in Clearwater, FL. The topic areas included footwear and tire evidence. The proceedings of the 2010 meetings are published on the Internet at the following links

2010 Symposium: http://projects.nfstc.org/ipes/ (no password is required)

2015 Impression Pattern and Trace Evidence Symposium

In August 2015 the National Institute of Justice sponsored a joint pattern and trace evidence symposium in San Antonio, Texas.

It is anticipated that links to the presentations of the 2012 and 2015 meetings will be available in the future.

Forensic Footwear Databases

A computer database is a regular part of many full service forensic laboratories. Footwear databases are designed and used for two separate purposes. One is to collect and categorize

---

[*] http://www.journals.elsevier.com/forensic-science-international
[†] http://www.forensic-science-society.org.uk/Publications/ScienceAndJustice
[‡] http://www.enfsi.eu/about-enfsi/structure/working-groups/marks

the manufacturer or source of outsole designs enabling a crime scene impression of unknown origin to be associated with a specific brand or style such as a Nike Air Force 1 or a New Balance 845. The other is to store crime scene impressions that have been recovered, and to categorize them by their outsole designs in a way that permits them to be linked with impressions of similar designs recovered in other crimes. This latter use is often referred to as footwear intelligence. Each is further discussed hereafter.

Databases for Footwear Intelligence

Footwear intelligence refers to the practice of linking different scenes of crime to each other based on the design and details of footwear evidence. Impressions that are recovered from scenes of crime are collected, encoded, and stored in a computer database, as well as known impressions of persons taken into custody. This practice works most effectively for linking repeatable offenses such as burglaries and robberies but is also effective in helping to identify those committing more serious crimes. Footwear intelligence is practiced successfully in many countries.[*,†,‡,§,¶] In the United States, it is practiced by a few localized jurisdictions but overall the concept of footwear intelligence is used far less. At least one police force has published the top 50 footwear designs collected from arrestees in custody each year, shown in Figure 21.1. They post this among the police forces to bring awareness to footwear evidence and the designs that most populate their footwear intelligence database.[**] This can serve as an incentive to scene-of crime-investigators who, upon seeing 1 of these top 50 designs at their crime scene, will realize that the design is in the database and might contribute to linking their scene with others.

One newer automated system produced by Dalian Everspry includes the option of using a pressure-sensitive pad that records a detailed image of the outsole impression of a shoe when the person stands on it.[††,‡‡] Figure 21.2 depicts this pressure-sensitive device and how the outsole design instantly appears on the computer screen. An automated search could follow. Technology such as this is beginning to be applied in situations at local police departments to instantly record and enter footwear designs of arrestees into a searchable database to see if their outsole design has appeared at recent crime scenes.

In 2015 the Metropolitan Police Force created the National Footwear Database (NFD). The NFD uses the automated digitized footpad produced by Everspry that captures an instant digital scan of the outsole design of arrestees. The footwear design information obtained from the scan permits investigators to search the arrestee's outsole design in the NFD against similar designs already entered in the NFD and National Footwear Reference Collection (NFRC) systems. This search can be performed while the arrestee or suspect is

[*] Davis, R., An intelligence approach to footwear and tool marks, *J. Forensic Science Society*, 21:183–193, 1981.

[†] Mashiter, K., Footwear Intelligence Guidance for Scientific Support, August 2007, Lancashire, UK.

[‡] Ribaux, O., Girod, A., Walsh, W., Margot, P., Mizrahi, S., and Clivaz, V., Forensic intelligence and crime analysis, *Law Probability and Risk* 2:47–60, 2003.

[§] Girod, A., Computerized classification of the shoeprints of burglar's soles, *Forensic Science International* 82(1):59–65, 1996.

[¶] Mikkonen, S., Suominen, V. Heinonen, P., Use of footwear impressions in crime scene investigations assisted by computerized footwear collection system," *Forensic Science International* 82(1):67–79, 1996.

[**] Provided courtesy of Jonathan Goodyear, Lancashire Constabulary, Preston, UK, 2014.

[††] Li, B., Everspry automated shoeprint recognition, Everspry Science and Tech Co., Ltd., presented at the ENFSI SPTM 2014 meeting, Prague, Czech Republic, October 22, 2014.

[‡‡] http://www.footprintmatcher.com, Dalian Everspry Science and Tech Co. LTD, Dalian, China.

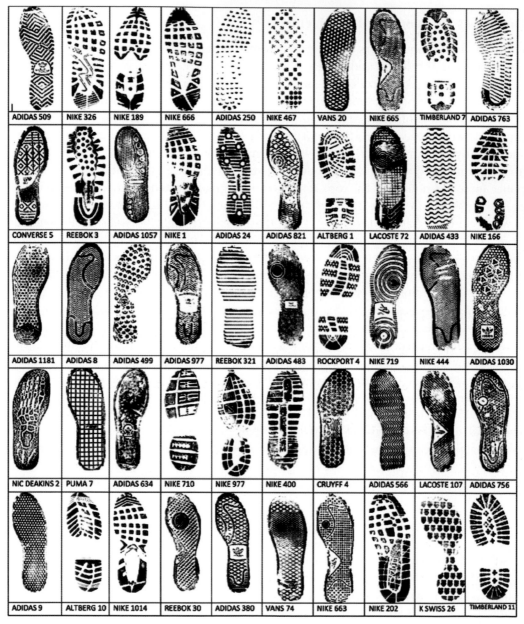

Figure 21.1 The Lancashire Constabulary's top 50 footwear patterns for 2013. (Courtesy of Jon Goodyear.)

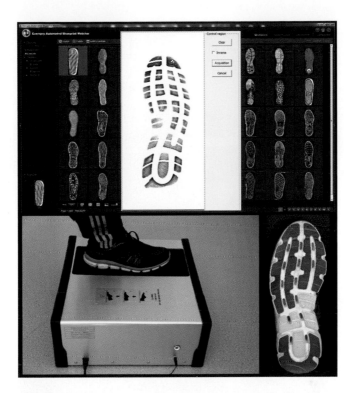

Figure 21.2 The Dalian Everspry footwear database showing the pressure plate that records the shoe print of a shoe. (Photographs courtesy of Bo Li.)

still in custody. The digitized scanner is cost effective and provides better detail than conventional paper impression methods. The future use of scanners that are capable of auto coding and searching databases within seconds will provide police forces with the ability to use footwear information to link arrestees with other crime scenes and provide greater footwear intelligence capabilities than previous manually operated systems.[*]

Databases to Determine Footwear Design or Manufacturer

Some databases are used only to store brand and outsole design information. The association of a specific brand or style of footwear with impressions recovered from a scene can aid some investigations in various ways. Having a photograph of impressions recovered from the scene and/or knowing the brand name and style enable the investigation to more efficiently use that evidence. In an occasional case, even when this is not known for some time after the date of the crime, information concerning the brand and style of footwear can provide critical information leading to the identity of the perpetrator. In one case a jewelry burglary was believed to be an inside job committed by an employee. The database provided information about the shoe brand and design that produced the shoe marks that enabled the discreet identification of the employee involved.

[*] Henderson, Julie, Digitized Capture of Custody Footwear Impressions for Integration with the National Footwear Database and Real-Time Intelligence within the London Metropolitan Police Service, IAI 100th Educational Conference, Sacramento, CA 8/7/15.

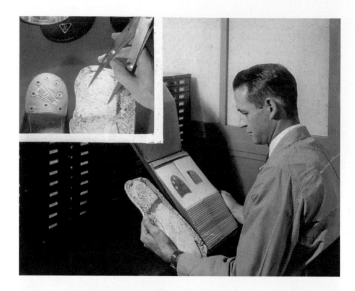

Figure 21.3 An FBI footwear examiner manually searches the Rubber Heel and Sole reference collection in the 1950s.

Figure 21.4 The FBI's first computerized footwear database in 1981.

Collections of footwear outsole designs have been used for a long time. In December 1937, the FBI Laboratory began collecting the outsole and heel designs of footwear. These were housed in metal file drawers that had to be manually searched as shown in Figure 21.3. In 1981, the FBI's first footwear database was created on a mainframe computer, the terminal of which is shown in Figure 21.4. A new system was designed and improved considerably in 1991. Shown in Figure 21.5, the newer system utilized numerous design element icons and a drag and drop system allowing outsole design information to be added or searched simply by dragging various design element icons onto the shoe palette of the screen. Since the vast majority of footwear impression evidence is athletic footwear, the reference collection focused on the collection of outsole designs of athletic shoes made by the major footwear

Figure 21.5 The FBI's computerized database utilizing design icons and the drag and drop search and entry method.

companies but also included photographs of outsoles and shoes collected from case sources. It was successful in identifying the brand and style of shoe in a high percentage of cases.

Similar computerized footwear databases have been created and used by law enforcement agencies in many countries for many years.[*,†,‡,§,¶] Maintaining any footwear database is not an easy task and requires dedicating the necessary budget and time to collect and populate the database. Collecting samples of existing footwear designs is time consuming and designs are constantly being supplemented and replaced due to competitive marketing reasons. A database that is not constantly maintained will quickly fail to produce results. Consequently, many laboratories purchase a database and pay for regular updates of the outsole designs to keep the information current. One commercially available database is known as SICAR Solemate.[**] The acronym SICAR stands for Shoeprint Image Capture and Retrieval. Solemate is a reference database that contains tens of thousands of outsole images. Those who purchase the database can obtain periodic updates to keep it current. An agency can also use the system to add and code additional images as well. A photograph of the SICAR computer screen is provided in Figure 21.6.

Some footwear database systems store images of shoes and outsole designs while others store only impressions made from shoe outsoles. The various systems are designed according to the needs of the respective organizations. Whereas databases have traditionally involved

[*] Ashley, W., What shoe was that? The use of computerized image database to assist in identification, *Forensic Science International*, 82(1):1–5, 1996.

[†] Girod, A., Computerized classification of the shoeprints of burglar's soles, *Forensic Science International*, 82(1):59–65, 1996.

[‡] Mikkonen, S., Suominen, V., and Heinonen, P., Use of footwear impressions in crime scene investigations assisted by computerized footwear collection system, *Forensic Science International*, 82(1):67–79, 1996.

[§] Geradts, Z., and Keijzer, J., The image database REBEZO for shoeprints with developments on automatic classification of shoe outsole designs, *Forensic Science International*, 82(1):7–20, 1996.

[¶] Chochól, A., and Świętek, M., Characteristics of forensic shoe sole databases, *Problems of Forensic Sciences*, 90:164–177, 2012, Institute of Forensic Research, Krakow, Poland.

[**] Foster and Freeman, http://www.fosterfreeman.com/trace-evidence/357-sicar-6-solemate-2.html.

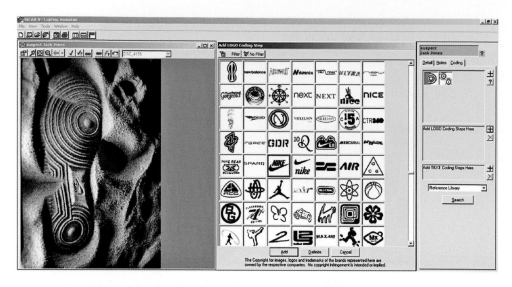

Figure 21.6 A screen shot of the SICAR Solemate database. This particular screen is showing various logo coding choices.

manual coding and searching, newer systems are now being explored and developed to permit more automated processing, either assisted by the examiner or totally automated.[*,†,‡]

In those cases where all efforts and database searches have been exhausted to identify the brand and style of footwear responsible for a crime scene impression, there are other sources known as the Wanted Page and Tread Typer. Both involve informal submissions of the crime scene impression and rely on the voluntary response of other examiners. The Wanted Page is operated by ENFSI Marks Working Group. Tread Typer is accessible through the SWGTREAD website.[§]

UK National Footwear Reference Collection (NFRC)

In the UK, there are approximately 45 police forces throughout England, Wales, Scotland and Ireland. On average, footwear evidence is found at approximately 25% of crime scenes. In April 2009, the United Kingdom's National Police Improvement Agency (NPIA) started the National Footwear Reference Collection (NFRC) to provide a national coding for footwear patterns. The database contains tens of thousands of designs in a searchable format. Each sole pattern is assigned a code that includes the manufacturer as shown in Figure 21.1. Thus, a particular Nike design may be coded Nike 189 while an Adidas design may be coded Adidas 509. This allows various police forces throughout the UK to communicate with each other regarding footwear outsole designs of a specific pattern and get cross-border hits. The impressions entered into this database are primarily collected in casework and from the footwear of persons taken into custody by the various participating police forces. Custody

[*] Pasquier, J., Automatic footwear mark pattern retrieval: results and perspectives, presented at the ENFSI SPTM 2014 meeting, Prague, Czech Republic, October 21, 2014.

[†] Kortylewski, A., Automated footwear impression analysis and retrieval based on periodic patterns, presented at the ENFSI SPTM 2014 meeting, Prague, Czech Republic, October 21, 2014.

[‡] Koller, T., A better approach for footwear retrieval systems: computer assisted shoe track matching, presented at the ENFSI SPTM 2014 meeting, Prague, Czech Republic, October 21, 2014.

[§] http://swgtread.org/footwear/make-model-determination.

impressions can be searched against the crime scene database, often in real time, to see if a person arrested has a sole design found at other crime scenes. The searches can be targeted at offense types, geographical areas, and over certain dates. The fact the arrestee happens to have a footwear design that was found at other crime scenes does not mean they committed that crime, but may allow the police force to seize the footwear for examination. The police forces in the UK have a very proactive approach to footwear intelligence and have realized many successes. Foster and Freeman have incorporated the NFRC pattern numbers into SICAR. A more recent article has perhaps indicated a newer effort to combine information in databases from prior crime scenes with scans of footwear of suspects that could provide instant information to link them with prior crimes.[*]

Webster Groves High School

Often commercial and police databases include more popular athletic brand outsole designs, leaving a gap when searching for footwear outsole patterns sold through other sources. Since 2001, the Advanced Forensic Science Program at Webster Groves High School has photographed the outsoles and collected manufacturing data from shoes at Payless and Wal-Mart stores twice a year. Starting in 2014, they created a website that contains the most recent four years of this data, which is available upon request to any member of law enforcement. They also take requests from any member of law enforcement to search this data and the Internet for possible outsole pattern matches. Contact Jeanette Hencken at henckenj@hotmail.com for more information.[†]

Logos

Many name brand athletic and other footwear have logos, names, or other trademarked or registered words. Logos commonly appear on different areas of both the uppers and outsoles of footwear. In some cases, these logos appear as part of the outsole design that is replicated and visible in the crime scene impression. Some popular logos are illustrated in Figure 21.7. Some databases have incorporated logos and brand names into their entry and search criteria.

Labels and Date Information

In most cases, shoes are seized a short time after the crime. Thus, it is common sense the shoes had been manufactured prior to the crime. There are occasional cases where the shoes are not seized for months or years after the crime and the question of whether those shoes actually existed when the crime occurred becomes relevant. Labels found in athletic and other footwear often contain dates or date codes that indicate the month and year they were manufactured. Although some manufacturers include a full date of manufacture on their labels, information about labels and potential information is not always

---

[*] Bassett, T., Shoe dunnit: Burglars being nabbed by new forensic evidence found in their footprints, www.mirror.co.uk, April 7, 2015.
[†] Personal communication with Jeanette Hencken, May 2015.

Figure 21.7 Some logos found on popular brands of athletic shoes.

that obvious. One study provided information about label dates and included many brand names and information on how manufacturers sometimes encode date information.[*] That study noted that some manufacturers have more than one label format due to production and sales in different countries. A comparison of the information provided in that study to present day footwear labels reveals some manufacturers have redesigned their labels and the information they contain. Thus providing extensive examples of label information for

---

[*] Banks, R., and Hamburg, C., Deciphering the symbols and codes on footwear labels, presented at the Pattern and Impression Symposium, Clearwater, FL, 2012.

Figure 21.8 Some labels found on the tongue of athletic shoes that include manufacturing date information. The Nike label shows the order date on the left and label printing date on the right; the New Balance label shows a date of 8/2014; the K-Swiss label shows a manufacturing date code of J12, for which J is the tenth letter of the alphabet, thus the tenth month is October and 12 is the year; Converse has the date code of 1404 for the year (2014) and month April (04); Skechers provides the entire date of 4/2/14; and Saucony provides 01/14 for January 2014.

manufacturers in this chapter is not practical, as it would likely become dated. Instead, some illustrations to provide a general understanding and awareness of dating information labels may contain is provided in Figure 21.8, which depicts labels of six athletic shoe brands obtained in late 2014 along with some explanation of their date information. When considering information relating to dating on labels that is significant in casework, this information should be confirmed with the respective manufacturer as well as confirmation the shoe and attached label are not counterfeit. There is no guarantee that date information on a counterfeit label and shoe is accurate.

Bar Codes

Bar codes on a shoebox may help determine if a shoe is real or counterfeit. A bar code on a shoebox should be identical to any bar code on the shoes it contains. If only the box is found, the bar code and information on the box may provide reliable information about the style and color of the shoes that were sold in it, in the event that information is not otherwise published on the box.[*] Bar codes will not provide information about distribution or in what stores the shoes were sold.

---

[*] Herb Hedges, Nike, Inc., personal communication, November 2, 2014.

Website Resources

A variety of general footwear industry websites are offered below with brief descriptions. Some provide information that may be of use while others provide more general footwear industry information.

Industry Websites

Brannock Device Company (www.brannock.com)
This is the website of the Brannock Company, which produces the Brannock devices used for measuring feet used in footwear stores. The site provides source and usage information about those devices as well as information about measuring the foot with this device.

Footwear Insight Magazine (www.footwearinsight.com)
Footwear Insight Magazine is a free subscription website magazine that covers new products, key trends, and news regarding the changing retail landscape.

American Apparel and Footwear Association (www.apparelandfootwear.org)
The American Apparel and Footwear Association is a trade organization that represents more than 1000 name brands.

Footwear News (www.wwd.com/footwear-news)
Footwear News website covers news and footwear fashion trends.

Trendy Websites

The following Internet sites contain unofficial news and photographs of shoe styles and some history. They may serve some purpose if you are looking for photographs of older name brand athletic shoes and styles or simply want to learn more about the culture of footwear.

    http://sneakers.pair.com
    www.flightclubny.com
    www.sneakerhead.com
    www.kicksonfire.com
    http://www.sneakerfiles.com
    http://sneakernews.com

Merchant Websites Useful for Casework

Many websites that sell large quantities of footwear also provide a potential resource for examiners, as many of them provide excellent photographs of outsole designs. Examples are websites like www.zappos.com, www.shoes.com, www.amazon.com, www.shoebacca.com, and www.pickyourshoes.com. Sites like www.ebay.com can provide access to old used shoes of a certain design that are no longer sold. It sells legitimate new footwear but also is a site where counterfeit footwear is commonly found. Some websites of casual shoes, many that contain flip flops and cut outsoles, include www.flipflopshops.com, www.quiksilver.com, www.reef.com, and www.sanuk.com.

Materials and Supplies Sources

There are a large number of forensic suppliers in the United States and other countries. Most listed below are based in the United States and are accessible through their websites. The following list is provided alphabetically and is not intended to be a recommendation or an all-inclusive list of every source of forensic supplies or materials. Forensic examiners should rely on first-hand information regarding products and materials and whenever possible inquire about or test those products to assure they work satisfactorily.

Arrowhead Forensics
http://www.crime-scene.com

BVDA America Inc.
http://www.usa.bvda.com

CSI Equipment
www.csiequipment.com (UK)

CSI Forensic Supply
http://www.csiforensic.com

Evident
https://www.shopevident.com

Forensics Source
http://www.safariland.com/products/forensics

Foster and Freeman
http://www.officer.com/company/10029101/foster-freeman-usa

Kjell Carlsson Innovations
http://www.carlssoninnovation.se

Lynn Peavey Company
https://www.lynnpeavey.com

Sirchie
http://www.sirchie.com

SPEX Forensics
http://www.spexforensics.com

Tri-Tech Forensics
http://tritechforensics.com

Dental Suppliers

Pearson Dental
www.pearsondental.com

Dentsply International
https://www.dentsply.com/en-us/search.html?q=dental+stone

Glossary

Abrasion: An injury from a scraping action that results in removal of portions of the top layers of the epidermis, often with minimal or no bleeding.

Accidental Characteristics: Same as Randomly Acquired Characteristics.

Acid Etching: A process wherein a gooey substance in the form of a textured pattern is applied to selected areas of a mold surface, after which the mold is dipped in an acid bath that etches the pattern into the portion of mold surface not protected with the gooey substance. Acid-etched patterns are unique to a specific mold.

Adhesive Lifter: Any clear or opaque material coated with an adhesive substance that is used for the purpose of lifting impressions. There are adhesive lifters made specifically for lifting footwear impressions and those created for fingerprint lifting but used by some to lift footwear impressions as well.

Air Bubble: A globule of air trapped within a solid material such as a shoe sole. Air bubbles found in polyurethane shoes will typically have a glossy surface.

Ambient Light: The available or existing light that surrounds an object.

Anatomic: Relating to the shape of the body or parts of the body. As it relates to the foot, the natural shape of the foot.

Arch Area: The area of the sole of the shoe immediately below the longitudinal arch of the foot.

Athletic Shoes: Any of a number of shoes used for a variety of athletic or casual athletic activities, most commonly including running, walking, basketball, tennis, and other sport footwear.

Ball: The part of the foot just behind the large toe, beneath the intersection of the first metatarsal phalangeal joint.

Bio-Foam®: A commercial product composed of collapsible foam used primarily for the recording of anatomical impressions of a foot. It is sometimes used to take known three-dimensional impressions of shoe soles.

Biscuits of Rubber: Premeasured pieces of soling compound that are placed in molds and pressed into the shape of a shoe sole or heel in a compression molding machine. Also known as Preforms.

Blades: Thin pieces of metal in molds that result in thin grooves or imitated sipes. Also, a sharp replaceable blade that is used in a siping machine to cut genuine sipes into existing molded soles.

Blocker: An oversized outsole made of one or more outsole and/or midsole components that is later cut or trimmed to size.

Blowing Agent: A soling compound material used to produce gas by chemical or thermal action, resulting in the expansion of a molded outsole to a size larger than its mold cavity. The expansion occurs the instant the mold opens.

Blunt Force Pattern Injury: A direct and forceful injury (contusion) to the skin by a blunt object such as a shoe that results in the replication of a portion of that object's pattern because of subcutaneous hemorrhaging.

Brannock Device®: The registered name of a foot-measuring device that can measure the length of the foot in two ways and can provide an estimate of the foot width. There are many similarly designed devices now produced by other companies.

CAD/CAM: Acronym for Computer-Aided Design/Computer-Aided Manufacture.

Calendering: A process where a soft blended unvulcanized rubber compound passes between a series of large steel calender rollers. The final calender roller contains the outsole design that is impressed into the soft rubber and later cut into outsoles.

Cast: The result of filling a three-dimensional impression with an appropriate liquid casting material that hardens and retains the impression's features.

Casting Material: Dental stone, sulfur, snow print plaster, or other suitable materials specifically used to accurately recover (cast) three-dimensional impressions.

Characteristics: When pertaining to footwear examination, this is a general term that refers to the features of the outsole included in a particular examination, such as the overall design and dimension, general and specific wear, specific mold features such as texture, and randomly acquired characteristics.

Chart Board: A solid laminated board, also called mounting board or Crescent board. This board is available in various qualities with a white lamination on at least one side. In more expensive forms, it will have a white lamination on both sides. It is used in the art world as well as to mount photographs. In forensics, it is used to provide a firm and smooth backing when obtaining known inked tire impressions or inked barefoot impressions. It should not be confused with foam core board.

Classic Outsole Design: An outsole design that has continued to be made by a manufacturer for many years due to its popularity.

Class Characteristic: A manufactured feature of design and/or dimension that is shared by a group of two or more shoes. The outsole design and a foxing strip are examples of class characteristics. Agreement of class characteristics between a crime scene impression and a shoe does not establish identification but reduces the number of shoes that could have made an impression by allowing for exclusion of shoes having different class characteristics.

Clicker: A hydraulic machine that forces a steel die through outsole and/or midsole materials in a cookie-cutter fashion to cut outsoles from sheet stock, from calendered material, or from oversized outsole blocker units.

Coating: The process of completely coloring a snow impression with Krylon Gray body primer or Snow Print Wax to allow for better photography.

Cold Cement Process: A general term in the footwear industry to describe any cold bonding adhesive process for attaching outsole and midsole components and/or outsoles to uppers.

Color Bleeding: The inadvertent crossing or bleeding of a molding compound of one color into an adjacent color during compression molding.

Compression Molding: A very common method for producing outsoles. The premeasured outsole compound, referred to as a preform or biscuit of rubber, is placed into an open mold, which is then closed. Through heat and pressure, the biscuit of rubber is pressed into an outsole. Soles made in this manner are often referred to as "pressed soles" or "compression molded soles."

Confirmation Bias: The tendency to look for features in the examination that support one's preconceptions and possibly ignore other features.

Consistency: The amount of water in the powder-to-water ratio (P:W) recommended for mixing a gypsum product such as dental stone. In this ratio, the powder will always be 100. As an example, a dental stone having a P:W ratio of 100/30 has a consistency of 30.

Contusion: The product of a blunt force trauma that has caused subcutaneous hemorrhaging (bruising) and the associated discoloration beneath the skin. See Blunt Force Pattern Injury.

Correspond: A word often used to describe agreement of class and other characteristics in the context that supports an item of footwear is capable of having produced those respective features in the crime scene impression.

Counterfeit Shoe Outsoles: Outsoles made that violate another shoe company's trademark and patent rights.

Degree of Wear: The extent to which a shoe outsole has been worn away or eroded. Examples of degree of wear range from a shoe outsole that is in a new or relatively unworn condition to those that have extensive wear. The degree of wear continues to change as a shoe outsole continues to be worn.

Dental Stone: A gypsum product made for the dental industry, generally having a dry compressive strength of 8000 psi or higher. Dental stone is commonly used throughout the world to cast footwear impressions.

Design: See Outsole Design.

Design Element: Single components of a footwear outsole distinguished by their shape features, such as a circle, parallel line, herringbone, wave, lug, and so forth. The specific shape and size of a design element may or may not change as it is graded through the size range.

Design/Size Relationship: The tendency for an outsole design to have more design elements, larger design elements, or a combination of both, as the overall outsole dimensions increase throughout the size range.

Die Cut: A process where outsoles are created or cut to size by forcing a sharp steel die through preformed outsole material with the assistance of a hydraulic clicker machine.

Difference: A characteristic or feature that is so clear and significant that it, in itself, can be attributed to a different shoe and thus indicates nonidentity. Usually a difference will present itself in an examination as a different class characteristic, such as the specific design or specific physical size of that design. It is noted that normal variations in the impression process, the absence of cuts evident in a questioned impression that appear on the shoe, or the additional advancement of wear over time do not constitute a comparative difference as defined here.

Dimension: The physical size of a shoe outsole or outsole component.

Direct Attach: A manufacturing process where a lasted shoe upper is lowered onto a sole design plate, after which the mold cavity is closed and the midsole and/or outsole material is injected directly onto the upper. This term also applies to *open pour polyurethane molding* where the lasted shoe upper is lowered into a mold containing a poured polyurethane outsole, directly attaching them together.

Dissimilarity: A possible difference that may or may not be attributed to a different shoe.

Distortion: An unclear or inaccurate representation of the shoe outsole in the impression it makes due to anything that prevents or interferes with a true recording or retention of its characteristics during the impression-making process.

Dry Casting: A method of sifting three thin layers of dental stone over a snow impression to protect the detail, followed by the addition of a dental stone mixture. The process works in snow that contains sufficient moisture. Dry casting relies on absorption of moisture into the first sifted layer from the underlying snow.

Dry Origin Impressions: Impressions formed under dry conditions such as occur during the transfer of dry dust and dry residue to a dry two-dimensional substrate.

Electrical Discharge Machine (EDM): A machine used to produce molds by running electric current through a designed electrode that burns away selective areas of metal, subsequently transferring that design into the metal.

Electrostatic Detection Apparatus (ESDA): An instrument used primarily to detect indented writing on documents. This instrument can also be used to detect indented footwear impressions on paper items in a small percentage of cases.

Electrostatic Dustprint Lifter: An instrument that utilizes an electrostatic charge as a means of transferring dry origin footwear impressions from a substrate to a piece of black lifting film. Also referred to as Electrostatic Lifting Apparatus (ESLA), Dustmark Lifting Kit (DLK), and other names.

Electrostatic Lifting: The process of using an electrostatic dustprint lifter to transfer dry origin impressions from the substrate to a black film.

Elimination Prints: Documentation of the footwear of first responders, the victim(s), and others who potentially innocently contributed footwear impressions at the scene. These are obtained so the footwear of those individuals can be excluded from impressions recovered from the scene and, in doing so, allow for focus on the unaccounted for impressions that may be those of the perpetrator. Originally obtained in the form of hard copy test prints known as elimination prints, most outsole elimination information is now obtained with a digital camera.

Enhancement: Improving the ability to visualize an impression through physical, photographic, digital, or chemical methods.

Ethylene Vinyl Acetate (EVA): A soling compound often produced in an expanded form.

Exclusion: The conclusion of an examiner without reservation that a shoe did not and could not have produced an impression.

Exemplar: Another name used for known test impressions of a shoe or foot.

Expanded Soling Materials: In compression molding, a sole that is produced with a special blown rubber compound that results in the expansion of the outsole to a size larger than its mold cavity. The outsoles literally burst and expand the instant the mold opens. Also known as blown rubber.

Examination Quality Photographs: High quality photographs taken from directly over an impression in a prescribed manner with a scale. These are taken and used specifically to capture a high degree of detail and to permit the enlargement of the crime scene impression to its natural size.

Exemplar: See Known Test Impression.

Feathering: See Schallamach pattern.

Fixative: Substance that stabilizes blood prior to enhancement so it is not degraded during the application of a reagent. The most commonly used fixative is 5-sulphosalicylic acid. Also refers to any product that will stabilize a three-dimensional impression prior to casting.

Flash: Small amounts of outsole rubber that have seeped between mold components during the footwear molding process.

Flat Foot: A foot with a dropped or unsupportive longitudinal arch.

Flex Grooves: A general term to describe larger grooves sometimes included in an outsole design that allow the outsole to flex more easily. They are most common across the forefoot region of the outsole.

Foot Impression: Impressions made by the naked or sock-clad human foot.

Foot Size: The actual dimensions of the foot that define its length and width. Foot size is measured with devices like the Brannock Device®, Ritz Stick®, or other devices that in turn convert the foot size to a suggested shoe size.

Foot Stance: Position of the feet while standing or walking. The feet may be turned inward or outward.

Footwear: Any apparel worn on the foot, such as shoes, boots, sandals, slippers, sneakers, etc.

Footwear Impression: A general term used to describe the result of contact of the outsole of a shoe that produces a two-dimensional or three-dimensional replication of that outsole on a surface. Also referred to as a footwear mark or shoeprint when referring to two-dimensional impressions.

Forensic Light Source: A filtered light source that may be fixed or tunable to a variety of spectral ranges. Also referred to as an **Alternate Light Source (ALS)**.

Foxing Strip: A strip of rubber that is usually hand-wrapped around the lower part of some shoes to cover the gap or seam that exists between the upper and the outsole.

Fragmented Impression: A very small and isolated impression made by footwear that contains insufficient information to associate with a specific design or brand of footwear. Examples would be very small and isolated portions of herringbone, parallel lines, hexagonal shapes, etc.

Full Impression: A two- or three-dimensional impression that represents all, or nearly all, of the outsole.

Gelatin Lifter: A tacky gelatin material applied to a pliable backing that can be used to lift two-dimensional impressions.

General Crime Scene Photographs: Photographs taken at a crime scene to document the position of evidentiary objects such as footwear impressions.

General Sole Design: A looser definition of a footwear outsole design, such as a herringbone or wave pattern, a parallel line pattern, a square or diamond-shaped pattern, a lugged sole pattern, a textured pattern, and so forth. Different brands and styles of footwear may share similar general sole designs.

General Wear: The gradual changes to the outsole as a shoe is worn that are due to the erosive effects of friction between it and the substrate that result from both vertical and horizontal forces. General wear ranges from outsoles that are in a new and unworn condition, to those with moderate wear, to those that have extreme wear. Ragged edges of holes or tears that have resulted from extreme wear, as well as abrasion patterns, although products of wearing a shoe, involve random events and are considered randomly acquired characteristics and not general wear characteristics.

Grading: The gradual increase or decrease in physical size and design content throughout the size range that a manufacturer uses for each size they produce, typically achieved with computer systems that use algorithms. In general, the standard throughout the industry for each half size will result in an approximate heel to toe measurement change of 4.23 mm in the length of an outsole.

Hand Milled: In the mold making operation, the process of guiding the milling of metal by hand during the manufacture of a mold, as opposed to the milling operation being directed by a computer.

Handiprint®: A quality white adhesive material used to lift powdered fingerprints and shoe prints and also used with fingerprint powder to make known impressions of footwear.

Heel Counter: A reinforcement or stiffener placed between the outside and the lining at the back of the shoe to prevent the upper from collapsing around the heel.

Highlighting: The process of coloring the high points of a snow impression with Krylon Gray body primer or Snow Print Wax to add contrast for photography.

Holes: The result of extreme erosion and degradation of a shoe outsole in isolated areas that has resulted in complete removal of the outsole or outsole/midsole combination, often accompanied by randomly formed irregular edges.

Horizontal Forces: Forces that occur laterally in regard to movement of the outsole in relation to the substrate. Different horizontal forces that occur because of different activities, especially athletic activities, can affect the position of general wear.

Identicator®: A product that combines a chemically soaked pad containing a clear solution that turns black when it comes into contact with chemically treated paper, used to produce known ink quality footwear impressions without ink. Often referred to as an inkless method of producing known footwear impressions, the shoe first steps on the pad and then onto the treated paper to produce an instant black impression much like an ink impression.

Identification: The highest degree of association expressed by a footwear impression examiner. When reaching a conclusion of identification, an examiner is opining the known footwear was the source of and produced the crime scene impression.

Identifying Characteristics: See **Randomly Acquired Characteristics**.

Impression: The product of direct physical contact of an item such as a shoe with a substrate, resulting in a two- or three-dimensional transfer of the characteristics of that item.

Individual Characteristics: See **Randomly Acquired Characteristics**.

Industry Open Mold: A mold that can be used by a third-party outsole manufacturer to produce outsoles for more than one shoe brand. Open industry molds are often accompanied by rectangular, oval, or circular logo areas that accommodate production of outsoles from the same molds accompanied by switching of the logo names. In some cases, the logo area remains defined on the outsole but contains no name. The presence of this logo area on a shoe, in itself, does not mean the mold is an industry open mold, but merely suggests the possibility. The absence of this defined area or a logo on an outsole does not mean the molds are not industry open molds.

Injection Molding: A manufacturing method where the sole and/or midsole is made by forcing (injecting) a heat softened or mixed liquid material into a closed mold through a small channel or port. Injection molded outsoles can be molded individually as unit soles or directly onto the shoe upper as direct attached soles.

Insole: A cushioned liner that occupies the inner surface of a shoe where the foot rests and is placed there for comfort and/or protection. The insole may or may not be removable. Also referred to as an inner sole or liner.

Known Impression: See **Test Impression**.

Known Shoe: A shoe whose owner or source is known that is compared to a crime scene shoe impression.

Label (manufacturer's sizing label): A cloth, paper tag, or stamp placed on the tongue or other inner surface of the shoe that contains information including but not limited to the manufacturer's name, shoe size, country of manufacturer, style number, dating information, barcodes, etc.

Latent Impression: An impression not readily visible to the naked eye.

Lateral: Refers to the outer side of the foot or shoe.

Last: A form made of wood, metal, or synthetic material that approximates the shape of a foot. The upper of the footwear is stretched over a last that holds its specific shape and size throughout the manufacturing process. The size on a manufacturer's label is directly related to the size of the last. Lasts may be straight or curved or somewhere in between.

Lift: A transfer of an impression from its original surface to a film or gel or other material for recovering it from the crime scene and usually providing better contrast.

Lividity: The settling of blood into the lowermost blood vessels after death when circulation has ceased due to gravitational forces.

Logo: A name, design, or pattern that is a trademark of a manufacturer. Logos may appear on the shoe upper and/or on the outsole.

Logo Area: The area of the shoe most commonly in the center of the outsole where a company name or trademark is placed. In some cases, this area may be defined in a shoe sole in the form of a rectangle, circle, or oval, yet not contain an actual symbol or name.

Manufacturer's Shoe Size: The shoe size that a particular manufacturer has assigned to a particular shoe as indicated on the shoe and/or shoebox.

Manufacturing Defect: Damage, flaws, or other unplanned characteristics on the shoe outsole that have occurred during manufacturing. Many of these are randomly acquired. Examples would be some air bubbles, nicks, or other damage to unvulcanized soles, mold damage, etc.

Manufacturing Variable: Variations that occur during the manufacturing process that do not appear on all of the shoe outsoles of a particular design and size but appear on more than one. Examples would be the precise positioning of foxing strips, the precise cutting of die cut or Wellman cut soles, the precise positioning of stitching that is added to the bottom of some soles, etc.

Medial: Refers to the inner side of the foot or shoe.

Microcellular Soling Compound: Soling compound that is not solid and has a density of less than 1. Outsoles that are microcellular have small closed cells that make the material lighter and shock absorbent. The vast majority of microcellular outsoles are molded in exact sizes that do not change; however, some microcellular outsole compounds actually expand to a size larger than the mold in which they were pressed (see **Blown Rubber**).

Midsole: A component positioned between the upper and the outsole on some shoes to provide cushioning and/or support. Not all footwear have a midsole.

Mikrosil™: A silicone-based casting material commonly used to lift footwear and fingerprint impressions that have been treated with fingerprint powder.

MikroTrack™: A soft reusable material designed for producing three-dimensional known impressions of footwear.

Mold (Outsole Mold): A hollow cavity containing the design of the outsole and possibly the midsole. Molds for footwear may have a sole plate and top plate, or may be more complex with more parts as used for direct attach injection systems.

Mold Characteristic: A general term often used to refer to a feature that relates to a specific mold such as texture or how a specific portion of the design interfaces with the perimeter or in relation to other design elements.

Mold Dams: Very thin vertically oriented metal blades used in a mold as borders to separate areas of design, often for separating different color soling compounds during the molding process. Mold dams result in a small groove in the outsole.

Mold Defect: Damage to a mold such as a nick, dent, or scratch. A molded outsole will reflect these characteristics as raised areas on the outsole as the damage area fills with outsole material during molding.

Mold Warp: A term used to define the twisting or warping of a solid compression molded outsole as a result of it being stacked on top of or beneath other outsoles while still soft and hot immediately after being removed from a compression mold. When the outsole cools, it may retain some of the twisted or uneven features. In some cases, this unevenness may be evident in two-dimensional impressions during the first days or weeks of wear.

Natural Crepe Rubber: A crude form of coagulated natural rubber having a crinkled or knobby texture.

Natural Rubber: A natural product derived from latex that is tapped from rubber trees.

Negative Impression: An impression that has resulted from a shoe outsole removing a substance from a two-dimensional substrate.

Oblique Lighting: Illumination from a light source that is at a low angle of incidence, or even parallel, to the surface of the item. Also known as side lighting.

Open-Pour Molding: A method of making outsoles by pouring polyurethane into an open mold cavity and then closing the mold. Both unit soles and direct-attach soles can be made utilizing this process.

Outsole/Sole: The bottom portion of the shoe that makes contact with the substrate and provides traction and durability that also produces an impression.

Outsole Design/Sole Design: A term used to describe a specific pattern or arrangement of design elements on the bottom of an outsole, often associated with a manufacturer and/or having a name and/or style number.

Oversize Outsoles: Solid or microcellular outsoles that are intentionally produced larger than their final size and must later be die cut and/or trimmed prior to or after assembly to the shoe upper. Some manufacturers refer to oversize soles as blocker unit soles.

Partial Impression: An impression that does not represent the majority of the shoe outsole.

Patent impression: An impression visible to the naked eye.

Pattern: See **Outsole Design**.

Physical Size and Shape (of design): The specific dimensions of a design, noting that these are distinguishable in various ways as they are graded throughout the size range. The terms physical size and shape do not refer to the manufacturer's shoe size such as size 9 or size 10.

Plasters: A very general term that includes all gypsum casting materials. Also used to define the softer gypsum materials having lower compressive strengths.

Plaster of Paris: A gypsum casting material produced by heating crushed gypsum in an open oven at high temperatures. Although used for years as a casting material for footwear impressions, it is no longer regarded as an acceptable material due to its softness.

Polyurethane (PU): A reaction polymer used in both the outsoles and midsoles of shoes. Its microcellular characteristics are used to produce a variety of microcellular shock absorbing and lightweight midsoles ranging to more solid and durable outsoles.

Polyvinylsiloxanes: Condensation silicones that come in a variety of forms produced for the dental industry, but also used in forensics for producing known three-dimensional impressions and for recovery of powdered impressions and tool marks.

Polyvinyl Chloride (PVC): A thermoplastic polymer used in shoe outsoles.

Position and Orientation of Wear: The location and direction of an area of erosion on a shoe outsole.

Position of Wear: The location or locations of visible general wear on an outsole. An area of erosion on a footwear outsole that stands out against areas of less erosion. Examples of position of wear include wear along the medial edge of the shoe outsole, wear on the outside of the heel, or a small area of worn stippling on a footwear outsole.

Positive Impression: A two-dimensional transfer impression that represents the portion of the outsole that made contact with the substrate.

Pressed sole: A sole formed (pressed) in a compression mold.

Printer's Ink: A highly toned oil-based black ink. Printer's inks that set up in 2 to 4 hours are often used in the production of known shoe, barefoot, or tire impressions.

Qualitative: Refers to the clarity and detail present in an impression.

Quantitative: Refers to the amount of information in an impression such as its size and completeness.

Questioned Impression: An impression of a shoe recovered from a crime scene whose origin is unknown.

Randomly Acquired Characteristics (RACs): Features that have occurred unsystematically and unintentionally on a footwear outsole during its use. Examples of randomly acquired characteristics include cuts, scratches, tears, stone holds, abrasions, and the acquisition of debris stuck to or in the outsole. The position, orientation, size, and shape of randomly acquired characteristics contribute to the uniqueness of a shoe outsole. Randomly acquired characteristics are essential for an identification of a particular shoe as the source of an impression. (Synonymous with accidental, individual or individualizing, and identifying characteristics.)

Release Agent: A product applied to a three-dimensional impression prior to casting to prevent soil from adhering to the cast.

Retro Design: An outsole design that has been reissued by a manufacturer, often years after the original design was produced. The term has both specific meaning, such as in the case where the exact same molds are used to produce the retro design and a looser meaning when a new set of molds is made to mimic a prior or generic version of a prior design.

Ritz Stick®: Device for measuring foot length and width. The Ritz stick for measuring foot sizes has been replaced with the Brannock Device and other similar devices.

Roller Transport Film: A seven-mil ESTAR base nonsilver gelatin-coated film designed to clean roller transport mechanisms in photo-processing machines. Many examiners use fingerprint powder on outsoles to produce known impressions on this clear film. This film was once produced by Kodak but is no longer commonly available.

Rough Rounder Machine: A machine that cuts away excess solid rubber soling to conform to the outline of the shoe upper. Used in cases involving the use of solid rubber oversized outsoles.

Schallamach Pattern: Microscopic abrasion pattern that develops as ridges on rubber outsoles because of repeated frictional forces. These patterns are very similar in their size and appearance to skin friction ridges and are highly individual. The pattern continues to change as it is affected by additional abrasions to the outsole. Schallamach patterns are randomly acquired characteristics. The name Schallamach originates from the researcher of the same name. Also known as **Feathering**.

Shoe Perimeter: The outer border or edge of the shoe sole that defines an outsole's physical size and shape. Some borders may be solid and part of the molded design, some may be composed of an added foxing strip, and others will have an open-ended design that terminates at the perimeter.

Shoe Size: The size a manufacturer designates for an item of footwear to accommodate a foot of a certain dimension. Shoe sizes are placed on a label within the footwear and/or on the shoe sole and shoebox. Due to various shoe construction types and styles, there is not a strict dimensional relationship between a manufacturer's shoe size and the length and width of an outsole.

Shoe Size Grading: The gradual increase or decrease in physical size and content that a manufacturer chooses for each half size of a particular design. In general, each larger half size will result in an approximate increase of 4.23 mm in the heel-to-toe length of the outsole.

Side-by-Side: A comparison method performed by placing two or more objects next to one another, sometimes assisted with a divider or caliper and low magnification.

Similar: An observation that an impression shares a general likeness with a known shoe outsole. Similar should not be equated with correspondence and does not infer the sole designs in an impression are the same as a particular shoe outsole.

Sipes: Thin slits cut into a shoe outsole to create better traction. True sipes are those that are cut into a shoe outsole after it is molded and require the shoe sole to flex before the sipes open. Imitation sipes are molded because of a thin metal blade in the mold design and are always open. Sipes were named after John Sipe.

Snow Print Plaster™ (aka Snow Stone): A modified plaster product that is first sifted over a snow impression followed by a mixture of the plaster and water poured on top. It works in all types and conditions of snow and sets quickly.

Snow Print Powder™: A bright orange powder that can be used with a fingerprint brush to colorize heavy slushy or frozen snow impressions, providing better contrast for photography.

Snow Print Wax™ or Snow Impression Wax™: Bright red or brown aerosol waxes, used to both highlight snow impressions to create contrast in photography and completely coat the surface of snow impressions prior to casting.

Specific Location of Wear: A defined area of erosion on a shoe outsole. An example of a specific location of wear would be a small area where texture on a shoe outsole was worn away. Specific locations of wear may allow for a greater level of discrimination or association between questioned impressions and known shoes.

Specific Sole Design: The precise arrangement of design elements of part or all of a shoe outsole. The precise size/shape and arrangement of design elements in an outsole of one style and manufacturer's size are normally distinguishable from other sizes of the same manufacturer's style. See **Design/Size Relationship**.

Spotting: The process of positioning an oversized outsole onto a shoe upper so the shoe upper falls entirely within the perimeter of the outsole.

Sprue: A piece of material that remains attached to the rear or bottom of the outsole after injection molding that represents the passageway where the molding material was injected into the mold. It will be trimmed away in the finishing process.

Stippling: A pattern hand struck into the surface of a mold using a steel die containing a selected design with the use of a hammer. The tip of the die is small and requires numerous, often overlapping, strikes. These multiple strikes produce a textured pattern or fine design on the surface of the mold that is transferred to all outsoles that come from that mold. Because of the random manner in which hand-struck stippling is applied, its pattern is unique to each specific mold.

Stitching: Characteristic marks left by a tool used when joining the soft unvulcanized rubber components of a shoe prior to vulcanization in an autoclave. These are occasionally found on Wellman produced outsoles and shoes made with unvulcanized parts. Stitching also refers to the application of thread through the bottom (bottom stitched) or side (side stitched) of an outsole to fasten the outsole to the upper.

Stitching Wheel: A circular wheel with raised ribs that is rolled over parts of unvulcanized rubber components to secure them prior to their vulcanization in an autoclave. The stitching wheel will leave linear indentations in the rubber.

Stone Hold: A stone held in a groove or other recessed area of a shoe outsole that may or may not be replicated in an impression.

Styrene Butadiene Rubber (SBR): A rubber compound commonly used in the compression-molding process.

Subcutaneous: Beneath the skin. Subcutaneous hemorrhaging is the bleeding from blood vessels beneath the skin.

Substrate: The surface upon which a shoe makes contact, normally composed of wood, tile, concrete, asphalt, carpet, soil, sand, snow, and the like. The term also extends to any other surface on which a shoe may contact and leave its mark, such as a door that was kicked, a piece of paper on the floor, skin, etc.

Sulfur: A yellow elemental substance available in powder or prill forms that can be melted and used for casting snow impressions.

Sulfur Cement: A black reinforced modified sulfur material, available in flake form that is a safer, stronger alternative to using pure yellow sulfur for casting snow impressions.

Superimposition: A comparison method performed by placing one object over the other. In footwear examinations, this normally involves the use of a transparent version of a known test impression of a shoe that is placed over the crime scene impression to assist in the comparison process.

Synthetic Rubber: Any artificial elastomer that simulates the qualities of natural rubber.

Tears: Fractures that have occurred in shoe outsoles that reflect irregular edges. The features of tears are randomly acquired characteristics.

Test Impression: An impression made from a shoe or foot used as an aid for comparison purposes. (Synonymous with known impression, or exemplar.)

Texture: A rough surface or shallow design added to surfaces of a mold through the process of acid etching or hand-struck stippling. This texture will be transferred to each outsole during the molding process. Texture is unique to a specific mold to which it is applied.

Three-Dimensional Impression: An impression made on given substrates such as soil, sand, snow, and mud that contains depth in addition to length and width.

Toe Box: The portion of the shoe upper that surrounds the toes.

Toe Bumper Guard: A thick strip of rubber that, in some shoe designs, is placed around the front perimeter of the shoe surrounding the toe area.

Transfer Impression: Any impression made as a result of a shoe outsole acquiring dust, residue, blood, mud, or other materials, followed by the deposition or transfer of that same material back to the substrate in the form of a two-dimensional impression.

Two-Dimensional Impression: An impression on a firm, nongivable subtrate, often called a shoeprint or shoe mark.

Unit Sole: An individual sole or heel/sole unit that must be glued and/or stitched to the upper.

Upper: The area of the shoe that encloses the foot exclusive of the midsole and outsole.

Variations: Slight deviations that exist between successive impressions of a shoe including those produced at crime scenes and those produced as known test impressions. Variations are normal and unavoidable.

Vertical Forces: Those transmitted from the wearer down through the shoe as related to things like body weight and foot morphology.

Vulcanization: An irreversible process during which a rubber compound is heated under pressure, resulting in a chemical change transforming it from a soft, tacky substance to a tough, hard rubber.

Wear: The effects of erosion of the surfaces of a footwear outsole caused by frictional and abrasive forces between the outsole and the ground.

Wear Characteristics: General term for any change on the surface of the outsole that is observable in the impression and/or known shoe and that occurred due to the erosion of portions of the surface of that outsole.

Wellman Outsole Cutting Machine: A machine used to cut outsoles from soft unvulcanized calendered outsole material. The machine is controlled by an operator and utilizes a small replaceable knife blade that rapidly runs around a template to cut the soling material.

Wet Origin Impression: Impressions formed in the presence of moisture either from the shoe or the substrate. Some examples would be impressions made by or in wet residue, blood, and mud.

Bibliography

A method of reproducing footmarks, etc. from certain objects, *Police J.*, 9, 1936, Philip Allan & Co. LTD, London.

Abbott, J. R., *Footwear Evidence*. Germann, A. C., Ed. Charles C Thomas, Springfield, IL, 1964.

Abbott, J. R., Reproduction of footprints, *RCMP Quarterly*, 9(2):186–193, 1941.

Abbott, J. R., Reproduction and identification of impressions and marks, *RCMP Gazette*, 3–8, August 1952.

Adair, T., Casting two-dimensional bloody shoe prints from concrete, fabric and human skin, *I.A.B.P.A. News*, March 2005.

Adair, T., Electrostatic dust lifting on metallic surfaces using automotive window tinting film as a nonconductive barrier, *JFI*, 55(5), 2005.

Adair, T., Experimental detection of blood under painted surfaces, *Int. Assoc. Bloodstain Pattern Analysts*, Mar. 2006, 12–19.

Adair, T., and Tewes, R., Strengthening sulfur casts with plasti-dip, *Information Bulletin for Shoe Print/Tool Mark Examiners*, 12(2), August 2006.

Adair, T., Tewes, R., Bellinger, T., and Nicholls, T., Characteristics of snow and their influence on casting methods for impression evidence, *JFI*, 57(6):807–822, 2007.

Adair. T., and Shaw, R., The dry-casting method: a reintroduction to a simple method for casting snow impressions, *JFI*, 57(6):824–831, 2007.

Adair, W., LeMay, J., McDonald, A., Shaw, R., and Tewes, R., The Mount Bierstadt study: an experiment in unique damage formation in footwear, *JFI*, 57(2):199–205, 2007.

Adair, R., and Dobersen, M., Lifting dusty shoe impressions from human skin. a review of experimental research from Colorado, *JFI*, 56(3), 2006.

Adam, J., and Adam, J. C., *Criminal Investigation: A Practical Handbook for Magistrates, Police Officers, and Lawyers*, Sweet & Maxwell, Ltd., London, 1924, pp. 483–552. (Translated and adapted from the *System Der Kriminalistik* of Dr. Hans Gross, University of Prague.)

Adelaar, R. S., The practical biomechanics of running, *Amer. J. Sport Med.*, 14:6, 1986.

Albrecht, H., Über die Chemiluminescenz des Aminophthalsäurehydrazids (On the chemiluminescence of aminophthalic acid hydrazide), *Zeitschrift Physik. Chem.*, 136:321–330, 1928.

Allen, J. W., Making plaster casts in snow, *International Criminal Police Review*, 89:171–174, 1955.

American Apparel and Footwear Association, Textile outsoles on footwear: The impact of the 1205 rule changes on your bottom line, updated November 15, 2013.

American Orthopaedic Foot and Ankle Society, The National Shoe Retailers Association, and the Pedorthic Footwear Association, When the Shoe Fits: The Basics of Professional Shoe Fitting, a course manual, 1997.

American Shoemaking Directory, Shoe Trades Publishing Co., Cambridge, MA, 1996 (published annually).

Andriacchi, T. P., Ogle, J. A., and Galante, J. O., Walking speed as a basis for normal and abnormal gait measurements, *J. Biomechan.*, 10:261–268, 1977.

Anonymous, An electrostatic method for lifting footprints, *International Criminal Police Review*, 272:287–292, 1973.

Anusavice, K. J., *Phillip's Science of Dental Materials*, Elsevier Science, St. Louis, MO, 2003, Chap. 10.

Ashley, W., Shoe and tyre impression evidence within Australian state and territory jurisdictions, presented at the International Symposium on the Forensic Aspects of Footwear and Tire Impression Evidence, FBI Academy, Quantico, VA, June 27–July 1, 1994.

Ashley, W., What shoe was that? The use of computerized image database to assist in identification, *Foren. Sci. Int.,* 82(1):1–5, 1996.

Aspegren, B., Palmgren, T., and Carllson, K., Identification of prints from stockinged feet, Swedish National Police College, February 1997.

Baker, H., Marsh, N., and Quinones, I., Photography of faded or concealed bruises on human skin, *JFI,* 63(1), 2013.

Bandey, H., Footwear mark recovery, presentation before the Scientific Working Group for Shoe Print and Tire Track Evidence (SWGTREAD), March 2010.

Bandey, H., and Bleay, S., Fingerprint and Footwear Forensics Newsletter, Home Office Scientific Development Branch, Hertfordshire, UK, February 2010, Publication No. 6/10.

Banks, R., and Hamburg, C., Deciphering the symbols and codes on footwear labels, presented at the Pattern and Impression Symposium, Clearwater, FL, 2012.

Barnett, C. H., Bowden, R. E., and Napier, J. R., Shoe wear as a means of analyzing abnormal gait in males, *Annals of Physical Medicine,* 3, October 1956.

Bassett, T., Shoe dunnit: Burglars being nabbed by new forensic evidence found in their footprints, www.mirror.co.uk, April 7, 2015.

Beaudoin, A., New technique for revealing latent fingerprints on wet, porous surfaces: Oil Red O. *J. Foren. Ident.,* 54(4):413–421, 2004.

Beecroft, W., Enhancement of physical develop prints, *RCMP Gazette,* 51(2):17, 1989.

Beheim, C. W., and Wolfe, J. R., The use of Luminol for visualizing latent footwear impressions during crime-scene investigations, presented at the International Symposium on the Forensic Aspects of Footwear and Tire Impression Evidence, FBI Academy, Quantico, VA, June 27–July 1, 1994.

Belkin, R., and Korukhov, Yu., *Fundamentals of Criminalistics,* USSR English Translation by Progress Publishers, 1986, pp. 65–66.

Belser, Ch., Ineichen, M., and Pfefferli, P., Evaluation of the ISAS system after two years of practical experience in forensic police work, *Foren. Sci. Int.,* 82(1):53–58, 1996.

Benedict, I., Corke, E., Smith, R., Maynard, P., Curran, J., Buckleton, J., and Roux, C., Geographical variation of shoeprint comparison class correspondences, *Sci. Justice,* 2014.

Bilo, R. A. C., Oranje, A. P., Shwayder, T., and Hobbs, C. J., *Cutaneous Manifestations of Child Abuse and Their Differential Diagnosis: Blunt Force Trauma,* Springer, Heidelberg, 2013, pp. 41–42.

Bily, C., and Maldonado, H., The application of Luminol to bloodstains concealed by multiple layers of paint. *J. Foren. Ident.,* 56(6):896–905, 2006.

Birkett, J., Variations in Adidas 'Kick' and related soles, MPFSL Report #34, Metropolitan Police Forensic Science Laboratory, June 1983.

Birkett, J., Scientific scene linking, *J. Forensic Science Society,* 29(4):271–284, 1989.

Bischoff, M. A., *La Police Scientifique* (translated from French), Payot, Paris, 1938, pp. 72–81.

Black, J. P., An interesting case involving footwear distribution information, *JFI,* 55(4), 2005.

Bleay, W., Bandey, H., Black, M., and Sears, V., The gelatin lifting process: an evaluation of its effectiveness in the recovery of latent fingerprints, *JFI,* 61(6), 2011.

Blitzer, H., Hammer, R., and Jacobia, J., Effect of photographic technology on quality of examination of footwear impressions, *JFI,* 57(5):641–657, 2007.

Bodziak, W. J., Back to basics (Douthit, J. D., coordinator), *J. Foren. Ident.,* 47(3), May–June, 1997.

Bodziak, W. J., Evidence photography of shoe and tire impressions, *The Professional Photographer,* 43–44, September 1985.

Bodziak, W. J., *Footwear Impression Evidence: Detection, Recovery, and Examination,* Elsevier Science Publishing Co., New York, 1990.

Bodziak, W. J., The examination of barefoot impression evidence, presented at the First International Conference on Forensic Human Identification in the Millennium, London, 1999.

Bodziak, W. J., *Footwear Impression Evidence: Detection, Recovery, and Examination,* 2nd ed., CRC Press, Boca Raton, FL, 2000.

Bodziak, W. J., Manufactured and acquired sole surface characteristics found on shoe soles, presentations at International Association for Identification meetings, Greensboro, NC, July 1996, and Danvers, MA, July 1997.

Bodziak, W. J., Manufacturing processes for athletic shoe outsoles and their significance in the examination of footwear impression evidence, presentation at American Academy of Forensic Sciences meeting, Anaheim, CA, February 1984.

Bodziak, W. J., Manufacturing processes for athletic shoe outsoles and their significance in the examination of footwear impression evidence, *J. Foren. Sci.*, 31(1):153–176, 1986.

Bodziak, W. J., Shoe and tire impression evidence, *FBI Law Enforcement Bulletin*, 53(7):2–12, 1984 (revised 1986).

Bodziak, W. J., Use of Leuco-crystal violet to enhance shoe prints in blood, *Foren. Sci. Int.*, 82(1):45–52, 1996.

Bodziak, W. J., Traditional conclusions in footwear examinations versus the use of the Bayesian approach and likelihood ratio: A review of a recent UK appellate court decision, *Law, Probability and Risk*, 11:279–287, 2012.

Bodziak, W. J., A final comment, *Law, Probability and Risk*, 11:363–364, 2012.

Bodziak, W., and Hammer, L., An evaluation of dental stone, Traxtone, and Crime-Cast, *JFI*, 56(5), 2006.

Bodziak, W., Hammer, L., Johnson, G., and Schenck, R., Determining the significance of outsole wear characteristics during the forensic examination of footwear impression evidence, *JFI*, 254/62(3), 2012.

Bodziak, W., and Monson, K., Discrimination of individuals based on their barefoot impressions, presentations at the International Association of Forensic Sciences meeting, Vancouver, B.C., August 1987, and American Academy of Forensic Sciences, Las Vegas, NV, February 1989.

Borkowski, K., *Kryminalistyczna Identyfikacja Śladów Stóp*, Centralnego Laboratorium Kryminalistycznego Policji, Warzawa, 2013.

Boyd, F. M., Shoe box and side labeling—A most valuable piece of evidence when shoes are missing, presented at the International Symposium on the Forensic Aspects of Footwear and Tire Impression Evidence, FBI Academy, Quantico, VA, June 27–July 1, 1994.

Brabant, P. R., Developing footwear evidence, *Identification News*, 25(9):14–15, 1975.

Bradford, W. R., Light on the invisible footprint, *Spectrum* (British Science News), 140:1–4, 1976.

Brand, C., *Heaven Knows Who*, Charles Scribner's Sons, New York, 1960.

Bratton, R., Hemaglow, presented at the 82nd Educational Conference of the International Association for Identification, Danvers, MA, July 1997.

Brennan, J. S., Dental stones for casting depressed shoemarks and tyremarks, *J. Forensic Science Society*, 23:275–286, 1983.

Brennan, J. S., The visualization of shoe marks using the electrostatic detection apparatus, *MPFSL Report #10*, Metropolitan Police Forensic Science Laboratory, October 1981.

Bright, J., and Petricevic, S., Recovery of trace DNA and its application to DNA profiling of shoe insoles, *Foren. Sci. Int.*, 145:7–12, 2004.

Brown, K., Bryant, T., and Watkins, M., The forensic application of high dynamic range photography, *JFI*, 60(4):449–459, 2010.

Brooks, J., Identifying and sharing class characteristics of outsole impressions, *JFI*, 56(5), 2006.

Brun-Conti, L., and Stoeffler, S., Homemade gelatin lifters, presented at the International Symposium on the Forensic Aspects of Footwear and Tire Impression Evidence, FBI Academy, Quantico, VA, June 27–July 1, 1994.

Brundage, D. J., Ammonium thiocyanate: a successful technique for dusty footwear impressions, presented at the International Symposium on the Forensic Aspects of Footwear and Tire Impression Evidence, FBI Academy, Quantico, VA, June 27–July 1, 1994.

Brundage, D. J., Current use of 8-hydroxyquinoline for enhancing footwear impressions, presented at the International Symposium on the Forensic Aspects of Footwear and Tire Impression Evidence, FBI Academy, Quantico, VA, June 27–July 1, 1994.

Brundage, D. J., Physical developer: a chemical enhancement technique for footwear impressions, presented at the International Symposium on the Forensic Aspects of Footwear and Tire Impression Evidence, FBI Academy, Quantico, VA, June 27–July 1, 1994.

Burggraff, J. C., The use of forensic photography to record and enhance impression evidence, presented at the International Symposium on the Forensic Aspects of Footwear and Tire Impression Evidence, FBI Academy, Quantico, VA, June 27–July 1, 1994.

Burns, M., Non-weightbearing cast impressions for the construction of orthotic devices, *J. Am. Podiatry Assoc.*, 67:790–795, 1977.

Bulbulian, A. H., A professional look at plaster casts, *FBI Law Enforcement Bulletin*, 34(9):2–7, 1965.

Bullock, J. L., Footwear photographic techniques, *AFTE Journal*, 15(2):91–94, 1983.

BVDA, How to use Hungarian Red, information sheet, http://www.bvda.com/EN/prdctinf/pf_en_hu_red.html

Cantu, A., Silver physical developers for the visualization of latent prints on paper, *Foren. Sci. Rev.*, 13(1):29–64, 2001.

Cairnduff, R., Design, development and evaluation of a model portable cyanoacrylate fuming chamber to develop and enhance shoe impressions on immovable surfaces, Specialist Project Report, Diploma of Applied Sciences, Canberra Institute of Technology, New South Wales Police Service, 1996.

Carlsson, K., A new method for securing impressions in snow, *Crime Laboratory Digest*, 1–4, December 1982.

Carlsson, K., Comparison of lifting shoeprints with gelatin lifter versus with electrostatic method, *Information Bulletin for Shoeprint/Toolmark Examiners*, 4(1):109–120, 1998.

Carlsson, K., Snow Print Plaster, information sheet, Kjell Carlsson Innovation, Sundbyberg, Sweden.

Carlsson, K., and Maehly, A. C., New methods for securing impressions of shoes and tyres on different surfaces, *Int. Criminal Police Rev.*, 299:158–167, 1976.

Cassidy, M. J., *Footwear Identification.* Canadian Government Printing Centre, Quebec, Canada, 1980.

Castle, D., Cinderella analysis—or does the shoe fit? Metropolitan Police Laboratory, London, England, *Contact Magazine*, No. 23, 10/1/95.

Caussé, Sév. *Annals of Public Health and Forensic Medicine*, 1(2):175–189, 1854.

Cavannah, P. R., The biomechanics of lower extremity action in distance running, *Foot and Ankle*, American Foot and Ankle Society, 1987.

Cayton, J. C., Recent footwear identification innovations reviewed, *AFTE J.*, 16(3):123–125, 1984.

Cayton, J. C., Procedure for recovery of flooring with shoeprints, *AFTE J.*, 16(3):119–122, 1984.

Champod, C., Girod, A., and Sjerps, M., The meaning of conclusion in the identification context, presented at the first European Meeting of Forensic Science, Lausanne, Switzerland, September 1997.

Chabert, S., and Girod, A., LCV enhancement of a shoeprint's sequence, presented at the First European Meeting of Forensic Science, Lausanne, Switzerland, September 1997.

Chase, M. T., The making of the Vibram sole: Quabaug's manufacturing process, presented at the International Symposium on the Forensic Aspects of Footwear and Tire Impression Evidence, FBI Academy, Quantico, VA, June 27–July 1, 1994.

Chan, C. W., and Rudins, A., Foot biomechanics during walking and running, *Mayo Clinic Proc.*, 69:448, 1994.

Chee, H. W., and Wilson, S. J., A modified method of plaster casting, *Foren. Sci. Society J.*, 83–84, 1963.

Chen, J., and Donovan, J. A., The relation of Schallamach pattern to rubber properties and wear conditions, *Rubber World*, 211(2), 1984.

Cheskin, M. P., *The Complete Book of Athletic Footwear*, Fairchild Publications, New York, 1987.

Chochól, A., and Świętek, M., Shoe prints on the human body – An analysis of three cases, *Problems of Forensic Sciences*, Institute of Forensic Research, Krakow, Poland, 78:239–247, 2009.

Chochól, A., and Świętek, M., Characteristics of forensic shoe sole databases, *Problems of Forensic Sciences*, 90:164–177, 2012, Institute of Forensic Research, Krakow, Poland.

Chung, J., Enhancement of difficult to capture two-dimensional footwear impressions using the combined effects of overhead lighting and the perspective control lens, *JFI*, 57(5), 2007.

Classification of footprints, *FBI Law Enforcement Bulletin*, September–October, 1971.

Cold weather cast, *FBI Law Enforcement Bulletin*, 31(4):20, 1962.

Colbeck, S., et al., The international classification for seasonal snow on the ground, prepared by the Working Group on Snow Classification and issued by the International Commission on Snow and Ice of the International Association of Hydrology, and the International Glaciological Society, 1985.

Cole, G., Your sneaker is a slipper—wacky tax Wednesday, March 25, 2015, http://www.avalara.com/blog/2015/03/25/your-sneaker-is-a-slipper-wacky-tax-wednesday.

Collins, J., and Jarvis, J., The wrongful conviction of forensic science, *Forensic Science Policy & Management*, 2009.

Cooke, C. W., Comparative analysis (footprint and tire identification), *Identification News*, 29(4):3–6, 1979.

Cooke, C. W., *A Practical Guide to the Basics of Physical Evidence*, Charles C Thomas, Springfield, IL, 1984, pp. 101–136.

Cooke, C. W., Footprint identification, *Fingerprint and Identification Magazine*, 57(6):9–10, 1975.

Cooke, C. W., Footprints and tiretracks, *Identification News*, 31(7):7–10, 1981.

Craig, R. G., *Restorative Dental Materials*, 6th ed., C.V. Mosby Company, St. Louis, 1980.

Craig, C., Hornsby, B., and Riles, M., Evaluation and comparison of the electrostatic dust print lifter and the electrostatic detection apparatus on the development of footwear impressions on paper, *J. For. Sci.*, 51(4):819–826, July 2006.

Creer, K. E., Some applications of an argon ion laser in forensic science, *Foren. Sci. Int.*, 20:179–190, 1982.

Curran, W. J., McGarry, A. L., and Petty, C. S., *Modern Legal Medicine, Psychiatry and Forensic Science*, 1980.

Cushman, B. Q., and Simmons, N. J., A cyanoacrylate fuming method for the development of footwear impressions, *Journal of Forensic Identification*, 412/46(4), 1996.

Davis, R. J., Current perspectives in footwear identification, *Identification News*, 36(10):8–11, 1986.

Davis, R. J., The enhancement of two-dimensional footwear impressions using electrostatic lifting, ESDA and gel lifting, presented at the International Symposium on the Forensic Aspects of Footwear and Tire Impression Evidence, FBI Academy, Quantico, VA, June 27–July 1, 1994.

Davis, R. J., Footwear training seminar, Michigan State Police Training Academy, Lansing, MI, 1985.

Davis, R. J., An intelligence approach to footwear marks and toolmarks, *Journal of the Forensic Science Society*, 21:183–193, 1981.

Davis, R. J., Notes on the use of chemical reagents for footwear-mark enhancement, presented at the Florida Department of Law Enforcement, Tallahassee, FL, 1988.

Davis, R. J., Scientific bureau: electrostatic lifting, *Fingerprint Whorld*, 9(36):114, 1984.

Davis, R. J., A systematic approach to the enhancement of footwear marks, *Canadian Society Forensic Science Journal*, 21(3):98–105, 1988.

Davis, R. J., UK trends in the examination of footwear impression evidence, presented at the International Symposium on the Forensic Aspects of Footwear and Tire Impression Evidence, FBI Academy, Quantico, VA, June 27–July 1, 1994.

Davis, R. J., and Birkett, J., A new footwear-pattern coding scheme, *MPFSL Report No. 48*, Metropolitan Police, London, 1984.

Davis, R. J., and DeHaan, J. D., A survey of men's footwear, *Journal of the Forensic Science Society*, 17(4):271–285, 1977.

Davis, R. J., and Keeley, A., Feathering of footwear, *Science & Justice*, 40:273–276, 2000.

DeBroux., S., McCaul, K., and Shimamoto, S., Infrared photography, http://www.crime-scene-investigator.net/Infrared_Photography_research_paper.pdf, January 2007.

DeHaan, J., Clark, J., Spear, T., Oswalt, R., and Barney, S., Chemical enhancement of fingerprints in blood: an evaluation of methods, effects on DNA, and assessment of chemical hazards, CA Department of Justice, Bureau of Forensic Services, Sacramento, CA.

DeHaan, J. D., Wear and accidental characteristics of men's footwear, presented to the International Association of Forensic Scientists, Zurich, Switzerland, 1975.

DeHaan, J. D., Wear characteristics of men's footwear, presented at International Association of Forensic Science meeting, Vancouver, BC, August 1987.

DeHaan, J. D., Footwear evidence: an update, 1982, unpublished.

The Dictionary of Shoe Industry Terminology, Footwear Industries of America, Philadelphia, PA, R. J. Schacter, Ed., 1986.

Dilbeck, L., Use of Bluestar forensic in lieu of Luminol at crime scenes, *JFI*, 56(5), 2006.

Dinkins, L. S., Development and enhancement of footwear impressions on non-porous surfaces, presented at the International Symposium on the Forensic Aspects of Footwear and Tire Impression Evidence, FBI Academy, Quantico, VA, June 27–July 1, 1994.

Doller, D. W., Interpretations of shoe and tire impressions, presented at the International Symposium on the Forensic Aspects of Footwear and Tire Impression Evidence, FBI Academy, Quantico, VA, June 27–July 1, 1994.

Downey, A. J., and Bone, R. G., The application of protein stains and protein transfer media to the recovery and enhancement of footwear impressions in blood on both porous and non-porous surfaces, presented at the International Symposium on the Forensic Aspects of Footwear and Tire Impression Evidence, FBI Academy, Quantico, VA, June 27–July 1, 1994.

Dovci, J. R., The application of computer graphic technology to tire tread comparisons and expert testimony, presented at the International Symposium on the Forensic Aspects of Footwear and Tire Impression Evidence, FBI Academy, Quantico, VA, June 27–July 1, 1994.

Drexler, S. G., Test impressions of footwear outsoles using biofoam, presented at the International Symposium on the Forensic Aspects of Footwear and Tire Impression Evidence, FBI Academy, Quantico, VA, June 27–July 1, 1994.

Duffy, K., Hammer, L., Fraser, J., and Nic Daéid, N., A study of the variability in footwear impression comparison conclusions, *JFI*, 63(2), 2013.

DuPasquier, E., Hebrard, J., Margot, P., and Ineichen, M., Evaluation and comparison of casting materials in forensic sciences. Applications to tool marks and foot/shoe impressions, *Foren. Sci. Int.*, 82(1):21–31, 1996.

de Puit, M., Koomen, L., Bouwmeester, M., Gijt, M., Rodriquez, C., Wouw, J., and de Haan, F., Use of physical developer for the visualization of latent fingerprints, *JFI*, 61(20), 2011.

Eade, J. F., Frost, footprints and photography, *The Police Journal*, 27(1):27–30, 1954.

Ellis, J., The match game: finding the right shoe for your biomechanics and running gait, *Runners World*, October 1985.

ENSFI Expert Marking Group, Conclusion scale for shoeprint and tool marks examination, *JFI*, 56(2), 2006.

Evett, I. W., Lambert, J. A., and Buckleton, I. S. A Bayesian approach to interpreting footwear marks in forensic casework, *Science & Justice*, 38:241–247, 1998.

Facey, O. E., Hannah, I. D., and Rosen, D., Analysis of the reproducibility and individuality of dynamic pedobarograph images, *Journal of Medical Engineering & Technology*, 17(1):9–15, 1993.

Facey, O. E., Hannah, I. D., and Rosen, D., Shoe wear patterns and pressure distribution under feet and shoes, determined by image analysis, *Journal of Forensic Science Society*, 32(1), 1992.

Farrar, A., Porter, G., and Renshaw, A., Detection of latent bloodstains beneath painted surfaces using reflected infrared photography, *J. Fors. Sci.*, 57(5):1190–1198, 2012.

Farrugia, K., An evaluation of enhancement techniques for footwear impressions made on fabric, PhD Thesis, University of Strathclyde, 2011.

Farrugia, K., Bandey, H., Dawson, L., and Nic Daéid, N., Chemical enhancement of soil based foot-wear impressions on fabric, *Foren. Sci. Int.*, 219:12–28, 2012.

Farrugia, K., Nic Daéid, N., Savage, K., and Bandey, H., Chemical enhancement of footwear impressions in blood on fabric—Part 1: Protein stains, *Science & Justice*, 51:99–109, 2011.

Farrugia, K., Savage, K., Bandey, H., Ciuksza, T., and Nic Daéid, N., Chemical enhancement of footwear impressions in blood on fabric—Part 2: Peroxidase reagents, *Science & Justice*, 51(4):110–121, 2011.

Farrugia, K., Nic Daéid, N., Savage, K., and Bandey, H., Chemical enhancement of footwear impressions in blood on fabric—Part 3: Amino acid staining, *Science & Justice*, 53:8–13, 2013.

Farrugia, K., Savage, K., Bandey, H., and Nic Daéid, N., Chemical enhancement of footwear impressions in blood deposited on fabric—Evaluating the use of alginate casting materials followed by chemical enhancement, *Science & Justice*, 50(4):200–204, 2010.

Farrugia, K. J., Bandey, H. L., Bleay, S., and Nic Daéid, N., Chemical enhancement of footwear impressions in urine on fabric, *Foren. Sci. Int.*, 214(1–3):67–81, 2012.

Fawcett, A. S., The role of the footmark examiner, *Journal of the Forensic Science Society*, 10(4):227–244, 1970.

Federal Bureau of Investigation, *Handbook of Forensic Science*, U.S. Government Printing Office, March 1995.

Federal Rules of Criminal Procedure, Rule 16, December 1, 2013, 26-30 (as printed for the use of The Committee on the Judiciary House of Representatives).

Fertgus, D. A., Ardrox staining for wet footwear tracks, Florida State Division of the International Association for Identification, July–September, 1993.

Fischer, J. F., An aqueous leucocrystal violet enhancing reagent for blood impressions, presented at the International Symposium on the Forensic Aspects of Footwear and Tire Impression Evidence, FBI Academy, Quantico, VA, June 27–July 1, 1994.

Fischer, J. F., Forensic light sources and their application to tire and shoe examination, presented at the International Symposium on the Forensic Aspects of Footwear and Tire Impression Evidence, FBI Academy, Quantico, VA, June 27–July 1, 1994.

Fischer, J. F., and Green, E., A technique for the enhancement of shoeprints by painting with UV light, *Identification News*, 30(3):7–8, 1980.

Fischer, J. F., and Miller, W. G., The enhancement of blood prints by chemical methods and laser-induced fluorescence, *Identification News*, 34(7):2, 14–15, July 1984.

Fischer, J. F., and Trozzi, T. A., Chemical blood enhancement techniques workshop, handout and presentation at the International Association for Identification Educational Conference, July 19–25, 1998, Little Rock, AR.

FMI Shoe Size Report, Footwear Market Insights, Nashville, TN, 1995.

Footprint and tire impressions, *RCMP Gazette*, 15–19, 1965.

Footprint examinations and the FBI rubber footwear file, *FBI Law Enforcement Bulletin*, 14(3):2–12, 1945.

Footprints and tire treads, *FBI Law Enforcement Bulletin*, 10(8):21–30, 1941.

Footwear Comparisons (A Training Manual Developed by the RCMP), "L" Directorate, Canadian Police Services (undated).

Forsythe-Erman, J. C. A., Footwear identification recognition of 'invisible' evidence, *RCMP Gazette*, 52(6), 1990.

Fox, R. H., and Cunningham, C. L., *Crime Scene Search and Physical Evidence Handbook*, U.S. Government Printing Office, Washington, DC, 1973 pp. 134–149.

Freedman, A., Huntington, E., Davis, G., Magee, R., Milstead, V., and Kirkpatrick, C., *Foot Dimensions of Soldiers: A Survey of Foot Measurements and the Proper Fit of Army Shoes*, U.S. Armored Medical Research Laboratory, Ft. Knox, KY, March 1946.

Freels, R. H., Improved test impressions and prints, presented at the FBI Technical Conference on Footwear and Tire Tread Impression Evidence, Quantico, VA, April 1984.

Fregeau, C., Germain, O., and Fourney, R., Fingerprint enhancement revisited and the effects of blood enhancement chemicals on subsequent *Profiler Plus* fluorescent short tandem repeat DNA analysis of fresh and aged bloody fingerprints, *J. Fors. Sci.*, 45(2):354–380, 2000.

Frisbie, T., and Garrett, R., *Victims of Justice Revisited*, Northwestern University Press, Evanston, IL, 2005.

Fruchtenicht, T., Herzig, W., and Blackledge, R., The discrimination of two-dimensional military boot impressions based wear patterns, *Science & Justice*, 42, 2002.

Gamboe, T. E., Identification of footwear impressions in soil by comparison to silicone rubber mold of outsole, presented at the International Symposium on the Forensic Aspects of Footwear and Tire Impression Evidence, FBI Academy, Quantico, VA, June 27–July 1, 1994.

Gayer, G. W., *Foot Prints; An Aid to the Detection of Crime for the Police and Magistracy*, 1909.

Geller, J., Are we adequately trained in footwear/tire tread identification? *Florida Division International Association for Identification News*, 10–12, March 1988.

Geller, J., Casting on road surfaces, 73rd Annual Educational Conference, International Association for Identification, July 1988.

Geller, J., Dental stone verses plaster of Paris, presented at the 74th Annual Educational Conference, International Association for Identification, Pensacola, FL, June 1989.

Genna, R., Doller, D., Burhans, D., and Tuffy, W., The utilization of the electrostatic lifting apparatus with roll lumar window film in the collection of two-dimensional shoeprints at the crime scene, presented at the International Symposium on the Forensic Aspects of Footwear and Tire Impression Evidence, FBI Academy, Quantico, VA, June 27–July 1, 1994.

Gent, A. N., and Pulford, C. T. R., Mechanisms of rubber abrasion, *Journal of Applied Polymer Science*, 28:943, 1983.

Geradts, Z., and Keijzer, J., The image database REBEZO for shoeprints with developments on automatic classification of shoe outsole designs, *Foren. Sci. Int.*, 82(1):7–20, 1996.

German, E. R., A microscopic footwear identification on cloth, *Identification News*, 31(1):10–12, 1981.

Gervais, R., Footwear impression on ice, *Identification Canada*, 144–145, December 2006.

Giles, E., and Vallandigham, P., Height estimation from foot and shoeprint length, *J. Foren. Sci.* 36(4):1134–1151, July 1991.

Gimeno, F. E., Fill flash color photography to photograph Luminol bloodstain patterns, *Journal of Forensic Identification*, 39(5):305–306, 1989.

Gimeno, F. E., and Rini, G. A., Fill flash photo luminescence to photograph Luminol blood stain patterns, *Journal of Forensic Identification,* 39(3):149–156, 1989.

Girod, A., Shoeprints: coherent exploitation and management, presented at the First European Meeting of Forensic Science, Lausanne, Switzerland, September 1997.

Girod, A., Computerized classification of the shoeprints of burglar's soles, *Foren. Sci. Int.*, 82(1):59–65, 1996.

Glattstein, B., Shor, Y., Levin, N., and Zeichner, A., Improved chemical reagents for the enhancement of footwear marks, presented at the International Symposium on the Forensic Aspects of Footwear and Tire Impression Evidence, FBI Academy, Quantico, VA, June 27–July 1, 1994.

Glattstein, B., Shor, Y., Levin, N., and Zeichner, A., pH Indicators as chemical reagents for the enhancement of footwear marks, *JFS*, 41(1):23–26, 1996.

Gordon, C., and Buikstra, J., Linear models for the prediction of stature from foot and boot dimensions, *J. Foren. Sci.*, 37(3):771–782, May 1992.

Gorn, M., A history of footwear evidence, presented at the IAI International Educational Conference, Minneapolis, MN, August 13, 2014.

Gorsuch, L., Distortion in the class characteristics of footwear impressions made in water-saturated soils, presented at the International Symposium on the Forensic Aspects of Footwear and Tire Impression Evidence, FBI Academy, Quantico, VA, June 27–July 1, 1994.

Gould, J. et al., Predicting erroneous convictions: a social science approach to miscarriages of justice, February 2013, NIJ award 2009-IJ-CX-4110 (see http://nij.ncjrs.gov/multimedia/video-gould.htm).

Graham, G. D. Sr., Distortion in two-dimensional shoe impressions: a tool for inclusion, exclusion and identification, National University, Master of Forensic Science Thesis, San Diego, 1997.

Grimes, D. P., Three year old cast impressions of footwear from an unsolved rape case assist police in obtaining confessions in ten rape cases, presented at the International Symposium on the Forensic Aspects of Footwear and Tire Impression Evidence, FBI Academy, Quantico, VA, June 27–July 1, 1994.

Grispino, R., Luminol and the crime scene, FBI Laboratory, undated.

Groom, P. S., and Lawton, M. E., Are they a pair? *Journal of the Forensic Science Society*, 27:189–192, 1987.

Gross, S., Jeppesen, D., and Neumann, C., The variability and significance of class characteristics in footwear impressions, *JFI*, 332/63(3):332–351, 2013.

Guigui, K., and Beaudoin, A., The use of Oil Red O in sequence with other methods of fingerprint development, *JFI*, 57(4):550–581, 2007.

Gupta, S. R., Footprint and shoeprint identification, *International Criminal Police Review*, 205:55–61, 1967.

Hamamatsu, Fingerprint detection and recording with Hamamatsu intensifier ultraviolet viewer, *Hamamatsu Application Bulletin*, November 1987.

Haque, F., Westland, A., and Kerr, F. M., An improved non-destructive method for detection of latent fingerprints on documents with iodine-7,8-benzo-flavone, *Foren. Sci. Int.*, 21:79–83, 1983.

Hague, F., Physical developer after 13 years, *Identification News*, 37(8):10–12, August 1987.

Hamer, P., and Price, C., Case report: a transfer from skin to clothing by kicking—the detection and enhancement of shoeprints, *Journal of the Forensic Science Society*, 33(3):169–172, 1993.

Hamilton, D., Traces of footwear, tyres and tools, etc., in criminal investigation, *The Police Journal*, 22: January-March, 42–49 and April-June, 128–137, 1949.

Hamm, E., Chemical developers in footwear prints, *Fingerprint Whorld*, 9(6):117–118, 1984.

Hamm, E., Enhancement of bloody footwear prints by physical and chemical methods, presentation to 35th Annual Meeting, American Academy of Forensic Sciences, Cincinnati, OH, February 18, 1983.

Hamm, E., Footwear evidence, paper presented at 67th Annual Educational Conference of the International Association for Identification, Rochester, NY, July 1982.

Hamm, E., The individuality of class characteristics in Converse All-Star footwear, *Journal of Forensic Identification*, 39(5):277–292, 1989.

Hamm, E., Tire tracks and footwear identification, *Identification News*, 3–6, January 1975.

Hamm, E., Track identification: an historical overview, *JFI*, 39(6):333–338, 1989.

Hamm, E., A unique outsole as a result of the die cut method of outsole production, presented at the International Symposium on the Forensic Aspects of Footwear and Tire Impression Evidence, FBI Academy, Quantico, VA, June 27–July 1, 1994.

Hamm, E., The value of shadow in footwear and tire track evidence recovered by photographic techniques, *JFI*, 38(3):91–97, 1988.

Hammell, L., Deacon, P., and Farrugia, K., Chemical enhancement of soil-based marks on nonporous surfaces followed by gelatin lifting, *JFI*, 64(6):583–608, 2014.

Hammer, L., A study of the comparison of inked barefoot impressions to barefoot impressions inside the shoe, Master's Thesis, University of Strathclyde, Glasgow, Scotland, 2007.

Hammer, L., Duffy, K., Fraser, J., and Nic Daéid, N., A study of the variability in footwear impression comparison conclusions, *JFI*, 63(2), 2013.

Hammer, L., and Wolfe, J., Shoe and tire impressions in snow: Photography and casting, *JFI*, 53(6):647–655, 2003.

Hammer, L., Nic Daéid, N., Kennedy, R., and Yamashita, A., Preliminary study of the comparison of inked barefoot impressions with impressions from shoe insoles using a controlled population, *JFI*, 62(6):603–622, 2012.

Hansen, M., Believe it or not, *ABA Journal*, 79:64, June 1993.

Hardwick, S. A., User guide to physical developer—a reagent for detecting latent fingerprints, Home Office, Scientific Research and Development Branch, Sandridge, December 1981.

Harnum, W., and Stanley, G., Amido Black presumptive false-positive tests, Royal Newfoundland Constabulary Forensic Identification Unit, RNC File #2007-3299.

Harris, R. I., Army foot survey. An investigation of foot ailments in Canadian soldiers, No 1574, Ottawa, National Research Council, Canada, 1947.

Hart, R. P., The south Florida footwear industry, presented at the International Symposium on the Forensic Aspects of Footwear and Tire Impression Evidence, FBI Academy, Quantico, VA, June 27–July 1, 1994.

Harvey, A. J., *Footwear Materials and Process Technology*, New Zealand Leather and Shoe Research Association, Palmerston North, 1983.

Hayes, A. J., Factors that influence wear on shoes, presented at the International Symposium on the Forensic Aspects of Footwear and Tire Impression Evidence, FBI Academy, Quantico, VA, June 27–July 1, 1994.

Hebrard, J., Dupasquier, E., Romanello, P., and Poully, G., Experimental and comparative study of new casting materials, presented at the International Symposium on the Forensic Aspects of Footwear and Tire Impression Evidence, FBI Academy, Quantico, VA, June 27–July 1, 1994.

Hegvold, A. E., Effective presentation of expert shoe testimony, Term Paper, George Washington University, Washington, DC, 1971.

Hegvold, A. E., Relationships between document and footwear examinations, presentation to American Academy of Forensic Sciences, Washington, DC, 1976.

Henderson, J., Digitized capture of custody footwear impressions for integration with the National Footwear Database and real-time intelligence within the London Metropolitan Police Service, IAI 100th Educational Conference, Sacramento, CA 8/7/15.

Herold, L. D., How much is enough for a conclusive footwear impression comparison? presented at the International Symposium on the Forensic Aspects of Footwear and Tire Impression Evidence, FBI Academy, Quantico, VA, June 27–July 1, 1994.

Hickman, G. M., Iodine sensitized paper technique for test impressions, presented at the FBI Technical Conference on Footwear and Tire Tread Impression Evidence, 1984.

Hilderbrand, D., *Footwear, The Missed Evidence: A Field Guide to the Collection and Preservation of Forensic Footwear Impression Evidence*, Staggs Publishing, Temecula, CA, 1999.

Hillier, E., Dixon, P., Stewart, P., Yamashita, B., and Lama, D., Recovery of DNA from shoes, *Can. Soc. Forensic Science Journal*, 38(3):143–150, 2005.

Hirschi, F., Tell-tale soles, *International Criminal Police Review*, 240:219–222, 1970.

Hofstede, J. C., Convicted by his shoes, *RCMP Gazette*, 27:6–11, 1965.

Hofstede, J. C., and Verzijden, D. J., The relation of foot to shoe as a means of identification, Leiden, The Netherlands (undated) (translated from Dutch).

Holtslag, H., and Keijzer, J. *Sporen Onderzocht, Handboek 2, Recherchetechniek, Vergelijkende Onderzoeken* (Footprints Investigated, Manual 2, Investigative Techniques, Comparative investigations) (tranlated from Dutch), Lelystad, 1990.

How to make walking shoes run, *Footwear News Magazine*, 4–9, Summer 1988.

Howard, M., and Nessan, M., Detecting bloodstains under multiple layers of paint. *JFI*, 60(6):682–717, 2010.

Hudson, S., Use of the ESDA to visualize latent shoe sole pattern impressions on paper, presented at the International Symposium on the Forensic Aspects of Footwear and Tire Impression Evidence, FBI Academy, Quantico, VA, June 27–July1, 1994.

Hueske, E. E., The examination of Goodyear Neolite cowboy walking boot heels, *SWAFS Journal*, 14(1):21–25, March 1992.

Hueske, E. E., Photographing and casting footwear & tiretrack impressions in snow, *Journal of Forensic Identification*, 41(2):92–95, 1991.

Hueske, E. E., A superior method for obtaining test prints from footwear and tires, *Journal of Forensic Identification*, 41(3):165–167, 1991.

Hueske, E. E., The use of videomicroscopy in footwear comparisons, *SWAFS Journal*, 14(2):25–34, September 1992.

Hussain, J. I., and Pounds, C. A., The enhancement of marks in blood. Part I, 5-sulphosalicylic acid: a convenient and effective fixative for marks made in blood, *Central Research Establishment*, report #649, London, February 1988.

Hussain, J., and Pounds, C. A., The enhancement of marks in blood Part II. A modified amido black staining technique, *Central Research Establishment,* report # 685, London, June 1989.

Hyzer, W. G., and Krauss, T. C., The bite mark standard reference scale, ABFO No. 2, *J. Foren. Sci.*, 33(2):498–506, 1988.

Hyzer, W. G., Scales and perspective-revisited, *Photomethods*, 10–11, July 1988.

Ineichen, P. W., The discriminating power of a computerized shoeprint reference collection system, presented at the International Symposium on the Forensic Aspects of Footwear and Tire Impression Evidence, FBI Academy, Quantico, VA, June 27–July 1, 1994.

Inlow, V., Use of forensic light sources in the detection of impression evidence on deceased persons, presented at the International Symposium on the Forensic Aspects of Footwear and Tire Impression Evidence, FBI Academy, Quantico, VA, June 27–July 1, 1994.

International Seminar on Barefoot Impression Evidence, FBI Academy, Quantico, VA 2/17–20/1998

Instructions for operating the Brannock scientific foot-measuring device, The Brannock Device Company, Syracuse, NY.

Iten, P. X., Recovery of shoe and fingerprint impressions by means of electrostatic transfer, *Kriminalistik* 10:468–470, 1986.

Izraeli, E., Wiesner, S., and Shor, Y., Computer-aided courtroom presentation of shoeprint com parison, *JFI*, 61(6):549–559, 2011.

Jacobia, J., and Blitzer, H., Photographic quality for examination of footwear impressions, presented at the IAI Educational Conference, 2007.

Jakovich, C., STR analysis following latent blood detection by Luminol, Fluroescein, and Blue Star, *JFI*, 57(2), 2007.

Jasuja, O. P., Harbhajan, S., and Anupama, K., Estimation of stature from stride length while walking fast, *FSI*, 86:181–186, 1997.

Jasuja, O., Jasvir, S., and Jain, M., Estimation of statute from foot and shoe measurements by multiplication factors: a revised attempt, *FSI*, 50:203–215, 1991.

Jay, C., and Grubb, M. J., Defects in polyurethane soled athletic shoes—their importance to the shoeprint examiner, *Journal of the Forensic Science Society*, 25:233–238, 1984.

Jay, D. R., A method for preparing high resolution test impressions for footwear comparison, *Identification News*, 23(10):5, 1983.

Johnson, A. P., Stun gun dust print lifting device, presented at the International Symposium on the Forensic Aspects of Footwear and Tire Impression Evidence, FBI Academy, Quantico, VA, June 27–July 1, 1994.

Johnson, M., Use of gelatin lifters for forensic footwear evidence, presented at the IAI Annual Educational Conference, Spokane, WA, July 2010.

Joling, R. J., Shoeprints: quantum of proof, *J. Foren. Sci.*, 13(2):223–235, 1968.

Jonasson, L., The EWG marks collaborative test 1, *The Information Bulletin for Shoeprint/Toolmark Examiners*, 15(1), 2009.

Joseph, A., and Harrison, C. A., *Handbook of Crime Scene Investigation*, Allyn and Bacon, Inc., Boston, MA, 1980, 84–93.

Jurgens, E., Hainey, A., Shaw, L., and Andries, J., Chemical enhancement of footwear impressions in blood recovered from cotton using alginate casts, *JFI*, 65(3), 2015.

Kainuma, A., Manufacturing variations in a die-cut footwear model, *JFI*, 55(4):503–517, 2005.

Kainuma, A., The significance of class characteristics of die cut footwear, presented at the 2010 Pattern and Impression Symposium, Clearwater, FL, August 2010.

Karlmark, E. (Scientific Assistant of the National Central Bureau of the Swedish State Police, Stockholm, Sweden), The taking of casts in the snow, submitted to and published in the *F.B.I. Law Enforcement Bulletin*, 8, 1939.

Katona, G., The impact of the development in the technology on the examination of footwear impressions, presented at the International Symposium on the Forensic Aspects of Footwear and Tire Impression Evidence, FBI Academy, Quantico, VA, June 27–July 1, 1994.

Katterwe, H., About the identification value of imperfections in shoes with polyurethane soles, *Kriminaltechnik,* 66, February 1984.

Katterwe, H., Current usage of footwear and tire tread evidence in Germany, presented at the International Symposium on the Forensic Aspects of Footwear and Tire Impression Evidence, FBI Academy, Quantico, VA, June 27–July 1, 1994.

Katterwe, H., Forensic-physical investigations of polyurethane treads, *Archiv für Kriminologie,* 174:89–95, September/October 1984.

Katterwe, H., Modern approaches for the examination of toolmarks and other surface marks, *Forensic Science Review*, 8(1):45–72, 1996.

Kazlauskas, J., Teamwork and photography win confession, *Fingerprint and Identification Magazine*, 57(1):4–5, 1975.

Kearney, J., *Tracking: A Blueprint for Learning How*, Pathways Press, El Cajon, CA, July 1983.

Keedwell, E., Birkett, J., and Davis, R. J., Chemical methods for the enhancement of footwear marks, Metropolitan Forensic Science Laboratory Report, January 1988.

Keereweer, I., The Nike project—results of barefoot identification, Information Bulletin for Shoeprint/Toolmark Examiners, 4(1):129–138, 1998.

Keereweer, I., Guidelines for drawing conclusions regarding shoeprint examinations, *Information Bulletin for Shoeprint/Toolmark Examiners*, 6(1), 2000.

Keijzer, J., Identification value of imperfections in shoes with polyurethane soles in comparative shoeprint examination, *Journal of Forensic Identification,* 40(4):217–223, 1990.

Keijzer, J., Keereweer, I., van der Heuvel, H., and Geradts, Z., The use of gelatin lifters for the recovery of footwear impressions in combination with latent fingerprint powders, presented at the International Symposium on the Forensic Aspects of Footwear and Tire Impression Evidence, FBI Academy, Quantico, VA, June 27–July 1, 1994.

Kennedy, R. B., Uniqueness of bare feet and its use as a possible means of identification, *Foren. Sci. Int.*, 82:81, 1996.

Kennedy, R., Barefoot Comparison and Identification Research, Forensic Identification Research and Review Section, RCMP, funded by the Canadian Police Research Centre, March 1997.

Kennedy, R., and Yamashita, A., Barefoot morphology comparisons: a summary, *JFI*, 57(3):383–413, 2007.

Kennedy, R. B., Pressman, I. S., Sanping, C., Petersen, P. H., and Pressman, A. E., Statistical analysis of barefoot impressions, *J. Foren. Sci.*, 48(1):55–63, 2003.

Kennedy, R., Chen, S., Pressman, I., Yamashita, A., and Pressman, A., A large-scale statistical analysis of barefoot impressions, *J. Foren. Sci.*, 50 (5):1071–1080, 2005.

Kennedy, R., Gehl, S., Massey, S., and Saunders, G., Use of barefoot morphology in criminal investigations, *Identification Canada*, 25(4):4–6, 2002.

Kennedy, R. B., Bare footprint marks. In: *Encyclopedia of Forensic Sciences*, Volume 3, Siegel, J. A., Saukko, P. J., and Knupfer, G. C., Eds., Academic Press, London, 2000, pp. 1189–1195.

Kenny, R. L., Identification of a footwear impression in the snow, presented at the International Symposium on the Forensic Aspects of Footwear and Tire Impression Evidence, FBI Academy, Quantico, VA, June 27–July 1, 1994.

Kerr, F. M., Barron, I. W., and Westland, A. D., Organic-base fluorescent powders for fingerprint detection on smooth surfaces, Part I, *Can. Soc. Forensic Sci. J.*, 16, 1983.

Kerr, F. M., Barron, I. W., Hague, F., and Westland, A. D., Organic-base fluorescent powders for latent fingerprint detection on smooth surfaces, Part II, *Can. Soc. Forensic Sci. J.*, 16, 1983.

Kirk, P. L., *Crime Investigation*, 2nd ed., John Wiley & Sons, New York, 1963.

Knecht, W., The shoes only fit the murderer, *Kriminalistik*, December 1987, pp. 673–681 (translated from German).

Koehler, J. R. G., Footwear evidence, *RCMP Gazette*, 48(9), 1986.

Koller, T., A better approach for footwear retrieval systems: computer assisted shoe track matching, presented at the ENFSI SPTM 2014 meeting, Prague, Czech Republic, October 21, 2014.

Kortylewski, A., Automated footwear impression analysis and retrieval based on periodic patterns, presented at the ENFSI SPTM 2014 meeting, Prague, Czech Republic, October 21, 2014.

Krauss, T. C., and Warlen, S. C., The forensic science use of reflective ultraviolet photography, *J. Foren. Sci.*, 30(1):262–268, 1985.

Lafrance, G., Reproduction of impressions, *RCMP Gazette*, 38(1):12–13, 1976.

Lake, S., and Ganas, J., Optical enhancement of leucocrystal violet treated impressions in blood, Victoria Police State Forensic Science Laboratory, Macleod, Australia, 1995.

Larkin, T., and Gannicliffe, C., Illuminating the health and safety of Luminol, *Science & Justice*, 48:71–75, 2008.

Laskowski, G. E., and Kyle, V. L., Barefoot impressions—A preliminary study of identification characteristics and population frequency of their morphological features, *J. Foren. Sci.*, 33,(2):378–388, 1988.

Last: the birthplace of shoe fashion, *Leather and Shoes*, 36–42, May 1974.

Lee, H. C., TMB as an enhancement reagent for bloody prints, *Identification News*, 10–11, March 1984.

Lee, H. C., and Gaensslen, R. E., Electrostatic lifting procedure for two-dimensional dustprints, *Identification News*, 8–11, January 1987.

Lee, T., The case of the counterfeit Nike, presented at the 2010 Impression and Pattern Symposium, Clearwater, FL, August 2010.

Lehar, Dr. A. F., and Preston, Dr. F. H., Digital manipulation of scene of crime images, Police Scientific Development Branch, Sandridge, 72–73 (undated).

Leishman, S., If the shoe fits, *RCMP Gazette*, 53(9), 1991.

LeMay, J., Accidental characteristics in a footwear outsole caused by incomplete blending of fillers in the outsole rubber, *JFI*, 63(5), 2013.

LeMay, J., If the shoe fits: An illustration of the relevance of footwear impression evidence and comparisons, *JFI*, 60(3), 2010.

LeMay, J., Making three-dimensional footwear test impressions with Bubber, *JFI*, 60(4):439–448, 2010.

LeMay, J., Adams, S., and Stephen, A., Validation of vinyl static cling film for the collection and preservation of dust impressions, *JFI*, 61(4):317–327, 2011.

Li, B., Everspry automated shoeprint recognition, Everspry Science and Tech Co., Ltd., presented at the ENFSI SPTM 2014 meeting, Prague, Czech Republic, October 22, 2014.

Liukkonen, M., Majamaa, H., and Virtanen, J., The role and duties of the shoeprint/toolmark examiner in forensic laboratories, *Foren. Sci. Int.*, 82(1):99–108, 1996.

Litchfield, P., Reebok manufacturing techniques, International Symposium of the Forensic Aspects of Footwear and Tire Impression Evidence, FBI Academy, Quantico, VA, 1994.

Llewellyn Jr., P., and Dinkins, L., A new use for an old friend, *JFI*, 45(5):498–503, 1995.

Lohnes, R. C., Infant footprint identification by flexure creases, *Identification News*, 36(8):10, 13, August 1986.

Lovejoy, O., *Methods of Footprint Analysis*, prepared by Dr. Owen Lovejoy, Professor of Anatomy, Kent State University, for presentation at the FBI Academy, April 1984.

Loveridge, F. H., Shoe print development by silver nitrate, *Fingerprint Whorld*, 10(38):58, 1984.

Lucock, L. J., Identifying the wearer of worn footwear, *Journal of the Forensic Science Society*, 7(2):62–70, April 1967.

Ludas, J. M., and Leonard, J. L., Why 'no scale' photographs are not always a dead-end! presented at the International Symposium on the Forensic Aspects of Footwear and Tire Impression Evidence, FBI Academy, Quantico, VA, June 27–July 1, 1994.

Lytle, L., and Hedgecock, D., Chemiluminescence in the visualization of forensic bloodstains, *J. Foren. Sci.*, 550–562, 1978.

MacMullan, J., The shoe fits, *Review—The Magazine of Eastern Airlines*, 77–81, April 1987.

Maltais, L., and Yamashita, A., A validation study of barefoot morphology comparison, *JFS*, 362/60(3), 2010.

Majamaa, H., The state of footwear/tire track evidence in the Nordic countries, presented at the International Symposium on the Forensic Aspects of Footwear and Tire Impression Evidence, FBI Academy, Quantico, VA, June 27–July 1, 1994.

Majamaa, H., The recovery methods of shoeprints in Finland during ten years (1986–1995), *Information Bulletin for Shoeprint/Tool Mark Examiners*, 4(1):97–107, 1998.

Majamaa, H., and Ytti, A., Survey of the conclusions drawn of similar footwear cases in various crime laboratories, *Foren. Sci. Int.*, 82(1):109–120, 1996.

Mankevich, A., Chemical enhancement of clay residue footwear impressions, presented at the 78th Annual Educational Conference, International Association for Identification, Orlando, FL, July 27, 1993.

Mankevich, A., Geologic, climatic and chemical weathering considerations in the application of footwear/tire track enhancement techniques, presented at the International Symposium on the Forensic Aspects of Footwear and Tire Impression Evidence, FBI Academy, Quantico, VA, June 27–July 1, 1994.

Manual of use for BVDA (gelatin) lifters, prepared by BVDA International, Amsterdam, Holland, distributed at the first European Meeting of Forensic Science, Lausanne, Switzerland, 1997.

Manning, J. R., and Smith, Alison M., Mondopoint grading and size ranges, The Shoe and Allied Trades Research Association, Ref: IP 119, May 1973.

Mansfield, E. R., Footwear impressions at scenes of crimes, *The Police Journal*, 43(2):93–96, 1970.

Manual of Shoemaking, C&J Clark Ltd., England, 1980.

Marchant, B., and Tague, C., Developing fingerprints in blood: a comparison of several chemical techniques, *JFI*, 57(1):76–93, 2007.

Martin, F. W., A simple method of taking footprints, *The Police Journal*, 9:450–452, 1936.

Mashiter, K., *Footwear Intelligence Guidance for Scientific Support*, August 2007, Lancashire, UK.

Massey, S. L., Persistence of creases of the foot and their value for forensic identification purposes. *JFI*, 54(3):296–315, 2004.

Massimilliano, F., Doiron, T., Thompson, R., Jones II, J., Ballou, S., and Neiman, J., Dimensional Review of Scales in Forensic Photography, August 2013, NCJRS award 2010-DN-R-7121, US Department of Justice.

McBrayer, W. S., Dust shoe prints on plexi-glass, *AFTE Journal*, 13(4):26–28, 1981.

McCafferty, J. D., The shoe fits, *The Police Journal*, 28:135–139, 1955.

McConaghey, D., Resting gelatin lifters prior to use, *JFI*, 63(6):653–659, 2013.

McGonigle, C., Tracking: an ancient skill makes a comeback, *Law and Order*, 36(2), 1988.

McNeil, K., and Knaap, W., Bromophenol Blue as a chemical enhancement technique for shoe-prints, *JFI*, 62(2):143–153, 2012.

McPoll, T., Schuit, D., and Knecht, H., Comparison of three methods used to obtain a neutral plaster foot impression, *Physical Therapy*, 69(6), June 1989.

McVicker, B., Advanced photoshop techniques for the enhancement of footwear impression evidence, presented at the IAI International Educational Conference, Minneapolis, MN, August 13, 2014.

Meisler, K., What your old shoes say about your running, *Runner's World*, 45–80, November 1984.

Menzel, E. R., Pretreatment of latent prints for laser development, *Forensic Science Review*, 1(1), June 1989.

Mikkonen, S., and Astikainen, T., An image related databased classification system for identification of partial footwear impression found at a crime scene, presented at the International Symposium on the Forensic Aspects of Footwear and Tire Impression Evidence, FBI Academy, Quantico, VA, June 27–July 1, 1994.

Mikkonen, S., Suominen, V., and Heinonen, P., Use of footwear impressions in crime scene investigations assisted by computerized footwear collection system, *Foren. Sci. Int.,* 82(1):67–79, 1996.

Milne, R., The pathfinder wireless electrostatic mark lifting machine and the electrostatic lifting of shoe, tyre and finger marks at crime scenes, *Fingerprint Whorld*, April 1997.

Milne, R., The development of a wireless electrostatic mark lifting method and its use at crime scenes, *JFS*, 154/62(2), 2012.

Moran, B., Physical match/tool mark identification involving rubber shoe sole fragments, *AFTE Journal*, 16(3):126–128, 1984.

Morgan-Smith, R., Elliot, D., and Adam, H., Enhancement of aged shoeprints in blood, *JFI*, 59(1):45–50, 2009.

Moreau, D. M., *Fundamental Principles and Theory of Crime Scene Photography*, Forensic Science Training Unit, FBI Laboratory (undated).

Moriarty, C. C., Taking casts of footprints, *Police Journal* (London), 5:229–232, 1932.

Morris, J. L., Biomechanical implications of hammertoe deformities, *Clinics in Podiatric Medicine and Surgery*, 3:2, 1986.

Morton, S., Shoe print development by physical developer treatment, *Fingerprint Whorld*, 9(34):60–61, 1983.

Mueller, R., Utilizing the electrostatic dust lifter on concrete surfaces, presented at the IAI International Educational Conference, Minneapolis, MN, August 15, 2014.

Mullner, H., and Kaempfer, L. J., The Mullner Moulage method, *J. Crim. Law Crim.*, 23(2):351–355, 1932.

Murdock, J. E., Photography of Luminol reaction in crime scenes, *The Criminologist*, 10(37):14–19, 1966.

Musgrave, J. H., and Hareja, N. K., The estimation of adult stature from metacarpal bone length, *American Journal of Physical Anthropology*, 48:113, 1978.

Music, D., and Bodziak, W. J., A forensic evaluation of the air bubbles present in polyurethane shoe outsoles as applicable in footwear impression comparisons, *J. Foren. Sci.*, 33(5), September 1988.

Myers, D. A., *A Reference Guide for Law Enforcement Personnel*, S.O.L.E. Publications, Beaverton, OR, 1982.

Napier, T. J., and Thompson, L. R., Transfer and back-transfer of electrostatic lifts between film and folder, 1987 (unpublished).

National Shoe Manufacturers Association, The foot inside the shoe, New York.

Nayar, P. S., and DasGupta, S. K., Personal identification based on footprints found on footwear, *International Criminal Police Review*, 326:83–87, 1976.

Nause, L. A., Casting footwear impressions in snow: snowprint-wax vs. prill sulphur, *RCMP Gazette*, 54(12):1–7, 1992.

Nause, L. A., Footwear impressions on glass, *RCMP Gazette*, 47(5):9–14, 1985.

Neuner, J. K., Selection criteria for utilizing amido black, coomassie blue and luminol for the development/enhancement of bloody footwear impressions, presented at the International Symposium on the Forensic Aspects of Footwear and Tire Impression Evidence, FBI Academy, Quantico, VA, June 27–July 1, 1994.

Nigg, B. M., Bahlsen, H. A., Luethi, S. M., and Stokes, S., The influence of running velocity and midsole hardness on external impact forces in heel-toe running, *Journal of Biomechanics*, 20(10):951–959, 1987.

Niremberg, M. S., Forensic methods and the podiatric physician, *Journal of the American Podiatric Association*, 79(5), May 1989.

Nordanstig, R., Short observations about stretching of gell lifter, presentation at 11th European Shoe Print and Tool Mark Meeting, Prague, Czech Republic, October 22, 2014.

Nubar, G. W., Biomechanics of the foot and ankle during gait, *Foot and Ankle Injuries: Clinics in Sports Medicine*, 7:1, 1988.

O'Hara, C. E., and Osterburg, J., *An Introduction to Criminalistics*, The MacMillan Company, New York, 1949, pp. 103–120.

O'Hara, C. E., *Fundamentals of Criminal Investigation*, Charles C. Thomas, Springfield, IL, 1956, pp. 726–735.

Ojena, S. M., A new improved technique for casting impressions in snow, *J. Foren. Sci.*, 29(1):322–325, 1984.

Ojena, S. M., New electrostatic process recovers visible and invisible dust particles at crime scenes, *Law and Order*, 3:31–33, 1988.

Oliver, W. R., The pathology and interpretation of blunt force pattern injuries to the skin, presented at the International Symposium on the Forensic Aspects of Footwear and Tire Impression Evidence, FBI Academy, Quantico, VA, June 27–July 1, 1994.

Olsen, R. D. Sr., Sensitivity comparison of blood enhancement techniques, *Identification News*, 36(8):5–11, 1986.

Olsen, R. D., Need for defining nomenclature of class and individual characteristics, FBI Technical Conference on Footwear and Tire Tread Impression Evidence, Quantico, VA, April 1984.

Osborn, S., and Wilson, K., Digital enhancement of latent prints using Adobe Photoshop black and white adjustments, *JFI*, 59(4):373–385, 2009.

Osterburg, J. W., *The Crime Laboratory*, Indiana University Press, Bloomington, IN, 1967, pp. 37–47.

Owen, F., A latent heel impression, *Police Journal* (London), 27:221–223, 1954.

Paine, N., The use of cyanoacrylate fuming and related enhancement techniques to develop shoe impressions on various surfaces, *JFI*, 48(5):585–601, 1998.

Pagliano, J., Last stop: the shoe shop, *Runners World*, 20(10):70–71, 1985.

Pasquier, J., Automatic footwear mark pattern retrieval: results and perspectives, presented at the ENFSI SPTM 2014 meeting, Prague, Czech Republic, October 21, 2014.

Paulisick, J. F., Class and identifying characteristics: the identification, presented at the International Symposium on the Forensic Aspects of Footwear and Tire Impression Evidence, FBI Academy, Quantico, VA, June 27–July 1, 1994.

Perkins, M., The application of infrared photography in bloodstain pattern documentation on clothing, *JFI*, 55(1), 1–9, 2005.

Peterson, H., Chucks! *The Phenomenon of Converse Chuck Taylor All Stars*, Skyhorse Publishing, New York, 2007.

Petraco, N., Antoci, P., Deforest, P. R., and Pizzola, P. A., The enhancement of fine two dimensional residual soil and dust footwear prints encountered on low contrast surfaces, presented at the International Symposium on the Forensic Aspects of Footwear and Tire Impression Evidence, FBI Academy, Quantico, VA, June 27–July 1, 1994.

Petraco, N., A rapid method for the preparation of transparent footwear test prints, *J. Foren. Sci.*, 27(4):935–937, 1982.

Petty, C. S., Smith, R. A., and Hutson, T. A., The value of shoe imprints in automobile crash investigations, *Journal of Police Science and Administration*, 1–10, March 1973.

Phillip, T. A., Reconstruction of stature from foot outline and foot print size, *Journal of Indian Academy of Forensic Medicine*, 11:1, 1989.

Pick up the trail from impressions found on firm surfaces, *FBI Law Enforcement Bulletin*, 20(6):12–15, 1951.

Pick up the trail with plaster casts, *FBI Law Enforcement Bulletin*, 20(5):6–10, 1951.

Potter, D. R., Two types of outsole manufacturing techniques and their influence on footwear impression variations, presented at the International Symposium on the Forensic Aspects of Footwear and Tire Impression Evidence, FBI Academy, Quantico, VA, June 27–July 1, 1994.

Preservation of impressions in earth, *Ohio Law Enforcement Training Bulletin*, 1(1), 1959.

Preserving prints of shoes and tires on hard surfaces, *FBI Law Enforcement Bulletin*, 30:6, 7–10, June 1961 (revised April 1974).

Proescher, R., and Moody, A., Detection of blood by means of chemiluminescence, *J. Lab. Clin. Med.*, 24:1183, 1939.

Professional Shoe Fitting, National Shoe Retailers Association, New York, 1984.

Puri, D., Footprints, *International Criminal Police Review*, 187:106–111, 1965.

Putnam, B. A., Powder, prints and the effects of wear, presented at the International Symposium on the Forensic Aspects of Footwear and Tire Impression Evidence, FBI Academy, Quantico, VA, June 27–July 1, 1994.

Qamra, S., Sharma, B., and Kaila, P., Naked foot marks—A preliminary study of identification factors, *Foren. Sci. Int.*, 16:145–152, 1980.

Raymond, J., and Sheldon, P., Standardizing shoemark evidence–An Australian and New Zealand Collaborative Trial, *JFI*, 65(5):868–881, 2015.

Rao, V. J., Patterned injury and its evidentiary value, *J. Foren. Sci.*, 31(2):768–772, April 1986.

Rawji, A., and Beaudoin, A., Oil Red O versus physical developer on wet papers: a comparative study, *JFI*, 56(1):33–54, 2006.

Recommended course of study for footwear and tire track examiners, IAI Footwear and Tire Track Subcommittee, International Association for Identification (revised 2006).

The reproduction of original evidence in the third dimension, *FBI Law Enforcement Bulletin*, 5(12):3–9, 1936.

The reproduction of shoeprint and tiretread impressions, *FBI Law Enforcement Bulletin*, 16(6):5–11, 1947.

Reynard, J. N., Footprints—the practical side of the subject, *The Police Journal*, 30–34, January-March, 1948.

Ribaux, O., Girod, A., Walsh, W., Margot, P., Mizrahi, S., and Clivaz, V., Forensic intelligence and crime analysis, *Law Probability and Risk* 2:47–60, 2003.

Richards, A., and Leintz, R., Forensic reflected ultraviolet imaging, *JFI*, 63(1), 2013.

Roberts, A. D., Theories of dry rubber friction, *Tribology International*, April 1976.

Robert, L., Converse manufacturing techniques, Converse Rubber Company Inc., North Reading, MA, International Symposium of the Forensic Aspects of Footwear and Tire Impression Evidence, FBI Academy, 1994.

Robbins, L. M., *Footprints*, Charles C. Thomas, 1985.

Robbins, L. M., The individuality of human footprints, *J. Foren. Sci.*, 23(4):775–778, 1978.

Robbins, L. M., Estimating height and weight from size of footprints. *J. Foren. Sci.*, 31:143–152, 1986.

Robinson, H. M., *Science Catches the Criminal*, Blue Ribbon Books, New York, 1935.

Rodowicz, L., Polish methodology of forensic shoeprint identification, *Information Bulletin for Shoeprint/Toolmark Examiners*, 4(1), March 1998.

Rossi, W., The high incidence of mismated feet in the population, *Foot & Ankle*, 4:2, 1983, American Orthopaedic Foot and Ankle Society, Inc.

Rossi, W., How shoe sizes grew, *Footwear News Magazine*, 34–35, March 1988.

Rossi. W., The foot: a masterpiece of engineering, *Pedoscope*, 12, Feb/Mar 1991.

R v T, Case No: 2007/03644/D2 in the High Court of Justice Court of Appeal from the Crown Court, Royal Courts of Justice, Strand, London, WC2A 2LL October 26, 2010.

Rummelhoff, J. Von, Does the print belong to the perpetrator? *Association of Firearms and Toolmarks Examiners Journal*, (15)2, April 1983.

Russell, J. R., Matharu, S. S., and Brennan, J. S., A new, portable device for the electrostatic lifting of marks, *MPFSL Report No. 55*, Metropolitan Police, London, June 1985.

Saferstein, R., *Criminalistics: An Introduction to Forensic Science,* 6th ed., Prentice-Hall, Englewood Cliffs, NJ, 1997.

Salama, J., Shaheen, A., Lennard, C., and Roux, C., Evaluation of the fingerprint reagent Oil Red O as a possible replacement for physical developer, *JFI*, 58(2):203–237, 2008.

Salmons, R., Identification by flexion creases, *RCMP Gazette*, 48(11), 1986.

Samen, C. C., Major crime scene investigation: casting (shoe and tire impressions), *Law and Order Magazine*, 52–57, March 1972.

Schachter, R. J., *The Art and Science of Footwear Manufacturing*, Footwear Industry of America, 1983.

Schallamach, A., *Friction and Abrasion of Rubber*, The British Rubber Producers' Research Association, Vol. 1, 384, 1957–1958.

Schallamach, A., Abrasion, fatigue and smearing of rubber, *Journal of Polymer Science*, 12:281, 1968.

Schallamach, A., Abrasion of rubber by a needle, *Journal of Polymer Science*, 9(5):385, 1952.

Schallamach, A., How does rubber slide? *Wear*, 17:301, 1971.

Schallamach, A., A theory of dynamic rubber friction, *Wear*, 6:375, 1963.

Schallamach, A., The adhesion and friction of smooth rubber surfaces, *Wear*, 33:45, 1975.

Scheller-Sheridan, C., *Basic Guide to Dental Materials*, Wiley-Blackwell, 2010, p. 222.

Schmitz, A., Uber das hydrazid der trimensinaure und die hemimellitsaure, Inaug. Dissertation Heidelberg, 1902; cited in Curtius T. and Semper A. *Ber. Btsch. Chem. Ges.* 46:1162, 1913.

Sears, V. G., and Prizeman, T. M., Enhancement of fingerprints in blood—Part 1: The optimization of Amido black, *JFI*, 50(5), 470–480, 2000.

Sears, V. G., Butcher, C. P. G., and Prizeman, T. M., Enhancement of fingerprints in blood—Part 2: protein dyes, *JFI*, 51(1):28–38, 2001.

Sears, V. G., Butcher, C. P. G., and Fitzgerald, L. A., Enhancement of fingerprints in blood—Part 3: reactive techniques, Acid Yellow 7, and process sequences, *JFI*, 55(6):741–763, 2005.

Segura, M. A., Footprints and tire marks, *Forensic Science Digest* (U.S. Air Force), 7(1):1–17, 1981.

Selection and Application Guide to Police Photographic Equipment, U.S. Department of Commerce, National Bureau of Standards, NBS Publication 480-23, Washington, DC, 1980.

Serpa, J. F., Identification of amido black enhanced footwear impressions in blood, presented at the International Symposium on the Forensic Aspects of Footwear and Tire Impression Evidence, FBI Academy, Quantico, VA, June 27–July 1, 1994.

Sharein, R., Rainy day ident, *RCMP Gazette*, 55(7 & 8): 15–17, 1993.

Sharma, B. R., Foot and footwear evidence, *Journal of the Indian Academy of Forensic Sciences*, 9(1):9–13, 1970.

Sharma, B. R., *Footprints, Tracks and Trails in Criminal Investigation and Trials*, Central Law Agency, Allahabad, India, 1980, pp. 61–77.

Sheets, D. H., Gross, S., Langenbury, G., Bush, P., and Bush. M., Shape measurement tools in footwear analysis: A statistical investigation of accidental characteristics over time, *Foren. Sci. Int.*, 232:84–91, 2013.

Shoe and tire impressions, *FBI Law Enforcement Bulletin*, 24(1):15–17, 1955.

Shoe and tire impressions put the suspect at the scene of the crime, *Forensic Bulletin* (Commonwealth of Virginia Bureau of Forensic Science), 4(4):2–4, 1975.

Shoe buyers guide—footnotes—an A to Z guide to shoe terminology, *Runners World*, 25(10), October 1990.

Shoe size conversion research results and recommendations, Footwear Industry Team, U.S. Department of Commerce, Contract No. 41 USC 252C (3), July 31, 1979.

Shoeprint on rug links man to house robbery, *FBI Law Enforcement Bulletin*, 18–19, June 1961.

Shor, Y., Cohen, A., Wiesner, S., and Weiss, R., Recovering dusty shoe prints from skin: comparative research, *The Open Forensic Science Journal*, 7:1–5, 2014.

Shor, Y., and Weisner, S., A survey on the conclusions drawn on the same footwear marks obtained in actual cases by several experts throughout the world, *J. Fors. Sci.*, 44(2):380–384, 1999.

Shor, Y., Belser, C., and Wiesner, S., A comparative study: gelatin lifter vs. electrostatic lifter, presented at the European Meeting for SP/TM examiners, May 2007, Copenhagen, Denmark.

Shor, Y., Vinokurov, A., and Glattstein, B. The use of an adhesive lifter and pH indicator for the removal and enhancement of shoeprints in dust. *J. Forensic Science*, 43(1):182–184, 1998.

Shor, Y., Tsach, T., Wiesner, S., and Meir, G., Removing interfering contaminations from gelatin lifters, *J. For. Sci.*, 50(6), November 2005.

Shor, Y., and Wiesner, S., Why should we make several test impressions, presented at the 11th European Shoeprint/Toolmark Meeting, Prague, Czech Republic, October 21–23, 2014.

Shor, Y., Wiesner, S., Chaikovsky, A., and Tsach, T., Methods for improving problematic footwear prints, presented at the SPTM Meeting, Stavern, Norway, May 2005.

Shor, Y., Tsach, T., Vinokurov, A., Glattstein, B., Landau, E., and Levin, N., Lifting shoeprints using gelatin lifters and a hydraulic press. *J. Forensic Sci.*, 48(2):368–372, 2003.

Shuler, R., *Small Town Slayings in South Carolina*, History Press, Charleston, SC, 2009, pp. 113–136.

Slater, J., *Techniques for the Enhancement of 2-Dimensional Footwear Impressions in Blood*, diploma thesis, Canberra Institute of Technology, Canberra, Australia, December 1993.

Smerecki, C. J., and Lovejoy, C. O., Identification via pedal morphology, *International Criminal Police Review*, 186–190, August 1985.

Smith, J., Computer fingerprint enhancement: the joy of lab color, *JFI*, 62(5):464–475, 2012.

Smith, M. B., Using the manufacturer's information of the Nike Air Force 1 to assist in the examination process, presented at the Impression and Pattern Symposium, Clearwater, FL, August 2010.

Snyder, C., The ability of footwear to produce impressions of good detail in sandy soil substrates, *JFI*, 65(3), 2015.

Snyder, C., A comparison of photograph and casting methods of footwear impressions in different sandy soil substrates, *JFI*, 66(1), 2016.

Sodermann, H., and O'Connell, J. J., *Modern Criminal Investigation*, 5th ed., Funk & Wagnalls, New York, 1945, pp. 156–168.

Someha, S., Chemical techniques for the enhancement of footwear and tire impressions in Japan, presented at the International Symposium on the Forensic Aspects of Footwear and Tire Impression Evidence, FBI Academy, Quantico, VA, June 27–July 1, 1994.

The soul of a running shoe, *Science '82*, 3(6):104–105, 1982.

Soule, R. L., Reproduction of foot and tire tracks by plaster of Paris casting, *Identification News*, 8–12, January 1961.

Spear, T., Barney, S., Khoshkebari, N and Silva, A., The impact of body fluid identification and fingerprint reagents on PCR-based typing results, presented at the CAC Seminar, May 2002.

Speiden, R., *Foundations for Awareness, Signcutting and Tracking*, Natural Awareness Tracking School, Christiansburg, VA, 2009.

Speller, H. C., The identification of crepe-rubber sole impressions, *The Police Journal*, 22:269–274, 1949.

Spilker, J. G., Luminol reaction, presentation at the FBI Technical Conference on Shoeprint and Tire Tread Examinations, FBI Academy, Quantico, VA, April 1983.

Sport Research Review, Adult Foot Structure, August/November, 1990, Nike, Inc. Beaverton, OR.

Stature Estimation, Scientific Working Group for Forensic Anthropology, August 2, 2012.

Stene, I., Shimamoto, S., Gabel, R., Tewes, R., and Adair, T., Using Luminol to detect blood in soil eight years after deposition, *J. Assoc Crime Scene Reconstruction*, 19(1):1–4, 2013.

Stone, R. S., Mathematical probabilities in footwear comparisons, presented at the FBI Technical Conference on Footwear and Tire Impression Evidence, Quantico, VA, April 1984.

Stone, R. S., Footwear examinations: mathematical probabilities of theoretical individual characteristics, *JFI*, 56(4):577–599, 2006.

Strauch, H., Wirth, I., Taymoorian, U., and Geserick, G., Kicking to death—forensic and criminological aspects, *Foren. Sci. Int.*, 123:165–171, 2001.

Subotnick, S. I., The biomechanics of running: implications for the prevention of foot injuries, *Sports Medicine*, 2, 144, 1985.

Taroni, F., and Aitken, C., Correspondence: Interpretation of scientific evidence, *Science & Justice*, 37(1):64–65, 1997.

Tart, M. S., Downey, A. J., Goodyear, J. G., and Adams, J., The appearance and duration of feathering as a feature of wear, *Forensic Science Society Report No. RR 786*, August 1996.

Tart, M. S., and Adams, J., Transient wear features, The Forensic Science Service, Birmingham, UK, Report No. TN824, October 1997.

Tart, M. S., Adams, J., and Ohene, A., Wear patterns: location and rate of advancement, The Forensic Science Service, Birmingham, UK, Report No. RR801, June 1999.

Tart, M. S., Adams, J., and Ohene, A., Variations in size of footwear impressions with increasing wear, The Forensic Science Service, Birmingham, UK, Report No. TN819, September 1996.

Tart, M. S., Adams, J., Downey, A. J., Goodyear, J. G., and Ohene, A., Feathering, transient wear features and wear pattern analysis: A study of the progressive wear of training shoe outsoles, *Information Bulletin for Shoeprint/Toolmark Examiners*, 4(1):51–68, 1998.

Taylor, A., *Principles and Practice of Medical Jurisprudence*, 2nd ed., Vol 1, Henry C. Lea, Philadelphia, 1873.

Theeuwen, A., Barneveld, S., Drok, W., Keereweer, I., Limborgh, J., Naber, W., and Velders, T., Enhancement of footwear impressions in blood, *Foren. Sci. Int.*, 95:133–151, 1998.

Theeuwen, A., van Barnevald, S., Drok, J., Keereweer, I., Lesger, B., Limborgh, J., Naber, W., Schrok, R., and Velders, T., Enhancement of muddy footwear impressions, *Foren. Sci. Int.*, 119(1):57–67, 2001.

Theeuwen, A., van Barnevald, S., Drok, J., Keereweer, I., Limborgh, J., Naber, R., and Velders, T., Enhancement of footwear impressions in blood, *Foren. Sci. Int.*, 95(2):133–151, 1998.

Thompson, R. W., Sulfur casting, *AFTE Journal*, 12(2):15–16, 1980.

Thornton, J., and Maloney, R., The chemistry of the Luminol reaction—where to from here? *CAC Newsletter*, 9–17, September 1985.

Tiller, C. D., Examination of footprints at crime scenes, *RCMP Gazette*, 24:12, 1962.

Tips on making casts of shoe and tire prints, *FBI Law Enforcement Bulletin*, 18–22, October 1963.

Timmons, K., Ackeren, J., Rushton, C., and Staton, P., Detection and documentation of bloodstains concealed by paint: a practical approach, Marshall University Forensic Science Center, Huntington, WV.

The true story of shoe sizes, Sterling Last Corporation, Long Island City, NY, 1979.

Tobe, S., Watson, N., and Nic Daéid, N., Evaluation of six presumptive tests for blood, their specificity, sensitivity, and effect on high molecular-weight DNA, *J. Forensic Science*, 52(1), Jan. 2007.

Toso, B., and Girod, A., Evolution of random characteristics (appearance and disappearance), presented at the First European Meeting of Forensic Science, Lausanne, Switzerland, September 1997.

Tovar, R., The use of electrostatic equipment to retrieve impressions from the human body, *JFI*, 54(5):530–533, 2004.

Tripathi, R. S., and Jogulamma, M. R., Individualization from footwear—a case report, *Medicine, Science & Law*, 22(2):115–118, 1982.

Trotter, M., and Gleser, G. C., A re-evaluation of estimation of stature based on measurements of stature taken during life and of long bones after death, *American Journal of Physical Anthropology*, 16, 1958.

Trozzi, T. A., Developing bloody footwear impressions with the use of diaminobenzidine, presented at the International Symposium on the Forensic Aspects of Footwear and Tire Impression Evidence, FBI Academy, Quantico, VA, June 27–July 1, 1994.

Tryhorn, F. G., Scientific aids in criminal investigation, Part V, marks and impressions, *Police Journal* (London) 10:19–27, 1937.

Truszkowski, G. J., Daylight flash photography of three dimensional impressions, *Journal of Forensic Identification*, 38(3):83–90, 1988.

Tuthill, H., and Graeme, G., *Individualization: Principles and Procedures in Criminalistics*, 2nd ed., Lightning Powder Company, Jacksonville, FL, 2002.

Valmassy, R., *Clinical Biomechanics of the Lower Extremities*, Mosby, St. Louis, MO, 1996.

Vandiver, J. V., Casting materials, *Identification News*, 30(12):3–9, 1980.

Vandiver, J. V., Easier casting and better casts, *Identification News*, 30(5):3–10, 1980.

Vandiver, J. V., and Wolcott, J. H., Identification of suitable plaster for crime scene casting, *J. Foren. Sci.*, 23(3):607–614, 1978.

Vandiver, J. V., Silicone rubber casting problems and very few solutions, *Identification News*, 31(1):7–9, 1981.

Vandiver, J. V., Tests of polysulfide, silicone rubber and polyether, *Identification News*, 31(2):3–8, 1981.

Vandiver, J. V., Toolmark and shoe, tire impression utilization by criminal investigators, Research Paper for George Washington University, April, 1975, unpublished.

Van Hoven, H., A correlation between shoeprint measurements and actual sneaker size, *J. Foren. Sci.*, 30(4):1233–1237, 1985.

Velders, M. J. M., Fluorescing traces in blood on white gelatin lifters with Hungarian red, presented at the 81st Educational Conference of the International Association for Identification, Greensboro, NC, July 1996.

Velders, M. J. M., Mud prints on paper activated for DFO with black gelatin lifters, presented at the 82nd Educational Conference of the International Association for Identification, Danvers, MA, July 1997.

Velders, M. J. M., Fluorescing mud prints with Safranin 0, presented at the 82nd Educational Conference of the International Association for Identification, Danvers, MA, July 1997.

Velders, T., New insight into the chemical improvement of shoeprints and fingerprints placed with blood on non-porous surfaces, Brabant South-East Department, Eindhoven, the Netherlands, Research Report 2011–2012.

Volckeryck, G., and Van Dijck, B., A method to obtain test prints from footwear, International Association for Identification Meeting, Danvers, MA, 1997.

Walker, S. A., *Sneakers*, Scholastic Book Services, New York, 1978.

Walls, H. J., *Forensic Science, An Introduction to Scientific Crime Detection*, Praeger Publishers, New York, 1959, pp. 17–18.

Walsh, K. A. J., and Buckleton, J. S., An aid for the detection and correction of inaccuracies in photographic reproduction of shoeprints, *AFTE Journal*, 19(3), 1987.

Walter, E., and Wilson, D., Joint forces research and resource unit physical developer, *Identification Canada*, 8(2):13–16, 1985.

Wang, Y., Weiping, Z., and Janping, M., Eosin Y detection of latent blood prints, *JFI*, 57(1):54–58, 2007.

Warren, D. F., Briner, R. C., and Longwell, C. R., Visualization of latent shoeprint impressions by the freeze-thaw technique or freeze-thaw III, *Crime Laboratory Digest*, August 1983.

Warren, D. F., Lemonds, A. T., Longwell, C. R., and Briner, R. C., Photography of footwear latents using ultra-high contrast techniques, *AFTE Journal*, 16(3):113–118, 1984.

Warren, G., Snowprint-wax casting material information, *AFTE Journal*, 15(2):77–78, 1983.

Watson, J., A method of lifting and photographing for evidence, *J. Criminal Law, Criminology and Police Science*, 49:89–90, 1958.

Watson, J., The technique of lifting and photographing shoe prints left in dust, *Fingerprint and Identification Magazine*, 1–6, May 1958.

Wayne, L., Nike purchasing Converse, A legend on the blacktop, NY Times.com, July 10, 2003.

Weise, E., Body may be key to a foolproof ID, *USA Today*, April 8, 1998.

Weiser, W., Analysis of shoe prints, *Kriminalistik*, 494–499, November 1979 (translation from German).

Whitlock, J. K., and Santamaria, R., Cracks in the sidewall of a Nike, presented at the International Symposium on the Forensic Aspects of Footwear and Tire Impression Evidence, FBI Academy, Quantico, VA, June 27–July 1, 1994.

Whittle, M. W., *Gait Analysis*, 2nd ed., Butterworth-Heinemann, Oxford, England, 1996.

Wiesner, S., Cohen, A., Shor, Y., and Grafit, A., A new method for casting three-dimensional shoe-prints and tire marks using dental stone, poster presented at the Pattern and Impression Symposium, Clearwater, FL, August 2010.

Wiesner, S., Cohen, A., Shor, Y., and Weiss, R., A comparative research on recovering dust shoeprints from bodies, presented at the Pattern and Impression Symposium, Clearwater, FL, August 2012.

Wiesner, S., Tsach, T., Belser, C., and Shor, Y., A comparative research of two lifting methods: electrostatic lifter and gelatin lifter, *JFS*, 56(1), January 2011.

Wiesner, S., Izraeli, E., Shor, Y., and Domb, A., Lifting bloody footwear impressions using alginate casts followed by chemical enhancement, *J. For. Sci.*, 58(3):782–788, 2013.

Wilgus, F., Latent shoeprint recovery on human skin, *JFI*, 54(4):428–432, 2004.

Wilson, H., Comparison of the individual characteristics in the outsoles of thirty-nine pairs of Adidas supernova classic shoes, *JFI*, 62(3), 2012.

Winkelmann, W., The evaluation of human footprints, especially the ball and toes, for identification in forensic medicine, *Z. Rechtsmed.*, 99:121–128, 1987 (translated from German).

Wisbey, D., Counterfeit Nike sneakers, *JFI*, 60(3):337–351, 2010.

Witzke, D., RAW benefits in forensic science, *Evidence Technology Magazine*, May–June 2014, pp. 10–15.

Wolfe, J. R., Photographing and casting snow impression evidence, presented at the IAI International Educational Conference, Minneapolis, MN, August 15, 2014.

Wolfe, J. R., Sulfur cement: a new material for casting snow impression evidence, presented at the 92nd IAI Educational Conference, San Diego, CA, July 2007, *JFI*, 58(4), 2008.

Wolfe, J. R., and Beheim, C. W., Dental stone casting of snow impressions, presented at the International Symposium on the Forensic Aspects of Footwear and Tire Impression Evidence, FBI Academy, Quantico, VA, June 27–July 1, 1994.

Wojcik, R. J., and Sahs, P. T., Reproducing footwear evidence impressions, *Identification News*, 34(7):6–7, 1984.

Wyatt, J., Duncan, K., and Trimpe, M., Aging of shoes and its effect on shoeprint impressions, *JFI*, 55(2):181–188, 2005.

Xiang-Qing, S., Estimation of stature from intact long bones of Chinese males, *Canadian Society J. Foren. Sci.*, 22:2, 1989.

Yamashita, A., Forensic barefoot morphology comparison, *Canadian Journal of Criminology and Criminal Justice*, 49(5), Dec 2007.

Yamazaki, M., Footwear print reference system using an optical disc, presented at the International Symposium on the Forensic Aspects of Footwear and Tire Impression Evidence, FBI Academy, Quantico, VA, June 27–July 1, 1994.

Yeomans, R. E., A non-classic perspective on footwear identification, *RCMP Gazette*, 47(6):10–15, 1985.

Young, P. A., Electrostatic detection of footprints, *Police Research Bulletin*, 21:11–15, 1973.

Young, T., A photographic comparison of Luminol, Fluorescein and Bluestar, *JFI*, 56(6), 2006.

Ytti, A. I., Enhancement of shoeprints with Polilight—A case report, presented at the International Symposium on the Forensic Aspects of Footwear and Tire Impression Evidence, FBI Academy, Quantico, VA, June 27–July 1, 1994.

Ytti, A., Majamaa, H., and Virtanen, J., Survey of the conclusions drawn of similar shoeprint cases, Part II, *Information Bulletin for Shoeprint/Toolmark Examiners*, 4(10):157–169, 1998.

Yu, A., Knaap, W., Milliken, N., and Bognar, P., Evaluation and comparison of casting materials on detailed three-dimensional impressions, *JFI*, 59(6), 2009.

Zeldes, Ilya, Footwear and tire track examination in the Soviet Union, *Journal of Forensic Identification*, 39(6), 1989.

Zercie, K. B., The role of footwear evidence in the reconstruction of a crime scene, presented at the International Symposium on the Forensic Aspects of Footwear and Tire Impression Evidence, FBI Academy, Quantico, VA, June 27–July 1, 1994.

Zmuda, C. W., Identification of crepe sole shoes, *Journal of Criminology, Criminal Law and Police Science*, 44(3):374–378, 1953.

Zmuda, C., and Brodie, T., Limitations in the identification of foot and shoe impressions, Miami, FL (undated).

Zugibe, F., and Costello, J., Identification of the murder weapon by intricate patterned injury measurements, *J. Foren. Sci.*, 31(2):773–777, 1986.

Zweidinger, R. A., Lytle, L. T., and Pitt, C. G., Photography of bloodstains visualized by Luminol, *J. Foren. Sci.*, 18(4):296–302, Oct. 1973.

Index

S